No matter what storms may come...

You Can Survive!

**A book designed for people
preparing for the end times.**

by
Jere Franklin

Published by Jere Franklin, P.O. Box 840, Chetwynd, British Columbia, Canada, V0C 1J0

Ordering information for **You Can Survive!** Send $19.95 (US) plus $5.00 shipping and handling to:

> Ruth Maddy, 43 Mill Drive, Wahkiacus, WA 98670, 1-509-369-3735 or youcansurvive@juno.com

Inquiries regarding seminars please contact:

> Jere Franklin, P.O. Box 840, Chetwynd, BC, Canada, V0C 1J0
>
> Phone/Fax: 1-250-788-2944 Website: youcansurvive.org
>
> Printed by: R&H Graphics

Franklin, Jere. C.

You Can Survive! No matter what storms may come......./Franklin, Jere C.

1. Survival skills. 2. Christian life. 3. End time events

I. Title.

BT877.F73 2001

ISBN 0-9688901-0-5

Printed in United States of America

Acknowledgments

I give gratitude to God for His love and His call to prepare us for His second coming.

To my wife, Linda, who wrote the chapter "Broken in Heart" and who did extensive editing. Her beautiful illustrations, including the cover, add greatly to this book.

To my son, Jed, for his interest in this book and in log cabin building.

Many thanks to Cresta Woodruff for typing this manuscript and for her interest in this project. Thanks to Don and Ruth Maddy for their editing and distribution.

Editing thanks to: Bessie Callahan who, at this writing, is 97 years young, helped with valuable editorial contributions, Delma Miller for her detailed copy editing, and Lincoln Steed, editor of *Liberty* magazine, for his advice during the editing process.

Thanks to Earlane Polen for all her hard work in formatting and her interest in this project.

I would also like to thank several people who have challenged me to be ready for Jesus' second coming: Elder W. D. Frazee, in his books Another Ark to Build and Enoch's Outpost, Elder James Lee, in Three Lines of Defense, and Elder Gordon Collier for his Closing Events chart.

Thanks to doctors Calvin and Agatha Thrash, who wrote chapter 13 on medical preparation, and to Wilbur Atwood for his work on accreditation in chapter 18. Thank you to Earl Qualls for his contribution regarding edible wild plants.

I am thankful to Jim Buller of Bakersfield, California, and Ellis Howard of Tumbler Ridge, British Columbia, for their contributions to the chapter on wilderness survival.

I am grateful to the staff and students at Sanctuary Ranch Academy for their "no buy-no sell" work in the class "Preparation for Coming Events."

Thanks to all of those who, with words or finances, supported and encouraged this production.

Lastly, I wish to thank my parents for early infusing me with a love for nature.

Jere Franklin

Table of Contents

CONTENTS

Section Three: Our Destiny Calls

Appendix

INTRODUCTION

*"A storm is coming, relentless in its fury.
Are we prepared to meet it?"* (8T 315)

Introduction

Storms Are Already Here

What storms? Why do people need a book on spiritual survival? While many people have expectations of cataclysmic events soon to come to this earth, what events could threaten human survival? Biblical prophecies draw back the dark curtain covering the future and reveal plans that could intimidate your school, church, and family. Is there something you can do to get ready for threatening events that will catch many by surprise?

The almighty God has a plan to counteract the evil one. This book gives spiritual and practical advice outlining God's intentions for your survival. If you want to respond to God's way and prepare your family for what is ahead, then you have many reasons to read this book. Here are some of the threats we need to survive:

* According to the American Society of Suicidology, suicides in the US in the year 2003 totaled 31,484 (all races, both sexes).
* Cancer cases in the US in the year 2002 totaled 557,271. A large portion of cancer cases can be prevented.
* AIDS current cases, as of December 2002 worldwide 38 million. Many of these cases are avoidable.
* Heart disease in the US in the year 2002 took 696,947 lives. While this is the world's biggest killer, a large portion of heart disease is preventable. (* Time Almanac 2006; pp. 137, 213)

Other societal threats include: drug addiction, alcohol and associated highway slaughter, sexually transmitted disease, unwanted pregnancies, abortions, crime (robbery, rape, and murder), animal and human abuse, prostitution, terrorism, hunger, hurricanes, tornadoes, volcanoes, floods, conflagrations, earthquakes. All of these threaten our churches, schools, and families. But, no matter what storms may come, **YOU CAN SURVIVE!**

I Was Prepared

Not long ago, I was on the shores of Sanctuary Lake in the Northern Canadian Rockies. It was mid-March, and snow was everywhere. The ice on the lake was about two feet thick. A storm front was developing behind the mountain, and from the color of the clouds, it appeared to be a snowstorm. I watched as it moved over and down the mountain, across the lake toward the shore on which I sat. It was a windy ten degrees below zero Fahrenheit, but instead of feeling threatened, I felt the goodness of the wilderness pressing into my heart, energizing me to meet the challenge of the storm.

My son and I enjoyed camping for those few days at the log cabin we built on the shores of Sanctuary Lake. We had some good friends with us and a two-week supply of food. Wood was stacked on the porch, and with our warm

Introduction

sleeping bags we could weather any snowstorm. So I just sat there watching the storm approach. The snow came across the lake toward me. I lifted my face to meet the storm. I felt safe. Why was I not afraid? Because, in this case, I was prepared. One Naval Academy cadet recently expressed it this way, "If you are prepared, you will not fear the future."

Several years ago, I taught a class to our Sanctuary Ranch seniors entitled "Preparation for Coming Events" as a part of their senior Bible sequence. The class of about 12 was divided into four groups: (1) Spiritual, (2) Food, (3) Shelter, and (4) Medical. Each group was instructed to submit a thesis on the topic assigned as if they were living a life-style without money (based on the warning in Revelation 13:17 which tells of a time when no man can buy or sell). The Bible and Spirit of Prophecy were the students' main source books, although they did use a few medical, carpentry, and agricultural texts. As they prepared their papers, the students told me that they were inspired to make personal preparations for the future. I have used parts of their reports in preparing this book.

Although I have incorporated some aspects of every area of survival, this book is not all-inclusive. End-time survival will ultimately depend upon your degree of commitment, intervention by God, and your willingness to spend time preparing for the coming of Jesus. This book cannot cover all circumstances or all situations. If this book serves only to overcome the inertia that binds us to business-as-usual, it will have served its purpose. Every person will know a personalized journey. "Noticing small changes early helps you to adapt to the bigger ones that are coming" (Who Moved My Cheese? Spencer Johnson, MD [Penguin-Putnam Books], p. 68). The earlier we detect our need for change and adapt to small changes in life-style, the more readily will we be able to face the larger issues that will confront us in the time of trouble.

Promises for All

We will have to claim promises from the Bible and other inspired writings for that which we cannot provide. It took a considerable amount of faith for the slaves leaving Egypt to abandon even the little security they had. The Lord blessed what they could not replace; their clothes and shoes did not wear out. When they ran out of food, they were fed miraculously. Why did God work these miracles? Because they were doing what He wanted them to do: escape from bondage.

"And I have led you forty years in the wilderness: your clothes are not waxen old upon you, and thy shoe is not waxen old upon thy foot" (Deuteronomy 29:5).

"He humbled you by letting you get hungry, then He fed you with manna, which no one had ever heard of, to teach you that man is not sus-

Introduction

tained by bread alone but by feeding on the word that comes from God" (Deuteronomy 8:3, Clear Word).

The Elderly, Part of the Team

An older sister came to me after one of our seminars shaking her head, "I don't want to think about these problems, Brother Jere. Elderly people can't maintain a country home and do the hard work demanded. There was a time I lived out of the garden. Not any more." By way of encouragement to her, I related this story.

"Several Waldensian families were fleeing from their homes under persecution. Among them was an aged barb (pastor). He made it just fine up the first climb to a level plateau and sat down on a rock making this declaration, " 'You young people go ahead. I have lived a full life. I am ready to close my ministry. I don't want to hold you up from fleeing from these angry persecutors.' The young people looked at each other and declared. " 'Not so Pastor! We need you. We need your faith, your courage, and your spiritual knowledge to help us during these times.' " Two men made a figure-4 chair, picked up their beloved minister, and continued their flight.

"In the last days we need each other. We need to make provision for those who cannot make provision for themselves. You who are elderly are part of the team!"

The history of John affords a striking illustration of the way in which God uses aged workers. *"And it was after John had grown old in the service of his Lord that he received more communications from heaven than he had received all the former years of his life* (Acts of the Apostles, p. 572-573).

Following the Blueprint

Noah followed God's plan for building the ark in every particular, but God's intervention was required to protect the ark through the catastrophic flood. The deluge of events soon to descend upon us will be much like the waters that descended upon the antediluvians. *"Angels that excel in strength guided the ark and preserved it from harm. Every moment during that frightful storm of forty days and forty nights the preservation of the ark was a miracle of almighty power"* (The Story of Redemption, p. 68). God will bless our ark of safety only if we follow His plan.

"In Noah's day the inhabitants of the old world laughed to scorn what they termed the superstitious fears and forebodings of the preacher of righteousness. He was denounced as a visionary character, a fanatic, an alarmist. 'As it was in the days of Noah, so shall it be also in the days of the Son of Man.' Men will reject the solemn message of warning in our day, as they did in Noah's

Introduction

time" (<u>Testimonies for the Church</u>, vol. 4, p. 308).

Noah's call to build the ark was not a call to hoard supplies. He was more than willing to share with his friends and neighbors. Survival means sharing. Though we are called to be a peculiar people, God does not want us to be hermits. He does not call on us to isolate ourselves merely for isolation's sake. The reason we need to study survival for these last days is to help each other survive. Much as Enoch shared his provisions with those who came out from the ancient cities, so we shall share God's provisions with those who come to us.

There are some things we must do in order to prepare. There will be no preparation for the time of trouble after the close of probation. We understand this from <u>Early Writings</u>, page 56, *"The Lord has shown me repeatedly that it is contrary to the Bible to make any provision for our temporal wants in the time of trouble. I saw that if the saints had food laid up by them or in the field in the time of trouble, when sword, famine, and pestilence are in the land, it would be taken from them by violent hands and strangers would reap their fields. Then will be the time for us to trust wholly in God and He will sustain us. I saw that our bread and water will be sure at that time, and that we shall not lack or suffer hunger; for God is able to spread a table for us in the wilderness. If necessary He would send ravens to feed us, as He did to feed Elijah, or rain manna from heaven, as He did for the Israelites."*

Noah did not forget evangelism while building the ark. It should be so with us. During the "no buy - no sell" mentioned in Revelation 13, mercy still exists for those who have not heard the good news of salvation. The loud cry will be at its peak. We are now commissioned to reach out to help others prepare for the second coming of Jesus, regardless of the hardships that we might be called upon to endure.

Simplify

Though we are counseled not to bring an early time of trouble upon ourselves, there are some things we can and should do to prepare for the future. A country life style encourages us to appreciate simple pleasures and helps us focus on preparations for end times. We are getting ready for the greatest event since the dawn of time, the return of Jesus and the beginning of eternity!

We recommend that each family practice a "nature day"—a day devoted to healthy activities and family interaction when the lights and the electronics go off for 24 hours. During your "nature day," use a wood- stove for cooking and heating, no television, computer, or electric lights—nothing that would ordinarily in-

Introduction

volve the utility web. It is a "back to the land" day. Do it one day a week, or maybe one day a month.

You might want to consider altering your diet, for in the last days animal products will not be used. A simple vegetarian diet, with plenty of raw food, is a means of improving health. *"Among those who are waiting for the coming of the Lord, meat eating will eventually be done away; flesh will cease to form a part of their diet"* (Counsels on Diet and Foods, pp. 380-381).

For ten years we operated a small school where we cooked with wood, heated with wood, and had kerosene or gas lamps. We were off the utility web. We built log houses. We grew the much of our own food, canning some, and storing the root crops in cellars for the winter. Life was simple, but busy. The young people really appreciated that lifestyle! It is true that *"A return to simpler methods will be appreciated by children and youth"* (Testimonies for the Church, vol. 6, p. 179). If we can do it for a whole school, you can do it, too!

"Let none sit in calm expectation of the evil, comforting themselves with the belief that this work must go on because prophecy has foretold it, and that the Lord will shelter His people. We are not doing the will of God if we sit in quietude, doing nothing to preserve liberty of conscience. Fervent, effectual prayer should be ascending to heaven that this calamity may be deferred until we can accomplish the work which has so long been neglected. Let there be most earnest prayer, and then let us work in harmony with our prayers" (ibid. vol. 5, pp. 713-714).

Although there are some basic tools we should have before we cannot buy and sell, spiritual preparation is far more important. Spiritual submission to God will lead us into cheerful obedience where we can begin to enjoy what God has prepared for us in the country. With very little study, one will come to realize that we need to leave the cities as soon as possible. God knew Noah would follow the blueprint. Noah was a survivor because he trusted in God, not because he trusted in the ark.

Great Soul Capacity

The best compliment one could give another is, "You have a great soul." A person with a great soul has a large capacity to love and care for other people as well as for their own family. In order to survive the end times, one needs to develop this "great soul" capacity. This requires special attention to growth in the whole person, both inside and out. This book is designed to help develop that capacity. You will find discussions about: practical skills for country living, how to build a log cabin with no money, how to grow a garden that will supply sufficient

Introduction

food for an entire year, wilderness survival skills, medical preparations for emergency response, and how to get your finances in order, and several chapters on spiritual preparation in these last days.

Our objective is not just to survive, but to help others survive, not because we trust in our own preparations, but because we have followed God's direction. This is the large capacity of a great soul, to share with others and help them get to heaven. Noah would not have survived without the ark, neither will we survive the end times without having followed the blueprint. We, too, have an ark to build. Our trust in God and following His plans are all-important. It means eternal survival. I like to think of survival as "making it to heaven to be with Jesus." We aren't preparing to live forever here on earth—heaven is our home. We can all be survivors. Some survivors may lose their life here, while others may never see death.

You may find this book a challenge to your present life-style. It is based on the writings of prophets. Truth must be applied one step at a time; God will help with the timing and providences where change is needed. Consider these references as you contemplate preparation:

"The time has come, when, as God opens the way, families should move out of the cities. The children should be taken into the country. The parents should get as suitable a place as their means will allow. Though the dwelling may be small, yet there should be land in connection with it, that may be cultivated" (Adventist Home, p. 139).

"Parents can secure small homes in the country, with land for cultivation where they can have orchards and where they can raise vegetables and small fruits to take the place of flesh-meat, which is so corrupting to the lifeblood coursing through the veins. On such places the children will not be surrounded with the corrupting influences of city life. God will help His people to find such homes outside of the cities" (Medical Ministry, p. 310; emphasis supplied).

"Those who have felt at last to make a move, let it not be in a rush, in an excitement, or in a rash manner, or in a way that hereafter they will deeply regret that they did move out..." (Country Living, p. 25).

Sharing What I Most Need

I have written this book as I would prepare a sermon—I study what I most need, hoping others will benefit. I am in need of these counsels as much as anyone. Together we may ask forgiveness, make restitution, resolve hurt feelings, and make a deeper commitment to God and move forward with His plans.

As I sat on the shores of Sanctuary Lake and watched the approaching storm I did not panic, because I was ready. My peace was a result of my preparation and trust in God. Over the years the Lord has brought to my attention things that we can do in order to be ready for the crisis ahead. I felt I should write about my experiences and how I have seen the hand of God leading in my life. I want the Lord to say of us what He said to Mary, *"She has done what she could, "* (Mark 14:8).

"A great crisis awaits the people of God. A crisis awaits the world. The most momentous struggle of all the ages is just before us.... Have we faithfully discharged the duty which God has committed to us of giving the people warning of the danger before them?" (Testimonies for the Church, vol. 5, p. 711).

"Christians should be preparing for what is soon to break upon the world as an overwhelming surprise, and this preparation they should make by diligently studying the word of God, and striving to conform their lives to its precepts.... . God calls for a revival and a reformation" (Prophets and Kings, p. 626).

Please write and tell us of blessings you receive in reading this book. Also, please let us know of corrections or additions we might make or if you are interested in having a Survival Seminar in your church. You may contact Jere Franklin, Box 840, Chetwynd, B. C., V0C 1J0, Canada. Phone 1-250-788-2944. God bless you as you continue your preparations for the crisis ahead.

SECTION ONE:
Spiritual Preparation

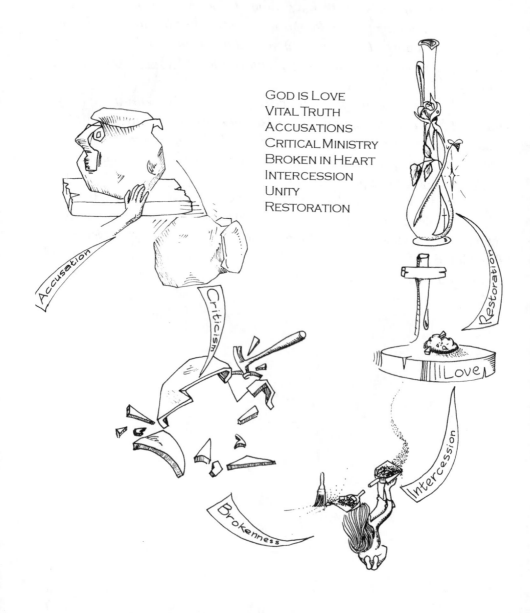

GOD IS LOVE
VITAL TRUTH
ACCUSATIONS
CRITICAL MINISTRY
BROKEN IN HEART
INTERCESSION
UNITY
RESTORATION

Accusation

Criticism

Brokenness

Intercession

Love

Restoration

Chapter One

God Is Love: Love Is Healing and Life

"The power of love was in all Christ's healing, and only by partaking of that love, through faith, can we be instruments for His work" (<u>Counsels on Health</u>, p. 31).

"Fight! Fight!" came loud yells from the boys' basement. It was recess at Belmont School and the children had to play inside because of rain.

The teachers on duty rushed to the rescue, clapping their hands for attention; but to no avail. The 9-year-old champion, the central figure of the warfare, was deaf to their entreaties.

Just when the teachers had given up in despair the young boyish-appearing principal stepped in, and after mustering all his forces, the fight was finally brought to an end.

"Come up to the office with me, boys."

Five guilty boys, headed by the champion, walked behind the man, and were soon arraigned before the court of justice. Eventually each one was disposed of—leaving the leader of the battle alone with the dispenser of punishments.

Something about the lone little figure drew Paul Day to him and made him wish to know more about him. It might have been the brown eyes beneath a shock of tousled brown curls, or it might have been the grotesque costume he wore. His slim little body was clad in faded tan trousers that were miles too big for him and sagged down over his thin knees almost to his ankles, and a tight little coat of plaid material that had apparently been made for a girl.

"Now, tell me your name and where you live."

The boy's brown eyes looked defiantly into the man's blue ones.

"It's Garvis Wilson, and I live … live …"

The defiance changed to wistfulness, and the little voice broke as he finished.

"I live … Fesser, I live … at the …orphans' home."

"Oh, I see. You've had several fights before, haven't you?"

"Yes, Fesser, me an' the fellers has been a-fightin' purt near ever recess since I bin a-comin' to this school."

"How long have you been coming to school?"

"More'n a week, Fesser, ever since I bin t' th' orphans' home."

The young man's manner was sympathetic as he drew the tiny bunch of wistfulness toward him.

"Why do you fight so much, Garvis?"

The expression in the boy's eyes changed once more, and a sudden angry fire lit them.

" 'Cuz the fellers call me 'Dub.' They called me 'Double' at first and then jist begin to call me 'Dub.' They do that 'cuz I ain't got no fittin' clothes; the britches is allus too big an' the coat's allus too tight an' I allus look funny jist like I was two fellers–a big un an' a little un."

Paul Day sat at his desk, silent for a moment, looking steadily at Garvis. Presently the hurt, angry look in the boy's eyes turned to triumph.

"But I lick 'em ever' time, Fesser, even 'f I am a 'Dub.' 'Spect it's 'cause I'm two fellers reason I can lick 'em! I'm a-goin' tu keep a-lickin' 'em too, long's they keep a-callin' me 'Dub.' "

"I wouldn't do that, Garvis. I'd be a man and not lower myself to fighting. Don't you know that if you fight, you will always find somebody else to fight with you, and you will grow up to be a bad sort of man?"

"But, Fesser, I haven't got nobody t' b'long to an' I hafta fight so's the fellers won't run over me. These big ol' britches an' this little ol' streaked coat jist makes me feel like I want t' jist fight, 'n' fight, 'n' fight 'n' jist keep a-fightin'!"

Paul Day was not much more than a boy himself, and something in his nature and experience made him long for some way to reach the small soldier's aching little heart and heal the wound that was there.

"I am not going to punish you very much today, Garvis, but the next time it will be severe. But you won't need it after this, will you? You are going to be a brave little man, aren't you?"

"Yes, Fesser, I'll try t' be a big, brave man an' not fight, but sometimes these big ol' britches a-floppin' 'round on me jist makes me s' mad they jist make me be bad. But I'll try t' be good 'cuz I like you. I wisht I wuz your little boy so's I c'd b'long."

For some time after the boy had gone, Paul Day pondered over the situation. His mind went back to the days when he had not "b'longed." He had not been an inmate at an orphans' home, but he had lived in the home of a cold, selfish, unsympathetic aunt. He had not had to wear "big ol' britches," but his aunt had made him stay dressed up all the time, and worst of all, he had had to wear Windsor ties! How he had hated them! What money could buy he had. But he had not "b'longed," as Garvis had termed his lack of love and sympathy.

The next day the sun shone and the playground at the Belmont School was alive with hundreds of happy voices and radiant with flashes of color.

"Fight! Fight!" There it was in spite of the splendor of the sunshine and the crisp freshness of the winter air.

Garvis and his opponents in battle were brought into Paul Day's office. This time the champion was in tears, and he barely stepped inside the door, standing there hanging his head in shame—the defiant spirit was gone. As before, the young principal sent the other boys out first.

"Come here, Garvis." The voice was tender, with a suggestion of hidden tears.

The tearful, shame-stricken little champion came forward, head hanging, not even glancing up. His ragged shoes that were not mates scraped the floor. He edged toward his hero. As he came near, his eyes glued to the floor, the shoes he had expected to see were not shiny, black man-sized shoes. They were tiny, tan pumps, and above each one was a slender silken ankle, then a soft, silky golden brown dress.

His eyes, traveling upward, stopped at a pair of sympathetic brown eyes, soft and sweet and smiling. Then he found Paul Day's blue eyes just above and behind the glorious brown ones.

"Oh, there you are, Fesser." A little sigh of relief escaped his lips. Then the sweetest voice he had ever heard came to him like an angel's:

"Don't mind me. I'm just Mrs. Fesser, and I have come to school today to get a glimpse of Fesser's boys. He has told me about you."

Paul Day smiled approvingly at his pretty little wife, then looked earnestly at Garvis.

"So you have been fighting again?"

The boy dropped his head, and in spite of his brave attempts to keep the tears back, they just would come.

"Yes, … it jist seems like I git all het up when the fellers call me 'Dub' an' I don't know whuther I'm more mad at the fellers er this ol' tight coat an' these big ol' britches. Now 'f I b'longed I don't b'lieve I'd keer one speck. But," he sobbed, " 'Taint no fun tu wear 'em when you don't b'long."

Two loving motherly arms went around the weeping little "Dub." A sweet voice that sounded like heaven said things that made him forget the sorrow of not belonging.

"We want you to come and be our little boy, dear. God took our little son away and He has sent you to take his place. We need you. You belong to us."

Then "Fesser" came nearer, his blue eyes misty.

"I never did belong, Garvis, until Mrs. Fesser took me. Now we'll both belong to her."

3

The curly head lifted itself, and two happy eyes smiled through their tears into the eyes of Mr. and Mrs. "Fesser."

"We'll both b'long to her, Fesser, an' I'll b'long to both of you. I'll be half yours an' half hers. I don't keer if I do hafta wear th' little ol' tight coat 'n' th' big ol' britches now, 'cuz I'll hafta be two fellers t' b'long t' both of you, won't I, Mis' Fesser?"

God's love for us is beautifully illustrated in this story by Kathryn Kimball about Little Dub. As Dub belonged to Mr. and Mrs. "Fesser," so we belong to God. Our Father can do for us what Dub's new parents did for him. God loves us so much that He created us. We wander away, then He redeems us, embraces us, and adopts us into His family.

There are several other acts that our Father performs even more wonderful than Dub's new parents could do for him. These acts are all based on, and are a direct result of, His love.

Love Is Healing

"There went virtue out of him, and healed them all" (Luke 6:19). There is a vital power that comes from love. But in order to be able to give this powerful love to others we must be connected to Jesus and His love.

"I am the vine, ye are the branches: He that abideth in me, and I in him, the same bringeth forth much fruit: for without me, ye can do nothing" (John 15:5). To be connected with Jesus opens a whole new realm of ministry.

The Desire of Ages, pages 262-266, tells of the leper who, ignoring taunts and shouts of "unclean," pressed through the crowd to get to Jesus. The disease had made frightful inroads and made him a loathsome figure. The isolation from his family had caused them great pain. Leprosy itself was considered a symbol of sin, and hence he was looked upon by all as a great sinner.

He falls at Jesus' feet and in a pleading voice says, "Lord, if Thou wilt, Thou canst make me clean." No one had been healed of leprosy since Elisha's experience with Naaman. How could he expect that Jesus could heal him now? He saw how people with other diseases had been restored to health. Maybe he could be healed, too. Hope sprang up in his heart, lifting his faith to new heights.

"And Jesus put forth his hand, and touched him, saying, I will; be thou clean. And immediately his leprosy was cleansed" (Matthew 8:3).

Immediately his skin became soft with the glow of a healthy child. Joy inexpressible spilled from his soul. Soon he would be restored to his family. The curse was gone. The name-calling would end. Accusations would be extinguished. He was a whole new person. Praise God!

GOD IS LOVE

How did it happen? The book Education gives us insight into how Jesus was able to heal. *"Only the love that flows from the heart of Christ can heal. Only he in whom that love flows, even as the sap in the tree or the blood in the body, can restore the wounded soul. Love's agencies have a wonderful power, for they are divine.... Would we learn the lesson, with what power for healing would our lives be gifted! How life would be transformed, and the earth become a very likeness and foretaste of heaven!"* (p. 114; emphasis supplied).

If we could love like Jesus loves, we would see more healing in this worldly lazar house. We can love enough if we connect with Him!

"Not all that this world bestows can heal a broken heart, or impart peace of mind, or remove care, or banish disease. Fame, genius, talent—all are powerless to gladden the sorrowful heart or to restore the wasted life. The life of God in the soul is man's only hope. The love which Christ diffuses through the whole being is a vitalizing power. Every vital part—the brain, the heart, the nerves—it touches with healing" (The Ministry of Healing, p. 115; emphasis supplied).

"The power of love was in all Christ's healing, and only by partaking of that love, through faith, can we be instruments for His work. If we neglect to link ourselves in divine connection with Christ, the current of life-giving energy cannot flow in rich streams from us to the people" (Counsels on Health, p. 31).

"You cannot exert an influence that will transform others until your own heart has been humbled and refined and made tender by the grace of Christ" (Thoughts From the Mount of Blessing, p. 128).

God asks us to believe that through sensing our need, obtaining the gifts of forgiveness and repentance, we can become channels of His love and healing for others.

"That love they knew not until they saw the suffering and death of Jesus Christ upon the cross of Calvary. The new commandment of love was given in behalf of the weak, the wretched, the helpless" (Medical Ministry, p. 121).

By giving our whole heart over to Christ, learning to love unconditionally, we can become a healing power in this hurting world. Jesus' hands reach out, anxious to sanctify the pain we have known into healing for others who are hurting as we have been. When He chooses us to share His pain, He can more easily grant us the gift of healing. Or we can choose to rebel:

Shall I Crucify My Saviour?

Oh, the kindly hands of Jesus,
Pouring blessings on all men
Bleeding, nail scarred, hands of Jesus,
Shall I crucify again?

—Anonymous

Love Is Reconciliation

He was standing on the porch of the courthouse. He was discouraged. His best friend had just been sentenced to death. He had been asked to testify as a character witness, but he said that he didn't want to be involved. Now he wished he had done more to help his friend. People wondered why he hadn't been more supportive. But when questioned about it, he stubbornly answered, "No, I don't even know him very well."

Unknown to him, his friend found out that he would not speak for him. The friend felt keen anguish over his lack of support. It added an almost overwhelming load to his death sentence. The condemned man thought that his best friends would be there for him, but they weren't.

The man standing on the porch decided to cover up his appearance by mingling in the crowd of onlookers after his friend was sentenced. He did not want anyone to recognize him as an associate of the condemned man.

Someone nearby asked him, "Aren't you a friend of the accused?"

He answered him angrily, with swear words, "No, I don't know who he is."

The man who had asked the question then knew he was mistaken, for it was commonly known that anyone who was a friend of the accused did not use such language.

Just as he was finished uttering his expletives, his attention was drawn to a small crowd of soldiers escorting the accused to the place of execution. His eyes fell on the face of his friend, who was looking directly at him. His friend showed no hatred in his expression and it broke the man's heart, for it was in that instant that he knew his friend had discovered the betrayal.

"In that gentle countenance he read deep pity and sorrow, but there was no anger there" (The Desire of Ages, p. 713). The man's mind was flooded with memories of how his friend, Jesus, had forgiven so many and in that gaze, Peter knew he had been forgiven and had been reconciled to Jesus. He felt sorrow in his heart for denying Jesus and sensed that he had not been separated from him as a friend. Though forgiven, Peter would remember always (repentance) this night of reconciliation.

It was in the glance of Jesus that Peter knew he was forgiven and reconciled. The Bible, in its thorough coverage of this topic, has anticipated that some reconciliations are not as easy as Peter's. It outlines steps that one can follow that will lead to reunion or separation. These counsels are directly related to our survival. In our relationship to Jesus and to others, our only safe course is prayer.

"It is a perilous thing to allow an unchristlike trait to live in the heart. One cherished sin will, little by little, debase the character, bringing all its nobler powers into subjection to the evil desire. The removal of one safeguard from the conscience, the indulgence of one evil habit, one neglect of the high claims of duty, breaks down the defenses of the soul and opens the way for Satan to come in and lead us astray. The only safe course is to let our prayers go forth daily from a sincere heart, as did David, 'Hold up my goings in thy paths, that my footsteps slip not' (Psalm 17:5)" (Patriarchs and Prophets, p. 452).

If we have one sin of commission toward a brother or a sister, we need to make it right.

"If we have in any manner defrauded or <u>injured our brother, we should make restitution</u>. If we have unwittingly borne false witness, if we have misstated words, if we have <u>injured his influence in any way</u>, we should go to the ones with whom we have conversed about him, and <u>take back</u> all our injurious misstatements" (Thoughts From the Mount of Blessing, p. 59; emphasis supplied).

The Spirit of Prophecy gives us guidelines on the attitude of heart we should have as we approach individuals with our concerns and burdens.

"Not until you feel that you could sacrifice your own self-dignity, and even lay down your life in order to save an erring brother, have you cast the beam out of your own eye so that you are prepared to help your brother. Then you can approach him and touch his heart. <u>No one has ever been reclaimed from a wrong position by censure and reproach</u>" (Thoughts From the Mount of Blessing, pp. 128, 129; emphasis supplied).

Reconciliation uses the principle of love and not censure. According to this reference, no one has been restored who was censured or reproached. When a church board is working on a problem, considering or recommending disfellowship of a member to the church at large, the principle of love should be followed in preference to the principle of enforcement. A church board should **never** disfellowship anyone. It must be the church that performs this uncomfortable task according to Matthew 18:17. As the process unfolds, much time should be spent with the person or people involved before such a terrible conclusion is reached.

Matthew 18:15-17 outlines the procedure for reconciliation in Jesus' own words. First, go to that person alone. Second, if that fails, take someone with you. Third, take it to the church and if that person doesn't hear the church, then keep trying to win him.

The Clear Word expresses it this way in verse 17: *"If he doesn't listen to the church, then treat him as an unbeliever who needs to be brought back to the Lord."*

"Brethren, if a man be overtaken in a fault, ye which are spiritual, restore such an one in the spirit of meekness; considering thyself, lest thou also be tempted. Bear ye one another's burdens, and so fulfil the law of Christ" (Galatians 6:1, 2).

"Meekness" means "I am no better than you." "Bear" means to carry, not "bare" one another's burdens to someone else. We don't expose others' faults or condemn them, thereby making the load heavier. We don't embarrass, but love them, knowing but for God's love, I would have done the same thing. We settle things with our brothers and sisters outside a court of law.

"God will guard the interests of those who love and fear Him, and with confidence we may commit our case to Him who judges righteously" (Christ's Object Lessons, p. 249).

"Everyone who has been free to condemn or discourage will in his own experience be brought over the ground where he has caused others to pass; he will feel what they have suffered because of his want of sympathy and tenderness. It is the love of God toward us that has decreed this" (Thoughts From the Mount of Blessing, p. 136).

It is important that we be careful how we treat others because God, in His love, has told us that we will be brought over the same ground that we have caused others to pass.

"In reforms we would better come one step short of the mark than to go one step beyond it. And if there is error at all, let it be on the side next to the people" (Testimonies for the Church, vol. 3, p. 21).

Forgiveness

From the old sanctuary service comes the concepts of forgiving intentional sins and sins of ignorance. The Spirit of Prophecy clarifies this even further by referring to these sins as ones of commission and omission. A sin of commission is one of intentional occurrence, while a sin of omission is one of "I didn't know" or "I forgot."

In some cases, the only measurement for sins of omission is the person we offended when we didn't mean to. If they are hurt by what we say, then it becomes a sin of omission because we said it wrong and we didn't know it would hurt. We ask forgiveness. They may also ask us to forgive them because they now see that we did not intend to hurt them. Addressing your sin of omission leaves you forgiven by God, and your brothers and sisters.

This work of reunion is a delicate work. <u>Evangelism</u>, page 348, says *"To deal with human minds is the nicest work ever committed to mortal man."* The word "nicest" means delicate, careful, and loving.

We need to remember that open sin cannot exist in the church without heavy responsibilities falling on the leadership. *"The plain, straight testimony must live in the church, or the curse of God will rest upon His people as surely as it did upon ancient Israel because of their sins. God holds His people, as a body, responsible for the sins existing in individuals among them. If the leaders of the church neglect to diligently search out the sins which bring the displeasure of God upon the body, <u>they become responsible for these sins</u>"* (<u>Testimonies for the Church</u>, vol. 3, p. 269; emphasis supplied).

It is imperative that these sins be eliminated from among us, or else we are held responsible by God for their existence. This work **must** be done in love. Not everyone can do it. *"<u>All are not fitted to correct the erring</u>. They have not wisdom to deal justly, while loving mercy. They are not inclined to see <u>the necessity of mingling love and tender compassion with faithful reproofs</u>"* (<u>ibid</u>., emphasis supplied).

The Elijah Message

"Behold, I will send you Elijah the prophet before the coming of the great and dreadful day of the Lord: and he shall turn the heart of the fathers to the children, and the heart of the children to their fathers, lest I come and smite the earth with a curse" (Malachi 4:5, 6).

There are no more moving stories of reconciliation than those involving parents and children. One such story comes from France. Sitting on a public bench under the burning sun was a young man with his face buried in his hands. His attitude expressed complete despair. Evangelist Charvet, who had just retired after 34 years' service, entered into a conversation with him, finally offering him a New Testament. "I don't want it," was the reply. "I used to have one, but it was too big to carry, and I threw it into the water." The evangelist felt by intuition that this was not the real reason he had thrown the book away.

After a little more conversation and a few tactful questions, the young man opened his heart and told the evangelist his story. "Several months ago, I left my parents and went to the town to live my own life in my own way. But things did not go as I had expected. My hope and my money gradually disappeared. Now I have nothing left. I intended to return home—that is my home there, the white house you see in the valley—but having gone so far, I am ashamed to go any farther. I am afraid, too; for if my parents should refuse to forgive me, there would be nothing left but death."

After listening to this sad confession, M. Charvet, profoundly touched by the story, opened his New Testament and read the parable of the prodigal son. The young man saw the application of the parable to himself, and began to weep over his sinful past. Suddenly the evangelist conceived a great idea. He told the prodigal to remain where he was while he went to the house in the valley that had been pointed out to him. Knocking at the door, he offered the New Testament to the man, who opened it and was soon joined by his wife. Asked what kind of book it was, he read to them the story of the prodigal (Luke 15:11-32).

Moved to the very depth of his being by the powerful story, which in the course of the ages has brought tears to so many eyes, the father opened his heart and told Charvet his story. "We had a son once, and he was everything to us," he said. "Unfortunately, we did not get on well together, and he went away. We have heard nothing from him since. We would gladly forgive him if he would return, but we do not know where to find him." Then Charvet told them everything. "I know where your son is," he began. "He is quite near here, humble and repentant, and has sent me to ask your pardon. He wants but a word from you to return home."

A few moments later the overjoyed mother was weeping on her son's neck, and the father, after kissing him on both cheeks, was shaking his hands. Then they all gave thanks to God for His goodness, and gladly bought a Testament, in which they could read together of the reconciled life (Bible Society Record, as quoted in "Treasured Gleanings" from The Quiet Hour Echoes). Oh, that we could each become as sensitive to the heart cries of others as was M. Charvet!

"And he shall go before him in the spirit and power of Elias [Elijah], to turn the hearts of the fathers to the children, and the disobedient to the wisdom of the just: to make ready a people prepared for the Lord" (Luke 1:17).

"In this age, prior to the second coming of Christ in the clouds of heaven, God calls for men who will prepare a people to stand in the great day of the Lord. Just such a work as that which John did, is to be carried on in these last days. The Lord is giving messages to His people, through the instruments He has chosen, and He would have all heed the admonitions and warnings He sends.... With the earnestness that characterized Elijah the prophet and John the Baptist, we are to strive to prepare the way for Christ's second advent" (The Seventh-day Adventist Bible Commentary, Ellen G. White Comments, vol. 4, p. 1184; emphasis supplied).

What is the Lord asking you to do in reconciling yourself with your friends, family, and church? He is coming. Will you survive? You will if you make right that which you know is wrong in your own life. You will if you let God make a demonstration of His love through you. Not only will His perfect love cast out your fear of becoming what He wants you to be, but you will also have perfect joy. The Elijah message will have the effect of restoring family relationships. "If the Lord be God, follow Him."

The Path of Healing

Sam was frustrated. It seemed like everything he did was not quite good enough. His wife wanted him to do more. Pamela just wanted him to keep his motivation at a high level for she knew he was a fast, efficient, hard worker. Ever since the injury to his leg, Sam wanted to take it easy, but when his wife prodded him to fix things around the house he felt she was unsympathetic and cold. The frustration built so intensely that Sam became violently angry, surprising himself, his friends, and Pamela. He decided he needed help with anger management and came to see me at my office.

As Sam told his story, beginning in his childhood, he revealed that he had been sexually abused during his early teens. He explained how he had harbored feelings of hatred and anger at the person who inflicted this mistreatment and made him feel so inferior to everyone else. When I suggested that this abuse might be the roots of his surprise anger and violence, he bowed his head in admission.

"How can I fix this, Jere?" Sam asked.

In my counseling practice I attend seminars to keep abreast with new techniques, and, as providence would have it, I had become acquainted with what I thought was just the help that would start Sam on a path of healing.

Sam and Pamela were both Christians. Introducing the concept of forgiveness was relatively easy. The clinical procedures are listed below:

1) Write a letter to the person who abused you.

2) In this letter you should list all the abuses: physical, sexual and verbal.

3) Mention how those abuses hurt you.

4) Take some time, at this point, to ask yourself, "Am I able, with God's help, to forgive this person and tell them?" If so, offer them your forgiveness.

5) Explain to them, in closing your letter, that in spite of how bad these abuses hurt, you forgive them.

6) Amen, and thank you, Lord.

Should the person be deceased, write the letter and throw it in the fire or give it to a friend or relative who had knowledge of the abuse. At a youth ranch where I was principal, one evening we lit a fire in a huge pile of brush. The young people were encouraged to write experiences from which they wanted to be free. They were asked to grant forgiveness to those who caused them pain, wad up the papers, and toss them into the fire. Victories were gained that night because some of the students sent their letters to the people who had hurt them. Experience has taught me that this concept of forgiveness really works, both in and out of the clinical setting.

As good as forgiveness is, it is just a short distance up the path of healing. We might think of this as the Christian's walk to complete restoration, but many travel no further than the "cliff of conviction" or the "overlook" of forgiveness. Jesus invites us to travel the path of healing and experience the love he has for us. At the "cliff of conviction" comes the invitation to healing that is essential to our survival in the last days.

Responsibility or Justification?

In our dealings with others we face a multitude of pleasant interactions that strengthen the bonds of friendship and affinity. Others are negative, hurtful experiences. Someone causes us pain or we cause trauma to others. The negative reactions tend to divide families and friends. They can be hard to resolve and reconcile partly because we justify our own feelings. When resolving conflict no one should infer in any way that someone is emotionally unstable because they are hurt.

The ideal way to resolve conflict is to deal with it in a Biblical, healthy, and therapeutic way. Properly conducted, this is the first step in a healing pilgrimage. This healing journey is as long as we choose to make it.

The first viewpoint along the journey to higher ground is the Cliff of Conviction. Thousands die here. Seeing no hope, they plunge into the abyss below. Despondent and discouraged, they often seek comfort among the unstable and destructive rocks of dependency: alcohol, illicit or prescription drugs, and other indulgences. When the rock upon which they choose to stand topples, they tumble toward the edge. Unless someone is there to rescue them, their fall will culminate in hopeless oblivion and, eventually, another needless suicide. It is while the victim is seeking comfort among the boulders, that a fellow traveler might come along and invite them to look higher. If the victim is willing to look, he will catch a vision of the trail he thought had ended at the point of conviction.

The next viewpoint on this trail is the Overlook of Forgiveness. It is the place where many lives are saved that would have been lost. From this overlook, the Pinnacle of Victory comes into view. It's yet a little higher up the trail. From Forgiveness, we can see on Higher Places a radiant group of people called Overcomers.

Let's examine a strategy that will help us relate to events at the first viewpoint, the one we have named Conviction. Conviction helps us gather momentum toward healing, for conviction always brings us to a choice; to continue traveling the upward path, or traveling the slippery trail downward to great loss.

As we meditate on our convictions pertaining to damaged personal relationships, we will see that we have either been hurt or have hurt someone else. Where we detect that we have hurt someone, we sense conviction, the need to resolve differences. We must choose to go to the one we hurt and apologize to them. As if by a miracle, we are at the second viewpoint of our healing journey, Forgiveness. If we linger too long at the viewpoint of Conviction and do not respond to its beckoning call, we fall easy victim to the shale slide toward discouragement and despondency. Seeking to salve our hurt when others do not apologize to us, we might seek indulgences to ease our pain. Most, if not all, suicides occur at this viewpoint of Conviction. It is essential to our survival that we move on from Conviction toward the overlook of Forgiveness, further up the trail.

Achieving the heights of Conviction and Forgiveness, however, are not enough. Who would want to repeat that cycle over and over again and not be free? We must travel on to yet higher ground, at the Rest Area of Victory. During these interactions with others that lead to forgiveness, we introduce the three R's, namely: Restitution, Resolution, and Reconciliation. In order to achieve this rest at the Viewpoint of Victory, we must be willing to follow the healing guidelines left along the path. We discover in the first message box along the trail that we must take responsibility for the hurts we have caused others. Remember, they are the expert on their feelings. If they say we have hurt them, we must say, "I am sorry."

13

We need to ask forgiveness.

In the atmosphere of Responsibility, the three R's can be nurtured, but if we justify our actions, then the person we hurt is still in pain. No resolution or reconciliation can take place. Without excuse, we need to take responsibility for the pain that we have caused others. Justification of our actions or words does not heal anyone, but continues to cause them pain and may actually encourage them to take further steps on the downward trail to discouragement and hopelessness. The Responsibility or Justification decision, as a measure of reconciliation, is a valid guidepost.

What happens when someone doesn't take responsibility for the hurt they have caused? We then must forgive them, for our sake, even if they continue to justify their behavior and do not acknowledge our pain. God acknowledges our effort to resolve and reconcile. He forgives us, even when they will not accept our apology (Matthew 18:35).

The first steps on the path of healing are the most difficult. It often seems as if we are alleviating those who have hurt us from accountability. We leave vengeance with God, where it belongs. When we are harboring a hurt we are only damaging ourselves, not the person who hurt us.

"That which we do to others, whether it be good or evil, will surely act upon ourselves, in blessing or in cursing... Everyone who has been free to condemn or discourage, will in his own experience be brought over the same ground where he has caused others to pass; he will feel what they have suffered because of his want of sympathy and tenderness" (Thoughts from the Mount of Blessing, p. 136).

Time of Jacob's Trouble

Years ago, at Sanctuary Ranch, in northern British Columbia, we had a "make it right meeting." They were usually held during our Friday night vespers service. We would sing hymns while those who needed to make things right with each other would absent themselves and make things right between them, asking forgiveness. Staff and students alike had been coached by counsels from the Bible and the Spirit of Prophecy about the proper procedure to follow, according to Matthew 19:15. Only public sins were to be confessed to the group. We sensed the Holy Spirit's presence. I recommend this type of meeting to any church who needs the balm of reconciliation. Nothing can be hidden if we expect to gain heaven. We must learn how to give our problems, sins, troubles and trials to Jesus. He is the only one who can solve our problems.

Ahead of us is a time referred to as Jacob's Trouble. During this time, imagine yourself in a group of people awaiting Jesus' return. Your group will probably be located in a remote, uninhabited place or in a prison awaiting the execution of your sentence. You find yourself unconcerned for your own life, but deeply burdened about others around you. You have a deep sense of your own past mistakes that could prevent you from gaining heaven. You wonder if you have made everything right, but you can't remember anything for which you have not made restitution and been forgiven, by others, and by God. You also realize that you have forgiven all those who have mistreated you, whether they have asked for it or not. It is some comfort to realize that your forgiveness may have aided others, unknown to them, in being ready for this great day.

The Great Controversy, p. 620, reveals a picture of people who will be awaiting Jesus' return during the time of Jacob's Trouble. They have been tested severely and yet have not had recent failure. They see only their past weaknesses and they plead with God for deliverance. *"So in the time of trouble, if the people of God had <u>unconfessed sins</u> to appear before them while <u>tortured with fear and anguish</u>, they would be overwhelmed; despair would cut off their faith, and they could not have confidence to plead with God for deliverance. But while they have a deep sense of their unworthiness, <u>they have no concealed wrongs to reveal</u>. Their sins have gone beforehand to judgment, and have been blotted out; and <u>they cannot bring them to remembrance</u>"* (emphasis supplied).

Notice the expressions "unconfessed sins," "while tortured," and then finally, "cannot bring them to remembrance." If they have no unconfessed sins to reveal then they have received forgiveness from God and are healed of their past mistakes. Their past is reconciled and resolved and their abuse of others has been forgiven. As a final step, God has forgiven them, as He has promised in 1 John 1:9

"If we confess our sins, he is faithful and just to forgive us our sins, and to cleanse us from all unrighteousness." Healing is victory.

In the heat of anger, let us remember that if God can give us time and a view of the outcome, we can have victory. Victory is an objective, another viewpoint on the path of healing. It is essential to our survival.

"He that overcometh shall inherit all things; and I will be his God, and he shall be my son" (Revelation 21:7).

Most people feel that anger needs to be responded to immediately. Victory over anger is obtained by thoughtfully focusing on new choices.

Testimonies to Ministers, p. 18; *"He [Jesus] is affecting transformations so amazing that Satan, with all his triumphant boasting, with his confederacy of evil united against God and the laws of His government, stands viewing them* [human hearts] *as a fortress impregnable"* (emphasis supplied). These human hearts have traveled the path of healing.

Psalm 147:3 *"He heals the brokenhearted and binds up their wounds"* (NKJV). From my experience, the path of healing is the same path on which we experience justification and sanctification (growth in the Christian walk). It is the same path as conversion and maturation, and it begins in the special sense of our need. Such experiences as acceptance, help, companionship, appreciation, and sorrow for our mistakes are examples of our needs being met. Many there are who jump off the cliff of conviction at only the first step on the path of healing. At that point we may become discouraged by people's comments about our search for something better, or by the denial of others to our request for forgiveness. It may be that they see things another way when we tell them we forgive them for what they did that hurt us. Do not be discouraged. Take courage, press on, even in the atmosphere of the painful reactions of others. Hebrews 13:5, *"I will never leave you nor forsake you."*

Many battles will be fought at or near the edge of this cliff of conviction until we reach one of the most beautiful viewpoints on the trail of healing. It is the scene of forgiveness. Victory is a distance up the trail, but it allows such freedom as we have not yet experienced. We see new colors in our human experiences that we never knew were in the spectrum. Such colors as empathy, calmness, peace, tolerance, forgiveness, are a vivid part of our new rainbow. The victory viewpoint will be over alcohol, drug addictions, anger, cheating, gossip, bitterness, and abuse. No victory is more precious as the one over our past. A destiny emerges into view that we never realized before and how thrilled we are. New colors have been added to our rainbow at the viewpoint of victory but color bands are missing that are still needed.

As we turn back to the trail, we see a sign: "For more colors to add to your rainbow, please move upward." The arrow on the sign points to higher places and other viewpoints of victory. There are people there, and even at this distance we can see that they are on their knees thanking God for their deliverance. Such a scene encourages me to press on, but sadly, as I turn around and look down the trail, many are still at the cliff of convictions, preparing to jump into oblivion rather than risk embarrassment and humiliation that results in conviction. How I wished they would press on. I begin singing, determined to sing until God and I will remember nothing of my past mistakes (Jeremiah 31:34).

"Beloved, now are we the children of God; and it has not been revealed what we shall be, but we know that when He is revealed we shall be like Him, for we shall see Him as He is. And everyone who has this hope in him purifies himself, even as He is pure" (1 John 3:2, 3, NKJV; emphasis supplied).

16

GOD IS LOVE

Love Is Life

When I was in college, a class in genetics was required for a biology major. Our teacher had a knack for getting us to think; he took it for granted that we would understand the basic chemical and physical concepts of cell division, anatomy, and the accompanying physiology. He wanted us to climb to a level above mere recall to the application and interrelationship of the sciences.

One day he challenged us to a thought question, "What is life?" We had just studied how amino acids had been formed in the lab and how the direction of such research was to determine the origin of life and then eventually create it. We knew that we could reduce living cells into the chemical components of life and that the only measurable loss from these cells was water. But if we added water back to this tube of cell parts and chemicals there were no living cells regenerated. Something else had been lost from the living cells that we could not recover in order to make new cells.

What is life? What a question! It has perplexed people for centuries. The answers, if only partial, must exist outside the laboratory. Let's examine a few inspired statements to gain some insight into the nature of life.

"For with thee is the fountain of life: in thy light shall we see light" (Psalm 36:9). As simple as this song sounds, it is very profound; there is no bottom to its pool of thought. The next verse connects thoughts of Psalm 36:9 to the great God of the universe. *"For God is love"* (1 John 4:8). God is the fountain of life. He is love also. Can we not, then, conclude that love is life?

"I am come that they might have life" (John 10:10). Jesus wants us to have life "more abundantly." What is this life? We have already seen that God is life, but has He told us any more?

"Not only is He the originator of all, but He is the life of everything that lives. It is His life that we receive in the sunshine, in the pure, sweet air, in the food which builds up our bodies and sustains our strength. It is by His life that we exist, hour by hour, moment by moment. Except as perverted by sin, all His gifts tend to life, to health and joy" (Education, p. 197; Psalm 36:9, quoted; emphasis supplied).

God keeps us alive moment by moment. This helps to explain why we couldn't just rehydrate or reassemble cells and bring them back to life. Life comes from God in a constant stream.

"He is caring for us every moment; He keeps the living machinery in action; if we were left to run it for one moment, we should die" (Counsels on Diet and Foods, p. 56).

His care is as constant as His love. Satan claimed that he had a better plan. Under the devil's plan, our lives are interrupted. God had to allow "the killer"

17

to demonstrate his plan. But in the end, God's love will triumph, showing His love has always been constant, even in this demonstration of Satan's plan.

"Day by day, hour by hour, minute by minute, God works by His infinite power to keep you alive. It is He who supplies the breath which keeps life in your body. Did God neglect man as man neglects God, what would become of the race?" (<u>Counsels on Stewardship</u>, p. 224).

Aren't you glad that our lives are dependent upon God's love and not our love to each other or even to God?

"Selfishness is death. No organ of the body could live should it confine its service to itself. The heart, failing to send its lifeblood to the hand and the head, would quickly lose its power. As our lifeblood, so is the love of Christ diffused through every part of His mystical body. We are members one of another, <u>and the soul that refuses to impart will perish</u>" (<u>The Desire of Ages</u>, p. 417; emphasis supplied).

Selfishness is the opposite of love. It is death. The word opposite of death is life, so love is life! Our body is an example of how life is sustained by unselfishness. Can't you hear the stomach saying to the legs, "I am keeping all the food because I need it and I might not get any more"? Or the small intestine saying to the rest of the body, after the stomach shared food with it, "I am keeping all the nourishment for myself"? You say, "How ridiculous!" Our selfishness only proves how shortsighted and prone to death we are!

<u>Christ's Object Lessons</u>, page 258, tells the parable of a selfish man who said, *"I will tear down my barns and build greater"* (Luke 12:18-20). Inspired commentary on this verse is, *"In living for self he has rejected that divine love which would have flowed out in mercy to his fellow men. Thus he has rejected life. For God is love, and <u>love is life</u>"* (emphasis supplied).

Love is not obtainable in a test tube from a laboratory yet it is the one ingredient that makes life function. That love from God gives life every day but also "more abundantly." Love is not only life, but healing; and we may experience that healing by connecting with Jesus to become a channel of His love to others. When nothing else will break the barriers, God uses His gift of love through us, as demonstrated in this true story by Melanie Show:

None of us liked to take care of Jessica. She was 18, beautiful, and completely unconscious. Oh, she would cry out when we washed and combed her beautiful long hair. And she would fuss and thrash about in bed from time to time. But that was all. She had lovely eyes, but I could never meet their wordless gaze.

Her story was familiar. She had been in a car accident, was brought to the hospital in comatose condition, and had more or less stayed that way ever since.

At first she couldn't breathe on her own. In that one way she had improved since coming to our unit—she no longer needed the respirator, and her tracheotomy wound was well healed. But she still had casts on both legs from toes to knees. Her jaws were wired together. And she responded to no one.

Jessica used to be a model. I knew that because of the pictures her mother showed me on her infrequent visits. She lived in Jessica's past, unable to grasp the present. Sometimes she would ask whether Jessica's legs couldn't be positioned better, or whether her hair couldn't be arranged differently. But that seemed to be as far as she could come to coping with the now. When the whole family visited, they awkwardly gathered around Jessica's bed or wheelchair, not knowing quite what to do with someone who couldn't talk back. We told them to speak to her as though she could hear and understand, but it never came naturally to them. It really didn't to us, either.

The only person who seemed comfortable with her was Val, a new graduate nurse. She talked to Jessica like the peer she was, braided her hair, discussed the latest fashions and music.

And she sang to her.

Val sang, no matter who her patients were. But we couldn't help thinking her a bit eccentric to sing for Jessica.

Jessica's "progress" was typical. After a few weeks she had to be sent to a nursing home because we could do no more for her. And besides, the hospital needed her bed for someone more acutely ill. It was with some relief that we transferred her and turned our attention to those who could at least mumble to us.

Several months later we received a note from her mother. Prepared for a funeral announcement, we read that Jessica had awakened one day, looked at her mother and said, "I love you." The leg casts had come off, she was learning to walk again, and she was able to eat solid food. We just looked at one another, dumbfounded.

Then her mother wrote us of the day when Jessica was able to go home, although she was still under her doctor's observation. She had to relearn some things, such as history, French, and chemistry. But her mind was alive! She was doing all right!

About then I think we each began praising ourselves for our good care. At least she hadn't had to fight bedsores. We wanted to see her and hear from her own lips how great we'd been.

One day she did pay us a visit. And we learned that Jessica remembered nothing about us or our diligent care: the tube feedings, the hair washings, the every-two-hour turnings, the baths. She didn't remember anything.

Except someone singing.

YOU CAN SURVIVE!

Val's love came through loud and clear, even when Jessica could not respond. God desires for us to respond to His love letters, the truths in His Word. A knowledge, and acceptance, of vital truth is essential to survival. It is a love letter from God. Love, as expressed in singing, created a response in Jessica even when she was in a coma.

The Love of God

The love of God is greater far
Than tongue or pen can ever tell;
It goes beyond the highest star,
And reaches to the lowest hell;
The guilty pair, bowed down with care,
God gave His Son to win;
His erring child He reconciled,
And pardoned from his sin.

O love of God, how rich and pure!
How measureless and strong!
It shall forevermore endure
The saints' and angels' song.

When years of time shall pass away,
And earthly thrones and kingdoms fall,
When men, who here refuse to pray,
On rocks and hills and mountains call,
God's love so sure, shall still endure,
All measureless and strong;
Redeeming grace to Adam's race—
The saints' and angels' song.

Could we with ink the ocean fill,
And were the skies of parchment made,
Were every stalk on earth a quill,
And every man a scribe by trade,
To write the love of God above,
Would drain the ocean dry.
Nor could the scroll contain the whole,
Though stretched from sky to sky.

—by Frederick Lehman

GOD IS LOVE

FOR FURTHER STUDY

Testimonies for the Church, volume 6, page 121

"The Lord wants His people to follow other methods than that of condemning wrong, even though the condemnation be just. He wants us to do something more than to hurl at our adversaries charges that only drive them further from the truth. The work which Christ came to do in our world was not to erect barriers and constantly thrust upon the people the fact that they were wrong."

The Desire of Ages, page 189

"While the very purity of His presence condemned her sin, He had spoken no word of denunciation, but had told her of His grace, that could renew the soul."

The Desire of Ages, page 462

"In His act of pardoning this woman and encouraging her to live a better life, the character of Jesus shines forth in the beauty of perfect righteousness. While He does not palliate sin, nor lessen the sense of guilt, He seeks not to condemn, but to save."

The Desire of Ages, page 808

"Jesus did not overwhelm Thomas with reproach, nor did He enter into controversy with him. He revealed Himself to the doubting one. Thomas had been most unreasonable in dictating the conditions of his faith, but Jesus, by His generous love and consideration, broke down all the barriers. Unbelief is seldom overcome by controversy."

The Ministry of Healing, page 495

"Until the judgment you will never know the influence of a kind, considerate course toward the inconsistent, the unreasonable, the unworthy. When we meet with ingratitude and betrayal of sacred trusts, we are roused to show our contempt or indignation. This the guilty expect; they are prepared for it. But kind forbearance takes them by surprise and often awakens their better impulses and arouses a longing for a nobler life."

Medical Ministry, page 210

"If, after a course of provocation and injustice on their part, you

treat them [the unreasonable, and unworthy] as you would an innocent person, you even take pains to show them special acts of kindness, then you have acted the part of a Christian; and they become surprised and ashamed, and see their course of action and meanness more clearly than if you plainly stated their aggravated acts to rebuke them."

In Heavenly Places, page 290

"We should remember that all make mistakes; even men and women who have had years of experience sometimes err. But God does not cast them off because of their errors; to every erring son and daughter of Adam He gives the privilege of another trial. The true follower of Jesus manifests a Christlike spirit toward his erring brother. Instead of speaking in condemnation, he remembers the words, 'He which converteth the sinner from the error of his way shall save a soul from death, and shall hide a multitude of sins' (James 5:20)."

Testimonies for the Church, volume 5, page 95

"Satan exults over the condition of God's professed people. While many are neglecting their own souls, they eagerly watch for an opportunity to criticize and condemn others. All have defects of character, and it is not hard to find something that jealousy can interpret to their injury. 'Now,' say these self-constituted judges, 'we have facts. We will fasten upon them an accusation from which they cannot clear themselves.' They wait for a fitting opportunity and then produce their bundle of gossip and bring forth their tidbits. ...

"Is there no law of kindness to be observed? Have Christians been authorized of God to criticize and condemn one another? Is it honorable, or even honest, to win from the lips of another, under the guise of friendship, secrets which have been entrusted to him, and then turn the knowledge thus gained to his injury? Is it Christian charity to gather up every floating report, to unearth everything that will cast suspicion on the character of another, and then take delight in using it to injure him? Satan exults when he can defame or wound a follower of Christ. He is 'the accuser of our brethren.' Shall Christians aid him in his work?"

Testimonies for the Church, volume 5, page 169

"Love is unsuspecting, ever placing the most favorable construction upon the motives and acts of others. Love will never needlessly expose the faults of others. It does not listen eagerly to unfavorable reports, but rather seeks to bring to mind some good qualities of the one defamed."

Our High Calling, page 237

"*We must learn to place the best possible construction upon doubtful conduct of others.... If we are ever suspecting evil we are in danger of creating what we allow ourselves to suspect.... We cannot pass along without sometimes having our feelings hurt and our temper tried, but as Christians we must be just as patient, forbearing, humble, and meek as we desire others to be.*"

Our High Calling, page 239

"*There is light in following Jesus, talking of Jesus, loving Jesus, and I will not allow my mind to think or speak ill of my brethren. 'Inasmuch,' said Christ, 'as ye have done it unto one of the least of these my brethren, ye have done it unto me' (Matt. 25:40). I would not feel unkindness or hatred to anyone. I would not be an accuser of my brethren. Satan will try to stir up my mind to do this, but I cannot do it. I will cherish the forgiving Spirit of Jesus.*"

Review and Herald, March 12, 1895

"*He who opens his heart to the suggestions of the enemy, taking in evil surmisings, and cherishing jealousy, frequently misconstrues this evil-mindedness, calling it special foresight, discrimination, or discernment in detecting guilt and fathoming the evil motives of others. He considers that a precious gift has been vouchsafed to him, and he draws apart from the very brethren with whom he should be in harmony; he climbs upon the judgment-seat and shuts his heart against the one he supposes to be in error, as though he himself were above the temptation. Jesus separates from him, and leaves him to walk in the sparks of his own kindling. Let no one among you glory any longer against the truth by declaring that this spirit is a necessary consequence of dealing faithfully with wrongdoers and of standing in defense of the truth. Such wisdom has many admirers, but it is very deceptive and harmful. It does not come from above, but is the fruit of an unregenerated heart. Its originator is Satan himself. <u>Let no accuser of others credit himself with discernment</u>; for in so doing he clothes the attributes of Satan with the garments of righteousness. I call upon you, my brethren, to purify the soul-temple of all these things that defile; for they are roots of bitterness*" (emphasis supplied).

The Upward Look, page 59

"*The presence of Christ's love in the heart will lead to love the very ones who are astray and who are in the wrong.*"

Testimonies to Ministers and Gospel Workers, page 150

"*If a person is in error, be the more kind to him; if you are not cour-teous, you may drive him away from Christ. Let every word you speak, even the tones of your voice, express your interest in, and sympathy for, the souls that are in peril. If you are harsh, denunciatory, and impatient with them, you are doing the work of the enemy.*"

The Spirit of Prophecy, volume 4, pages 337-340

"*As the people of God approach the perils of the last days, Satan holds earnest consultation with his angels as to the most successful plan of overthrowing their faith.... 'We must cause distraction and division. We must destroy their anxiety for their own souls, and lead them to criticize, to judge, and to accuse and condemn one another, and to cherish selfishness and en-mity. For these sins, God banished us from His presence, and all who follow our example will meet a similar fate'*" (emphasis supplied).

Chapter Two

Vital Truth: End Time Events Revealed

"The instruction that was given in the early days of the message is to be held as safe instruction to follow in these its closing days" (<u>Selected Messages</u>, book 1, p. 41).

The story is told about a man who had a beautiful, faithful collie dog named Laddie. The two lived alone at the edge of town in an old shack. The man was drunk most of the time. Laddie would accompany his master to town, many times helping the man return home if he was too inebriated. One day, in a drunken rage, the man decided to kill Laddie. He picked up a club and began swinging it at the dog. Since his coordination was slowed by the alcohol, Laddie was able to sidestep the blows. As the dog thwarted his efforts, the man's anger increased until, finally, he decided to drown Laddie. The man staggered toward the lake and the collie willingly followed, thinking they were going on one of his beloved walks. This time the dog's trust would be severely tested, for the man was leading Laddie to his death.

The man managed to get into the boat with Laddie, and rowed with some difficulty to the middle of the lake where he tied a large weight around the dog's neck and dumped him overboard. Laddie sank rapidly, but worked free of the rope and popped to the surface not far from the boat. Further enraged at yet another failure, the man grabbed an oar, stood up, and swung it at Laddie's head. Missing Laddie, he lost his balance, and fell into the water. Unfortunately, the man could not swim, even when he was sober.

Laddie, sensing trouble, quickly swam to his master, sank his teeth into the collar of his coat and towed him toward the boat. Pulling himself into the boat, the man collapsed and slept off his stupor. Hours later, when he was finally able to row back to shore, head aching, eyes inflamed, he was surprised to see Laddie waiting for him on the shore, wagging his tail. Touched by Laddie's unconditional love, the man wrapped his arms around Laddie's neck and, weeping, cried out, "Oh Laddie, I am so sorry. I am so glad you are still here. Thank you for saving my life!"

Isn't that how it is with us? Though we might try to put Him out of our boat, Jesus is the only way our little craft will make a safe harbor. Though we may try to dethrone Him, He saves us in our time of difficulty. When we most need Him, He is there. It is in reading the stories recorded in the Bible that our trust in His faithfulness is strengthened. Like Laddie, He saves us in spite of the stupor of sin and hatred in our lives.

Has the Bible, God's own collection of stories and letters, been changed in any way so as to weaken its truths for our present generation? Does the Bible, correct in every past prophecy, also forecast a time of trouble before Christ returns to earth? Could it be possible that the Bible also gives us some instructions about how to survive the end times? Our faith will increase as we study this ultimate survival manual–the Bible.

The Validity of the Bible

In 1947 a young Bedouin shepherd boy threw a rock into a cave opening just to see if he could hit it. As the rock fell inside the cave the boy heard the sound of shattering pottery. Curious, he entered the cave, and discovered some large clay pots containing scrolls. He sold some to his relatives, who then sold them to archaeologists, who in turn identified the scrolls as manuscripts that dated back to about AD 70. Coins were also found with the scrolls in the clay pots, identified as being minted about 134-104 BC.

Up to AD 1947 science versus religion debates centered around the question of the origin of the Bible. Hand-copied manuscripts created a host of questions as to whether these copies were flawed with copy errors. Before 1947 the oldest manuscripts were dated AD 900. These were not close enough to the original writings to eliminate the questionings of those who felt the Bible was full of errors. It was these transcriptions, dated AD 900, that were used in the first King James edition of the Bible in AD 1611.

After the discovery of the Dead Sea scrolls, written in AD 70, scientific eyebrows were raised. Quite miraculously, the wording of these ancient translations was almost identical to the Bible we hold in our hands today. They also established the validity of the copies dated AD 900.

In May of 1844, a scholar by the name of Constantin von Tischendorf determined to find more of the ancient scrolls that he knew must exist. Through a series of providences, he discovered additional manuscripts and scrolls at St. Catherine's Monastery at the foot of Mount Sinai. In 1859, on his third visit to St. Catherine's, he found 346 parchments (all in the same handwriting), including all of the Old and New Testaments! The complete Bible! These were discovered to be older than manuscripts used by Tyndale in his Bible, and others who wrote the King James Version in 1611! This discovery at St. Catherine's was named Codex Sinaiticus. It was dated as having been written very early in the Christian era (AD 300-350). This was much earlier than Tyndale's materials, dated AD 900. They also substantiated the scrolls found in the Dead Sea caves.

Comparisons were made between the Codex Sinaiticus, Tyndale's later originals, and the Dead Sea scrolls with the King James Version of the Bible. The conclusions by the scholars indicated that only minute errors existed and that each manuscript read essentially the same. Sir Fredrich Kenjoi in 1939 said, "Our Bible as we have it today, represents as closely as may be the actual words used by the authors of the sacred books" (The Battle for the Book, by David Marshall, p. 74). Soon after 1939, the Dead Sea scrolls further confirmed Sir Fredrich's conclusion. For further study, I recommend David Marshall's book. What a thrilling journey of discovery is portrayed there!

The Essenes meticulously copied the manuscripts that have been handed down as a precious legacy: the Bible we have today. Later, the Mesoretes carried on the same work from around AD 900. The legacy of the 40 men who wrote the original text was protected by these ancient transcribers. The accidental discovery of the Dead Sea scrolls by the Bedouin shepherd boy, coupled with Constantin von Tischendorf's determination to find the manuscripts he knew existed, eventually revealed the validity of the Holy Bible.

Over the centuries, war has been waged over of the Bible. People throughout all ages have either passed God's word along verbally or laboriously copied texts from the original manuscripts. Their efforts have handed down the legacy of the word of God we treasure today.

We discover that the Bible we hold in our hands is the same Word that came to the 40 writers of the 66 books over a span of 1,600 years. But the real confirmation of the Bible is in our own experience. We may find prophecy fulfilled accurately, careful transcriptions from early times, and testimony of God's interaction in men's lives, but the real confirmation is in our own experience with the Bible promises and how God keeps His Word.

Other Sources of Inspired Information on Survival

The Bible is now, and always will be, our only ultimate source and final authority of faith and survival counsel. It is an *a priori* (original) source. It is interesting to discover that the Bible mentions other sources of inspired information.

"Now the acts of David the king, first and last, behold, they are written in the book of Samuel the seer, and in the book of Nathan the prophet, and in the book of Gad the seer" (1 Chronicles 29:29). Two books are mentioned that are not included in the Bible but are inspired and written by two prophets: Nathan and Gad ("seer" is another name for a prophet according to 1 Samuel 9:9). Perhaps these books were not included because we already have the same information in the book of Samuel.

It is of interest that there were at least two books not included in the Bible that were inspired by God and written by prophets and seers. Might God have something more to share with us during the "time of the end" when there will be a "time of trouble" worse than all others in the history of the earth (Daniel 12:1)?

There were also prophetesses: Huldah and Anna. In 2 Kings 22:14 and in Joel 2:28 the Bible mentions that there will be more prophets.

Tests of a Prophet

As I studied, I discovered that the gift of prophecy was granted to God's people of old, to both men and women, and that there will be prophets in the end times. Here are the tests of a true prophet:

1. **Words agree with the Bible:** *"To the law and to the testimony: if they speak not according to this word, it is because there is no light in them"* (Isaiah 8:20). (See also 1 Corinthians 14:37.)

2. **Confesses that Jesus Christ is come in the flesh and is God:** *"Beloved, believe not every spirit, but try the spirits whether they are of God: because many false prophets are gone out into the world. Hereby know ye the Spirit of God: Every spirit that confesseth that Jesus Christ is come in the flesh is of God: and every spirit that confesseth not that Jesus Christ is come in*

the flesh is not of God: and this is that spirit of antichrist, whereof ye have heard that it should come; and even now already is it in the world" (1 John 4:1-3).

3. **Speaks God's words:** *"But the Lord said unto me, Say not, I am a child: for thou shalt go to all that I shall send thee, and whatsoever I command thee thou shalt speak... Then the Lord put forth his hand, and touched my mouth. And the Lord said unto me, Behold, I have put my words in thy mouth"* (Jeremiah 1:7-9).

4. **Is humble:** *"And whosoever shall exalt himself shall be abased; and he that shall humble himself shall be exalted"* (Matthew 23:12).

5. **Reproves sin:** *"Preach the word; be instant in season, out of season; reprove, rebuke, exhort with all longsuffering and doctrine. For the time will come when they will not endure sound doctrine; but after their own lusts shall they heap to themselves teachers, having itching ears; and they shall turn away their ears from the truth, and shall be turned unto fables"* (2 Timothy 4:2-4).

6. **Produces good fruit:** *"Beware of false prophets, which come to you in sheep's clothing, but inwardly they are ravening wolves. Ye shall know them by their fruits. Do men gather grapes of thorns, or figs of thistles? Even so every good tree bringeth forth good fruit; but a corrupt tree bringeth forth evil fruit. A good tree cannot bring forth evil fruit, neither can a corrupt tree bring forth good fruit. Every tree that bringeth not forth good fruit is hewn down, and cast into the fire. Wherefore by their fruits ye shall know them"* (Matthew 7:15-20). (See also Galatians 5:22-24.)

7. **Will receive visions and dreams from the Lord:** *"And he said, Hear now my words: If there be a prophet among you, I the Lord will make myself known unto him in a vision, and will speak unto him in a dream"* (Numbers 12:6).

8. **Has no breath while in vision:** *"And, behold, one like the similitude of the sons of men touched my lips: then I opened my mouth, and spake, and said unto him that stood before me, O my lord, by the vision my sorrows are turned upon me, and I have retained no strength. For how can the servant of this my lord talk with this my lord? for as for me, straightway there remained no strength in me, neither is there breath left in me"* (Daniel 10:16, 17).

9. **Words come to pass:** *"And if thou say in thine heart, How shall we know the word which the Lord hath not spoken? When a prophet speaketh in the name of the Lord, if the thing follow not, nor come to pass, that is the thing which the Lord hath not spoken, but the prophet hath spoken it presumptuously: thou shalt not be afraid of him"* (Deuteronomy 18:21, 22).

"The prophet which prophesieth of peace, when the word of the prophet shall come to pass, then shall the prophet be known, that the Lord hath truly sent him" (Jeremiah 28:9).

10. **Keeps all of God's commandments:** *"Ye shall walk after the Lord your God, and fear him, and keep his commandments, and obey his voice, and ye shall serve him, and cleave unto him"* (Deuteronomy 13:4).

This is a rigorous test, and will eliminate all false prophets and establish the true. The question remains: Does the Bible really forecast that there will be prophets arising in the last days?

"And it shall come to pass afterward, that I will pour out my spirit upon all flesh; and your sons and your daughters shall prophesy, your old men shall dream dreams, your young men shall see visions" (Joel 2:28).

The context of the preceding reference refers to the last days in which we live: *"And also upon the servants and upon the handmaids in those days will I pour out my spirit. And I will shew wonders in the heavens and in the earth, blood, and fire, and pillars of smoke"* (Joel 2:29-31). We will have prophets in the last days.

"Now concerning spiritual gifts, brethren, I would not have you ignorant" (1 Corinthians 12:1). *"God hath set some in the church, first apostles, secondarily prophets, thirdly teachers, after that miracles, then gifts of healings, helps, governments, diversities of tongues"* (verse 28; emphasis supplied).

These verses indicate that God will have prophets in His New Testament church. In fact, God will make the keeping of His commandments and the gift of prophecy, by the Holy Spirit, two special marks of His remnant church.

Revelation 12:17 states, *"And the dragon* [devil] *was wroth with the woman* [true church], *and went to make war with the remnant of her seed, which keep the commandments of God, and have the testimony of Jesus Christ."* What is the testimony of Jesus? Revelation 19:10 answers that question: *"Worship God: for the testimony of Jesus is the spirit of prophecy."* Keeping the commandments of God and having the testimony of Jesus are two special marks for the church that the devil hates. Why? Because they proclaim a message against Satan and encourage the survivors to hang on!

Let's cite an example: Does Mrs. Ellen G. White, wife of James White, one of the founders of the Seventh-day Adventist Church, fit the requirements of a true prophet? The following indicates that she passes the tests of a true prophet.

Characteristics of a Prophet

Test 1: **Words agree with the Bible:** Does she have visions of the truth

30

that agree with the Bible? Comparing her books with the Bible, as we are instructed in Isaiah 8:20, I have not been able to find an instance where her visions disagree with the Bible. She consistently points to the Bible as our source of all truth.

Test 2: **Confesses Jesus:** She affirms over and over that Jesus Christ is God and our only Saviour. (See The Desire of Ages, a book on the life story of Jesus.)

Test 3: **Speaks God's words:** She does speak what God says to her in vision. Much of her writings begin with "I saw," or "I was shown."

Test 4: **Humility:** She prayed that God would keep her humble, and though she never claimed humbleness, she sought the gift and urged it in the lives of others. *"God help us to humble our proud hearts, and bring Jesus into our midst"* (Review and Herald, December 23, 1884).

Test 5: **Reproves sin:** Testimonies for the Church, which Ellen White wrote, are nine volumes of examples of reproof of sin in church members. The ancient prophets all reproved sin. Nathan's relationship with David is one example (2 Samuel 12:1-12).

Test 6: **Produces good fruit:** Spiritual fruit is produced as a result of a conversion experience. Examples will be given in this book regarding the good produced by her work. Even the world now recognizes the value of her counsels. And the fruits were evident in her personal life.

Test 7: **Will have visions from God:** (See Early Writings, pages 13 and 14). There were witnesses to this at her first vision.

Test 8: **Has no breath while in vision:** She had many visions during which she had no breath. *"Then Ellen came and sat down by me. She was in vision one and a half hours, in which time she did not breathe at all"* (Life Sketches, p. 112).

Test 9: **The word of the prophet comes to pass:** Here are a few examples that have not only come to pass, but when heeded produced a better quality of life. Paul Harvey, national commentator for ABC News, refers to these fulfillments from the pen of Ellen White. Many of these statements were written by Mrs. White while the followers of modern medicine were still practicing bloodletting and performing surgery with unwashed hands.

Over 100 years ago she wrote: *"Tobacco is a slow, insidious, but most malignant poison"* (Ministry of Healing, p. 327). Today, we have volumes of evidence supporting her early testimony.

She wrote: *"Grains, fruits, nuts, and vegetables constitute the diet chosen for us by our Creator"* (Counsels on Diet and Foods, p. 81). Today we know that we should eat at the base of the food pyramid for health reasons.

She wrote: *"From the standpoint of health the smoke and dust of the cities are very objectionable"* (Testimonies for the Church, vol. 7, p. 82). Air pollution is found to be linked to respiratory disease.

She wrote: *"Both the blood and fat of animals are consumed as a luxury. But the Lord gave special directions that these should not be eaten"* (Counsels on Diet and Foods, p. 393). A diet high in fat is now known to cause obesity, heart disease, and many other complications. Ellen has written so much information on this subject that booklets are now available from the E. G. White Estate that itemize her fulfilled prophecies. Many statements are also available from the medical community addressing the dangers of eating animal fat.

Test 10: **Keeps all of God's commandments:** Ellen White advocated keeping all 10 commandments. *"He demands obedience to all of His commandments"* (Manuscript Releases, vol. 10, p. 102).

The impressive thought remains: although she has written so much that has been fulfilled, what about those things she wrote that have not been fulfilled? What about those things that have been forecast to happen in the future? Because past prophecies have been fulfilled the ones for the future will too.

In the last 11 chapters of her book, The Great Controversy, she wrote that severe weather disasters are coming. This will lead to spiritual intolerance of large groups against those who wish to worship on Sabbath. There will be pressure to appease the perceived wrath of God:

"In accidents and calamities by sea and by land, in great conflagrations, in fierce tornadoes and terrific hailstorms, in tempests, floods, cyclones, tidal waves, and earthquakes, in every place and in a thousand forms, Satan is exercising his power. He sweeps away the ripening harvest, and famine and distress follow. ... These visitations are to become more and more frequent and disastrous. ... It will be declared that men are offending God by the violation of the Sunday sabbath; that this sin has brought calamities which will not cease until Sunday observance shall be strictly enforced; and that those who present the claims of the fourth commandment, thus destroying reverence for Sunday, are troublers of the people, preventing their restoration to divine favor and temporal prosperity" (The Great Controversy, p. 590).

To be ready for these times spiritual and practical preparations are essential. *"Some of us have had time to get the truth and to advance step by step, and every step we have taken has given us strength to take the next. But now time is almost finished, and what we have been years learning, they will have to learn in a few months. They* [new converts] *will also have much to unlearn and much to learn again"* (Early Writings, p. 67).

The Testimony of Jesus: Safe Instruction

Wouldn't it be wonderful to have assurances that the Spirit of Prophecy by Ellen White is an inspired commentary on the Bible? Harmony between inspired writings is one mark of the remnant church (see Revelation 12:17). The Bible is made up mostly of the testimony of Jesus. Isaiah 8:20 says, *"To the law and to the testimony: if they speak not according to this word, it is because there is no light in them."* This text divides inspired writings into two parts; that which is written by God directly, such as His law, in Exodus 20:2-17 (the Ten Commandments), and those portions of inspiration that are written by man by visions from God (testimonies).

Psalm 93:5 states, *"Thy testimonies are very sure,"* and Psalm 19:7 says that *"the law of the Lord is perfect, converting the soul: the testimony of the Lord is sure, making wise the simple."* If we follow inspired information we are promised wisdom so that we will not be deceived and we will survive. Second Chronicles 20:20 says it all: *"Believe in the Lord your God, so shall ye be established; believe his prophets, so shall ye prosper."* In John 14:16, 17, Jesus promises a comforter: *"And I will pray the Father, and he shall send you another Comforter, that he may abide with you forever; even the Spirit of truth."* This Comforter, the Holy Spirit, has come and has given us all the gifts in 1 Corinthians 12, including the gift of prophecy.

One question still lingers: Were these laws and testimonies done away with after they were written or do they apply to our time? Are these counsels written for our day or are they for another day? The Bible indicates that they are relevant for our day.

Paul puts it this way, *"Now all these things happened unto them for ensamples: and they are written for our admonition, upon whom the ends of the world are come"* (1 Corinthians 10:11). This verse assures us that what was written so long ago was written specifically for those of us who live at the end of time. In the writings of Ellen White, note the agreement with Scripture on this point and how she amplifies the classic principle of "truth for all time."

"The instruction that was given in the early days of the message is to be held as safe instruction to follow in these its closing days" (Selected Messages, book 1, p. 41).

"Satan will work ingeniously, in different ways and through different agencies, to unsettle the confidence of God's remnant people in the true testimony.... Satan cannot have so clear a track to bring in his deceptions and bind up souls in his delusions if the warnings and reproofs and counsels of the Spirit of God are heeded" (ibid. p. 48).

"All our health institutions, all our publishing houses, all our institutions of learning, are to be conducted more and more in accordance with

the instruction that has been given" (Counsels to Parents, Teachers, and Students, p. 57; emphasis supplied).

Our survival will not depend upon our genius, our carefully laid plans, or how well we can sidestep disaster. Our survival will depend on our obedience to God's counsels.

Special Creation

We have verified the validity of the Bible by its ancient manuscripts and by our own experience. We can experience this validity in our own lives by claiming more of its promises. As we experience the Bible in our hearts let us see what it says about the origin of life and the life-style he wants us to live.

Colossians 1:16 says, *"For by him were all things created, that are in heaven, and that are in earth, visible and invisible, whether they be thrones, or dominions, or principalities, or powers: All things were created by him, and for him."*

Genesis 1:1 backs this simple declaration of God's creative power. *"In the beginning God created the heavens and the earth."*

The Bible states that God created everything. This flies in the face of evolution. Evolution claims to have science behind its tenets, but the truth is that special creation is strongly supported by scientific evidence. (Origin by Design, Harold Coffin) The concepts of creation are also supported by the word of God and the complexity of nature.

A farmer and a scientist were walking in the farmer's field. As they talked a discussion came up about how life began. The scientist waxed eloquent about the biochemical ooze that with time generated human beings. Presently they came to a cross fence in the field. As they were climbing through the fence the farmer, though profoundly impressed by the scientist, had a question.

"How did this fence get here?" He asked.

"Well," said the scientist emphatically, "You or somebody probably built it."

"Why do you say that?" asked the farmer. "If I give it enough time won't it build itself?"

The scientist got the point. A fence is a relatively simple structure yet it required a design, while we who are so totally complex, allegedly happened by accident. The Psalmist says, *"I will praise thee; for I am fearfully and wonder-fully made: marvelous are thy works; and that my soul knoweth right well"* (Psalm 139:14).

There are prominent world leaders in religion who believe the origin of life is by a gradual process. We must know for ourselves what is truth. We should anchor our faith in Scripture and let scientific evidence add to but not be the soul support of our faith. Be careful to sort speculation and opinion from evidence when reading scientific literature.

I find it comforting to know that I have a Designer and Creator who has a great destiny planned for me. The Bible, inspired by God, gives great pictures of this inheritance. We will build the temple of our lives on the foundation of belief in God as a Creator. Going back to the gospel of John we find that the Creator is Jesus.

"All things were made by him" (John 1:3).

This Jesus is described by Matthew, chapter 1 verse 21, when He was born in Bethlehem, *"...And you shall call His name Jesus, for He will save His people from their sins."* Sin has killed us, but He came to save our lives. Now we have the knowledge that he has created and rescued us. This is the basis of thankfulness that leads to a religion (relationship) in God.

We find He created the garden in Eden, Genesis 2:8, *"The Lord God planted a garden eastward in Eden, and there He put man whom he had formed."* Verse 15 mentions the basis for a simple life-style that was given to man for all time, *"Then the Lord God took the man and put him in the Garden of Eden to tend and keep it."*

Finally, the Bible says that He created all things in six literal, 24 hour days. Genesis 1:5, 8, 13, 19, 23, and 31 all say that the evening and the morning composed each day of creation. The Bible's original language indicates a literal 24 hour day.

Something special happened on the seventh day as a result of His creation. Genesis 2:2, 3, *"And on the seventh day God ended His work which He had done, and rested on the seventh day. Then God blessed the seventh day and sanctified it, because in it He rested from all His work which God created and made."* The Bible tells us that this day is the Sabbath that we should keep because it was the day God took time to appreciate His work. If God blessed the Sabbath then there is in it a special blessing for us.

In my counseling practice, a client came in who said he just dreaded doing anything for his wife. When the job was finished he wanted to take time to enjoy the work he had done and be appreciated for it, but as soon as one job was finished, she wanted to move onto the next with no time to appreciate previous accomplishments.

Even God needed time to appreciate His work and we should take time to appreciate His work, our successes, and lessons learned during the week. It is essential that we rest and worship on the day He blessed. Then we will get the blessing He promised. This blessing is guaranteed in the Ten Commandments in Exodus 20:8-11, and Isaiah 56:1 and 2. Because there is a great blessing in keeping the Sabbath, the adversary was anxious that the blessing not be realized by God's people. He began to contest this by persecuting those who kept it. This climaxes in Revelation 13 with a "no buy-no sell" and a death decree. Thus special creation becomes the foundation of our belief in a Creator-Redeemer and the resolution of the final issues of this world's history.

"Fear God and give glory to Him, for the hour of His judgment has come; and worship Him who made heaven and earth, the sea and springs of water" (Revelation 14:7; emphasis supplied). Creation is an issue in final apocalyptic events. Worship is also contested in these closing days of earth's history. In order to worship Him who made heaven and earth we will need to be loyal to the day of worship that He blessed at creation.

The devil will oppose this truth with counterfeits that will be forced upon the conscience. This sets the stage in opposition to the plain statements of Scripture.

The Day of Rest

The more we use the Scripture as our guide to survival, the more confidence we will have in the truths contained in the Bible. We will begin to understand that God, the Creator, provided for His creation. He provided the earth and all the things therein that we, His crowning act of Creation, might know Him. Included in these gifts was the Sabbath, a special day that God set aside for communion with His children. The day of worship we observe will play a vital role in identifying the remnant who keep the commandments of God.

Did God really bless one particular day of the week above another?

"Thus the heavens and the earth were finished, and all the host of them. And on the seventh day God ended his work which he had made; and he rested on the seventh day from all his work which he had made. And God blessed the seventh day, and sanctified it: because that in it he had rested from all his work which God created and made" (Genesis 2:1-3; emphasis supplied). Other versions of the Bible use the terms "holy" and "set apart" as a synonym of "blessed."

Moving on through the Old Testament we find that God directed Israel and her prophets to keep the Sabbath long before He wrote the law in stone for Moses on Mount Sinai. While leading them in the wilderness, God reminded the children of Israel to keep the Sabbath by giving them a double portion of manna on the sixth day and withholding it on the seventh.

"And it came to pass, that on the sixth day they gathered twice as much bread.... This is that which the Lord hath said, Tomorrow is the rest of the holy sabbath.... Six days ye shall gather it; but on the seventh day, which is the sabbath, in it there shall be none" (Exodus 16:22-26). God wanted them

to rest and worship on the Sabbath as a special sign that His people loved Him and were thinking of Him.

At Sinai, God gave them a special token that would help them remember the Sabbath when they were no longer in the wilderness. Among the Ten Commandments, given to Moses on two tables of stone, was the fourth, in which God asked us to remember the Sabbath day: *"Remember the sabbath day, to keep it holy. Six days shalt thou labour, and do all thy work: but the seventh day is the sabbath of the Lord thy God: in it thou shalt not do any work.... For in six days the Lord made heaven and earth, the sea, and all that in them is, and rested the seventh day: wherefore the Lord blessed the sabbath day and hallowed it"* (Exodus 20:8-11).

Some Christians feel that the ten commandment law was repealed, but even those who subscribe to that theory are keeping the other nine! Jesus says that He kept the Law in Matthew 5:17, 18: *"Think not that I am come to destroy the law, or the prophets: I am not come to destroy, but to fulfill. For verily I say unto you, Till heaven and earth pass, one jot or one tittle shall in no wise pass from the law, till all be fulfilled."* James 2:10, 11 speaks about breaking even one law in the Ten Commandments, *"For whosoever shall keep the whole law, and yet offend in one point, he is guilty of all. For he that said, Do not commit adultery, said also, Do not kill."*

If we violate one of the commandments we are guilty of violating all of them. This scripture in James, mentions two of the Ten Commandments law, adultery and killing. Jesus said that He did not come to do away with the law; so who did?

Who Changed the Sabbath?

Someone changed the Sabbath from the seventh day to another day. The Roman Catholic Church will not deny having changed the seventh-day Sabbath to Sunday, calling the first day of the week "The Lord's Day" on their own authority. Though admitting no scriptural authority for such a change, the Catholic church says it was a command from Christ. The rest of Christendom followed her lead and "Protestants" also began keeping Sunday as their day of worship. A recent declaration by the Catholic Church leaves no doubt as to this claim.

"Perhaps the boldest thing, the most revolutionary change the Church ever did, happened in the first century [actually it happened in the fourth century] the holy day, the Sabbath, was changed from Saturday to Sunday. 'The Day of the Lord' [Dies Domini] was chosen, not from any direction noted in the Scriptures, but from the church's sense of its own power.... People who think the Scripture should be the sole authority, should logically become [Seventh-day] Adventists, and keep Saturday holy" (Saint Catherine Catholic Church Sentinel,

Algonac, Michigan, May 21, 1995). (See also The Apostolic Letter Dies Domini, by Pope John Paul II, pp. 17, 27, 34, 55, 75.)

What day is the true Sabbath? Can it be confused with any other day? Let's look at Luke 23:52-24:2: *"This man went unto Pilate, and begged the body of Jesus. And he took it down, and wrapped it in linen, and laid it in a sepulchre that was hewn in stone, wherein never man before was laid. And that day was the preparation, and the sabbath drew on. And the women also, which came with him from Galilee, followed after, and beheld the sepulchre, and how his body was laid. And they returned, and prepared spices and ointments; and rested the sabbath day according to the commandment. Now upon the first day of the week, very early in the morning, they came unto the sepulchre, bringing the spices which they had prepared, and certain others with them. And they found the stone rolled away from the sepulchre"* (emphasis supplied).

Notice that the preparation day is mentioned, just as when Israel gathered manna, only now, it is in the New Testament among Jesus' followers. Jesus has just been crucified and is in the grave. You would think that He would have told them of any change of worship day, but He did not. The only evidence of change of the Ten commandments was by the Roman Church. (Samuele Bacchiocchi, Ph.D., From Sabbath to Sunday [Pontifical Gregorian University Press, Rome, 1977]).

The day after the preparation day was the Sabbath on which they rested according to the commandment. The seventh-day Sabbath was kept by His followers after Jesus' death.

On the first day of the week (Luke 24:1), the stone was rolled away. Thank God for that empty tomb! We all know what day that was, don't we? It was Easter Sunday! So all we have to do is look at the day before Easter Sunday. It was Saturday! And the day before that was the preparation day, Friday. So the Bible is very clear about which day His disciples honored as the Sabbath: the seventh day! The day before Sunday!

Did this day of worship continue through the New Testament? Read Acts 13:42, 44; 16:13; 17:2; and 18:4. The apostles met on the Sabbath many times.

Will the Sabbath be important in heaven? Yes. Isaiah 66:22, 23: *"For as the new heavens and the new earth, which I will make, shall remain before me, saith the Lord, so shall your seed and your name remain. And it shall come to pass, that from one new moon to another, and from one sabbath to another, shall all flesh come to worship before me, saith the Lord."*

Satan will make the Sabbath a point of controversy to try to destroy the blessing of that special day and establish his own day of worship. We must choose the sign of loyalty to God or choose the false sabbath. This will set the stage for the last scenes of history on earth. Our eternal survival depends upon our allegiance to God's will!

The Sunday Law

In planning and praying for survival, we should take a look at the future from the prophets' viewpoint. Joseph could plan for survival in Egypt 3,000 years ago because God gave him a prophet's view of what was coming.

Let's take a look at Revelation 13:15-17, especially verse 16. There the scripture refers to *"a mark"* given by the beast to allow people to buy and sell (verse 17). Further, it says that people who do not have this mark, and thereby worship the beast, will be killed. *"And he had power to give life unto the image of the beast, that the image of the beast should both speak, and cause that as many as would not worship the image of the beast should be killed. And he causeth all, both small and great, rich and poor, free and bond, to receive a mark in their right hand, or in their foreheads: and that no man might buy or sell, save he that had the mark, or the name of the beast, or the number of his name."*

We need to know the meaning of this mark. The Bible reveals that the issue surrounding the mark involves worship. If I don't worship the beast, then I will be killed. If I do worship the beast, then God counts me as disloyal to Him (Revelation 14:9-11), and I will lose eternal life.

Verse 12 says that we should keep the commandments of God. Is it possible that the issue could be over the Ten Commandments? If I am faithful and I know the issue, I can make my decision now. *"Those who would not receive the mark of the beast and his image when the decree goes forth, must have decision now to say, Nay, we will not regard the institution of the beast"* (Early Writings, p. 67; emphasis supplied).

One of the final acts in the great controversy between God and Satan is the arrival of the mark of the beast. Revelation 13:15 and 17 mentions that those who do not worship the beast or his image will be killed. Using modern language, I would say it this way; "If I don't worship the way these beasts dictate, I will be killed or cut off from doing business for my livelihood. I will not be able to buy or sell, hence, I will need to grow my own food to survive. But if I receive the mark from the beast and his image, I can perform my business as usual."

On page 36 we learned that the last-day issues for Christendom involves a dispute over the proper day of worship. Those who wish to take their stand on the side of literal interpretation of Bible truth will face the fierceness of the wrath of the beast. The beast, in turn, will face the wrath of God. God says to remember His Sabbath; others say the day has been changed. Those who follow God's truths, keeping His Sabbath will be saved eternally. *"And I saw as it were a sea of glass mingled with fire: and them that had gotten the victory over the beast, and over his image, and over his mark, and over the number of his name, stand on the sea of glass, having the harps of God"* (Revelation 15:2). For further study about this victory, I recommend: Sunday Is Coming, by G Edward Reid and the King James version of Revelation.

The enforcement of worship by the beast will involve a union of church and state, with the church urging the state to enforce its dogmas. It may seem improbable, in light of all the current legislation aimed at religious tolerance, that a religious law could be enacted, but Sunday laws have existed for years. There were Sunday laws in the 13 Colonies. There was one in the 1890s in the United States when people were fined and jailed if they violated the Sunday worship day. (See The Great Second Advent Movement, by J. N. Loughborough, pp. 451- 452.) Eventually, before the end of time, those laws will again be enforced by death (see Revelation 13:15).

What will make church and state unite to legislate a Sunday Law and violate freedom of worship? The Great Controversy states the answer clearly, *"In accidents and calamities by sea and by land, in great conflagrations, in fierce tornadoes and terrific hailstorms, in tempests, floods, cyclones, tidal waves, and earthquakes, in every place and in a thousand forms, Satan is exercising his power. He sweeps away the ripening harvest, and famine and distress follow. He imparts to the air a deadly taint, and thousands perish by the pestilence. These visitations are to become more and more frequent and disastrous...*

"Then the great deceiver will persuade men that those who serve God are causing these evils. The class that have provoked the displeasure of Heaven will charge all their troubles upon those whose obedience to God's commandments is a perpetual reproof to transgressors. It will be declared that men are offending God by the violation of the Sunday sabbath; that this sin has brought calamities which will not cease until Sunday observance shall be strictly enforced; and that those who present the claims of the fourth commandment, thus destroying reverence for Sunday, are troublers of the people, preventing their restoration to divine favor and temporal prosperity" (pp. 589- 590; emphasis supplied).

"Although church and state will unite their power to compel, 'all, both small and great, rich and poor, free and bond' (Rev. 13:16) *to receive 'the mark of the beast,' yet the people of God will not receive it"* (ibid. p. 450).

The remnant of true believers will refuse to pay homage to the false sabbath.

Church and State

The history of the Christian Church from the late 1100s to the landing of the pilgrim fathers on North American soil, reveals many examples of injustices that occurred during the control of the state by the church. The experience of the Waldenses, the martyrdom of millions during the middle ages, and the fines and imprisonment of early colonists of different faiths by the Pilgrim church, demonstrate irrefutably that the church is blindly cruel when it has the power of the state to enforce its wishes. (For further study I recommend the book, The Great Controversy, by E. G. White.)

As we examine the religious politics of the thirteen original colonies in early American history, we find the Pilgrim fathers in control. Laws were made to enforce their beliefs. It is interesting to note that the reason these Pilgrim/Puritan people came to America was to have religious freedom and to flee persecutors of their faith in England. It was soon revealed that they were unwilling to grant these same freedoms to others of different faiths.

Soon after they arrived, laws were enacted that restricted religious freedom. One such law required people to be church members in order to have a voice in civil government. A state church was formed and all people were required to contribute to the support of the clergy regardless of the fact that some beliefs were different. Another law required all people to attend Puritan church services under penalty of fine or imprisonment.

When Roger Williams came to America, he too sought religious freedom. He was a Puritan minister and highly respected by his church and its parishioners. He had a much more tolerant attitude toward those who differed with him in spiritual matters. In fact, he believed that this tolerance was the recognition of an inalienable right to worship God according to the dictates of one's conscience. His own faith was not threatened by others of different beliefs. He may have disagreed with their views, but he would defend their right to have them.

The Puritan elders could not tolerate such a belief as freedom of conscience and banished him from the colonies. He was forced to flee to the wilderness in the winter. This could have been a death sentence but for the providence of God on behalf of His servant. For 14 weeks Williams wandered in the forest suffering greatly from cold and hunger until an Indian tribe took care of him. They had benefited from his previous ministry and it was with affection that they provided him food and shelter. Many members of the tribe had become Christians through his ministry.

After his stay with the Indians he made his way to the shores of Narragansett Bay and formed a colony that he named Rhode Island where freedom of conscience would be a God-given right. Williams was the first person in modern times that established a civil government on the idea of liberty of conscience and the equality of opinions. Roger Williams' ideas on freedom spread through Europe and others came to America seeking religious liberty. This freedom granted in Rhode Island attracted the oppressed and those yearning to be free. It had a profound influence on the other colonies and they too became bastions of spiritual freedom. This principle was at last to be incorporated into the Declaration of Independence and the U. S. Constitution. These words still stir the hearts of all those who are thankful for religious liberty and freedom of conscience.

"We hold these truths to be self-evident, that all men are created equal; that they are endowed with certain inalienable rights; that among these are life, liberty and the pursuit of happiness. ...No religious test shall be required as a qualification of office of public trust under the United States." This is what made America great in the eyes of God.

"The Lord has done more for the United States than for any other country upon which the sun shines. Here he provided asylum for his people, where they could worship Him according to the dictates of conscience. God designed that this country should ever remain free for all people to worship Him in accordance with the dictates of conscience. He designed that its civil institutions in their expansive productions should represent the freedom of gospel privilege" (Maranatha, p. 193).

Other countries followed this example and they too became great. Some did not, and the results were devastating to the conscience.

"Thus again was demonstrated the evil results, so often witnessed in the history of the church from the days of Constantine to the present, of attempting to build up the church by the aid of the state, of appealing to the secular power in support of the gospel of Him who declared, 'My kingdom is not of this world,' John 18:36" (The Great Controversy, p. 297).

A Word from the Pope

Pope Pius IX, in his Encyclical Letter of August 15, 1854 said, *"The absurd and erroneous doctrines or ravings in defense of liberty of conscience, are a most pestilential error—a pest of all others most to be dreaded in the state. ...As Rome asserts that the church never erred; nor will it, according to the Scriptures, ever err, how can she renounce the principles which governed her course in past ages"* (The Great Controversy, p. 564).

We need to understand what the beast of Revelation 13 represents. To be able to cooperate with God's plan in maintaining liberty of conscience is a privilege. It is not without risks, or the possibility of persecution, but here is a cause to which we can give our life. The smile of Jesus will be upon us. It's a matter of survival.

Christians First

Who are the first to be tested on the mark of the beast and asked to accept it? What is the consequence of accepting this mark? When people accept the mark, can they change their mind? These questions relate directly to our survival. Our eternal destiny depends upon our understanding of the importance of the answers to these questions.

Ezekiel 9:4-6 reads, *"And the Lord said unto him, Go through the midst of the city, through the midst of Jerusalem, and set a mark upon the foreheads of the men that sigh and that cry for all the abominations that be done in the midst thereof. And to the others he said in mine hearing, Go ye after him through the city, and smite: let not your eye spare, neither have ye pity: slay utterly old and young, both maids, and little children, and women: but come not near any man upon whom is the mark; and begin at my sanctuary. Then they began at the ancient men which were before the house."*

The judgments of God will begin at the church. In Testimonies for the Church, volume 5, page 211, this issue is made very clear. *"Here we see that the church— the Lord's sanctuary—was the first to feel the stroke of the wrath of God."*

Peter explains how God's judgments begin with the house of God—His church. First Peter 4:17: *"For the time is come that judgment must begin at the house of God: and if it first begin at us, what shall the end be of them that obey not the gospel of God?"*

Ellen White comments on Revelation 13:14-17, explaining how God's people will be first to close their probation. *"The Lord has shown me clearly that the image to the beast will be formed before probation closes: for it is to be the great test for the people of God, by which their eternal destiny will be decided"* (Seventh-day Adventist Bible Commentary, vol. 7, p. 976; emphasis supplied). Notice that the people of God (the church) will make their final decision first, while probation is open for the rest of the world.

"The 'image to the beast' represents the form of apostate Protestantism which will be developed when the Protestant churches will seek the aid of the civil power for the enforcement of their dogmas" (The Great Controversy, p. 445).

Probation is closed for those who have already rejected the light, while the hand of mercy is still extended to those who have not yet heard and understood the truth of the issues involved. Clearly, there are two groups explained in Testimonies for the Church, volume 9, page 97: *"The time of God's destructive judgments is the time of mercy for those who have had no opportunity to learn what is the truth. Tenderly will the Lord look upon them. His heart of mercy is touched; His hand is still stretched out to save, while the door is* _closed_ to those who would not enter" (emphasis supplied).

"But I speak not my own words when I say that God's Spirit will pass by those who have had their day of test and opportunity, but who have not distinguished the voice of God or appreciated the movings of His Spirit. Then thousands in the eleventh hour will see and acknowledge the truth. 'Behold, the days come, saith the Lord, that the plowman shall overtake the reaper; and the treader of grapes him that soweth seed' (Amos 9:13)" (Selected Messages, book 2, p. 16).

Clearly, Christians will face eternal decisions before the rest of the world.

The Seal of God

When we neglect God's call in preparing for the Lord's return, succumbing to the pleasures of the world without remorse, we shall be left without the seal of God.

"The class who do not feel grieved over their own spiritual declension, nor mourn over the sins of others, will be left without the seal of God" (Testimonies for the Church, vol. 5, p. 211).

"Those who have in their foreheads the seal of the infinite God will regard the world and its attractions as subordinate to eternal interests" (Seventh-day Adventist Bible Commentary, Ellen G. White Comments, vol. 7, p. 978).

"The seal of the living God is placed upon those who conscientiously keep the Sabbath of the Lord. ... It is a life and death question" (ibid. p. 980).

"Sundaykeeping is not yet the mark of the beast, and will not be until the decree goes forth causing men to worship this idol sabbath. The time will come when this day will be the test, but that time has not come yet" (ibid. p. 977; emphasis supplied).

"When the test comes, it will be clearly shown what the mark of the beast is. It is the keeping of Sunday" (ibid. p. 980).

"John was called to behold a people distinct from those who worship the beast and his image by keeping the first day of the week. The observance of this day is the mark of the beast" (ibid. p. 979).

If we are greatly surprised by the Sunday law, we will not have as much preparation time as those who have lived for and loved the true Sabbath. But when the decision comes to us, our survival depends upon our loyalty to the Sabbath truth. God will then have a people ready to help others at the eleventh hour.

The Remnant People, Who are They?

The Bible refers to the remnant in both the Old and the New Testament and each time it represents people who are loyal to God and His plan for their lives. In Isaiah 1:9 a remnant is mentioned whose influence deferred God's judgments. In chapter 11, verse 11 gives evidence that God's protecting care is over the remnant. The remnant will know that God's Word will guide them through their experience. Joel 2:32 states that the remnant is a group of people who will be called to do a special work in the end times. Paul says that there is a remnant who choose the grace of God (Romans 11:4, 5) while the apostle John wrote in Revelation 11:13 about how the remnant gave glory to God for their safety in times of trouble.

The remnant of Revelation 11 is mentioned again in Revelation 12 as having two identifying characteristics (verse 17). This remnant is the last one on this earth. It is a remnant of which we all will want to be a part. We will be welcomed to this remnant because we have a love of the truth as expressed in the commandments of God and the testimony of Jesus. While the commandments are found in Exodus 20, Jesus told us that the foundation of these ten precepts is love to God and love to fellow man (Matthew 29:37-40).

The testimony of Jesus is identified in Revelation 19:10 as the Spirit of Prophecy. Those people who keep the commandments and have the Spirit of Prophecy are the remnant of Revelation 12:17 to whom the devil is violently opposed. God is inviting us to be a member of this remnant group. All He needs is our decision and then He will empower us to be faithful.

"War is coming against the remnant because they keep the commandments of God and have the testimony of Jesus. ... Don't yield your sacred peculiarities which distinguish you from the world, from the nominal church and backslidden Adventists. ..." (<u>Manuscript Releases</u>, vol. 5, p. 290).

The promise of God is sure, *"Now unto him that is able to keep you from falling and to present you faultless before the presence of his glory with exceeding joy,"* (Jude 24)

Time of "No Buy-No Sell" Prophesied

In Revelation 13:16, 17 an economic embargo in conjunction with the mark of the beast is prophesied against God's people before the end. *"And he causeth all, both small and great, rich and poor, free and bond, to receive a mark in their right hand, or in their foreheads: and that no man might buy or sell, save he that had the mark, or the name of the beast, or the number of his name."* Notice the clause *"that no man might buy or sell."* This refers to a time when, if we compromise with the world and receive the mark of the beast, we will be able to buy and sell. If we don't compromise, then we will receive the seal of God, and not be able to buy and sell.

It would be helpful to know the sequence of events leading to this embargo against the remnant (see the Closing Events chart in back of this book). As the Sunday law is enacted, enforcement is mild at first. For Sundaybreaking, referred to as violating "Blue Laws," fines are administered, then imprisonment, inducements, "no buy-no sell," and finally the death decree.

Enforcement of the national Sunday law will occur. *"As the movement for Sunday <u>enforcement</u> becomes more bold and decided, the law will be invoked against commandment keepers. They will be threatened with <u>fines</u> and <u>imprisonment</u>, and some will be offered positions of influence, and other rewards and advantages, as <u>inducements</u> to renounce their faith. But their steadfast answer is: 'Show us from the word of God our error,' the same plea that was made by Luther under similar circumstances"* (<u>The Great Contro-versy</u>, p. 607; emphasis supplied).

Severity of Sunday law enforcement will increase. *"Fearful is the issue to which the world is to be brought. The powers of earth, uniting to war against the commandments of God, will decree that <u>no man may buy or sell</u>, save he that has the mark of the beast, and, finally, that whoever refuses to receive the mark shall be put to <u>death</u>"* (<u>The Spirit of Prophecy</u>, vol. 4, p. 422; emphasis supplied).

"No buy-no sell" occurs before the enforcement of the death decree and before the seven last plagues begin to fall. *"I saw that the four angels would hold the four winds until <u>Jesus' work was done in the sanctuary</u>, and then will come the seven last plagues. These plagues enraged the wicked against the righteous; they thought that we had brought the judgments of God upon them, and that if they could rid the earth of us, the plagues would then be stayed. A decree went forth to slay the saints, which caused them to cry day and night for deliverance"* (<u>Early Writings</u>, pp. 36, 37).

Because the death decree occurs at the final close of probation, then the time for "no buy-no sell" is in the latter end of the probationary time; that is, probation is still open and God's merciful hand is still extended.

During this time we will need to be in the country or have a friend that has an outpost; a place where we will be able to grow food, etc. Far better to heed the instruction now and plan for what is ahead. It is a matter of survival. Remember Lot and Abraham; Abraham already had a farm, but Lot waited and left the city at the last minute, barely surviving. Some of his family didn't make it.

Have you thought about what it will mean not to be able to buy or sell anything and experience "no money" living? We will have no money to pay utilities, buy gasoline, pay insurance, or purchase food. We can't sell anything to earn money either. It will be too late to sell, and we cannot spend! We will have to have alternate systems for our families, friends, and others who come out to live with us. No need to have a paying job. Money is of no use to us.

This next reference further explains how the Sunday law is more severely enforced at the time of the "no buy-no sell." It is safe to trust God when it appears that we will have to sever all our earthly supports.

"'Man shall not live by bread alone, but by every word of God.' Often the follower of Christ is brought where he cannot serve God and carry forward his worldly enterprises. Perhaps it appears that <u>obedience to some plain requirement of God will cut off his means of support</u>. Satan would make him believe that he must sacrifice his conscientious convictions. But the only thing in our world upon which we can rely is the word of God. 'Seek ye first the kingdom of God, and his righteousness; and all these things will be added unto you' (Matthew 6:33). *Even in this life it is not for our good to depart from the will of our Father in heaven. When we learn the power of His word, we shall not follow the suggestions of Satan in order <u>to obtain food</u> or to save our lives. Our only questions will be, What is God's command? and what His promise? Knowing these, we shall obey one, and trust the other* (this counsel is repeated in <u>Prophets and Kings</u>, p. 184).

"In the last great conflict of the controversy with Satan those who are <u>loyal to God will see every earthly support cut off</u>. Because they refuse to break His law in obedience to earthly powers, <u>they will be forbidden to buy and sell</u>. It will <u>finally be decreed that they shall be put to death</u>. But to the obedient is given the promise, 'He shall dwell on high: his place of defense shall be the munitions of the rocks: bread shall be given him; his waters shall be sure' (Isaiah 33:16). *By this promise the children of God will live.... They shall not be ashamed in the evil time; <u>and in the days of famine they shall be satisfied</u>* (Psalm 37:19)" (<u>The Desire of Ages</u>, pp. 121, 122; emphasis supplied).

As in all else, God has a plan. We have the opportunity to prepare now by moving to the country. *"Again and again the Lord has instructed that our people are to take their families away from the cities, into the country, where they can raise their own provisions; for in the future the problem of <u>buying and selling will be a very serious one</u>"* (<u>Country Living</u>, pp. 9, 10; emphasis supplied).

"It is no time now for God's people to be fixing their affections or laying up treasure in the world. The time is not far distant, when, like the early disciples, we shall be forced to seek a refuge in desolate and solitary places. As the siege of Jerusalem by the Roman armies was the signal for flight to the Judean Christians, so the assumption of power on the part of our nation in the decree <u>enforcing</u> the papal sabbath will be a warning to us. It will then be time to leave the large cities, preparatory to leaving the smaller

ones for <u>retired homes in secluded places among the mountains</u>" (<u>Testimonies for the Church</u>, vol. 5, p. 464; emphasis supplied).

When the death decree is first enforced, it is the last opportunity to flee. While in flight, we will be dependent on God because we cannot then grow our own food. This is the time we claim the promise in Isaiah 33:16, which tells us that our bread and water will be sure, even when we are in the most desolate places. We need to make haste to get all things ready for the coming crisis (see <u>Country Living</u>, p. 21).

Do the Dead Reappear?

Another common deception of the day put forward in religious groups and in the entertainment media is the belief that the dead exist as spirit forms. It is natural to have questions about "ghosts." The belief that when we die we go to heaven, purgatory, or come back to haunt and advise people is false according to the Scripture. Satan will try to threaten our spiritual survival by assuming we will listen to his deceptions if we hear them from the lips of deceased loved ones.

Can the dead return to communicate with the living? Job 7:9, 10: *"As the cloud is consumed and vanisheth away: so he that goeth down to the grave <u>shall come up no more</u>. He shall return no more to his house, neither shall his place know him any more."* It is a good practice, in Bible study, to line up two or more texts on the same topic. Even though one scripture is very plain, a better position can be secured when more than one text is cited. On this subject, two more texts follow: Ecclesiastes 9:5, 6: *"For the living know that they shall die: but <u>the dead know not any thing</u>, neither have they any more a reward; for the memory of them is forgotten. Also their love, and their hatred, and their envy, is now perished; neither have they any more a portion for ever in any thing that is done under the sun."*

Psalm 146:4: *"His breath goeth forth, he returneth to his earth; in that very day his thoughts perish."*

In the light of these scriptures, it is clear that when we die we remain in the grave. According to 1 Thessalonians 4:14-18, we remain in the grave until Christ's return. *"For if we believe that Jesus died and rose again, even so them also which sleep in Jesus will God bring with him. For this we say unto you by the word of the Lord, that we which are alive and remain unto the coming of the Lord shall not prevent them which are asleep."*

Can we assume that Satan is the source for the appearances of dead people to those who are yet living? There are many reports of spirit apparitions giving counsel to the living, but the Lord calls these familiar spirits abominations. Deuteronomy 18:10-12: *"There shall not be found among you any one that maketh his son or* *his daughter to pass through fire, or that useth divination, or an observer of times, or an enchanter, or a witch, or a charmer, or <u>a consulter with familiar spirits</u>, or a wizard, or <u>a necromancer</u>* [magic, communication with the dead]. *For all that do these things are an abomination unto the Lord: and because of these abominations the Lord thy God doth drive them out from before thee."* The NIV states that "familiar spirits" means "consults the dead," just as the word <u>necromancer</u> refers to communication with the dead.

It seems clear from the Scripture that those who consult with "spirits of the dead" are not in harmony with God and that the spirits are not from God, however consoling or wise they may appear. What these spirits say to us would not be counsel from God and should be rejected as originating with the evil one. Ecclesiastes 9:10: *"For there is no work, nor device, nor knowledge, nor wisdom, in the grave, whither thou goest."*

Secret Rapture

The belief in a secret rapture has been accepted by various churches. It states that at some future time Jesus will select worthy people and take them suddenly from their workplace, home, or places of recreation. He may take pilots from airliners, or drivers from cars, so suddenly and secretly that the airplanes crash and the cars run off the road. Books have been written and movies made that describe the results of such a secret rapture.

Will Christians escape the time of trouble by being raptured? The Bible does not mention the word rapture nor does it support the idea of a secret exiting of God's people from the earth. The concept of a secret rapture, as usually presented, is said to occur before Jesus' second coming. The Scripture is clear that the Lord comes back to get His people, not secretly or separately.

"For the Lord Himself will descend from heaven with a <u>shout</u>, with the <u>voice of an archangel</u>, and with the <u>trumpet</u> of God. And the <u>dead in Christ will rise first</u>. Then <u>we who are alive</u> and remain shall <u>be caught up together with them</u> in the clouds to meet the Lord in the air. And thus we shall always be with the Lord. Therefore <u>comfort one another with these words</u>" (1 Thessalonians 4:16-18 [NKJV]; emphasis supplied).

Paul here refers to a shout, the voice of an archangel, the trumpet of God—powerful non-secretive ways of declaring His coming. Notice the two groups who meet Him are the resurrected ones and those who are alive; no one else will be going to heaven to be with the Jesus. The Scripture says to comfort one another with this hope. We must not confuse this hope for to do so is to lose it, and

49

be out of step with Jesus.

Concerning the wicked the Scripture is clear about them as well. *"And then shall that Wicked be revealed whom the Lord shall consume with the Spirit of His mouth and shall destroy with the brightness of His coming."* (2 Thessalonians 2:8). The righteous people are with Jesus as they meet in the air while the wicked are destroyed by the non-secret brightness of His coming. Revelation 1:7 says *"Behold He is coming with clouds and <u>every eye shall see Him</u>."* Matthew 24:27; *"For as the lightning comes from the east and flashes to the west so also will the coming of the Son of Man be"* (NKJV). These Scriptures all refer to a very obvious second coming.

Second Peter 3:10 is used by some who believe in the rapture, *"But the day of the Lord will come as a thief in the night, in which the heavens will pass away with a great noise and the elements will melt with fervent heat; both the earth and the works that are in it will be burned up."*

This cannot be a secret appearing of Jesus through rapture, or any other coming, because there is a great noise and the elements are melting. His coming as a thief is **not secret** as a thief but as the **surprise** of a thief.

The text in Matthew 24:40 is also used to support the idea of a secret rapture. This Scripture, in context, states that it is the surprise of Christ's return and not the secrecy of it that is important. The verses from 36-44 emphasize the suddenness and unexpected nature of the second coming. This idea of a secret rapture must be measured by the Scripture so that we are not deceived. Since the rapture does not exist, it would be eternally fatal not to be prepared.

Psalm 50:3, *"Our Lord shall come, and shall not keep silence."*

Martyrs for Jesus Are Survivors

"In all ages Satan has persecuted the people of God. He has tortured them and put them to death, but, in dying they became conquerors.... He could incarcerate in prison walls, but he could not bind the spirit. They could look beyond the gloom to the glory.... Through trials and persecution, the glory—character—of God is revealed in His chosen ones" (<u>Thoughts From the Mount of Blessing</u>, pp. 30, 31).

I love, so much, a paragraph on page 7 from the preface to <u>Martyr's Mirror</u>, by Thielman J. Von Braght, an account of the experiences of martyrs from the days of Christ until 1660.

"Many of them [martyrs] would not have exchanged the darkest and severest dungeons, or the caves of the earth, in which they had to hide themselves, for royal palaces. The wilderness to them was a delightful pleasure garden, the howling of wild beasts which surrounded them, as sweet music or the songs of birds; and water and roots or dry bread delighted them more than the daintiest viands and drink from the tables of the great." These faithful ones are true survivors—they survived the ultimate test; making a gift of their lives to God.

The dictionary definition of a martyr is a "person who chooses to suffer death rather than to renounce his convictions." When studying the subject of martyrs, we need to remember there are other people who die for the wrong cause and lose eternal life. It is imperative that if we are martyred, that we die for Jesus and His word, not for an opinion or mistaken interpretation. John 16:2: *"They shall put you out of the synagogues: yea, the time cometh, that whosoever killeth you will think that he doeth God service."*

There have been martyrs through all past ages. Able was the first martyr. Will martyrdom continue right up until Christ returns?

Observe this scene in heaven where all those who have survived from all ages are gathered: *"Nearest the throne are those who were once zealous in the cause of Satan, but who, plucked as brands from the burning, have followed the Saviour with deep, intense devotion. Next are those who perfected Christian characters in the midst of falsehood and infidelity, those who honored the law of God when the Christian world declared it void, and the millions of all ages who were martyred for their faith"* (The Great Controversy, p. 665). Notice it says "all ages." Would this "all ages" include the last days?

"When this grand work is to take place in the battle, prior to the last closing conflict, many will be imprisoned, many will flee for their lives from cities and towns, and many will be martyrs for Christ's sake in standing in defense of the truth" (Maranatha, p. 199; emphasis supplied). Yes, there will be martyrs in the last days.

You may say, "I could never be a martyr. I hate confrontation, pain, and suffering. How will I ever survive?" The disciples were also tempted along these lines: *"The disciples were not endowed with the courage and fortitude of the martyrs until such grace was needed"* (The Desire of Ages, p. 354; emphasis supplied). **You will have the courage when you need it!**

Let us consider what it is going to take to survive the onslaught ahead of us as Christians. *"Those who would rather die than perform a wrong act are the only ones who will be found faithful"* (Testimonies for the Church, vol. 5, p. 53; emphasis supplied).

Part of what made the Dark Ages so dark was the persecution. We are now part of a society who prides itself in its religious freedom. How could the fires

YOU CAN SURVIVE!

of persecution be rekindled? The answer is found in The Great Controversy, page 48: *"There is another and more important question that should engage the attention of the churches of today. The apostle Paul declares that 'all that live godly in Christ Jesus shall suffer persecution' (2 Tim. 3:12). Why is it, then, that persecution seems in a great degree to slumber? The only reason is that the church has conformed to the world's standard and therefore awakens no opposition. The religion which is current in our day is not of the pure and holy character that marked the Christian faith in the days of Christ and His apostles. It is only because of the spirit of compromise with sin, because the great truths of the word of God are so indifferently regarded, because there is so little vital godliness in the church, that Christianity is apparently so popular with the world. Let there be a revival of the faith and power of the early church, and the spirit of persecution will be revived, and the fires of persecution will be rekindled"* (emphasis supplied).

But there will be no martyrdom **after** the close of probation. *"If the blood of Christ's faithful witnesses were shed at this time, it would not, like the blood of the martyrs, be as seed sown to yield a harvest for God. Their fidelity would not be a testimony to convince others of the truth; for the obdurate heart has beaten back the waves of mercy until they return no more. If the righteous were now left to fall a prey to their enemies, it would be a triumph for the prince of darkness"* (The Great Controversy, p. 634).

The witness of martyrdom will serve no purpose when every person has made a final decision. Then the promise in Isaiah 33:16 will apply: *"Bread shall be given him; his waters shall be sure."* We will no longer, on this premillennial earth, raise our own provisions or build our houses even with no money. "No buy-no sell" is past and the death decree has been enforced. We will flee for our lives or be in prison awaiting Christ's return. *"After Jesus rises up from the mediatorial throne, every case will be decided, and oppression and death coming to God's people will not then be a testimony in favor of the truth"* (Selected Messages, book 3, p. 399).

"God would not suffer the wicked to destroy those who were expecting translation and who would not bow to the decree of the beast or receive his mark" (Early Writings, p. 284).

In vision, Ellen White observed a chosen few in heaven whose robes were edged in red. When she asked Jesus who this company was *"He said they were martyrs that had been slain for Him. With them was an innumerable company of little ones; they also had a hem of red on their garments"* (ibid. p. 19).

The following song, The Border of Red, was written by my friend Warren Wilson, who was intrigued by Ellen White's reference regarding the hem of red.

52

VITAL TRUTH

The Border of Red

There's a border of red on his garment,
His robe is a glistening white;
He lives on a street that's called holy,
His star-studded crown glitters bright;
He walks with the ransomed of ages,
Beloved of all Heaven, it's said;
Why is he so honored in Heaven?
Tell me, why is the border of red?

He was slain in the valleys of Piedmont,
Killed at the door of his home,
And pursued o'er the Waldensian mountains
To be slain by the legions of Rome.
Despised for his simple religion,
For Jesus he suffered and bled,
And now he will wear through the ages
The robe with the border of red.

He was found in the cruel Inquisition,
Slain with his Bible in hand,
He was dragged through the streets of the city
And burned for his heresy grand.
Condemned to the rack and the dungeon,
By torture his lifeblood they shed,
And now he will wear through the ages
A robe with a border of red.

He was hated, despised, and tormented,
Wandering, an outcast from men,
Oh, the fires will soon be rekindled
And martyrs will die once again!
By faith you may live to see Jesus,
And watch as He wakens the dead,
Or maybe you'll wear through the ages
The robe with the border of red.

—*Warren C. Wilson*

"Christ will restore the life taken; for He is the Life-giver: He will beautify the righteous with immortal life" (Maranatha, p. 199).

Righteousness by Faith

Whether we are called by God to endure the last days of time or are laid to rest before Jesus' return, the covering of Christ's righteousness is essential. In a special way, as God's wrath is poured out in plagues, the remnant will receive protection. The acceptance of the blood-bought gift of righteousness offered by Jesus to replace our unworthiness is a major pillar of spiritual survival. Paul has some of the best discussion on this diamond of truth. Romans 5:1 says, *"Therefore being justified by faith, we have peace with God through our Lord Jesus Christ."* Being justified by faith is the first step in Christian growth and preparation for survival. This is all made possible by Christ Jesus, according to Romans 8:1. Think about it! You are justified when you accept Jesus.

Some of us tend to confuse this special gift with indulgence rather than the discipline required for survival. We allow ourselves to continue in sin while supposing to enjoy the covering of Christ's righteousness. In The Desire of Ages, pages 555, 556, we read, *"No repentance is genuine that does not work reformation. The righteousness of Christ is not a cloak to cover unconfessed and unforsaken sin; it is a principle of life that transforms the character and controls the conduct. Holiness is wholeness for God; it is the entire surrender of heart and life to the indwelling of the principles of heaven"* (emphasis supplied).

"The righteousness of Christ will not cover one cherished sin" (Christ's Object Lessons, p. 316).

A reference that integrates much of the Bible comments on the conditions of acceptance of righteousness by faith is found in the August 28, 1894, Review and Herald, and reads as follows, *"It is not the grace of Christ that makes void the law of God. Christ declared, 'I have kept my Father's commandments, and abide in his love.' To those who are making void the commandments of God, the True Witness says, 'I counsel thee to buy of me gold tried in the fire, that thou mayest be rich; and white raiment, that thou mayest be clothed, and that the shame of thy nakedness do not appear.' Christ's white robe of righteousness will never cover any soul that is found in sin unrepented of and unforsaken. 'Sin is the transgression of the law.' Therefore those who are trampling upon the law of God, and teaching others to disregard its precepts, will not be clothed with the righteousness of Christ"* (emphasis supplied).

This covering of Christ's righteousness is referred to in the context of the last days in Early Writings, page 44. How necessary it is that we have this covering for survival? *"I saw that Satan was at work in these ways to distract, deceive, and draw away God's people, just now in this sealing time. I saw some who were not standing stiffly for present truth. Their knees were trembling, and their feet sliding, because they were not firmly planted on the truth, and the covering of Almighty God could not be drawn over them while they were thus trembling.*

"Satan was trying his every art to hold them where they were, until the sealing was past, until the covering was drawn over God's people, and they left without a shelter from the burning wrath of God, in the seven last plagues. God has begun to draw this covering over His people, and it will soon be drawn over all who are to have a shelter in the day of slaughter. God will work in power for His people" (emphasis supplied).

Romans 6:1, 2 says, *"What shall we say then? Shall we continue in sin, that grace may abound? God forbid. How shall we, that are dead to sin, live any longer therein?"* To be honest in heart with God is the essence of survival in these last days. First Corinthians 15:57 says that God has made it possible for us to have victory through Christ. *"But thanks be to God, which giveth us the victory through our Lord Jesus Christ."* Jude 24, 25 reemphasizes this: *"Now unto him that is able to keep you from falling, and to present you faultless before the presence of his glory with exceeding joy, to the only wise God our Saviour, be glory and majesty, dominion and power, both now and forever, Amen."* Jesus can keep us from falling!

"We may be clothed with the righteousness of Christ, but His righteousness will not be a covering for the least iniquity" (Signs of the Times, July 29, 1889, p. 12). For an excellent synopsis of present truth on this subject that is entirely Bible-based, I refer you to Seventh-day Adventists Believe (Review and Herald Publishing Association, HAGERSTOWN, Maryland).

To be committed enough to accept this gift and to allow God to work in our lives is a struggle. It is a struggle because of our nature and our choices. Notice this reference from Signs of the Times: *"But many of you say, 'I have prayed, I have tried, I have struggled, and I do not see that I advance one step.' What is the trouble? Have you not thought you were earning something, that you were by your struggles and works paying the price of your redemption? This you can never do. Christ has paid the price of your redemption. There is only one thing that you can do, and that is to take the gift of God. If you feel that you are poverty-stricken in spirit, you can come in all your need, and plead the merits of a crucified and risen Saviour. But you cannot come expecting that Christ will cover your wickedness, cover your indulgence in sin, with His robe of righteousness. He has come to save His people from their sins. The people of God are to be as branches grafted into the living Vine, to be partakers of the nature of the Vine. If you are a living branch of the True Vine, Jesus will prove you by affliction, that you may bring forth fruit more abundantly"* (May 9, 1892; emphasis supplied).

Early Writings, page 47, outlines the struggle we will have with the bitter cup given us in the last days. *"God has shown me that He gave His people a bitter cup to drink, to purify and cleanse them. It is a bitter draught, and they can make it still more bitter by murmuring, complaining, and repining. But those who receive it thus must have another draught, for the first does not have its designed effect upon the heart. And if the second does not effect the work, then they must have another, and another, until it does have its designed effect, or they will be left filthy, impure in heart. I saw that this bitter cup can be sweetened by patience, endurance, and prayer, and that it will have its designed effect upon the hearts of those who thus receive it, and God will be honored and glorified"* (emphasis supplied).

In order to survive, we will have to practice patience and endurance. This promise assures us of growth: *"Patience is a plant that will make rapid growth if carefully cultivated"* (My Life Today, p. 97).

Selected Messages, book 1, page 363, says, *"If you would stand through the time of trouble, you must know Christ, and appropriate the gift of His righteousness, which He imputes to the repentant sinner."* Without Christ's gift of righteousness, no one can stand. This covering is described in Early Writings, page 44. It is only through Christ and His grace that the last-day ark will survive the flood of evil and the disasters to come.

God promises our survival. *"He is watching those who are climbing, ready, when the grasp relaxes and the steps falter, to send help. Yes, tell it in words full of cheer, that no one who perseveringly climbs the ladder will fail of gaining an entrance into the heavenly city"* (Messages to Young People, p. 95; emphasis supplied).

We are guaranteed survival, if we overcome and endure to the end. *"And ye shall be hated of all men for my name's sake: but he that endureth to the end shall be saved"* (Matthew 10:22).

The Sanctuary Message

God's love is shown very graphically in the sanctuary. God made a request that His people build Him a sanctuary. Exodus 25:8: *"And let them make me a sanctuary; that I may dwell among them."* I think of friends that I enjoy being close to. I want them with me. This is the way God felt. He wanted to be closer to those He loved. He wanted to show them how He was hurting over the sins that caused separation.

Psalm 77:13: *"Thy way, O God, is in the sanctuary: who is so great a God as our God?"* Besides being with His people, He wanted them to see what the sin problem cost and how valuable people are to Him.

The typical or ancient sanctuary service involved offerings for sin given by the people who had hurt God and each other. By giving these sacrifices (lambs without defects), God thought that His people would understand to the depth of their souls the agony that sin had brought to Him. He wanted also to let us know that the Lamb of God was coming to atone forever and for all the sins torturing God.

When the Baptist said in powerful witness, *"Behold the Lamb of God, which taketh away the sin of the world"* (John 1:29), he was announcing that the great Lamb was now here to replace the animal sacrifices. God was saying through John that He was giving His Son for man and that man was as valuable as His own Son! *"Thou hast loved them, as thou hast loved me"* (John 17:23).

What need have we to ever place a low value on ourselves? God was willing to give Himself for man, valuing man as high as His own Son. A King died in our place after being hurt for thousands of years. If we can hasten His coming (see chapter 17, "Hastening Our Lord's Return"), then we can stop the Father's suffering, the Son's suffering, the angels' suffering, and our suffering. We were so valuable to God, that in the face of the high cost to Himself, He paid! He wants us in fellowship with Him, freed from the disease of sin. *"I will come again, and receive you unto myself"* (John 14:3).

How important is it for us to understand our worth? It is the difference between surviving or not.

"All need to become more intelligent in regard to the work of the atonement, which is going on in the sanctuary above. When this grand truth is seen and understood, those who hold it will work in harmony with Christ to prepare a people to stand in the great day of God, and their efforts will be successful. By study, contemplation, and prayer God's people will be elevated above common, earthly thoughts and feelings, and will be brought into harmony with Christ and His great work of cleansing the sanctuary above from the sins of the people. Their faith will go with Him into the sanctuary, and the worshipers on earth will be carefully reviewing their lives and comparing their characters with the great standard of righteousness. They will see their own defects; they will also see that they must have the aid of the Spirit of God if they would become qualified for the great and solemn work for this time which is laid upon God's ambassadors" (Testimonies for the Church, vol. 5, p. 575; emphasis supplied).

God wants us to understand and appreciate His work in the sanctuary, and by doing so we will be ready for the crisis times ahead. When Israel made the sanctuary on earth according to God's specific instructions, God came and manifested His presence as the Shekinah glory.

"The Lord commanded Moses.... So Moses finished the work. Then a cloud covered the tent of the congregation, and the glory of the Lord filled

the tabernacle" (Exodus 40:32-34).

Just like Noah's ark, the sanctuary was built as God specified and His blessing was placed upon it. If we do not follow God's plan, then we cannot expect our plans to receive God's blessing. This is vitally important to all of our preparation for end time events. Receiving God's blessing is the difference between success or misery and failure.

"Behold, I set before you this day a blessing and a curse; a blessing, if ye obey the commandments of the Lord your God, which I command you this day: and a curse, if ye will not obey the commandments of the Lord your God, but turn aside out of the way which I command you this day, to go after other gods, which ye have not known" (Deuteronomy 11:26, 27).

The sanctuary on earth during Biblical times was composed of three parts. A courtyard immediately surrounded the sanctuary. Inside this beautiful building was a first compartment called the Holy Place and in the second compartment, the Most Holy Place. These two compartments were separated by a beautiful curtain, or veil.

The sacrifices were made in the courtyard and the blood was ministered in the Holy Place on a daily basis for forgiveness of sins. But once a year this typical service was replaced by ministry in the Day of Atonement. The ministry of the first compartment provided for forgiveness and symbolic separation of sin from the sinner. The death of the lamb and its blood mediated the transfer of sin from the penitent to the sanctuary's Holy Place.

On the Day of Atonement sins were separated from the sanctuary and placed on the head of a scapegoat. The people fasted and prayed for victory as they were forever separated from their past sins. This was called the cleansing of the sanctuary. Only the high priest ministered on this day.

In the antitypical service in heaven, which was the pattern for services (typical) on earth (Hebrews 8:5 and 9:23), no sacrifice could be found except Jesus (Hebrews 8:1 and 7:25). So He is the one that we should honor. He is the one that saved us! He became the Sacrifice and the Priest of His own life. The cross of Jesus was antitypical to the altar of burnt offering and was the place of agony. A place where the innocent died for the guilty at the hand of the guilty.

"The cross is a revelation to our dull senses of the pain that, from its very inception, sin has brought to the heart of God" (Education, p. 263). God wanted us to feel with Him the truth of the cost of sin. This brings true victory.

While carrying a vase for a potter, Ed dropped and broke it. In his generosity, Ed offered to pay him $20 to replace it. The potter's head dropped and tears filled his eyes. Ed was surprised at the potter's behavior. Hadn't he gone the second mile by offering more than the vase was worth? The potter then explained, "I made the vase in a class I attended. My instructor said that it was the best he had ever seen and asked if he could have permission to show it in a gallery. A man came along and offered me $2,500 for it. I told the man 'No, I want to keep it because my teacher said it was good.'"

We will never gain the victory over sin until we know the cost. Even with our best guess we underestimate the cost of a soul to Jesus.

"It's impossible to bring back to repentance those who have fallen away from Christ if they reject Him and continue to mock the Christian faith. By doing this, they're crucifying Christ all over again and holding Him up to public shame" (Hebrews 6:6, The Clear Word). When we sin Jesus pays the price again; we crucify Him afresh. Since Jesus is our high priest and makes intercession for us in the heavenly sanctuary (Hebrews 7:25-27), we can pray effectively.

The cleansing of the sanctuary marked the Day of Atonement, and, in 1844, was a sign that showed the time of the end. This work of Jesus during our Day of Atonement is very important to Him, and He wants it to be important to us. Daniel 8:14 states, *"Unto two thousand and three hundred days; then shall the sanctuary be cleansed."*

I invite you to study this important subject for your own spiritual joy. Jesus' way is in the sanctuary! He wants us to survive by Him and in Him. For the best study on this subject, see Exodus 25-40, Leviticus 1-6, the book of Hebrews, Christ In His Sanctuary, by Ellen White, and chapter 16 of this book.

The Heavenly Sanctuary and the Intercession of Jesus

A few years ago I was challenged by a learned theologian to consider that the sanctuary in heaven does not exist, that the intercession of Jesus was not necessary or in existence, and that everything needed for man's salvation was completed at the cross. For many years I had believed that there was a sanctuary in heaven and that Jesus was interceding for us there. I believed it because that was how I was taught. Now, I was faced with establishing this truth or rejecting it for myself. This experience of research was a very great blessing to me and I recommend it to all who have accepted traditional thoughts without examination.

My search began with the Bible in Exodus 25:8 where Moses was asked by God to build a sanctuary on earth. *"And let them make me a sanctuary; that I may dwell among them."* The next verse says that God showed him a pattern that he was to follow in the construction of this earthly sanctuary.

"According to all that I show you, that is, the pattern of the taber-

nacle... " (Exodus 25:40, NKJV). It goes on to list all of the furniture of the sanctuary including the ark, candlestick, censor, table of shewbread and the altar.

Hebrews 8:5 repeats that Moses followed a pattern. *"Who served unto the example and shadow of heavenly things, as Moses was admonished of God when he was about to make the tabernacle: for, See, saith he, that thou make all things according to <u>the pattern showed thee in the mount</u>."*

"It was therefore necessary that the patterns of things in heaven... For Christ is not entered into the holy places made with hands which are the figures of the true; but into heaven itself, now to appear in the presence of God for us" (Hebrews 9:23-24).

If the patterns of the earthly sanctuary are in heaven, then there is a sanctuary in heaven from which Moses' pattern was derived.

In Revelation 11:19 John saw the ark of the testament. In Revelation 1:12 the candlestick was also seen by him. In Revelation 8:3 the altar and censor were observed. This is more evidence that there is a sanctuary in heaven.

Jesus' intercession is mentioned in Hebrews 7:25, *"<u>Wherefore He was able to save them to the uttermost that come unto God by Him, seeing He ever liveth to make intercession for them</u>."*

Romans 8:34 emphasizes the great love manifested in Jesus' intercession, *"Who is he that condemns? It is Christ that died, yea rather, that is risen again, who is even at the right hand of God, who also makes intercession for us."*

The Spirit of Prophecy is a master artist in painting word pictures of the work of the Father and the Son in the sanctuary in heaven. *"<u>The intercession of Christ in man's behalf in the sanctuary above is as essential as His death on the cross</u>"* (The Great Controversy, p. 489; emphasis supplied).

In this reference, Christ is interceding for us in the heavenly sanctuary. This reference answers two questions; 1) is there a heavenly sanctuary? and 2) does Jesus intercede for us? But, did you notice that this intercessory work for us is as important as His death on the cross? That really says something, doesn't it? The devil is attacking, using well-meaning, well-educated people, to dislodge the anchors of our faith in the ministry of Christ and the existence of the heavenly sanctuary.

Selected Messages, book 2, p. 170, states it another way, *"The perfect work of Christ was consummated in His death upon the cross. In <u>His sacrifice and His intercession</u> at the right hand of the Father <u>is our only hope of salvation</u>"* (emphasis supplied).

To just have the sacrifice is not enough, we must have both the blood of

VITAL TRUTH

Jesus at the cross and the intercession of His death as our only hope. Let's thank God for such work and not let it be undermined by anyone.

This statement puts it all in a grand panorama and builds a solid foundation for the temple of our faith. *"The Scripture which above all others had been both the foundation and central pillar of the Advent faith was the declaration, 'Unto two thousand and three hundred days; then shall the sanctuary be cleansed"* (The Great Controversy, p. 409). This sanctuary that was to be cleansed at the end of this great prophetic period is the heavenly sanctuary and the beginning of the great day of atonement.

"Now this is the main point of the things we are saying: we have such a High Priest, who is seated at the right hand of the throne of the Majesty in the heavens a minister of the sanctuary and of the true tabernacle which the Lord erected and not man" (Hebrews 8:1, 2 NKJV).

"Here [Hebrews 8:1, 2 quoted] is revealed the sanctuary of the new covenant, The sanctuary of the first covenant was pitched by man, built by Moses; this is pitched by the Lord, not man. In that sanctuary the earthly priests performed their service; in this, Christ our great High Priest ministers at God's right hand. One sanctuary was on earth, the other in heaven" (The Great Controversy, p. 413).

"The sanctuary in heaven, in which Jesus ministers in our behalf, is the great original, of which the sanctuary built by Moses was a copy" (The Great Controversy, p. 414).

While I was studying this subject a miracle began to happen in my heart. The ministry of Jesus is not just an event but an experience that we, by faith, can enter into with Him and even listening to what He is saying on our behalf. Early Writings, page 55, *"He [Jesus] stepped into the chariot and was borne to the holiest, where the Father sat.... Those who rose up with Jesus would send up their faith to Him in the holiest, and pray, 'My Father, give us Thy spirit.' Then Jesus would breathe upon them the Holy Ghost."* How clear that Jesus is receiving our prayers in the most holy place of the heavenly sanctuary and that our faith goes up to Him there. In that act of faith we receive the Holy Spirit. The devil would wish us not to have this experience. We must determine not to let Satan have his way and that the Holy Spirit may be received by us, by faith, in the Most Holy Place of the heavenly sanctuary.

"I saw the incense in the censor smoke as Jesus offered their confessions and prayer to the Father. And as it ascended a bright light rested upon Jesus and upon the mercy seat; and the earnest praying ones who were troubled because they had discovered themselves to be transgressors of God's law, were blessed,

and their countenances lighted up with hope and joy" (Early Writings, page 256)

As I studied, I saw why this intercession of Jesus' sacrifice was our only hope. The question arose: "What does Jesus say to the Father?" [John 17] *"This chapter contains the intercessory prayer offered by Christ to His Father just before His trial and crucifixion. This prayer is a lesson regarding the intercession that the Saviour would carry on within the veil when His great sacrifice in behalf of men, the offering of himself, should have been completed. Our mediator gave his disciples this illustration of His ministration in the heavenly sanctuary in behalf of all who will come to Him in meekness and humility, emptied of all selfishness, and believing in His power to save"* (The Seventh-day Adventist Bible Commentary, Ellen G. White Comments, vol. 5, p. 1145; emphasis supplied).

This great prayer of Jesus in the seventeenth chapter of John is His prayer for our unity. He is also praying that we will not be of the world. Verse 14, *"I have given them my word; and the world hath hated them, because they are not of the world, even as I am not of the world."* To be not of the world is not to follow worldly policies in our lives, in our families, or in our churches and schools.

Just how great is this chapter? *"God's family on earth have many lessons to learn in order to answer the prayer of Christ—His last prayer with His disciples before His humiliation. The seventeenth chapter of John, which contains this prayer, comprehends more than any other chapter in the New Testament"* (Spalding-Magan Collection, p. 387; emphasis supplied). I have often thought that the other chapters in the New Testament might be more significant but not so, according to inspiration. This intercessory prayer by Jesus in our behalf, before the Father for unity and separation from the world comprehends more than any other chapter of the New Testament.

"Christ has not a casual interest in us but an interest stronger than a mother for her child. ...Our Saviour has purchased us by human suffering and sorrow, by insult, reproach, abuse, mockery, rejection and death. He is watching over you, trembling child of God. He will make you secure under His protection. ...Our weakness in human nature will not bar our access to the heavenly Father, for He [Christ] died to make intercession for us" (Sons and Daughters of God, p. 77; emphasis supplied).

Preparation

The Bible is insistent regarding the necessity of preparation for the coming crisis. Note how, in 1 Corinthians 14:8-10, there is an emphasis not only on preparation but also on doing the right kind of preparation; *"For if the trumpet give an uncertain sound, who shall prepare himself to the battle? So likewise ye, except ye utter by the tongue words easy to be understood, how shall it be known what is spoken? for ye shall speak into the air. There are, it may be, so many kinds of voices in the world, and none of them is without signification."*

"Be thou prepared, and prepare for thyself, thou, and all thy company that are assembled unto thee, and be thou a guard unto them (Ezekiel 38:7).

The testimony of Jesus on the subject of preparation is also urgent. *"God has revealed what is to take place in the last days, <u>that His people may be prepared</u> to stand against the tempest of opposition and wrath. Those who have been warned of the events before them are not to sit in calm expectation of the coming storm, comforting themselves that the Lord will shelter His faithful ones in the day of trouble"* (<u>Testimonies for the Church</u>, vol. 5, p. 452; emphasis supplied). God wants us to prepare for these last days based upon what He has revealed will take place.

"What are you doing, brethren, in the great work of preparation? Those who are uniting with the world are receiving the worldly mold and preparing for the mark of the beast.... Now is the time to prepare" (<u>ibid</u>; p. 216). Our survival depends upon rejecting worldly influences in our lives. The warning is clear: If we allow worldly influences to creep in, we are preparing to receive the mark of the beast and we will not survive.

"Ministers and people are unprepared for the time in which they live, and nearly all who profess to believe present truth are unprepared to understand <u>the work of preparation for this time</u>. In their present state of worldly ambition, with their lack of consecration to God, their devotion to self, they are wholly unfitted to receive the latter rain and, having done all, to stand against the wrath of Satan, who by his inventions would cause them to make shipwreck of faith, fastening upon them some pleasing self-deception. They think <u>they are all right</u> when <u>they are all wrong</u>" (<u>ibid.</u>, vol. 1, p. 466; emphasis supplied). Christian people, who in their profession and understanding of truth, are still unprepared to understand the work of preparation for this time and are wrong when they think they are right.

"Satan leads many to believe that God will overlook their unfaithfulness in the minor affairs of life; but the Lord shows in His dealings with Jacob that He will in no wise sanction or tolerate evil. <u>All who endeavor to excuse or conceal their sins, and permit them to remain upon the books of heaven, unconfessed and unforgiven, will be overcome by Satan</u>. The more

exalted their profession, and the more honorable the position which they hold, the more grievous is their course in the sight of God and the more sure the triumph of their great adversary. <u>Those who delay a preparation for the day of God cannot obtain it in the time of trouble, or at any subsequent time. The case of all such is hopeless</u>.

"Those professed Christians who come up to that last fearful conflict unprepared will, in their despair, confess their sins in words of burning anguish, while the wicked exult over their distress" (<u>The Great Controversy</u>, p. 620; emphasis supplied). The message is clear that to delay preparation for the day of God, thinking that we can "do it later," threatens our survival. The sentence in a previous reference says "**Now** is the time to get ready" and not to say, as did King Agrippa, *"Almost thou persuadest me"* (Acts 26:28).

"Study Revelation in connection with Daniel, for history will be repeated.... <u>We, with all our religious advantages, ought to know far more today than we do know</u>.... As we near the close of this world's history, the prophecies relating to the last days especially demand our study. The last book of the New Testament Scriptures is full of truth that we need to understand" (<u>Testimonies to Ministers</u>, p. 116; emphasis supplied).

The testimonies are here pointing back to the Scripture for special study as we near the end of time. We ought to know more, and we ought to be better prepared than we are. To those of you who are living in any city of the seven continents, begin a work now to prepare for survival and move to the country!

"<u>Those who are engaged in service for the Master need an experience much higher, deeper, broader, than many have yet thought of having</u>. Many who are already members of God's great family know little of what it means to behold His glory and to be changed from glory to glory. Many have a twilight perception of Christ's excellence, and their hearts thrill with joy. They long for a fuller, deeper sense of the Saviour's love. Let these cherish every desire of the soul after God. <u>The Holy Spirit works with those who will be worked</u>, molds those who will be molded, fashions those who will be fashioned. <u>Give yourselves the culture of spiritual thoughts and holy communings</u>. You have seen but the first rays of the early dawn of His glory. <u>As you follow on to know the Lord, you will know that 'the path of the righteous is as the light of dawn, that shineth more and more unto the perfect day'</u>" Proverbs 4:18, R. V., margin (<u>The Ministry of Healing</u>, p. 503; emphasis supplied).

The promise is, and let it be said with encouraging words, that if we will make a beginning, God will bless us. If we neglect to make a beginning, the end will be a hardened heart and the mark of the beast. God in His great love is pleading with us to get to know Him and then, with His arm around us, He points the way. *"Every act of transgression, every neglect or rejection of the grace of Christ, is reacting upon yourself; it is hardening the heart, depraving the will, benumbing the understanding, and not only making you less inclined to yield, but less capable of yielding, to the tender pleading of God's Holy Spirit"* (Steps to Christ, p. 33).

We have been warned that there is a storm coming from which we must have shelter in order to survive. *"The storm is coming, relentless in its fury. Are we prepared to meet it? Are we one with Christ as He is one with the Father? Are we heirs of God and joint heirs of Christ? Are we working in copartnership with Christ?"* (Evangelism, p. 199; emphasis supplied).

Continuing our study of vital truth, consider a reference in Selected Messages, book 2, page 142: *"The work of the people of God is to prepare for the events of the future, which will soon come upon them with blinding force"* (emphasis supplied). It is clear that our work is to prepare ourselves and help others to be ready for the Lord's soon return.

Survival

Our spiritual and practical preparation must have goals. Why should we prepare? To what end? The Bible states in Matthew 10:22, *"And ye shall be hated of all men for my name's sake: but he that endureth to the end shall be saved."* This verse specifically challenges last-day survivors to endure to the end. There will be a temptation to compromise the truths of the Bible.

"The last great delusion is soon to open before us. Antichrist is to perform his marvelous works in our sight. So closely will the counterfeit resemble the true that it will be impossible to distinguish between them except by the Holy Scriptures. By their testimony every statement and every miracle must be tested. Those who endeavor to obey all the commandments of God will be opposed and derided. They can stand only in God. In order to endure the trial before them, they must understand the will of God as revealed in His word. ... None but those who have fortified the mind with the truths of the Bible will stand through the last great conflict. To every soul will come the searching test: Shall I obey God rather than men? The decisive hour is even now at hand" (The Great Controversy, pp. 593, 594; emphasis supplied). *"Fearful sights of a supernatural character will soon be revealed in the heavens, in token of the power of miracle-working demons. ...As the crowning act in the great drama of deception, Satan him-*

self will personate Christ" (The Great Controversy, p. 624).

In order to endure we must understand and experience the Scriptures. We can only survive these last days if we make the Bible our guide book. God's Holy Word will help us test the sayings of these demons in disguise.

When we begin to live by faith, we may lose old friends, maybe even our own family. But all should be tempered with the joy and peace of forgiveness. Does the Bible, our ultimate survival manual, have any practical advice to help us endure the terrible trials we will face if we are to survive? Yes, it does! God's love is the bridge between heaven and earth.

The Only Argument Against the Truth

You may think it strange to say that there is an argument against the truth. We have confirmed the fact that the truth has a strong evidence-based existence. However, there is an argument that neutralizes the effect of truth, and, hence, affects our survival. Romans 8:18 gives us insight into this irony: *"For I reckon that the sufferings of this present time are not worthy to be compared with the glory which shall be revealed in us."*

Second Corinthians 4:17 makes a similar statement, *"For our light affliction, which is but for a moment, worketh for us a far more exceeding and eternal weight of glory."* We give up too soon!

Thoughts From the Mount of Blessing, page 30, comments upon the verse in Deuteronomy 33:25 *"As thy days so shall thy strength be." "Those who love their Redeemer will rejoice at every opportunity of sharing with Him humiliation and reproach. The love they bear their Lord makes suffering for His sake sweet."*

"Beloved, think it not strange concerning the fiery trial which is to try you, as though some strange thing happened unto you: but rejoice, inasmuch as ye are partakers of Christ's sufferings; that, when his glory shall be revealed, ye may be glad also with exceeding joy" (1 Peter 4:12, 13). Notice that it says we should rejoice for every trial. This is indeed advanced Christianity. When you consider such trials as false accusations, scorn, ridicule, misjudged motives, and slander, you see how they may set the stage for the only argument against the truth.

In Acts 26:27, 28 Paul had been called to appear before King Agrippa, and appeal to him to become a Christian. Agrippa's answer was, *"Almost thou persuadest me to be a Christian."*

The Acts of the Apostles, page 438, says, *"But Agrippa put aside the proffered mercy, refusing to accept the cross of a crucified Redeemer."* "Almost," but not quite, was Agrippa's response to Paul's invitation.

Acts 24:25 tells some of the story of Felix and Drusilla. *"Felix trembled, and answered, Go thy way for this time; <u>when I have a convenient season, I will call for thee.</u>"* Felix and Drusilla did not want to make a decision about spiritual things when Paul appealed to them, but wanted to wait until later.

The Acts of the Apostles, page 426, comments on their experience: *"But instead of permitting his convictions to lead him to repentance, <u>he sought to dismiss these unwelcome reflections</u>. The interview with Paul was cut short. 'Go thy way for this time,' he said; 'when I have a convenient season, I will call for thee'"* (emphasis supplied).

King Agrippa and his household, along with Felix and Drusilla, exemplify the attitude of those who decide to put off responding to Christ's invitation to eternal survival. Some may have hurt feelings regarding some bad experiences or reproofs. This is expressed in Testimonies for the Church, volume 3, page 266: *"The spirit of hatred which has existed with some because the wrongs among God's people have been reproved has brought blindness and a fearful deception upon their own souls, <u>making it impossible for them to discriminate between right and wrong</u>. They have put out their own spiritual eyesight"* (emphasis supplied).

For whatever reason, if we reject truth, we find that the heart hardens and we become less responsive. This is done at our eternal peril and threatens our survival. Testimonies for the Church, volume 5, page 681, describes this spiritual condition, which effectively neutralizes the effect of the truth, *"Let ministers and people remember that gospel truth <u>hardens when it does not save</u>. The rejection of light leaves men captives, bound about by chains of darkness and unbelief. '<u>The soul that refuses to listen to the invitations of mercy from day to day can soon listen to the most urgent appeals without an emotion stirring his soul</u>'"* (emphasis supplied).

The best summary of the arguments against the truth is expressed in The Great Controversy, page 460. Here it mentions the great obstacles and barriers to the effects of truth upon our lives and how we can have an effective argument against our own survival. *"<u>The great obstacle both to the acceptance and to the promulgation of truth is the fact that it involves inconvenience and reproach. This is the only argument against the truth which its advocates have never been able to refute</u>"* (emphasis supplied).

It is a serious matter to put off carrying out our convictions. The following poem explains just how serious it is.

Almost

A leper sat beside a cave
In upper Galilee;
His form was wasted and his grief
Was pitiful to see.

No future stretched inviting arms,
His hopes were for release,
For quiet in the mossy tomb
And rest of dreamless peace.

Of late, uneasy were his thoughts,
Hope reared its weary head;
One who could heal the leprosy
Lived south, so rumor said.

Some told of demons exorcised,
Some said He raised the dead,
And changed some water into wine,
And multiplied the bread.

"Soon will I rise and go to Him,
And see what can be seen,
Perhaps He'll see my hopeless state,
Perhaps He'll make me clean."

With languor he began to plan
To put away his sorrow;
He'd say, as every morning dawned
"I'm tired, I'll go tomorrow."

But days and weeks and months passed by,
His eyes were growing dim;
He knew that he must haste to Christ,
Or death would haste to him.

His journey was a painful one
And, as its end drew nigh,
He saw three crosses etched in black
Against a darkening sky.

—Josephine Cunnington Edwards

VITAL TRUTH

FOR FURTHER STUDY

The Battle for the Book, David Marshall, 1991, Stanborough Press, Grantham, England.

Bible Sabbath, Ned Ashton, Review and Herald Publishing Association, Hagerstown, MD, 21740

Christ in His Sanctuary, Ellen White, 1969, Pacific Press Publishing Association, Nampa, ID.

Country Living, Ellen White, 1946, Review and Publishing Association, Hagerstown, MD, 21740.

Day to Remember, George Vandeman, Review and Herald Publishing Association, Hagerstown, MD, 21740.

Early Writings, Ellen White, Pacific Press Publishing Association, Nampa, ID pp. 250-253.

Ellen G. White, Prophet of Destiny, Rene Noorbergen, Keats Publishing, Inc., New Canaan, CT.

Fox's Book of Martyrs, John Fox, Hurstad Co., NY.

From City to Country Living, Arthur L. White and E. A. Sutherland, 1983, Review and Herald Publishing Association, Hagerstown, MD,

The Great Controversy, Ellen G. White, Pacific Press Publishing Association, Nampa, ID, 1911.

History of the Reformation of the 16th Century, J. H. Merle D'Aubigne, Baker Book House, Grand Rapids, MI 1976.

History of the Waldenses, J. A. Wylie, Pacific Press Publishing Association, Nampa, ID, 1977.

Martyrs Mirror, Thielman J. Van Braght, Harold Press, Scottsdale, PA, 1979.

Protestant Dilemma, Richard Lewis, Pacific Press Publishing Association, Nampa, ID.

Ransom and Reunion, W. D. Frazee, Pioneers Memorial, Box 102, Wildwood, GA, 30757.

Roger Williams: Freedom's Forgotten Hero; Videotape available from Freedom Research, Inc. 7631 Southcliff Drive, Fair Oaks, CA, 95628. $19.95 plus S&H, 1-916-967-6584.

Seventh-day Adventists Believe . . . A Biblical Exposition of Fundamental Doctrines, Review and Herald Publishing Association, Hagerstown, MD, 21740.

YOU CAN SURVIVE!

There is a strong connection between the third angel's message and medical missionary work:

"As religious aggression subverts the liberties of our nation, those who would stand for freedom of conscience will be placed in unfavorable positions. For their own sake, they should, while they have opportunity, become intelligent in regard to disease, its causes, prevention, and cure. And those who do this will find a field of labor anywhere. There will be suffering ones, plenty of them, who will need help, not only among those of our own faith, but largely among those who know not the truth" (Counsels on Health, p. 506).

"John was a representative of the people of God in the last days, to whom God has committed important and solemn truths. The world at large are given to gluttony and the indulgence of base passions. The light of health reform is opened before the people of God at this day, that they may see the necessity of holding their appetites and passions under control of the higher powers of the mind. This is also necessary, that they may have mental strength and clearness, to discern the sacred chain of truth, and turn from the bewitching errors and pleasing fables, that are flooding the world. Their work is to present before the people the pure doctrine of the Bible. Hence health reform finds its place in the preparatory work for the second appearing of Christ" (The Spirit of Prophecy, vol. 2, p. 44).

Chapter Three

Accusations: Words Can Hurt

"Neither do I condemn thee. . . " (John 8:11).

Her eyes looked down, but she knew that they were all staring at her. She could hear the whispers. The fingers they were pointing at her may as well be jabbing into her back. Their tongues were wagging. Her aching heart wished for someone who really understood. Her accusers had brought her to the temple, and cast her down in front of the Teacher. The accusers loudly flaunted her sin and bragged of their own cleverness in discovering her. "Moses and the law says she should be stoned!" yelled one man above their jeers and shamings. "What do *you* say?"

She suddenly knew that they were using her actions to trap the Teacher. There was no way He could meet their accusations without accusing others Himself. But, He said nothing. Neither yes or no. He merely wrote in the dirt, as if He were deaf to their taunts. Quietly, amid the dying accusations and whispered musings, Jesus said, *"He that is without sin among you, let him first cast a stone at her"* (John 8:7). He continued marking in the dirt. And, one by one, reading their own dirt, the accusers left.

At last, Jesus looked at her. "Where are your accusers; has no man condemned you?" She could hardly find her voice when she realized the concern in His tone. She looked into His eyes—eyes reflecting the love she felt—and said, *"No man, Lord."* He replied, *"Neither do I condemn you. Go and sin no more."*

Here we have a picture of people accusing this woman and also using it as a trap so they could accuse Jesus. Accusing people, whether they are guilty or not, is a habit that is easy to form. This woman was actually guilty, and yet, not accused by Christ. If Jesus did not accuse when guilty, what place is there to accuse the innocent? In each case, the vital issue is whether or not we should accuse one another at all. I think you will see that as we enter further into this study, that to accuse someone is to do a work other than what God would have us to do. Let's look at a definition for the word "accusation." The definition reads simply, "charged with a fault; to blame someone."

One well-known text in Matthew 18:7 puts things in perspective. This view is somewhat different than we ordinarily take but, as usual, the Bible reveals the true light. *"Woe unto the world because of offences! for it must needs be that offences come: but woe to that man by whom the offence cometh!"* We need to be very careful with our accusations, and with our offenses because the Bible says, "Woe to them." It's a mistake to be offended, but a greater one to offend.

Am I Offended?

So far, we have found that the one who offends has committed the greater sin than the one who is offended (Matthew 18:7). Let's take a look at the fate of the offended. Is it a sin to be offended?

Proverbs 18:19 says, *"A brother offended is harder to be won than a strong city: and their contentions are like the bars of a castle."* There is extreme danger in being offended. An offended person is harder to be won than a strong city. Evidently when we are offended, we put up arguments that are irrefutable and our position hardens our hearts and puts us in a position where no one can help us (Matthew 18:15-17).

In Matthew 24:9-13 we read about what some offended people do. *"Then shall they deliver you up to be afflicted, and shall kill you: and ye shall be hated of all nations for my name's sake. And then shall many be offended, and shall betray one another, and shall hate one another…. But he that shall endure unto the end, the same shall be saved."*

Here we see one result of being offended. The offended person is being set up to betray and hate others and that makes it a sin. Matthew 10:21-23 says that the offended will betray family members to death. *"And the brother shall deliver up the brother to death, and the father the child: and the children shall rise up against their parents, and cause them to be put to death. And ye shall be hated of all men for my name's sake: but he that endureth to the end shall be saved. But when they persecute you in this city, flee ye into another: for verily I say unto you, Ye shall not have gone over the cities of Israel, till the Son of man be come"* (emphasis supplied). It is a terrible thing to be offended. We need to do whatever we can to make it right, as soon as possible, to forgive them and seek forgiveness from God.

Note the chain of evil: someone says something or accuses someone else and that person becomes offended. That person, in turn, is setting themselves up to be a persecutor because they are offended.

"But because offenses will come, we should be careful not to stir up the natural temperament of those who love not the truth, by unwise words and by manifestations of an unkind spirit" (Manuscript Releases, vol. 16, p. 159).

ACCUSATIONS

When we are offended we become unforgiving. Notice this statement regarding a person in that situation. *"He who is unforgiving cuts off the very channel through which alone he can receive mercy from God. We should not think that unless those who have injured us confess the wrong we are justified in withholding from them our forgiveness. It is their part, no doubt, to humble their hearts by repentance and confession; but we are to have a spirit of compassion toward those who have trespassed against us, whether or not they confess their faults. However sorely they may have wounded us, we are not to cherish our grievances, and sympathize with ourselves over our injuries; but, as we hope to be pardoned for our offenses against God, we are to pardon all who have done evil to us"* (Mount of Blessing, p. 113; emphasis supplied). Think of it! By being offended and unforgiving we cut off the very channel of mercy and recovery.

Long ago Sister F. was offended. Notice what spirits raced into her heart. *"Sister F. moves from impulse, and finds fault, and has had too much to say against her brethren and sisters. This will cause confusion in any church. If she could control her own spirit, a great victory would be gained.... Unless she is converted and an entire change is wrought in her, unless she educates herself to be slow to speak and slow to wrath, and cultivates true Christian courtesy, her influence will prove injurious, and the happiness of others connected with her will suffer. She manifests an independence which is a damage to her and alienates her friends. This independence has caused her much trouble and has wounded her best friends"* (Testimonies for the Church, vol. 2, p. 51).

Sometimes it is little things that offend our human nature. Things like being jostled in a crowd or driving on a street or highway. Brother P. had this problem. *"Your hasty temper often causes you sincere and painful regret and self-condemnation. This passionate spirit, unless subdued, will increase to a peevish, faultfinding spirit; indeed, this is already upon you in a degree. You will be ready to resent everything. If jostled upon the sidewalk, you will be offended, and a word of complaint will spring to your lips. When driving in the street, if full half the road is not given you, you will feel stirred in a moment. If asked to put yourself out of your course to accommodate others, you will chafe and fret, and feel that your dignity is imposed upon. You will show to all your besetting sin. Your very countenance will indicate an impatient spirit, and your mouth will seem always ready to utter an angry word. In this habit, as in tobacco using, total abstinence is the only sure remedy. An entire change must take place in you"* (ibid. p. 424; emphasis supplied).

73

Being offended is a fault. If we didn't become offended, we could stop a cycle of events perpetrated by Satan and the offender would be in a much better position of recovery. *"Christ has given direction for their guidance, declaring that they are to show Christian interest in one another. If one commits sin, do not talk of it among yourselves. Go first to the one who has offended. 'Tell him his fault between thee and him alone: if he shall hear thee, thou hast gained thy brother.' 'If thou bring thy gift to the altar, and there rememberest that thy brother hath aught against thee; leave there thy gift before the altar, and go thy way; first be reconciled to thy brother, and then come and offer thy gift.' Do church members obey this word? <u>Suppose that in every institution established among us, in publishing houses, sanitariums, and schools, God's people had sought to understand and follow His plan, as it is outlined in the Old and New Testaments</u>. Suppose that the instruction given by Christ to the children of Israel had been woven into the life-practice. <u>Would not we as a people stand today on vantage ground</u>?"* (<u>Review and Herald</u>, April 1, 1902; emphasis supplied).

In conclusion to the matter of being offended, this reference states our need of conversion. *"But truth will bear away the victory. Those who will maintain the truth, irrespective of consequences, will offend some whose hearts are not in harmony with the truth as it is in Jesus. These persons cherish theories of their own, which are not the truth. <u>The truth does not harmonize with their sentiments, and rather than give up their own ideas, they walk away from those who obey the truth. But there are men who will receive the truth, and these will take the places made vacant by those who become offended and leave the truth</u>"* (<u>Manuscript Releases</u>, vol. 7, p. 180; emphasis supplied).

Remember Matthew 18:7 and this counsel in 1 Corinthians 10:32: *"Give none offense, neither to the Jews, nor to the Gentiles, nor to the church of God."* Let us safeguard our Christian experience by not becoming offended. Our own long-suffering is our indication of a connection to heaven! *"The highest evidence of nobility in a Christian is self-control.... Lowliness of heart is the strength that gives victory to the followers of Christ; it is the token of their connection with the courts above"* (<u>The Desire of Ages</u>, p. 301).

What if I Offend?

Let's notice again the same Bible verse, Matthew 18:7, *"Woe unto the world because of offences! For it must needs be that offences come; but woe to that man by whom the offence cometh!"*

In his recent book <u>The Wounded Spirit</u>, Frank Peretti reveals how his mistreatment and rejection by schoolmates scarred his spirit. It is his belief that the shootings at Columbine High School might have been averted if someone had detected and helped to treat the wounded spirits of the boys who did the shooting. He claims that bullying is often the root cause of many of those wounds.

NBC news anchor Stone Phillips reported on March 6, 2001, in regard to the shooting at Santana High School near San Diego, California, that since 1974 two out of three perpetrators in school shootings felt bullied.

As Christians, we should each study to make ourselves a committee of one to seek out these hurting youngsters and let them know someone cares. They will be the very ones who try us most; they question our authority, they say nothing matters to them. But what they really mean is, "No one cares enough about me to be my friend." Teenagers need to be aware that their words and actions carry an impact.

This philosophy seems to be supported by Ellen White: *"In one moment, by hasty, passionate, careless words, may be wrought evil that a whole lifetime's repentance cannot undo. Oh, the hearts that are broken, the friends estranged, the lives wrecked, by the harsh, hasty words of those who might have brought help and healing!"* (Messages to Young People, p. 135).

We are called to be comforters, not to cause offense. When our pain seems important enough to inflict discomfort upon another, we are representing the enemy of souls. We must speak, even God's truths, in love, in cases where we find our brother in error. Our words can easily offend. When in doubt, silence is better than gold.

"Words spoken in reply to one who is angry usually act as a whip, lashing the temper into greater fury.... The religion of Christ brings the emotions under the control of reason and disciplines the tongue" (ibid. p. 136). We are called to be inoffensive as well as unoffended, as wise as serpents and as harmless as doves.

Scripture states exactly how we should react when accused, whether we are guilty or innocent. Romans 8:33, 34 asks that very question: *"Who will lay anything to the charge of God's elect? It is God that justifieth. Who is he that condemneth? It is Christ that died, yea rather, that is risen again, who is even at the right hand of God, who also maketh intercession for us.*

"How shall we react?" is indeed to ask the question, "How does God react toward us?" In Romans 8:1, He says, *"There is therefore now no condemnation* [or accusation] *to them which are in Christ Jesus. "*

The Zacchaeus Principle

The story of Zacchaeus is about a tax collector hated by most of the people in the community. There were many dishonest things that tax collectors did in those days, including overcharging and paying the government the tax and keeping a hefty override. So, Zacchaeus is in town one day and he notices that Jesus is coming to where he is doing business. Being a short man, he climbs up into a tree to view Jesus over the crowd. As Jesus comes by, He sees Zacchaeus in the tree. Jesus tells him that He wants to come to his house for dinner. The people then accuse Jesus of associating with crooks and fraudulent people. If He was truly the Messiah, He wouldn't do that!

True to His word, Jesus came to Zacchaeus' house, and Zacchaeus made a decision as a result of that visit to become a follower of Christ. Then he made this speech in Luke 19:8: *"Behold, Lord, the half of my goods I give to the poor; and if I have taken any thing from any man by false accusation, I restore him fourfold. And Jesus said unto him, This day is salvation come to this house."* This verse ties in neatly with our scripture in Matthew 18:7, which says to be careful how you offend someone and be careful how you are offended, but "woe to them who offend you." Here, Zacchaeus is saying that if he has offended anyone by false accusation he will repay fourfold.

The Scripture admonition to those who have made false accusations, false charges, fraudulent dealings, is a fourfold repayment. As a result of Zacchaeus' commitment, Jesus says in Luke 19:9, *"This day is salvation come to this house."* This gave the seal to Zacchaeus' promise. Because of his false charges, Zacchaeus chose to make fourfold repayment. This is a hefty restitution, but it still does not cover all of the damage.

Guilt or Innocence—Judge Not

Some soldiers came to John the Baptist because they were interested in the life-style that He recommended. They asked Jesus this question in Luke 3:14, *"And the soldiers likewise demanded of him saying, And what shall we do? And he said unto them, Do violence to no man, neither accuse anyone falsely, and be content with your wages."* Three things Jesus told them, one of which was not to accuse anyone falsely. Accusation is an offense that brings woe upon those who make it.

Joseph, in Genesis 39, was running for his life. He held a shredded piece of his coat, the other half was held by the wife of Potiphar, Joseph's employer. Potiphar's wife had falsely accused Joseph of adultery with her. As a result of her accusations, Joseph was put into prison. He remained there, but he didn't go to prison with a hateful attitude toward anyone; he knew he was innocent. So he continued to work for God in prison and gained the attention of many of the prisoners that were there. The word spread about Joseph and his wisdom.

ACCUSATIONS

One day the king had a dream, and Joseph was called from prison to interpret it. He gave the interpretation, and the plan of implementation, given him by God. There would be seven years of good crops, followed by seven years when there wouldn't be any harvest. Joseph helped a whole nation, indeed, helped supply a lot of the then-known world with food, during a time when it was really difficult to get food. As a result, Joseph was made prime minister of the country.

In the example of Joseph there is a promise of vindication that will assure us that we can afford to be calm and quiet under accusation. *"And if like Joseph they suffer calumny and false accusations, Providence will overrule all the enemy's devices for good, and God will in His own time exalt as much higher, as for a while they were debased by wicked revenge"* (The Seventh-day Adventist Bible Commentary, Ellen G. White Comments, vol. 1, p. 1097; emphasis supplied). What a promise for those who have been accused! Romans 8:28 says, *"And we know that all things work together for good to them that love God, to them who are the called according to his purpose."*

Matthew 7:3 talks about judging other people, and here's how it reads, *"Why beholdest thou the mote* [the little splinter] *that is in thy brother's eye, but considerest not the beam that is in thine own eye?"*

Thoughts From the Mount of Blessing, page 125, comments on this verse in a powerful way. *"According to the figure that our Saviour uses, he who indulges a censorious spirit is guilty of greater sin than is the one he accuses, for he not only commits the same sin, but adds to it conceit and censoriousness"* (emphasis supplied). There's not much room to accuse, is there?

Matthew 7:1 says, *"Judge not, that ye be not judged. For with what judgment ye judge, ye shall be judged: and with what measure ye mete, it will be measured to you again."* As we deal with one another, in a manner that accuses some other person, or talk about them, or gossip about them, the judgment that we give to somebody else is the judgment that is going to be passed upon us. In a more practical application, the path that we take others over, we'll have to go over ourselves.

In Thoughts From the Mount of Blessing, pages 136, 137 we read: *"Everyone who has been free to condemn or discourage, will in his own experience be brought over the same ground where he has caused others to pass; he will feel what they have suffered because of his want of sympathy and tenderness."* We will learn to guard our tongue more closely, and as a result, we will more tenderly value our friends. .So we need to be very careful about how we deal with one another in an accusing way. *"'Thou that judgest doest the same things,' does not reach the magnitude of his sin* who presumes *to criticize and condemn his brother.... His words describe one who is swift to discern a defect in others.... But Jesus declares that the very trait of character developed in doing this un-Christlike work is, in comparison with the fault criticized, as a beam in proportion to a mote"* (ibid., p. 125; emphasis supplied).

When we make accusations intended to hurt others, we are promoting our own fall.

The Spirit of Persecution

In the Garden of Eden, when Adam and Eve first did that which God had told them not to do, one of the first things they did was to accuse each other. This is found on page 126 in Thoughts From the Mount of Blessing: *"It was through sin that men gained the knowledge of evil; no sooner had the first pair [meaning Adam and Eve] sinned than they began to accuse each other."* And this is what human nature will inevitably do when uncontrolled by the grace of Christ. As soon as we sin ourselves, we accuse.

As the spirit of accusation continues to grow, we will see more restrictive measures put on individuals. Notice this statement: *"When men indulge this accusing spirit, they are not satisfied with pointing out what they suppose to be a defect in their brother. If milder means fail of making him do what they think ought to be done, they will resort to compulsion. Just as far as lies in their power, they will force men to comply with their ideas of what is right"* (ibid. p. 126; emphasis supplied).

Accusation begins the spirit of compulsion and then develops persecution. That example is given at the top of page 127 in Thoughts From the Mount of Blessing. Finally, let's look at the remedy on page 128, *"Not until you feel that you could sacrifice your own self-dignity, and even lay down your life in order to save an erring brother, have you cast the beam out of your own eye so that you are prepared to help your brother. Then you can approach him and touch his heart. No one has ever been reclaimed from a wrong position by censure and reproach; but many have been thus driven from Christ and led to seal their hearts against conviction. A tender spirit, a gentle, winning deportment, may save the erring and hide a multitude of sins. The revelation of Christ in your own character will have a transforming power upon all with whom you come in contact"* (emphasis supplied). It is wrong to reproach anyone, even if they are guilty!

The spirit that should be manifested when we are accused, or the spirit that we should manifest toward each other is best expressed in two texts. The first one is Romans 12:15: *"Rejoice with them that do rejoice, and weep with them that weep."* In this verse, it points out that we should be so closely identified with the interests and concerns of each other, that when one weeps, we weep with them, and when they rejoice, we rejoice with them. Certainly there is no spirit of accusation, condemnation, criticism, in this attitude. A similar statement is found in 1 Corinthians 12:26: *"And whether one member suffer, all members suffer with it; or one member be honoured, all the members rejoice with it."* Speaking of members, it sounds like a church group, doesn't it? He could be a member of a business, or a member of an organization of any kind. When one of us suffers, we are so closely identified with them that we suffer too. Or, if someone is accused, maybe a friend of ours, we suffer with them as though it were happening to ourselves.

One of the most tragic stories in the Bible is of Jesus during His trial. He was accused of wrongdoing, and yet everything that He had done was right. He was accused of treason, of causing insurrection, of being associated with the wrong people. His accusers hated Him. The people who were accusing Him wanted to use the law of the land to force Him to do things that they were promoting. Finally they killed Him because He wouldn't comply with their wishes.

His example gives us the best response to accusations. Matthew 27:12-14 says, *"When he was accused of the chief priests and elders, he answered nothing. Then said Pilate unto him, Hearest thou not how many things they witness against thee? And he answered him to never a word."*

The Desire of Ages, page 750, states, *"For long hours of agony, reviling and mockery have fallen upon the ears of Jesus. As He hangs upon the cross, there floats up to Him still the sound of jeers and curses. With longing heart He has listened for some expression of faith from His disciples. He has heard only the mournful words, 'We trusted that it had been He which should have redeemed Israel.' How grateful then to the Saviour was the utterance of faith and love from a dying thief! While the leading Jews deny Him, and even the disciples doubt His divinity, the poor thief, upon the brink of eternity, called Jesus Lord. Many were ready to call Him Lord when He wrought miracles, and after He had risen from the grave; but none acknowledged Him as He hung dying upon the cross save the penitent thief"* (emphasis supplied).

Many of His friends left Him, forsook Him, but here is a thief who is honest in heart and wants to declare his confidence in Jesus. He just asked the Master if He would save him in His kingdom. This brought encouragement to our Lord. Think about it. All the church people, all the leaders of the nation, the leaders of the community accused and forsook Him. But this guilty thief saw something that no one else beheld in Christ and asked Him for help. Amid all the accusations, here is the accused thief coming through for God. That is truly an amazing story.

YOU CAN SURVIVE!

Let It Pass

Be not swift to take offense, let it pass.
Anger is a foe to sense, let it pass.
Brood not darkly for a wrong which will disappear erelong,
Rather sing this cheery song, let it pass.

Echo not an angry word, let it pass.
Think how often you have erred, let it pass.
Any vulgar souls that live, man condemns without reprieve,
'Tis the noble who forgives, let it pass.

If for the good you've taken ill, let it pass.
Oh be kind and gentle still, let it pass.
Time at last makes all things straight, let us not resent but wait,
And our triumph shall be great, let it pass.

Bid your anger to depart, let it pass.
Take these homely words to heart, let it pass.
Follow not the common throng, better to be wronged than wrong,
Therefore sing the cheery song, let it pass, let it pass.

—Unknown

The above poem points out the examples of how we should react to accusations. By acting this way, we are practicing faith, trusting that God will take care of us. God always operates on balanced books. He will see to it that the accusations that come to us will work out for our best good and for the good of the accuser.

In The Seventh-day Adventist Bible Commentary, Ellen G. White Comments, vol. 3, pages 1162, 1163, we discover the steps that accusations bring to cause disunity in the church, and in any organization. *"Brethren sometimes associate together for years, and they think they can trust those they know so well just as they would trust members of their own family. There is a freedom and confidence in this association which could not exist between those not of the same faith. This is very pleasant while mutual faith and brotherly love last; but let the 'accuser of the brethren' gain admittance to the heart of one of these men, controlling the mind and the imagination, and jealousies are created, suspicion and envy are harbored; and he who supposed himself secure in the love and friendship of his brother, finds himself mistrusted and his motives misjudged. The false brother forgets his own human frailties, forgets his obligation to think and speak no evil lest he dishonor God and wound Christ in the person of His saints, and every defect that can be thought of or imagined is commented upon unmercifully, and the character of a brother is misrepre-*

sented as dark and questionable.

"There is a betrayal of sacred trust. The things spoken in brotherly confidence are repeated and misrepresented; and every word, every action, however innocent and well-meaning, is scrutinized by the cold, jealous criticism of those who were thought too noble, too honorable to take the least advantage of friendly association or brotherly trust. *Hearts are closed to mercy, judgment, and the love of God; and the cold, sneering, contemptuous spirit which Satan manifests toward his victim is revealed.*

"The Saviour of the world was treated thus, and we are exposed to the influence of the same malicious spirit. The time has come when it is not safe to put confidence in a friend or brother.

"As in the days of Christ spies were on His track, so they are on ours now. *If Satan can employ professed believers to act as accusers of the brethren, he is greatly pleased; for those who do this are just as truly serving him as was Judas when he betrayed Christ, although they may be doing it ignorantly.* Satan is no less active now than in Christ's day, and those who lend themselves to do his work will represent his spirit.

"Floating rumors are frequently the destroyers of unity among brethren. There are some who watch with open mind and ears to catch flying scandal. They gather up little incidents which may be trifling in themselves, but which are repeated and exaggerated until a man is made an offense for a word. Their motto seems to be, 'Report and we will report it.' *These talebearers are doing the devil's work with surprising fidelity, little knowing how offensive their course is to God*.... The door of the mind should be closed against 'they say' or 'I have heard.' *Why should we not, instead of allowing jealousy or evil-surmising to come into our hearts, go to our brethren, and, after frankly but kindly setting before them the things we have heard detrimental to their character and influence, pray with and for them*? While we cannot love and fellowship with those who are bitter enemies of Christ, we should cultivate the spirit of meekness and love that characterized our Master, a love that thinketh no evil and is not easily provoked" (The Seventh-day Adventist Bible Commentary, Ellen G White Comments, vol. 3, page 1163; emphasis supplied).

Notice one place here in the previous reading, that it is not safe to put confidence in a friend or a brother. We need to continue to grow in our friendships and our trusts and use good judgment as to how much confidential information we share with each other.

But at the same time, notice this quote entitled "The Value of a Friend" from The Seventh-day Adventist Bible Commentary, volume 3, page 1163,

YOU CAN SURVIVE!

"Things will go wrong with every one, sadness and discouragement press every soul; then a personal presence, <u>a friend who will comfort and impart strength, will turn back the darts of the enemy that are aimed to destroy. Christian friends are not half as plentiful as they should be</u>. In hours of temptation, in a crisis, what a value is a true friend! Satan at such times sends along his agents to cause the trembling limbs to stumble; but <u>the true friends who will counsel, who will impart magnetic hopefulness, the calming faith that uplifts the soul</u>, ...oh, such a help is worth more than precious pearls!" (emphasis supplied).

When we have friends who are being accused, that is the time they need us the most. We can stand by them and encourage them, and let them know that we don't think those things are true. If the accusations **are** true, we can do what we can to help and comfort them, not accusing, condemning, or neglecting them. If accused, how special is that friend who will "be there" for us, even if we are wrong.

In <u>The Great Controversy</u>, pages 519, 520, we read, *"There has ever been a class professing godliness, who, instead of following on to know the truth, make it their religion to seek some fault of character or error of faith in those with whom they do not agree. <u>Such are Satan's right-hand helpers. Accusers of the brethren are not few, and they are always active when God is at work</u> and His servants are rendering Him true homage. They will put a false coloring upon the words and acts of those who love and obey the truth. They will represent the most earnest, zealous, self-denying servants of Christ as deceived or deceivers. It is their work to misrepresent the motives of every true and noble deed, to circulate insinuations, and arouse suspicion in the minds of the inexperienced. In every conceivable manner they will seek to cause that which is pure and righteous to be regarded as foul and deceptive. But none need be deceived concerning them. It may be readily seen whose children they are, whose example they follow, and whose work they do. 'Ye shall know them by their fruits'* (Matt. 7:16). <u>*Their course resembles that of Satan, the envenomed slanderer, 'the accuser of the brethren'*</u>*"* (emphasis supplied).

The new phrase there, *"accuser of the brethren,"* is a quotation from the Bible, which is in Revelation 12:10: *"And I heard a loud voice saying in heaven, Now is come salvation, and strength, and the kingdom of our God, and the power of his Christ: for the <u>accuser of our brethren is cast down</u>, which <u>accused them</u> before our God day and night."*

Further, Biblical mention is found in Zechariah 3:1, 2: *"Then he showed me Joshua the high priest standing before the angel of the Lord, and Satan standing at his right hand to <u>accuse him</u>. And the Lord said to Satan, 'The*

ACCUSATIONS

Lord rebuke you, O Satan! The Lord who has chosen Jerusalem rebuke you! Is not this a brand plucked from the fire?" (RSV). Joshua is standing before the angel and before God in judgment, as we all will be, and the devil is right there to accuse him and us. The accusations are all true because we've all made mistakes. Accusing is not part of our work; this is the devil's work. He's accusing Joshua, and God rebukes him. God doesn't want us to accuse each other, either.

Stoning System Continued Today

In Old Testament times, there were some offenses punishable by death. The punishment dealt out was by stoning. This "stoning system" has been used to vividly illustrate, the harmful effects of accusations and gossip.

"I had a dream. I saw A in close conversation with men and with ministers. He adroitly would make statements born of suspicion and imagination to draw them out, and then would gain expression from them. I saw him clap his hands over something very eagerly. I felt a pang of anguish at heart as I saw this going on. I saw in my dream yourself and B in conversation with him. You made statements to him which he seemed to grasp with avidity, and close his hand over something. I then saw him go to his room, and there upon the floor was a pile of stones systematically laid up, stone upon stone. He placed the additional stones on the pile and counted them up. Every stone had a name—some report gathered up—and every stone was numbered.

"The young man who often instructs me came and looked upon the pile of stones with grief and indignation, and inquired [of A] what he had and what he supposed to do with them. A looked up with a sharp, gratified laugh. 'These are mistakes of C. I am going to stone him with them, stone him to death.' The young man said, 'You are bringing back the stoning system, are you? You are worse than the ancient Pharisees. Who gave you this work to do? The Lord raised you up, the Lord entrusted you with a special work. The Lord has sustained you in a most remarkable manner, but it was not for you to degrade your powers for this kind of work. Satan is an accuser of the brethren. ... You have a higher calling, a more important work. Leave all such work of gathering stones for the enemies of God's law. You brethren must love one another, or you are not the children of the day, but of darkness'" (Manuscript Releases, vol. 12, p. 10-11; emphasis supplied).

The Lights Come On

Another graphic illustration shows the effect of our words and action on each other. In Testimonies for the Church, volume 9, pages 28, 29, is outlined the story of two maps. The first map Ellen White saw in vision, *"I saw jets of light shining from cities and villages, and from the high places and low places of the earth. God's word was obeyed, and as a result there were memorials for Him in every city and village. His truth was proclaimed throughout the world.*

"Then this map was removed and another put in its place. On it light was shining from a few places only. The rest of the world was in darkness, with only a glimmer of light here and there. Our instructor said: 'This darkness is the result of men's following their own course. They have cherished hereditary and cultivated tendencies toward evil. They have made questioning and faultfinding and accusing the chief business of their lives. Their hearts are not right with God. They have hidden their light under a bushel.' If every soldier of Christ had done his duty, if every watchman on the walls of Zion had given the trumpet a certain sound, the world might ere this have heard the message of warning. But the work is years behind. While men have slept, Satan has stolen a march on us" (emphasis supplied).

Notice the reference to the two maps; one has lights everywhere, lights in every village. There are very few lights on the second map where there is cherished a spirit of questioning, faultfinding, and accusing. These traits have taken the lights out of the map.

If we really want to be evangelistic as Christian people, we need to cherish the spirit of love and concern for each other, not accusing and finding fault. Then we will have a profound positive evangelistic effect on others.

Notice this reference in Christ's Object Lessons, pages 340, 341: *"That our influence should be a savor of death unto death is a fearful thought; yet this is possible. Many who profess to gather with Christ are scattering from Him. This is why the church is so weak. Many indulge freely in criticism and accusing. By giving expression to suspicion, jealousy, and discontent, they yield themselves as instruments to Satan. Before they realize what they are doing, the adversary has through them accomplished his purpose"* (emphasis supplied). Why is the church so weak today? Here we have the answer: they yield themselves to suspicion, jealousy, discontent, criticism, and accusation.

In John, chapter 17, Christ prayed for; unity among His people here on earth. This closeness would be an example to the world. It seems this lack of unity is one of the biggest reasons why the Christian church is so ineffective at present. Instead of unity, there is so much accusation and misunderstanding among our people.

"If we have a sense of the long-suffering of God toward us, we

shall not be found judging or accusing others. When Christ was living on the earth, how surprised His associates would have been, if, after becoming acquainted with Him, they had heard Him speak one word of accusation, of faultfinding, or of impatience. Let us never forget that those who love Him are to represent Him in character" (The Ministry of Healing, p. 489; emphasis supplied).

Jesus never spoke one word of accusation. The previous reference says that those who accuse others are actuated by the spirit of Satan.

There is a promise also found in The Ministry of Healing on page 90, *"The souls that turn to Him for refuge, Jesus lifts above the accusing and the strife of tongues"* (emphasis supplied). A promise that when we are subjects of accusations of any kind, the Lord will help us to rise above these and have a plan and strategy to cope with them. Jesus never accused; *"Jesus is our example in all things"* (Fundamentals of Christian Education, p. 50; emphasis supplied).

Paul in his experiences, when he was preaching, ran into a similar experience: *"Jealousy, evil surmising, and accusation had closed the hearts of many of the Corinthian believers against the full working of the Holy Spirit which searched all things, yea, the deep things of God"* (The Acts of the Apostles, p. 271; emphasis supplied). Accusations will undo the work of loving relationships and much of what God purposes to do on this earth in evangelism.

"More love is needed, more frankness, less suspicion, less evil thinking. We need to be less ready to blame and accuse. It is this that is so offensive to God" (Testimonies for the Church, vol. 7, p. 212; emphasis supplied). What really hurts God is our accusations against each other.

"Is there no law of kindness to be observed? Have Christians been authorized of God to criticize and condemn one another? Is it honorable, or even honest, to win from the lips of another, under the guise of friendship, secrets which have been entrusted to him, and then turn the knowledge thus gained to his injury? Is it Christian charity to gather up every floating report, to unearth everything that will cast suspicion on the character of another, and then take delight in using it to injure him? Satan exults when he can defame or wound a follower of Christ. He is 'the accuser of the brethren.' Shall Christians aid him in his work?" (ibid. vol. 5, p. 95; emphasis supplied).

Black Balls

There is an interesting story by Ellen White in volume 1 of Testimonies for the Church about accusations: *"I then saw a company pressing through the crowd*

with their eyes intently fixed upon the heavenly crown. As they earnestly urged their way through the disorderly crowd, angels attended them, and made room for them to advance. As they neared the heavenly crown, the light emanating from it shone upon them and around them, dispelling their darkness, and growing clearer and brighter, until they seemed to be transformed, and resembled the angels. They cast not one lingering look upon the earthly crown. Those who were in pursuit of the earthly mocked them, and threw black balls after them. They did them no injury while their eyes were fixed upon the heavenly crown, but those who turned their attention to the black balls were stained by them. The following scripture was presented before me, 'Lay not up for yourselves treasures upon earth'" (p. 349; emphasis supplied).

The "black balls" were thrown from one group who were seeking the earthly crown, toward a group who were seeking the heavenly crown. What were these black balls? <u>Testimonies for the Church</u>, volume 1, page 696, explains what they are: *"Angels flee from the dwelling where words of discord are exchanged, where gratitude is almost a stranger to the heart, and <u>censure leaps like black balls to the lips, spotting the garments, defiling the Christian character</u>"* (emphasis supplied).

These black balls, then, are censure, criticism, and accusations which spot our garments **only** if we pay attention to them. We now have a clue that would save us from these black balls. We do not give them any attention or become offended. We keep our eyes on the heavenly crown when under attack.

"Every man who praises himself, brushes the lustre from his best efforts. <u>A truly noble character will not stop to resent the false accusations of enemies; every word spoken falls harmless; for it strengthens that which it cannot overthrow</u>. The Lord would have His people closely united with Himself, the God of patience and of love. All should manifest in their lives the love of Christ. <u>Let none venture to belittle the reputation or position of another</u>; this is egotism. It is saying, 'I am so much better and more capable than you, that God gives me the preference. You are not of much account'" (<u>Testimonies for the Church</u>, vol. 4, p. 607; emphasis supplied). (See also chapters 16, "Treasures in the Trash," and 17 "Hastening Our Lord's Return" for more

ways to prepare the way for the return of Jesus.)

Consider the words of this poem by Margaret Bruner, entitled "The Monk and the Peasant." My wife, Linda, added a few lines about the joy of forgiveness.

The Monk and the Peasant

A peasant once unthinkingly spread lies about a friend
But later found the rumors false and hoped to make amends.
He sought the counsel of a monk, a man esteemed and wise
Who heard the peasant's story through and felt he must advise.

The kind monk said, "If you would have a mind again at peace,
I have a plan whereby you may from trouble seek release.
Go fill a bag with chicken down and to each door yard go,
And lay one fluffy feather where the streams of gossip flow."

The peasant did as he was told and then to the monk returned
Elated that his penance was a thing so quickly earned.
"Not yet," the old monk sternly said, "Take up your bag once more
And gather up the feathers that you placed at every door."

The peasant, eager to atone, went hastening to obey
But not one feather met his sight, the wind had blown them all away.

—Margaret Bruner

His feathers then forever free, released upon the wind
Brought him dismay and sorrow once he recognized his sin.

The man had learned, to his dismay, his unkind words could end
The precious love and friendship, the trust of his dear friend
His mother said, "Boys flying kites haul in their white winged birds,
But you can't do that way when you are flying words."

Then helplessly, the peasant to his friend, the monk, did say
"I never shall forget the hopeless lesson learned today."
The monk said, "Courage brother mine, there is yet hope—return
And ask forgiveness of your friend, so prove the lesson learned."

With shame he shuffled slowly back, knocked at his friend's abode,
Confessed his accusation, and there left his guilty load.
At first his friend was angry, but knew he must forgive,
For he, too, had been guilty but now could, in freedom, live.

"Arise, my friend, it was not me that you offended here
But Christ Himself, the crucified, who sheds another tear."
The accused and the accuser then knelt in one accord
To plead for the forgiveness of their understanding Lord.

—Linda Franklin

Please consider the references included under "For Further Study."

YOU CAN SURVIVE!

Perhaps you will conclude, as I did, that there is little, if any, room for placing an accusation against anyone; be it true or false. There are many have advocated reform and have lived it many years. Making changes in our lives that would eliminate accusations is a call to reform for all. **It is reform for reformers.** This cannot be neglected if we are to survive.

In the next chapter we will consider a problem that results from accusations toward church leadership. Groups of accusers form, focusing their attention on the church's shortcomings. These "splinter groups" criticize and, in the name of reformation, do great harm. Certainly we have no need to accuse anyone. The devil does it just fine through those who are willing to accept his principles of condemnation!

FOR FURTHER STUDY

Selected Messages, book 1, pages 411, 412
"No one is able to explain the Scriptures without the aid of the Holy Spirit. But when you take up the Word of God with a humble, teachable heart, the angels of God will be by your side to impress you with the evidences of the truth. When the Spirit of God rests upon you, there will be no feeling of envy or jealousy in examining another's position; there will be no spirit of accusation and criticism, such as Satan inspired in the hearts of the Jewish leaders against Christ" (emphasis supplied).

The Publishing Ministry, page 309
"The Lord lives and reigns. Soon He will arise in majesty to shake terribly the earth. A special message is now to be borne, a message that will pierce the spiritual darkness and convict and convert souls. 'Haste thee, flee for thy life,' is the call to be given to those dwelling in sin. We must now be terribly in earnest. We have not a moment to spend in criticism and accusation. Let those who have done this in the past fall on their knees in prayer, and let them beware how they put their words and their plans in the place of God's words and God's plans" (emphasis supplied).

In Heavenly Places, page 288
"When the Holy Spirit moves upon human minds all petty complaints and accusations between man and his fellow man will be put away. The bright beams of the Sun of Righteousness will shine into the chambers of the mind and heart. In our worship of God there will be no distinction between rich and poor, white and black. All prejudice will be melted away. When we approach God it will be as one brotherhood. We are pilgrims and strangers, bound for a

better country, even a heavenly. There all pride, <u>all accusation</u>, all self-deception, will forever have an end. Every mask will be laid aside, and we shall 'see him as he is'" (emphasis supplied).

Testimonies for the Church, volume 5, page 339
  "Zacchaeus declared: '<u>If I have taken anything from any man by false accusation</u>, I restore to him fourfold.' You could at least have made efforts to correct your acts of injustice to your fellow men. You cannot make every case right, for some whom you have injured have gone into their graves, and the account stands registered against you. In these cases the best you can do is <u>bring a trespass offering</u> to the altar of the Lord, and He will accept and pardon you. <u>But where you can, you should make reparation to the wronged ones</u>" (emphasis supplied).

Patriarchs and Prophets, page 520
  "<u>Even under false accusation those who are in the right can afford to be calm and considerate</u>. God is acquainted with all that is misunderstood and misinterpreted by men, and we can <u>safely leave our case in His hands</u>. <u>He will as surely vindicate the cause of those who put their trust in Him as He searched out the guilt of Achan</u>. Those who are actuated by the spirit of Christ will possess that charity which suffers long and is kind" (emphasis supplied).

Manuscript Releases, volume 18, pages 361, 362
  "Every heart that is controlled by these principles in 1896 will be loyal. <u>When those who are in God's service resort to accusation, they are adopting Satan's principles</u> to cast out Satan. <u>It will never work</u>. Satan will work. He is working upon human minds by his crooked principles. These will be adopted and acted upon by those who claim to be loyal and true to God's government. How shall we know that they are untrue, disloyal? 'By their fruits ye shall know them'" (emphasis supplied).

The Advent Review and Sabbath Herald, October 24, 1893
  "O that the mercy and love of God were cultivated by every member of our churches! <u>O that brotherly love might be revived, never to wane, but to grow more and more fervent</u>! It is true that words of admonition and counsel are frequently needed in the church, but they are never to be given by those who are filled with suspicion and distrust, who are eager to weigh others in the scales of their own opinions. No one can do the work of reproving and counseling in the way that Christ would have it done, whose heart is not filled with

peace and love. <u>We are near the end, there is no time to waste in educating</u> <u>ourselves in the line of accusation of brethren</u>, and we are not to take up a reproach against our neighbor. Deal tenderly and graciously with every soul, and <u>especially deal tenderly with those who are liable to err.</u> They, of all others, need your help the most. Never take up a report against a brother or a neighbor, or harbor evil surmisings against him. Thou shalt not imagine evil in thy heart against thy brother" (emphasis supplied).

<u>The Second Advent Review and Sabbath Herald</u>, August 28, 1883
   "<u>Envy and jealousy loose the blood-hounds of suspicion, and minds</u> <u>that love the sport join in hunting down the fair fame of Christ's ambassa-</u> <u>dors</u>. An unjust insinuation is started, a conjecture is set afloat; and it gathers strength as it passes from one to another of those who desire it to be true. These evil reports are received with great satisfaction by some who have been reproved for heinous sins or grave defects of character. They smarted under the reproof, and yet did not reform. <u>Now their consciences are eased; they</u> <u>learn that the reprover cannot be trusted; somebody has circulated a damag-</u> <u>ing report; somebody has brought an accusation.</u> They leave the distasteful work of caring for their own souls and repenting of their own sins, and climb upon the judgment seat to condemn another" (emphasis supplied).

<u>The Home Missionary</u>, September 1, 1894
   "He who is a follower of Christ will distinguish between the sacred and the common, and will cling to the true evidence of a man's character and work, for Christ has said, 'By their fruits ye shall know them.' The Christian will move forward amid all manner of opposition. He will despise flattery because it is born of Satan. <u>He will detest accusation because</u> <u>it is the weapon of the evil one</u>. They will not cherish envy or indulge in self-exaltation because these are the characteristics of the adversary of God and man. They will not be found as spies; for Satan used the despised Jews in doing this work against Jesus. They will not follow their brethren with a flood of questions as the Jews followed Christ for the purpose of entangling him in his words, and provoking him to speak of things in order that they might make him an offender for a word" (emphasis supplied).

<u>Patriarchs and Prophets</u>, page 417
   "The water gushed forth in abundance to satisfy the host. But a great wrong had been done. Moses had spoken from irritated feeling; his words were

an expression of human passion rather than of holy indignation because God had been dishonored. 'Hear now, ye rebels,' he said. This accusation was true, but even truth is not to be spoken in passion or impatience. When God had bidden Moses to charge upon Israel their rebellion, the words had been painful to him, and hard for them to bear, yet God had sustained him in delivering the message. But when he took it upon himself to accuse them, he grieved the Spirit of God and wrought only harm to the people. His lack of patience and self-control was evident. Thus the people were given occasion to question whether his past course had been under the direction of God, and to excuse their own sins. Moses, as well as they, had offended God. His course, they said, had from the first been open to criticism and censure.

They had now found the pretext which they desired for rejecting all the reproofs that God had sent them through His servant" (emphasis supplied).

The Desire of Ages, page 354

"The servants of Christ will be brought before the great men of the world, who, but for this, might never hear the gospel. The truth has been misrepresented to these men. They have listened to false charges concerning the faith of Christ's disciples. Often their only means of learning its real character is the testimony of those who are brought to trial for their faith. Under examination these are required to answer, and their judges to listen to the testimony borne. God's grace will be dispensed to His servants to meet the emergency. 'It shall be given you,' says Jesus, 'in that same hour what ye shall speak. For it is not ye that speak, but the Spirit of your Father which speaketh in you.' As the Spirit of God illuminates the minds of His servants, the truth will be presented in its divine power and preciousness. Those who reject the truth will stand to accuse and oppress the disciples. But under loss and suffering, even unto the death, the Lord's children are to reveal the meekness of their divine Example. Thus will be seen the contrast between Satan's agents and the representatives of Christ. The Saviour will be lifted up before the rulers and the people" (emphasis supplied).

Education, pages 89 and 90

"If the look that Jesus cast upon him had spoken condemnation instead of pity; if in foretelling the sin He had failed of speaking hope, how dense would have been the darkness that encompassed Peter! How reckless the despair of that tortured soul! In that hour of anguish and self-abhorrence, what could have held him back from the path trodden by Judas? ...

"Human beings, themselves given to evil, are prone to deal untenderly

91

with the tempted and the erring. <u>They cannot read the heart, they know not its struggle and pain</u>. Of the rebuke that is love, of the blow that wounds to heal, of the warning that speaks hope, they have need to learn" (emphasis supplied).

The Desire of Ages, page 441
"Christ's instruction as to the treatment of the erring repeats in more specific form the teaching given to Israel through Moses: 'Thou shalt not hate thy brother in thine heart: thou shalt in anywise rebuke thy neighbour, that thou bear not sin for him'(Lev. 19:17). That is, if one neglects the duty Christ has enjoined of trying to restore those who are in error and sin, he becomes a partaker in the sin. <u>For evils that we might have checked, we are just as responsible as if we were guilty of the acts ourselves</u>" (emphasis supplied).

Gossip
These six things doth the Lord hate: yea, seven are an abomination unto him: A proud look, a lying tongue, and hands that shed innocent blood, An heart that deviseth wicked imaginations, feet that be swift in running to mischief, A false witness that speaketh lies, and he that soweth discord among brethren" (Proverbs 6:16-19).

The Upward Look, page 363
"Christians will be tested and tried. But if they are sincerely trying to serve God, strength will be given them for every conflict. <u>They are not to listen to false reports that come to their ears</u>, but are to go straight forward in the path of duty. They are to learn to think for themselves, and their actions are ever to be in accordance with the Word of God. ...
"Often difficulties may be healed by silence. Let the evil talker alone. Go about your work as one who has a sacred trust to fulfill. When you are criticized, move on as one who hears not. <u>Your heart may be wounded; nevertheless, do not allow yourself to be turned aside from your work</u>. Give your time and attention to matters of eternal interest" (emphasis supplied).

Additional references on the subject of gossip:

Education, page 235 (gossip compared to cannibalism)
Fundamentals of Christian Education, page 487 (Christ grieved by gossip)
In Heavenly Places, page 88 (counsel about gossip)
Our High Calling, page 359 (we will not escape gossip)

ACCUSATIONS

Chapter Four

Critical Ministry: An Oxymoron?

"Enfeebled and defective as it may appear, the church is the one object upon which God bestows in a special sense His supreme regard" (The Acts of the Apostles, p. 12).

The spirit of criticism is sometimes mislabeled as reformation. We discovered in Chapter Three that we should neither accuse nor be offended. How should we relate to organizations who accuse and criticize, especially when their accusations are aimed at the church?

In Luke 6:37 Jesus says, *"Judge not, and ye shall not be judged: condemn not, and ye shall not be condemned: forgive, and ye shall be forgiven."* According to this verse, if we engage in a spirit of condemnation, we also are condemned. If we want to avoid the spirit of condemnation toward us, we must not condemn anyone else.

Thoughts From the Mount of Blessing tells us that the path that we take others over is the path we will have to tread ourselves. *"That which we do to others, whether it be good or evil, will surely react upon ourselves, in blessing or in cursing. Whatsoever we give, we shall receive again"* (p. 136).

Critical Ministry or Supporting Ministry?

In self-supporting work, there are two main groups of people. The first group, now labeled "supporting ministries," is comprised of organizations and people that work as a support to the church in witnessing to the world field. There are others, "independent ministries," who feel called upon to take the mistakes and failures of the church to the pulpit. True, there are mistakes and failures in any organization, but God has given us a way to handle them personally and responsibly. We are not to carry on a critical ministry or have a condemning attitude, which is the principle of Matthew 18:15-17. If someone in the church does something that offends you, discuss it, but only with that person. Gain your brother if you can. If you can't, and you feel it is a matter of his salvation or life and death, take one or two others to hear him. If this person refuses to listen to anyone, the counsel is to treat him as one who needs to be won to Christ. Take it to the church. These verses give no license for you to let an offense stand between you and fellowship.

John 3:17 states clearly that *"God sent not his Son into the world to condemn the world; but that the world through him might be saved."*

Romans 2:1 states: *"Therefore thou art inexcusable, O man, whosoever thou art that judgest: for wherein thou judgest another, thou condemnest thyself: for thou that judgest doest the same things."* Brothers and sisters, we need to be very careful how we judge others because the Bible says that, automatically, the things we condemn in others are the very things we do ourselves. Invariably, the path over which we take others is the path we will have to tread. This truth, if followed, saves heartache and pain down the road. Any of us who have been too critical will have to pass over the road of being criticized ourselves. The love of God that has ordained that experience is a most unforgettable lesson book.

"Everyone who has been free to condemn or discourage, will in his own experience be brought over the same ground where he has caused others to pass; he will feel what they have suffered because of his want of sympathy and tenderness" (Thoughts From the Mount of Blessing, p. 136; emphasis supplied).

Romans 8:1 says, *"There is therefore now no condemnation to them which are in Christ Jesus, who walk not after the flesh, but after the Spirit."* This verse emphasizes the positive path members of the church should follow. We must walk "after the Spirit." Ellen G. White elaborates on this pathway of the church in The Acts of the Apostles, page 9: *"The church is God's appointed agency for the salvation of men. It was organized for service, and its mission is to carry the gospel to the world. From the beginning it has been God's plan that through His church shall be reflected to the world His fullness and sufficiency.... The church is the repository of the riches of the grace of Christ; and through the church will eventually be made manifest, even to the 'principalities and powers in heavenly places,' the final and full display of the love of God"* (emphasis supplied).

"Enfeebled and defective as it may appear, the church is the one

object upon which <u>God bestows in a special sense His supreme regard</u>" (<u>ibid</u>., p. 12; emphasis supplied). Why, then, would we ever want to engage in a critical ministry of the very thing that is the closest to the heart of God? It really doesn't make any spiritual sense. In fact, it is devastating to our own personal spiritual experience. This idea is clearly stated on page 11: *"The church is God's fortress, His city of refuge, which He holds in a revolted world. <u>Any betrayal of the church is treachery to Him</u> who has bought mankind with the blood of His only begotten Son"* (emphasis supplied).

Isaiah 56:7 tells us what we are to call the church: *"For mine house shall be called an house of prayer."* Each member is to recognize that God's church is a house of prayer. It is open to all people, those who criticize and those who don't. There is a place in every heart to gain victory over this treacherous sin.

Critical ministries are actually supporting Satan's work. *"Divisions, and even bitter dissensions which would disgrace any worldly community, are common in the churches, because there is so little effort to control wrong feelings, and to repress every word that Satan can take advantage of. As soon as an alienation of feeling arises, the matter is spread before Satan for his inspection, and the opportunity given for him to use his serpentlike wisdom and skill in dividing and destroying the church. <u>There is great loss in every dissension</u>....*

"Worldlings look on, and jeeringly exclaim, 'Behold how these Christians hate one another! If this is religion, we do not want it.' And they look upon themselves and their irreligious characters with great satisfaction. Thus they are confirmed in their impenitence, and Satan exults at his success" (<u>Selected Messages</u>, book 1, p. 123; emphasis supplied). The reason for separating should not be because of our criticism of others. Rather than condemning one another, let us turn our spiritual weapons on the world around us and work toward gaining more souls for the kingdom by bringing them into fellowship with Christ.

In volume 3 of <u>Testimonies for the Church</u>, Mrs. White expresses severe warnings to those who wish to vent in public feelings of condemnation toward the church in general or toward particular individuals. She says, *"It is worse, far worse, to give expression to the feelings in a large gathering, firing at anyone and everyone, than to go to the individuals who may have done wrong and personally reprove them. The offensiveness of this severe, overbearing, denunciatory talk in a large gathering is of as much more grave a character in the sight of God than giving personal, individual reproof as the numbers are greater and the censure more general. It is ever easier to give expression to the feelings before a congregation, because there are many present, than* *to go to the erring and, face to face with them, openly, frankly, plainly state their wrong course. But bringing into the house of God strong feelings against individuals, and <u>making all the innocent as well as the guilty suffer, is a manner of labor which God does not sanction and which does harm rather than good</u>. It has too often been the case that criticizing and denunciatory discourses have been given before a congregation. These do not encourage a spirit of love in the brethren. They do not tend to make them spiritually minded and lead them to holiness and heaven, <u>but a spirit of bitterness is aroused in hearts</u>"* (pp. 507, 508; emphasis supplied).

God never sanctions a critical ministry. If the spirit of God dwells in our hearts, His love is perfected in us and we will never indulge in a spirit of condemnation or criticism. The Bible in 1 John 4:7-12 tells us that love is of God and if we do not love others, we do not know Him.

Sometimes people excuse their criticism because they think they are going to set things right, especially regarding leadership that they consider weak and ineffective. But we are told to leave this to God. *"<u>There is no need to doubt, to be fearful that the work will not succeed</u>. God is at the head of the work, and He will set everything in order. <u>If matters need adjusting at the head of the work, God will attend to that</u>, and work to right every wrong. <u>Let us have faith that God is going to carry the noble ship which bears the people of God safely into port</u>"* (<u>Selected Messages</u>, book 2, p. 390; emphasis supplied).

Campaigns to criticize the leadership of our church need not be made public, because condemnation and criticism only make their burdens heavier. Let us support them and help all we can so that unity and the grace of Christ may be found in each heart.

"Let the men standing as watchmen and as shepherds of the flock proclaim the solemn truth, sound the notes of warning to all people, nations, and tongues. Let them be living representatives of the truth they advocate, and honor God's law by strict and holy compliance with its requirements, walking before the Lord in purity" (ibid. p. 378). Who among us want to be watchmen on the walls of Zion? Let those, then, urge the true reformation—that of conversion and coming back to God, not criticizing and causing dissension and division.

When people have true conversion and loyalty to Christ, they will see that *"the church is organized for service; and in a life of service to Christ, <u>connection with the church is one of the first steps</u>. Loyalty to Christ demands the faithful performance of church duties. This is an important part of one's training; and in a church imbued with the Master's life, it will lead directly to* *effort for the world without"* (Education, pp. 268, 269; emphasis supplied). Can you see the vision? As we become connected with Christ, we do not focus on criticism and condemnation of each other, but in the united effort of reaching the world for Christ.

How to Deal With Error

Elder W. D. Frazee says it this way in his book Another Ark to Build, page 126: "When God chooses men to deal with errors among His people, He desires them to go about this work in the right way, and the right way does not include circulating reports that are derogatory to the church and its leaders. But this is the very thing the criticizers do. When a leader makes a mistake, they pounce upon it like a buzzard on a corpse and call all the other buzzards to come and enjoy it with them. If we love the church as Jesus loves it, we will not be eager to promote reports that reflect on the church and its leadership or even listen to them."

But what happens if the reports are true? Have we any inspired counsel on this? Elder Frazee also quotes from Letter 48, written by Ellen G. White to a church elder. *"You have undertaken to point out the defects of reformers and pioneers in the cause of God. No one should trace the lines which you have done. You have made public the errors and defects of the people of God, and in so doing have dishonored God and Jesus Christ. I would not for my right arm have given to the world that which you have written. You have not been conscious of what would be the influence of your work.... Let God by inspiration trace the errors of His people for their instruction and admonition; but let not finite lips or pen dwell upon those features of the experience of God's people that will have a tendency to confuse and cloud the mind.... God will charge those who unwisely expose the mistakes of their brethren with sin of far greater magnitude than He will charge the one who makes the misstep. Criticism and condemnation of the brethren are counted as criticism and condemnation of Christ"* (Selected Messages, book 3, pp. 343-345; emphasis supplied). So those who criticize others are in greater sin than those whose sin is being magnified!

How much more plain can it be? Why would we ever want to criticize our church, each other, or Christ? Still there are groups who do this, mistakenly labelling themselves as reformers. Mrs. White has this to say of them: *"There is a class who profess to believe the truth, but who cherish secret feelings of dissatisfaction against those who bear the burdens in this work.... Such readily receive, cherish, and circulate reports which have no foundation in truth, to destroy the influence of those who are engaged in this work. All who wish to* *draw off from the body will have opportunity. Something will arise to test everyone. The great sifting time is just before us. <u>The jealous and faultfinding, who are watching for evil, will be shaken out</u>"* (<u>Testimonies for the Church</u>, vol. 1, p. 251; emphasis supplied).

When we criticize and condemn, we are setting ourselves up to be shaken out of the church! We must give a solemn and clear warning about this–this is not the spirit or the type of activity in which God wants to see us engaged. The sad part is that those who want only to criticize and condemn not only destroy themselves, but may also destroy others' chances of heaven.

Mrs. White also elaborates on the end result of criticism. She writes, *"There are two opposing influences continually exerted on the members of the church. One influence is working for the purification of the church, and the other for the corrupting of the people of God.... <u>Although there are evils existing in the church, and will be until the end of the world, the church in these last days is to be the light of the world that is polluted and demoralized by sin</u>.... <u>There is but one church in the world who are at the present time standing in the breach, and making up the hedge, building up the old waste places; and for any man to call the attention of the world and other churches to this church, denouncing her as Babylon, is to do a work in harmony with him who is the accuser of the brethren</u>"* (<u>The Faith I Live By</u>, p. 305; <u>emphasis supplied</u>). If we find ourselves involved in that sort of work, we must consider ourselves to be in league with Satan as identified in Revelation 12:10.

Tearing Down or Building Up?

We are not to turn our accusations against the church; rather, we are to join forces with her against the tide of evil.

"Those who start up to proclaim a message on their own individual responsibility, who, while claiming to be taught and led of God, still make it their special work to tear down that which Christ has been for years building up, are not doing the will of God. <u>Be it known that these men are on the side of the great deceiver. Believe them not</u>" (<u>Testimonies to Ministers</u>, p. 51; emphasis supplied). We see pamphlets and hear messages that tear down the church. We should not to give ear to or read these materials.

In the October 3, 1893, issue of the <u>Review and Herald</u>, Mrs. White again affirms that the remnant church is not to be identified with Babylon. She wrote: *"The Lord has sent messages of warning and entreaty, messages of reproof and rebuke, and they have not been in vain. <u>But we have never had a message that the Lord would disorganize the church. We have never had the prophecy con-</u>*

cerning Babylon applied to the Seventh-day Adventist Church, or been informed that the 'loud' cry consisted in calling God's people to come out of her; for this is not God's plan concerning Israel" (emphasis supplied).

Angel Tears

Home is where the angels linger
Listening to the words we say.
Are they saddened by our anger—
Happy when they hear us pray?
Angels smile at calm and order
Joyous, heavenward they fly.
But a harsh, unloving spirit,
Always makes the angels cry.

Does your angel smile beside you
In the Sabbath meeting-place?
Whispering fears and cruel doubtings
Put a tear upon his face.
Worldly musings, love of pleasure,
Those who love and make a lie,
Bickering brother's tongues of fire
Wound and make the angels cry.

Sickness, death can leave you weeping,
Premature those last good-byes.
When you're lonely, torn by sorrow,
That is when your angel cries.
All too soon, time will be over,
When the angels in the sky
Bring the Lord to claim His children—
Nevermore will angels cry.

—Linda Franklin

Tithe

It is clear that we do not have the message to leave the church. Let us not give heed to seducing spirits that would suggest otherwise. We can discern mistakes in the church, but that is not the reason to send our tithe money to any other organization. *"Cannot you see that it is not best under any circumstances to withhold your tithes and offerings because you are not in harmony with everything that your brethren do? The tithes and offerings are not the property of man, but are to be used in doing a certain work for God; unworthy ministers might receive some of the means thus raised; but dare anyone, because of this, withhold from the treasury and*

100

brave the curse of God. I dare not" In <u>Sermons and Talks</u>, vol. 2, p. 74; (emphasis supplied).

We often hear from various pulpits and papers that because there is so much evil in the church we should withhold our tithe. Each of us must seriously reconsider this position advocated by certain organizations that engage in critical ministry.

The Lord needs each of us to be a supporting, not a critical ministry. Notice this special counsel from <u>Counsels to Writers and Editors</u>: *"Do not understand me as approving of the recent action of the <u>General Confer-ence</u> Association, of which you write; but in regard to that matter it is right that I should speak to them. <u>They have many difficulties to meet, and if they err in their action, the Lord knows it all, and can overrule all for the good of those who trust in Him</u>"* (pp. 156, 157; emphasis supplied). God is in charge of His church. His work is to lead His church. Our work is to go to one another when we see a problem, but not to accuse, criticize, or condemn. Ellen White knew many more errors in the church than we do, yet she maintained her connection with the church.

"We cannot now enter into any new organization; for this would mean apostasy from the truth" (<u>Selected Messages,</u> book 2, p. 390).

We are survivors only as we trust God to overrule every mistake for good. Why would we want to be an exception to Romans 8:28 *(all things work together for good)*, when the rubber of our heart hits the rocky road of life? What about those painful personal experiences which tend to challenge our trust? The following chapter is a discussion of how others have not only survived, but have allowed God to transform the broken pieces of their lives into healing ministries.

Chapter Five

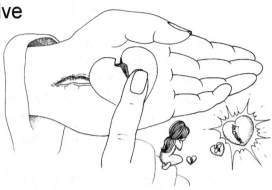

Broken in Heart:
A Purpose in Pain

by Linda Franklin

"The tears of the penitent are only the raindrops that precede the sunshine of holiness" (The Desire of Ages, p. 300).

Harry brought more joy to the angels than any of us realized. After the altar call at our old-fashioned gospel meetings, adults and children alike would ask each other, "Who stood tonight?"

"Just Harry." Our group shrug confirmed the ineffective effort of our minister to save anyone's soul that night. Harry was a sort of consolation prize; he had a slight mental handicap, but he was a friendly soul with innocent puppy-dog eyes framed in a timeless face. It was hard to tell if Harry was an aged 30-year-old or a well-kept man in his 60s. He was always clean; his slacks and white shirt sharply pressed, his rosy cheeks and balding head always shiny, as if to overcompensate for his shortcomings.

Harry's dedicated caregiver, an ancient mother in Israel, always sat in the back row. Not so, her son. Chin forward, head listing slightly starboard, Harry clutched his tattered Bible tightly with both hands in front of him, giving the impression of being propelled to his pew by the Word itself. His broad, reverent smile almost made one forget his hunched shoulders and deformed body.

Though I don't remember hearing him speak, Harry must have understood the minister's words, for he was always ready to stand when the altar call was extended. I would sometimes muster up enough nerve to sit at the side of the room where I could watch Harry, though I was painfully shy and was uncomfortable walking to the front. But it was worth it, once in a while, to watch Harry. He would direct his fixed smile at the speaker from the first word of the sermon and then, when he knew the call was about to be made, Harry would lift his eyes toward heaven, an angelic glow irradiating his otherwise homely features. Then Harry would stand up, clutching his Bible as if he knew what he was doing.

Though I tried focusing where Harry looked, I could see nothing—except the fear that held me in my seat, keeping me from standing or saying anything about my convictions. For instance, I knew I should have told the other children my age who mocked Harry behind his back, "You shouldn't laugh at Harry." But I didn't.

The sticks and stones of thoughtlessness others directed by a knowing glance, a shake of the head, a cluck of the tongue behind Harry's back never bothered him; Harry had no enemies because he acknowledged none. He was a committed Christian. Like Stephen of old, he chose to look above and beyond, toward heaven. I can see that clearly now, though the truth evaded me at the time. Harry would be old now, but if he can still hear and if he can still grip his Bible, I am sure it is still pulling him to his feet answering altar calls.

I had forgotten about Harry, but as I sat quietly considering the subject of submission recently a thought-picture of Harry sped across my inmost soul, and it suddenly seemed clear to me that Harry, better than all the rest of us at those old gospel meetings, had understood surrender. His weaknesses were obvious, his strength was in surrender. Harry was happy in service. He always smiled, his rosy cheeks glowed more with the joy of service than with the stifling summer heat of the big tent where he was regularly found washing thousands of dishes at our yearly conventions.

In Jesus' sermon on the mount, in Matthew 5, the first people to whom He directs the attention of the multitude are the poor in spirit: *"Blessed are the poor in spirit: for theirs is the kingdom of heaven"* (verse 3). Many times I have come to that place in life where the Lord has arranged for me to know the blessing of brokenness. It is as if He is saying to me, "My child, take My Spirit and you will not have to continue to sacrifice your own."

Shadows in the Valley

Our son's burn accident was the most consuming fire of surrender we have yet endured. He was only 8 when he suffered third-degree burns over a significant portion of his body. As parents, Jere and I almost begged his physician to promise us that he would live. As Jed's life hung in the balance, I finally came to the place of surrender where I knew I had to sacrifice my will for His and say those dreadful words, "Not my will but Thine be done." As soon as I breathed this prayer, my sorrow was reduced to a bearable level. Today, whenever I am tempted to grasp for my "rights," I have only to look at my son's scars to realize the price my Father paid to claim my will, my rights, my all.

Unless I had known that valley of surrender those many years ago, I could not have experienced the mountaintop of gratitude for the sacrifice God made for me in allowing the death of His only Son.

Jed's scars keep me in a constant attitude of gratefulness for intervening in what could have been a tragedy. What my heart has borne helps me to lift up others who suffer. Just the other day, as he was chauffeuring us to church, Jed's upbeat philosophy of life emerged when he observed, "Mom, have you ever noticed how the shadows always point to the rainbows?" Instantly, I was back in the valley of the shadow of death holding his little burned hands in mine, desperately wanting to put the words of his survival into my Father's mouth. But, it was in that valley where, instead, I came to the cross and saw a weeping Father give His only begotten Son to an unappreciative world. And, because of my Father's heart of sacrifice, I have a chance at immortality. Truly, tears of submission compose the rainbows of serenity.

Jed's observations about the shadows pointing to the rainbows launched me on an in-depth study of the power in surrender as revealed in the light of the cross. The light of the cross may help explain that place of brokenness to which we all must come before we know the joy of victory:

"Therefore I take pleasure in infirmities, in reproaches, in necessities, in persecutions, in distresses for Christ's sake: for when I am weak, then am I strong" (2 Corinthians 12:10).

Life's Negatives: Developing a Perfect Picture of His Image

Like me, you may have had the privilege of having one of those sparkling acquaintances, maybe a friend or a child, who blessed your life through their acceptance of a physical, emotional, or mental challenge. Is there a brighter torch for truth than a heartbroken, heart-healed warrior for Christ? Far from acting as if they expect others to treat them as a hero or martyr, they live above the darkness, blessing others with the atmosphere of heaven by living beyond their pain. Like Harry, these gems, because of their beauty in surrender, send a gleam of hope from heaven's gates to those who reach toward them in times of despair. Faith is borne of adversity– when we trust the hand of God to dip us in the solution He sees will best develop His image in our dark lives.

"The fact that we are called upon to endure trial shows that the Lord Jesus sees in us something precious which He desires to develop" (The Ministry of Healing, p. 471; emphasis supplied).

"When trials and tribulations come to you know that they are sent in order that you may receive from the Lord of glory renewed strength and increased humility, so that He may safely bless and support and uphold you.... We

miss very much because we do not grasp the blessings that may be ours in our afflictions. All our sufferings and sorrows, all our temptations and trials, all our sadness and griefs, all our persecutions and privations, and in short all things, work together for our good. All experiences and circumstances are God's workmen whereby good is brought to us" (My Life Today, p. 185; emphasis supplied).

Georgia Senator Max Clelland, triple amputee and veteran of Vietnam, in his book Strong in the Broken Places, assures us, "It is possible to become strong in the broken places ... most people discover that adversity does make them stronger."

Becky Conway was only 15 when she lost her leg to cancer. But Jesus had been the center of her life, the "trunk of her tree" as she puts it. When she lost her leg, it was merely a pruning of a limb, so to speak, that seemed to cause the nutrients of her soul to concentrate within the remaining portion of her body, resulting in a deeper and stronger relationship with God. It was an exposure to the world of others' pain such as she had never known. At the time she was hospitalized, Becky befriended a young lady who was dying of intestinal cancer; the same cancer which had taken her sister the year before and from which her father was also suffering. They had in-depth discussions about living and dying, with each feeling sorry for the other's lot. By accepting their own plight, the girls made the burden much easier for their parents knowing that whatever happened, they were each resigned and even joyful in the will of God.

Becky's father, Jim, says, "It is out of the experiences of life, when God comforts us, that we learn to comfort others. We can't continue to say, 'God, get me out of this!' It is through the experiences God allows to come to us that He is saying, 'Time to grow up, Jim.' And we have only two choices: to become angry at God, continue to try to control each crisis, praying against His will, or accept the working out of God's will. Like Job, we need to admit that we don't know all of the purposes God has in mind, *'Though he slay me, yet will I trust in him'* (Job 13:15). Jim goes on to say that throughout Becky's ordeal, he rebelled, prayed against God's will, and was a miserable person. But when he came to the point of saying, "Not my will, but Thine be done," he found peace. Though he does not yet understand why it happened, he knows that God often has higher purposes to accomplish than human eyes are willing to see.

Keith Miller claims, "Every problem in my life has become a bridge across which I have helped another."

Trials are our opportunity to accept God's comfort. Perhaps it is in the darkest valleys that those who would be pure in heart learn to trust God by looking toward the light, trusting by faith, that all things will work together for good.

Ellen White understood trials, pain, adversity, and hardship–the most common roads toward brokenness: *"The whole universe of heaven are watching the conflict, and if our eyes could be opened we would see angels in the ranks, for the Holy Spirit is promised to all who fight manfully the battles of the Lord. There are soldiers engaged in the battle who are not perfect, compassed with infirmities, falling into sin, ignorant, and needing instruction at every step; but to feel their need, to sense their poverty is essential before they can be helped. When they fall upon the Rock and are broken then the everlasting arms are around the helpless. Heavenly agencies are employed to do their work, fit them as vessels of honor, overpowering the enemies, piercing the cloud and shadow of Satanic agencies. ... A conqueror stands at your head, victory is sure"* (The Ellen G White 1888 Materials, vol. 2 p. 794; emphasis supplied).

Life will bring, in the wake of its sunshine, a few drops of rain, sometimes a shower or two, once in a while a deluge of trouble above which we struggle to keep from being swept into a flood of total despair. God's child must remember that from the shadows of earth is being written the greatest story ever told. We are not just watching the great controversy unfold from eternity past to eternity future, we are part of the story. We can even read between the lines, if we choose to accept the eyesalve He wants to give us!

The drama of the ages does not just involve Christ, Satan, and those few giants of faith of whom we read in Hebrews 11; it involves you and me. Each one of us is a piece of the unfinished puzzle, a small, but indispensable, portion of the total picture, though it often seems our days appear in the negative rather than the positive we desire to see. Our Father, the great artist, knows just how much of the darker hues to allow in the lives of each of His children so that their canvas is completed for the world to see. No one knows how important one swipe of His brush across the canvas of our life may be to those observing our faith, but that part is important to the whole picture because Someone is watching, and He is all-wise.

Next time you think things are just not developing properly, remember that it is quite impossible to have a fully developed picture without a negative, the timing of which and the solutions of which are in God's hands. The world watches to see how we are going to react when the rinsing process begins and the rain falls. In accepting life's negatives, however broken they may leave us, we endure only a few years of earthly life. Should He call upon us to suffer, we can do so with our head high, for His sake. We can stand up, like Harry. We have been chosen, among those called, to fall on the Rock.

Step by step, day by day, I must test Him with the burden of my tears. Maybe you are tired of crying as you wonder about elusive victories. There are practical applications—what does a service of surrender really mean?

All for the Best

Things mostly happen for the best.
However hard it seems today,
When some fond plan has gone astray
Or what you've wished for most is lost
An' you sit countin' up the cost
With eyes half-blind by tears o' grief
While doubt is chokin' out belief,
You'll find when all is understood
That what seemed bad was really good.

Life can't be counted in a day.
The present rain that will not stop
Next autumn means a bumper crop.
We wonder why some things must be—
Care's purpose we can seldom see—
An' yet long afterwards we turn
To view the past an' then we learn
That what once filled our minds with doubt
Was good for us as it worked out.

I've never known an hour of care
But that I've later come to see
That it has brought some joy to me.
Even the sorrows I have borne,
Leavin' me lonely an' forlorn
An' hurt, an' bruised, an' sick at heart,
In life's great plan have had a part.
An' though I could not understand
Why I should bow to Death's command,
As time went by I came to know
That it was really better so.

Things mostly happen for the best.
So narrow is our vision here
That we are blinded by a tear
An' stunned by every hurt and blow
Which comes today to strike us low.
An' yet some day we turn an' find
That what seemed cruel once was kind.
Most things, I hold, are wisely planned
If we could only understand.

–Edgar Guest

Little Things, Like Money

Sometimes, like Job, we may be called upon to face trials in order to test our connection with our Father. But we can also choose to fall on the rock of surrender by relinquishing our hold upon the things of earth. Some of these are by requirement, this is called obedience. God calls for volunteers, but once we are in the army, we follow His rules. Tithe-paying demonstrates our induction into boot camp. As we learn to surrender 10 percent, by habit, we will eventually discover that all of our money is rightfully His and will find ourselves volunteering for service above and beyond His promise of 10 percent joy. Our puny cash flow is merely a single wave upon the shoreline of His endless ocean of riches. He sends a wave of income, we toss a portion back upon the waters. Inevitably the next wave is bigger, but our faith, having been blessed by surviving the last trial, lifts our vision above mere earthly treasures.

Once we understand the ebb and flow of His blessings we can understand why He would counsel us to *"shun debt like the leprosy"* (Testimonies for the Church, vol. 6, p. 217). Debt imprisons us from becoming the blessing we could be to others. If you are in debt, He cannot call upon you to help His church, the apple of His eye, the object of His supreme regard. Surrender may be as simple as slicing up that credit card, allowing it to be consumed upon the altar if that is what keeps us from being debt free. If you have not yet experienced the freedom He longs for you to have with regard to debt, test Him. It may be one of the hardest tests you have yet endured, but get ready for blessings to pour from the windows of heaven. By those blessings with which He blesses us, just so are we in debt to our needy brother. Financial surrender means that we become and remain an open channel of blessing. He may call upon you to help your brother, in secret, someday.

The Word shares stories hinting about finances to help steady those of us upon whom the ends of the earth are come: Ananias and Sapphira, the widow's mite, the parable of the talents. Surrendering our talents, our things—these are merely practice runs until we come to the place where we can totally surrender our broken heart. The heart we have so long salved ineffectively with our selfish indulgences. Money is not the only giant challenging us from across our valley of Elah (where a young shepherd boy defeated a giant).

Satan has a "designer comfort" for each of us, a comfort which, when indulged, begins, deceptively, to anaesthetize that longing within us for our Creator. Like a customized hammock, our need for comfort lures us into the sleep of Laodicea, where, upon Satan's enchanted ground, we lie in blissful ignorance of our true state. We begin to think that all the references we read apply to others.

We know we must arise, someday, but the hammock is so comfortable. Can it compare to the mansion He's gone to prepare? For any amount of discomfort we are called on to endure, heaven will be cheap enough. We will be more than compensated by our Father for anything we suffer here. He asks of us nothing but that which is in our best interest to surrender. If only we could see the bright ending when we are in the dark valley. God wants to build our faith, and not fear to fight the Goliath that stands between us and victory.

Giants for God

Beyond our own mountain ranges of painful surrenders are those giants for God who have actually laid their hearts and lives on the altar of surrender. These stories amaze me. Some people have managed to surrender rejection, painful memories, even illness. "Wait!" you say. "Why would anyone want to hang on to those things, anyway? What would they have to lose?"

We have nothing to lose except our grip on the ineffective solutions we keep rubbing into the pain from which we are unable to escape. He takes the heart we give Him, broken and bleeding, and heals us. How does healing, the growth of the soul, interface with the struggles of everyday life? If surrendering our pain is so good for us, why is it so hard? The other day my husband's prayer in this regard caught my attention: "... and thank You, Lord, for everything You send to save us from ourselves." It occurred to me as he prayed, that this is the principal purpose of trials; pain, brokenness–to save us from ourselves and to perfect His image within us. Like the vessel marred, He breaks us and reshapes us–and fires us in the heat until we are cured or choose to be destroyed. Our survival depends upon escaping from ourselves.

In The Blessings of Brokenness, Charles Stanley explores the apparent oxymoron in his book's title: "Broken. Blessed. The two words don't seem to go together. If anything, they seem to be exact opposites. We all know what it means to be broken–to be shattered, to feel as if our entire world has fallen apart, or perhaps been blown apart. We all have times in our lives when we don't want to raise our heads off the pillow, and when we feel the tears will never stop flowing. Brokenness is often accompanied by emptiness–a void that cannot be filled, a sorrow that cannot be comforted, a wound for which there is no balm. Nothing feels blessed about being broken.... The blessing comes only if we experience brokenness fully and confront why it is that God has allowed us to be broken. If we allow God to do His complete work in us, blessing will follow brokenness."

Catherine Marshall, in her book, A Man Called Peter, reveals her struggle with tuberculosis. To her, it was not just a disease. She had grown up believing TB to be the most dreaded and loathsome degradation imaginable! When, as a young mother, she discovered she had contracted the very disease she most dreaded, she sank into grief and despair. She had always considered herself a dedicated Christian, but it was impossibly hard for her to accept the fact that a loving God would allow her to suffer from that which she dreaded most. She prayed, studied, tried to repent of everything that might be standing in the way of her being healed, for she felt it was not God's will that she die from the disease.

It was not until she read a booklet her husband gave her as she left for her parents' home to rest for several months that the "law of brokenness" began to dawn upon Catherine. In the pamphlet was the story of a missionary who had been bedridden for eight years. During those long years, she had persistently asked God why she had been laid on the shelf when she had been doing God's work? There was rebellion in her heart—she must be returned to active duty. God should make her well. But nothing happened. Exhausted with the failure of her prayers and with a desperate resignation, she finally prayed, "All right, Lord, I give in. If I am to be sick for the rest of my life, I bow to Thy will. I want Thee even more than I want health. It is for Thee to decide." Thus leaving herself entirely in the Lord's hands, she began to know the peace that had evaded her all during her illness and she soon returned to active duty.

To Catherine, health had seemed to be her right. She had never stopped rebelling against her illness. What a revelation to her that submission and surrender may be the only way! Finally, with tears eloquent with what she was about to do, she prayed, "Lord, I've done everything I've known how to do, and it hasn't been good enough. I'm desperately weary of the struggle of trying to persuade You with what I want. I'm beaten, I'm whipped through. If You want me to be an invalid for the rest of my life, all right, here I am. Do anything You like with me and my life."

When Catherine discovered and prayed that prayer of resignation she says, "There was no trace of graciousness about the gift of my life, my will, nothing victorious and expectant. I had no faith left, as I understood faith. Nevertheless, a strange deep peace settled into my heart." The next time her lungs were X-rayed, it became evident that the disease was losing its grip. Within weeks, Catherine was completely well. But the healing of her body was obviously subservient to the greater accomplishment–the wellness of her soul. Whatever stands between God and His child, that thing which stands where brokenness should stand–is the very thing from which He seeks to release our grip. It may even stand between us and survival!

I had a similar experience when I was in my early 20s. I remember what a revelation it was to me when I learned that there was a possibility that it might be God's will for me to experience health. From birth I suffered with "incurable" allergies, asthma, bronchitis, fevers of unknown origin, and fearful bouts of pneumonia. Because so many doctors had said so, I believed that I was incurable. Illness was my heritage. It became my excuse for weakness, my replacement for exercise, my reason for even shunning spiritual growth. It took some time to reach the altar where I was willing to open myself up to the possibility of releasing, like Christian in Pilgrim's Progress, the familiar, but uncomfortable burden upon my back.

I cannot, now, understand why it was difficult for me to surrender my brokenness to His healing touch except that I had become comfortable with my disability. Christian friends and physicians were patient with me, speaking faith when I expressed doubt, until, miracle of miracles, I began to believe that if He willed it, I, too, could have the gift of health. It seems so simple, now—I had but to release my grasp on illness to accept His gift of health. I am vibrantly healthy, now, and so thankful, for health is important to survival.

Healing is Forgiveness

I was once asked to help with a seminar for abused women. The weekend course was designed to create a comfortable environment for church women to experience release from emotional pain. The last exercise was one that will remain forever etched in my mind.

I sat at the back of the room near a huge stone fireplace praying that these women could be free from the pain they had suffered. The women who sought freedom from their past were asked by the facilitator to list everything they had lost, because of their abuse, on a piece of paper. She then asked those who desired to begin their healing journey to toss their list of losses into the flames. The cedar logs crackled invitingly, ready to receive the sacrifice I was sure each woman wanted to submit. But, to my amazement, very few women could perform this exercise. They had been shown the way, but could not submit their pain to the healing flame. They sat immobilized by fear and frustration. Most of them had tears streaming down their cheeks as they clutched their familiar list. To burn it would mean to open themselves up to the yawning chasm of forgiveness, healing and peace–so foreign to their pain. It seemed obvious to me, as an onlooker, that though Jesus was willing to take their pain, they could not give it to Him.

But what a witness for God's goodness are those who have walked through the flames of submission and tasted the sweet victory of forgiveness! Broken healers, having known the divine touch, bring us those amazing stories that so inspire us to lay our helpless soul on the Rock and be broken. He is able to save us, even from ourselves.

Most of us are familiar with the fascinating stories of Corrie ten Boom's experiences in Nazi concentration camps during World War II. Few Christians have been called to endure as was Corrie. Her messages of faith and forgiveness are so inspirational because she was so misused, but also because she was so willing to ask for healing. Though she did not find the path to forgiveness easy, she endeared herself to countless thousands by making her humanity transparent in her book, The Hiding Place.

One night in a Munich church, where she had just delivered a sermon on forgiveness, Corrie recognized, walking down the aisle toward her, a former German S. S. guard, one especially loathed by the prisoners at Ravensbruck. She didn't think the man recognized her, but that was no real comfort. This man had "despitefully used" Corrie and her sister during their imprisonment. Corrie's sister, Betsy, had died at Ravensbruck, but not before challenging Corrie to give her heart to Jesus and to be thankful for everything (even the lice), and to be forgiving of those who tormented and abused them in the concentration camps.

As this former S. S. guard approached and extended his hand toward her, asking for her forgiveness, Corrie's arm became ramrod stiff. She tried to smile and shake his hand and at least appear to believe the message she had just delivered, but vengeful thoughts boiled within her. She found herself totally helpless to practice what she had preached! In that instant she called upon her Source of strength, as she had done in so many times and in so many hard circumstances. She offered a quick inward prayer, "Jesus, I cannot forgive him. Give me Your forgiveness!" Immediately, she says, it was as if a weight had been removed from her arm, and she lifted it toward the man. As her hand touched his, there sprang into her heart such a joyful love as she had not believed possible.

Is Corrie's experience unique? Yes, but no more unique than what our story can add to the great controversy when we come to the Gethsemane of our experience and say, "Not my will, but Thine be done." Only because He sought and found that place of brokenness was Christ able to carry out the plan of salvation by which we are assured of eternal life today. Wrung from a heart of unconditional love, Christ's final blessing upon those at whose hands He was dying proves the depths of His surrender. He was the intercessor unrecognized by those who counted Him an enemy. He sought to erase the curse they had brought upon themselves with His final blessing, "Father, forgive them, for they know not what they do."

Our Weakness, His Strength

Even Christ did not trust His own strength, choosing rather to submit to His Father's will in Gethsemane. Perhaps this is why the cross has become such a symbol of hope for Christians through the ages. In order to prove our own weakness, God allows that to come to us which we cannot bear in our own strength. Christ, though perfect in every respect, was helpless to drink the cup. He could not see beyond the cross. An angel came from heaven, assigned to lift the bitter cup to His lips.

Often, in our spiritual development, God's will is obvious, but unbearable. Our eyes are often blinded with tears of bitterness, loneliness, or anger so that we cannot see the need for our trials. It is a difficult lesson to learn to trust that some-day we will understand. It is in the valley that we must look to where we last saw the light and speak hope and faith to our brothers and sisters while we are in the trial. We overcome by the blood of the Lamb and the word of our testimony (Revelation 12:11).

A true survivor will speak words of hope into the sneer of adversity. Like Harry, we will look beyond our affliction and stand for the right, even when it looks wrong. Even when we stand alone.

"When perplexities arise, and difficulties confront you, look not for help to humanity. Trust all with God. The practice of telling our diffi-culties to others only makes us weak, and brings no strength to them.... Talk and act as if your faith was invincible" (Christ's Object Lessons, pp. 146, 147; emphasis supplied).

"Nothing is apparently more helpless, yet really more invincible, than the soul that feels its nothingness and relies wholly on the merits of the Saviour. By prayer, by study of His word, by faith in His abiding pres-ence, the weakest of human beings may live in contact with the living Christ, and He will hold them by a hand that will never let go" (The Minis-try of Healing, p. 182; emphasis supplied).

We are told that we can strengthen each other when difficulties weaken us. *"If you cannot rely on your own faith, rely upon the faith of others. We believe and hope for you. God accepts our faith in your behalf"* (Testimonies for the Church, vol. 2, p. 319; emphasis supplied). God has helped others in times of trouble. After all, we only need just enough strength to become weak and weakness to stay strong. We grow by the things we choose to put under our feet. As we fall on the Rock, He begins to perfect His image within us. Sooner or later, His will becomes our will. If we allow ourselves to be fully broken, His love can completely heal.

"He is watching those who are climbing, ready, when the grasp re-

laxes and the steps falter, to send help. Yes, tell it in words full of cheer, that no one who perseveringly climbs the ladder will fail of gaining an entrance into the heavenly city" (<u>Messages to Young People</u>, p. 95; emphasis supplied).

Young David rejected the armor Saul thought would help save his life from the giant Goliath. Why? Because David had not proved it. David altared his fear of the unknown enemy by allowing his trust to overpower his fear. He overcame the giant by that which he had proven of God's care for him in his daily life. He simply grasped the familiar Rock, and claimed victory over the giant in the Valley of Elah. The Rock upon which we choose not to fall will be the one which crushes us at last. He can only save those who have chosen to trust Him through the breaking. What if no one else is falling—or standing—when they should?

What if everyone around us looks at us as if we are not quite "all there," as if we are hearing voices they cannot hear? Is surrender too difficult?

Harry surely didn't think so!

SUGGESTED READING

<u>Beyond Ourselves</u>, Catherine Marshall, McGraw-Hill Books Company, 1961.
<u>Hind's Feet On High Places</u>, Hannah Hurnard, Tyndale House Publishers, 1977.
<u>The Blessings of Brokenness</u>, Charles Stanley, Zondervan Publishing House, 1973.
<u>The Christian's Secret of a Happy Life</u>, Hannah Whitall Smith, Spire Books, New Jersey, 1980.
<u>The Hearing Heart</u>, Hannah Hurnard, Tyndale House, 1977.
<u>The Hiding Place</u>, Corrie ten Boom, Fleming H. Revell, 1996.

Chapter Six

Intercession: Praying for Others Effectively

"Bear ye one another's burdens, and so fulfil the law of Christ" (Galatians 6:2).

Arriving in an unfamiliar city early one cold winter morning, a man got off the train and entered the train station. The station was much like any other with the crowds milling about—except that everybody was barefoot. Even the cab driver he hailed was barefoot.

"Pardon me," the man asked his driver, "I was just wondering why you don't wear shoes. Don't you believe in shoes?"

"Sure we do," said the driver.

"Why don't you wear them?"

"Ah, that's the question," came the reply. "Why don't we wear shoes? Why don't we?"

It was the same at the hotel. The clerk, the bell boys, everybody was barefoot. In the coffee shop he noticed a nice-looking fellow at a table opposite him who was also barefoot. He said, "I notice you aren't wearing any shoes. I wonder why? Don't you know about shoes?"

The man replied, "Of course I know about shoes."

"Then why don't you wear them?"

"Ah, that's the question. Why don't we? Why don't we?"

After breakfast the man walked out on the street in the snow, but every person he saw was barefoot. He asked another man about it, and pointed out how shoes protect feet from the cold. The man said, "We know about shoes. See that building yonder? That is a shoe factory. We are proud of that plant, and every week we gather there to hear the man in charge tell about shoes and how wonderful they are."

"Then why don't you wear shoes?"

"Ah, that's the question."

Don't we believe in prayer? Don't we know what it could mean in our lives? Then why don't we pray? Ah, that is the question. Why don't we? (from City of Everywhere, by H. P. Hughes).

This little story sounds as ridiculous to our ears as our actions must appear to the angels who stand in awe at our lack of prayer and its practical application to our lives. This reference shows us clearly that God wants us to pray and ask things of Him.

"It is a part of God's plan to grant us, in answer to the prayer of faith, that which he would not bestow did we not thus ask" (The Great Controversy, page 525).

It seems that there are packages in heaven, ready for delivery, including prayers answered for other people, that will not be delivered unless we ask. Yes, we believe in prayer, we know about it, we know it can protect us, we even meet once a week at prayer headquarters. But until we touch the throne of God with our petitions, we may be as ignorant of its worth as were the barefoot residents in the City of Everywhere, who wore no shoes. If we were to really grasp the concept of the power of prayer to change lives, we would be putting on not only our shoes, but our boots. We would be partakers of the divine nature by walking with God, empathizing prayer with and for others, and mending hearts as did Enoch, Dorcas, and Christ.

"The world in Enoch's time was no more favorable to a growth in grace and holiness than it is now, but Enoch devoted time to prayer and communion with God, and this enabled him to escape the corruption that is in the world through lust. It was his devotion to God that fitted him for translation.

"We are living among the perils of the last days, and we must receive our strength from the same source as did Enoch. We must walk with God. A separation from the world is required of us. ... But how many are slaves to the lust of the flesh, and the lust of the eye, and the pride of life. This is the reason they are not partakers of the divine nature, and do not escape the corruption that is in the world through lust. They are serving and honoring self. ...

"If they were partakers of the divine nature, the same spirit that dwelt in their Lord would dwell in them. The same tenderness and love, the same pity and compassion, would be manifested in their lives. They would

not then have to wait to have the needy and unfortunate come to them, and be entreated to feel their woes. It would be as natural for them to aid the needy and minister to their wants as it was for Christ to go about doing good.... If each would realize this, and take hold of the work, we should be as mighty as an army with banners" (Christ Triumphant, p. 44; emphasis supplied).

We learned in chapter 5 about how the experiences of life bring us to that place of brokenness where we let God reach down into the depths of our pain, and obtain healing. Our own experience then helps us empathize with those around us whom God puts in our path. Nothing comes to us but can be used to help someone else. Have you been helped by reading about or knowing someone who has had a similar experience to yours? Perhaps someone you know prayed for you while you were in the valley of despair. Perhaps they phoned you, or dropped you a note just to say, "I am praying for you." If you have not had that experience, perhaps God is calling upon you to tread a little more closely in His steps and let someone who is despairing lean upon you. Your prayer could be crucial to their survival.

Sometimes we turn our backs on the very ones who most need help–those who reject or accuse us, or hurt a friend, or complain and murmur constantly. This type of commentary emerges from the lips of those whose hearts are filled with pain. Being able to understand another person's pain is a special gift of the Holy Spirit referred to as the gift of intercession. The Holy Spirit can enable us to sense another's pain even though we have not had their experience. Being human, Jesus deeply understood the needs of humanity, and now He is with the Father interceding for us.

The gift of intercession is available as a ministry. God calls us to pray for others rather than to accuse them or ignore them. Although He never experienced sin, Christ knows how much it hurts, because our sins were all laid upon Him as He suffered the crucifixion for us. As we open our hearts to His intercession for us, we are healed. As we begin our healing journey, He calls us to help heal others. The gift of intercession may mean allowing Jesus to use us to help heal another's pain by praying for them and allowing Him to love them through us.

Mystery of Intercession–He Who Knew No Sin Became Sin for Us

In order for us to be effectual in our prayers for each other, we are going to have to know, as did Jesus, the pain of the other person. Jesus knows the pain of divorce–His people have divorced themselves from Him. Jesus knows the pain of third party relationships–we have left Him for another. The book of Hosea is a story illustrating how Christ feels about our separation from Him and His knowledge of our adulteries. Even though we may not feel the regret, He does. Hebrews 4:15 states, *"For we have not an high priest which cannot be touched with the feeling of our infirmities; but was in all points tempted like as we are... ."* What does it mean to feel? Was He a drug addict, was He an alcoholic, adulterous? How could He know the feeling of our infirmities? *"For He hath made him to be sin for us, who knew no sin; that we might be made the righteousness of God in him"* (2 Corinthians 5:21). *"He, the sin-bearer, endures judicial punishment for iniquity and becomes sin itself for man"* (The Story of Redemption, p. 225).

    "While the city was hushed in silence, and the disciples had returned to their homes to obtain refreshment in sleep, Jesus slept not. His divine pleadings were ascending to His Father from the Mount of Olives that His disciples might be kept from the evil influences which they would daily encounter in the world, and that His own soul might be strengthened and braced for the duties and trials of the coming day. All night, while His followers were sleeping, was their divine teacher praying. The dew and frost of night fell upon His head bowed in prayer. His example is left for His followers" (Testimonies for the Church, vol. 2, p. 508; emphasis supplied). We are to follow Him as an example in being touched by the feelings of others and entering into intercessory prayer. *"We may expect to suffer; for it is those who are partakers with Him in His sufferings, who shall be partakers with Him in His glory"* (Review and Herald, June 9, 1896).

    "In your association with others, put yourself in their place. Enter into their feelings, their difficulties, their disappointments, their joys and their sorrows. Identify yourself with them, and then do to them as, were you to exchange places with them, you would wish them to deal with you" (Thoughts from the Mount of Blessing, p. 136; emphasis supplied).

    I have to feel the pain of my brother in order to properly pray for him. How can I feel the pain if I haven't actually experienced it? It is a gift of the Holy Spirit.

Entering In

    There are several Bible texts that support the idea of entering into the feelings of others, both in joy and in pain as Jesus did. Galatians 6:2 tells us, *"Bear ye one another's burdens, and so fulfil the law of Christ."* *"Whether one member suffer, all the members suffer with it; or one member be honoured, all the members rejoice with it"* (1 Corinthians 12:26). We rejoice with them, we suffer with them–we enter into their feelings. This is proper preparation for being an effectual intercessor. Paul, strong, steadfast, and independent in Christ, who, though imprisoned, was appreciative of sympathy, *"Notwithstanding ye have well done, that ye did communicate with my affliction"* (Philippians 4:14).

Jesus, Himself sweating blood in Gethsemane, desired that someone would enter into His sufferings and understand His feelings and pray for Him. *"Hitherto He had been as an intercessor for others;* now He longed to have an intercessor for Himself.... The human heart longs for sympathy in suffering.... *The One who had always had words of sympathy for them* [the disciples] *was now suffering superhuman agony, and* He longed to know that they were praying for Him *and for themselves.... If He could only know that His disciples understood and appreciated this, He would be strengthened"* (The Desire of Ages, pp. 686-688; emphasis supplied). None of His apostles, church leaders, or even His immediate family, shared His sorrow as the shadow of the cross loomed over Him. Jesus is still agonizing today, still longing for intercession from us.

Instead of accusing our leaders for their failures and shortcomings, we should enter into their burdens and their feelings. *"There must be by the church as a whole and by its individual members a* spirit of intercession *and wrestling with our covenant-keeping God in behalf of themselves and also for the watchmen on the walls of Zion and the workers in the cause of God.... God* will answer the earnest supplications that are sent to Him in faith" (Ellen G White 1888 Materials, pp. 755, 756; emphasis supplied).

Jesus was encouraged by the understanding and compassion that the thief on the cross manifested. *"To Jesus in His agony on the cross, there came one gleam of comfort. It was the prayer of the penitent thief"* (The Desire of Ages, p. 749).

What potential we have to bear one another's burdens and become an intercessor! We must learn not just to sympathize, but to empathize with others. *"Rejoice with them that do rejoice, and weep with them that weep"* (Romans 12:15). How can we rejoice or weep when we don't **feel** with the people who are rejoicing and weeping?

Moses had the gift of intercession when he prayed in Exodus 32:32: *"Lord, forgive their sin." "As Moses interceded for Israel, his timidity was lost in his deep interest and love for those for whom he had, in the hands of God, been the means of doing so much. The Lord listened to his pleadings, and granted his unselfish prayer.... God was pleased with his faithfulness"* (Patriarchs and Prophets, p. 319).

In Ezra 9, we read that Ezra pleaded for Israel in the same manner as did Moses. Jacob was an overcomer because he did not cease his intercession (see Genesis 32:24-30). In the example of Pentecost, we see the church gathered together and praying in one accord (Acts 2:1).

Reconciliation

During the 1844 reform movement, people spent time interceding for each other, making things right, entering into one another's spiritual problems, not resting until their hearts were right with God. *"Often was heard the <u>sound of earnest intercession</u>. Everywhere were souls in deep anguish, pleading with God. <u>Many wrestled all night in prayer</u> for the assurance that their own sins were pardoned, or for the conversion of their relatives or neighbors. That earnest, determined faith gained its object.... Every morning they felt it was their <u>first duty</u> to secure evidence of their acceptance with God. Their hearts were closely united, and <u>they prayed much with and for one another</u>. They often met together in secluded places to commune with God, and the <u>voice of intercession</u> ascended to heaven from the fields and groves. The assurance of <u>the Saviour's approval was more necessary to them than their daily food, and if a cloud darkened their minds, they did not rest until it was swept away</u>"* (The Story of Redemption, pp. 359, 371; emphasis supplied).

Apparently history will be repeated when the Spirit returns in the power of Pentecost: *"In visions of the night, representations passed before me of a great reformatory movement among God's people.... <u>A spirit of intercession was seen</u>, even as was manifested before the great Day of Pentecost. Hundreds and thousands were seen visiting families and opening before them the Word of God. Hearts were convicted by the power of the Holy Spirit, and a spirit of genuine conversion was manifest.... Great blessings were received by the true and humble people of God. I heard voices of thanksgiving and praise, and there seemed to be a reformation such as we witnessed in 1844"* (Testimonies for the Church, vol. 9, p. 126; emphasis supplied).

"We must be much in prayer if we would make progress in the divine life. When the message of truth was first proclaimed, how much we prayed. How often was the <u>voice of intercession</u> heard in the chamber, in the barn, in the orchard, or the grove. Frequently we spent hours in earnest prayer, two or three together claiming the promise; often the sound of weeping was heard and then the voice of thanksgiving and the song of praise.... <u>Our perils are greater now than then</u>. Souls are more hardened. We need now to be imbued with the spirit of Christ, and <u>we should not rest until we receive it</u>" (ibid., vol. 5, pp. 161, 162; emphasis supplied).

Are we concerned deeply enough to storm Heaven for each other? We are now closer to the end than we have ever been. We are to be more zealous than the early Christians were. We should express more concern and understanding, as we are called, again, into the spirit of intercession.

INTERCESSION

How? This is nothing we can invent. We are not born with it. It does not naturally occur within our carnal heart. Again, it is a gift of the Holy Spirit. *"The Father has given His Son for us that through the Son the Holy Spirit might come to us, and lead us unto the Father. Through divine agency, we have the spirit of intercession, whereby we may plead with God, as a man pleadeth with his friend"* (Signs of the Times, Oct. 3, 1892; emphasis supplied). With the outpouring of this gift will come the ability to enter into, through Jesus, the hurts and joys of others–in the spirit of intercession.

Our calling is to care for one another, love one another, and enter into one another's joys and sorrows as if they were our own. We would see more conversions to the truth if we could claim and receive this gift. *"If we would humble ourselves before God, and be kind and courteous and tenderhearted and pitiful, there would be one hundred conversions to the truth where now there is only one"* (Testimonies for the Church, vol. 9, p. 189). To be pitiful means that we are able to enter into another's disappointments, hopes, and joys. As we do this, we become effectual intercessors and soul winners through Jesus alone.

"As we see souls out of Christ, we are to put ourselves in their place, and in their behalf feel repentance before God, resting not until we bring them to repentance" (The Seventh-day Adventist Bible Commentary, E. G. White Comments, vol. 7, p. 960; emphasis supplied).

Oh, that we could care enough! One of the greatest gifts of the Holy Spirit is that we may be effectual servants of Christ through intercessory prayer, that we may care and love each other effectively. We must weep when others weep, rejoice when others rejoice, just as if we were in their shoes. Or, according to the little allegory at the beginning of this chapter, as if we were **wearing** shoes! Perhaps when they see the way the Lord protects our feet, **others** will wear shoes, too! When the Holy Spirit is poured out in a mighty measure, it will change us, it will change others. It is a gift; the promised Comforter.

"Would that there were today more earnest intercession with God, greater humility, greater purity, and greater faith" (Testimonies for the Church, vol. 5, p. 88; emphasis supplied).

"Satan is playing the game of life for every soul. He knows that practical sympathy is a test of the purity and unselfishness of the heart, and he will make every possible effort to close our hearts to the needs of others, that we may finally be unmoved by the sight of suffering. He will bring in many things to prevent the expression of love and sympathy" (ibid., vol. 6, p. 264; emphasis supplied).

YOU CAN SURVIVE!

The Seeing Heart

O God, cut eyes into my callous heart and brain
So I can see, along each street or road or lane
The broken hearts that form the human map of pain.
God, help me see!

O God, carve ears into my heart of stone, I plead,
That I may hear the anguished cries of human need,
And by my loving service verify my creed.
God, help me hear!

Dear God, since Thou didst love this world with love so kind,
Since Jesus came to show us how to seek and find,
How can our hearts be still so cold and hard and blind?
God, help me feel!

O God, give me a heart of flesh so I can feel,
Anoint my lips–these languid lips that sin doth seal–
That I may speak, in love and power, time's last appeal!
God, help me speak!

—Adlai Albert Esteb

We cannot learn the prayer of intercession without first receiving the gift of empathy. Neither can we pray for someone without learning to love them. The gift of unity will only be poured out upon those who have learned to pray for and love others. It is this spirit of unity by which the world will identify the true believers. It will be this spirit that marks potential survivors.

FOR FURTHER STUDY

Rees Howells: Intercessor, Norman P. Grubb, Christian Literature Crusade, Fort Washington, PA, 1952.

Chapter Seven

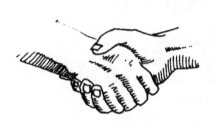

The Miracle of Unity: "That the World May Believe. . ."

"Behold how good and how pleasant it is for brethren to dwell together in unity" (Psalm 133:1).

I t was a small western town with the usual bickerings and feuds. Not everyone agreed with everyone else. One day a little girl named Susie was lost. Search parties with the family had looked everywhere, but she was not to be found. A large field was scanned, but not as thoroughly as could be done with a larger group. Someone suggested, "Let's all hold hands and comb the field." So they did. The field was one and a half miles long and a mile wide. About two-thirds of the way down the field, a cry went up, "Here she is!" But elation quickly turned to sorrow. The little girl would not respond to their calls.

At Susie's funeral, a young person, one of the searchers, who had known her and whose heart had been broken by the suffering of the family stood up and said, "If only we had joined hands sooner."

Are there any members in our own family and circle of friends who are suffering because we, who are concerned for their spiritual welfare, have not yet joined hands, uniting our forces, in the search to secure their soul for heaven? Maybe they will be lost because we do not have the power of unity Christ promised. Unity is essential to our witness for Christ. However good our sanitarium, hospital, school, church, or family may be, it is essential that we, its members or staff, be unified. It is even more essential that you and I know unity with Christ as our personal Saviour. Complete unity in Christ guarantees unity at organizational levels. *As long as we hold to our own ideas and opinions with determined persistency, we cannot have the unity for which Christ prayed"* (<u>Testimonies to Ministers and Gospel Workers</u>, p. 30).

With all the possibilities for misunderstanding, reactions, and disagreement, unity is a miracle. Do you know of someone with whom you are not in unity? Go to them and make it right. We all have some of this work to do, but, even at best, unity will require a miracle. Can we expect miracles in this day? Let's explore this possibility.

YOU CAN SURVIVE!

The Bible says, *"... endeavoring to keep the unity of spirit in the bond of peace"* (Ephesians 4:2, 3). The chapter also tells us to walk worthy of the vocation to which we are called; with all lowliness, meekness, long-suffering, and forbearance. Those traits of character are prerequisites to unity. Most of us have not developed these traits of character enough. Verse 13 says, *"Till we all come in the unity of the faith, and of the knowledge of the Son of God, unto a perfect man, unto the measure of the stature of the fulness of Christ."* We must "endeavor," or make an effort (verse 3) "till we all come into the unity of the faith" (verse 13).

Working Together

Reading between verses 3 and 13 of Ephesians 4, we discover many expressions of unity: one Lord, one faith, one baptism, one God and Father of all, one body, one Spirit, one hope. Verse 7 points out our different gifts expressed in apostles, prophets, evangelists, pastors, and teachers. We're all gifted differently, but as we come into the unity of the faith, these differing gifts will blend.

When our spiritual eyes are opened, the industrial worker is going to say that the medical work is as important as the industrial work, while a teacher will understand that the medical work is just as important as the educational work. The miracle begins to happen, triggering a chain reaction of blessings, and the Holy Spirit begins to be poured out without measure. Every one of these workers who claim that the work of others is as important to God as is his own, is working for unity. If we all come into unity of the faith, we will reflect Christ's character.

One of the most beautiful verses in all the Bible is 1 John 3:2: *"Beloved, now are we the sons of God, and it doth not yet appear what we shall be; but we know that, when he shall appear, we shall be like him; for we shall see him as he is."*

In His life, Christ combined the educational work, the ministerial work, and the medical work in perfect unity. *"And Jesus went about all Galilee, teaching in their synagogues, and preaching the gospel of the kingdom, and healing all manner of sickness and all manner of disease among the people"* (Matthew 4:23).

"Those who disparage the ministry and try to conduct the medical missionary work independently are trying to separate the arm from the body. What would be the result should they succeed? We should see hands and arms flying about, dispensing means without the direction of the head. The work would become disproportionate and unbalanced. That which God designed should be the hand and arm would take the place of the whole body, and the ministry would be belittled or altogether ignored. This would unsettle minds and bring in confusion, and many portions of the Lord's

vineyard would be left unworked" (<u>Testimonies for the Church</u>, vol. 6, pp. 288, 289; emphasis supplied).

John 17:18-23 read, *"As thou hast sent me into the world, even so have I also sent them into the world. And for their sakes I sanctify myself, that they also might be sanctified through the truth. Neither pray I for these alone, but for them also which shall believe on me through their word; <u>that they all may be one</u>; as thou, Father, art in me, and I in thee, that they also may be one in us: ... <u>That the world may know that thou hast sent me</u>"* (emphasis supplied). If we are one with God the Father, one with Jesus Christ, and with each other, the world will believe that we have been sent by heaven.

Let's look at some evidence calling for unity among all departments of church work. The Spirit of Prophecy says John 17, Christ's prayer for unity, comprehends more than any other chapter in the New Testament. *"God's family on the earth have many lessons to learn in order to answer the prayer of Christ–His last prayer with His disciples before His humiliation. The seventeenth chapter of John, which contains this prayer, <u>comprehends more than any other chapter in the New Testament</u>"* (<u>Spalding Magan Collection</u>, p. 387).

Gossip or Unity?

In Jesus' prayer of John 17, we have evidence that we are sent from Christ if we are one in Him and one with each other. Unity cannot be neglected. Though we are all different, we must be together. The ability to be one is the significant difference between the beast and God's remnant. True unity is based on Christ and the love that we have for one another. Union through conformity, as found in the beast is a misrepresentation of unity.

"Even as we are one" (verse 22). Who is we? God the Father, God the Son. Can we have unity like that? It will take a miracle! Think about that—unity like God the Father and God the Son. How often would tales be told about someone in a gossipy way if we had this kind of unity? How often would we speak disrespectfully or purposely provoke one another?

The Father and the Son don't gossip about us? But could They? Would They see anything that needs to be changed in our closets at home, the ones with the skeletons in them? Do They gossip? No. Yet they know all about us! If we are one with Christ, neither will we gossip about each other.

The love of Christ cannot be counterfeited. When we love as He loves, the character traits that are unlike Him will fall away. We cannot cherish His love without losing gossip.

Unity is Evidence of Christianity

In His mercy, the Lord sent us the gift of unity at a personal level. *"This unity of the believers is to be as a testimony to the world that He has sent us, and that we bear the evidence of His grace"* (My Life Today, p. 252; emphasis supplied). The testimony that Jesus has sent us is that we should love one another as He loved us, and in that we have unity. What an evangelistic tool this is!

"Unity existing among the followers of Christ is an evidence that the Father has sent His Son to save sinners. It is a witness to His power, for nothing short of the miraculous power of God can bring human beings with their different temperaments together in harmonious action their one aim being to speak the truth in love" (Testimonies for the Church, vol. 9, p. 194; emphasis supplied). If we don't have unity in Christ, then there is no evidence of our Christianity.

"If you who have engaged in this work of bruising and condemning have not heartily repented, then light, and peace, and joy will not come into your souls. When you are careful, kind, and tender to your brethren in the same degree that you have been hard, unforgiving, and oppressive you will confess your faults and make restitution as far as possible; and when you have done all on your part you may ask the Lord to do that which it is impossible for you to do—heal the wounds you have made, forgive you, and blot out your transgression" (Testimonies for the Church, vol. 5, p 343; emphasis supplied).

We are to expect miracles of healing through our love relationship with Jesus and the application of God's plan. We can expect an even greater miracle as we allow God to manifest His power through us, not only for healing the body but for healing the soul. Wouldn't it be wonderful to assist the breeze of the Holy Spirit into the window of the soul, blowing all the trash out the other side; the trash of differences that keep us apart? At the time of the miraculous outpouring of the Holy Spirit we will have unity. But we must specifically seek Him. We must plead for Him. He is vital to our survival!

Power for Churchgoing Unity

Imagine being able to come to church and go home a better person than you were before you came. Then, there is evidence that Christ came to save us. What a tremendous challenge and calling we have. *"Behold, how good and how pleasant it is for brethren to dwell together in unity!"* (Psalm 133:1). When you have that experience, you will be a powerful witness. How important is it to have harmony among brothers and sisters?

THE MIRACLE OF UNITY

"As we approach the last crisis, it is of vital moment that harmony and unity exist among the Lord's instrumentalities" (Testimonies for the Church, vol. 7, p. 182; emphasis supplied).

What are vital signs? Respiration rate, blood pressure, stimulus response, temperature; these are indications of life. So is unity a vital sign of spiritual life among the Lord's instrumentalities. We are either dead or alive. The difference is unity. What if we don't have it? What are our vital signs?

"The world is filled with storm and war and variance. Yet under one head–the papal power–the people will unite to oppose God in the person of His witnesses. This union is cemented by the great apostate. While he seeks to unite his agents in warring against the truth he will work to divide and scatter its advocates" (ibid.). The enemy's strategy is to divide and scatter its advocates, leaving them with the attitude that they do not need each other, that they are the proverbial island unto themselves. Have we experienced Satan's diversionary tactics at church? It is our responsibility to experience the comfort everyone needs when in unity with their church family?

The apostate will use the tools of disunity against the people of God: *"Jealousy, evil surmising, evilspeaking, are instigated by him* [Satan] *to produce discord and dissension. The members of Christ's church have the power to thwart the purpose of the adversary of souls"* (ibid.; emphasis supplied).

Power to thwart Satan? Picture the last crisis; the enemy uniting his forces to set you and me at variance. But we have the power to wage war against the effects of the enemy—with unity, which is a gift from God. What if we don't have the unity that gives us the power to thwart the devil's tools?

"At such a time as this let them not be found at variance with one another or with any of the Lord's workers. Amidst the general discord let there be one place where harmony and unity exist because the Bible is made the guide of life" (ibid.; emphasis supplied). The prophet pleads here for just one place of unity. *"Let the people of God feel that the responsibility rests upon them to build up His instrumentalities"* (ibid.).

If we don't have unity, then the devil's tools are going to be applied to us— they are going to be applied successfully and we will be defeated. Unity is a vital sign that we are alive and not dead. Our survival depends on having unity. We cannot accuse each other, we do not repeat gossip, we don't attend church to display the latest fashions, and we sing from a committed heart. We go to church, seeking that experience of oneness with the Father, the Son, and each other. The church family is designed like a body; members accomplishing a common goal. If someone is hurting, the family needs to know and send support. Are we really listening? Unity of heart and mind will help us see and hear the heart cries of those in need. Church friends are not just acquaintances, they are the body of Christ. It is our duty to make our church home a haven where the wounded spirits of our brothers and sisters can cry, and be comforted with Christ's words and the acts of His children. We must make the church home, that one place, that safe place where we can all, as family members, love and be loved, not because of, but in spite of, who or what we are. Church is one place where we need never be reluctant to lend a helping hand, speak a word of encouragement, or take time to listen to the heart cry of a friend or family member.

Angels Are Waiting

The angels are waiting with longing desire,
Waiting to work with your hands.
A soul who is dying might soon live again,
With just the touch of your hands.
No other hands can ever restore;
What if they fail to be true?
He'll miss all the glories of heaven's fair shore—
Angels are waiting for you.

Angels are waiting to speak through your lips,
Waiting with longing desire.
A soul is just waiting the message to hear
From lips touched with heavenly fire.
Only your voice can speak to his heart;
Tell him of Jesus, I pray.
For angels are longing to speak through your lips—
Why do you longer delay?

Angels are waiting with longing desire;
Heaven is waiting for you.
Jesus bows low on His glorious throne,
Watching to see what you do.
Please go to work with the angels, my friend.
Lend them your hands and be true.
Angels are waiting with longing desire;
Angels are waiting for you.
—Warren C. Wilson

"One of Christ's last commands to His disciples was,' 'Love one another as I have loved you'(John 13:34). *Do we obey this command, or are we indulging sharp, unchristlike traits of character?* <u>*If we have in any way grieved or wounded others, it is our duty to confess our fault and seek for reconciliation*</u>. *This is an* <u>*essential preparation*</u> *that we may come before God in faith, to ask His blessing"* (<u>Christ's Object Lessons</u>, p. 144; emphasis supplied).

Our Offerings—A Sign of Unity

"Therefore if thou bring thy gift to the altar, and there rememberest that thy brother hath aught against thee, leave there thy gift before the altar, and go thy way; first be reconciled to thy brother, and then come and offer thy gift" (Matthew 5:23, 24).

A Biblical study of this aspect of church service would reveal that our offerings are a sign of our unity. The Bible says if we have an offering and yet have aught against someone, we are not to give it until we have made things right. Go and be reconciled first. When we give our offering to God's cause, we are telling Him and everyone that we are in unity!

When we give an offering but are not in unity, we have violated one of Christ's commands. The offering in the 11 o'clock service symbolizes our unity in Christ, and that testifies that we have been sent by Him: that we are going to have an impact on the world and that the work is soon going to be finished. Are our offerings beneficial if we are not in unity? Worship is not a simple, superficial "fix" for the week, not like a doctor's appointment where we can request: "Give me a pill, give me a shot, but don't ask me to humble my own ideas!" The plan is *"Press together; press together; press together"* (<u>Testimonies for the Church</u>, vol. 6, p. 293). Let us make our offerings a greater blessing by being in unity.

The Witness of Disunity

<u>*"If there is disunion among those who claim to believe the truth, the world will conclude that this people cannot be of God because they are working against one another*</u>. *When we are one with Christ, we shall be united among ourselves. Those who are not yoked up with Christ always pull the wrong way. They possess a temperament that belongs to man's carnal nature, and at the least excuse passion is wide awake to meet passion. This causes a collision; and* <u>*loud voices are heard in committee meetings, in board meetings,*</u> *and in public assemblies,* <u>*opposing reform methods. Obedience to every word of God is another condition of success*</u>*"* (<u>ibid</u>., p. 139; emphasis supplied).

What is our witness in disunity? Our witness is that we cannot be of God.

YOU CAN SURVIVE!

Unity is not something we just keep praying for and never experience in the working laboratory of life. We must work to answer our own prayers. We need to welcome Christ's divine intervention. God is in charge. He doesn't need our ideas. He needs for us to be willing to be in unity, not pulling against each other. No team of horses can plow effectively if they pull against each other.

Allegory of the Tools

Someone has imagined the Carpenter's tools holding a conference. Brother Hammer presided. Several suggested he leave the meeting because he was too forceful. Replied the Hammer, "If I have to leave this shop, Brother Screw must go also. You always have to turn him to get him to accomplish anything."

Brother Screw then spoke up, "If you wish, I'll leave, but Brother Plane must leave too. All his work is on the surface. His efforts have no depth."

To this, Brother Plane responded, "Brother Rule will also have to withdraw, he is always measuring folks as though he were the only one who is right."

Brother Rule then complained against Brother Sandpaper, "You ought to leave too because you are so rough and always rubbing people the wrong way."

In the midst of all this discussion, in walked the Carpenter of Nazareth. He had arrived to start His day's work. Putting on His apron, He went to the bench to make a pulpit from which to proclaim the Gospel. He employed the hammer, screw, plane, rule, sandpaper and all the other tools.

After many days of work, when the pulpit was finished, Brother Saw remarked, "Brethren, I observe that all of us are workers together with the Lord" (Gleanings From Thomas Watson, p. 87 [Morgan, PA: Soli Deo Gloria Publications, 1995]).

Disunity Affects the School

"Until the spirit of criticism and suspicion is banished from the heart the Lord cannot do for the church that which He longs to do for the establishment of schools; until there is unity, He will not move upon those to whom He has entrusted means and ability for the carrying forward of this work" (Testimonies for the Church, vol 6, p. 202).

Is it possible that parents could stand in the way of their children's education, even while paying a church school to educate them in the ways of the Lord? Who has not shaken their head in shame at the immature behavior of parents of Little Leaguers? The young players often get along with each other just fine, while their parents yell obscenities at the officials, the coach, even their children. I wonder if the Lord might not look down upon His church, the apple of His eye, and shake His head in shame and disappointment when they are bickering.

THE MIRACLE OF UNITY

Testimonies for the Church, volume 8, page 212 explains the urgency of this matter, *"Behold, the Bridegroom cometh; go ye out to meet Him"* (Matthew 25:6). *Lose no time now in rising and trimming your lamps. Lose no time in seeking perfect unity with one another."* How much time can we afford to lose? Not one more day. Do you know of anyone in your experience with whom you have a hard time getting along? If there is someone like that, please realize that the experience of disunity is affecting your witness. Christ says, "Come now and lose no more time." Unity is vital to our survival, now and forever. When we join hands and sweep the world for the lost, they will see, by our unity, that we belong to Christ. There will be no regrets, as there was at little Susie's funeral when her friend lamented, "If only we had joined hands sooner!"

Maybe we could join our prayer with the little four-year-old who put the preacher's sermon into his own words, "And forgive us our trash as we forgive those who put trash in our baskets."

Our unity demonstrates to others that God is restoring us, physically and spiritually, into His image. *"... we shall be like him for we shall see him; as he is"* (1 John 3:2).

FOR FURTHER STUDY

God's plea for unity is for all departments of the church work:

1. People with varied dispositions (Testimonies for the Church, vol. 8, pp. 242, 243).

2. Ministers with ministers (Testimonies for the Church, vol. 6, p. 50).

3. Church members with each other (Testimonies for the Church, vol. 6, pp. 292, 293).

4. Medical missionaries with other Christian workers (Testimonies for the Church, vol. 6, pp. 235-242).

5. Medical Missionaries with gospel ministry (Testimonies for the Church, vol. 8, p. 46; Selected Messages, book 1, p. 199).

6. Physicians and ministers (Medical Ministry, pp. 46, 47).

7. Publishing house to publishing house (Testimonies for the Church, vol. 7, p. 171).

8. Sanitariums and schools (Counsels to Parents, Teachers, and Students, p. 522).

9. Teachers and students (Testimonies for the Church, vol. 6, p. 139).

Chapter Eight

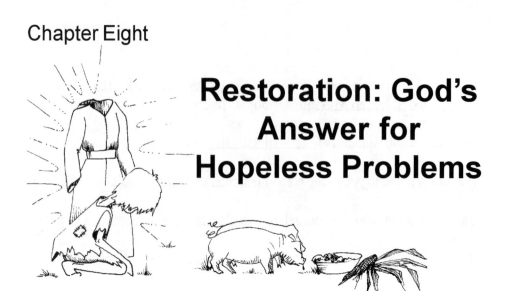

Restoration: God's Answer for Hopeless Problems

"Christ's character stands in the place of your character, and you are accepted before God just as if you had not sinned" (Steps to Christ, p. 62).

I remember when I was about 9 years old when I had gone by myself to a little corner grocery store. While I was in there, I saw a candy bar that just looked too good. I decided to take it. No one would know. This was back when candy bars were a nickel, and I hadn't had a nickel for some time.

When I got home, my mother asked, "Where did you get the candy bar?" I stammered and stuttered until she finally asked the ultimate question, "Did you take it without paying for it?" That was the day I began to realize that she, as my mother, had the gift of insight that enabled her to see right into my guilty soul. How else could she know that I had stolen the candy? I, of course, was unaware of the chocolate bordering my lips.

Mom took me by the hand, and we went back down to the corner store. It was one of the longest trips of my young life. I knew I would have to confess my sin of theft and make arrangements to pay for the candy bar. The store manager was very nice, and accepted my mother's offer of having me work to make amends for the stolen sweets. She paid the nickel that I owed the store manager, then I worked for a few days sweeping floors and lifting boxes. Finally, the store manager said, "Okay, Jere, that's enough. You can go home now." My lesson was learned. My debt was paid. My restitution was accomplished.

Accepted, Just as if I Had Never Sinned

Restitution for some things is relatively easy. However, such things as wasted time, divorce, sexual misconduct, loss of purity, angry words, accusa-

133

tions, drug abuse, physical and verbal abuse, gossip, judging, bad influences, and broken promises, cannot be paid for as easily as my stolen candy bar. Have you ever made a mistake in any of these areas? We have all done something in our past that we wish we had not done. They linger in our subconscious, those skeletons in our closet, weighing us down with guilt. Can we get rid of them? Unless we have God's intervention we will never recover from these kinds of hopeless mistakes. The good news of the gospel is that Christ has made provision even for incurable wounds!

Even if we are victims of accusations, or worse, if we have victimized others by our words, we can still have restoration as though we had never sinned: *"Christ's character stands in place of your character, and you are accepted before God just as if you had not sinned"* (Steps to Christ, p. 62; emphasis supplied).

"It was Satan's purpose to bring about an eternal separation between God and man; but in Christ we become more closely united to God than if we had never fallen" (The Desire of Ages, p. 25; emphasis supplied). This reference in The Desire of Ages was difficult for me to understand. How could we be more closely united with God than Adam was when he was perfect? Then I had a very special insight as the result of an experience with my young son, Jed, who brought the deeper understanding home to my heart.

Jed had gotten himself into trouble. As his father, I had to apply discipline. But before I did, he hugged me and said, "Dad, I'm sorry for what I did." At that moment, I realized the truth of the mystery. As I enjoyed Jed's embrace and apology, I realized that we were closer than if he had just been playing outside and had not made a mistake. So it is with our heavenly Father. We will be closer to Him because of our errors and His mercy toward us than if we had never fallen. Errors do not earn this relationship, but God's love overrules our mistakes. Our guilt and His mercy draws us nearer than before.

"If we confess our sins, he is faithful and just to forgive us our sins, and to cleanse us from all unrighteousness" (1 John 1:9).

This verse contains two promises. The first promise is God's forgiveness to the repentant sinner. The second promise, "to cleanse us from all unrighteousness," contains the generous offer by our loving God to re-create us in His image, to purify, to perfect, to sanctify, and to restore.

Many people stop with the first promise of forgiveness, glad to have "the peace of heaven," forgetting that heaven will not be populated by sinners who are just forgiven, but inhabited by those who have been cleansed and restored.

The thief on the cross did not have time to complete the process of restoration on this earth, but he had the desire to be like Jesus. That thief was, at the last possible moment, forgiven and accepted as if he had never sinned! His restoration will take place at the second coming of Jesus and in heaven.

Wasted Years

Throughout the Bible, there are many promises that indicate God is willing and able to restore our non-repairable lives. In Joel 2:25, God says, *"I will restore to you the years that the locust hath eaten."* How is it possible that God can restore the time we have wasted? In The Desire of Ages, page 330, we are told, *"Our Heavenly Father has a thousand ways to provide for us, of which we know nothing."*

Let me tell how God was able to demonstrate to me, personally, His power to restore my own wasted years. When I was 13 years old, I was heavily involved in athletics. For the next 20 years or so, sports were an integral part of my life: they helped keep me off the street, out of jail, and may have even saved my life. But as I began to study what the Lord had in mind for me, the Holy Spirit convicted me that I needed to give up sports because they had such a grip on me. A recovering alcoholic must stay away from taverns. I began to understand that this was the way it had to be with me and my involvement in ball games.

But how could God restore the years I had wasted in sports? Some time ago, an evangelist and I were on stage in dialogue before 3,000 young people in some youth meetings in Hope, British Columbia, Canada. We discussed how sports can become an addiction. To be so focussed on pitching a great game can "shut out" God.

After the meeting, a mother and her son came walking down the center aisle. "May we talk with you, Brother Franklin?" asked the mother. She told me that her son, much taller than she and obviously very strong, even at 13 years of age, was already an all-star on the local baseball team. "My boy and I have been discussing sports and athletics recently. He is right now trying to make a choice between serving God as a minister or pursuing an athletic career."

We sat down and I began telling about some of my experiences in baseball; some things that I had been told to do by my coaches, some of what I had seen, and what he might expect if he chose a career in sports.

At the conclusion of our discussion he said, "You know, Mr. Franklin, it doesn't sound like Jesus enjoys competitive sports, does it?"

I admitted to him that I didn't think so either. After we had talked a little longer, he said, "I really feel that maybe the Lord wants me to plan for the ministry." We had prayer together and it was a wonderful experience. I believe Scott left with a deeper commitment to God.

What does this have to do with wasted time and restoration? Just this—every year that Scott remains faithful to his commitment restores one of my years! As we become involved in witnessing from our own experience, we can restore, "the years the locust hath eaten." No experience will be wasted, for God will send us those who are struggling just as we once struggled. Our victory is a witness to others of God's power to restore wasted years.

Impurity

It is never too late. But what about impurity of all kinds that does irreparable damage to one's life? Virtue is gone because of immorality. How does the gospel deal with such a condition? Part of the answer is found in Jeremiah 2:20: *"For of old time I have broken thy yoke, and burst thy bands; and thou saidst, I will not transgress; when upon every high hill and under every green tree thou wanderest, playing the harlot."* Shortly after God called Israel a harlot, there was a period of spiritual revival in Israel, and God calls His same people, through the same prophet, a virgin; *"Turn again, O virgin of Israel"* (Jeremiah 31:21). How can a person go from a harlot to a virgin? Will there be harlots in heaven? Oh, yes. But only harlots that have experienced God's generous offer of restoration. How can purity be restored?

About 6,000 years ago, the Lord stooped over a pile of dirt. He was creating a man. God created a man who was pure and undefiled. If the Lord can do that with a pile of dirt, what can He do with you, a living person? You are much better than any pile of dirt! Harlot to virgin? Those who have struggled with this problem, take courage! The Lord can restore you if you desire restoration, just as though you had never sinned (see Steps to Christ, p. 62). Only God can do this!

Notice this reference in The Desire of Ages: *"None but Christ can fashion anew the character that has been ruined by sin"* (p. 38). If something is ruined, can you fix it? No. By definition, if something is ruined, you can't fix it. Only God can fashion anew something that has been ruined. When we repent and give God all the pieces, He works a miracle and makes us a clean and usable vessel. And our reformation can become the means of rescuing others.

Health

The same is true for broken health caused either by living a sin-damaged life or living in a sin-damaged world. In Jeremiah 30:12-17, we find this spiritual diagnosis: *"For thus saith the Lord, Thy bruise is incurable, and thy wound is grievous"* (verse 12). Here we find a description of our condition: incurable bruises and wounds from which we are dying: *"There is none to plead thy cause, that thou mayest be bound up: thou hast no healing medicines"* (verse 13). No one will stand with us to be our attorney and there are no healing medicines for this type of worldly wound: *"All thy lovers have forgotten thee... because thy sins were increased"* (verse 14). Those that we thought loved us, love us no longer. The reason for all of these hopeless conditions is our many sins which have caused non-repairable damage to ourselves and others. *"Thy sorrow is incurable"* (verse 15). Our sorrow is incurable; we weep because of our hopeless mistakes.

Now let's look at the good news from God that promises to heal all of the incurable bruises and sorrows. *"For I will restore health unto thee, and I will heal thee of thy wounds, saith the Lord"* (verse 17). Those same wounds that were incurable, grievous, the wounds from which we were dying, no physician could cure, will be healed. No pharmacist could issue us a medicine. No attorney would take our case or plead our cause. Everybody who loved us was gone. But the Lord says, "I will restore health unto thee."

Entanglements

Have you ever been embarrassed by a social situation, and were sure the results would last a lifetime? Have you been involved in business deals in which you were so entangled you felt helpless and hopeless to improve the situation? Have you done anything of which you were later ashamed? Have you said words you would give anything to retract? What about your mountain of debts that look so impossible to pay? Is there help for the "impossible," even for you?

Listen again to the gospel's response expressed in the chapter "The Invitation" in The Desire of Ages, page 329: *"Whatever your anxieties and trials, spread out your case before the Lord. Your spirit will be braced for endurance. The way will be opened for you to disentangle yourself from embarrassment and difficulty"* (emphasis supplied).

Expanding on this idea of release from personal, permanent entanglements, the same book says, *"Those who decide to do nothing in any line that will displease God, will know, after presenting their case before Him, just what course to pursue"* (p. 668; emphasis supplied).

If we have been involved in accusing others, creating dissension, gossiping, leading an impure life, or been subject to dependencies, we must take courage! Though we recognize mistakes that cannot, humanly, be made right, God can take all the sins that have done irreparable damage and not only repair, but make life better than it was.

"It was Satan's purpose to bring about an eternal separation between God and man; but in Christ we become more closely united to God than if we had never fallen. ... By love's sacrifice, the inhabitants of earth and heaven are bound to their Creator in bonds of indissoluble union" (The Desire of Ages, p. 25-26).

RESTORATION

Restoration is God's most generous offer to all who desire to be made whole. Accusing, criticizing, condemning, and gossiping will require a special plea for victory, but He desires for us to be victorious even more than we do! *"He desires to restore you to Himself, to see His own purity and holiness reflected in you"* (Steps to Christ, p. 64).

There is a special promise in The Ministry of Healing, page 516, which will cover any and all impossible circumstances that stem from the mistakes and failures of our past. *"Whatever the mistakes or failures of the past, we may, with the help of God, rise above them."*

Skeletons in the Closet

For those of us who have experienced forgiveness and continue to live out our lives on this earth, it is imperative that we move on to the "cleansing from all unrighteousness." What about those proverbial skeletons in your upstairs hall closet? True, no one else may know about them. They are well hidden. We have locked the door. Yet their bones rattle in the night and the stench of their decay causes unacceptable Christian behavior: unprovoked defensiveness, angry words, unexplained fears, a dread of punishment to come, profound rebellion, and an embarrassing lack of self control. Those skeletons deaden the colors of happiness that our loving Father desires for us even in this life. Have you done something that you think cannot be forgiven? Begin your journey of restoration. God will complete it, in His time.

Ephesians 3:17, *"...Christ may dwell in our hearts by faith."* But Christ will not cohabit with evil. *"We are to empty the heart of everything that defiles the soul temple, that Christ may dwell within"* (That I May Know Him, p. 153). To dwell means to live in our hearts, or to be at home. A home has many different rooms: a kitchen, living room, dining room, den, library, bedroom, bathroom and closets. I may have given all of the activities associated with these rooms to God: such as my diet in the kitchen, my choice of entertainment in the den, my wardrobe in the closet, even the more private functions of the bathroom and bedroom. Maybe I even went so far as to vow to meet him in the living room every morning and evening (Isaiah 50:4). Then comes that one fateful morning when I see Him walk right past me, as I wait upon His presence in the living room.

Leaving me to dread what He might uncover, He goes straight upstairs, right on up to the attic and stands in front of an old closet. Odors from the closet fill the attic with a horrid stench. He tries the door of the closet, but it is locked bolted, barred and chained. A sign, in bold red letters reads Do Not Enter! Breathlessly, I arrive in time to warn Him away. He turns to me with a look of sadness and leaves the house.

I wait in the living room the next day, but He does not come. Sometimes it looks as if He is coming, but He goes right on out the back door. He cannot dwell where evil is harbored (3 John 1: *"Beloved, follow not that which is evil, but that which is good. He that doeth good is of God: but he that doeth evil hath not seen God"*). Morning after morning it is the same: he goes up to the closet, asks that I let him in. Every morning I deny Him entrance. I tell Him that no one must know about the skeletons I am hiding there. It is just too awful for words.

"I already know what is in there," He says kindly. "Please let me clean it up!"

"No!" I shout. "Absolutely not!"

For years we are at a standoff. Oh, He comes and visits on a regular basis, but my first love has waned. The relationship is no longer growing. Though I desire to have Him help me overcome my tendencies to defensiveness, anger, and depression, I still resist whenever He even looks toward my closet. I deny that there is any relationship between my actions today and the secrets of my past. "Besides, I believe they are all insoluble. There is no possibility of resolution. They can't be made right!"

The sadness on his face is hard to look upon. I turn away, leaving Him standing there alone. As I leave, there is an awful emptiness in the pit of my being, as if I might be rejecting the Only One who can help me solve the unsolvable mysteries and problems in my life, but, surely I am not completely helpless! I still have some tricks up my sleeve that will help me forget my troubles, even if I can't solve them. There are tricks that many of my friends are using. Sleep comes with difficulty, sometimes requiring a pill or two. I must keep some background noise around me all the time, lest the Voice of Truth break through to my guilty heart. Yet, try as I might, I cannot completely silence the voice of conscience. Gradually I am wearing out, my nerves are on edge, the burden is too great for me to carry.

I finally admit to myself that my agony of guilt and resistance to the truth has left me spiritually and physically weak. In the empty darkness of the midnight, I realize that I can no longer live the lie. Sooner or later I will face my Judge. If I consider Him an enemy in this life, how can I expect His friendship in the next life. I am guilty of His innocent blood. He was once my friend. He was only trying to help me when I pushed Him away. I remember His smile, His compassion, His love and patience. I sense He is just waiting for me to come to the end of myself that He might show me the way to healing. I am tired of resisting His friendship. I crave His smile of acceptance even more than my own will, my own selfish privacy.

"I can't go on without You, Lord! Go ahead and open the doors of that horrid closet!" I offer him the key, but he says He doesn't need them. In a single bound he stands before the closet. At the touch of His nail-scarred hand, the bars fall off, the chains break, the lock falls open and the doors swing wide. The odor is overpowering. I turn from the sight, cover my face in shame, and sink to my knees.

"Lord, this is so bad! What can be done? Please take it away!" I experience the hallowed joy of total surrender. Death and decay vanish at His touch. He gives me a promise about untangling the knots of my life and before I know it He lays His hand on my on shoulder and says, "It is done."

I lift my tear-dimmed eyes to find that the skeletons have vanished. Conviction has lead me to repentance and forgiveness. My heart is softened, my spirit cleansed. Miracle of miracles, my heart is more full of joy than if the skeletons had never existed! My love returns with a train of blessings I had never dreamed possible. I am open to experiencing friendships with those whom I considered enemies. I am more patient. A spirit of hope dispels my gloomy attitude. Joyfully I take up the work He asks of me. Family problems appear to solve themselves.

Once again, I have the joy of togetherness, morning by morning. I can hardly wait to join Him in the living room day by day where the time with Him flies by. He shares with me from His word and His testimony what I need to do. I joyfully continue the work He has begun in me: conviction, forgiveness, and victory. I am now a friend of God.

The Great Controversy, p. 619, tells about the close of probation when God's people are in prison or gathered together in small groups in desolate and solitary places. They are fearful that not every sin has been repented of. They are afraid there is some room in their life where they have not allowed Jesus entrance and granted permission to clean. Oh, the condescension of our Lord, waiting for us to allow Him entrance! We must not wait until it is too late! Thankfully, God's people in the Time of Jacob's Trouble have no wrongs to reveal. They have made everything right and allowed the Lord to heal them of their incurable wounds (Jeremiah 30:17).

We need nothing less than the touch of the Master's hand. Myra Brooks Welch elegantly captures the essence of the gospel in her well-known ballad about a "worthless" violin. In 1921, although badly crippled with arthritis, Myra, by holding a pencil with both hands, captured the essence of the gospel in The Touch of the Master's Hand. The poem was completed in 30 minutes!

The Touch of the Master's Hand

'Twas battered and scarred, and the auctioneer
Thought it scarcely worth his while
To waste much time on the old violin,
But held it up with a smile:

"What am I bidden, good folks," he cried,
"Who'll start the bidding for me?"
"A dollar, a dollar"; then, "Two" "Only two?
Two dollars, and who'll make it three?

Three dollars, once; three dollars, twice;
Going for three—" But no,
From the room, far back, a gray-haired man
Came forward and picked up the bow;

Then, wiping the dust from the old violin,
And tightening the loose strings,
He played a melody pure and sweet
As sweet as an angel sings.

The music ceased, and the auctioneer,
With a voice that was quiet and low,
Said: "What am I bid for the old violin?"
And he held it up with the bow.

"A thousand dollars, and who'll make it two?
Two thousand. And who'll make it three?
Three thousand, once, three thousand, twice,
And going, and gone," said he.

The people cheered, but some of them cried,
"We do not quite understand
What changed its worth." Swift came the reply:
"The touch of a master's hand."

And many a man with life out of tune,
And battered and scarred with sin,
Is auctioned cheap to the thoughtless crowd,
Much like the old violin.

A "mess of pottage," a glass of wine;
A game— and he travels on.
He is "going" once, and "going" twice,
He's "going" and almost "gone."

But the Master comes, and the foolish crowd
Never can quite understand
The worth of a soul and the change that's wrought
By the touch of the Master's hand.

"The very essence of the gospel is restoration, and the Saviour would have us bid the sick, the hopeless, and the afflicted take hold upon His strength" (The Desire of Ages, pp. 824, 825; emphasis supplied).

FOR FURTHER STUDY

The Ministry of Healing, page 17

"It was His mission to bring men to complete restoration; He came to give them health and peace and perfection of character."

The Ministry of Healing, page 451

"As the sacrifice in our behalf was complete, so our restoration from the defilement of sin is to be complete."

The Desire of Ages, page 568

"Freely will He pardon all who will come to Him for forgiveness and restoration."

1 Corinthians 15:51-58: Promise of complete restoration to all who persevere.

SECTION TWO
Practical Preparation

Chapter Nine

Financial Preparation: Escaping the Leper Colony

"We should shun debt as we would shun the leprosy" (<u>Testimonies for the Church</u>, vol. 6, p. 217).

Two boys, were each given a box of chocolates by their grandfather. The first boy took the package to his bedroom and stuffed the candies into his mouth until he was one big mess of smeared chocolate. The other boy unwrapped the package in front of his grandfather. He opened the box and looked at all the different candies, then, with a big smile, he lifted the box up to his benefactor and said, "Thank you, Grandfather. Here, you have the first piece."

The boy, in letting his grandfather choose the first chocolate, demonstrated determined giving. This attitude is a choice we, as potential survivors, must begin practicing today. Determined giving reflects heaven's economy. Perhaps that is one reason the Lord will allow the dollar to phase out with the "no buy-no sell"—to reveal the ultimate financial integrity of the remnant. Often a new Christian's faith is increased when he learns the value of tithe. There are numerous stories written about the blessings we receive when we are willing to return ten percent of our income to the author of our financial blessings. However, tithe will not be the issue addressed in this chapter. We must develop an attitude such as the survivors of the death camps understood in World War II.

Studies of prisoners in Nazi concentrations camps have revealed that an attitude of determined giving was one of the things that distinguished survivors

144

from those who would likely die in the camp. If a prisoner, though on the verge of starvation himself, had a crust of bread or scrap of potato, and he shared it with a fellow inmate he became psychologically and spiritually stronger, and more capable of surviving. A survivor of Treblinka described it this way: "In our group we shared everything, and the moment one of the group ate something without sharing it, we knew it was the beginning of the end for him."

The accumulation of debt is a spiritual decision. To develop an attitude of determined giving with regard to money as well as other earthly blessings, we must acknowledge God as the author of all our financial blessings. In thankfulness, we can safely ask Him to show us how to manage that with which He has blessed us, thus becoming persons of financial integrity. We must not only be debt free in the crisis ahead, but in such a financial position that we can support the Lord's work when it will be most needed. By rendering to Caesar, paying our debts, and laying aside funds in reserve, we are better able to render service to God, giving faithful account of our stewardship.

"*You can and should make determined efforts to bring under control your disposition to spend means beyond your income*" (Counsels on Stewardship, p. 255; emphasis supplied).

Financial Depression: Is it Really Coming?

What is man predicting for the world in terms of financial crisis? What can we do? What does God say about it? Will it really happen? The last depression was bad. Will the next one be the same—or worse? Back in 1929-1936 we had soup lines, 25 percent unemployment, dust bowl in the grain belt, and banks failed. If you had a garden you could eat.[17,19,20] Most people lost everything on which they owed money. Experts are predicting another financial crisis in the form of a depression.[8,10,37,38] Some of you went through the last depression. Your experience is invaluable to those of us headed for the coming crisis.

A Russian economist by the name of Nicholai Kondratief studied history in the light of economics. According to Kondratief, the economic woes of the world are repeated in a typical cycle of 45-60 years.[1] This cycle is one of slow "controlled" inflation followed by depression. This has proven to be an accurate prediction over the last few hundred years.[2,33] In further study, the parallels between our current day and the day of the last financial crash are unbelievably similar except for one factor—there is a greater danger today than there ever has been.[3]

In the late 1920s there was a period of financial prosperity. Everything was going fine, interest rates were at the highest level known (6 percent), wages had never been better.[3] Today, we are on a peak of even higher prosperity than has ever been duplicated in the history of the world. Let's look at a few economic indicators, then zero in on the spiritual implication of these indicators.[42]

Economic Indicators
• An increased number of businesses are going bankrupt.[16]
• Consumer credit is at a record level; 300 billion dollars plus in the United States.[4, 17]
• Over 50 percent of Americans depend on the government for some form of income.[6]
• Personal bankruptcies in the United States in 1981 were 350,000 a year.[7, 43, 40] There has been very little reduction in this figure to date.
• Most people are completely dependent on the grocery store. (In 1930, 40 percent of the population lived on the farm as compared to 4 percent today.)[8, 31]
• Loss of value of the American dollar; in 1945 it was worth 100 cents; now it is worth less than 24 cents.[9]
• Banks are failing.[10, 11, 35]
• The usual bank safety net (FDIC) could be in hard times.[35, 38, 42, 46]

It would be interesting for you to read some of the library literature on the economic situation today that parallels the Great Depression of 1929-1936.[3, 17, 20] After reading these articles, you will be impressed that businesses are grappling with huge financial problems, many of which cannot be solved.

"But there are not many, even among educators and statesmen, who comprehend the causes that underlie the present state of society. Those who hold the reins of government are unable to solve the problems of poverty, pauperism, and increasing crime. They are struggling in vain to place business operations on a more secure basis" (The Ministry of Healing, p. 183; emphasis supplied).

It is hard to realize that we are struggling in vain, isn't it? What, then, should we do with our property and funds? The Lord counsels that if we would have we must learn to give:

"Your means are far safer there [in the Lord's work] *than if deposited in the bank or invested in houses and lands"* (Counsels on Stewardship, p. 41).

Bank Failure
The economic predictions that men can supply are fallible, but from Dr. Kondratief's cycle and economic indicators of the day, coupled with divine predictions, it becomes clear that we are headed for financial difficulties.[40, 41] We are also headed for financial hard times as social groups and churches. A series of events predicted by inspiration will hasten an economic depression. Again, our survival may depend upon how well prepared we are.

FINANCIAL PREPARATION

"The land boom has cursed this country, extravagant prices have been paid for lands bought on credit; then the land must be cleared and more money is hired; a house to be built calls for more money, and then interest with open mouth swallows up all the profits. Debts accumulate, and then come the <u>closing and failure of banks</u>, and then the foreclosure of mortgages. Thousands have been turned out of employment; families lose their little all, they borrow and borrow, and then have to give up their property and come out penniless. Much money and hard labor have been put into farms bought on credit, or inherited with an encumbrance. <u>The occupants lived in hope of becoming real owners, and it might have been so, but for the failure of banks throughout the country</u>" (Fundamentals of Christian Education, pp. 317, 18; emphasis supplied).

In Haggai 1:6, we read, *"Ye have sown much, and bring in little; ye eat, but ye have not enough; ye drink, but ye are not filled with drink; ye clothe you, but there is none warm; <u>and he that earneth wages earneth wages to put it into a bag with holes</u>. "* Have you found that true with your funds today? There are so many holes in the bag you cannot hold onto your income!

Sunday Law and Financial Depression

The national Sunday law will be established in an attempt to return to temporal prosperity. *"It will be declared that men are offending God by violation of the Sunday sabbath; that this sin has brought calamities which will not cease until Sunday observance shall be strictly enforced; and that those who present the claims of the fourth commandment, thus destroying reverence for Sunday, are troublers of the people, <u>preventing their restoration to divine favor and temporal prosperity</u>"* (The Great Controversy, p. 590; emphasis supplied).

The tragedy of natural calamities will eventually require funds our nation does not possess. People's losses will not be covered by the insurance upon which they depend. First there was Hurricane Andrew. Katrina, then Rita, swept through the southern U. S. at a cost of billions of dollars and many lives. These disasters have been followed by devastating earthquakes worldwide. If these natural disasters are to become more frequent and disastrous, it will cost our government more and more money until there is none left. People will lose their homes and possessions and there will be no money to rebuild. This could lead to a severe depression. Then the nation will become spiritually concerned and want to please an offended God. It is not God but the devil who brings these miseries to us.

The world will be tempted to think that God's people are preventing

147

them from gaining divine favor and economic prosperity. For this reason, we must be urgent in our preparation. *"The Protestant world have set up an idol sabbath in the place where God's Sabbath should be, and they are treading in the footsteps of the Papacy. For this reason I see the necessity of the people of God moving out of the cities into retired country places, where they may cultivate the land and raise their own produce. Thus they may bring their children up with simple, healthful habits. I see the necessity of making haste to get all things ready for the crisis"* (Country Living, p. 21; emphasis supplied).

God has many ways of protecting His people from financial ruin just as He protects them from cataclysmic events. In His mercy, God sees that we are not prepared for that crisis. The winds of strife are beginning to blow. Others have heard His voice in stormy times. What did they do?

The Church in the Depression

In an article entitled "God Was Ready the Day the Banks Closed," from the Review and Herald, September 13, 1979, and reprinted August 31, 2000, Elder Williams, undertreasurer for the General Conference, was impressed to ask his secretary to place several envelopes containing $1,000 each into the office safe. Elder Williams, himself, did not fully understand the implications of why he was transferring this money from the operating funds and placing it in reserve.

Then, on March 3, 1933, he felt pressure on his shoulder and a clear voice commanded, "Go to New York City tonight." Elder Williams responded instantly. He was instructed by the Lord to withdraw three months' overseas payroll from their accounts in New York and send it to the division leaders in the mission field. That Friday evening he returned home with the peace of God in his heart and went to bed. On Sabbath morning, March 4, he was awakened to the newsboy proclaiming, **'Banks fail nationwide!'** Elder Williams dropped to his knees and thanked God that he had a small part in preserving the funds of God during a critical time. If His people listen to His instruction, God will protect them from financial ruin.

"As soon as it was sundown, Elder Shaw, treasurer for the General Conference, phoned Elder Williams arranging an emergency meeting. All the committee members felt that it was a day of gloom and doom for General Conference operations, except Elder Williams, who said: "I noticed that as the treasurers entered Elder Shaw's office, everyone was tense, and all were talking in subdued tones. All were especially concerned for our overseas workers. 'With the banks closed there will be no funds with which to support the missionaries in the field, neither will there be money with which to bring them home,' Elder Shaw explained. At that point, I requested permission to speak, and I quietly related to them my story. We had a prayer session that evening instead of a business meeting. Instead of agonizing for help there were prayers of praise and gratitude for God's wonderful guidance. Nor did we forget to beseech Him to keep us humble in the future. Oh, that He might always lead us as He had in this instance, we prayed.

"'As we rose from our knees, someone remarked that we had been so concerned for our overseas missionaries that we had given no thought to the need of our workers at headquarters. How would we provide for them? How long would the banks be closed? Then I remembered the thousand-dollar items in the safe in my office. Quickly we counted the envelopes and with care, there would be enough cash in which to meet our payroll for the next three months, the same length of time for which we had sent funds for our overseas divisions.'

During the time the banks were closed, workers were paid from the dated and marked envelopes in the little safe in Elder Williams' office. As a result of the 1933 experience, the General Conference adopted a policy stated in the Review and Herald, April 9, 1981: "The treasurer of the General Conference is required by policy to maintain in cash and readily available securities a working fund equal to 20 percent of the operating expenses for the previous 12 months so as to provide for the regular operations of the General Conference and to tide over a possible financial depression."

Banks follow this procedure too![39] I would like to ask you two serious questions. First, Would it not be of extreme importance that we, in our personal finances, have a similar policy? Second, What is the source of the cash reserve in the church? It is our offerings! Cash reserves by families will help God's work in a time of crisis.

Interest Loss Insignificant

You say, "Cash reserves cause a loss of interest!" But, if you have a cash reserve on hand when the depression hits, you will see your interest loss drop into insignificance compared to the buying power you can have at that time. When a bank fails, the loss is larger than just the interest, the principal is gone, too!

My prayer is that everyone of us will consider, on our knees and with hearts open to the Holy Spirit, what we have discussed in this study. I am sure much of it is new and different, but I believe our church is in the forefront in providing this counsel to us in regard to our personal finances. As has been mentioned, our biggest obstacle is our attitude toward our personal indebtedness. May God help each one of us to be free, not only of the indebtedness today, but of its ultimate destiny. May we stand free in Christ as practical Christians in every financial aspect of our Christian living. *"Owe no man any thing."* (Romans 13:8).

"When you can stand forth a free man again, owing no man any-thing, you will have achieved a great victory" (Adventist Home, p. 393-4; emphasis supplied).

Good financial preparedness is for all, especially for those who want to be true to God. There are a few debts which may be incurred of which the Lord approves: God cosigns for these debts, but never leaves us in them (see Counsels on Stewardship, p. 278). Most of the debt problems we incur have nothing to do with the Lord's work. The debts that God approves usually are for building a church or fulfilling pledges of special needs if there are indications of God's providence.

Inspired Financial Counsel

King Solomon understood the essence of time. In Ecclestiastes 3:1, *"To everything there is a season, and a time to every purpose under heaven."* In the times ahead, we will have to be in step with God.

"I saw that if any held on to their property and did not inquire of the Lord as to their duty, He would not make duty known, and they would be permitted to keep their property, and in the time of trouble it would come up before them like a mountain to crush them.... Then, as the cause needs it, their duty is to sell.... The object of selling is not to give to those who are able to labor and support themselves, but to spread the truth" (Early Writings, p. 57; emphasis supplied).

"All that he [Noah] possessed, he invested in the ark" (Patriarchs and Prophets, p. 95).

God's people will be found having all their stewardship invested in the ark and deposited in the bank of heaven. We save money in order to give money, or use it for personal and church emergencies.

"The time is coming when we cannot sell at any price.... Now is our opportunity to work" (Testimonies for the Church, vol. 5, p. 152; emphasis supplied).

"If the love of Christ were found burning in the hearts of His professed people, we would see the same spirit manifested today. Did they but realize how near is the end of all work for the salvation of souls, they would sacrifice their possessions as freely as did the members of the early

church" (Counsels on Stewardship, pp. 40, 41; emphasis supplied).

You may ask, "How will I know when to sell my goods and put my stewardship into the Lord's work?" First, let's consider this inspired counsel:

"If they [God's people] *have their property on the altar and earnestly inquire of God for duty, He will teach them when to dispose of these things. Then they will be free in the time of trouble and have no clogs to weigh them down. "* (Early Writings, p. 57; emphasis supplied). God will teach us when to liquidate and put our funds in God's cause. They will be of no use to us during "no buy-no sell," as described in Revelation 13.

Our leadership is ready to lead. *"When large sums of money are given to the work, let a portion of the means be laid by; for there will be emergencies to meet in the Lord's great vineyard"* (Evangelism, p. 89).

As church members, our personal financial plan should include reserve funds as well. Our motivation is not just personal survival. Our motivation is to be a benefit and a help to the work of our church, the cause of God, the work of helping others. *"Every week you should lay by in some secure place $5 or $10 not to be used up unless in case of sickness"* (Selected Messages, book 2, p. 329).

"Get your means where you can handle it for the benefit of the cause of God" (Testimonies for the Church, vol. 5, p. 465). When you put a handle on something, you can get your hands on it, right? But, remember the motivation, *"for the benefit of the cause of God. "* There will come a time when our *"possessions cannot be disposed of to advance the cause of present truth. "* (Counsels on Stewardship, p. 57).

Debt—The Most Deadly Enemy to Economic Preparation

In review, we have learned how the land boom cursed the country because we borrowed money to buy the land, we borrowed money to clear the land, we borrowed money to build the house, and then we borrowed money to plant the crop. Interest compounds debt. Interest swallows profit, tending to make our wages appear to be falling through the holes in our pockets. Is there danger in this need versus debt cycle?

Consider the possibility of a depression; property values would decrease greatly.[45] However, if God's people have cash on hand obtained during prosperity, that same money (gained from liquidation of their inflationary property) could be used in purchasing, debt-free, a less expensive country property enabling them to grow their own provisions.

God may use a depression to help His people leave the cities.[31] Purchasing and selling at the right time is all-important.[13]

The Leper Colony

"We should shun debt as we should shun the leprosy" (<u>Testimonies for the Church</u>, vol. 6, p. 217). Who among us would choose leprosy over good health? Yet, today, many are living in modern leper colonies by incurring debt. Think how ridiculous our justification must sound to the great cloud of witnesses in heaven.

"Oh, I have always wanted leprosy. To be able to live in a leper colony—how mah-velous! I absolutely love the landscaping around the hovels, and the interiors are ultramodern! I can cover up my leprosy for a while, and maybe all the other lepers in the colony will think I'm rich. Oh yes, someday I'll have to pay for it, but for now, I'm really going to get a kick out of living in the leper colony. What a lifestyle! And maybe someone will have figured out a cure by the time the disease starts to show. Even if leprosy does come with the deal, it's thrilling! Well, actually, I've always wanted to help lepers, but now I find myself enjoying the disease!"

What if we do wake up and realize we have leprosy and desire healing from the disease? How do we get out of the colony? Is bankruptcy an option of escape for the Christian?

Bankruptcy—A Christian's Cure for Debt?

Satan spins such a comfortable web around his unsuspecting victims, so totally anesthetizes them, that they sometimes don't even want to get out of debt. *"When one voluntarily becomes involved in debt, he is entangling himself in one of Satan's nets which he sets for souls"* (<u>Counsels on Stewardship</u>, p. 254).

But the counsel is strong. We must break his hold. *"Redeem every pledge unless sickness lays you prostrate. Better deny yourself food and sleep than be guilty of keeping from others their just dues"* (<u>ibid</u>., pp. 253, 254).

Indulging in debt effectively neutralizes our peace of mind. *"It* [the eighth commandment] *forbids overreaching in trade, and requires the payment of just debts or wages"* (<u>ibid</u>. p. 254). Not paying just debts and wages is stealing, and a violation of the eighth commandment, and what Christian could sleep well knowing he had stolen something? We are morally obligated to pay our debts.

Bankruptcy, for the Christian, is not a viable option. Can you begin to see why debt is likened to a leprosy? Failure to pay debts compromises our spiritual health because there is an increased chance that we will fail to pay increased indebtedness, thereby breaking the eighth commandment. Let's say, for example, in times of prosperity we incur debt. If a depression hits, everything drops in value except the dollar bill and your debt. **The policy of having cash on hand in case of emergency is sound economic advice,** but debts accumulated in inflationary times cannot be paid with dollars earned during a depression because our debt is so much more than our earning power. Christians are morally obligated to pay inflationary debts, even during times of depression. Ignoring the claims of honest debt compromises our spiritual integrity.

"The practice of borrowing money to relieve some pressing necessity, and making no calculation for canceling the indebtedness, however common, is demoralizing. The Lord would have all who believe the truth converted from these self-deceiving practices. They should choose rather to suffer want than to commit a dishonest act" (ibid. p. 255).

Forgiveness of Debt

The Lord's Prayer is a possible solution to impossible economic problems, *"And forgive us our debts, as we forgive our debtors"* (Matthew 6:12). Forgiveness involves more than emotional release of our sins against God and our brothers and sisters. It is a financial option as well.

The gospel includes a story of compassion when a debt holder forgives his debtor millions of dollars! *"The lord of that servant was moved with compassion, and loosed him, and forgave him the debt* [money]*"* (Matthew 18:23-35). If we are called upon to forgive, we should forgive from our hearts. We are not obliged to forgive a debt, but if someone is sincerely trying to free themselves of the chains of slavery, we might consider releasing him if it is within our power to do so.

We can forgive debts and we can be forgiven debts. According to Luke 7:41, 42, and 16:5-7 we can forgive large or small debts. The Golden Rule, in Matthew 7:12, says that whatever we would like to have done to us is what we should do to others. The principle of forgiveness of debt was part of the lifestyle of God's people for centuries. Every seventh year was called a year of release (see Deuteronomy 31:10 and 15:1-3), in which the debts of poor brethren were remitted. During the Jubilee year (which was every fiftieth year) slaves were freed and lands which had been lost through debt were returned to their rightful owners. In Leviticus 25:8, 10, 35 we see that the debt holder completely relieves the debtor. *"Take thou no usury of him"* (verse 36). According to Scripture, the debt holder forgave the debt as well as the interest accumulated.

These celebrations of the Sabbatical and the Jubilee were not only joyous because people were free of debts, but also because the debt holders had the pleasant task of doing good for someone else. Those love most who are forgiven most (see Luke 7:43).

As a balance, remember that we should always pay our debts, even *"if we have to live on porridge and bread"* (Counsels on Stewardship, p. 257). To forgive a debt is only an emergency measure and an act of love, not a requirement. (See Christ's Object Lessons, p. 247). There should be no oppression by debt holders or cheating by debtors where love dwells in the heart. None need fear that their liberality will bring them to want. *"Obedience to God's commandments would surely result in prosperity"* (Patriarchs and Prophets, p. 533). We can have complete faith that God will keep this promise (Hebrews 10:23). God has forgiven us great debts that we owe Him, more than we can ever pay. These debts include money (Counsels on Stewardship, p. 100), time (Christ's Object Lessons, p. 342), and sin (ibid. p. 249). No matter how far we have strayed from His plan for us, we can always humble ourselves and say, "Lord, forgive my sin." He will reward the honest and willing heart.

From Debt to Slavery—Literal?

Historically, people have sold themselves, becoming what was known as indentured servants, because of indebtedness. In the troublous times ahead Christians may be facing this slavery again for the same reasons.[24, 25]

Slavery has come about through two main avenues: through conquest and through the sale of life in order to pay a debt. Indebtedness could put us in a position to sell what we have in order to pay our debt. We might be required to supply the only thing we have left: our potential to work for the rest of our lives! It has happened in the past and it may happen again!

"In ancient times criminals were sometimes sold into slavery by the judges; in some cases, debtors were sold by their creditors; and poverty even led persons to sell themselves or their children" (Patriarchs and Prophets, p. 310; emphasis supplied).

"As the defenders of truth refuse to honor the Sunday-sabbath, some of them will be thrust into prison, some will be exiled, some will be treated as slaves" (The Great Controversy, p. 608).

"But many of all nations and of all classes, high and low, rich and poor, black and white, will be cast into the most unjust and cruel bondage" (ibid. p. 626).

"But," you say, "would slavery be all that bad?" Patriarchs and Prophets, p. 211 says of past history that *"To become a slave was a fate more to be feared than death."*

Have you ever heard someone say, "Everybody does it!" or "It's not really a debt, it's just a monthly payment! I can always get my money back out of my house and even more than what I paid for it!"? These are all common arguments justifying indebtedness.

Let's say it another way, "Well, maybe I do have leprosy, but I can always get healed." I fancy I can hear flies on a flypaper carrying on the same conversation! One brother, stuck by a wing, says to one who is stuck by five legs, "I can get off anytime!" If a depression comes and you are still in debt, you are still obliged to pay. **It is best to get out and stay out of debt, now.**

VICE

Vice is a monster
Of so frightful a mien
As to be hated,
Needs but to be seen
But, seen too oft,
Familiar with her face
We first endure,
Then pity, and embrace.

— Alexander Pope

Wouldn't it be presumptuous to think that even if we accumulate debt the Lord will swoop in and rescue us? The character that we shape today, by our choices, will be ours for eternity. The Lord counsels us to **shun debt like the leprosy.** Our health, spiritually and physically, may depend upon our financial response to God's counsel.

"How many have become insane over the loss of their bank deposits, or their failure in business! How many have devoted life and soul to acquiring wealth, but were not rich toward God; and when adversity came upon them, and their possessions were swept away, they had nothing laid up in heaven. They had lost all–both temporal and eternal riches. In despair and cowardice, they have taken their own lives, and put an end to the opportunities and privileges that had been purchased for them at an infinite cost to the Son of God" (The Review and Herald, Sept. 18, 1888; emphasis supplied).

The Cleansing of the Leper

Down the street a cry was heard, "Unclean! Unclean!" Word spread rapidly ahead of the leper as he was coming to Jesus. Some of the people were close enough (without getting contaminated) to yell, "Go back! Go back to your hovel! Go back to your leper colony!" But he would not be refused. His disease caused him to seek healing. He proceeded right through the crowd. It parted. Jesus did not try to avoid him. The poor wretch dropped at Jesus' feet and said, *"If thou wilt, thou canst make me clean"* (Luke 5:12). Jesus touched him, and immediately the leprosy was gone.

The cure for the modern leprosy of debt is the same—approaching Jesus. As you look at your financial condition you may just have to say, "Unclean!" When you look at your preparedness for what's ahead you may also have to say, "Unclean!" But, by God's grace, as you come to Jesus, personally, with your needs, you can be made as clean as was that man centuries ago. Jesus is still in the business of healing lepers, even leprosy due to debt! And He does it in a miraculous way! *"The work of Christ in cleansing the leper from his terrible disease is an illustration of His work in cleansing the soul from sin"* (The Desire of Ages, p. 266). This same Jesus who, in Matthew 8:3, said, *"I will, be thou clean,"* can work miracles for you.

"Whatever your anxieties and trials, spread out your case before the Lord. Your spirit will be braced for endurance. The way will be opened for you to disentangle yourself from embarrassment and difficulty. The weaker and more helpless you know yourself to be, the stronger you will become in His strength. The heavier your burdens, the more blessed the rest in casting them upon the Burden Bearer. The rest that Christ offers depends upon conditions, but these conditions are plainly specified. They are those with which all can comply. He tells us just how His rest is to be found" (The Desire of Ages, p. 329; emphasis supplied). Pray and then get up and do the work to answer your prayer (see Amazing Grace, p. 166).

Go ahead, make your way through the crowd. Hear their taunts, hear their teasing. Endure. Make your way to Jesus. If you find yourself suffering from the leprosy of debt, unload your burden and all of its complications at Jesus' feet. Jesus is the **only** sure cure; He is the WAY. It will call for no small sacrifice to get our financial situations where they should be before the impending crises, but it will be worth it. Work to answer your own prayer for victory over debt.

"Let there be most earnest prayer, and then let us work in harmony with our prayers" (Testimonies for the Church, vol. 5, p. 714). Our prayer should include freedom from sin and debt, as well as the disease of selfishness that infected us in the beginning. We can forgive, and we can be forgiven of debt. Freedom follows faith.

Steps in Financial Preparation

There will be as many plans for debt reduction as there are people, but a few simple principles can be followed by everyone. Remember, placing God first in your personalized financial plan is the best guarantee of success.

FINANCIAL PREPARATION

1. To the best of your ability, total up your debt.
2. Record the interest rates on each debt.
3. Record your monthly/yearly income.
4. Record the value of what you might sell to raise money to pay debts, especially those with the highest interest rates.
5. Pay small debts first so you begin to feel free!
6. If your debts are overwhelming, consult a debt consolidation expert.
7. In any circumstance, make double and triple payments if possible without penalty.
8. Pray that God will help you providentially to be free of this leprosy.
9. Develop a savings plan that includes having liquid assets in your possession.
10. Allow a place in your financial plan for determined giving, including tithe-paying. *"Bring ye all the tithes into the storehouse, that there may be meat in mine house, and prove me now herewith, saith the Lord of hosts, if I will not open you the windows of heaven, and pour you out a blessing, that there shall not be room enough to receive it"* (Malachi 3:10; emphasis supplied).

    "It has ever proved that nine tenths are worth more to them [God's people] *than ten tenths"* (Testimonies for the Church, vol. 3, p. 546).
11. Once you're free of debt, don't use credit cards; this could be a temptation to get into debt again.

FOR FURTHER STUDY

1. Testimonies for the Church, vol. 9, p. 131, "Money will perish"
2. The Advent Review and Sabbath Herald, May 27, 1902, "Higher interest rate"
3. Manuscript Releases, vol. 17, p. 286, "Not in banks"
4. Counsels on Health, p. 493, "Love Him supremely and our neighbor as ourselves"
5. It's Your Money, Isn't It?, G. Edward Reid, Review and Herald Publishing Association, Hagerstown, Maryland.
6. Margins, Swenson, Richard, A. M. D., Nav Press, Colorado Springs, Colo. (see especially chapter 10, "Margin in Finances").

Footnotes

[1] Futurist, Oct. 1979, p. 353.
[2] Levy-Pascal, Ehud. An Analysis of the Cyclical Dynamics of Industrialized Counties. Published by the U.S. Central Intelligence Agency, 1976.
[3] U.S. News, Oct. 29, 1979, p. 32.
[4] U.S. News, Mar. 31, 1980, p. 29.
[5] Business Week, June 23, 1980, p. 122.
[6] U.S. News, Mar. 9, 1981, p. 73.
[7] U.S. News, May 25, 1981, p. 87.
[8] Futurist, June 1980, p. 32.
[9] U.S. News, Oct. 29, 1979.
[10] Clark, Douglas. How to Survive the Money Crash. Harvest House Publishing, Irvine, Calif., pp. 95, 98-104.
[11] Edmonton Journal, Jan. 29, 1980.
[12] White, Ellen G., Early Writings, p. 33.
[13] ———, Early Writings, p. 57.
[14] ———, Counsels on Stewardship, pp. 40-41.
[15] ———, Testimonies for the Church, vol. 5, p. 154.
[16] U.S. News, Mar. 31, 1980, p. 25.
[17] U.S. News, Oct. 29, 1979, p. 35.
[18] White, Ellen G., Testimonies for the Church, vol. 6, p. 217.
[19] National Review, Nov. 9, 1979, p. 1419.
[20] Newsweek, Oct. 22, 1979, p. 40.
[21] White, Ellen G., Country Living, p. 21.
[22] Cooper, Emma Howell. Review and Herald, Sept. 13, 1979, "God Was Ready the Day the Banks Closed," p. 4.
[23] White, Ellen G., Testimonies for the Church, vol. 6, p. 209.
[24] ———, The Great Controversy, p. 608.
[25] ———, ibid., p. 626.
[26] ———, Counsels on Stewardship, p. 254.
[27] ———, ibid., p. 254.
[28] ———, ibid., p. 254.
[29] ———, Early Writings, p. 85.
[30] U.S. News, Feb. 9, 1981, p. 53.
[31] White, Ellen G., Country Living, pp. 9, 10.
[32] ———, Counsels on Stewardship, p. 41.
[33] Futurist, December 1978, "A Great Depression Ahead."
[34] Bartlett, John. Familiar Quotations, Toronto, Little, Brown & Co., 1968 (14th Ed.), p. 409.
[35] U.S. News, Mar. 25, 1985, p. 73.
[36] Time, Jan. 10, 1983, p. 42.
[37] The Oregonian (Portland, Oreg.), July 17, 1986, "Economists Fear Repeat of '29 Crash.."
[38] The Oregonian (Portland, Oreg.), June 30, 1986, "Failing Banks Leave FDIC to Peddle Millions in Assets."
[39] MacLeans, Apr. 11, 1988, p. 5.
[40] Time, Sept. 28, 1992, p. 18.
[41] Newsweek, May 21, 1990, p. 20.
[42] Newsweek, Dec. 31, 1990, p. 20.
[43] Vancouver Sun, Apr. 23, 1991.
[44] Chattanooga News Free Press, Feb. 12, 1992, and Mar. 7, 1991.
[45] Newsweek, Nov. 19, 1990, p. 54.
[46] Time, Sept. 24, 1990, p. 46.
[47] Vandeman, George. "The Day the Dollar Dies," Signs of the Times, June 1988, p. 3.

Chapter Ten

Country Living:
A Taste of Elegance

"Fathers and mothers who possess a piece of land and a comfortable home are kings and queens" (<u>Country Living</u>, p. 18).

The following plea appeared among the letters to the editor in the May 28, 1998, edition of <u>USA Today</u>; "Will someone help me save my son? My son is two years old and is a reflection of complete innocence. His vulnerability to this harsh, violent, ignorant and uncaring world just rips my heart apart. He knows nothing of the killing within the schools.... He knows nothing of the abuse that happens within homes of children just his age. As he plays with his toys, he is oblivious to the tragedies that occur every day across the country. As he clutches his blanket, sleeping soundly, dreaming of the mommie and daddy who love him, he has no idea of the complete social and moral decay of our society.

"Does anyone care anymore? Will someone please, please help me save my son?" —Edward Moats, Belleair Beach, Florida.

I know, personally, of no better advice to give Mr. Moats when he asks for help in saving his son than to advise him to move to the country.

Protection by Escape

Pollution comes in many forms. Social pollution is nearly impossible to escape in our cities today. Who among us has not longed for the refreshment of solitude? Our children, growing up in an artificial environment display modern diseases that reflect the lifestyle in which they are expected to perform. True, Satan can wedge himself into our quiet time no matter where we live, but where

159

do our city children go to watch spectacular sunset? How often are they up with the dawn and hear a bird song above the roar of engines and voices? Why do we see so much violence, hyperactivity, and a lack of respect? Who among our young people can feel comfortable sitting beside a quiet stream for an afternoon, cleansing his soul of artificial stimuli, without feeling obligated to accomplish something measurable? I love the country for I have seen it work miracles in the lives of emotionally disturbed and artificially overburdened youth.

In his autobiography, the late well-known naturalist John Muir states, "Thousands of tired, overcivilized people are beginning to find out that going to the mountains is going home; that **wildness is a necessity**; and that mountain parks and reservations are useful not only as fountains of timber and irrigating rivers, but as fountains of life" (The Story of My Boyhood and Youth, page 459).

Mark R. Rosenzweig, in his article "Brain Changes in Response to Experience," (Scientific American, February 1972) records a comparison study between two groups of genetically similar rats raised in two different environments. The first environment was crowded, stacked cage conditions. The second was referred to as a seminatural environment in a large enclosure with more space, logs, sand, plants, burrows, limbs, etc. At the end of the experiment it was found that the brain synapses were 50 percent larger and the brain weight was increased 6.4 percent in the rats living in the seminatural environment as compared to animals living in crowded cage conditions. The parallel to human development was noted.

Mark Reisner wrote an article for the L. A. Times on October 19, 1989 entitled "In Fifteen Seconds We Are Humbled." The summation of his article can be expressed in these words: **the more complex our society, the more subject we are to natural disasters.** His words make a strong appeal to a simpler life.

He continues, "The Ohlone Indians, who lived around San Francisco Bay for thousands of years, must have experienced earthquakes far more powerful than the World Series quake of 1989.... . But to people living at that level of simplicity, earthquakes are just a terrifying curiosity. Their society is not utterly incapacitated by collapsing overpass pylons and falling bridge decks. They do not risk months without water when aqueducts break, or neighborhood conflagrations when water pressure disappears. ...

"As a species we can't resist flaunting our profound ability to defy nature with our dams, skyscrapers, freeways, and nuclear power plants. And the more spectacular this ability becomes, **the more vulnerable we make ourselves.** That is the oldest cliché in the world—the higher you rise, the farther you fall—but it seems we keep having to relearn it, and we never really learn from it.

"Freeways, bridges, tunnels, aqueducts, dams and all the rest—for this whole century we have been fascinated by such gargantuan wizardry, partly because it snubs nature (or what we used to call reality) so wondrously; but mainly, and quite simply, because we could build it.

"How do you tell a society like ours that wisdom lies in reaching backward for old ideas?"

Is it really reaching backward? Are the "good old days" truly outdated? We are told, that *"... the old, old times will be back* (Series B, #7, p. 63)." Frenzied men and women long for a time of escape from the hectic pace of life. How often can a person's innocence be bombarded and not become calloused to even the most sensational reports? Does it matter to God how and where our character is formed?

Roberta Donovan, in "Victory in the Mountains," published in <u>Listen Magazine</u>, June 1985, quotes a young person who participated in their youth ranch program conducted in a wilderness setting: "I left the old me out in the woods, and I am a new person. I am going to make it."

Glimpse of a Better World

Let me tell you about my high school years. I was born in a large northwestern city. Self- preservation was a necessary art form. I was fourteen as I began my studies at a secondary church school. I looked up to my PE teacher, Mr. V. because he was so strong! He could do anything we boys could do and twice as easily; if we could lift one end of something, he could lift the whole thing! It seemed we were always comparing our strength to his. Mr. V. never raised his voice, but he could sure get our attention! I remember when he broke up a fist fight between two teenagers by lifting them each off the ground at the same time!

Back then I was classed among the troublemakers and it was Mr. V. who, one day, decided to do something about us rebels. He took six of us on a five-day camp out. It seemed to us that he picked the worst weekend he could find; mixed rain and snow, barely above freezing. Those of us he had chosen to attend the camp had never worked together on anything. When we arrived, we began doing things in our own way, independent as usual, and everything began to unravel. Before long, two of us were in a fist fight.

"Now boys," said Mr. V., pulling us away from each other by our wet coat collars as easily as we peeled the bananas in our lunch bags. "Let's be about this business of survival." So we did. We were all in the same boat—a wet sleeping bag, no shelter, and no skills with which to change our situation.

It soon became obvious to us that, next to loving rebels, Mr. V.'s very favorite thing was camping. That long weekend, he tried to teach us everything he knew, and his enthusiasm eventually rubbed off on us. It's hard to build a fire in the rain, but Mr. V. took us under a big fir tree and showed us how to snap off the dry limbs. He explained fire building step by step. Our spirits soared with the flames. He explained things that I have never forgotten. During that weekend I glimpsed a better world. I began to learn to get along with others.

That camping trip was my first survival experience and my first glimpse of the person that Mr. V. believed I could be. It was the turning point of my life. True, it was five days of misery, but, oh, what I learned! I wonder if Mr. V. ever knew how much that weekend really meant to me. Those lessons of hardship, discipline, and trust I learned on that camping trip helped me begin to understand some things about God's character that I had never considered, all because Don Van Tassel persevered and was patient with six young rebels. Those days spent camping with Mr. V. brought me out of the woods and marked the beginning of my love for the wilderness and for the character of God. I can look back on that weekend as the days that ignited my desire to enjoy the great outdoors. After that camping trip, I knew I wanted to live in the country, as far from the confines and corruption of the city as I could get.

God's Plan to Protect Our Children

Living in the country does require what some might classify as sacrifice, but if we truly see the need and long for a country home with our whole heart, the Lord will provide a way of escape. Leaving the city behind us is the only way to escape its pollution. Lot had left his Uncle Abraham's farm to live in Sodom, perhaps justifying his move with the desire to evangelize the town. Instead of saving Sodom, he sacrificed his own spiritual purity and the innocence of his daughters. His wife remains the virtual reminder of the ultimate sacrifice of those whose heart is enamored with that which God will destroy.

"The children and youth should be carefully guarded. They should be kept away from the hotbeds of iniquity that are to be found in our cities" (Country Living, p. 12). *"Out of the cities is my message for the education of our children"* (ibid., p. 13).

162

COUNTRY LIVING

It has always been God's call for His people to live a simple lifestyle in the country. From these locations, families were educated to do missionary work in the cities. Many of God's ambassadors received their training in a country environment. God felt it imperative that some of these men and women be examples of what we are to be when the last message is given, for *"there are Enochs in this our day"* (Sons and Daughters of God, p. 314.) These people found elegance in simple living. As we look at examples of Bible characters, we see that they experienced an ever increasing awareness of their need of preparation. Such plans produced sons and daughters of God, joint heirs with Christ, members of the royal line, and happy people.

True, you might have to sacrifice a few conveniences, but country living need not remove your appreciation of elegance. Even amid the practical virtues of work one can glimpse the truly elegant touches of the hand of God; a spider web's sparkling beauty as it collects dew, numberless diamonds strewn across a meadow glittering in the first light of dawn, the moments of blazing glory as the sun sets, the pastel sunrise, an autumn harvest, a snow-capped peak.

❋ *"When we are converted, our desire for ease and elegance will be changed"* (The Upward Look, p. 330). Country living encourages a converted heart—our tastes change, almost imperceptibly—for we are closer to His works.

Principle of Separation

One of the ways God can protect our families is found in 2 Corinthians 6:14-18; *"Be ye not unequally yoked together with unbelievers: for what fellowship hath righteousness with unrighteousness? and what communion hath light with darkness? And what concord hath Christ with Belial? Or what hath he that believeth with an infidel? And what agreement hath the temple of God with idols? for ye are the temple of the living God; as God hath said, I will dwell in them, and walk in them; and I will be their God, and they shall be my people. Wherefore come out from among them, and be ye separate, saith the Lord, and touch not the unclean thing: and I will receive you, And will be a father unto you, and ye shall be my sons and daughters, saith the Lord Almighty."* The principle of separation is a safety net for our families, churches, and schools.

There are several questions asked of us by God. It is His attempt to invite us to respond to His counsel affirmatively. Don't be affiliated with unbelievers. Come out and be separate, He advises. If we follow God's counsel then He will dwell in us and we will be His people. He will be our Father if we separate from the world. This is an irrefutable principle of living that will affect our survival. We must not be influenced by the world to the detriment of our spiritual life. Yes, there is balance to this principle. We must not isolate ourselves in a hermit's existence but give the message of truth to the world.

"The followers of Christ are to be separate from the world in principles and interests, <u>but they are not to isolate themselves from the world</u>. The Saviour mingled constantly with men, not to encourage them in anything that was not in accordance with God's will, but to uplift and ennoble them" (Counsels to Teachers, p. 323; emphasis supplied). While we are to mingle with the world in mission work we are to be separate in attitude and in principles of living.

"The great Head of the church, who has chosen His people out of the world, requires them to be separate from the world" (Counsels to Teachers, p. 329).

Jesus' example and words are in clarion tones *"Come out from among them and be ye separate."*

"The baleful influence of sin poisons the life of the soul. <u>Our only safety</u> is in separation from those who live in its darkness. The Lord has enjoined upon us to come out from among them and be separate, and to touch not the unclean thing, and He will receive us and will be a Father unto us, and we shall be His sons and daughters. If we wish to be adopted into the family of God, to become children of the heavenly King, we must comply with His conditions; we must come out from the world and stand as peculiar people before the Lord, obeying His precepts and serving Him" (Testimonies For the Church, vol. 4, p. 109).

What is true for ourselves and our families is also true for our schools. They must also be separate from the world and its standards.

"Many have so far shown their lack of wisdom from above as to join with the enemies of God and the truth in providing worldly entertainments for the students. In doing this they bring upon themselves the frown of God, for they mislead the youth and do a work for Satan. <u>This work, with all its results, they must meet at the bar of God</u>. ...When the Lord requires us to be distinct and peculiar, how can we crave popularity or seek to imitate the customs and practices of the world?" (Testimonies for the Church, vol. 6, p. 143; emphasis supplied).

Taste of Elegance

Living in the country can ennoble and refine us, which is as God would have it. The dictionary defines the word **elegance**: "richly ornamental; a refinement pleasing to good taste, graceful, neat, refined, nice." What is more richly ornamental, a Ming vase or a mountaintop? A Renaissance painting or a sunset? Greek architecture or a log home you built yourself? A fountain downtown or a waterfall in the wilderness? A polluted city river or a mountain cataract? The best preparation for the lifework of the minister and the gospel worker takes place on the farm, in the country, and in the wilderness communicating with God. *"The usefulness learned on the school farm is the very education that is most essential for those who go out as missionaries to many foreign fields"* (Series B, no. 11, [The Madison School], p. 29). In living a simple lifestyle, we learn essential knowledge free of encumbrances dictated by city living. Health, both physical and spiritual, is built right in to country life.

"There are life-giving properties in the balsam of the pine, in the fragrance of the cedar and the fir healing in the spruce and pine..." (The Ministry of Healing., p. 264).

"All who are under the training of God need the quiet hour for communion with their own hearts, with nature, and with God. In them is to be revealed a life that is not in harmony with the world, its customs, or its practices; and they need to have a personal experience in obtaining a knowledge of the will of God. We must individually hear Him speaking to the heart when every other voice is hushed, and in quietness we wait before Him, the silence of the soul makes more distinct the voice of God. This is the effectual preparation for all labor for God" (ibid. p. 58; emphasis supplied).

The same principles that applied to early Christians apply to us today. Spirit of Prophecy explains that the training outlined by God cannot be bypassed by modern gadgets and technology.

"A return to simpler methods will be appreciated by children and youth. Work in the garden and field will be an agreeable change from the wearisome routine of abstract lessons, to which their young minds should never be confined" (Testimonies for the Church, vol. 6, p. 179). The simple lifestyle and training of the early days is needed for our children today. Parents and teachers wish to provide conveniences for young people that end in a softening which diminishes the pioneering experience they so desperately need and deeply desire. All children, including those with ADD and other nervous disorders, will benefit spiritually and psychologically from a life in the country. Parents can consider the option of home school when they move to the country. This training is extremely productive of growth, both spiritually and academically. We found this to be true with our own son as we home-schooled him through grade twelve.

"Children should virtually be trained in a home school from the cradle to maturity" (Child Guidance, p. 26).

Country living is a central training for our young people from the cradle to the grave. It is a truly classical experience, relevant to all ages. In God's book of nature, all may easily be taught by the Holy Spirit.

The rest of this chapter will report about great champions of truth and how they used the principle of separation and country living to live a life of purity. Because of this they were effective witnesses for God and His message.

Country Living From Creation to the Flood

God has always used simple, beautiful methods to train His leaders and His people. The Godhead always planned the best for humans (see 1 Corinthians 3:11; Hebrews 4:3; and Ephesians 1:4). God set Adam and Eve in a garden to dress it and keep it (Genesis 2: 7-15). God will restore the same program in heaven (Isaiah 65:17, 21-25).

The Bible states that God has planned a garden home both before and after 6,000 years of sin. I wonder if His best plan for us during the 6,000 years since Eden has changed? Has he said anything about it? During sin's reign, is tending a garden in the country important? Is it just for our enjoyment or is the training gained from country living **essential** to spreading the gospel? Does country living really offer more educational potential? We can answer these questions from inspired sources and discover some reasons God wants His people in the country.

As we look at the lives of the characters in the Bible story we will discover some of the answers to our questions. From Eden lost to Eden restored God has not nor will He ever deprive His people; He has ever kept before them the true taste of elegance. *"So with the great majority of the best and noblest men of all ages. Read the history of Abraham, Jacob, and Joseph, of Moses, David, and Elisha. Study the lives of men of later times who have most worthily filled positions of trust and responsibility, the men whose influence has been most effective for the world's uplifting. How many of these were reared in country homes"* (Country Living, p. 15).

Adam

Adam and Eve were placed by God in a garden, the splendor of which we can only imagine. Sky blue ceilings, a living carpet, tree lined walls, a surround-sound-system which they not only heard but with which they conversed! Untouched by decay or disease, the Garden of Eden must have been a wonder to behold. The first school was their garden home.

"Men, in their pride, delight in magnificent and costly edifices and

166

glory in the works of their own hands; but <u>God placed Adam in a garden</u>. This was his dwelling. The blue heavens were its dome; the earth, with its delicate flowers and carpet of living green, was its floor; and the leafy branches of the goodly trees were its canopy. Its walls were hung with the most magnificent adornings—the handiwork of the great Master Artist. <u>In the surroundings of the holy pair was a lesson for all time</u>—that true happiness is found, not in the indulgence of pride and luxury, but in communion with God through His created works. If men would give less attention to the artificial, and would cultivate greater simplicity, they would come far nearer to answering the purpose of God in their creation" (<u>Patriarchs and Prophets</u>, p. 49; emphasis supplied).

"<u>In the beginning He placed our first parents amidst the beautiful sights and sounds He desires us to rejoice in today. The more nearly we come into harmony with God's original plan, the more favorable will be our position to secure health of body, and mind, and soul</u>" (<u>The Ministry of Healing</u>, p. 365; emphasis supplied).

Seth

Adam and Eve had to leave their garden home after sin entered. Their oldest son, Cain, killed their second son, Abel. The principle of separation emerged as wickedness spread. God's people chose to live separate from the followers of Cain.

"For some time the two classes remained separate. The race of Cain, spreading from the place of their first settlement, dispersed over the plains and valleys where the children of Seth had dwelt; and the latter, in order to escape from their contaminating influence, withdrew to the mountains, and there made their home. <u>So long as this separation continued, they maintained the worship of God in its purity.</u> But in the lapse of time they ventured, little by little, to mingle with the inhabitants of the valleys. <u>This association was productive of the worst results</u>" (<u>Patriarchs and Prophets</u>, p. 81; emphasis supplied).

Enoch

Separation of lifestyle and geography was not the total answer to spreading the good news of the gospel. God used Enoch to exemplify His plan to do missionary work. We may gain spiritual and physical strength by communion with God in nature so that we can minister to those in the cities. Enoch accented the principle that if you love the cities, you are not ready to work them.

"He [Enoch] *did not make his abode with the wicked. <u>He did not locate in Sodom, thinking to save Sodom.</u> He placed himself and his family*

where the atmosphere would be as pure as possible. Then at times he went forth to the inhabitants of the world with his God-given message. Every visit he made to the world was painful to him. He saw and understood something of the leprosy of sin. After proclaiming his message, he always took back with him to his place of retirement some who had received the warning. Some of these became overcomers, and died before the Flood came. But some had lived so long in the corrupting influence of sin that they could not endure righteousness" (The Seventh-day Adventist Bible Commentary, Ellen G. White Comments, vol. 1, pp. 1087, 1088; emphasis supplied).

"He [Enoch] did not become a hermit, shutting himself entirely from the world; for he had a work to do for God in the world. ... Distressed by the increasing wickedness of the ungodly, and fearing that their infidelity might lessen his reverence for God, Enoch avoided constant association with them, and spent much time in solitude, giving himself to meditation and prayer" (Patriarchs and Prophets, p. 85; emphasis supplied).

It is interesting to see how God helped Enoch solve his dilemma. He did not want to leave his country home to go to the city where he witnessed crime and sin, yet he felt an urgency from God to minister. Let's look back over the centuries to see how Enoch did it.

"The greater and more pressing his labors, the more constant and earnest were his prayers. He continued to exclude himself, at certain periods, from all society. After remaining for a time among the people, laboring to benefit them by instruction and example, he would withdraw, to spend a season in solitude, hungering and thirsting for that divine knowledge which God alone can impart. Communing thus with God, Enoch came more and more to reflect the divine image. His face was radiant with a holy light, even the light that shineth in the face of Jesus. As he came forth from these divine communings, even the ungodly beheld with awe the impress of heaven upon his countenance" (ibid., p. 86; emphasis supplied).

"The godly character of this prophet represents the state of holiness which must be attained by those who shall be 'redeemed from the earth' (Rev. 14:3) *at the time of Christ's second advent"* (ibid, pp. 88, 89; emphasis supplied).

"And there are Enochs in this our day" (Christ's Object Lessons, p. 332; emphasis supplied).

"Enoch, separating himself from the world, and spending much of his time in prayer and in communion with God, represents God's loyal people in the last days, who will be separate from the world" (The Story of Redemp-

168

tion, p. 60; emphasis supplied).

"By faith Enoch was translated that he should not see death; ... for before his translation he had this testimony, that he pleased God" (Gospel Workers, p. 54). *"To such communion God is calling us. As was Enoch's so must be their holiness of character who shall be redeemed from among men at the Lord's second coming"* (Maranatha, p. 65; emphasis supplied). (See also Spiritual Gifts, vol. 3, pp. 53-60).

Enoch brought people back with him to an environment more nurturing to spiritual growth. Some made spiritual progress and some did not. Those that didn't, couldn't because of having lived in the filth of the cities too long. God's plan for Enoch was for him to live outside of the contaminated cities in a place as pure as possible, communing with God, working hard to support his family, and even though it was painful to him, to witness in the cities. If there are Enochs in this our day, then there are some people following Enoch's plan today.

Noah

Noah's call emphasizes God's plan for the training of His people in all ages and especially for the last days. *"But as the days of No'e were, so shall also the coming of the Son of man be"* (Matthew 24:7).

"As in the days of Noah and Lot, there must be a marked separation from sin and sinners" (Patriarchs and Prophets, p. 167). Noah was aware of the principle of separation.

"For a time the descendants of Noah continued to dwell among the mountains where the ark had rested. As their numbers increased, apostasy soon led to division. Those who desired to forget their Creator and to cast off the restraint of His law felt a constant annoyance from the teaching and example of their God-fearing associates, and after a time they decided to separate from the worshipers of God" (ibid. p. 118).

The Flood itself separated the wicked from those who were dedicated to God's plan.

Country Living From the Flood to Jesus

Abraham and Lot

Abraham was a man who experienced great blessings from the hand of God. Abraham knew he could trust Him in all circumstances. He knew, by a practical personal experience that God always keeps His word. By studying what composed Abraham's farm, perhaps we can get an idea of God's plan for His people today (see Testimonies for the Church, volume 6, page 177).

Abraham was called by God to go to a strange country. He didn't know where or how. He only knew that God asked him to go, and trusted God to show him.

"Who will accept new duties and enter untried fields doing God's work with firm and willing heart, for Christ's sake counting his losses gain? He who will do this has the faith of Abraham" (Patriarchs and Prophets, p. 127).

Abraham had a nephew by the name of Lot who came with him in his journey to the land of promise. Strife and division occurred between the two families, so Abraham proposed a solution. Separation was obviously needed, and Lot chose the rich, fertile valley near the cities. Dazzled by the potential of financial gain, Lot overlooked the moral and spiritual evils that existed there.

Abraham chose the hills and upland plains, but he did not shut himself away from witnessing to his neighbors. *"In the free air of those upland plains, with their olive groves and vineyards, their fields of waving grain, and the wide pasture grounds of the encircling hills, he dwelt, well content with his simple, patriarchal life, and leaving to Lot the perilous luxury of the vale of Sodom"* (ibid. p. 133).

Abraham's farm grew. *"Those who were led by his teachings to worship the true God found a home in his encampment; and here, as in a school, they received such instructions as would prepare them to be representatives of the true faith."* (ibid. p. 141; emphasis supplied).

In Patriarchs and Prophets, page 142, we read that Abraham's farm was a witness to all around. Members of Abraham's family were characterized by integrity, honesty, and mutual respect by all members of the family. Meanwhile, the cities of the valley where Lot dwelt were having severe problems. Evil was everywhere, and God decided to destroy them. Messengers were sent to Lot asking him to leave the cities and escape to the mountains. To Lot this was a severe trial. To leave all of his possessions and not even look back was almost more than he could bear. Lot's hesitancy caused his wife and family to lightly regard the warning. Lot's wife perished at the border of Sodom. The strong tide of evil influenced Lot by dimming his faith and paralyzing his spiritual perceptions while Abraham prospered and influenced many for God living in the hills (see Patriarchs and Prophets, p. 133 and 161).

The flames of the consumed cities of the plain flashes a warning beacon to our day. In these last days, there will be a movement, by God's people, from their properties in the city to homes in the country. We need to separate from evil where we can live free from their influence. When Lot entered Sodom, he fully intended to keep separate from similar evils. By a simple choice of where we live, our families will be influenced for good or evil. *"Lot could have preserved his family from many evils had he not made his home in this wicked, polluted city. All that Lot and his family did in Sodom could have been done in a place some distance away from the city"* (Evangelism, p. 78; see also Testimonies for the Church, vol. 4, p. 112).

Joseph

With the passage of time, God's promise to Abraham was realized. Their numbers increased, even when they were captured as slaves. Their bondage in Egypt was a result of their rebellion against God. When famine threatened the survival of Egypt as a nation, Joseph was God's man of the hour, thwarting the devil's purposes in his own life and averting a catastrophe for the entire nation. Joseph had learned lessons of integrity as a boy having been raised in a country setting before he was sold into slavery by his brothers.

"How was Joseph enabled to make such a record of firmness of character, uprightness, and wisdom? In his early years he had consulted duty rather than inclination. ... A pure and simple life had favored the vigorous development of both physical and intellectual powers. Communion with God through His works, and the contemplation of grand truths entrusted to the inheritors of faith had elevated and ennobled his spiritual nature, broadening and strengthening the mind as no other study could do" (Patriarchs and Prophets, p. 222; emphasis supplied). This was Joseph's secret; it should be and can be ours (see Education, p. 52).

Moses

Moses was one of God's greatest leaders (see Deuteronomy 34:10). How and where did Moses obtain the training that prepared him for the huge task God had planned for him? In the mighty military school in Pharaoh's palace?

"In the military schools of Egypt, Moses was taught the law of force, and so strong a hold did this teaching have upon his character that it required forty years of quiet and communion with God and nature to fit him for the leadership of Israel by the law of love" (Education, p. 65; emphasis supplied).

One of God's greatest leaders had to unlearn what he had been taught, exchanging man's intellectual strategies for God's wisdom. Where did he do this? In quiet communion with God and nature. But it took 40 years for Moses to unlearn the worldly ways.

YOU CAN SURVIVE!

"Amidst the solemn majesty of the mountain solitudes Moses was alone with God. Everywhere the Creator's name was written. Moses seemed to stand in His presence and to be overshadowed by His power. Here his self-sufficiency was swept away. In the presence of the Infinite One he realized how weak, how inefficient, how shortsighted is man" (ibid., p. 63).

There are many lessons we can learn from Moses' experience. *"Before God could talk with Moses, He educated him in the mountains, among the sheepfolds. Exiled from the courts of Egypt and from the temptations of city life, Moses held communion with God. ... For forty years Moses dwelt in the wilderness, receiving from God an education that made him a wise, tender, humble man. When this time was ended, his self-confidence was gone; he was meek and lowly, so divested of self that God could communicate to him His will in regard to the people He had chosen, and whom He designed to educate and discipline in their wilderness life, while He was preparing for them a home in the land of Canaan"* (The Youth's Instructor, Dec. 13, 1900; emphasis supplied).

God's wilderness curriculum for Moses' education in ministry might well have been overlooked or counted as useless, a waste of time.

"And there were other lessons that, amid the solitude of the mountains, Moses was to receive. In the school of self-denial and hardship he was to learn patience, to temper his passions. ... Man would have dispensed with that long period of toil and obscurity, deeming it a great loss of time" (Patriarchs and Prophets, p. 247; emphasis supplied). God did not see the wilderness education as a loss of time. His plan for Moses is a plan we can follow today. In close contact with nature, our families may commune with God as did Moses.

"If many who are connected with the work of the Lord could be isolated as was Moses, and could be compelled by circumstances to follow some humble vocation until their hearts became tender ... they would not be so prone to magnify their own abilities, or seek to demonstrate that the wisdom of an advanced education could take the place of a sound knowledge of God" (Counsels to Parents, Teachers, and Students, p. 417; emphasis supplied).

Moses' example shows us that to skip a spiritual preparation or substitute a worldly education for the proper spiritual preparation is not God's plan. We must have our time of conversion, a time of wilderness solitude, a time of communion with nature and with God in order to rightly discern our calling. (See The Ministry of Healing, p. 58).

Because of his training in the wilderness, Moses was able to lead God's people out of Egypt. Why do you suppose that Israel had to have a similar experience before going into the Promised Land?

"The history of the wilderness life of Israel was chronicled for the benefit of the Israel of God to the close of time.... The varied experience of the Hebrews was a school of preparation for their promised home in Canaan. God would have His people in these days review with a humble heart and teachable spirit the trials through which ancient Israel passed, that they may be instructed in their preparation for the heavenly Canaan" (<u>Patriarchs and Prophets</u>, p. 293).

God again chose separation from the world to train His people for higher spiritual attainments.

"God desired to take His people apart from the world and prepare them to receive His word. From Egypt He led them to Mount Sinai, where He revealed to them His glory. Here was nothing to attract their senses or divert their minds from God; and as the vast multitude looked at the lofty mountains towering above them, they could realize their own nothingness in the sight of God" (<u>Testimonies for the Church</u>, vol. 6, p. 9).

Samson

Samson's story contrasts obedience to the requirements of God and the results of poor choices and close association with worldly youth.

"The town of Zorah being the country of the Philistines, Samson came to mingle with them on friendly terms. Thus in his youth, intimacies sprang up, the influence of which darkened his whole life.... <u>Whoever</u> voluntarily <u>enters into such relations will feel it necessary to conform, to some degree</u>, to the habits and customs of his companions.... Thoughts are entertained... that tend... to weaken the citadel of the soul" (<u>Conflict and Courage</u>, p. 131; emphasis supplied).

Samuel

Samuel, like David and Daniel, was influenced by the teachings of nature.

"The stars of heaven, the trees and flowers of the field, the lofty mountains, the babbling brooks, all spoke to him [the Hebrew student], and the voices of the prophets, heard throughout the land, met a response in his heart. Such was the training of Moses in the lowly cabin home in Goshen; of Samuel, by the faithful Hannah; of David, in the hill-dwelling at Bethlehem; of Daniel, before the scenes of the captivity separated him from the home of his fathers" (<u>Fundamentals of Christian Education</u>, p. 96).

YOU CAN SURVIVE!

David

The influence of seclusion and nature was very important in David's life. *"The Lord was preparing him* [David] *in his solitary life with his flocks, for the work He designed to commit to his trust in afteryears"* (<u>The Seventh-day Adventist Bible Commentary</u>, Ellen G. White Comments, vol. 2, p. 1018).

"The history of David affords one of the most impressive testimonies ever given to the dangers that threaten the soul from power and riches and worldly honor—those things that are most eagerly desired among men. <u>Few have ever passed through an experience better adapted to prepare them for enduring such a test</u>. David's early life as a shepherd, with its lessons of humility, of patient toil, and of tender care for his flocks; the communion with nature in the solitude of the hills, developing his genius for music and poetry, and directing his thoughts to the Creator; the long discipline of his wilderness life, calling into exercise courage, fortitude, patience, and faith in God, <u>had been appointed by the Lord as a preparation</u> for the throne of Israel. David had enjoyed precious experiences of the love of God, and had been richly endowed with His Spirit; in the history of Saul he had seen the utter worthlessness of mere human wisdom. And yet worldly success and honor so weakened the character of David that he was repeatedly overcome by the tempter" (<u>Patriarchs and Prophets</u>, p. 746; emphasis supplied).

"Notwithstanding the high position which he was to occupy, he quietly continued his employment, content to await the development of the Lord's plans in his own time and way. As humble and modest as before his anointing, <u>the shepherd boy returned to the hills</u> and watched and guarded his flocks as tenderly as ever. But with inspiration he composed his melodies and played upon his harp. Before him spread a landscape of rich and varied beauty. The vines, with their clustering fruit, brightened in the sunshine. The forest trees, with their green foliage, swayed in the breeze. He beheld the sun flooding the heavens with light, coming forth as a bridegroom out of his chamber and rejoicing as a strong man to run a race. There were the bold summits of the hills reaching toward the sky; in the faraway distance rose the barren cliffs of the mountain wall of Moab; above all spread the tender blue of the overarching heavens. And beyond was God. He could not see Him, but His works were full of His praise. <u>The light of day, gilding forest and mountain, meadow and stream, carried the mind up to behold the Father of lights</u>, the Author of every good and perfect gift. Daily revelations of the character and majesty of his Creator filled the young poet's heart with adoration and rejoicing. <u>In contemplation of God and His works, the facul-</u>

ties of David's mind and heart were developing and strengthening for the work of his afterlife. He was daily coming into a more intimate communion with God.... Who can measure the results of those years of toil and wandering among the lonely hills? The communion with nature and with God, the care of his flocks, the perils and deliverances, the griefs and joys, of his lowly lot, were not only to mold the character of David and to influence his future life, but through the psalms of Israel's sweet singer they were in all coming ages to kindle love and faith in the hearts of God's people, bringing them nearer to the ever-loving heart of Him in whom all His creatures live. ... His opportunities of contemplation and meditation served to enrich him with that wisdom and piety that made him beloved of God and angels" (ibid, pp. 641, 642; emphasis supplied). David was a man after God's own heart, due largely to his early training, communing with God out in nature.

Elijah

Elijah was one of the greatest prophets in Israel. He reestablished the schools of the prophets (see Prophets and Kings, pp. 224, 225) and was God's representative of reform on Mount Carmel, challenging the children of Judah with the classic Christian question, *"How long halt ye between two opinions? if the Lord be God, follow him"* 1 Kings 18:21.

Let's look at how Elijah lived. *"Among the mountains of Gilead, east of Jordan, there dwelt in the days of Ahab a man of faith and prayer whose fearless ministry was destined to check the rapid spread of apostasy in Israel. Far removed from any city of renown, and occupying no high station in life, Elijah the Tishbite nevertheless entered upon his mission confident in God's purpose to prepare the way before him and to give him abundant success. The word of faith and power was upon his lips, and his whole life was devoted to the work of reform. His was the voice of one crying in the wilderness to rebuke sin and press back the tide of evil"* (Prophets and Kings, p. 119; emphasis supplied).

Elisha

The prophet Elisha desired a double portion of Elijah's spirit to carry on the work of God. What was his early training and where did he live? *"Elisha did not live in the thickly populated cities. His father was... a farmer. Far from city and court dissipation, Elisha had received his education. He had been trained in habits of simplicity, of obedience to his parents and to God"* (Sons and Daughters of God, p. 93; emphasis supplied). We can see, again, how early training with God in the country was the best training, even for a prophet.

"*The early years of the prophet Elisha were passed in the <u>quietude of country life, under the teaching of God and nature and the discipline of useful work</u>*" (<u>Education</u>, p. 58; emphasis supplied).

Solomon

Solomon was the wisest king who ever wielded a scepter (1 Kings 3:12) and yet he failed horribly in his conduct. To what does inspiration attribute these failures in the life of Solomon?

"*Compare the early history of David with the history of Solomon and consider the results.... The discipline of David's early experience was lacking in that of Solomon*" (<u>Education</u>, p. 152). Even the wisest man on earth, a man whom God blessed with great knowledge, would have been a better Christian witness had he had the early training his own father, King David, received but neglected to give his son.

Country Living from Jesus to the Apostles

John the Baptist

Jesus said of John the Baptist that there had not risen a greater born of woman (Matthew 11:11).

"*An angel from heaven came to instruct Zacharias and Elizabeth as to how they should train and educate their child, so as to work in harmony with God in preparing a messenger to announce the coming of Christ. As parents they were to faithfully co-operate with God in forming such a character in John as would fit him to perform the part God had assigned him as a competent worker.*

"*John was the son of their old age, he was a child of miracle, and the parents might have reasoned that he had a special work to do for the Lord and the Lord would take care of him. But the parents did not thus reason; <u>they moved to a retired place in the country</u>, where their son would not be exposed to the temptations of city life, or induced to depart from the counsel and instruction which they as parents would give him. They acted their part in developing a character in the child that would in every way meet the purpose for which God had designed his life*" (<u>Child Guidance</u>, p. 23; emphasis supplied)

"<u>*The experience of Enoch and of John the Baptist represents what ours should be*</u>" (<u>Testimonies for the Church</u>, vol. 8, p. 329; emphasis supplied).

"*In this age, just prior to the second coming of Christ in the clouds of heaven, such a work as that of John is to be done"* (ibid. p. 332).

"In order to give such a message as John gave, we must have a spiritual experience like his. The same work must be wrought in us. We must behold God, and in beholding Him lose sight of self" (ibid. p. 333). All of God's people are called to live in the country for purposes of education, spiritual growth, safety and food (see Country Living, pp. 9, 10).

"God had directed John the Baptist to dwell in the wilderness, that he might be shielded from the influence of the priests and rabbis, and be prepared for a special mission" (The Desire of Ages, p. 150).

"John did not feel strong enough to stand the great pressure of temptation he would meet in mingling with society. He feared his character would be molded according to the prevailing customs of the Jews; and he chose to separate himself from the world, and make the wilderness, his home. He denied himself the ordinary comforts of life; his food was simple; his clothing, a garment made of camel's hair, and confined about the waist by a leather girdle. But although John passed his childhood and youth in the desert, he was not unreconciled to his life of hardship and seclusion. So far from being lonely, gloomy, or morose, he enjoyed his life of simplicity and retirement, and his temperate habits kept all his senses unperverted" (The Youth's Instructor, Jan. 7, 1897; emphasis supplied).

To gain a spiritual experience like John's, we must have an education like his. *"He [John] chose rather to have his home in the wilderness, where his senses would not be perverted by his surroundings. Should we not learn something of this example of one whom Christ honoured and of whom He said: 'Among them that are born of women there hath not risen a greater than John the Baptist?'* (Matthew 11:11)*"* (Testimonies for the Church, vol. 4, p. 109).

How effective was John's ministry? *"The whole nation was stirred. Multitudes flocked to the wilderness"* (The Desire of Ages, p. 104).

How did he do it? *"In solitude, by meditation and prayer, he sought to give up his soul for the lifework before him.... John found in the wilderness his school and his sanctuary"* (ibid. p. 102).

"I was pointed down to the last days and saw John represented those who should go forth in the spirit and power of Elijah to herald the day of wrath and the second advent of Jesus" (Early Writings, p. 155; emphasis supplied).

John's preparation included witnessing to, but separation from, the world. He spent much time in meditation and prayer in the beautiful expanse of natural solitude.

Jesus

Jesus was born in the humble surroundings of a barn, His first bed a manger. Our Father had an eternity to plan the life and education of Jesus and decided on a home in the Galilean hills.

"What were the conditions chosen by the infinite Father for His Son? A secluded home in the Galilean hills; a household sustained by honest, self-respecting labor; a life of simplicity; daily conflict with difficulty and hardship; self sacrifice, economy, and patient, gladsome service; the hour of study at his mother's side, with the open scroll of Scripture; the quiet dawn or twilight in the green valley; the holy ministries of nature; the study of creation and providence; and the soul's communion with God—these were the conditions and opportunities of the early life of Jesus. (The Ministry of Healing, p. 365).

Jesus' education was not in the schools of His day. From His mother He learned Scripture; from His father He learned the carpenter's trade, and He learned to communicate with His heavenly Father from His simple life in the country.

Jesus' greatest happiness was found in communion with His Father and in nature and creation. *"He studied the word of God and His hours of greatest happiness were found when He could turn aside from the scene of His labors to go into the fields, to meditate in the quiet valleys, to hold communion with God on the mountainside or amid the trees of the forest"* (The Ministry of Healing, p. 52).

Isn't it amazing? He had made it all, and yet He learned from it and loved it! (John 1:10). Even as a child, Jesus *"could not be persuaded to change His habits of contemplating the works of God and seeking to alleviate the suffering of men or even... animals.... He shared their burdens and repeated to them* [people] *the lessons He had learned from nature, of the love, the kindness, the goodness of God"* (The Desire of Ages, p. 90).

He wants us to follow His example. *"The life and spirit of Christ is the only standard of excellence and perfection, and our only safe course is to follow His example"* (Testimonies for the Church, vol. 1, p. 408).

This He found to be *"more in harmony with the lessons of self-abnegation. He desired to teach them* [the disciples].... *By communion with God in nature, the mind is uplifted, and the heart finds rest"* (The Desire of Ages, p. 291).

Jesus, our example, obeyed His Father's plan and grew up in the country. He had a "school" for His disciples there. Those of us who read this counsel can look at it three ways. **First,** we can **reject** it like Samson did and reap the consequences. **Second**, we can **wait** like Lot did (and barely make it) losing part of our family in the last-minute escape (see Patriarchs and Prophets, pp.

160, 161). **Third**, we can **accept** it as a gift from God as did Enoch, and, in our love for Him, enjoy it. Jesus is the focus of the ages, and as in all things else He desires us to have a higher experience. This, then, makes Him the Desire of Ages, whom we can hear speaking to us along the streams and in the hills of His own creation. No one had a larger or higher calling than did He, yet His education and His life were free of complexity and so-called "higher education." He did not live in the cities, but He did work there.

"His education was gained from heaven-appointed sources, from useful work, from the study of the Scriptures and of nature, and from the experiences of life–God's lesson books, full of instruction to all who bring to them the willing heart, the seeing eye, and the understanding heart" (Testimonies for the Church, vol. 8, pp. 222, 223).

Paul

Paul was a highly educated man with many talents. Before His conversion, he occupied a high position in the Jewish hierarchy. He was zealous in defense of the faith and felt it was an offense to God to believe in a Messiah that was his contemporary. He obtained letters of authority from Jerusalem to bring people back, bound as prisoners, who followed this Messiah. He set out to Damascus to enforce the edict when our Lord appeared to him and asked him to stop hurting Him. Paul arose blind, was led to Damascus, and eventually became converted to the Messiah, whom he had once persecuted.

There was yet a preparation he had to make. The Lord saw that he needed a wilderness experience to adequately train him to be a powerful spokesman for Him. An angel appeared to him and told him to leave Damascus. So he went to Arabia, where he found a retreat (see The Acts of the Apostles, p. 125). Here in the solitude of the desert Paul could study and meditate with Jesus. In such communion is found the highest education. (see The Acts of the Apostles, p. 126). In The Story of Redemption, page 274, we find that this preparation was, for Paul, of lasting comfort to him throughout his ministry.

"He went into Arabia; and there, in comparative solitude, he had ample opportunity for communion with God and for contemplation" (Education, p. 65). To Paul, nature's solitudes became a school whose Teacher was the source of truth.

John

The apostle John, just after being rescued by God from a cauldron of boiling oil, was banished to the island of Patmos. It was a barren, rocky island where criminals were removed from society. To John it was the gate of heaven.

"Here, shut away from the busy scenes of life, and from active labors of former years, he had the companionship of God and Christ and the heavenly angels, and from them he received instruction for the church for all future time" (The Acts of the Apostles, p. 570).

In his isolated home, John was able to study more closely than ever before the manifestations of divine power as revealed in the book of nature and in the pages of inspiration (see Courage and Conflict, p. 362).

"To him it was a delight to meditate on the work of creation and to adore the Divine Architect" (The Acts of the Apostles, p. 571).

"The history of John affords a striking illustration of the way in which God can use aged workers.... Even in Patmos he made friends and converts" (ibid. pp. 572, 573; emphasis supplied).

"And it was after John had grown old in the service of his Lord that he received more communications from heaven than he had received all the former years of his life" (ibid. p. 573) We find in The Acts of the Apostles, page 572, that the visions of the book of Revelation were given to John as he enjoyed his banishment in nature.

Even in our sunset years, God may give us a wilderness experience, such as He did for John, in order to deepen our relationship with Him. *"Among the cliffs and rocks of Patmos, John held communion with his Maker.... Peace filled his heart"* (The Acts of the Apostles, p. 571; emphasis supplied).

Country Living from the Apostles to the Reformation

Columba

In the early centuries, after the passing of John, the last of the twelve apostles, God continued to have witnesses who prepared the way and operated according to His plan.

"From Ireland came the pious Columba and his co-laborers, who, gathering about them the scattered believers on the lonely island of Iona, made this the center of their missionary labors. Among these evangelists was an observer of the Bible Sabbath, and thus this truth was introduced among the people. A school was established at Iona, from which missionaries went out, not only to Scotland and England, but to Germany, Switzerland, and even Italy" (The Great Controversy, p. 62).

Columba believed in having the school separated from contaminating influences so that the students might have an experience with God. The school operated for many years and sent missionaries to many lands and was a long-lasting influence for good.

"For hundreds of years after the churches of England submitted to Rome, those of Scotland maintained their freedom" (ibid. p. 249).

The Waldenses

From the high mountain valleys of the Alps came words of truth sounded by the Waldenses. Picture beautiful snow-capped peaks surrounding each valley of northern Italy and southern France. In these valleys were small villages and farms with flocks and vineyards. The Waldenses believed that it was necessary to live in these secluded glens and rocky fastnesses of the mountains to maintain separation from the world. The wilderness church maintained its integrity in the face of extreme persecution for many, many years.

"Behind the lofty bulwarks of the mountains,—in all ages the refuge of the persecuted and the oppressed,—the Waldenses found a hiding place" (The Great Controversy, p. 65).

"God had provided for His people a sanctuary of awful grandeur, befitting the mighty truths committed to their trust.... The mountains that girded their lowly valleys were a constant witness to God's creative power, and a never-failing assurance of His protecting care.... They were never lonely amid the mountain solitudes" (ibid. p. 66; emphasis supplied)

"Thoughts of God were associated alike with the sublime scenery of nature and with the humble blessings of daily life.... Every spot of tillable land among the mountains was carefully improved; the valleys and the less fertile hillsides were made to yield their increase. ... The process was laborious and wearisome, but it was wholesome, just what man needs in his fallen state, the school which God has provided for his training and development" (ibid., pp. 67, 68; emphasis supplied).

"Far from the monuments of human pomp and pride the people assembled, not in magnificent churches or grand cathedrals, but beneath the shadow of the mountains, in the Alpine valleys, or, in time of danger, in some rocky stronghold, to listen to the words of truth from the servants of Christ" (ibid. p. 68)

The youth received instruction in this wilderness setting and it had a protecting influence on them and a profound effect on their ministry. *"From their schools in the mountains some of the youth were sent to institutions of learning in the cities"* (ibid. p. 70). They were *"exposed to temptation, they witnessed vice, they encountered Satan's wily agents, who urged upon them the most subtle heresies and the most dangerous deceptions. But their education from childhood had been of a character to prepare them for all this"* (ibid., emphasis supplied). What a wonderful formula for saving our youth today! Yes, it required sacrifice for them, as it will for us, but God's plan will be as successful today as it was for the Waldenses.

"Thus the Waldenses witnessed for God centuries before the birth of Luther. Scattered over many lands, they planted the seeds of the Reformation that began in the time of Wycliffe, grew broad and deep in the day of Luther, and is to be carried forward to the close of time by those who are willing to suffer all things for 'the Word of God, and for the testimony of Jesus Christ'" (ibid. p. 78; emphasis supplied).

We are counseled to study the history of the Waldenses because we will need the training and the experience they received. *"It would be well for all our workers to study the history of the Waldensian missionaries and to imitate their example of sacrifice and self-denial"* (Testimonies for the Church, vol. 5, p. 400). (See also the chapter entitled "Waldenses" in The Great Controversy and J. A. Wylie's History of the Waldenses.)

Huss and Jerome

During the days of Huss and Jerome, persecution was rampant. They were teaching the truth that Wycliffe had advocated. *"The fears of the hierarchy were roused, and persecution was opened against the disciples of the gospel. Driven to worship in the forests and the mountains, they were hunted by soldiers, and many were put to death"* (The Great Controversy, pp. 97, 98). Again the trail of truth leads to the forests and mountains where God's people are taking a stand (ibid., p. 65). A new church called the United Brethren was formed.

"Forced to find refuge in the woods and caves, they still assembled to read God's word and unite in His worship" (ibid. p. 119).

Martin Luther

Martin Luther spent his early years in a miner's cabin with his German parents. Hardship, privation, toil, and strict discipline were the schools where Luther was trained. Luther's preparatory work here outlined gave him strength for the great work God had planned for him (see The Great Controversy, pp. 120, 121).

Ulrich Zwingli

Ulrich Zwingli was born in a herdsman cottage situated in the Alps. He early learned an appreciation for the elegance of the alpine valleys. *"Zwingli's surroundings in childhood, and his early training, were such as to prepare him for his future mission. <u>Reared amid scenes of natural grandeur, beauty, and awful sublimity, his mind was early impressed with a sense of the greatness, the power, and the majesty of God</u>. The history of the brave deeds achieved upon his native mountains kindled his youthful aspirations"* (<u>ibid</u>. pp. 171, 172; emphasis supplied).

As we study the lives of those who, in the past, committed themselves wholeheartedly to God, we can readily discern that His plan for training workers is in the beautiful school of nature where one can sense God's presence. Surrounded by true elegance, our eyes are more readily opened to that which He desires us to see, and our hearts are more readily weaned from that which will perish. Such training will produce strong people for God (see <u>Education</u>, p. 211).

Healing in the Hills

I feel the lure of the mountains,
As day after day it calls;
I hear the voice of the fountains—
The music of waterfalls.

I love the air of the mountains
The scent of the fragrant pine;
And there by the flowing fountains
On nature's green carpet recline.

There's therapy on a mountain,
While gazing on snow-crowned peaks;
You cleanse your soul in the fountain,
When the God of nature speaks.

If ever men needed a mountain,
They need it much more today;
O come and plunge in the fountain
And wash your worries away!

—Adlai A. Esteb

Country Living from the Reformation to the Present

William Miller

William Miller was an honest-hearted farmer. He had early learned the essential lessons of self-denial and morality. These lessons he combined with integrity and benevolence. His life on the farm, living in the country, taught him the value of practical work and perseverance. His work climaxed in the interpretation of the great 2300-day prophecy that affected most of the world. God had prepared William Miller for his work.

When God's people sensed the nearness of His coming in 1844, they spent much time in prayer communing with God in retired places. They did not rest until they were right with God and with each other. They chose a retired place in the country because they could commune with God much easier. They were in such earnestness that they would do without food and sleep in order to be right with God and with each other (see The Story of Redemption, p. 371).

"In the movement of 1844, when we believed the coming of Christ was at hand, night after night, when bidding good night to those of like-faith we would grasp their hands, feeling we might not clasp them again until we meet in the Kingdom of Glory. Thus it will be again as we draw near to the close of time. I urge our people to make it their lifework to seek for spirituality. Christ is at the door. This is why I say to our people, do not consider it a privation when you are called to leave the cities and move into country places. Here there awaits rich blessings for those who will grasp them. By beholding the scenes of nature, the work of the Creator, by studying God's handiwork, imperceptibly you will be changed into the same image" (Manuscript 85, 1908, portion in Country Living, p. 14).

Ellen White

Through visions, God used Ellen White to guide the early Seventh-day Adventist church. Her work load of writing, traveling, speaking, and resolving conflicts of opinion was tiring. Her health was not robust, but God continually strengthened her.

Ellen and her husband, James, kept a secluded cabin in the Rocky Mountains entirely surrounded by God's created works. There she was refreshed and strengthened. The mountain solitudes put her in touch anew with her Creator. In her words, *"From our cottage I could look out upon a forest of young pines, so fresh and fragrant that the air was perfumed with their spicy odor. ... Through the works of creation we communed with Him who inhabiteth eter-*

nity. As we looked upon the towering rocks, the lofty mountains, we ex-claimed, 'Who is so great a God as our God?'" (Life Sketches, p. 256).

"But when we considered God's love and care for His creatures, as revealed both in the book of nature and on the pages of inspiration, our hearts were comforted and strengthened. Surrounded by the evidences of God's power and overshadowed by His presence, we could not cherish distrust or unbelief. Oh, how often have peace, and hope, and even joy, come to us in our experience amid these rocky solitudes!" (ibid. p. 257; emphasis supplied). Such an experience always lifts the spirit and invigorates the soul. Brother and Sister White felt the need to spend many weeks in succession at their mountain cabin. All of us in modern society need this experience. The call of Jesus is, *"Come ye yourselves apart into a desert place, and rest a while"* (Mark 6:31).

Schools that Chose a Rural Setting

Oberlin College

The founders of Oberlin College prior to 1844 chose land of unbroken forests in Ohio. "The founders of Oberlin were guided by a wisdom higher than human, since a location, almost forbidding in its physical aspects, and for years quite difficult of access, was a condition indispensable to the formation of the character and the performance of the work to which Oberlin was clearly called" (Studies in Christian Education, E. A. Sutherland, p. 36).

Madison College

Madison College was located on a farm near Nashville, Tennessee. *"The usefulness learned on the school farm is the very education that is most essential for those who go out as missionaries to many foreign fields"* (Madison School, p. 29). This program was so successful that it was lauded by the world as the correct model of education in The Reader's Digest, May 1938.

Avondale College

The pioneers of Avondale College, with counsel from the Lord to Sister White, chose a spot in a retired country location. Various questions were asked by church leaders, "Do we need workers for the foreign fields? Do we need missionary nurses and young people who love God and who love to minister?" Sister White responds publicly in the church newspaper:

"What can we do in response to these demands? Shall we go into the city, and build up our school where there will be the most ease and comfort? Shall we use the circumstances and surroundings of the country as a means

of developing, as far as possible, the traits and characteristics required? We have chosen the country, and we do not regret the choice" (The Review and Herald, Oct. 11, 1898). But why be so isolated?

In a later issue of The Review and Herald, Mrs. White told the students, *"In His providence the Lord had directed us to this place, and had established us here in the woods, away from the large cities and their influences, which are constantly ensnaring the young"* (Oct. 25, 1898).

This school was located in the forest a quarter of a mile from the road. One hundred students gathered there (see The Review and Herald, Oct. 11, 1898).

"As we draw near to the close of time the cities will become more and more corrupt, and more and more objectionable as places for establishing centers for our work. The dangers of travel will increase, confusion and drunkenness will abound. <u>*If there can be found places in retired mountain regions where it would be difficult for the evils of the cities to enter, let our people secure such places for our sanitariums and advanced schools"*</u> (Manuscript Releases, vol. 10, p. 260; emphasis supplied). This counsel will help us today.

Present to the Future

We have seen, in our scan of the past, that God has trained His men and women through practical work, communion with God in nature, in the experiences of life, and by studying the pages of inspiration. These were essentials in God's plan in the past, and so it is today.

"But in Joseph and Daniel, in Moses and Elijah, and many others, we have <u>*noble examples of the results of the true plan of living. Like faithfulness today will produce like results"*</u> (Testimonies for the Church, vol. 9, p. 165; emphasis supplied).

COUNTRY LIVING

The Out-Doors Man

He must come back a better man,
Beneath the summer bronze and tan,
Who turns his back on city strife
To neighbor with the trees;

He must be stronger for the fight
And see with clearer eye the right,
Who fares beneath the open sky
And welcomes every breeze.

The man who loves all living things
Enough to go where nature flings
Her glories everywhere about,
And dwell with them awhile,

Must be, when he comes back once more,
A little better than before,
A little surer of his faith
And readier to smile.

—Edgar Guest

God's Plan Unchanged

God's plan today is the same as it has always been, and that plan will produce results such as it produced when God needed leaders among His past remnant. Persons of character like Joseph, Daniel, Moses, Ruth and Elijah who stood for truth when forces all around were against them, will again be produced.

As did Ellen and James White, so we may have to seek a retreat for a time to get our perspective on life adjusted back to God. By making God first in this enjoyable way, we begin to be changed into His image. Then, as God opens the way, we should make our permanent move into the country. We will have troublous times ahead (see Country Living, pp. 9, 10), which will include persecution, imprisonment, and martyrdom (see Maranatha, p. 199). We will then want to leave the cities and not be able (see Country Living, p. 11).

If we decide to make this move, we are preparing *"for a place on the Lord's farm in the earth made new"* (Testimonies for the Church, vol. 6, p. 177). *"The more nearly we come into harmony with God's original plan, the more favorable will be our position to secure health of body, and mind, and soul"* (Country Living, p. 6; emphasis supplied). Our need for God's plan will not decrease but increase as we near the end of time.

"Well," you might say, "that was written for another time–long past, but now

187

it doesn't apply." This is not true, according to the Lord. *"All our health institutions, all our publishing houses, all our institutions of learning, are to be conducted more and more in accordance with the instruction that has been given"* (Counsels to Parents, Teachers, and Students, p. 57; emphasis supplied).

"Time and trial have not made void the instruction given, but through years of suffering and self-sacrifice have established the truth of the testimony given. The instruction that was given in the early days of the message is to be held as safe instruction to follow in these its closing days" (Selected Messages, book 1, p. 41; emphasis supplied). (See also Selected Messages, book 1, p. 48 and Selected Messages, book 3, pp. 83, 84).

The impact of this next statement requires a serious second look. *"It is Satan's purpose to attract men and women to the cities, and to gain his object he invents every kind of novelty and amusement, every kind of excitement"* (Selected Messages, book 2, p. 355).

A Call to Agrarian Living is a Call to be Spiritually Prepared

The dictionary defines the term **agrarian** as; "rural and agricultural, related to land, the advancement of agriculture." Not long ago, I came across an article in which a comparison was made between two farms. The first one was operated by a farmer of the Amish religion and the other was a large, individually owned, commercial farm. The Amish property was cultivated and harvested with horses, while the second one was tilled and harvested with engine-powered machinery.

The Amish farmer had all of his equipment paid for, while the second farmer owed $250,000.00 on his equipment. The Amish farmer owned his 160 acres, while the second farmer had one and a half sections of inherited land.

The conclusion of the article included some salient comments. When an Amish farmer buys a piece of land, it takes him three years to loosen the soil that has been packed by the weight of tractors and combines. The Amish farmer, using horses, made $30,000.00 per person in his family in one year, while the second farmer lost money and incurred further indebtedness. Simple farming pays in many ways. I am not trying to make a case for horse-drawn machinery or diesel powered machinery, but only to point out that a simple lifestyle will pay dividends.

We, like the Amish, Hutterites, and other similar religious groups, are called to be an **agrarian** church. We may differ in our beliefs regarding the sanctuary, the Sabbath, and health reform, but we are agrarian. Psalm 104:14 states, *"...and herb for the service of man: that he may bring forth food out of the earth."*

It has always been God's plan for His children to eat the fruit of their own hands. When the prophet saw heaven in vision, he recorded what he saw in Isaiah 65:21, 22: *"And they shall build houses, and inhabit them; and they shall plant vineyards, and eat the fruit of them. They shall not build, and another inhabit; they shall not plant, and another eat."* In heaven we are going to be planting and eating what we grow. From Eden to Eden it has been God's plan for His people; even the kings He sets up and takes down are to be served from the field. Ecclesiastes 5:9 says, *"Moreover the profit of the earth is for all: the king himself is served by the field."*

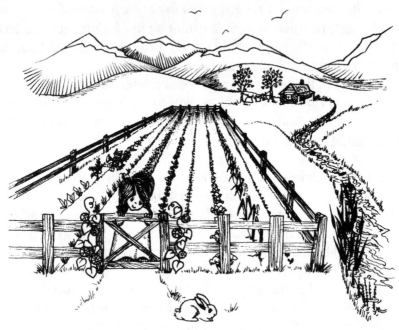

We should have a knowledge of how to grow our own food and preserve it. If agriculture is the A, B, and C of our education, then we can conclude that we should be an agrarian church (see Testimonies for the Church, vol. 6, p. 179). We can actually use agriculture as part of our missionary work.

"There are multitudes of poor families for whom <u>no better missionary work</u> could be done than to assist them in settling on the land and in learning how to make it yield them a livelihood" (<u>The Ministry of Healing</u>, p. 192; emphasis supplied).

How can we be sure that we can depend on the soil to feed us?

"If the land is cultivated, it will, with the blessing of God, supply our necessities" (<u>Testimonies for the Church</u>, vol. 6, p. 178).

"God can bless twenty acres of land and make them as productive as one hundred" (<u>Testimonies for the Church</u>, vol. 5, p. 152). A promise like this is worth remembering.

We have assurance that, as we work and cultivate the land, He will supply our necessities. But gardening involves much more than just providing food for our table. Gardening protects our health in many ways; it improves our diet, it is good outdoor exercise, and it keeps us from spending time in less spiritual pursuits.

"Exercise in the open air should be prescribed as a life-giving necessity. And for such exercises there is nothing better than the cultivation of the soil" (The Ministry of Healing, p. 265).

Schools—Vital Part of the Church

"It is God's plan that agriculture shall be connected with the work of our sanitariums and schools. Our youth need the education to be gained from this line of work. It is well, more than well,—it is essential,—that efforts be made to carry out the Lord's plan in this respect." Counsels on Health, p. 223; emphasis supplied).

"The usefulness learned on the school farm is the very education that is most essential for those who go out as missionaries to many foreign fields" (Series B, No. 11, p. 29; emphasis supplied).

Valuable lessons are learned when teachers, students, and families work together with God.

"Look at nature. There is room within her vast boundaries for schools to be established where grounds can be cleared and land cultivated. This work is essential to the education most favorable to spiritual advancement; for nature's voice is the voice of Christ, teaching us innumerable lessons of love and power and submission and perseverance. Some do not appreciate the value of agricultural work. These should not plan for our schools, for they will hold everything from advancing in the right lines. In the past their influence has been a hindrance" (Testimonies for the Church, volume 6, page 178; emphasis supplied).

Sanctuary Ranch School Song

Chorus:
The wilderness, so wild so free,
Holds secrets of eternity.
Lord, take my hand, how dear to me,
This sanctuary then will be.

—Linda Franklin

"Nature Day" Activities

Those of you who plan to move to the country may enjoy scheduling "nature days"; days in which family activities include only non utility-based projects. Ideally, this would be a day when the whole family is home. There are many activities to enjoy together. Here are a few suggestions:

1. Use a wood cook stove for meals and baking.
2. Practice using a crosscut saw and a splitting maul for firewood.
3. Hand carpentry.
4. Camping.
5. Story time; children especially love stories about when their parents and grandparents "made-do" with what they had.
6. Hiking and picnicking.
7. Gardening—use only hand tools, paint and/or print row markers, order seeds, plan a layout.
8. Singing (with nonelectrical instruments).
9. Write letters.
10. Trim and fill kerosene lamps and use them for light.
11. Dry clothes outdoors.
12. Take a "bird bath."
13. Use your wood heater.

Overcoming inertia is the hardest part of this decision. Far from being a "boring" day, children find it exciting to learn skills from their parents. It is especially rewarding to begin the day with prayer together that the Lord will use the experiences of the day to strengthen family bonds and help us to be ready for the coming of Jesus.

Guidelines for Moving to the Country

Even though it is late in earth's history and God wanted us out of the cities years ago, we should move no faster than God opens the way. There are guidelines for our move to the country. You will recognize providence when you begin to act on God's plan. Pray often for help.

"Get out of the cities as fast as possible" (Medical Ministry, p. 310).

"For years we have been instructed that our brethren and sisters, and especially families with children, should plan to leave the cities as the way opens before them to do so. Many will have to labor earnestly to help open the way" (Country Living, pp. 24, 25; emphasis supplied).

"Those who have felt at last to make a move, let it not be in a rush, in an excitement, or in a rash manner or in a way that hereafter they will deeply regret that they did move out. Do nothing without seeking wisdom of God.... All that anyone can do is to advise and counsel, and then leave those who are convicted in regard to duty to move under divine guidance, and with their whole hearts open to learn and obey God" (Country Living, p. 25; emphasis supplied).

"The parents should get as suitable a place as their means will allow.

Though the dwelling may be small, yet there should be land in connection with it, that may be cultivated" (Country Living, p. 24).

By choosing a dark area and setting up a family outpost in the country, we can work the cities as did Enoch.

"Choose some locality where you will have opportunity to let your light shine forth amid the moral darkness" (Fundamentals of Christian Education, p. 495).

"God will help His people find such homes outside the cities" (Medical Ministry, p. 310).

It will take some work and determination, but no move you have ever made will be more rewarding than moving your family to the country. (See pages 24-28 in Country Living, "Guided by God's Providences.")

Looking for Property

Every property has advantages and disadvantages. It might be a good idea to make a list, in order of importance, of what you envision as being the best for you. Do not feel obligated to make a certain property work which is not right for you.

1. **Clean air** is vital.
2. **Good water**–A spring that arises on the property will reduce the possibility of contamination from adjoining parcels. The best location for water is at a higher elevation than the house; this enables gravity flow without the need for pumping. Other water sources are useful and desirable; creeks, rivers, lakes, or ponds for irrigation.
3. **Good soil**–River or creek bottom for growing food.
4. **Wood**–Your property should have hardwood or evergreen trees. Wood is essential as a fuel source for cooking and heating. Log cabins can be built and/or lumber can be cut by hand methods for use in construction.
5. **Location**–It is important that you choose a **quiet,** secluded place, an attractive country setting, a place you would love to visit or live. It should be a place of scenic beauty, if it is to no one else but you.
6. **Financial** consideration–Make arrangements to get your property **paid for** as soon as possible. Watch for a providence in price or provision from family and friends.
7. A place with **buildings** already on it is often advantageous (see Loma Linda Messages, p. 474).
8. **Invite others** to your new outpost.
9. **Seek counsel** of others who are experienced in country living.

Youth Ranches and Retreats

Rehabilitation centers have recognized, for some time, the value of using beautiful natural surroundings to enhance the educational process and to recover young people from the cesspools of city life.

Deep Springs College, located near the California/Nevada border, is a remote ranch, where the students are academically advanced, but where nature and practical work play a large part in their success (Campus Voice, 1986, p. 25).

The Wilderness Retreat is located on a 4,560-acre working cattle ranch in northwestern Montana. It is in a beautiful, remote location where the youth live in small cabins. The director had previous experience with witnessing first-hand how the wilderness had helped rehabilitate drug-addicted teens.

Richard Jeffries, in Countryside Ideals, July 1971, agrees: "If you wish your children to think deep thoughts, and to know the holiest emotions, take them to the woods and hills and give them the freedom of the meadows; the hills purify those who walk upon them."

"Here among the scenes of nature Christian character is more easily formed than amid the wickedness of city life" (Evangelism, p. 46; emphasis supplied).

"Send the children to schools located in the city, where every phase of temptation is waiting to attract and demoralize them, and the work of character building is tenfold harder for both parents and children" (Country Living, p. 13).

"Never can the proper education be given to the youth in this country, or in any other country, unless they are separated a wide distance from the cities. The customs and practices in the cities unfit the minds of the youth for the entrance of truth" (Life Sketches, p. 351; emphasis supplied).

Young people are quick to respond to nature. Cari was a student at Sanctuary Ranch when she wrote this poem reflecting her understanding of God's plan for survival.

Oh, Deep Still Hills

Oh, deep still hills of misty shade,
To blue infinity you fade,
The tranquil front that you display
Will be our hiding place someday.

When weary tears fall to the earth,
Fulfill the purpose of your birth,
And shield His hunted ones with care
So only God can see them there.

—Cari Strand-Mutch

YOU CAN SURVIVE!

Our choice of lifestyle and the location of our home affects our spiritual life. This is not a new thought. Country living has been a part of a higher plan for thousands of years. It is of special importance now that we move out of the cities to the country in order to survive. Before any move, plan well and ask God to help and to lead by His providences.

FOR FURTHER STUDY

Schools

1. Education, pp. 211-12: *"They lived close to the heart of nature.... Such training produced strong men.... It would be a great aid in educational work could every school be so situated as to afford the pupils land for cultivation and access to the fields and woods."*

2. Testimonies for the Church, vol. 8, p. 216: *"The Lord will make the wilderness a sacred place, as His people, filled with the missionary spirit, go forth to make centers for His work, to establish sanitariums, where the sick and afflicted can be cared for; and schools, where the youth can be educated in right lines"* (emphasis supplied).

3. Fundamentals of Christian Education, p. 325: *"It will take time to develop the true missionary spirit, and the farther they* [the young people] *are removed from the cities and the temptations that are flooding them, the more favorable will it be for them to obtain the true knowledge and develop well-balanced characters"* (emphasis supplied).

4. Counsels to Parents, Teachers, and Students, pp. 203-4: *"Intermediate schools are highly essential. In these schools thorough work is to be done; for many students will go forth from them directly into the great harvest field.... The Word of God is to lie at the foundation of all the work done in our intermediate schools. And the students are to be shown the true dignity of labor.... He will open ways before us to establish small schools in retired places for the education of our youth, not only in the Scriptures and in book learning but in many lines of manual labor"* (emphasis supplied).

5. Testimonies for the Church, vol. 6, p. 152: *"Our schools must be more like the schools of the prophets. They should be training schools, where the students may be brought under the discipline of Christ and learn of the Great Teacher. They should be family schools, where every student will receive special help from his teachers as the members of the family should receive help in the home"* (emphasis supplied)

7. Manuscript Releases, vol. 10, p. 260: *"If there can be found places in re-*

194

tired mountain regions where it would be difficult for the evils of the cities to enter, let our people secure such places for our sanitariums and advanced schools" (emphasis supplied).

8. Fundamentals of Christian Education, p. 526: *"In the night season these words were spoken to me: 'Charge the teachers in our schools to prepare the students for what is coming upon the world'"* (emphasis supplied).

9. Testimonies for the Church, vol. 7, p. 281: *"Young men and young women, gather a stock of knowledge. Do not wait until some human examination pronounces you competent to work, but go out into the highways and hedges, and begin to work for God…. Constantly improve…. Tax the powers of mind and body, ever keeping eternal realities in view…. Become more and more refined, more spiritually cultured. Then you will have the best diploma that anyone can have—the endorsement of God"* (emphasis supplied).

God's Promises for Country Living

Psalm 37:3: *"Trust in the Lord, and do good; so shalt thou dwell in the land, and verily thou shalt be fed."*

II Chronicles 7:14: *"If my people, which are called by my name, shall humble themselves, and pray, and seek my face, and turn from their wicked ways; then will I hear from heaven, and will forgive their sin, and will heal their land."*

Ecclesiastes 5:9: *"Moreover the profit of the earth is for all: the king himself is served by the field."*

Psalm 104:14: *"He causeth the grass to grow for the cattle, and herb for the service of man; that he may bring forth food out of the earth."*

Ezekiel 38:7: *"Be thou prepared, and prepare for thyself, thou, and all thy company that are assembled unto thee, and be thou a guard unto them."*

Education, p. 126: *"Every command is a promise; …God does not give commands without giving power to obey."*

Testimonies for the Church, vol. 6, p. 166: *"He will not give commands without giving with them power for their performance."*

Testimonies for the Church, vol. 6, p. 178: *"If the land is cultivated, it will, with the blessing of God, supply our necessities. …the blessing of God, which spreads a table for His people in the wilderness, will never cease."*

Country Living, p. 13: *"Send the children to schools located in the city, where every phase of temptation is waiting to attract and demoralize them, and the work of character building is tenfold harder for both parents and children."*

YOU CAN SURVIVE!

Country Living, p. 10: *"The work of the people of God is to prepare for the events of the future, which will soon come upon them with blinding force."*

Country Living, p. 21: *"I see the necessity of making haste to get all things ready for the crisis."*

Country Living, p. 9: *"Our cities are increasing in wickedness, and it is becoming more and more evident that those who remain in them unnecessarily do so at the peril of their soul's salvation."*

Testimonies for the Church, vol. 5, p. 152: *"Could our brethren remember that God can bless twenty acres of land and make them as productive as one hundred..."*

Country Living, p. 11: *"But erelong there will such strife and confusion in the cities, that those who wish to leave them will not be able. We must be preparing for these issues. This is the light that is given me."*

Medical Ministry, p. 310: *God will help His people to find such homes outside of the cities."*

Possible Home Industries

"My business is serving the Lord. I cobble shoes to pay expenses." William Carey

Gardening and Greenhousing: cut flowers, vegetables, herbs, dried foods
Yardwork: landscaping, tree trimming, tree planting, nursery
Wood: firewood, cabinet work, furniture making
Art: printing, photography, crafts, signs, carving, window painting, writing
Computer Arts: web page designs, bookkeeping, trouble-shooting
Tradesman: mechanic, electrician, plumbing
Carpentry: contracting, laborer, remodeling, house painting, drywall, roofing
Janitorial work: custom cleaning, window washing, carpet care
Teaching: home school, tutoring, specialty classes, music lessons
Sewing: upholstering, mending, customized

Books

History of the Waldenses, J. A. Wylie, Pacific Press Publishing Association, Nampa, Idaho, 1977.
Country Living, Ellen White, Pacific Press Publishing Association, Nampa, Idaho.
The Great Controversy, Ellen White, Pacific Press Publishing Association, Nampa, Idaho.
The Desire of Ages, Ellen White, Pacific Press Publishing Association, Nampa, Idaho.
Life Sketches, Ellen White, Pacific Press Publishing Association, Nampa, Idaho.
The Wilderness World of John Muir, Edwin Way Teale, Houghton-Mifflin, Boston, MA, 1954.
Experimenting With God in Families and Schools, Raymond and Dorothy Moore, Box 1, Camas, WA 98607, 2001.

Chapter Eleven

Log Cabin Building: You Can Do It!

"Go up to the mountain, and bring wood, and build the house..."
(Haggai 1:8).

Several years ago, I was invited to teach a log cabin seminar in western Tennessee. As I backed out of the driveway, I heard an ominous clunk. It took me about three hours to find and replace the rear universal joint in my old 4x4 Ford pickup. By then, I knew it would be impossible, even with a police escort, to meet my appointment on time.

With only one stop for fuel, we drove across the state, arriving at the National Guard Armory half an hour late. A uniformed army officer opened the razor-wired gate and signaled us into a parking lot. Another man motioned us to the other side of the building, and a third man signaled someone inside the building. A huge door opened. There, in front of us, sat the entire class of over 100 people waiting patiently for our arrival. Everyone pitched in and we unloaded our model cabin and tools in record time.

One message came through to me loud and clear: I was as ready as I could be—my tools were sharp and I knew how to use them. I had my notes and model cabin ready. I even knew the day and hour I would be needed. But without God's intervention and the help of many willing hands working in unity, I would not have been able to fill my place properly.

So it is with our end time survival preparations. No matter how well we prepare, we will never outgrow our need of each other and of God.

197

YOU CAN SURVIVE!

Invitation to Cooperate With God

There is a verse that makes me think God likes log cabins. *"Go up to the mountain, and bring wood, and build the house; and I will take pleasure in it, and I will be glorified, saith the Lord"* (Haggai 1:8).

In an article entitled "Cooperation" by Ellen G. White, (Review and Herald, May 28, 1908), building forest homes are considered a blessing. *"God desires every human being in our world to be a worker together with Him. This is the lesson we are to learn from all useful employment, <u>making homes in the forest, felling trees to build houses, clearing land for cultivation</u>. God has provided the wood and the land, and to man He has given the work of putting them in such shape that they will be a blessing"* (emphasis supplied).

A whole new frontier emerges for students, *"<u>Our schools should not depend upon imported produce</u>, for grain and vegetables, and fruit so essential for health. Our youth need an education in felling trees and tilling the soil as well as in literary lines"* (Testimonies for the Church, vol. 6, p. 179; emphasis supplied).

I consider these counsels an invitation to learn the joys of working with our hands in cooperation with God, in order that, even in building our home, He may be glorified. Here are a few reasons to consider learning to build a simple house made of logs:

First: People will be leaving the cities at the eleventh hour to escape persecution. They will be leaving because they have accepted the Sabbath truth in spite of the wrath of the beast (see Revelation 13).

Second: People will be leaving the cities; from streets, tenements, condos and even 50-floor apartments, penthouses and multi-million dollar homes; coming to our outposts with very few earthly possessions (Compendium of City-Outpost Evangelism, p. 229).

Third: They will need shelter, the first rule of survival. We will need to provide this shelter during a time when we can't buy and sell.

Fourth: With a little planning, practice and forethought, logs are one way to build in a time of financial strain.

Tools of the trade

Tools are of primary importance. Tools and materials can be purchased from a number of sources. Used tools can be found at yard sales and second hand shops. (For a picture of these tools see back cover and last page of this book.) It is a good plan to collect your tools before the crisis when you can't buy them.

1. Chain saw (speeds up building process but not used in "no buy-no sell")

2. Crosscut saw, one and two-man (for no buy-no sell situation)
3. Frow, for shake splitting (described later in this chapter)
4. Splitting axes, chopping axes, and hatchets
5. Splitting maul, six- or eight-pound, and wedges
6. Claw hammer
7. Hand drill with bits from 1/8 to 1 inch (metal)
8. Drawknives for peeling logs and planing
9. Four-or six-foot level
10. Plum bob
11. Scribe or locking tape
12. Hand plane
13. Wood chisels and gouges
14. Log tongs
15. Peavey
16. A rake (clean up)
17. A mattock, or grubbing hoe
18. Brace with bits from ¼ to 1-inch (wood)
19. Stoves, heater and cook
20. Chimney
21. Stovepipe
22. Hinges
23. Windows, clear plastic
24. Plastic water pipe
25. Alaska mill or pit saw

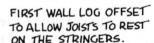

SCRIBE

PEAVEY

Preparing the Building Site

The property for your log cabin must be just right; it will have wood, water, and a good garden spot. Its view and location will be beautiful. It must be well drained; do not build on a low spot (Ministry of Healing p. 274). After you have chosen the place to build your cabin, prepare your site and begin the foundation by "squaring up."

Diagonals in any four-sided figure will determine its squareness. Use a long tape measure, a string, or rope.

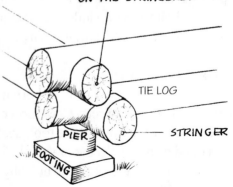

FIRST WALL LOG OFFSET TO ALLOW JOISTS TO REST ON THE STRINGERS.

TIE LOG

PIER

FOOTING

STRINGER

Compare the measurements. When the diagonals are equal, your building is square. Mark each corner with a stake so that you will know where to put your footings or foundation.

A simple way that footings may be constructed is by using flat rocks or concrete pads placed on the ground. Concrete building blocks may also be used as piers. Plan eight feet of distance between piers.

Falling Trees

Choosing timber, falling trees and getting them to the building site is a big job. I like to encourage beginners by telling them that when the logs are at the cabin site, stacked and peeled, the cabin is half finished.

Select trees that are straight and show the least amount of taper. Where we live, lodge pole pine is best for cabin building. Ideally, all the trees you cut should be of the same diameter or within one inch of the standard measurement you choose. Smaller logs are lighter in weight but do not insulate as well and it takes more logs to achieve the height of wall you desire. A simple method for maintaining proper diameter is to cut a length of string the circumference of the "ideal" tree you have selected. For example, if you select a 7-inch tree, your circumference would be 22 inches.

To determine the straightness of a tree, stand at the base of the tree and sight straight up from two different positions. Don't be concerned if it is leaning, just check to see if it is straight. Measure the circumference of the tree with your string to see if it meets your requirements for size. Next, check to see if there is at least one section in the tree the length of your cabin wall. If there are several limbs on the log, it will be harder to fit, but it can be used.

A tree will fall in the direction it leans. If it is standing straight, the side with the most limbs will determine the direction of fall. **Never fall trees when the wind is blowing!** With an ax or saw, make an undercut facing the direction in which you want the tree to fall. Then make a back cut, leaving a hinge of wood one inch thick to keep the tree connected **full width** of the stump. **Never cut the tree off the stump!** If the tree is large enough, adjustments can be made in directing the fall of a tree by inserting a wedge in the back cut.

Because this is dangerous work, be sure that no objects are in the falling path of the tree. You should clear all debris and brush from around the base of the tree so that it will not interfere with your saw or your escape route when the tree begins to fall. Make sure all of your helpers, including your dog, are far from the tree before you start to cut it.

As the tree is falling, step straight back about ten feet and then to either side of the tree butt so that you will be out of the way in case of a kick back. The tree could hang up on another tree and move to the left or right. You should wear ear protection against chainsaw noise, eye protection (goggles) and a hard hat to protect yourself from falling limbs. If you are using a chain saw, **always** be aware of the position of your saw tip, and inform your coworkers that you need a 5-foot working radius. **For safety's sake, no one should ever reach into your workspace trying to help you while you are operating a chain saw!**

Once the tree is on the ground, cut it to length and limb it. The length will be determined by your floor plans plus two feet; a foot beyond the notches at each end.

CAUTION: When using blowdown (trees ripped up by the roots during a previous windstorm) do not allow children to play in the hole left by the tree roots. The stump can fall back into the hole when the tree is cut off and cause serious injury!

Cabin logs should be cut and peeled in the late spring. Let them dry over the summer and then begin building your cabin in the fall. I have built log cabins using dry trees (dead standing) and I have used green ones. It is much easier to use dead trees than green! Be careful when you stack the logs as they can "belly" on you and become crooked when they dry out. One of the best methods to ensure straightness is to simply girdle the green tree in the early springtime (cut through the bark all the way around the tree to keep the sap from flowing) while it's standing and let it cure over the year; by the following spring it will be ready to cut down and the bark will peel easily. The tree remains straighter by leaving it to dry in an upright position. Your available time will determine which method to use.

In a single-room log cabin, you will need approximately 40 to 60 wall logs, plus purlins. The number of logs, will depend upon the size of your cabin, your floor plan, and the size of the logs you choose to use.

Piers, Stringers, and Tie Logs

You are now ready to place the stringers. These must be straight logs with a minimum diameter of 10 inches and hardly any taper. The stringers are placed directly over upright piers (**B**). Piers are sections of treated or untreated wood set on flat rocks or concrete blocks (**A**) to prevent contact with the ground. Inserting a piece of tarpaper between **A** and **B** will help prevent insect invasion and rot. Stringers are the logs on which you will place the two outside tie logs (**D**). Wall logs (**E**) are the first logs on the front and back of the cabin. The stringers (**C**) are held in place by the tie logs (**D**). Stringers should not be notched. A **slight bit** of flattening on the lower side of the stringers may be required so that they will sit firmly on the piers. The stringers should be eight feet apart. The tie logs (**D**) are doweled or nailed to the stringers (**C**).

Floor Joists and Flooring

Floor joists are constructed from smaller logs (approximately five inches in diameter) laid across the stringers on two-foot centers (see illustration on page 193). Floor boards are then laid across the joists. The quickest, most stable floor is constructed of two-by-six joists on edge. Floor boards can be applied at random lengths to center over the joists. I have used my Alaska Mill to cut boards for flooring, door sills, windowsills, window

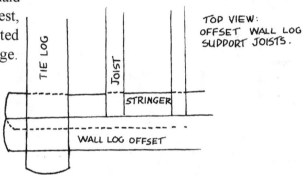

framing, and door framing, and it works well. This is one way to provide the boards for construction as needed. If no Alaska Mill is available, a one-man crosscut saw can also be used to cut lumber. A pit saw may be used, if available, as part of your survival tool kit.

Floor boards may be doweled, planed, and sanded for a nice rustic look which only improves with use. Finished flooring may also be applied as desired.

Moss sprinkled with lime and sulfur can be used for floor insulation and as a deterrent to vermin. This is a dry mixture requiring a second layer of floorboards (or plastic) beneath the floor to hold it in place.

Wall Logs

Now, you're ready to begin your first round of wall logs. There are many styles of log cabin construction; Hudson's Bay, stack log, cordwood, saddle notch, and dovetail, to name a few. We have chosen the saddle notch method to illustrate. In building your walls, it is worthwhile to take the time to fit the logs well to each other to increase the insulating factor. Saddle notching is a simple and sturdy way to fit logs together. But, for whatever style of notch you choose, the insulation factor is greatly enhanced if you take the time to fit the logs into the wall properly. Plumb the logs center over center.

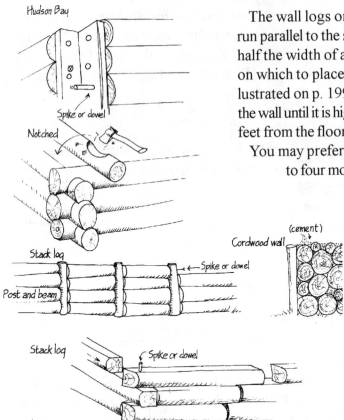

Hudson Bay

Spike or dowel

Notched

Stack log

Post and beam

(cement)

Cordwood wall

←Spike or dowel

Stack log

Spike or dowel

The wall logs on the sides of the cabin run parallel to the stringers, and are offset half the width of a log so as to have a sill on which to place your floor joists (as illustrated on p. 199 and 201). Add logs to the wall until it is high enough; at least seven feet from the floor for a finished wall.

You may prefer to continue on up two to four more rounds above the loft support logs before beginning the gables, thus giving more head room in the attic or loft. The gables are very simply constructed. Continue with your wall logs into the gables, tying them together with purlins running full length of the building. In determining the pitch of your roof and gable, you will need to consider geography. Any pitch less than a five-twelve pitch (5 inches of rise for every 12 inches of run) is not desirable in snow country. Two jigs may be constructed on each gable end of the cabin at a six-twelve pitch so that purlins may be moved against the inside of the jig to maintain an accurate pitch. At the desired pitch purlins are tied to the gable logs. Do not notch the purlins.

Continue on up with the gables and the purlins until the ridge pole is placed. The gable logs are notched and pinned to the purlins. Then the gable log ends are cut off flush with the angle of the roof pitch and you are ready to begin the roof.

The ridge pole should be your straightest log with the least taper of any log in the building. Choose your ridge pole early and set it aside. This will provide a good strong support for the roof of the cabin.

Saddle Notching

Always cut the notch from the under side of the upper log to prevent moisture retention. All notching and limbing can be done with an ax.

1) Determine the distance between log **A** and **C** with a locking tape measure.

2) The contour of the notch is dictated by the shape of the crosswise log, **B**. To create a notch pattern, keep the tape measure **perfectly vertical** following the contour across the top half of log **B**. Use the locked tape as a scribe, marking dots in several locations on the outside of log **A**. Connect the dots into a smoothly arched line.

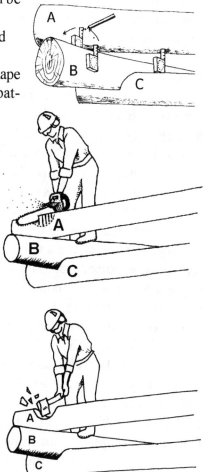

3) Repeat this pattern on the opposite side of log **A**.

4) Roll the log so that the portion to be notched faces upward.

5) Using your chain saw, cut 1 inch serial sections through the notch pattern. **Do not cut past your pattern marks.**

6) Using your ax, remove the slices of wood from log **A**.

7) Smooth the newly shaped notch with the tip of your chain saw.

8) Roll log **A** into place. Slide log **A** back and forth over log **B** to reveal high spots along the length of the log and in the notch.

9) While log **A** is resting on its new notch, run your chain saw full length between logs **A** and **C**. The approximate ¼ inch width of your saw blade indicates a good fit.

Lofts

A portion of the attic, or even the whole attic can be used as a sleeping loft or for storage. Loft beams are placed across the room on top of the last round of wall logs. The loft support beams are hefty logs, about 10 inches in diameter, placed on three- or four-foot centers. To secure these beams to the wall, flatten them where they rest on top of the wall so they won't roll then spike or dowel them into place. Place flooring over your loft joists, using two by six lumber.

After the roof is on your cabin, a decorative safety railing is constructed inside the cabin across the front of the loft supporting the overhead purlins. This railing strengthens the structure and assists in building the roof. A ladder can be provided for loft access. The ends from the loft support beam may be cut to the angle of the roof.

Porches

There are probably as many floor plans as there are log homes, but keep your first cabin simple. A beaver can cut down a pretty big cottonwood, but I have seen even that busy little animal leave a tree half finished because he bites off more than he can chew! Log building is not a difficult, but it is time-consuming and can get discouraging to the beginner. For the sake of simplicity, we have considered only a single room cabin. This could in-

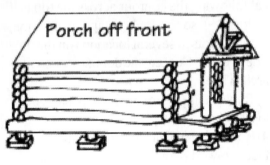

volve a porch off the gable end or off the side. Making a porch for a small cabin is relatively easy, and either style is widely used.

In the case of a porch off the front, using 18-foot logs, our cabin will end up with a room 16-feet square. When you begin to build, allow for the porch to be supported by the same stringers that support the cabin floor. This means the stringers will extend to 6 or 8 feet beyond the front gable end. Then, when you reach the top log of the cabin wall, allow it and the purlins to extend out in front of the cabin (to the same length as your stringers) to give roof support over the porch. The floor of the porch is constructed over stringers; the porch roof is built on the purlins. You will place upright posts on top of the porch floor to support the two outside purlins. On top of upright posts, a horizontal cross-tie is placed to support the front end of the ridge pole. Fasten the cross-tie by flattening it on the underneath side over the upright. Spike it or dowel down through the purlin, cross-tie and into the upright. Roof the porch as you would the rest of the cabin.

For a cabin with the porch off the side, extend the tie logs (that are notched over the stringers) six- to eight-feet beyond the outer wall of the cabin to support the porch floor. As the walls are finished, the top wall logs will be extended the same length as the

205

tie logs in order to support the porch roof. Upright posts are placed under these extended top wall logs and down to the porch floor to support the beam which forms the outer edge of the porch roof. These upright posts must be supported from beneath with a block and pier. Additional support for the porch floor can be built by adding a beam under the floor. These additional support beams may be attached to the cabin across the porch floor with dowels or heavy spikes. These additional beams are supported from the ground at the outer edge of the porch with a concrete block and pier. Attach rafters to outer log beam and cabin wall. Then strapping, such as one-by-fours are placed over the rafters in the porch in preparation for shake roofing.

Shake-splitting

The most inexpensive way to roof your cabin is to split your own shakes. This I have done from both western cedar and white oak, and I am here to testify that cedar is the easiest! Other species of wood can be used, but whatever you choose, be sure that it is straight-grained and free of knots.

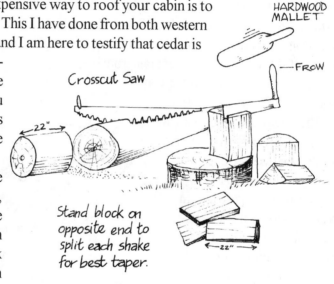

HARDWOOD MALLET

FROW

Crosscut Saw

22"

Stand block on opposite end to split each shake for best taper.

22"

To determine the length of the shake, measure the distance between the purlins in your roof and add six inches. If the purlins in your roof are 16 inches apart, plan on your shakes being 22 inches long. You need not use sheathing or any other material on your roof. Shakes may be applied directly to the purlins.

The art of shake-splitting begins with the selection of straight-grained wood, that is, wood without knots. Yellow or western cedar seems to be the best, but redwood, white oak, or any knot-free straight grain wood can be used. Select and peel the log you will be using for shakes, then cut the log into blocks that are the length of the shakes that will fit your roof. Then quarter the blocks.

Next, you will need a frow. A frow is an old-fashioned tool our grandfathers used in shake-making. A frow may be purchased or is easily made from a piece of steel attached to a 16-inch handle, as illustrated. The back edge of the frow is about ¼ inch thick and tapers to the edge of the blade. Place the sharp edge of the frow blade about ½-¾ inch into the block; this will be the thick edge of the shake. Experiment with the least amount of thickness that will allow a full-length shake. Use a wooden mallet to drive the frow into the shake block about the width of the frow blade. Then separate the shake from the block by pushing forward on the handle until the shake pops free of the block. Turn the quarter block over and place the edge of the frow at the ¾-inch thickness and repeat this process until the block is less than 4 inches in width. Use the remainder of the block for fuel in cooking or heating.

Roofing the Cabin

Lay shakes side by side across the bottom edge of the roof, in a random wide/narrow, thick/thin pattern. You may use either 3/8 inch hardwood dowels (if you do not have nails) or 1¼ inch ring-nails (preferably with a rubber washer) to attach the shakes to the purlins. Over the cracks (the spaces where your shakes meet), lay a second row of shakes, making sure each crack has at least a two-inch width of shake over it to prevent rain from seep-ing through. To say it another way, each row of shakes on your cabin will have two layers of shakes. Repeat this process on each row all the way to the ridge.

The easiest way to cap the ridge, to keep it from leaking, is to use flashing; aluminum is preferred. If aluminum flashing is unavailable, you may use one of two other methods for sealing the ridge. The first is to extend the last row of shakes on the windward side of your cabin over the shakes on the leeward side. The second method is to come down the center with overlapping, pre-fitted shakes. All of these methods can yield a leak-proof roof, and, properly done, a shake roof will last many years. The roof may be insulated with friction fit insulation between purlins under the shakes. A sod roof is financially inexpensive and relatively easy to build, too. Cover purlins with heavy plastic sheeting and tack boards or poles around the outside edge of the roof to hold the sod from slipping. Lay sod strips directly on the roof in a mat no less than 4 inches thick to give the roots room to grow. A sod roof is homey and artistic, but will need reworked every few years.

Doors and Windows

When cutting the doors and windows, nail a two-by-four, or some other straight edge, precisely opposite each other on the inside and the outside of the wall of your cabin in the exact location of the window or door you have chosen. Be sure these guides are straight up and down. Be sure to allow for two by six framing or casing material when you measure and mark your opening. With a chain saw, or crosscut saw, cut beside the two-by-fours so that the logs fall free of the opening. Let the cut logs fall outside the building. The two-by-fours that you first nailed to both the outside and inside as wall guides will continue to hold the loose ends of the wall from falling out while you prepare your framing or casing material. The framing material is constructed of two-by-sixes nailed or lag-screwed into the ends of the logs. Dowels may also be used. Lag screws or dowels are particularly valuable in a door casing because they hold more firmly.

A door may be made from hand-sawn lumber and doweled together as shown. Allow ¼ inch on each side of door opening to ensure closure. A door can then be shut from the outside, as in the case of a root cellar. Hinges may be made of heavy truck mud flap material.

A hook and eye type latch is easily constructed from bent nails which will enable closure from the inside or outside.

BENT NAILS FORM HOOK & EYE LOCK.

Unique handles can be made from limbs.

Windows are optional, but remember that log buildings tend to be dark inside, so additional light from windows adds cheer to your cabin. Having clear plastic on hand helps in the construction of simple windows. Plastic can be stretched over a frame and fastened by use of dowels and wooden strips. You can also use glass windows if available.

Once you have constructed your window, set your window in the opening against a window jamb constructed of ½ inch square wooden strips. When the window is inserted into the opening, another strip of wood may be nailed inside to hold the window in place.

In warmer climates, opening shutters can be built to allow light to come in through just an opening in the log walls. These shutters can be built as a scaled-down version of the door. They can also be built as two doors closing together.

The Chimney

You may want to build a chimney from chimney block and mortar (three parts sand, one part cement, no lime). These are simple to lay. Be sure to level each block. The use of concrete chimney blocks next to wood walls is safer than stovepipe. Many people find metal chimneys easiest to use. If a metal chimney is used, you will need flashing and a waterproof unit in the roof itself so that leaks are prevented and that the heat produced will not cause a fire hazard. You may wish to put such a 7-inch insulated chimney into your "tool box" before "no buy-no sell."

A chimney may also be built from "scratch" using 2- or 3-inch diameter logs, notched together in approximately a 2 by 3 foot rectangle and lined inside and out with clay. The pioneers used this method, but were troubled with chimney fires as the clay fell out. Yet another approach is to use the clay to set stones in a chimney form. Because of mass, the stones tend to hold heat. **Do not use river rocks as they may explode when heated.**

Whatever method of chimney construction you use, the chimney should be situated as near the peak (center of cabin) as possible. This keeps the heat in the cabin longer as it travels up the pipe inside the cabin and also allows you to get the chimney farther above the cabin without extra support outside. Locating the chimney above the peak will aid in drafting your stove. The chimney, outside the roof, should be extended at least two feet above the ridge **so that sparks do not fall down and ignite your roof.** Many cabins have burned down because there was simply not enough clearance between the roof level and the height of the chimney.

Log Preservation

The first step in preservation of logs is to remove the bark. If your cabin was built with the bark still on the logs, take a wide-blade chisel and remove all the bark you can, even the bark between the logs. If your cabin has already been permanently chinked, just remove the bark that shows.

Bark is very moisture absorptive and sets up wet conditions for rotting the logs. The removal of this bark is laborious but worthwhile. It is easier to peel logs before using them in your cabin. If the bark is left on the new cabin and is not yet dry, allow a little time for this drying to take place then use your wide-blade chisel to peel it off. After the bark is removed, you can paint the logs outside with any petroleum based-oil, such as diesel, kerosene, etc. Linseed oil is also a good preservative.

Chinking

No matter how tight your scribed or saddle notching may be, it is necessary to chink every crack where logs fit together to prevent drafts. However hot your fire, drafts will suck the heat out of your house. Even the scribing method of log building requires insulation between the logs. Chinking seals the outside and inside of the logs. The comfort factor of your cabin is greatly increased by your attention to this detail.

Chinking your cabin can be done in a number of ways. Mortar is made by mixing three parts sand, one part cement and ½ part lime. Lime will allow the cement to stick more readily. To be sure that it sticks properly, however, drive nails or pegs into the logs in the cracks to help hold the cement in the crack.

Another method I have used is packing fiberglass insulation into the log joints, and painting this with linseed oil. The oil causes the outside layer of fiberglass to dissolve, forming a waterproof crust.

You may also use a mixture of wet lime mixed in moss; this will stick to the wood as it dries. There are also many excellent commercial chinking compounds available.

The Finished Cabin

Your finished cabin, with stairs, ladders, furniture, kitchen decks, cabin skirting, along with customized finishing touches will give you a feeling of success like no other practical job that you've ever completed. Here is something you built yourself. It is solid, inexpensive, and something I believe is part of the Lord's plan; a simple means of construction where you can be comfortable in the wilderness, even at 40 below. You've learned many practical skills; from the falling of the trees to the finishing touches. You have learned perseverance when the work was hard. Spiritually, you have followed the Lord's plan in being as close to nature as possible.

"God desires every human being in our world to be a worker together with Him. This is the lesson we are to learn from all useful employment, making homes in the forest, felling trees to build houses, clearing land for cultivation" (The Advent Review and Sabbath Herald, May 28, 1908, p. 4).

The Cabin in the Trees

There's a little old log cabin
Tucked away among the trees
In a valley 'way up yonder;
It's as pretty as you please.

You can hear the birds a-singing
As they greet the morning sun.
And the chatter of the red squirrel
As he takes his morning run.

You'll hear the whispering breezes
And the laughter of the rill;
You can watch cloud shadows wander
Here and there along the hill.

So, friend, when troubles get you
And you find it hard to smile,
Just wend your way up yonder
And stay a little while.

You'll find your cares will vanish,
The sun will rise again
When you're at the old log cabin
In the pretty mountain glen.

--- George Clark

The Water System

It is important to keep your drinking water separate from the water you have used for cleaning. The simplest water system is easily constructed from two buckets and a shoulder yoke. A few trips to the spring and your indoor storage tank is full. If your well is not too deep, a hand pump may be installed. This pump may be hooked up to a storage tank in the cabin if your water source is not too far away. Thirty gallon plastic containers can be used for water storage.

For a simple drain, hook up a short pipe to the sink that drains into an open five-gallon pail. This bucket is then carried out and dumped in a dry well or previously prepared place. Since it is gray water, it will not help your compost pile as it has antibacterial agents in it.

Your water source was given consideration before you built. If your water source was located above the building site, you are fortunate to have the potential of a gravity-fed water system. With a gravity flow system, getting water into your cabin is quite simple. Plastic pipe requires less specialized skill to assemble than the old galvanized pipe assembly method. If you have a gravity-fed water system, many

211

laborious chores can be eased. You will then have pressured water at your sinks and toilets if you opt for indoor facilities. A gravity flow hot water system may be hooked up to a gas hot-water heater with a separate supply tank. The pressure of the gravity-fed water system will make hot-water accessible at your sinks. This system may be used as long as you can buy gas to heat the hot-water tank.

Another simple hot-water system is made from coils of copper pipe inside the firebox of your wood cook stove. The incoming cold water moves into the firebox from the bottom of the storage tank. A line from the top of the tank goes to the sink for your domestic hot water supply or recycled as cooled water, going back to the cook stove.

A gravity system provides water pressure for sinks and toilets which must be connected to a septic system. This system requires 4-inch lines to a septic tank. Connected to the septic tank is a drain field of perforated 4-inch line, 150 feet in length. Drain lines and drain fields need to be at least 150 feet from your water supply. In our country, drain fields need to be 8 feet underground to prevent freezing, so consider the climate factor when digging your field. Use at least 1 inch sized gravel or larger, covering the pipe gently so as not to damage it. Then finish by covering it with dirt.

The Use of Wood for Fuel

Picture this; it is evening on a beautiful lake. Your campfire begins to die down, but glows a little brighter as twilight descends. You stir the sticks and send a rush of sparks heavenward. It is cool outside, but, here beside your fire, you are warm.

A campfire is the most elegant of necessities. It cooks our food, warms us, burns our garbage, keeps us safe, and relaxes our over stimulated brains. Building a good fire is an art form. Fires, like love of family and friends, must be tended gently, steadily, but with purpose.

Consider the type of wood you will use to build this campfire. Although a campfire is often built from scrap wood, the same conditions that guide the selection of firewood for a campfire may be used in choosing firewood for home use.

Choose dry wood. Wet wood does not generate as much heat. Choose dry standing trees or leaners still off the ground. A tree is dry if it has a crack in the trunk and the bark is sloughing off.

Follow the same rules when falling a dry tree as when falling a green one, being sure to watch the top of a dry tree as it may break out easily and come straight down. A hard hat should always be worn during any work in the woods. Leave a little thicker "hinge" in a dry tree than in a green one. **Do not cut it free of the stump** or you will lose the direction of fall.

When the tree is on the ground, limb the tree with either an ax or saw and

212

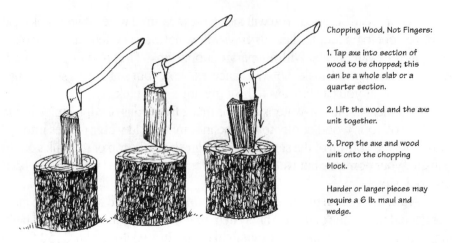

Chopping Wood, Not Fingers:

1. Tap axe into section of wood to be chopped; this can be a whole slab or a quarter section.

2. Lift the wood and the axe unit together.

3. Drop the axe and wood unit onto the chopping block.

Harder or larger pieces may require a 6 lb. maul and wedge.

cut the lengths of firewood you want. Wood cook stoves usually use shorter lengths of wood than do heaters. Use a power or crosscut saw for the larger parts of the tree nearer the butt.

Once the tree is cut to the desired lengths, splitting it into lengths which are easily handled is good exercise. It is said that "wood heat warms you twice: once getting it and once burning it." Set the blocks on end and use a 6- or 8-pound splitting maul or a combination of maul and wedges. Use wedges particularly when splitting hardwood that is not straight-grained or where knots occur.

If your tree had a crack in it, then split through the face of the block that connects with the crack. If no crack exists in your wood, then sight a line through the face of the block where no knots occur. Begin your splitting process on the outside edge and line each blow right across the block face, following your line of sight. With practice, you will be able to strike repeatedly in a straight line.

Wood may be stacked anywhere, but, if no woodshed is available, stack it between two trees or posts. If no such supports are available, "square-end" it. At the ends of your stacks, put the split pieces together as you would a log cabin, but fill in all spaces and then cross another layer of pieces at 90 degrees to the existing pile. This forms a pillar you can stack against, even up to 4 or 5 feet high.

It is good to keep your wood dry by putting a tarp or plastic over the top of the stack. I like to have a woodshed to keep snow and rain off my wood. Happy warming to you; it is a matter of survival!

Cooking and Heating

Since one of the reasons we build a log cabin is to decrease building expense, we may also keep down the heating cost by using wood stoves. Heaters are available that have a thermostat governing the damper. By placing a log or two in the firebox every few hours, heat may be produced all day. At night fill the stove with wood and turn the damper down. The stove will hold heat all night. These are attractive furnishings, in appearance much like any other heater. There are many models available, even with catalytic converters that definitely save on total wood consumption.

The Outhouse

When the children of Israel were wandering in the desert, learning all kinds of lessons, the Lord instructed them to be careful with waste. *"Thou shalt have a place also without the camp, whither thou shalt go forth abroad: And thou shalt have a paddle upon thy weapon; and it shall be, when thou wilt ease thyself abroad, thy shalt dig therewith, and shalt turn back and cover that which cometh from thee: For the Lord thy God walketh in the midst of thy camp, to deliver thee, and to give up thine enemies before thee; therefore shall thy camp be holy: that he see no unclean thing in thee, and turn away from thee"* (Deuteronomy 23:12-14).(Ministry of Healing, p. 277-286.)

Indoor facilities are easily taken for granted until a power failure deprives us of water. As in the previous discussion about gravity fed systems, toilets are easily maintained. But with a nongravity-fed water system the outhouse is used. Some folks find outhouses intimidating, but there are a few things that can be done to make them more comfortable. First, your outhouse must be located at least 150 feet, from your water supply.

The outhouse may be constructed similar to your cabin, with notched logs. If you have access to lumber, you can frame the structure. A knee-high bench built inside the outhouse sits over a three foot deep hole. Deeper holes can be dug, but for a family this is plenty of volume since the solids do break down. Odors are controlled, and the rate of disintegration increased, by adding wood ashes or lime.

When you cut the hole in the bench, be careful not to cut the hole too big; the usual diameter of a toilet seat is 8½ inches wide by 10 inches long. A toilet seat may be used to cover this hole or you may customize a piece of 1-inch Styrofoam for additional comfort against cold.

The Burn Barrel

In most every household located where neighbors are a half mile or more away, there is always refuse that is not recyclable yet burnable. Obtain one or two 55-gallon (45- gallon in Canada) metal barrels to burn this refuse. As the barrel accumulate ashes, lay the barrel on its side to keep moisture from activating the ashes and increasing the rate of rust. Be sure your burn barrel is in a location where the smoke does not come into the house and the ground is clear for an area of ten feet square. This will prevent the start of grass fires that could cause damage.

Tools

Selection of Tools

Good-quality tools are easy to choose. In general, "You get what you pay for," but that is not always true. I remember buying a drawknife from a farmer who had it hanging in his barn. It was well-worn, the handles were loose, and it was dull. He wanted $2 for it, and I took it home and removed the rust. I discovered a blacksmith mark on it. I smiled to myself as I sharpened it and tightened the handles. It is my favorite drawknife. The steel was hand-forged and tempered. It holds an edge better than any of the drawknives I bought at the hardware store for $25 to $40 each.

The Oxhead brand of chopping ax is excellent, though there may be other brands that are comparable. Here is a good test for chopping axes: thump the edge of the blade with your finger and see if it "rings." If it does, you have the best steel. If it does not ring but "thuds," you probably have a splitting ax or a poor-quality chopping ax. A chopping ax is thin, used for cutting cross grain as in chopping logs into lengths. A splitting ax is thicker, more wedge-shaped, making it easier to split wood. Consult with those who can share their experience about how to recognize tool quality.

Making Handles

In the south, hickory is the best wood for handles. In the north, hedge apple or alder is best. These choices are based on lightness in weight and length of tree fiber. If you have neither of these woods, choose a wood that has the aforementioned qualities. Be sure your selection is straight-grained and not curved. All wood used in handle-making should be thoroughly dry. For most tools, the carving of straight rather than curved handles is easiest to do. A straight handle works best for such tools as hatchets, hammers, frows, chisels, and saws. Handles are carved to fit the tool required. To learn the art of making handles, one must first attempt a relatively simple handle, such as a hammer.

Notice the shape and dimensions of the hole in the hammer head where the new handle will fit. Measure the entrance through the head and mark it out on the end of your dry, seasoned handle wood. Take note also of how far the handle goes through the hammer and mark it accordingly.

Using a drawknife and placing the handle wood in a vise or shave horse, remove wood down to your lines. You might want to practice making your handle on a piece of waste wood until you have mastered the skill.

Your new handle should have a snug fit on all sides. Snug enough so that it will have to be driven on with a wood mallet. Before you hammer it on, cut a slot in the top of the handle (the end which will go into the hammer) for inserting a hardwood wedge to expand the handle once it is in place. This will secure the handle in the tool.

Leave a definite hub ring so that the hammerhead cannot move down the handle, then shape and smooth the handle with your drawknife until it fits your hand. Then leave a smooth tapering knob at the end; a gradual thickening of the handle wood to the length desired. Cut the handle off there and save what is left to make another handle or some hardwood wedges. Sand smooth as desired.

The handles for larger tools such as splitting mauls, peaveys, rakes, shovels, and hoes are all straight handles. I recommend straight handles whenever possible because cutting a curve weakens the handle allowing it to break more easily along the grain lines. Some woods will bend allowing the integrity of the grain to remain intact. Such bending may be done with steam or soaking in hot water and applying pressure at each end of the handle wood.

An important object lesson comes from the Lord's carpenter shop 2,000 years ago. He made handles for tools as well as furniture and conveyances. The God of heaven had an eternity to plan the life of His Son on this earth and He chose carpentry for the education of His Son. He did not choose the schools of His day, but was educated at the feet of His mother, from the scrolls of the prophets, and from nature. (See The Desire of Ages, pp. 69, 70.) He did chores in the home and gained lessons from parables in nature and in the handling of tools in His father's shop. (See The Desire of Ages, p. 72.)

"Dear Lord, let me be a piece of handle wood in Your hand is my prayer. Amen."

Tool Repair and Sharpening

A loose handle is a common tool repair. This repair may be done by soaking the handle a few days in water or oil. If this doesn't tighten the handle sufficiently, remove the wedge and put in slightly larger wedge. If the handle is broken, it will need to be replaced (see section on handle-making). Save your old handles, as they may be used in smaller tools or reshaped if they are broken near the end.

Sometimes a small piece is broken out of the blade requiring the blade to be reground. This can be done with a hand grinder, but it requires two people: one to turn the crank and one to hold the tool. There are old-fashioned pedal grinders requiring only one person to run them—a worthwhile addition to the tool box. A new bevel angle will need to be cut the full length of the blade in order to eliminate the notch in the broken blade.

Steps in the sharpening process:

Step 1: Take a close look at the angle of the dull blade and maintain that angle as you file or grind.

Step 2: Take the angle to a new sharp edge. A burr will form on the opposite side.

Step 3: Take your file or stone and remove the burr. In some cases, blades are only sharpened on one side (broadax, draw knives, etc.). These must be sharpened only on the tapered side. The burr that is left on the back side must be removed holding your file or stone completely flat against the blade. Be sure to use water on the pedal grinders as you sharpen.

"Iron sharpeneth iron" (Proverbs 27:17). "Dear Lord, help me to be a usable tool in Your hands to give satisfaction to the Craftsman. In Jesus' name. Amen."

Blacksmithing

Blacksmithing may be used to repair metal straps, loops, or other parts of broken tools. A forge may be made from a discarded brake drum of a ¾-ton truck. A bellows may be constructed from two paddle-like pieces of wood hinged at the opposite end from the handles and the sides closed in with 6 mil plastic. Handles should be extended another 12 inches beyond the plastic. A spout may be made of 1-inch plastic pipe so that as the bellows are compressed, air will be forced through the tube into the forge containing charcoal. A set of metal tongs can be used to remove the red-hot metal from the forge so that it may be shaped on an anvil.

Welding may also be done by placing the two pieces of metal in the forge, heating to red-hot, and allowing them to melt together. Then remove and beat to shape on the anvil. A larger forge can be made from bigger brake drums. Tools may be repaired in this way. (Refer to page 271 on how to make charcoal. Before it is ground for medicinal purposes, the larger chunks may be used for fueling your forge.)

Lamps

It has always interested me that the children of Israel, at the time of the plague of darkness upon Egypt, had light in their dwellings (see Exodus 10:23). This leaves no doubt in my mind that the Lord can keep our dwellings filled with light in the end times. We can wean ourselves away from the need for utility web lighting. Simplifying our lifestyle, going to bed with the chickens and rising with the sun, we can become people of the day. Outside chores can be finished before dark.

I recall the heavenly glow of the little candle lanterns our students at Sanctuary Ranch used to construct from tin cans. They would cut little designs with tin snips, or pound a pattern with a hammer and nail through which the light would escape.

Candles, kerosene lamps, lanterns, and gas lamps are alternative sources of light. One candle in a dark room sheds an immense amount of light. Kerosene lamps can be a part of your basic tools in readiness for the future. Five gallons of kerosene will supply the needs of a family for quite some time. You should also obtain extra wick to fit your lamps. Wicks should be trimmed once a week if your lamps are used regularly. To trim your lamp, cut the corners ever so slightly at a 45 degree angle with a pair of scissors and then straight across the burnt wick. This will give you a rounded full flame inside the chimney. Keep lamp chimneys clean to ensure the best illumination. Be sure they are cool before washing.

If you don't have a lamp, you can make one by constructing a container made of clay in the shape of a Roman lamp and fill it with vegetable oil. This oil may be extracted from oil seeds such as sunflower, peanuts, canola, soybeans, etc.

To make oil, first, soak the seeds in warm water till soft, then place them in containers and apply pressure with a hydraulic car jack. Build a bracket in which the jack can be placed to apply pressure. The oil will come from the seeds and float on top of any water in your container.

Having obtained the oil, place it in your Roman lamp and insert a strip of clean rag in the oil. Allow the cloth to soak up oil for a couple of hours and light the end. It will yield a candle-like light.

At Home in the Woods

It is better to have cabins built before the crisis hits, but now you know what is necessary in order to build later, even without money. **Construction in the end times will require that certain tools and supplies are on hand in order to build without money.**

Your log cabin with its simple accessories may assist you in physical survival, but it is only a shell to support the lives within; much as our bodies were created to house our spiritual temple. You did not build the cabin just for yourself, you were thinking of others. Your house, no matter where it is, can only be a home when your Best Friend lives there with you. The best laid plans, open to His divine direction, can help your home to be a heaven on earth.

FOR FURTHER READING

Compendium of City-Outpost Evangelism, James Lee, HCR 77 Box 64, Coalmont, TN 37313

Country Woodcraft, Drew Langsner, Rodale Press, Emmaus, PA, 1978.

Handmade Hot Water Systems, Art Sussman and Richard Frazier, Garcia River Press, P.O. Box 527, Point Arena, CA 95468, 1978.

How to Build and Furnish a Log Cabin, W. Ben Hunt, Collier Books, New York, NY, 1974.

Chapter Twelve

Garden to Kitchen:
Food for the Future

"If my people, which are called by my name, shall humble themselves, and pray, and seek my face, and turn from their wicked ways; then will I hear from heaven, and will forgive their sin, and will heal their land" (II Chronicles 7:14).

She leaned on her hoe, removed her old straw hat, and fanned herself. Though she did not have robust health, I would often see this elderly lady tending the little plot of stubborn red Tennessee clay she called a garden.

"You must enjoy gardening," I said, coveting her love of the soil.

"On the contrary, Jere. I garden from principle!" She shook her head and took a drink from her water jug. "The little red books say it's **good** for me, so I **do** it. I do learn a spiritual lesson nearly every day and it's not as grueling as it once was, but I don't yet enjoy it. I hope to one day, though. I need to practice up for my **big** one," she said, pointing upward.

Maybe you, too, share the feelings of some who don't really enjoy spending time in the garden. Perhaps your parents forced you to hoe seemingly endless rows of corn, potatoes, sugar beets, and beans when you'd rather have been chasing grasshoppers. When I enter the garden and humble myself to the hoe, I get a valuable object lesson. Have you discovered, as have I, that produce from your own garden always tastes so much better? Miracle of miracles, now I find I must limit myself to an hour in the garden in order to accomplish the rest of my chores!

219

YOU CAN SURVIVE!

In the coming crisis, we may not only be responsible for feeding ourselves without money, but feeding others on our acreage. Sometimes I wonder how this will happen, then I read: *"...God can bless twenty acres of land and make them as productive as one hundred..."* (Testimonies for the Church, vol. 5, p. 152).

Throughout history, famines have occurred in which people who followed the Lord's instructions were fed. Our position, stature, or rank is irrelevant when it comes to our need for food—we are all served from the field.

"The king himself is served by the field" (Ecclesiastes 5:9).

What we grow will, both now and at the end of time, be a blessing to those who gather around our table. Very often, today, we depend upon others to grow our food. But, as we are learning in this book, the time is soon coming when this will change and we will need to know how to grow our own food; not to hoard it, but so that we will have something to share.

Solomon advised us a long time ago with these words recorded in Proverbs 24:27: *"Prepare thy work without, and make it fit for thyself in the field; and afterwards build thine house."* Solomon, the richest king ever to have lived, advised his people that their first **priority** was to provide a means for growing food, and then to build their house. Certain circumstances may dictate that your need for shelter is greater than your need for food. But we do need both.

In planning your move to the country, consider moving in the springtime, so as not lose a year's worth of produce. Then follow the counsel of the wisest man—plant your garden as soon as you can—even before you build your house!

Historical Gardens

The first gardening instructions were given to Adam and Eve regarding their diet as recorded in Genesis 1:29: *"Behold, I have given you every herb bearing seed, which is upon the face of all the earth, and every tree, in the which is the fruit of a tree yielding seed; to you it shall be for meat."* The last part of Genesis 3:18 says, *"Thou shalt eat the herb of the field."* The original diet consisting of fruits, nuts, grains, and then vegetables was the diet designed for man by God Himself. God made us and knows the best food for us.

An incident in history, when recorded in Jeremiah 29 contains admonition, in verses 5 and 28, regarding what the children of Israel were to do while they were in Babylonian captivity. *"For therefore he sent unto us in Babylon, saying, This captivity is long: build ye houses, and dwell in them; and plant gardens, and eat the fruit of them"* (Verse 28).

Where we can provide for ourselves, we must acquaint ourselves with the lessons and blessings the earth has to offer. When we eat from our garden, meals become very special.

"The cross of Christ is stamped on every loaf. It is reflected in every water spring. ... The family board becomes as the table of the Lord and every meal a sacrament." (The Desire of Ages, p. 660).

Preparation for the Future

There is a time coming in which God's people will not be able to buy and sell, as clearly stated in Revelation 13:17; *"And that no man might buy or sell save he that had the mark, or the name of the beast, or the number of his name."*

Preparations are needed. The instructions in this chapter will help us to be in harmony with God's plan for the future. The short time of trouble is soon to come. Country Living, p. 9-10 states the importance of being in the country where we can grow our own food. *"Again and again the Lord has instructed that our people are to take their families away from the cities, into the country, where they can raise their own provisions; for in the future the problem of buying and selling will be a very serious one."*

Can you imagine what it would be like not being able to go and buy food at the grocery store?

Unknown Bread

No discussion of diet would be satisfactory without at least mentioning our elder Brother's outlook on food. He was not gluttonous, though he was accused by some because he did not fear to be judged by association. He, on the other hand, appeared to be quite familiar with fasting. When His disciples voiced their concerned that he was not eating enough, He assured them, *"I have meat to eat that ye know not of. ... My meat is to do the will of him that sent me, and to finish his work"* (John 4:31-34). Perhaps, in the last days, God's chosen people will be more concerned, as was Jesus, about getting the work done than about their bread and water.

Hopefully, before troublous times are upon us, we will find that place of surrender where even our tongue, the most unruly member, will have been subdued. That special place is the point at which we sense that it is important to allow the Lord to fill us than to fulfill our own desires. Our survival will not be dependent upon the filling of our stomach, but the infilling of the Spirit. With our body temple properly yielded, might it not be possible for Him to supply even our physical needs in a spiritual manner?

One of the best ways to nourish our body temple is to eat as much of our food as possible just as it came from the hand of the Creator. Growing your food helps you appreciate it. Gardens are the foundation of the food chain!

YOU CAN SURVIVE!

Preparation of the Ground

The ideal spot for a garden is one that gently slopes to the southwest. Deep sandy loam is ideal because it warms up fairly fast, contains a good proportion of sand to clay, and usually has a good content of organic matter. Other ground soil types can be used but need more attention. Sand, clay, and gravel soils can be built up by using organic matter. To build soil, spread four inches of organic matter (deciduous leaves, grass, compost) over the surface of the garden to condition the soil and encourage microbial activity. Conditioning your soil helps prevent extremes such as drought and flooding.

Begin working with your soil as soon as possible in the spring. Allow plenty of time for it to warm up if you live in the Far North. You can encourage soil to earlier warmth by spreading black plastic over the area you want to use first. Thoroughly pick out roots and rocks. Make sure there are no trees within 20 feet of your garden. Try to situate your garden in such a way that there will be some sort of shelter-belt to protect it if wind is a problem. Keep the south side reasonably open to allow for plenty of sunlight.

Cultivating

"Whatsoever thy hand findeth to do, do it with thy might," Solomon tells us in Ecclesiastes 9:10. Of all the time spent in gardening, cultivating and weeding is the most demanding of our time. When we can see weeds, we wish they were gone, but it takes effort, on our knees, to rid both ourselves and our garden of that which is undesirable.

As in character building, so with the garden: weeds are most easily controlled when they are small. Planting the garden, and taking care of the weeds for the first few weeks is fun, but by the time August arrives, unless the garden is weeded regularly, it may be difficult to distinguish the potato vines from certain weeds.

One effective method of weed control is to cultivate your soil and allow the weed seeds to germinate, then torch them before you plant the garden seeds. This burning technique is especially helpful for carrots and beets, which take some time to germinate and whose tiny seedlings may tend to get lost in the faster-growing weeds. Continued cultivation will eliminate weeds.

"Man is not to fail of doing his part. ... The harvest is proportionate to the energy he has expended" (In Heavenly Places, p. 157). What is our part? – weeding, seeding, watering, cultivating, just as in the Garden of Eden, when Adam and Eve were appointed to dress and keep it. When we have done our best, God will take care of the rest and fulfill His promise. Here are some points to remember:

1. Every weed you leave is robbing the more valuable plants of what they need.
2. When hoeing avoid digging deep holes and cutting vegetable roots; hill (scoop dirt, building it up around the stem of) potato plants as you weed so as not to overexpose them. Hoeing while soil is dry will kill weeds faster.
3. Try to uproot all weeds at the seedling stage.
4. Hand weeding deeper roots is easiest in damp soil.
5. If you let weeds mature to seed stage, they will reseed themselves.
6. Rake the weeds so that they don't re-root. Put them on the compost pile.
7. Water daily; use a sprinkling can where a hose system is not available.
8. Be sure to pray for God's blessing before you begin your garden.

Garden Tools

1. Hoe–excellent for weeding, has an easily replaced handle. Keep it sharp.
2. Mattock–used for chopping out roots and digging out sod.
3. Pick–also used for grubbing out rocks.
4. Pitchfork–for spreading loose straw and compost.
5. Potato Fork–for digging potatoes, has heavy flat tines.
6. Rake–for leveling ground and piling weeds.
7. Pointed shovel–for digging.
8. String–for making straight rows.
9. Stakes–for marking rows.

Northern Garden Calendar (Zones 2 and 3)

January–Start planning your garden and calculating how much food you will need for the coming year. Seed catalogs help increase gardening enthusiasm during winter months.

February–Prepare your greenhouse, or starter area for planting. Start celery, tomatoes, and peppers in the house in seedling trays. Flowers such as marigolds and nasturtiums are good for bug control and may be started early for this purpose. The easiest way to start seeds is under grow lights in the house. Plant them rather thickly (less than ¼ inch apart). When the plants are an inch or two tall, transplant them into single pots or in small six-pack boxes. Water only in the morning to prevent fungus growth. Sunlight from a south window will substitute when grow lights are not available.

March–Start lettuce, herbs, onions, marigolds and other flowers to plant among your vegetables.

April–Start cucumbers, corn, cabbage, broccoli, and brussels sprouts.

Start squash at the end of the month.

May–At the beginning of the month, begin preparing the garden soil. You may preheat soil by covering the ground with plastic, either clear or black. Begin hardening the greenhouse plants by placing them outside in the shade on calm days; this will prevent them from wilting when you plant them in the garden. In northern climates, the last killing frost is usually toward the end of May. Seeds to plant early–peas, lettuce, onion sets. Seed the rest of your garden after the earth feels warm to your touch, otherwise beans, corn, and squash seeds will rot. Set out your bedding plants after getting them used to the sun for a few days and after frost danger is over. Another planting of lettuce, broccoli, onions, peas, beans, etc. will give you a second crop later in the season. Berries, rhubarb, asparagus, and some herbs are perennial and should have a portion of the garden that is undisturbed by the plow, but must be weeded early.

June–Weed, cultivate, thin carrots and beets; begin enjoying your harvest with young lettuce, herbs, green onions, and spinach.

July–Most lettuce, radishes, strawberries are picked now. Dry herbs. Can baby carrots and berries. Winter preparation should begin.

August–Pick raspberries. Begin food preservation.

September–Harvest root vegetables and store in root cellar.

November– Check the root cellar, making sure the temperature is right; as temperature decreases, you will need to plug root cellar vents with insulation. Set mouse traps.

December–Start thumbing through seed catalogs and dreaming of May!

Bug Trouble

Pests in many forms may attack your garden, but the attacks will often invade only the weaker plants. The best advice regarding "bugs" is prevention–keep the weeds away; keep the plants moist and growing well so that they have a good start. Here are some of the more common pests: slugs, snails, aphids, cutworms, fungus gnats (root maggots), and cabbage worms. Can they be controlled, naturally? Here are some suggestions:

1. If possible, plant a disease-resistant variety of plants.
2. Fungus gnats are discouraged by covering brassicas (broccoli, cauliflower, cabbage, kohlrabi, and Brussels sprouts) with a white row crop cover at least until mid-July. The cabbage butterfly may become a problem at that time, so some years it is best to keep the plants covered until harvest.
3. Remove unhealthy plants; sick plants can contaminate each other.

4.   Keep a tidy garden; pests thrive on garbage.
5.   Plant marigolds (seeds and mature flowers), garlic, onions, and hot peppers near the plants with which you usually have the most bug trouble; sometimes the strong smells make life miserable enough for them that the bugs will leave. Marigolds seem to help prevent root maggots.
6.   A spray made from garlic, hot pepper, and a little dish soap will help repel bugs.
7.   Remove larger bugs from your plants by hand and drop them into a bottle of alcohol. Aphids can be daily sprayed off of plants with a strong stream of water; natural enemies in the soil will often inhibit them from returning.
8.   Encourage children to catch the white cabbage butterflies by providing them with butterfly nets.
9.   Rotate crop types each year, on a three-year cycle, including one year of summer fallow.

Some growers claim that certain nematodes will attack tomato roots if grown in the same soil a second year, but we have not had this experience. The most serious threat currently, both indoors and outdoors, is the fungus gnat, which lays her eggs in the soil adjacent to cabbage, cauliflower, broccoli, and Brussels sprouts, turnips and rutabagas, as well as certain flowers. Growing these vegetables under a row crop cover usually saves the plants. The row crop cover admits water and enough light to permit growth.

Plant Nutrients
The chart below shows the three main foods that plants require for proper growth.

	Nitrogen	Phosphorus	Potassium
Effects	Promotes rapid growth	Promotes better fruit formation	Seed production and root growth
Signs of lack	Leaves turn yellow; stunted growth	Leaves dull green with purple tint. Stunted growth	Slow growth, yellow tips and edges look scorched
If in excess	Plants grow too fast; weak; produce too late in season	Little danger	Little danger
Organic sources	Animal manure, compost, green manure	Dry manure, fish fertilizer, rock phosphate	Wood ashes, manure, unwashed sand

Blood and bonemeal

New scientific discoveries regarding the use of blood bonemeal have revealed that users are at risk of exposure to **prions,** a protein known to cause mad cow disease. Manure may also have to be discarded as a fertilizer.

Fish Fertilizer

Fish may be used by allowing it to decompose in a covered bucket over winter. In spring, add some water and stir with a gyprock mud mixer attached to a half-inch drive drill. This slurry is then diluted in a barrel of water: 1-6 quarts in a 30 gallon plastic garbage can. Though is it smelly, and will attract animals, it grows good plants. Your garden should be fenced. If the fish you catch are from industrially polluted waters, you will have to discontinue its use as a source of soil nutrients.

Green Manure

Trace elements may also be supplied by green manure. Green manure results from turning under a crop that is allowed to break down in the soil. Such crops as peas, (many varieties) rye (before seed formation), clover, and alfalfa.

Compost

Layer compost (kitchen waste, grass cuttings, leaves) with straw and keep it watered and turned occasionally. Compost is valuable when it is completely rotted to the crumbly stage. This takes more time in colder climates because of lack of heat. Find a method that works for you. In any case, it is better to return these organics to the soil, even if you don't tend the pile. Be sure to keep your compost pile 100 yards from the house, unless you want wildlife close by!

Greenhouse Construction

Although you may never have the picture-perfect structure that you might desire, a greenhouse is of benefit. Certain crops, especially young bedding plants, need extra protection from spring frost. Later in the summer there are those that require a boost of heat in order to mature. There are a few simple facts to consider. Never be discouraged about having a greenhouse! Growing food in a greenhouse is fun and simple.

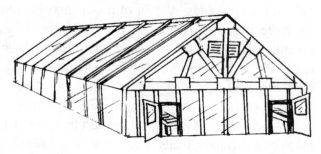

Build your greenhouse where water is readily available; a gravity flow system is ideal. Our first greenhouse was watered with a sprinkling can, but as we increased the size of our structures, we included a pump and hose in our design.

It is much easier to maintain even temperatures in a larger greenhouse (over 1000 square feet) than in a smaller structure. A greenhouse frame is easily constructed from two-by-fours. Plastic should be of a greenhouse grade and can be attached in a number of ways. Check out a plan at your local bookstore or garden shop. There are greenhouse kits available, using metal oval tubing which are very cost effective and much longer lasting than wooden structures.

In northern climates where permafrost or freeze-up occurs, 6 inches of gravel should be leveled under your greenhouse site if you are just using it for bedding plants. If you use it for growing produce, leave the dirt intact. If your greenhouse is constructed on unusable land, such as gravel, rocks, or sand, then build growing boxes in whatever design you like, at a height of one or two feet and fill with a the best organic soil you can find. We recommend a blend of dirt, and some well decomposed compost. The free use of chemical fertilizer kills the good bacteria in the soil and should never be used in the garden. Natural fertilizers accentuate growth; compost, kelp, and green manure crops (rye, clover, or peas) tilled under before they bloom are very helpful to your soil.

Bears especially are attracted to the smell of fish fertilizer. If used in the garden bury it several inches underground.

Greenhouses require no foundation. Long spikes are angled into the gravel to hold the upright supports in place. Side wall supports and rafters can be spaced at least four feet apart. The side walls should be high enough to allow you to work inside comfortably.

If you choose to build from wood, be sure to smooth the edges where the outer wood touches the plastic to prevent wearing when the wind blows. Attach the plastic only where necessary; raw edges at ground level may be stapled and rolled over a two-by-two, then pulled tight and tacked to the uprights at the bottom of the structure. The plastic need not be tacked on the ridge or the rafters, only at the very ends. A layer of plastic may be attached to the inside of the structure; the air space between the two layers will guard against extreme temperatures. Roof pitch should be of such an angle to encourage snow to slide off easily. Plastic, made especially for greenhouses, lasts at least ten years and, when properly installed, won't be ripped in the wind. Panels of fiberglass, make a satisfactory greenhouse covering, but they are expensive and not as resilient as regular greenhouse plastic. Glass is not the best material to use as it magnifies heat too much on sunny days, tends to burn plants, and filters out some UV.

YOU CAN SURVIVE!

If you use wood heat, keep a large pan of water directly on the stove for added moisture. The potential for fungus growth is decreased by; confining watering procedures to morning hours, and keeping your greenhouse clean and well ventilated. Water the soil, not the plants; moisture on plants tends to incubate unwanted growths such as molds. Any plant that enjoys a little extra heat will thrive in a greenhouse: tomatoes, squash, beans, corn, peppers. Supplement your garden with early produce from the greenhouse. By starting lettuce early and growing a few plants in the greenhouse, you will easily be eating salad by the first of June, even in northern Canada.

Growing food in the greenhouse is much the same as growing it in the garden. Our experience has been very rewarding in the north, for we can increase heat (without a heater) and extend both ends of the growing season just enough to mature our beans, corn, squash, and tomatoes: the hot weather crops. There are some vegetables that do better out-of-doors: cabbage, cauliflower, broccoli, and most root crops.

The greenhouse limits air circulation. Keep both front and rear doors open and/or a fan blowing during daylight hours. Open the greenhouse as soon as you can on warm days. On cool days, you should still open the doors for an hour or two to exchange the air. Fungus and bacterial infections are avoided in this way.

As your plants mature in the greenhouse, you will have to keep leaves to a minimum in order to allow for circulation around tomatoes, cucumbers, and squash. Keep suckers pruned off of tomato plants to divert all the energy possible into the fruit. To prevent the spread of fungi, plunge your scissors or knife into boiling water when you cut into moldy or rotten plants. Corn leaves never need pruned.

Preparing the greenhouse and garden, looking at seed catalogs, and making out seed orders is a good "nature day" activity for the family. Including your children as you plan the garden helps them to know that their input is valued. Their little hands are needed when weeding and harvesting approaches.

Saving Seed

A hybrid plant does not produce true to kind. Collect seeds from your best non-hybrid plants. In so doing you might refine a breed particularly suited to your region. Sometimes you'll have to buy seeds for the second year, even if you decide to grow your own, simply because your plants won't produce seed till their second year. There are many good books available on seed-saving techniques. Baby-food jars work well for seed storage by adding a desiccant, keeping them sealed, cool, and dark.

Such crops as spinach or leaf lettuce, where leaves are generally harvested, select a plant where leaves are not taken and allow that plant to go to seed. With root crops such as radishes and carrots, use those plants that go to seed first, since this could mean earlier crops the next year. Many seeds can be sprouted for winter salads: alfalfa, radish, broccoli, wheat, and lentils to name a few. Never eat treated seed!

Beets: If your winters are mild, beets can be left out in the garden. If not, store the best roots in sand in a cool, dark, damp place (root cellar). Come spring, replant the beets, and when the seed stalk develops, tie it to the stick to keep it from breaking off. Cover with cheesecloth as it matures; birds love beet seeds! Once the stalk is mature, break it off and hang it indoors with your seed onions. Remove the seeds when dry. On good years, you may have seeds in time for a late crop the same year. In any case, you'll have plenty for the following year. Store in a glass jar.

Cabbage: Cross-pollinates readily. If you want seeds to be true, grow only one species. Store the firmest, largest heads by hanging them individually in a root cellar or other cold spot over the winter. Replant cabbage the second year in order to obtain seed.

Cantaloupes and Muskmelons: Remove seeds from ripest fruit. Wash, making sure all pulp is removed from seed, and let seeds sit in a shallow dish of water for a day. Wash them again, pick out all the pulp, pat dry with clean, dry towel–not paper towels as they contain unfriendly chemicals. When absolutely dry, store in a tight glass container in a cool place. Check often to make sure no mold has started. If mold begins, discard the seeds.

Carrots: If your winters are mild, carrots can be left out in the garden. If not, store the best roots, set in sand, in the root cellar. In the spring, replant the carrots, and when the seed stalk develops, tie it to a stick to keep it from breaking off. Cover with cheesecloth as it matures as birds love carrot seeds. Once the stalk is mature, break it off and hang it indoors with your onions. Remove the seeds when dry. You'll have seed in time for a late crop the same year. In any case, you'll have plenty for the following year. Store seeds in a glass jar. Note: Don't try replanting if there are wild carrots in your region or you'll end up with worthless hybrids.

Corn: Select the earliest and best ears and let them ripen on the stalk. Then strip back the husks and hang the full cobs in a dry place. When the kernels have thoroughly dried, shell them out and store in tight glass jars.

Cucumbers: Let them vine-ripen to yellow-orange, even slightly musty.

Remove seeds, wash, and let them sit in shallow dishes of water to ferment for two days. Wash them again, pat dry in a clean towel, and dry further by air-drying. When seeds are absolutely dry, store them in a tight glass container in a dry place. Check often to make sure no mold has started.

Eggplant: Pollination is like peppers, so separate two varieties by the length of your garden or by a taller crop. Leave the best fruits on several of your plants for as long as possible. When fully mature, scrape out seeds, dry and store in a glass jar.

Kohlrabi: Grow and harvest same as turnips.

Lettuce: Cross-pollinates readily. If you want seeds to be true, grow only one species. The flower stalk will develop in the fall of the first year, so you don't have to replant the head the following spring. When the seed stalk develops, tie it to a stick to keep it from breaking off. Cover with cheesecloth as it matures. Once the stalk is mature, break it off and hang it indoors with your other seeds. Remove the seeds when dry. With luck, you should have seeds in time for a late crop the same year. In case you don't, you'll have plenty for the following year. Store seeds in a glass jar.

Okra: Okra is self-pollinating, so you may grow more than one variety without danger of crossbreeding. Leave several of your best plants completely alone. When the pods are dry, but before they open enough to drop the seeds on the ground, shell them out and save in a glass jar.

Onions: Most large onions are biennial. Save large, fully developed bulbs through the winter and set them out the following spring. Support the tall blossom stalks and harvest the seeds when they mature. Store dry.

Peas: Leave on the vine until the leaves turn color and begin to die. Pick the pods and shell the peas. Dry them for several days near the wood stove. Larger seeds take much longer to dry thoroughly. Watch closely for signs of mold. Store in dry glass jars.

Peppers: Peppers are mostly self-pollinating, although bees may cause some crossing. If growing both sweet and hot peppers (or more than one variety of either), separate them by the length of your garden, or with a tall crop, or you may be in for a hot surprise. Select several of your largest and best peppers from your best plants. Let them ripen on the plant until red and starting to soften, scrape out the seeds, dry and save in glass jar.

Potatoes: Pick your plumpest, best-shaped, scab-free tubers. Store whole, in burlap bags or buried in dry sand in your cold cellar. For planting, cut each piece, with an eye or two.

Pumpkins: After the pumpkins have vine-ripened in the field, remove seeds, wash, and let them sit in a shallow dish of water for one day. Wash them again, pat dry in an old towel, and dry for a few days at room temperature or beside the wood stove. When absolutely dry, store them in a tight glass container. Check once in a while to make sure no mold has started to grow on them.

Radishes: The flower stalk will develop in the fall of the first year, so you don't have to replant the radish root the following spring. When the seed stalk develops, tie it to a stick to keep it from breaking off. Cover with cheesecloth as it matures; birds love radish seeds. Once the stalk is mature, break off and hang it indoors with your other seeds. Remove the seeds when fully dry. You should have seeds in time for a late crop the same year, or to sprout indoors for salads. Store in a glass jar.

Rutabagas: Mulch heavily over the winter and uncover rutabagas early in the spring and collect seeds as you would for herbs. Rutabagas are hardy enough so that you don't have to transplant them if they are well mulched.

Spinach: Spinach cross-pollinates readily. If you want seeds to be true, grow only one species. The plant to save from is the last one to ripen. Cut the seed stalks after they reach full maturity, let them dry, and hull out the seeds.

Squash: Pick out the largest squash you want to save for seed and let vine-ripen. Then remove seeds, wash, making sure all pulp is removed, and set in a shallow dish of water for a day. Wash them again, removing any pulp that was left, pat them dry with clean towel and then let them dry near wood heat. When absolutely dry, store them in a tight glass container. Check once in a while to make sure no mold has started. Discard moldy seed.

Tomatoes: Let them vine-ripen to a slightly mushy stage. Remove seeds, wash, and set them in shallow dishes of water for two days until they get bubbly. Wash them again, pat dry in an old towel, and dry further by allowing to air-dry. When thoroughly dry, store them in a tight glass container and check them every so often to make sure no mold has started.

Turnips: Mulch heavily over the winter and uncover turnips in early spring. Collect seeds as for beets. Turnips are hardy enough so that you don't have to transplant them if they are well mulched.

Watermelon: Pick out your best watermelon–let it vine-ripen to a good size. Then remove the seeds. Wash, making sure all pulp is removed. Let seeds sit in shallow dish of water for one day. Wash again, pat dry between sheets of clean cotton toweling. When seeds are absolutely dry, store in a tight glass container. Check once in a while to make sure no mold has started.

Someday we may not be able to buy seed, and some of the old varieties are already extinct. There's no mystery to gathering your own seed except for the ever everlasting mystery of nature. Farming and gardening is truly the way to self-sufficiency and a better way of life.

How to Build a Root Cellar

Root cellars were a way of life for the early settlers. No winter was too harsh but that a tasty and nourishing meal could be collected from its earthy depths. Root cellars are very simple to build and well worth the effort. To begin, choose a south-facing bank if you live in northern climates, north-facing slopes if you live in the South. Choose your site where it is convenient and is easily accessible. In addition to storing fruits and vegetables, the cellar can be used 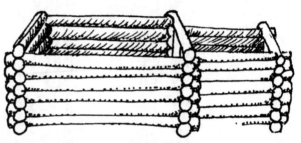 for emergency shelter in case of severe storms: tornadoes, hurricanes, etc. Storms will pass over a root cellar without doing damage because they are level with the ground. Cellars should be equipped with latches inside.

Dig a level-floored hole in the bank about 8 feet square plus a 4' x 8' entranceway. When the hole is ready, 6" x 6" log beams of wood or logs are stacked similar to a log cabin structure up to a height of 7 feet. Planks or gravel can be used for flooring. Bins and shelves can be built to suit your storage purposes before you build the roof. The roof consists of solid beams across the roof side by side. A vent is constructed of planks making a 10" x 10" chimney structure reaching from about 12 inches from the floor to about 3 feet above the ground and covered with an open tepee vent cover. This will help keep cool air at floor level allowing warm air to rise, keeping vegetables cool and dry. The roof beams are then covered with thick plastic sheeting (6 mm) before replacing four feet of dirt over the top and replanting the sod.

The front of the root cellar is constructed of the same solid beams used in the main walls and ceiling. Plumb in two two-by-fours vertically about 30 inches apart. These are used as guides for sawing two cuts on the wall for the inner door frame. When the two cuts are made, a 2' x 6' face plate (door frame) is nailed to the ends of the cut beams to hold them in place. They serve as a doorjamb against which the inner door will be attached.

The doors can be built of planking and a "Z" reinforcement. Frame them to fill the hole to about 1/4" from each edge: right, left, top and bottom. Insulate the door and cover the framework with plywood. The doorjamb may be insulated with sponge tape. This seals the door against drafts and light. The closing apparatus consists of two 1' x 4's sliding into a slots at the top and bottom of the door. This slot is at an angle to permit friction/lever closure.

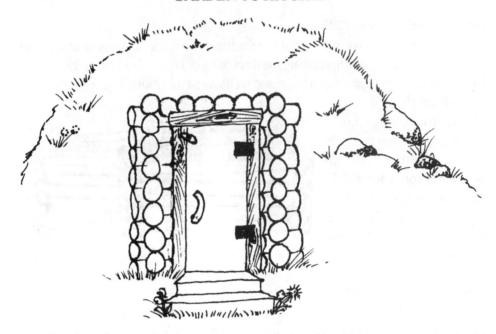

The entrance may be built using the same 6" x 6" beams or logs as in the main cellar. These beams should be 8 feet long, spiked to the main root cellar room, approximately 4' to 5' apart on either side of the inner door. These are stacked in the same manner as the main cellar room with a solid beam roof over the full 8 feet. This also is covered with 6 mil plastic and gently backfilled with dirt to insulate. In the construction of both the main room and the 4' x 8' entranceway, all corners should be lapped butt to joint. This is also true for the corners in the entranceway where the outer door is built in exactly the same manner as the inner door. This entranceway provides frost protection. In warmer climates the entranceway can be shorter.

Cautions: Store fruits and vegetables in separate cellars; apples can soon taste like potatoes if stored together! Root cellars are good hiding places, but **children should not play inside**. There is danger of being trapped and forgotten by their playmates. Before severe winter temperatures plummet, **plug the vent** with insulation to keep produce from freezing. Mice can do a great deal of damage in a short time; keep traps baited and set and a screen over the vents.

Planting a garden

There are many ways to plant a garden. One of the ways I recommend is the raised bed, double dig method. This is labor intensive, but will produce more food in less space, especially in hard packed soil. It is one way of keeping the topsoil "on top" while loosening the lower layers of dirt. To prepare such a bed, start at one end of the bed area and dig with a shovel or, better yet, a spade fork.

Push the fork into the ground the full length of the tines and lean back on the handle. This spadeful of surface dirt is then deposited at the opposite end of the bed. By sticking the fork into the bottom of the trench several times, you can loosen the soil in the second layer down. When this second layer of dirt (scoop number two forward) has been dug, it is placed in the first hole. Next, loosen the second layer down in hole number two. Continue this through the rest of the bed. This method loosens the soil to a two spade depth allowing the roots to go deeper and produce healthier plants. Be careful to replace dirt in their proper layer, and approximately their same position, with the topsoil on top, the subsurface soil in the bottom of the bed. Following the instructions on the package, or on spacing charts (next page), plant seeds or bedding plants a consistent distance in all directions.

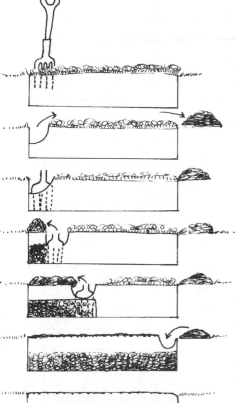

Spread a layer of compost over entire area to be dug.

Remove soil from upper part of first trench and place at far end of bed.

Loosen soil an additional 12".

Dig out upper part of second trench and throw forward into upper, open part of first trench. Loosen lower part of second trench.

Continue "double-digging" process (repeating step 4) for remaining trenches.

Place soil in mound at end of bed into open, upper of last trench.

The completed "double-dig" bed.

If you have plenty of garden space and the demand for food is not as high, planting in rows is much less demanding of your time in early spring. Rototillers cultivate approximately 4 to 6 inches below the surface, so if you are growing a crop that needs root room, you may want to loosen the soil a little deeper with your spade fork.

When you locate your new garden, use only soil that has not had commercial fertilizers or insecticides sprayed on it. The row method works especially well in new soil; root crops really reward first year gardeners.

To begin a row garden, use a string (small gauge nylon cord) fastened to two stakes. Press the stake into the ground at the beginning of the row, then walk the length of the row and press the second stake into the ground at the end of the row.

Necessary Spacing for Planting

Vegetable	Spacing (in inches)
Asparagus	11-17
Beans (green)	3-5
Beans (lima)	3-8
Beets	1-5
Broccoli	14-17
Brussels sprouts	14-17
Cabbage	14-17
Carrots	1-2
Cauliflower	14-17
Celery	5-8
Collards	11-14
Corn	17
Cucumbers	17-35
Eggplant	17-23
Garlic	14-17
Kale	1-5
Leeks	1-5
Lettuce (head)	9-11
Lettuce (leaf)	5-8
Melons	23-35
Okra	11-17
Onions (bulb)	3-5
Onions (bunching)	1-2
Parsnips	3-5
Peas	1-5
Peppers	11-14
Potatoes	12
Pumpkins	23-35
Radishes	1-2
Rhubarb	23-35
Spinach	3-5
Squash (summer)	23-35
Squash (winter)	23-35
Tomatoes	17-23
Turnips	3-5

Three feet is a handy measurement to lay out rows which will be tilled between. Two feet of width is plenty of space between the rows of a hand-hoed garden.

Just a few tips on planting once you have chosen a method. Potatoes have to be cut so that at least one "eye" appears on every piece of potato you plant. Plant about 12 inches apart. For carrots and other root vegetables plant seeds 2 inches apart. This is hard to do, so you will have to thin them later as they tend to come up much too thick to allow for proper maturation. Keep your garden soil loose and free of weeds, but don't forget to enjoy it!

"Brethren, when you take time to cultivate your garden, thus gaining the exercise needed to keep the system in good working order, you are just as much doing the work of God as in holding meetings" (Gospel Workers, p. 240).

The Gardener's Prayer

The kiss of the sun for pardon,
The song of the birds for mirth.
One is nearer God's heart in the garden
Than anywhere else on earth.

-Dorothy Frances Gurney

How Much to Grow?

No matter how well you plan, some foods will grow better than you might expect resulting in an abundance. Some may not grow quite as well as you may have hoped. Every day brings a new surprise from your garden. Make a habit of bringing at least a little something, if only a parsley garnish, from your garden to your kitchen every day. Not only will you realize that the food budget has been stretched but you will find your family asking, "Did we grow this ourselves?" Garden treats often tempt even the most finicky into eating more healthfully.

Planning meals around garden produce is a rewarding challenge. How much should you plant of each variety? Since you have chosen your property with the idea of growing your food, you want to prepare your garden considering what you want to harvest.

Most gardens grow certain plants better than others. Climate dictates some of the limitations you may experience. Ask the advice of some gardeners in your area if you are unfamiliar with frost patterns, but do not fear to experiment. Most of North America will grow everything we need. Your family's preferences may dictate that you grow more peas or less tomatoes than another family, but learning to live from the garden is a rewarding experience for the whole family.

Calculating how to grow enough food for your family from your own garden is a developing experience—allow for a few visitors as well as emergencies. For the sake of illustration, we will assume you live in a fairly severe climate, such as we experience here in northern British Columbia. Grow as many items on the following list as possible. Store the remainder in bulk. Planning a year-long menu is a challenge, but let's project some approximate needs for a family of about eight:

A Year's Supply for a Family of Eight

1. Fruit
>Apples.. 400-500 lb.
>Berries... 300 qt.
>Others as available in your climate.

2. Grains
>Wheat.. 1,200 lb.
>Brown Rice... 100 lb.
>Oats.. 225 lb.
>Barley... 150 lb.
>Rye... 100 lb.
>Flax.. 50 lb.
>Millet... 200 lb.

3. Herbs—Grow the ones you like best for flavorings, teas, and remedies. Many of these are perennials (grow every year without replanting, even in northern climates).

4. Legumes
>Kidney or Pinto Beans.. 75 lb.
>Other Dry Beans... 50 lb.
>Peas (dried, split)... 25 lb.

6. Vegetables
>A. Root Cellar (Plan on a 10 percent loss)
>>Potatoes... 500 lb.
>>Soybeans.. 100 lb.
>>Lentils (sprouting or cooking)............................. 20 lb.
>>Shelled Raw Peanuts.. 100 lb.

5. Seeds
>Alfalfa.. 20 lb.
>Sunflower... 75 lb.
>Radish, Broccoli, Mung Beans, etc...................... 20 lb.

Beets..100 lb.
Cabbage...50 heads
Carrots...500 lb.
Onions..200 lb.
Garlic...15 lb.
Parsnips..100 lb.
Squash..50 lb.

B. Canned Vegetables (Be careful to process 45 minutes)
Tomatoes..400 qt.
Green Beans..200 qt.
Greens...100 qt.
Corn (150 lb. dried)..100 qt.
Peas...100 qt.

Preserving Food

Canning Preparations

1. Clean and peel the fruits and/or vegetables. Peaches and tomatoes may be scalded in boiling water for one minute to more easily remove skins.
2. Wash jars in hot, soapy water, rinse, and set out to drain.
3. Pack food firmly into quart jars.
4. Add 2 to 3 tablespoons of sugar or other sweetener per quart of fruit. In place of sugar, apple juice or pineapple juice may be used. For vegetables use 1 teaspoon of salt per quart.
5. Fill jars with hot water or juice, leaving about one inch of space from the top.
6. Wipe jar rims clean.
7. Cover with warmed lids and twist ring firmly into place.
8. Invert gently back and forth until sweetening or salt no longer settles out.

Water Bath Method

In this method, the packed quart jars are placed in a large canner and barely covered with cool water (hot water will crack your jars, so always pour off enough boiling water from the last batch and add some cold water to the boiler). A rack should be placed in the bottom of the boiler so that the jars do not touch the bottom. Place the lid on the canner. Bring the canner to a rolling boil (this takes 15-20 minutes, depending on the intensity of your heat source). Maintain a rolling boil for 20 minutes when canning quarts of fruit, 30 minutes for two-quart jars. Jars will break if heat is too intense. For vegetables maintain a rolling boil for 45 minutes on quart jars. Canning two-quart jars of vegetables is not recommended.

Pressure Cooking Method

The pressure cooking method is the best way to can vegetables. Vegetable canning temperatures must reach 212° F in order to deactivate a toxin that causes food poisoning. Follow the directions that come with your specific pressure canner regarding the length of time and proper weight (10-15 lb.) on the pressure valve. By adding pressure, you can attain temperatures of 240° F. **Take care to follow the directions that come with your pressure cooker to avoid accidents. Never open a pressure canner until it has cooled and released its pressure.**

Always check your jars to be sure they are sealed before storing them. Refrigerate unsealed jars and use them the next day or reprocess them in another batch, using a new lid. Date your jars. Nothing will warm your heart quite like the beauty of your colorful rows of these summer memories throughout the cold winter months. Here's a colorful idea for using garden leftovers:

"Summer Rainbows"

Collect and wash your small or late vegetables from the garden: potatoes, carrots, onions, tomatoes, peas, beans, corn, celery, garlic—anything that is a little small for storage in the root cellar. Chop vegetables as for stew, filling several large serving bowls with a different type of vegetable. Layer the produce into several clean canning jars, contrasting colors against each other into a tasty, healthy and colorful instant winter stew. You may wish to add a clove or two of garlic to each quart along with a half teaspoon of salt. Process jars of stew the same as for vegetables, 45 minutes in hot water bath or 15 minutes at 15 pounds of pressure. When ready to serve, heat to boiling point and add flour or cornstarch dissolved in cold water to thicken it after it comes to a boil. Serve Summer Rainbow Stew hot with homemade crackers. These colorful jars look especially beautiful lined up on your pantry shelves. It is the ideal fast food on a cold winter's day.

Serving

After opening, always boil home-canned vegetables for at least 5 minutes before serving; this will deactivate the toxin that causes food poisoning. Be especially careful of high-protein and low-acid foods: gluten, beans, beets. Refrigerate leftovers immediately in shallow cooking pans, quart jars, or containers that will cool quickly and not culture bacterial growth.

Drying Foods

Don't overlook this simple method of food preservation. It takes a little planning. A drying rack is very easily made out of framed screen, suspended by a ¼ inch rope from the ceiling above your heating stove or cook stove. This is good for drying everything from apples, bananas, tomatoes, and celery, to herbs for tea and flavorings. Slice fruits thin and allow them to dry thoroughly. Herbs such as dill, mint, basil, et cetera, can be picked as a bouquet, washed, and hung outside in the sun and wind to dry. Store dried foods in large glass jars or plastic bags in a cool, dark area. A sheet of lightweight plastic draped over the food will prevent it 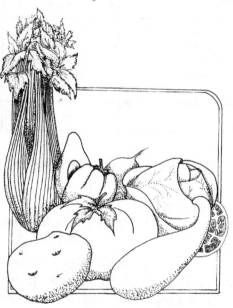 getting dusty while drying. Food may also be sun dried during hot weather.

Root Cellar Storage

Beets, carrots, potatoes, turnips, rutabagas, parsnips, can all be wintered successfully in the root cellar. Storage cabbage (tight heads) will keep well if hung by the root from the ceiling of the root cellar. Store fruit in a separate cellar or your apples will taste like potatoes! I recently visited a friend who kept his carrots in plastic 5 gallon buckets without sand or any other material. The carrots were nice and crisp after winter storage.

Vegetable Storage

Crop	Place	Humidity	Period
Cabbage	root cellar	dry	All winter
Cauliflower	root cellar	dry	3-4 months
Celery	roots in soil	dry	6-8 weeks
Onions	hung, in cool dry place	dry	fall and winter
Parsnips	basement	dry	fall and winter
Potatoes	root cellar	dry	several months
Pumpkins/Squash	cellar or basement	moderately dry	fall and winter
Carrots, Beets	root cellar in sand	dry	fall and winter

Harvest and Preparation of Common Vegetables

Artichokes

When Harvesting: Look for plump globes that are compact with fresh, green inner leaves.

To Prepare: Remove any discolored leaves and the small leaves at the base of the artichoke. Trim stem off, even with the base of the artichoke. Cutting straight across, slice 1 inch off top and discard top. Snip off points of the remaining leaves. Rinse artichoke in cold water. To prevent discoloration, invert in cold water with small amount of lemon juice.

To Boil: Heat 6 quarts of water to boiling in large kettle with 2 tablespoons of lemon juice and a clove of garlic which has been cut into fourths. Add artichokes. Simmer uncovered 30-40 minutes, rotating occasionally, until leaves pull out easily and bottom is tender when pierced. Remove artichokes carefully with tongs or two large spoons and place upside down to drain.

To Steam: Place steamer basket in ½ inch of water. Water should not touch the bottom of the basket. Place the artichokes in the basket. Cover tightly and heat to boiling; reduce heat. Steam 20-25 minutes or until the bottom of the artichoke is tender when pierced.

Asparagus

When Harvesting: Look for smooth, round, tender, medium-sized green spears with closed tips.

To Prepare: Break off tender ends where they snap easily. Wash asparagus; remove scales if sandy or tough. Remove sand particles with a vegetable brush if necessary. Asparagus may be cooked in spears or pieces.

To Boil: Place asparagus in 2 inches of boiling water. Boil uncovered for 5 minutes. Cover and boil 7-10 minutes longer or until stalk ends are crisp-tender; drain. Serve immediately. Asparagus may also be canned.

To Steam: Place steamer basket in ½ inch of water. Water should not touch the bottom of the basket. Place asparagus in basket. Cover tightly and heat to boiling; reduce heat. Steam 6-8 minutes or until crisp-tender.

Beans, Green and Wax

When Harvesting: Look for bright, smooth, crisp pods. Just-picked beans are crisp and velvety.

To Prepare: Wash beans and remove ends. Leave beans whole or snap into smaller pieces.

To Boil: Place beans in 1 inch of water, salted if desired. Heat to boiling; reduce heat. Boil uncovered 5 minutes. Cover and boil 5-10 minutes longer or until crisp-tender; drain.

To Steam: Place steamer basket in ½ inch of water. Water should not touch the bottom of the basket. Place beans in basket. Cover tightly and heat to boiling; reduce heat. Steam 10-12 minutes or until crisp-tender.

Beans, Lima

When Harvesting: Look for broad, thick, shiny pods that are plump with seeds.

To Prepare: Shell lima beans just before cooking. To shell beans, remove thin outer edge of pod with sharp knife. Slip out beans.

To Boil: Heat 1 inch of water, salted if desired, to boiling. Add beans. Heat to boiling; reduce heat. Boil uncovered 5 minutes. Cover and boil 15-20 minutes longer or until tender; drain.

Beets

When Harvesting: Dig with fingers around top of plant; if beet is large (more than 2 inches in diameter) it is ready for harvest. Store large beets in root cellar. Can smaller beets, as they do not store well.

To Prepare: Cut off all but 1 inch of beet tops. Wash beets; leave whole with root ends attached. Do not cut the skin in any way, or you will lose color and nutrition.

To Boil: Heat 6 cups water, salted if desired, to boiling. Add beets. Cover and heat to boiling; reduce heat. Boil 40-50 minutes or until tender; drain. Run cold water over beets; slip off skins and remove root ends. Slice, dice, or cut into julienne strips.

To Steam: Place steamer basket in ½ inch of water. Water should not touch the bottom of the basket. Place beets in basket. Cover tightly and heat to boiling; reduce heat. Steam 45-50 minutes or until tender. Add boiling water during the steaming process if necessary. Run cold water over beets; slip off skins and remove root ends. Slice, dice, or cut into julienne strips.

Broccoli

When Harvesting: Look for firm, compact dark green clusters. Cut or break clusters from plant. Most broccoli will continue to sprout tender heads through the summer, but the largest heads will be first.

To Prepare: Wash broccoli; peel if desired. Cut into pieces of desired size.

To Boil: Heat 1 inch of water, salted if desired, to boiling. Add broccoli. Cover and heat to boiling; reduce heat. Boil 10-12 minutes or until crisp-tender; drain.

To Steam: Place steamer basket in ½ inch of water. Water should not touch the bottom of the basket. Place broccoli in basket. Cover tightly and heat to boiling; reduce heat. Steam 10-11 minutes or until stems are crisp-tender.

Brussels Sprouts

When Harvesting: Wait until the heads are well formed, removing leaves to give the heads enough space to form. Look for unblemished, bright green sprouts with compact leaves.

To Prepare: Remove any discolored leaves; cut off stem ends. Watch for worms. Wash sprouts; cut large ones in half.

To Boil: Heat 1 inch of water, salted if desired, to boiling. Add Brussels sprouts. Cover and heat to boiling; reduce heat. Boil 8-10 minutes or until tender; drain.

To Steam: Place steamer basket in ½ inch of water. Water should not touch the bottom of the basket. Place Brussels sprouts in basket. Cover tightly and heat to boiling; reduce heat. Steam 20-25 minutes or until tender. Serve immediately.

Cabbage, Red and Green

When Harvesting: Look for firm heads. Depending on variety, most outer leaves should have good color. Cut head from plant at base unless storing in root cellar, at which time the cabbage is pulled and hung by the root. A good storage variety will keep all winter.

To Prepare: Remove outside leaves. Wash cabbage; cut into 4 wedges. Trim core to within ¼ inch of leaves, or shred cabbage to the core. Core may be peeled and used in stir fry as a replacement for water chestnuts.

To Boil: (wedges) Heat 1 inch of water, salted if desired, to boiling. Add cabbage. Cover and heat to boiling; reduce heat. Boil 10-17 minutes, turning wedges once, until crisp-tender; drain.

(Shredded): Heat ½ inch of water, salted if desired, to boiling. Add cabbage. Cover and heat to boiling; reduce heat. Boil 5-8 minutes or until crisp-tender; drain.

To Steam: (wedges) Place steamer basket in ½ inch of water. Water should not touch the bottom of the basket. Place cabbage in basket. Cover tightly and heat to boiling; reduce heat. Steam 18-24 minutes or until crisp-tender.

(Shredded): Place steamer basket in ½ inch of water. Water should not touch the bottom of the basket. Place cabbage in basket. Cover tightly and heat to boiling; reduce heat. Steam 5-7 minutes or until crisp-tender.

Sauerkraut: Finely shred 5 pounds cabbage into an earthen crock. Sprinkle with 3 tablespoons of non-iodized salt. Mash the cabbage, with a potato masher or wooden mallet, until it begins to form juice. Add layers of shredded cabbage generously sprinkled with salt in the same way until crock is full. Put a plate with a weight (a large clean rock) on top of the crock to keep cabbage submerged in the brine. Drape the crock with plastic: this prevents odors coming out and dust getting into your crock. Let set 5-6 weeks in a cool place. Pack into quart jars and process for 20 minutes. Note: kraut will not "work" in plastic buckets or with iodized salt.

Carrots

When Harvesting: Loosen the sides of the dirt with a garden fork and move the carrots from side to side until they pull easily from the ground. Clip tops if storing in root cellar. Carrots are delicious canned as pickles.

To Prepare: Pare carrots thinly and remove ends. Leave carrots whole, shred, or cut into julienne strips crosswise into ¼ inch slices.

To Boil: Heat 1 inch of water to boiling, salted if desired. Add carrots. Cover and heat to boiling; reduce heat. Boil whole carrots 25 minutes, shredded 5 minutes, julienne strips 18-20 minutes, slices 12-15 minutes or until tender; drain.

To Steam: Place steamer basket in ½ inch of water. Water should not touch the bottom of the basket. Place carrots (slender whole or slices) in basket. Cover tightly and heat to boiling; reduce heat. Steam whole carrots 12-15 minutes, slices 9-11 minutes or until tender. Serve hot.

Cauliflower
When Harvesting: Cut cauliflower head from plant at base.

To Prepare: Remove outer leaves and stalk; cut off any discoloration. Wash cauliflower. Leave whole, cutting cone-shaped center from core, or separate into flowerets.

To Boil: Heat 1 inch of water, salted if desired, to boiling. Add cauliflower, cover, heat to boiling, then reduce heat. Boil whole cauliflower 20-25 minutes, flowerets 10-12 minutes or until tender; drain.

To Steam: Place steamer basket in ½ inch of water. Water should not touch the bottom of the basket. Place cauliflower in basket. Cover tightly and heat to boiling; reduce heat. Steam whole cauliflower 18-22 minutes, flowerets 6-8 minutes or until tender.

Celery
Celery can be harvested at any stage for flavoring stir-fry, soups, patties, roasts, or fresh celery sticks. Simply wash and cut off root ends. Add to favorite recipe as instructed. Your garden celery may not mature as large as the grocery variety, but has the same amount of flavor. You may encourage a milder flavor and a larger plant by keeping celery "bound" with newspaper as it matures.

Corn
When Harvesting: Look for bright green, tight-fitting husks, peel husk back to see if ear is filled out. Ears will generally be filled to the tip when ready to eat. Corn may be hung to dry for long term storage as soon as it is ripe.

To Prepare: Corn is best when eaten as soon after picking as possible. Husk ears and remove silk just before cooking. (Husks can be used in making tamales.)

To Boil: Place corn in enough unsalted cold water to cover. (Salt toughens corn). Heat to boiling. Boil uncovered 2 minutes; remove from heat. Let stand uncovered 10 minutes before serving.

To Steam: Place steamer basket in ½ inch of water. Water should not touch the bottom of the basket. Place corn in basket. Cover tightly and heat to boiling; reduce heat. Steam 6-9 minutes or until tender.

Eggplant
When Harvesting: Look for smooth, glossy taut-skinned eggplant.

To Prepare: Just before cooking, wash eggplant; pare if desired. Cut eggplant into ½ inch cubes or ¼ inch slices.

To Boil: Heat small amount of water, salted if desired, to boiling. Add eggplant. Cover and heat to boiling; reduce heat. Boil 5-8 minutes or until tender; drain.

To Sauté: Heat 3-4 tablespoons of oil in 10-inch skillet over medium-high heat. Sauté eggplant 5-10 minutes or until tender.

To Steam: Place steamer basket in ½ inch of water. Water should not touch the bottom of the basket. Place eggplant in basket. Cover tightly and heat to boiling; reduce heat. Steam 5-7 minutes or until tender.

Greens: Beet, Chicory, Collards, Escarole, Kale, Lamb's Quarters, Mustard, Spinach, Swiss Chard, or Turnip.

When Harvesting: Look for tender, young leaves of bright green color.

To Prepare: Remove root ends and imperfect leaves. Wash **several times** in water, lifting out each time to inspect for dirt particles; curly varieties need more intense rinsing.

To Boil: Cover with a lid and cook with just the water that clings to the leaves until tender: beet tops 5-15 minutes; chicory, escarole, mustard and Swiss chard, 15-20 minutes; collards 10-15 minutes; spinach 3-10 minutes; kale and turnip greens 15-25 minutes; drain.

Kohlrabi

When harvesting: Look for the bulb forming above the ground. Harvest when bulb is 2-4 inches in size for best taste. Large ones tend to be woody.

To Prepare: Eat raw in stick form.

To freeze: cut in half-inch cubes, boil 15-20 minutes, place in freezer bags.

To Cook: Place steamer basket in half-inch of water. Cover with lid. Steam 15-20 minutes. May be boiled in salted water same as potatoes, turnips, carrots.

Leeks

When Harvesting: Look for white bulbs with pliable, crisp green tops. Bulbs less than 1½ inches in diameter are the most tender.

To Prepare: Remove green tops to within 2 inches of white part (reserve greens for soup or stew). Peel outside layer of bulbs. Wash leeks several times in cold water; drain. Cut large leeks lengthwise into fourths. Leeks are most often used as flavorings for roasts, soups, etc., but can be eaten as a cooked vegetable.

To Boil: Heat 1 inch of water, salted if desired, to boiling. Add leeks. Cover and heat to boiling; reduce heat. Boil 12-15 minutes or until tender; drain.

To Steam: Place steamer basket in ½ inch of water. Water should not touch the bottom of the basket. Place leeks in basket. Cover tightly and heat to boiling; reduce heat. Steam 13-15 minutes or until tender. Serve hot.

Lettuce

Wash and prepare fresh in salads. When storing leftover salad, rinse it with cold water, let drain as dry as possible, and place in an airtight container to keep it fresh for one day. This prevents oxidation and browning of leaves. Romaine lettuce is best kept fresh by separating the leaves, washing each and patting dry. Place dry leaves side by side on a dry dishtowel, roll firmly, refrigerate until ready to use.

Mushrooms

When Harvesting: Look for creamy white to light-brown caps, closed around the stems; if slightly open, gill should be light pink or tan. Know your mushrooms! **Never eat any mushroom which you cannot identify.**

To Prepare: Depending on variety, brush off dirt or peel as necessary or rinse mushrooms and trim off stem ends. Cut into ¼ inch slices if desired.

To Sauté: Heat 2 tablespoons of oil in 10-inch skillet over medium-high heat. Roll mushrooms in breading meal. Sauté mushrooms 6-8 minutes or until tender.

To Steam: Place steamer basket in ½ inch of water. Water should not touch the bottom of the basket. Place medium-sized whole mushrooms or pieces in basket. Cover tightly and heat to boiling; reduce heat. Steam 6-8 minutes or until tender.

Okra

When Harvesting: Look for tender, unblemished, bright green pods, less than 4 inches long.

To Prepare: Wash okra; remove ends and cut into ½ inch slices.

To Boil: Heat 1 inch of water, salted if desired, to boiling. Add okra. Cover and heat to boiling; reduce heat. Boil about 10 minutes or until tender; drain.

To Steam: Place steamer basket in ½ inch of water. Water should not touch the bottom of the basket. Place whole okra in basket. Cover tightly and heat to boiling; reduce heat. Steam 6-8 minutes or until tender.

To Fry: Roll in breading meal and brown for 5 minutes. Cover with lid and cook on low heat until tender.

Onions: White, Yellow, or Red

When Harvesting: Late summer, early fall or first frost, onions can be dug with a spade fork or pulled up by the tops.

To Prepare: Peel onions in cold water to help prevent eyes from watering.

To Boil: Heat several inches of water, salted if desired, to boiling. Add onions. Cover and heat to boiling; reduce heat. Boil small onions 15-20 minutes, large onions 30-35 minutes or until tender; drain.

To Sauté: Cut onions into ¼ inch slices. Heat 3-4 tablespoons margarine, butter, olive, or vegetable oil in 10-inch skillet over medium-high heat. Sauté onions 6-9 minutes or until tender. Serve as garnish over roasts, patties, mushrooms, etc.

To Steam: Place steamer basket in ½ inch of water. Water should not touch the bottom of the basket. Place small white onions in basket. Cover tightly and heat to boiling; reduce heat. Steam 15-20 minutes or until tender.

Onions may be used fresh in green salads, potato salads, and more.

Parsnips

When Harvesting: With a spade fork, dig as you would carrots. Late in the season, after first frost.

To Prepare: Scrape or pare. Leave whole or cut in half, fourths, ¼ inch slices or strips.

To Boil: Heat 1 inch of water, salted if desired, to boiling. Add parsnips. Cover and heat to boiling; reduce heat. Boil whole parsnips or halves 15-20 minutes, slices or strips 7-9 minutes or until tender; drain.

To Steam: Place steamer basket in ½ inch of water. Water should not touch the bottom of the basket. Place parsnips (whole or slices) in basket. Cover tightly and heat to boiling; reduce heat. Steam whole parsnips 20-25 minutes, slices 8-10 minutes or until tender.

Peas, Green

When Harvesting: Look for plump, tender, bright-green pods.

To Prepare: Wash and shell peas just before cooking.

To Boil: Heat 1 inch of water, salted if desired, to boiling. Add peas. Boil uncovered 5 minutes. Cover and boil 3-5 minutes longer or until tender. Drain.

To Steam: Place steamer basket in ½ inch of water. Water should not touch the bottom of the basket. Place peas in basket. Cover tightly and heat to boiling; reduce heat. Steam 10-12 minutes or until tender.

Sugar peas may be eaten fresh, whole.

Peppers, Bell

When Harvesting: Look for well-shaped, shiny, bright-colored peppers with firm sides.

To Prepare: Wash peppers; remove stems, seeds, and membranes. Leave whole to stuff and bake, cut into thin slices or rings to use fresh, chop for seasoning in salads.

To Sauté: Heat 1-2 tablespoons of margarine or oil in 10-inch skillet over medium-high heat. Sauté slices or rings 3-5 minutes or until crisp-tender.

To Steam: Place steamer basket in ½ inch of water. Water should not touch the bottom of the basket. Place peppers in basket. Cover tightly and heat to boiling; reduce heat. Steam 8-10 minutes or until tender.

Potatoes, Small New

When Harvesting: Dig with a spade fork.

To Prepare: Wash potatoes; do not peel.

To Boil: Heat 1 inch of water, salted if desired, to boiling. Add potatoes. Cover and heat to boiling; reduce heat. Boil slowly 20-25 minutes or until tender; drain.

To Steam: Place steamer basket in ½ inch of water. Water should not touch the bottom of the basket. Place potatoes in basket. Cover tightly and heat to boiling; reduce heat. Steam 18-22 minutes or until tender.

Potatoes

When Harvesting: First frost will kill the vines. Dig with a spade fork. Allow to air dry for several hours, put in burlap bags for root cellar storage. This procedure can be followed for any species of potato: reds often keep longer than the white varieties.

To Prepare for boiling: Scrub potatoes. Leave skins on whenever possible, or pare thinly and remove eyes. Leave whole or cut into large pieces.

To Prepare for baking: Scrub potatoes. Pierce with fork to allow steam to escape. To save time, potatoes may be cut in half and baked on cookie sheet.

To Boil: Heat 1 inch of water, salted if desired, to boiling. Add potatoes. Cover and heat to boiling; reduce heat. Boil whole potatoes 30-35 minutes, pieces 20-25 minutes or until tender; drain.

To Bake: Bake 350° F oven for 1 hour.

To Steam: Place steamer basket in ¾ inches of water. Water should not touch the bottom of the basket. Place whole potatoes in basket. Cover tightly and heat to boiling; reduce heat. Steam 30-35 minutes or until tender.

Rutabagas

When Harvesting: After first frost, dig with spade fork. If tops are green, they may be eaten, prepared like spinach. Rutabagas may be kept in a root cellar over winter.

To Prepare: Wash rutabagas; pare thinly. Cut into ½ inch cubes or 2 inch pieces.

To Boil: Heat 1 inch of water, salted if desired, to boiling. Add rutabagas. Cover and heat to boiling; reduce heat. Boil cubes 20-25 minutes, pieces 30-40 minutes or until tender; drain.

To Steam: Place steamer basket in ½ inch of water. Water should not touch the bottom of the basket. Place rutabaga cubes in basket. Cover tightly and heat to boiling; reduce heat. Steam 25-28 minutes or until tender.

May also be served raw.

Squash, Winter: Acorn, Buttercup, Butternut, or Spaghetti

When Harvesting: These may be gathered through the summer. Some varieties will keep well in the root cellar for two or three months.

To Prepare: Wash squash. For boiling, pare squash if desired; cut into 1 inch slices or cubes. Or, cut each squash lengthwise in half; remove seeds and fibers.

To Bake: Place squash halves in ungreased rectangular baking dish. Sprinkle cut sides with salt. Cover and bake in 400° F oven 30-40 minutes, or a 350° F oven about 40 minutes, in 325° F oven about 45 minutes or until tender. For spaghetti squash, remove strands with two forks, serve with spaghetti sauce.

To Boil (for large squash): Heat 1 inch of water, salted if desired, to boiling, then add squash (sliced, peeled, or cubed). Cover and heat to boiling; reduce heat. Boil 15-20 minutes or until tender; drain. Remove peeling if desired and reheat before serving.

To Steam: Place steamer basket in ½ inch of water. Water should not touch the bottom of the basket. Place squash (slices or cubes) in basket. Cover tightly and heat to boiling; reduce heat. Steam slices 12-15 minutes, cubes 7-10 minutes or until tender.

Squash, Summer: Chayote, Crookneck, Pattypan, Straightneck, or Zucchini

When Harvesting: These may be gathered through the summer. Smaller zucchini and crookneck are more tender than the larger squash.

To Prepare: Wash squash; remove stem and blossom ends but do not pare. If squash are small, cut in half. For larger squash, cut into ½ inch slices or cubes.

To Boil: Heat 1 inch of water, salted if desired, to boiling. Add squash. Cover and heat to boiling; reduce heat. Boil slices 5-10 minutes, cubes 3-6 minutes or until tender; drain.

To Steam: Place steamer basket in ½ inch of water. Water should not touch the bottom of the basket. Place squash (slices or cubes) in basket. Cover tightly and heat to boiling; reduce heat. Steam 5-7 minutes or until tender.

To Bake: Slice thinly, roll in savory breading meal, place on oiled cookie sheet. Bake at 375° F for 15 minutes on each side, until golden and crispy.

To Sauté: Chop onions, peppers and zucchini or crookneck squash and sauté together with a little oil until tender. Serve hot.

Tomatoes

When Harvesting: Look for nicely ripened, well-shaped tomatoes. Fully ripe tomatoes should be slightly soft but not mushy. Most varieties have a rich red color when ripe.

To Prepare: Wash tomatoes; cut into 8 wedges or ½ inch slices. Peel tomatoes before cutting if desired. To remove skin easily for canning, dip tomato into boiling water for 30 seconds, then plunge into cold water.

To Eat: Tomatoes are delicious raw, and very high in vitamin C. They may be sliced for sandwiches, diced for salads or cubed finely for fresh salsa (see recipe section). They may also be canned in a variety of ways.

Turnips

When Harvesting: Dig with spade fork, remove tops. Store in root cellar. If tops are green, they may be eaten, prepared like spinach.

To Prepare: Cut off tops. Wash turnips; pare thinly. Leave whole or cut into ½ inch pieces.

To Boil: Heat 1 inch of water, salted if desired, to boiling. Add turnips. Cover and heat to boiling; reduce heat. Boil whole turnips 25-30 minutes, pieces 15-20 minutes or until tender; drain.

To Steam: Place steamer basket in ½ inch of water. Water should not touch the bottom of the basket. Place turnip pieces in basket. Cover tightly and heat to boiling; reduce heat. Steam 15-20 minutes or until tender.

Turnips are also very good eaten as a raw vegetable.

Legumes: The Key to Complete Protein

Legumes grow in pod form and are often dried. They should be soaked, covered with water overnight, before cooking. Season as desired. There are many good recipes available for cooking beans. With the exception of lentils, all legumes should be boiled uncovered for a couple of minutes, with the first water drained off before cooking; this boiling period destroys the enzyme that causes illness in some people who feel they are allergic to beans. Some folks are surprised when their legumes triple in volume when they are soaked! Common legumes include: split peas, peanuts, lentils and all kinds of beans–lima, pinto, great northern, navy, kidney, soy, garbanzo, and black.

A vegetarian meal is more properly balanced if a legume is present. Eat at least one serving of any legume per day with any whole grain. This combination makes a complete protein.

Doctors Agatha and Calvin Thrash, in their book <u>Nutrition for Vegetarians</u>, address the challenge of a complete protein in the vegetarian diet: "In certain selected areas there are isolated traditions involving food items such as breads, pastas, food combinations, etc. These combinations either enhance or reduce the quality of food served on the table. Every ethnic group has a traditional legume/ grain combination. Orientals have rice and soybeans. Latins have tortillas and frijoles. Indians have chapatis and garbanzos. Americans have the peanut butter sandwich. Surely this wisdom about the desirability of combining legumes and grains came to the world through Inspiration to be a blessing to mankind before the science of nutrition had sufficiently developed to recognize the need for balancing amino acids." It is highly recommended that unless you eat your grains as sprouts, that they be thoroughly cooked.

Basic Grain Preparation

Grain	Water	Salt	Cooking Time
1 c. Barley	4 c.	½ t.	45 minutes
1 c. Brown Rice	2 ¾ c.	¼ t	50 minutes
1 c. Cornmeal	4 c.	1 t.	30 minutes
1 c. Millet	4 c.	1 t.	1 hour
1 c. Oats	3 c.	1 t.	30 minutes
1 c. Quinoa	2 c.	½ t.	15 minutes
1 c. Wheat	4 c.	½ t.	45 minutes
1 c. White Rice	2 ¼ t.	¼ t.	20 minutes

Simple Eating Plan

"Grains, fruits, nuts, and vegetables constitute the diet chosen for us by our Creator" (The Ministry of Healing, p. 296).

Once, not so long ago, there were no supermarkets, no oil refineries, no cars and trucks, and no gas stations. Life was quiet with the exception of bird songs, the clopping of horses hooves, and the squeak of a wagon wheel. When great-grandma made dinner, she didn't go to the freezer to get prepared meat substitutes or frozen mixed vegetables. She never added hot water to powder to create mashed potatoes; nor did she ever mix up a package of instant pudding for dessert. When she ran out of peanut butter, she didn't hop in the car and putt down to the local grocery store. She had to "make do" and wait until great-grandpa was ready to go to the city to bring back supplies. She went to the garden, root cellar, or the barn. But this never kept her from putting together a feast. Home cooking is one of the best parts of the "good old days."

The hub of the home was the kitchen and its hearth; living out of the orchard and garden required effort and planning. The time is coming when we will again be unable to buy from the supermarkets for there is a time prophesied when no man can buy or sell unless they compromise God's ideals and accept the mark of the beast. We will have to know how to prepare healthy meals in a simple way right from the garden.

Great-grandma juggled her time and talent between garden and kitchen with a skill that would leave most of us standing in awe. It was her way of life, so she did not consider it a hardship. It was all she had known, and the bigger the garden the more blessings she was able to share with her family and friends. Living from the garden was expected, but not taken for granted. Even very little girls were taught how to gather produce and peel potatoes and apples in those "good old days."

James and Ellen White's home was a very busy one. Ellen greatly valued her cook and has passed down a few words of encouragement to those who are skilled or seek to become knowledgeable in food preparation.

"Cooking may be regarded as less desirable than some other lines of work, but in reality it is a science in value above all other sciences. ... The one who understands the art of properly preparing food, and who uses this knowledge, is worthy of higher commendation than those who engage in any other line of work. This talent should be regarded as equal to ten talents; for its right use has much to do with keeping the human organism in health. ...it is the most valuable of all gifts" (<u>Counsels on Diet and Foods</u>, p. 251).

Cooking With Wood

My wife has learned the art of cooking on a wood cook stove, and, though she may claim to have once been totally without knowledge, she still laughs about one student's first attempt. Several of the girls who had previously helped her with the meals seemed to take quite naturally to their country kitchen duties. A few, however, had no knowledge of where food came from or how to prepare it; one girl had never been allowed in the kitchen and could not even use a can opener! One newcomer exuded an air of efficiency in the kitchen, so she was left to prepare scalloped potatoes, tripling the batch according to the recipe, for the 14 people eating in our home. My wife returned to reading her students' English papers and tending our then 3-year-old son, but was jolted to attention when the strong smell of smoke drifted through the house. Her terror melted into amusement when she opened the door from whence the smoke billowed. Her helper had built the fire in the oven instead of the firebox!

What is amusing today may be of grave consequence when we must depend upon our garden, our faithful cook stove, and our God. Among the many challenges great-grandmother faced, and among those we will also have to demonstrate, was cooking on a wood stove. Since great-grandmother grew up using this method, it was not such a challenge to her as it might be to most women today who have grown up with the electric range. Cooking with wood was a skill, like so many others, that was passed down from generation to generation. Even the simplest home had a stove on which to cook.

We, as a society, are used to having others do for us the things our ancestors did for themselves. Learning survival skills is not difficult, but they must be learned from someone familiar with these skills, and teaching may be challenging to an independent soul. Persevere, make friends with old timers who may share secrets when they realize you sincerely wish to preserve a heritage. These skills are invaluable and rapidly disappearing.

A practical lifestyle dictates certain requirements for survival; the simpler the life, the more we must depend upon practical skills. Children deprived of doing for themselves, of developing their imagination, of thinking for themselves, may have a poor survival rate. For those who have become dependent upon the utility web, simplifying cooking methods will require some time, patience and vision. Simple does not mean timesaving. Simple means doing for ourselves whatever we can learn to do. Here are a few simple pointers for learning to cook with wood:

1. Search for a good wood-burning cook stove (with an oven and firebox that is not rusted out) and set it up as soon as possible. A wood cook stove is a comforting addition to the family kitchen.
2. Empty ashes regularly—including those collected over the oven. Whisk ashes across the top of the oven to the right side, where they will fall down under the oven to be scraped out with the clean-out tool that comes with your stove. The oven will not heat if the ashes are insulating it.
3. Stove black and elbow grease will make your wood cook stove an attractive addition to the most modern kitchen.
4. Take time to master the art of maintaining a steady oven temperature for baking. Each stove is unique; you must learn when and how to damper your stove; when to admit more air under the firebox and when to damper the chimney to hold the fire at a more steady temperature. If your oven has no temperature gauge, you must buy one which will hang on the oven rack.
5. Know your wood: the size and type of wood you are using will dictate how hot your fire is and how long it will hold. Dry aspen and cottonwood burn hot and fast, leaving more ash than other wood. Spruce and pine leave less ash, tend to hold fire much longer and burn cooler. Birch holds the longest with the hottest flame, but takes a hot fire to get it started, especially if it is not completely dry. Learn what wood is best for your particular needs.
6. Design a large wood box that will last you through the cooking day. Encourage family members to keep the wood box filled during morning chore time.
7. If you use a wood cook stove you will have to live in the country.

When Mother Cooked With Wood

I do not quarrel with the gas,
Our modern range is fine,
The ancient stove was doomed to pass
From Time's grim firing line,
Yet now and then there comes to me
The thought of dinners good
And pies and cake that used to be
When mother cooked with wood.

The axe has vanished from the yard,
The chopping block is gone,
There is no pile of cordwood hard
For boys to work upon;
There is no box that must be filled
Each morning to the hood;
Time in its ruthlessness has willed
The passing of the wood.

And yet those days were fragrant days
And spicy days and rare;
The kitchen knew a cheerful blaze
And friendliness was there.
And every appetite was keen
For breakfasts that were good
When I had scarcely turned thirteen
And mother cooked with wood.

I used to dread my daily chore,
I used to think it tough
When mother at the kitchen door
Said I'd not chopped enough.
And on her baking days, I know,
I shirked whene'er I could
In that now happy long ago
When mother cooked with wood.

I never thought I'd wish to see
That pile of wood again;
Back then it only seemed to me
A source of care and pain.
But now I'd gladly give my all
To stand where once I stood,
If those rare days I could recall
When mother cooked with wood.

—Edgar Guest

Care of Ironware

The very best cookware, whether you cook with wood, electricity or gas, is cast iron. These are easy to care for and distribute heat evenly. They do not add chemicals to your food. Clean them after every use with warm water only (no soap) as soon as they are emptied (before the meal is served). Place the ironware back on the stove to dry during the meal. Hang it on the wall as soon as it dries. It is important that ironware not be allowed to rust. Keep it clean, dry, and cured.

Ironware must be cured when new or when the cure wears off. To cure a pot or pan, clean it thoroughly with soap, water, and a scratch pad to remove buildup or rust. After it is thoroughly dried (on the stove), wipe a thin layer of cooking oil over the entire surface, inside and out, then turn the pan upside down in the oven, and bake at 350° F. for one hour. An outdoor kitchen is ideal for curing ironware as it keeps the resulting smoke out of the house. Ironware should always appear to have a smooth finish that requires much less oil for cooking and prevents them from rusting.

Dutch Oven Cooking

A Dutch oven is a heavy cast iron pot with a lid. It can be used over an open fire to cook soup, beans, porridge, and bake vegetables. It can also be used for baking bread. To bake bread, place a three inch slab of your favorite bread dough in the well-cured Dutch oven. Let it rise, as usual, while you tend your coals. When the dough has risen properly, bury the Dutch oven in a bed of hot coals, placing a layer of coals over the container. Bake the same length of time as for oven-baked bread. Check it periodically. To decrease oven temperature about 25 degrees, remove a few coals from the top layer.

Keeping the inside of your Dutch oven seasoned, or cured is important, just as for any other ironware. Wash it in hot water, without soap, rinse it and lay it on the cook stove to dry as soon as you are finished using it.

Garden to Kitchen Cookbook

Think of your garden as your grocery store; watch it closely, for every day some new treat will appear along its aisles. Salt, bread yeast, oil, and other flavorings are necessary storage items to keep on hand. Since legumes are more difficult to grow in some areas, we suggest storing the items listed on page 237 under "legumes." Milling grains can be done at home; consider obtaining some hand-operated equipment for this purpose. The following recipes were designed for practicing for the time when your garden will be your paycheck. For a simple refrigeration system, consider using your water source or root cellar. The fruit of your own hand is as sweet as the rest it brings you.

Soups

Split Pea Soup

Soak 1 cup split peas in 4 cups of water overnight. Add 2 carrots (diced), 1 large onion (diced), 2 stalks celery (diced), 1 teaspoon salt. Simmer at least one hour until tender and creamy. For a creamier soup, mash the cooked ingredients with a potato masher.

"Miracle" Soup—The Gardener's Diet

This is a soup that burns more calories than it supplies; good for those who want to shed a few pounds. For weight loss, fast for the first day, drinking only water. Through days 2 and 3 drink a gallon of water with ½ cup of lemon juice and 2 teaspoons of salt added. On days 4 and 5, eat "Miracle" soup and raw veggies, then add raw fruit and bread as you ease back into regular food. This makes a large pot of soup.

> 3 large onions, chopped
> 1 head of cabbage, cut in bite-sized pieces
> 2 carrots, cut in bite-sized pieces
> 1 green pepper, chopped
> 1 bunch celery, chopped
> 2 whole tomatoes, canned or fresh

Cover with water, bring to a boil, add ¼ cup of soy sauce and other seasonings, such as garlic, as desired. Cook until tender.

Cresta's Simple Vegetable Stew

4 large potatoes
1 large onion
3 carrots
1 c. green beans
1 qt. canned tomatoes
1 T. salt

Clean and chop vegetables into soup kettle. Cover with water and cook until tender. Add tomatoes. Cook 5 minutes more. Serve with bread or crackers. For variation, add celery, omit tomatoes, or thicken with flour or cornstarch. Serves 6.

Summer Dillight

4 c. water (divided)	1/2 finely diced onion
1 c. raw cashew pieces* (if available)	1 clove finely diced garlic
1/2 T. salt	1/2 t. fresh dill
1/3 c. nutritional yeast flakes (if available)	1/8 c. pimientos (or red pepper)

In soup kettle, steam 4 cups finely chopped broccoli.

In blender: 1 cup of cold water plus all ingredients, except broccoli, until very smooth. Put all in a kettle and add remaining 3 cups of water. Cook very slowly on low heat, **stir often to prevent scorching,** until mixture boils. Simmer 15 minutes. Serves 4. *(½ c. flour may be substituted, or thicken with potatoes.)

Potato Soup

3 qt. water
6 c. peeled and cubed potatoes
2 large onions, diced
1 ½ t. salt
2 stalks celery (optional)

Simmer until tender. Variation: thicken with ½ c. flour dissolved in 1 c. cold water. Adding about 2 cups of creamed or canned corn turns this soup into a wonderful corn chowder. Serve with home made crackers (p. 261).

McClure's Lentil Soup

1 ½ c. lentils	1 clove garlic
2 qt. water	2 T. oil
2 medium onions	2 t. salt
2 stalks celery	3 T. lemon juice (optional)
1 carrot	½ c. tomatoes

Soak lentils ½ hour. Sauté diced vegetables, including garlic in oil. Combine all ingredients and bring to boil; simmer ½ hour. Add salt, lemon juice, and tomatoes. Served with whole wheat crackers this is a tasty and nutritious meal, satisfying all the requirements for complete protein.

Rushin' Borscht

2 qt. water	2-4 large tomatoes
4 beets	2 carrots, grated
2 c. shredded cabbage	½ c. celery, chopped
1 large onion, diced	3 cloves garlic
1 large potato, diced	1 c. precooked navy beans
1 t. lemon juice (optional)	½ t. dried dill (or fresh flower and leaves)
Salt to taste	

Combine ingredients in soup kettle; simmer 2 hours. A good way to use canned cabbage.

Navy Bean Soup

Soak 2 cups of navy beans overnight. Drain and parboil 15 minutes in fresh water. Drain off water to remove toxins. Rinse beans. Refill bean pot with 8 cups of water and 1 tablespoon of oil. Bring to boil and simmer at least 2 hours in covered pot. Add seasonings: 1 clove garlic, 1 large onion (diced fine), 1 ½ t. salt. Variation: 1 T. bacon flavored bits.

Breads

"It is a religious duty for every Christian girl and woman to learn at once to make good, sweet, light bread from unbolted wheat flour" (Counsels on Diet and Foods, p. 316)

The best way to learn to make good bread is to be taught by someone who has mastered the art. Copy a friend's recipe; there are as many bread recipes as there are folks who make bread! It just takes a little practice and perseverance to make a good loaf. Those who suffer from wheat allergies will be encouraged to know that other grains can be adapted to make good bread. The Lord has promised two provisions in the troublous times ahead: bread and water (Isaiah 33:16).

Easy Whole Wheat Bread (yield: 6 loaves)

1. **Mix water with flour**: In large mixing bowl, mix vigorously with potato masher: 6 cups of warm water with 10 cups whole-wheat flour until dough becomes stringy (gluten development). ½ cup of gluten flour will keep bread more limber.

2. **Yeast:** In small bowl: 1 cup warm water, 1 Tbs. sugar (not honey), then sprinkle 2 Tbs. of bread yeast into the water. DO NOT mix the yeast; let it rise, undisturbed, until foamy. Pour yeast mixture into the dough mixture.

3. **Salt, flour, seeds, grains:** Add 1 Tbs. salt, and seeds (sunflower seeds, fresh-ground flax, etc.) as desired. A cup of soy flour will make your bread a complete protein, as it is ground from a legume. 1-2 Tbs. lecithin and ¼ cup of molasses may also be added at this time if desired. Mix dough with a potato masher, adding remaining flour a cup at a time (total of 15 cups) until it is too stiff to beat.

4. **Kneading:** Pour 2 more cups of flour onto the countertop, place the dough on top and add another cup of flour. Fold the dough in upon itself repeatedly with the heel of your hand around the edge of the lump to work the rest of the flour, about 5 more cups, 1 cup at a time so that dough will not become heavy and dry. Knead for at least 10 minutes. If the dough is still sticky, add more flour until it feels like memory foam when pressed gently. The mass of

dough should be neither tough nor sticky, but should hold its shape and still be tender to the touch. (Adjust your height by standing on a stool and lean your weight into kneading.)

4. **Let rise:** Place the kneaded dough on counter top with your mixing bowl over the mass to keep it moist, warm, and free of contamination or drafts. Allow dough rise undisturbed for about 1 hour in a warm kitchen.

5. **Forming Loaves:** Divide the dough into 6 equal parts. Dough that squeaks when the bubbles escape as you flatten it before forming loaves will be good bread! Shape into 6 loaves with smooth tops, and place into oiled loaf pan. For a softer crust, roll loaf in the pan so that the top crust has some oil on it . Let rise until double in bulk in warm kitchen, but not too near a heat source as it will cause it to raise too quickly or pre-cook it and sour the bread. (Always discard soured dough.)

6. **Bake:** When bread has risen above the pans and no longer resists a gentle touch at the corner of a loaf (about 1 hour), bake the bread in preheated oven at 350° F. (When using a wood cook stove, be sure the oven has been at 350° F and holding constant temperature for a half hour or more and stoked with larger pieces of wood.) Oven racks should be centered so that the bread will bake evenly, top and bottom. Bake 25-30 minutes until well browned. Loaf will sound hollow when thumped. (In a wood cook stove rotate loaf positions after they have cooked for 15 minutes, or those nearest the firebox may burn while others may not be thoroughly cooked .)

7. **Cool:** Empty the loaves immediately out of the bread pans and allow to cool on a rack. Cover your bread with a designated towel (if flies are present) until it is cool enough to bag. Bread molds quickly when not refrigerated. Share it with a neighbor while it's fresh! Though it may require great self-denial, for the sake of health, let the bread remain uncovered for at least four hours before serving. Bread, eaten too fresh can be upsetting to the digestive system because of the alcohol content resulting from yeast growth. (Counsels on Diets and Foods, p. 316-321 for commentary on breads.)

8. **Clean-up:** Using cold or cool water for clean-up prevents "cooking" the dough into your dishcloth or sponge.

"There is more religion in a good loaf of bread than many think"
(Counsels on Diet and Foods, p. 316).

Honey Buns
Roll out a portion of whole wheat bread dough into a square, as for cinnamon rolls, drizzle with honey and nuts, roll into a log, slice, and bake as for rolls.

GARDEN TO KITCHEN

Sourdough Starter
Boil one minute: ¼ c. soy milk   ½ c. water   2 tsp. Oil
In separate bowl: ¼ C warm water   1 tsp. Sugar   2 Tbs yeast
When ingredients are cool, pour them all together in large mixing bowl and add:
       2 ½ C warm water   2 c. unbleached white flour   1 ½ tsp. salt
Mix and let stand at room temperature for 8 hours. Refrigerate until baking day.
To use: pour the whole culture into your bread bowl, mix it with warm water (5
cups for five loaves) and flour (5 cups) and remove a portion of this dough to save
as a refreshed starter in a clean jar. Mix the remainder as bread dough. . Keep
loaves warm (to activate growth) as this leavening agent will rise more slowly than
regular yeast. Refresh starter once every week or two and replace in a clean jar.

Pull-Aparts
Use the same amount of bread dough as for a regular loaf, but form dough into 12
balls. Mix a syrup of: 4 T. oil, 4 T. honey, 2 T. water, and pour into bread pan.
Nuts and/or berries may be added before the balls of dough. Let rise, then bake
the same as bread. Deliciously sweet, simple treat!

Squash Rolls
Blend: 1 c. cooked, peeled squash (butternut/pumpkin/acorn) with
½ c. sugar   1½ t. salt   1 c. scalded milk (soy or dairy)
Put 1 T. yeast in ¼ cup of warm water, let rise and add to the above mix. When cool,
add ½ cup of oil and 5 cup of flour. Mix, knead, and let rise to two times its original
size. Form into rolls, place on baking sheet, let rise again. Bake at 350° F for 20-25
minutes. This soft dough makes great dinner rolls or hamburger buns.

Crackers
Mix the following ingredients in blender, threading oil in last to make mix fluffy :
1 ½ c. cold soy milk   1 t. lecithin (if available)
1 ½ t. salt   1 c. oil
Add wet ingredients to 4 cups flour to form a stiff dough. Flatten onto cookie
sheet and bake for 10 minutes at 400° F.

Pie Crust or Simple Crackers (makes two pie crusts)
2 ½ c. flour (sifted whole wheat)   ½ c. oil
½ t. salt   ½ c. cold water
Mix flour and salt in mixing bowl. Add oil and stir with fork until well blended.
Pour in water and mix only until blended. Roll out the dough for pie crust, or press
into a cookie sheet for crackers. Bake 400° F 10 minutes, or until golden at edges.

Corn Tortillas (makes 6 tortillas)

1 c. fine cornmeal   1 t. salt
1 ½ c. white flour

Mix dry ingredients together and add 1 c. cold water. Knead slightly and divide into six equal parts. Form tortillas on floured surface with a rolling pin, as for pie dough, only much thinner. Bake on ungreased skillet, on low heat until golden spots appear. Eat while hot. May be used for burritos, or dipped in salsa. Older tortillas may be baked in oven and broken up as corn chips.

Breakfast Crepes (unleavened)

Blend together: 1 C cold water   ½ c. oats   ¼ C flour
                1 t. oil   1 t. honey   ½ t. salt
                ½ t. vanilla (when available)

In well-cured iron skillet, heated to 350°F (medium temp.), pour ¼ C of mixture and spread it quickly to about 7 inches in diameter. Cook for 3 minutes, or until it is tough enough to flip. Cook for another 3-5 minutes until done. Place on top of each other to keep moist and limber. Serving suggestion: Spread with nut butter or tofu cheese, roll up , three to a plate, and cover with hot fruit sauce, such as blueberries.

Croutons

To use old bread: dice, sprinkle with garlic/onion salt, stir in lightly oiled skillet until toasted, or baked slowly in oven. Serve with soup or salad. Store in tight container.

Zwieback: "Twice-baked Bread"

Slice older bread very thin and bake slowly until crispy. This bread will keep for months. It is good for camping, as it is lightweight and takes awhile to chew.

Entrées and Specialty Dishes

No Lump Savory Gravy

1 c. whole-wheat flour   ½ diced onion
6 c. cold water   salt to taste
1 T. soy sauce (if available)

Heat dry skillet and "brown" the flour by stirring it in the skillet on medium-high heat for 10 minutes, until it begins to smell toasty and turns brown. Be careful not to burn it. Stir in the 6 cups of cold water **all at once**; bring to a boil, stir; all the lumps disappear! Add flavorings. Simmer for 15 minutes. Add sautéed onion or meat substitutes for variety. Serve hot over biscuits, bread, potatoes, or patties.

Millie's Garden Gravy

In blender, combine:
3 cooked carrots
1 medium potato, cooked
1 raw onion
1 c. flour
And enough water to fill the blender. Pour contents of blender into a skillet or sauce-pan. Add water to thin gravy as it cooks; if you are cooking potatoes to go with the gravy, use the potato water to thin the gravy. Season with soy sauce or salt to taste.

Asparagus Toast

Edge a large serving platter with diagonally-sliced toast. Place steamed asparagus spears at each end of this arrangement and pour a white sauce over the center of the dish. Serve immediately. For white sauce: blend together 2 cups of cold water, 1/2 cup flour, 1 T. oil, 1/2 t. salt. Boil until thick.

Corn Tamale Casserole

Place 2 cups of cornmeal in dry skillet and stir constantly over medium heat till toasted. Place the hot, dry cornmeal in a mixing bowl, add 2 cups of water then add:

3 ½ c. whole canned tomatoes or 4-5 fresh tomatoes   ½ c. oil
2 c. black pitted olives (if available)   1 large onion, chopped
1 ½ c. corn off the cob after it has been cooked   2 t. salt
½ c. chopped green pepper
Mix well with cornmeal put in oiled casserole dish and bake 1-1 ½ hours at 350°F.

Don's Gluten Steaks

Mix 10 cups of warm water with 20 cups of high-gluten whole-wheat flour, or white flour. Knead into a firm bread-like dough. Cover this ball of dough with water and let it remain under water for at least four hours. Prepare broth:

2 gallons water   2 T. oil
1 c. soy sauce, or 3 T. salt   1 large onion, diced
Several celery leaves   2 cloves garlic

While broth comes to a boil, wash starch and bran out of the dough mass with repeated kneading under several changes of water. To keep gluten tender, leave a little starch; do not wash it completely clean. Shape gluten dough into a 2-inch log; slice dough very thin and press out thinner with your hands. Drop the dough, one piece at a time, into the boiling broth. Boil at least 15 minutes. Place steaks on deep cookie sheets and cover with broth. Bake at 400° F turning steaks occasionally, basting with remaining broth at 10 minute intervals. Bake until broth has been absorbed then remove from oven and serve hot. Store in refrigerator. Variation: After steaks are shaped, they may be rolled in breading meal and fried on each side until golden and crisp. Use within 2 days. Gluten has a high protein content. If it is canned, it should always be heated above boiling point for five minutes. Watch for puffy lid (indicating release of gas), and discard the contents of any unsealed jar.

Haystacks
Soak 2 cups of pinto beans overnight. Parboil 15 minutes. Pour off water. Cover beans with water and simmer at least 2 hours before serving. To make haystack: each person at the table builds their own stack. Favorite ingredients include corn chips (dried, broken tortillas), lettuce, tomatoes, onions, olives, salsa, pimiento cheese, and pickled beets. The beauty of this dish is that folks can create it as they like; an excellent choice for potluck dinners!

Lentil Sandwich Filling
Grind 1½ cups of dry lentils; set aside.
Bring to boil in saucepan:

4 c. water	2 t. salt
1 large onion, chopped	2 T. soy sauce (if available)

Pinch of each, garlic powder (or 1-2 fresh cloves), sage, dill, thyme.
When broth is just coming to a boil, add the dry lentil meal and stir while cooking for 3 minutes. Remove from heat and place in oiled container to slice after it has chilled overnight. Good for making sandwiches with alfalfa sprouts, pickles, leaf lettuce and/or onion slices.

Oat Burgers
Boil together:

8 c. water	½ c. nutritional yeast (if available)
5 cloves garlic	salt to taste
1 large onion, diced	fresh or dried herbs to taste (basil, sage)
¼ c. oil	8 c. oat flakes (regular or quick)

Mix and boil everything together **except oats** for 2 minutes. Add oats and stir only until moistened. Cover, set aside for ½ hour or until cool enough to handle. Form into patties with an oiled jar lid and ring, or dip lid and ring in warm water after each patty is formed. Bake or fry lightly on both sides. Serve with buns, ketchup, and mayonnaise, pickles and/or alfalfa sprouts. Sandwich idea: Sandwiches can be made from fresh garden produce, especially lettuce, tomatoes, and onions. An oat burger patty and some sprouts on whole wheat bread provides a quick, nutritious meal.

Scalloped Potatoes

Into shallow baking dish slice together: peeled potatoes, onions, garlic. Smother with uncooked gravy mixture (1 quart cold water to ½ c. flour with seasonings of choice; seasoned salts, or soy sauce.) Bake 375° F for 1 hour.

Vegetable Bake

In a casserole dish place clean, sliced fresh garden vegetables: potatoes, carrots, peas (in the pod are fun to skim through your teeth), green beans, onions, garlic, and some pre-flavored pieces of gluten. Drizzle with a little oil and season with your favorite herbs. Bake at 375° F for one hour. Serve hot with gravy.

Stir Fry

Simple, attractive, delicious way to use fresh garden produce. Clean and imaginatively cut cabbage (peel and slice as a water-chestnut substitute), broccoli, onions, carrots, cauliflower, and peppers. Heat a large iron skillet, rub with garlic and oil, stir in the vegetables until crispy-tender (about 5 minutes). When ready to serve, pour a seasoned thickening mix of 1 c. cold water, 3 T. cornstarch (or ¼ cup flour), 2 T. soy sauce (or salt to taste) over the cooked vegetables and stir until the mix thickens quickly to a glossy shine. Serve over rice with toasted sesame seeds or slivered almonds as a garnish .

Baked Garlic

Leave the garlic whole, trimming the tips off of each clove. Arrange garlic in a baking dish, pour in two inches of water, then bake at 400° F for 45 minutes. Serve as a spread for bread, a garnish for baked potatoes, or flavoring for pasta.

Zucchini Chips

Slice small to medium-sized zucchini into ¼ -inch rounds and dip in breading meal: 1 c flour, 1 c nutritional yeast (if available), 1 T salt, 1 T onion powder.
Bake on oiled cookie sheet for ½ hour at 375° F until golden. Flip chips over and bake until done. Serve hot or cold. They become more crisp as they cool if properly cooked.

Salads

Alfalfa Sprouts

Three tablespoons of alfalfa seeds in a quart jar will yield a quart of alfalfa sprouts in four to six days, depending upon temperature and germination rate. Special lids may be purchased for sprouting seeds, but a section of cheesecloth or a nylon stretched over the mouth of the jar with a rubber band works well. Fill jar about half full of warm water and let seeds soak overnight. Rinse thoroughly twice a day in cool water and leave on countertop until well-sprouted. Then place in a sunny windowsill until leaves form and turn the surface green. To remove sprouts from hulls and unsprouted seeds, place the contents of the jar in a large bowl of water and agitate with hands. Hulls will float off and unsprouted seeds will sink. This sprouting method can be used for lentils, wheat, mung beans, radish and broccoli seeds. **Always** use **untreated seed** for sprouting.

Taco Salad
To a tossed salad of lettuce, onions, tomatoes, and other vegetables as desired add: 2 c. Cooked and cooled kidney beans, some corn chips, and Catalina-type dressing or fresh salsa just before serving.

Simple Cabbage Salad
Cut 1½ inch cabbage wedge, serve with almonds or peanuts, either fresh or toasted. This is a unique, fulfilling taste combination requiring no dressing.

Everybody's Favorite Fresh Salsa
1 c. tomatoes (diced)
1 c. onions (diced)
½ c. green peppers (diced)
¼ c. lime juice (if available)
Mix all ingredients. Add salt and chili powder, and other favorite herbs (cilantro, parsley, etc.) to taste. Serve as a tasty and colorful garnish or dressing over any kind of beans, squash, potatoes, or salad. Keeps for one week in the refrigerator.

Quick Pickles (Don't like cukes? You'll like these! Makes a gallon of pickles)
Brine: Bring to boil 2 quarts water, ¼ c. salt, and 1 c. lemon juice.
In a gallon jar: layer sliced cucumbers, sliced onions, 3-5 cloves of whole garlic, fresh dill. Pour hot brine into jar, apply lid, cool until room temperature, then refrigerate 24 hours before serving. Keeps 2 weeks.

Substitutes
Soy Base
Blend, bring to boil, then simmer 30 minutes on medium heat, stirring occasionally.
2 1/2 c. water
1 c. soy flour (very finely ground soybeans)
1 t. salt

Egg Substitute

Soak 1 tablespoon of ground flaxseed in 1 cup of water for ½ hour, then simmer for 15 minutes. Strain immediately and store in refrigerator. ¼ cup equals 1 egg.

Soy Milk

Blend together for a nice cereal milk:

1 c. soy base
2 c. water
1 1/2 t. honey
1/2 t. vanilla
1/4 t. salt

Strain through a fine stainless steel mesh sieve. Chill and serve. For substituting soy milk in a savory recipe, omit the vanilla and honey.

Soy Kreem

Blend until creamy.

1/2 c. soy base
2 c. pears and pear juice
1 T. honey
1/4 t. salt
1/4 c. oil

This may be used as a topping over fruit sauces, waffles or desserts.

Fruit

Fruit Leather

Can you preserve food when you have no freezer or run out of jars? Yes! Leather is simple to make and is ideal for sack lunches. Any type of fruit may be used. The key to good leather is drying the paste slowly. A waxed paper inserted between layers or rolls prevents sticking. Recipe: Blend or mash any type of fruit to a paste. Make sure there are no lumps or whole berries, as they tend to mold because they do not dry properly. If fruit is not too runny when blended or mashed, it can be made into leather without using apples, though adding a fresh apple to any fruit blend will make the leather more pliable. Pour the paste, to about ¼-inch thickness, onto cookie sheet lined with plastic wrap or a lightly oiled glass casserole dish. Dry at about 100° F for a day until it is "tough enough" to lift. Turn it over for a few hours to assure that it is dry on both sides. Cut and roll it as you desire. May be cut into shapes or letters for special occasions. There are many types of drying racks available. (Keep in mind that you may not always have electricity!)

Breakfast Ideas

Wise man says, "Breakfast like a king, lunch like a prince, supper like a pauper."

Fruit Toast

Blend or slice canned fruit. Sauce may be thickened by stirring in a mixture of 3 Tablespoons of cornstarch or flour to ¼ cup of the cold juice. When sauce mixture is boiling, add thickening mixture, and then boil, stirring one minute, until thick. Serve hot over toast. Fresh apples may be sliced thin, cooked in water, sweetened and thickened. Leftover sauce may be used as pie filling for a quick dessert.

Fruit Crisp

In large mixing bowl, mix dry ingredients:

½ c. white flour	¼ c. whole-wheat flour
¼ c. honey	1 T. whole wheat flour

Mix wet ingredients separately:

1 t. vanilla (if available)	¼ c. oil
¼ c. water	

Sprinkle crisp over precooked, thickened fruit by dissolving 2 tablespoons of cornstarch in ½ cup cold fruit juice and bring to boil. Bake at 350° F.

Baked Apples

2 c. unbleached flour (half whole wheat), 2 T. honey, 1 t. salt, 1/3 c. oil Mix flour and salt. Add oil. Rub dough between fingers and thumb until well mixed. (A pastry tool can be used, as for pies, but this method works well.) Add enough soy milk ½ cup), forming a tender dough. Roll dough on a lightly floured board and cut into 4- or 5-inch squares. On each square of dough, place two or three peeled, cored, apple quarters with a teaspoon of honey, dates, nuts and/or dried currants. Wrap dough up around apples, place the balls in a covered casserole dish and bake for approximately 35 minutes at 350°F. Bake uncovered until golden brown. Serve hot, with soy milk, "soy kreem," eaten plain, hot or cold, for breakfast, as a lunchpail treat, or as a dessert.

Hot Cereal

See cooking chart in previous section entitled "Basic Grain Preparation." Bring the water to a boil, add salt and grain. Simmer undisturbed.

Toast and Gravy

Break the monotony of cold cereal breakfasts with your favorite leftover gravy served over toast or biscuits. Hot, savory and quick!

Linda's Granola
In large bowl, mix dry ingredients:

7 c. quick oats

½ c. nut pieces, (if available)

¼ c. whole wheat flour

½ t. salt

Mix together liquid ingredients in separate bowl and pour over dry ingredients:

½ c. water

½ c. oil

1½ t. vanilla (if available)

½ c. honey or brown sugar

Bake at 225° F for 1 hour, stirring occasionally, until very lightly toasted. Store in airtight container. Coconut, sunflower seeds, other nuts or grains may be added or substituted. Any granola recipe can be adjusted for food allergies. Substitute equal amounts of dry ingredients.

Oat Waffles
Blend together until creamy and let stand overnight in refrigerator:

5 c. water

1 t. salt

1 T. wheat germ

1 T. honey

3 T. oil

4 c. oats

½ c. cashews or sunflower seeds (if available)

Pour batter into waffle iron (these are available in ironware to be used with a wood cook stove). Cook until golden brown.

Baked Oatmeal
Mix together:

6 c. oatmeal

1½ c. chopped dates (if available)

¼ c. oil

2 T. honey

1 c. soy base (p. 236)

Put ingredients in shallow baking pan, pour in 4 cups of boiling water. Bake at 375° F for 30-40 minutes.

Meal Planning
Eating from the garden requires a planning and forethought, but it is not difficult. Think about what you have, and what makes a balanced meal, nutritionally and artistically. Remember to eat whole grains and legumes at least once a day in order to form a complete protein. When planning meals for your family, remember the rule of the green thumb cook: use what you have. The following is a sample menu. (B = breakfast, L = lunch, S = supper.)

YOU CAN SURVIVE!

Sunday
B: Hot oatmeal porridge with honey and soy milk, fresh strawberries.
L: Stir-fry with brown rice (if available)
S: Lentil soup, whole wheat crackers

Monday
B: Baked apples, soy kreem (p. 236), filberts
L: Gluten steaks, green beans, mashed potatoes, gravy, green salad
S: Summer Dillight soup, croutons

Tuesday
B: Bulger wheat cereal, toast, peanut butter (if available), hot applesauce
L: Cresta's Simple Vegetable Stew, crackers, carrot sticks
S: Canned fruit and toast

Wednesday
B: Oatmeal waffles, fruit sauce, peanut butter (if available)
L: Oatburgers, squash buns, pickles, onions, lettuce, and baked potatoes
S: Borscht and crackers

Thursday
B: Baked oatmeal, fresh or canned fruit, toast
L: Pinto beans, corn tamale casserole, fresh salsa, corn on the cob
S: Fresh or chilled canned fruit, whole wheat toast

Friday
B: Cornmeal mush, soy milk, dried currants
L: Sandwiches–lentil sandwich filling, dill pickles, tomato slices, lettuce, carrot
  sticks, baked squash
S: Potato soup and zwieback

Sabbath
B: granola, canned fruit, fruit juice or soy milk
L: haystacks (chips or tortillas, beans, lettuce, onions, salsa, etc.)
S: Fresh fruit and bread, hot apple juice

United States Recommended Daily Allowances (RDA)

Compound	Units /day	Adult males	Adult females	Children	Infants 7-12 months	Pregnant & lactating women
Protein	gram	63	50	28	14	65
Vitamin A	Re	1,000	800	700	375	1,300
Vitamin D	IU	200	200	200	200	200
Vitamin E	Mg alpha TE	10	8	7	4	12
Vitamin K	ug	80	65	30	10	65
Vitamin C	mg	60	60	45	35	95
Folate	ug	400	400	200	80	500-600
Thiamine (B_1)	mg	1.2	1.1	0.6	0.3	1.4
Riboflavin (B_2)	mg	1.3	1.1	0.6	0.4	1.4-1.6
Niacin	mg	16	14	8	4	17-18
Pyridoxine (B_6)	mg	1.3	1.3	0.6	0.3	1.9-2.0
Cyanocobalamine (B_{12})	ug	2.4	2.4	1.2	0.5	2.6-2.8
Biotin	ug	30	30	12	6	30-35
Pantothenic Acid	mg	5	5	3	1.8	6-7
Choline	mg	550	425	250	150	450-550
Calcium (Ca)	mg	1,000	1,000	800	270	1,000
Phosphorus (P)	mg	700	700	200	275	700
Iodine (I)	ug	150	150	120	50	200
Iron (Fe)	mg	10	15	10	10	30
Magnesium (Mg)	mg	420	320	130	75	320-360
Copper (Cu)	mg	1.5-3	1.5-3	1-2	0.6-0.7	1.5-3
Zinc (Zn)	mg	15	12	10	5	19
Selenium (Se)	ug	70	55	30	15	75
Chromium (Cr)	ug	50-200	50-200	50-200	10-60	50-200
Molybdenum (Mn)	ug	75-250	75-250	50-150	15-40	75-250
Manganese (Mn)	mg	2-5	2-5	2-3	0.3-1.0	2-5
Fluoride (F)	mg	4	3	1	0.5	3
Sodium (Na)	mg	500	500	400	120-200	500
Chloride (Cl)	mg	750	750	600	180-300	750
Potassium (K)	mg	2,000	2,000	1,600	500-700	2,000

Mg= milligrams (0.001g)
Ug= micrograms (0.000001g)
IU= International Units
RE= Retinol Equivalent (1 Retinol Equivalent is equal to 5 International Units)
Alpha TE= alpha Tocopherol equivalent
G= grams

Basic Food Values (Quantities based on 100 gram edible portion)

	Food Energy	Pro.	Fat	CHO	Cal.	Phos.	Iron	Sodi-um	Pota-ssium	Vit.A	Thi.	Ribo.	Nia.	Vit..C
	Calories	gm	gm	mg	gm	mg	mg	mg	mg	IU	mg	mg	mg	mg
Min. Daily Req.	3,000	20%	30%	50%	0.8	.88-1.5	12	500	750	5,000	1.2-2.0	1.6-2.6	12-20	75-100
Legumes:														
navy beans	118	7.8	0.6	21.2	50	148	2.7	7	416	---	0.14	0.07	0.7	---
kidney	118	7.8	0.5	21.4	38	140	2.4	3	340	---	0.11	0.06	0.7	---
lima	138	8.2	0.6	25.6	29	154	3.1	2	612	---	0.13	0.06	0.7	---
soy	130	11	5.7	10.8	73	179	2.7	2	540	30	0.21	0.09	0.6	---
Vegetables:														
green beans	24	1.4	0.2	5.2	45	25	1.5	236	95	470	0.03	0.05	0.3	4
yellow beans	24	1.4	0.3	5.2	45	25	1.5	236	95	100	0.03	0.05	0.3	5
raw beets	43	1.6	0.1	9.9	16	33	0.7	60	335	20	0.03	0.05	0.4	10
cooked beets	32	1.1	0.1	7.2	14	23	0.5	43	208	20	0.03	0.04	0.3	6
broccoli	26	3.1	0.3	4.5	88	62	0.8	10	267	2,500	0.09	0.2	0.8	90
Brussels sprouts	36	4.2	0.4	6.4	32	72	1.1	10	273	520	0.08	0.2	0.8	87
raw cabbage	24	1.3	0.2	5.4	49	29	0.4	20	233	130	0.05	0.05	0.3	47
cooked cabbage	20	1.1	0.2	4.3	44	20	0.3	14	163	130	0.04	0.4	0.3	33
raw carrots	42	1.1	0.2	9.7	37	36	0.7	47	341	11,000	0.06	0.05	0.6	8
cooked carrots	31	0.9	0.2	7.1	33	31	0.6	33	222	10,500	0.05	0.05	0.5	6
celery	14	0.8	0.1	3.1	31	22	0.2	88	239	230	0.02	0.03	3	6
chard	18	1.8	0.1	3.3	73	24	1.2	86	329	5,400	0.04	0.11	0.4	16
corn	84	2.6	0.8	19.8	5	49	1.8	236	97	350	0.03	0.05	0.9	4
cucumber	15	0.9	0.1	3.4	25	27	1.1	6	160	250	0.03	0.04	0.2	11
lettuce	18	1.3	0.3	3.5	68	25	1.4	9	264	1,900	0.05	0.05	0.4	18
onion	29	1.2	0.1	6.5	24	29	0.4	7	110	40	0.03	0.03	0.2	7
parsnip	66	1.5	0.5	14.9	45	62	0.6	8	379	30	0.07	0.08	0.1	10
peas	88	4.7	0.4	16.8	26	76	1.9	236	96	690	0.09	0.06	0.8	8
radish	17	1	0.1	3.6	118	31	1	18	322	10	0.03	0.03	0.3	26
spinach	24	2.7	0.6	15.4	28	26	2.6	236	250	8,000	0.02	0.12	0.3	18
squash	63	1.8	0.4	4.3	6	48	0.8	1	461	4,200	0.05	0.13	0.7	13
tomatoes	21	0.1	0.2	4.9	35	19	0.5	130	217	900	0.05	0.03	1.7	17
turnip	23	0.8	0.2	3.1	25	24	0.4	34	188	tr.	0.04	0.05	0.3	22
veg. marrow	15	1	0.2	3.6	25	25	0.4	1	141	444	0.05	0.08	0.8	11
veg. spaghetti	14	0.9	0.1	3.1	7	25	0.4	1	141	390	0.05	0.08	0.8	10
potatoes	76	2.1	0.1	17.1	7	53	0.6	3	407	tr.	0.09	0.04	1.5	16

Basic Food Values (Quantities based on 100 gram edible portion) Cont.

	Food Energy	Pr.	Eat	CHO	Cal.	Phos.	Iron	Sodium	Potas-sium	Vit. A	Thi..	Ribo.	Nia.	Vit. C
	Calories	gm	gm	mg	gm	mg	mg	mg	mg	IU	mg	mg	mg	mg
Minimum Daily Requirements	3,000	20%	30%	50%	.08	88-1.5	12	500	750	5,000	1.2-2.0	1.6-2.6	12-20	75-100
Fruit														
fresh apples	58	0.2	0.6	14	7	10	0.3	1	110	90	0.03	0.02	0.1	4
apple sauce	41	0.2	0.2	10.8	54	0.5	0.5	2	78	40	0.02	0.01	tr.	1
blueberries	39	5	2	9.8	10	9	0.7	1	60	40	0.01	0.01	0.2	7
sweetened cranberries	146	1	0.2	37.5	6	4	0.2	1	30	20	0.01	0.01	tr.	2
raspberries	35	0.7	0.1	8.8	15	15	0.6	1	114	90	0.01	0.04	0.5	9
rhubarb	141	0.5	0.1	36	78	15	0.6	2	302	80	0.02	0.05	0.3	6
strawberries	22	0.4	0.1	5.6	14	14	0.7	1	111	40	0.01	0.03	0.4	20
groundcherries	53	1.9	0.7	11.2	9	40	1	---	---	720	0.11	0.04	2.5	11
currants	50	1.4	0.2	12.1	32	23	1	2	257	120	0.04	0.05	0.1	41
gooseberries	26	0.5	0.1	6.6	12	10	0.3	1	105	200	---	---	---	11
cherries	43	0.8	0.2	10.7	15	13	0.3	2	130	680	0.03	0.02	0.2	3
plums	33	0.4	0.1	8.6	9	13	0.2	1	82	160	0.01	0.02	0.3	2
Grains:														
barley	348	9.6	1.1	77.2	34	290	2.7	---	296	0	0.21	0.07	3.7	0
oats, cooked	55	2	1	9.7	9	57	0.6	218	61	0	0.08	0.02	0.1	0
rye flour	327	16.3	2.6	63.1	54	536	4.5	1	860	0	0.61	0.22	2.7	0
rye, whole	334	12.1	1.7	73.4	38	376	3.7	1	467	0	0.43	0.22	1.6	0
wheat flour	333	13.3	2	71	41	372	3.3	3	370	0	0.55	0.12	4.3	0
wheat, whole	330	14	2.2	69.1	36	383	3.1	3	370	0	0.57	0.12	4.3	0
Seeds:														
sunflower	560	24	47.3	19.9	120	837	7.1	30	920	50	1.96	0.23	5.4	---

Brooms

Various sweeping devices were made by the pioneers: grasses, long pine needles, or rushes tied to the end of a stick. Brooms, similar to commercial varieties, can be made from broom corn where that plant has enough hot days to mature.

Useful Items in a Country Home

Kitchen

1. Bowls (set of stainless steel)
2. Containers
   a. glass or plastic ash container for lye
   b. burn barrel
   c. storage–plastic, gallon jars, garbage bins, jars
   d. slop buckets
   e. water containers–for heating, storage, pitcher, dipper
3. Dish-washing equipment
   a. sinks or dishpans (metal)
   b. dish drainer
4. Eating equipment
   a. containers–bowls, plates, saucers, cups, glasses
   b. utensils–forks, knives, spoons
5. Linens
   a. tablecloths
   b. hot pads
   c. drying towels, dishcloths, hand towels
   d. towels to cover bread
6. Baking pans
   a. bread pans
   b. cookie sheets
   c. casserole dishes
   d. pie pans
7. Pots and pans
   a. saucepans
   b. set of cast iron skillets and a Dutch oven
   c. teakettle
8. Preserving equipment
   a. pressure cooker and canner
   b. sealer jars, rings, lids (glass lids/reusable rubber rings)
   c. drying rack

9. Handy Utensils
   a. mixing spoons, serving spoons, and dippers
   b. spatulas, pancake turner
   c. eggbeater
   d. potato peelers
   e. knives, bread and paring
   f. rolling pin
   g. vegetable grater/chopper
   h. manual grain grinder
   i. manual blender

Other handy household equipment:
1. Cleaning
   a. broom and dustpan
   b. rug sweeper
   c. soap
   d. scouring pads, rags
2. Heating
   a. wood cook stove and heater
   b. wood box
   c. ash shovel and metal bucket
3. Sewing
   a. treadle sewing machine
   b. sewing kit: threads, needles, etc.
   c. spinning wheel
   d. treadle-type leather sewing machine (shoe repair)
   e. awl and heavy thread for leather repair
4. Laundry
   a. large boiler with lid for heating water
   b. washing machine–plunger type
   c. tubs
   d. scrub board
   e. hand operated wringers
   f. flat irons
   g. ironing board
   h. clothesline and clothespins
   i. laundry soap

Simplify

Many topics have been addressed in this chapter. The information that you have learned will allow you to grow a garden, construct a greenhouse and root cellar, preserve both food and seed, balance your diet, cook healthfully, obtain necessary kitchen equipment and garden tools. You have a few recipes to get you started using fresh and healthy produce from your own garden. Not only are these enjoyable activities, they will help reduce your fear of the time of "no buy-no sell" when you will be dependent upon what you grow.

We are told, in 1 John 4:18, that perfect love casts out fear; this applies to the fear of the unknown. Familiar with His Word, with what has been predicted, we can be prepared for the events of the future. As we learned in the introduction, preparation reduces the fear factor. When we have prepared our garden and grown our own food, we better appreciate it as it comes from the hand of the Creator: healthful, naturally delicious, and simple.

Nutrition, like life, need not be complicated. The simpler the better, in fact. To the benefit of our own health and those for whom we are responsible, we would do well to return, as close to "natural" as possible, in our choices: food, clothing materials, cleaning supplies, entertainment, and education.

One can begin simplifying at any time, by taking little steps. Simplify your home. Discard the clutter that has collected in the corners, in storage boxes, and book shelves. Eliminate what you don't need, or share items with friends who will appreciate them. Have a yard sale. Keep a bag or box for donations to your local thrift store or community service center. Your discards may bless someone in need. When we have less to dilute our time and attention, we can establish priorities with ease. Not only is it a comfort to realize that we can get along with less than most of us possess, it may eventually become an obligation to those who are anticipating a heavenly home.

"It is now that our brethren should be cutting down their possessions instead of increasing them. We are about to move to a better country, even a heavenly. Then let us not be dwellers upon the earth, but getting things into as compact a compass as possible" (Testimonies for the Church, vol. 5, p. 152; emphasis supplied).

Simplification is not meant to be overwhelming. Like any other chapter in life, simplification comes in stages. One such stage will be considered in the next chapter as we step into the realm of natural remedies.

GARDEN TO KITCHEN

FOR FURTHER READING

How to Grow More Vegetables, by John Jeavons, Ten Speed Press, P.O. Box 7123, Berkeley, CA 94707, 1979.

Silver Hills Cookbook, by Eileen Brewer, RR 2, Lumby, BC, Canada V0E 2G0.

Seed Saver's Catalogue (non-hybrid seed source), 3076 Winn Rd., Decorah, Iowa, 52101. www.seedsavers.org.

100% Vegetarian, a cookbook, by Julianne Pickle, Pickle Publishing, www.picklepublishing.com

Nutrition for Vegetarians, by Agatha Thrash, MD, and Calvin Thrash, MD, Thrash Publications, 1982, Yuchi Pines Institute, 30 Yuchi Pines Rd., Seale, Alabama 36875.

Composition of Foods, Agriculture Handbook #8, U.S. Dept. of Agriculture, Washington, DC 20402

Chapter Thirteen

Medical Preparation: Basic Skills and Natural Remedies

"It is far better to prevent disease than to know how to treat it"
(<u>Ministry of Healing</u>, p. 128).

Will and Louise were vital members of our staff at Sanctuary Ranch, a small school in northern British Columbia. When Louise had her first child, they were living in a log cabin that Will had planned and built. Louise had been nursing their new baby, Isaiah, for a few weeks when she contracted a breast infection that caused her temperature to rise to 104° F. We were all concerned, so Will took her to the hospital in town, a trip that took 45 minutes to an hour even though it was only 15 miles away. The jarring ride caused by the two-rut dirt road caused Louise severe pain.

When Louise arrived at the hospital, the doctor discovered that the milk glands in one breast were infected. He ordered bed rest and a prescription for a powerful antibiotic. But the infection progressed and her temperature did not decrease during the next two days. Because of the side-effects of the antibiotics, Louise quit taking her prescription. She was very ill and Isaiah was not getting proper nourishment. Will and I knelt beside her bed and prayed for her healing.

As we were praying together it occurred to us that a charcoal poultice might help Louise. Although I was familiar with the healing properties of charcoal, we did not have enough charcoal on hand for a large poultice. Will disclosed what he had been learning about charcoal's toxin-removing properties in the Natural Remedies class. I sensed that we were in unity about using charcoal on Louise.

We brazed up an old square galvanized washtub so it was airtight and fitted a piece of sheet metal over the top. We built an outdoor fire and gathered dead standing willow wood. Each piece of wood was no larger than 1 inch in diameter and broken into lengths that would fit into the tub. We filled the tub about half full of these willow "pencils," discarding the residual bark, and placed the tub over the fire with the lid on it. This created a reduced oxygen atmosphere inside the tub. We let it cook for one and one half hours.

At the end of the cooking time, we pulled the tub off of the fire and let it cool with the lid on. (If the lid is removed while the charcoal is still hot, it will burst into flame when the oxygen enters.) When it cooled, we found perfect little one-inch black "pencils" intact.

We then ground the charcoal into powder with a mortar and pestle. (Use a smooth flat rock and a thinner, elongated stone if these instruments are not available. These unground charcoal pencils can be used for drawing, or in blacksmithing as a fuel that will produce a hot flame when the bellows pumps air into the forge.)

After we had ground the charcoal pencils to powder, we made a poultice about six inches square. This poultice was made by taking a clean cotton cloth and placing the charcoal in the center of the material about one half inch deep and folding the cloth square. The poultice is moistened with water and placed on the affected area.

Louise had a high fever and was in great pain when Will placed the poultice on the infected breast. Will then joined our little group of concerned staff and students in prayer shortly after he had prayed with Louise. Trust in divine power offers the real healing when we follow God's plan and use His remedies.

The next half hour seemed like a miracle; Louise had relief from pain, the swelling was reduced, her fever decreased, and she slept soundly for the first time in several days!

Simple Remedies Needed

As we consider future opportunities for service, planning should be given to helping people in emergencies. Catastrophes are prophesied to happen in our world and in our community. We may sometimes be limited to simple remedies as we try to help disaster victims. The following references emphasize the fact that we need to prepare for calamities in ways that will provide caring emergency services.

"These calamities will increase more and more; one disaster will follow close upon the heels of another" (Christian Service, p. 155).

"In accidents and calamities by sea and land, in great conflagrations, in fierce tornadoes and terrific hailstorms, in tempests, floods, cyclones, tidal waves, and earthquakes, in every place and in a thousand forms, Satan is

exercising his power. He sweeps away the ripening harvest, and famine and distress follow. He imparts to the air a deadly taint, and thousands perish by the pestilence. These visitations are to become more and more frequent and disastrous" (The Great Controversy, pp. 589, 590; emphasis supplied).

"You hear of calamities by land and sea, and they are constantly increasing" (Selected Messages, book 2, p. 51).

"Disasters by sea and land follow one another in quick succession. How frequently we hear of earthquakes and tornadoes, of destruction by fire and flood with great loss of life and property" (Prophets and Kings, p. 277; emphasis supplied).

Some of these disasters could occur in your area. Accordingly, we need to prepare our emergency medical services to accommodate the possibility of disaster victims. We must learn what to do when they come.

The following statement accents the need for medical preparation: *"The ability to prepare food, to deal with accidents and emergencies, to treat disease, to build a house, or a church if need be–often these make all the difference between success and failure in his lifework"* (Education, p. 221; emphasis supplied).

In the following pages, written by physicians, you will discover the medical approaches to several emergencies. These approaches may be used as needed by people unacquainted with medical procedures. **We highly recommend training be obtained in local medical first aid courses and updated annually, especially those courses taught by physicians, nurses or emergency medical personnel.**

Resuscitation

Question: When is it appropriate to revive a person?

It will not be possible to revive persons who have died from germ diseases or those who have been dead quite some time prior to your arrival. You should merely pray for the comfort of the survivors. If, however, the person was healthy, and appeared to die of an acute injury or drowning, but not one otherwise having death-dealing significance, you should make every effort to revive them. Such is the case when the trauma is an electric shock, lightning bolt, head injury, drowning, etc.

Steps to Take in Reviving a Person

1. First, evaluate for level of consciousness and for signs of life. **"Shake and shout"** are the watchwords. With a gentle nudge at the shoulder or hand, say, "Are you all right!" or "Can you hear me?" Then, check for signs of breathing, or airway obstruction, and feel the pulse to be sure the heart is beating.

2. Be sure the airway is open. Since a person can live only 3 to 4 minutes

without breathing, it is mandatory that you make certain there are no airway obstructions. Tilting the head back will usually open the air passage in the throat. Press the back of the jaw forward to bring the back of the tongue forward. Then, listen at the nostrils for air exchange, and make sure the person can breathe. If you don't know, assume that there is a spinal column injury and follow C-spine procedures. (<u>Industrial First-aid Reference and Training Manual</u>, Workmen's Compensation Board of British Columbia, Canada, p. 16.)

3. Check the mouth, and as far as possible in the throat, for foreign bodies. Food, toys, cotton, plastic, etc.–anything that may interfere with breathing must be removed. If you suspect that the person has choked, or the victim grasps their throat to signify such, you may do the Heimlich maneuver. If the person is sitting, stand behind the chair, make a fist, and with both of the hands clasped just below the rib cage and over the stomach, thrust forcefully two times in the region described above (called the solar plexus). This thrust, known as the Heimlich maneuver, can also be performed when the victim is lying supine on the floor, by pushing up toward the heart in the stomach area. It will simulate a cough and often help the person dislodge the suffocating material out of the windpipe (trachea).

4. Only after the airway is cleared do you begin to pay attention to the heart and arteries. If there is no pulse or detectable heartbeat, strike the chest sharply two or three times with your closed fist. If an electrical shock of some kind stopped the heart's pacemaker, or if choking caused a cardiac arrest, this maneuver may start the heart beating again. If the rhythmic beating of the heart does not commence spontaneously, you can maintain a pulse by rhythmic compression of the chest (over the lower two-thirds of the sternum). It is pointless, however, to attempt to maintain a pulse unless you or your assistant is also maintaining artificial respiration. **All parents, and anyone interested in medical missionary work, should take a class in cardiopulmonary resuscitation (CPR), for training and practice are vital when preparing for accidents and emergencies.**

5. Next, examine the person for signs of hemorrhage. If bleeding has been evident before this time, while you were doing steps 1-4, ask someone to hold firm pressure on the spot where blood is seen to be flowing. You may use a clean handkerchief, a handful of facial tissues, or a folded cloth if these are available. If these are not available, use the hand or a finger to apply the pressure. Bear in mind the possibility of a transmissible disease from blood and other body fluids. You may want to slip on a latex glove, which is often found in first-aid and CPR kits. Advanced training in Life Support is valuable, too.

body fluids contaminate breaks in your skin or get into your nose, eyes, or mouth, you could get an infection. Remember, too, that blood flow always indicates some heart action, as bleeding stops at death.

American Heart Association materials in basic CPR are available.

Instant Guide to First Aid

Be calm! Examine the victim carefully. Stop arterial bleeding immediately! Don't touch wounds with fingers. Don't move the victim unnecessarily. Don't forget shock treatment. Compress firmly over wound to aid clot.

INJURY	SYMPTOMS	TREATMENT
ASPHYXIATION	Lips, earlobes, blue; breathing stopped; unconscious	Move to fresh air; give artifical respiration (CPR)
BLEEDING (from arteries)	Spurting, bright-red blood coming from wounds	Cover with pressure bandage. Apply hand pressure to nearest pressure point. Use tourniquet when other methods fail to stop bleeding. Once applied, it should be released by a physician.
BLEEDING (from veins)	Steady flow; dark red blood.	Apply sterile compress firmly over wound to aid clotting.
Bleeding (internal)	Pale face; faintness; thirst, sighing; weak rapid pulse.	Lay with head low; apply cold packs to point you think might be source of bleeding.
BURNS (thermal)	Redness; pain; blisters; charred or cooked tissue.	Exclude air by applying burn spray or other ointment, or cover with dry bandage.
BURNS (chemical)	Redness; pain.	Wash thoroughly eyes or skin with 8 to 32 ounces of NEUTRALIZE or irrigate with clean water for 10 to 15 minutes.
DROWNING	Unconscious, not breathing.	Remove from water; cleanse mouth; pull tongue forward. Loosen clothing. Give artifical respiration (CPR)
DISLOCATIONS	Deformity compared to uninjured limb; pain.	Bandage to stabilize in lines of deformity. Do not adjust dislocation unless trained to do so.
ELECTRIC SHOCK	Unconscious; breathing stopped; burns at contact point.	Insulate self and rescue the victim. Give artificial respiration (CPR) if indicated. Dress burns.
FAINTING	Unconscious; face pale; cold sweat; pulse weak and rapid.	Lay with head low; keep warm; loosen clothing; apply cool cloth to forehead; give water if thirsty.
FRACTURES (simple)	Pain; swelling; deformity; inability to move limb.	Support and stabilize above and below the fracture; apply well-padded splint.
FRACTURES (compound)	Open wound; possibly bone protruding, bleeding	Apply sterile compress to wound to control bleeding; apply padded splints to stabilize deformity. Do not attempt to replace bone or reduce fracture.
Fractures (skull)	Possibly clear fluid or bleeding from eyes, nose, mouth; unconscious or dazed.	Raise head keeping neck stable, dress wounds, do NOT give stimulants; keep warm and quiet.
Frostbite	Affected part is white; no sensation.	Thaw slowly with lukewarm (not hot) water, or by gently wrapping warm blanket or clothes. Make patient as warm as possible.
Gas Poisoning (carbon monoxide)	Yawning; giddiness; weariness; throbbing pulse; bright-red lips	Move to fresh air; give artificial respiration (CPR) if needed.
HEAT EXHAUSTION	Pale face; cold sweat; weak pulse; shallow breathing.	Keep warm; rub limbs toward heart; give stimulants.
SHOCK	Pale face; cold sweat; dazed condition; partly or totally unconscious.	Lay with head low and feet elevated; keep warm; rub limbs; give stimulants if conscious.
SNAKEBITE	Pain; swelling; fang marks.	Apply tourniquet above bite; open fang marks lengthwise; use suction. Keep quiet.
SUNSTROKE	Unconscious; face flushed; skin hot and dry; breathing labored; pulse rapid.	Raise head; reduce body temperature with cold packs; hydrate with water when conscious. Keep head cool.

MEDICAL PREPARATION

Special Kit of Supplies for Medical Emergencies

1. Large scissors for cutting away clothing, straps, etc.
2. Small scissors, one with rounded points, and another with very sharp points (almost needle sharp), for lancing boils, cleaning up wounds, etc.
3. Activated charcoal, two quarts of powder
4. Charcoal tablets, for use as lozenges
5. Elastic compression bandages, two or three different sizes
6. Black or white nylon and silk thread for suturing
7. Rubbing alcohol; hydrogen peroxide, tincture of iodine
8. Safety pins–about 10 large and 5 small
9. Tongue blades (usually made of wood)
10. Mirror, for signals, and to reflect light into body cavities, wounds, etc.
11. One large hemostat (Kelly clamp)
12. One curved and one straight hemostat, five to six inches long
13. Sewing needles, assorted sizes for suturing (or suture packs, if you can get them)
14. Tinctures, goldenseal, Echinacea, grapefruit seed extract, garlic, and Kyolic (garlic extract)
15. Old, well-worn bed sheet for bandage material
16. Adhesive tape, one inch wide, can be torn lengthwise for smaller strips
17. Rolls of gauze
18. A female urinal (works well for men also)
19. A pocketknife, such as a Swiss Army knife with a saw, scissors, and punch
20. Thumb forceps with and without teeth and/or eyebrow tweezers
21. Needle holders
22. Flashlight and extra batteries
23. Large towels (6-8) and washcloths, for fomentations and childbirth
24. Several rolls of toilet tissue, in wrapper
25. One roll of paper towels, in a wrapper
26. Blanket, one or more, washable
27. Two or three sheets–top sheets, not necessarily fitted sheets
28. Plastic sheet or shower curtain
29. A six-inch stack of clean newspapers for childbirth
30. Salt, two to three pounds
31. Epsom salts, one to two pounds (salts should be kept in tightly closed jars)
32. Curved needles, large and small for suturing
33. Bar soap and liquid soap

34. A small bottle of Lysol
35. A small bottle of bleach
36. Clean or new white shoestrings to tie cord at childbirth
37. Plastic bags, miscellaneous sizes, clean, 15-20
38. Box of facial tissues
39. Ear syringes
40. Washbasins and baby bathtub, plastic or metal
41. Vinegar, one gallon, as fungicide
42. Tea tree oil as antiseptic/fungicide

Suturing

Often, even for large lacerations, the wound can be closed quite satisfactorily by cleaning up the surrounding skin, drying it very carefully, pulling the wound edges together, perfectly matching the skin lines if they are visible, and taping the wound securely in place with adhesive tape or "butterfly" bandages. Space should be left between the tape "sutures" for the wound to be able to air dry; otherwise, the tape will be lifted off as the wound weeps, or the wound may become infected. Finally, put absorptive bandages over the wound, such as sterile gauze or torn strips from an old bed sheet that have been ironed to sterilize them.

Immobilize the laceration with tongue blades or splints until danger of its pulling apart is past–three to 10 days, depending on how much movement and tension will be placed on the wound. Wounds on the face need only about three days, but wounds over elbows or other moving parts may need immobilization for seven to 14 days, even longer over the knees. If bleeding cannot be stopped, or the wound edges cannot be pulled together satisfactorily without tension, you may need to put sutures in. Be sure the skin edges do not curl under, regardless of the kind of closure you do. The skin will not heal well if the edges curl under.

If you must put in sutures, there are a few points you should remember:

1. Remove all dirt, glass, foreign material, pieces of detached skin or flesh, and old blood clots from the wound before finishing the suturing and applying a bandage. If these objects are embedded in the tissue, irrigate the wound with clean water or saline if you cannot pick them from the wound. Sometimes, you may need to use sharp scissors and forceps with teeth to remove every particle of foreign matter. This may take a while. Fat and fibrous tissue may be trimmed to remove debris that is embedded. The wound will not heal well with foreign matter in it. However, do not cut away a lot of the tissue if it can be avoided, since a sunken area will be left if excess tissue is removed.

2. The skin may be tough, like soft leather. Quite a lot of effort is often needed to push the needle through.

3. Stabilize the skin by holding it as lightly as possible with the forceps (with small teeth, rather than mere grippers, if available), but firmly as needed to put counter pressure against the force of the needle.

4. Do not suture wounds that are more than six to 10 hours old. It is better to simply pull the edges together. On older wounds, place adhesive tape followed by a bandage and let them heal without suturing.

5. Put the needle through the skin about one-quarter to one-third inch from the wound edge. A curved needle held in a needle holder works best, but a regular sewing needle and thread can be used in an emergency. Sterilized materials are best, if they are available. Simply boil two needles and needle holders, with suture material, for five minutes to supply needed sterility precautions. If this is not possible, at least be sure they are clean, washed with water and soap.

6. Do not leave an air pocket in the base of the wound or blood clots will form inside the wound. If it is a deep space between the skin surface and the muscle below it, more than half to three quarters of an inch, it is best to take the first "bite" of muscle with a needle from the skin surface to the bottom of the wound and bring out the needle. Then take a second bite from the bottom of the wound to the top, making the needle come out of the skin about one quarter to one third of an inch from the edge of the wound. Make the sutures as neat as possible and pull the skin edges exactly, matching its position before laceration as well as you can. Do not allow the skin edges to curl. They have a tendency to do so.

7. Do not make the sutures so tight that the skin is pushed in or turns pale where you put in the sutures.

8. Leave the suture ends about ½ inch long so you can easily find them when it is time to remove the sutures.

9. Remove the sutures after three days on the face, but up to 10 to 14 days over knees and elbows.

10. A laceration on the hairy areas or scalp should not be shaved, but you should avoid letting the hair invert into the wound edges. On the scalp, you may be able to tie or braid the hair from one side of the wound across to hair on the other side of the wound. If you can do so, this will easily hold the wound edges together.

Note: You will find diagrams of various suture techniques in Dr. Richard Hansen's book, Get Well at Home. Study the chapter on accidents and injuries for a more in-depth discussion of this subject.

Women's Hygiene

Life for women changed considerably with the modern invention of disposable sanitary napkins. Baby diapers and feminine hygiene pads make life easier today, and we tend to take them for granted. But what about that time when we might not be able to get these necessities? Sometimes, under severe stress or continued physical exertion, a woman's hormones prevent her regular menses, and such may be the case in the end times. This is yet another way in which we should be prepared.

What did great-grandma do? Persecution may still dictate the use of ancient methods in developing countries. Though the Bible indicates that certain privileges were afforded to women during their menses, it is not clear as to how these women provided for their inconvenience. Though it is true that certain cultures make no special provisions today (gravity alone serves some women). With ingenuity, a few inexpensive, reusable, and environmentally friendly, alternatives are feasible.

Native women wore a leather thong padded with dried moss. Soft, absorbent, and disposable, these materials also served as baby diapers and bandages. The women harvested and piled the moss to dry for a few weeks before it was used. In earlier white cultures, each woman had her own set of "rags"–several sets of absorbent cloths which she kept clean and folded, ready for use. These were pinned or snapped into the underwear. These are still available, ready-made through certain stores. They are also easily handmade. Old rags should be rinsed as soon as a new one is applied since blood is good growth media for bacteria. Rinsed rags can be dried and accumulated until you have a load to wash. Rags are best rinsed in cold water to remove blood, then boiled, scrubbed with soap, rinsed again, and hung to dry in the sun. And, as with any preparation, the best plan is being ready before the need arises. Small amounts of blood may be removed from garments with one's own saliva.

Toilet Paper Alternatives

In times past, men and women who were voiding waste washed after each defecation. In later times, various plant leaves were used. In some societies, the cleansing after defecation was ignored altogether, causing disease problems.

In the hills of the Ozarks and Appalachians, specially treated corncobs were used. These cobs were treated with lye to soften them, rinsed clean, and dried. Small rags may be used which are washed and dried for reuse. It is important to keep the anal area washed and clean.

Childbirth

Most births should be allowed to progress without interference, simply keeping the labor environment clean and making the mother as comfortable as possible. You can rub her back, legs, and so forth, as she desires. Give her water and food as she desires. She should walk at intervals, and sit in a chair as long as she feels comfortable. She may wish to squat or kneel for the actual birth, or recline in bed with her legs drawn and spread. The assistant must use care to catch the baby and protect it from injury. Remember that the baby is very slippery and should be "caught" in a towel to prevent slipping or dropping. The baby will usually cry on its own. You do not need to spank the infant. Do not hold the baby by the heels, but keep the baby's head supported. Brain hemorrhage is more likely to occur if a prolonged head-down position is used.

Wipe the baby's mouth of mucus with a clean cloth or tissue. It is sometimes necessary to suction the nose and mouth with a bulb syringe, so be sure you have a clean syringe handy. Otherwise, use a dry cloth or tissue. As soon as the baby and placenta (sometimes called afterbirth) are born, have the mother lie in bed with her thighs together to retard bleeding. Massage the top of the uterus, which you can easily feel as a very firm lump in the lower abdomen. It may be almost as high as the umbilicus, but will get smaller in the first hours after birth. Rubbing it vigorously will retard hemorrhage and help stop bleeding.

These two measures are all one normally needs to do to prevent excessive bleeding in a home birth. Postpartum hemorrhage is not very common in home births, but when it occurs it can be serious. Dry the baby as soon as possible and wrap the baby in a warm blanket and give the baby to the mother for immediate nursing. As the baby nurses the breasts, a hormonal reflex (oxytocin) causes contraction of the uterus, which slows or stops bleeding. Vigorous assistance from the father will be additionally effective in stopping a serious postpartum hemorrhage by vigorously sucking on each nipple. Applying an ice pack over the uterus may also assist this process. The baby will usually nurse immediately, but will not have as much interest in nursing over the next 24 hours as during the first 10 minutes after birth. It needs rest, too, from the birth process.

You may now turn your attention to the baby, as the mother does not need much care for the next few minutes. Give the baby's skin a good rinsing in plain, lukewarm water. Be very careful not to allow the infant to get chilled or overheated immediately after birth. Chilling produces acidosis of the blood, which can depress respiration and depress the baby's nervous system. A lukewarm bath is very soothing to the baby. Wash the baby's face and irrigate the eyes to prevent complications of conjunctivitis. Rinse off all blood and amniotic fluid, and dry the infant all over, especially the hair. Dress the infant quickly, and again place the baby with the mother unless she is too tired to nurse again or to cuddle the newborn.

Check the mother frequently (every five to 10 minutes), to make certain there is not a lot of blood flowing from the vagina. A large ball of dry toilet tissue could be placed against the perineum, or you can use a sanitary napkin. The drainage should be reddish-pink but not bright red. If a gush of bright-red blood flows from the vagina, you will recognize a postpartum hemorrhage. Dark-red blood is due to pooling of blood in the vagina, and although it empties when she moves, the flow does not continue. Keep frequent checks on the pulse, and if the heart rate goes over 105 to 110, especially if it is normally closer to 80, apply an uncomfortably hot fomentation across the lower abdomen and upper thighs for two minutes. If the hot compress is kept on for more than three minutes, it will begin to dilate blood vessels rather than contract them. The fomentation must be quite hot (but not enough to blister), or it will not be effective. Such extremes in temperature will often slow down bleeding. As soon as the two minutes are up, put an ice-cold compress, squeezed from ice water, across the same area for precisely 30 seconds. Then dry the area and check again for continued bleeding.

Finally, if the bleeding is not checked by these simple means, you should insert your fist inside the vagina. Use that fist to make compression against the other hand on the abdomen, pressing against the top of the uterus, thus compressing the uterus between two hands to hinder the bleeding.

The pulse is a more sensitive indicator than the blood pressure as to the status of the hemorrhage or shock. If the mother complains of a loud ringing in her ears, this may also signify serious blood loss. Rarely, it may be necessary to transport the mother to a hospital if one is available. In an emergency, however, you may pack the vagina with clean strips of an old bed sheet or towels, pushing the strips tightly into the vagina to further stop the hemorrhage.

Natural Remedies

Healing Properties of Charcoal

One of our personal favorite remedies is charcoal. It has been around for years and is still standard procedure for poisoning even in well-equipped hospitals. The story of Will, Louise, and baby Isaiah introduced us to charcoal at the beginning of this chapter. We have had many interesting and amazing experiences with the healing properties of this simple remedy.

Aspirin

Aspirin is used medicinally for bringing down a fever, to relieve pain, and for anticoagulation. To perform the same functions, you can use a number of herbs—white willow bark, meadow sweet, wild lettuce, etc. You can also apply hydrotherapy—hot packs, hot foot baths, ice massage, etc. At times, massage or muscle stretches are useful in relieving pain. Pain in the abdomen or elsewhere can sometimes be eased by drinking a glassful of water every 10 minutes for an hour. Headaches can be relieved in this way as well.

For reducing a fever, very few things are as effective as a warm bath. Water temperature for this treatment should be slightly below the mouth temperature. The goal is to induce perspiration, which is nature's air conditioner, and this will lower the fever by evaporation of sweat from the skin.

Massage may also help to lower a fever by opening the pores, helping the skin to perspire. Drinking a glassful of water every 10 minutes for an hour helps bring the fever down.

Instead of taking aspirin as an anticoagulant, we should use some of the herbal or food anticoagulants such as five ounces of purple grape juice a day; garlic in moderation (one clove daily or four to eight tablets daily); hawthorne berry tea (four cups daily). Other herbal anticoagulants include feverfew and *Ginkgo biloba*.

Aspirin may be given to a patient suspected of having a heart attack. This may help break up potentially life-threatening clots.

Remedies for Colds
At the very first sign of a cold, elderberry extract can be taken to good advantage. It may help to stop a cold, even after symptoms begin. *Echinacea* and goldenseal can be taken to alleviate the symptoms of a cold, or shorten its course. These herbs may also make the person less likely to spread viruses to others but should not be taken other than for illness or preventive medicine. Tepid sponge baths and the wet sheet pack are recommended to help reduce fevers. For related headaches, take a hot foot bath, along with the herbs, feverfew, white willow bark, and valerian. Garlic blended in hot water along with lemon makes a valuable drink to treat viral infections.

Laxatives
For a laxative, ground flaxseed (one to two tablespoons daily), psyllium seed, slippery elm, and Epsom salts (magnesium sulphate) can be used. Herbal agents such as senna and *Cascara sagrada* should be used only for difficult cases of constipation, as they can be irritating and cause laxative habituation in some instances. Get medical advice, though, if your bowel habits change abruptly, or if you notice any bleeding from the rectum or blood in the stool.

Antiseptics
For an irrigation fluid, you may use goldenseal tea or garlic tea (one clove of

garlic in one cup of freshly boiled water blended until fine and three additional cups of boiling water added to the blender). When it has "cooked" until it is cool, it should not be irritating. The solution should not actually be boiled, only "cooked" in freshly boiled water, which is poured into the blender. These may be used as antiseptics. It should also be noted that soap and water can cleanse the skin sufficiently so that in most cases it is not necessary to use an antiseptic. Rubbing alcohol and hydrogen peroxide are two widely available chemicals for disinfecting wounds. Some microbes will survive both peroxide and alcohol.

Diet
The most beneficial diet for combating any affliction or disease is the total plant-based diet composed of fruits, nuts, grains, and vegetables. Starting this diet builds the immune system. You may use soy milk in place of dairy products, and tofu in place of eggs, for many dishes. Consult a good vegetarian cookbook or recipe guide for suggestions in meal planning, or, better yet, attend a class in vegan cooking for hands-on help in learning how to prepare both healthful and tasty dishes (see Silver Hills Cookbook under Further Reading at the end of this chapter).

Immunity
The eight natural laws of health do more to keep your immune system functioning properly than any drug. If an infection has occurred, *Echinacea* helps the immune defenses more than any other known herb. Other immune enhancers are contrast showers, mild fever baths, astragalus, and garlic. Remember to get plenty of sunshine, practice deep-breathing exercises, get extra sleep and rest, and avoid sugar and high fat foods. Sometimes a short-term fast can help cleanse the system and renew vigor and body defenses. The best way to enhance immunity is by building our general health. An ounce of prevention goes a long way in resisting disease.

Herbs
The use of herbs has been recommended by the Spirit of Prophecy.
"There are simple herbs and roots that every family may use for themselves and need not call a physician any sooner than they would call a lawyer" (Selected Messages, book 2, p. 279; see also pages 288, 294).
Here are some recommendations from inspired writings on the use of herbs.
"A cup of tea made from Catnip herb will quiet the nerves" (ibid., p. 297).
"Hop tea will induce sleep. Hop poultices over the stomach will relieve pain" (ibid.).

"When the head is congested, if the feet and limbs are put in a bath with a little mustard, relief will be obtained" (ibid.).

"For some forms of indigestion it [charcoal] is more effective than drugs. A little olive oil into which some of this powder has been stirred tends to cleanse and heal. I find it is excellent" (ibid., p. 298).

"For several days he has had a painful swelling on the knee, supposed to be from the bite of some poisonous insect. Pulverized charcoal, mixed with flaxseed was placed upon the swelling, and this poultice gave relief at once" (ibid., p. 300).

"I cannot advise any remedy for her cough better than eucalyptus and honey" (ibid.).

"Light was given that there is health in the fragrance of the pine, the cedar, and the fir. ... Let not such trees be ruthlessly cut down. Let them live" (ibid., p. 301)

For more detailed information on the use of herbs in healing and recovery, please see Get Well At Home, Richard Hansen, M. D., Chapter 18 "Medical Botany" and Home Remedies, by Agatha and Calvin Thrash (see For Further Study at the end of this chapter).

The Eight Natural Remedies

No discussion of simple recovery would be complete without a mention of the use of these health principles. They are useful for the prevention of disease as well as in the restoration of health.

"Pure air, sunlight, abstemiousness, rest, exercise, proper diet, the use of water, trust in divine power—these are the true remedies. Every person should have a knowledge of nature's remedial agencies and how to apply them. It is essential both to understand the principles involved in the treatment of the sick and to have a practical training that will enable one rightly to use this knowledge.

"The use of natural remedies requires an amount of care and effort that many are not willing to give. Nature's process of healing and upbuilding is gradual, and to the impatient it seems slow. The surrender of hurtful indulgences requires sacrifice. But in the end it will be found that nature, untrammeled, does her work wisely and well. Those who persevere in obedience to her laws will reap the reward in health of body and health of mind.

"Too little attention is generally given to the preservation of health. It is far better to prevent disease than to know how to treat it when contracted. It is the duty of every person, for his own sake, and for the sake of humanity, to

inform himself in regard to the laws of life and conscientiously to obey them. All need to become acquainted with that most wonderful of all organisms, the human body. They should understand the functions of the various organs and the dependence of one upon another for the healthy action of all. They should study the influence of the mind upon the body, and of the body upon the mind, and the laws by which they are governed" (The Ministry of Healing, pp. 127, 128; emphasis supplied).

These natural remedies are essential to the best recovery of health.

Hydrotherapy

Having had personal experience with the miracles of hydrotherapy, I can highly recommend this simple home remedy. There are a few instances when the simple application of hot and cold water is contraindicated, but most conditions will respond well to proper technique. Since it is a rather extensive subject, I highly recommend these books:

1. Home Remedies, by Calvin Thrash, M.D., and Agatha Thrash, M.D., Thrash Publications, Route 1, Box 273, Seale, AL 36875. (175 pages, illus).

2. Get Well at Home, by Richard Hansen, M. D., Shiloh Medical Publications, P.O. Box 1057, Creswell, OR, 97426. (464 pages, illustrated, $19.95).

Simple Home Hygiene

Clothing

When we first moved to Canada, our neighbors called us chechakos–I think that may be a Cree word for "white man who knows absolutely nothing about life." This title lasted until we had one winter behind us. One thing, among many we had to learn, was how to dress. We don't often think of our clothing as having much to do with our health, but tight restrictions, chilling of the extremities and exposure to filth by dragging portions of our clothing through the mud or dust, are things we must avoid Dressing comfortably and properly is part of caring for our body temple.

Although we have been given instructions regarding our dress throughout the Spirit of Prophecy, we are advised not to make it the main point of our religion. (For further study, see chapter in this book entitled "Education for the Future" a portion on dress reform.) There are a few practical principles in how we dress that can make our life in the country a little more pleasant.

Durable: Can you wear your clothes in the garden or sit on an unplaned bench? Will they protect you from hay and thistles? Can they be scrubbed clean

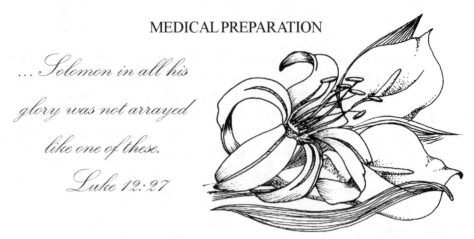

... Solomon in all his glory was not arrayed like one of these.
Luke 12:27

on a scrub board and hung in the sun to dry? Are they sturdy enough to last?

Comfortable: Does your clothing restrict natural movement and permit freedom of exercise? Cotton and wool tend to "breathe" best.

Modest: Clothing should cover you without undue exposure.

Neat and Clean: Garments should be kept repaired, clean, and unwrinkled. Flatten while hanging wet, and fold clothes as they come off the clothesline.

Healthy: Your body should be covered completely, preventing drafts. Women are especially prone to chilling; when women's extremities are covered as adequately as men's, a host of diseases are prevented. Clothes that drag in the dirt should be hemmed to prevent soiling and chilling of limbs.

Layers: One layer of clothing is adequate for warm weather. For cold weather, layer your clothing. A long skirt in winter is a good way for women to disguise how well-clad their limbs really are!

Color: Choose colors that match your complexion and complement each other. Avoid bold and loud prints. Consider the products your clothes advertise (T-shirts, hats with messages, etc.). Keep clothes simple so that others do not receive mixed signals as to your allegiance.

Sanitation

Study The Ministry of Healing, pages 277-286: "Hygiene Among the Israelites." This chapter outlines general principles of cleanliness as given to God's ancient people. (See also, Ministry of Healing, page 208

Soap Making

Always use rubber gloves and protective goggles when making soap. Do not allow children to help; lye burns deep! Neutralize lye burns with vinegar. It is relatively easy to make your own soap. It takes four to six weeks for soap to cure properly. We favor this recipe requiring no special weighing or measuring.

Equipment required: 9 ½ oz. lye crystals, 4 ½ pounds vegetable shortening, 5 cups distilled water, two candy thermometers, large stainless bowl, 2 quart glass jar, wooden spoon, Vaseline, rubber gloves, goggles, soap molds, and a picnic cooler.

Purely Simple Bar Soap Recipe

1) Prepare soap molds by greasing with Vaseline
2) Melt shortening over low heat
3) Slowly stir lye crystals into distilled water
4) Wait until respective thermometers register:
      Lye solution: 80-85 degrees F
      Shortening: 90-110 degrees F
5) Stir lye solution slowly into shortening
6) Stir 10-20 minutes, until soap solution thickens like pudding
7) Optional: Additives, such as essential oils for fragrance, herbs, spices, oats, almonds, Borax (degreaser), are added just prior to pouring the liquid soap solution into molds and placing them into the cooler.
8) Pour into Vaseline-greased soap molds or non-aluminum pans
9) Place soap molds immediately into your cooler and wrap with blanket
10) Let soap cool very gradually for two days, undisturbed
11) After 48 hours, open cooler, remove soap from molds, or cut into squares
12) Stack the fresh bars like bricks, as soon as they are removed from the molds, leaving space between bars so they can air dry for about four weeks before using or even wrapping them.

If you use the bars as gifts, scrape or trim the cured bars after drying (save the flakes), but while they are still a bit soft, then wrap each bar in waxed paper, plain brown paper, or in fancy gift wrap tied with rafia or ribbon.

Lamb's quarters may be used as a soap substitute by crushing the dried roots of the first green shoots in the spring.

Making Lye Water

Hardwood ashes are more alkaline than soft wood and, hence, produce stronger lye. Ashes (from the cook stove or heater) are suspended in a burlap bag, a nylon stocking or a layer of straw. By pouring rainwater through the ashes, a dilute solution of lye water is formed. Pour this solution back through the filtering process until the solution is strong enough. If tap water (from a treated source) is used, remember to allow for the fact that there are salts in the solution that will weaken the strength of the lye produced. When a freshly boiled egg will float in the lye solution, it is strong enough for soap-making. Lye is sodium hydroxide, a strong base, and will eventually eat out the bottom of a metal barrel. Never allow pets or children access to lye.

Larger volumes of lye may be produced in a wooden barrel in which tree limbs and a layer of straw are placed on the bottom to act as a rough filter. Burlap bags are then laid over the straw. The barrel, one third full of "filter" is then filled with hardwood ashes. A slight depression is made in the top of the surface of the ashes to catch water. Pioneers added two quarts of lime dissolved in boiling water to neutralize any salts that could affect soap making, then added jug after jug of cold soft water (rainwater) to effect leaching, sometimes taking all day. The barrel could then be drained by a spigot at or near the bottom.

For most people in a family setting, the burlap bag/nylon stocking method will produce enough lye for soap making. For larger groups of people, the barrel method may be used. It takes time to produce the ingredients for soap making, but cleanliness is important to survival.

Laundry

Here is a humorous recipe that an Alabama grandmother gave to the new bride (complete with spelling errors!):

"Warshin' Clothes-- Build fire in backyard to heat kittle of rain water. Set tubs to smoke so smoke won't blow in eyes if wind is pert. Shave one hole cake of lie soap in boilin' water. Sort things. Make three piles; 1 pile white, 1 pile colored, 1 pile work britches and rags. To make starch, stir flour in the water to smooth, then thin down with boilin' water. Take white things, rub dirty spots on board, scrub hard, and boil, then rub colored, but don't boil just wrench and starch. Take all things out of kittle with broom stick handle, then wrench and starch. Hang old rags on fence. Spread tea towels on grass. Pore wrench water on flower bed. Scrub porch with hot soapy water. Turn tubs upside down. Put on clean dress. Smooth hair with combs. Brew cup of tea, set and rock a spell and count yore blessings."

Keeping clothes clean is essential in order to eliminate germs and toxins given off and gathered as we work. This skill in a simple lifestyle will require some practice to get clothes free of ground-in dirt from outdoor work. We have all wondered how women in third world countries can actually get their clothes clean by scrubbing them on rocks. We depend on our automatic washers, but what if we were no longer able to plug in our washer? The following discussion will help you approach wash day much as great-grandma did.

To wash your clothes, you need a couple of large, square, galvanized wash tubs. Fill one wash tub about one-third to one-half full of warm to hot water. Put your scrub board in the tub and lean it back against the side closest to you. Place your bar of laundry soap on the tray at the top of the scrub board. If you can find scrub boards with a Pyrex glass scrubbing surface, they would be superior to metal surface scrubbers. But get one or two of any kind.

Start with the less soiled, white clothes. Different clothes get different treatments on the scrub boards. If you are doing underwear, scrub harder on places that absorb perspiration. Place the garment to be cleaned in your tub of hot water. Soap the whole garment, top to bottom, front and back. Then place a portion of the garment full length of the scrub board. Gripping the top of the garment, push repeatedly down and up and down again until that part is clean. Then grip another handful of the garment and repeat the same rhythm on the scrubbing surface. Keep going until you have gathered up the whole garment, then flip it over full length and repeat–"scrub, gather, up, down, scrub, gather, up, down."

Jeans, coveralls, and heavy clothing will require more scrubbing and a new start on your grip-and-gather method as you move down the garment. The reason for this is that you cannot hold the whole garment in your hands while scrubbing. Removing greasy spots or grass stains will require additional scrubbing on those areas.

Your rinse tub, the second tub mentioned at the first of this discussion, will be where the rinsing of each garment occurs. One or two rinses in the lukewarm water will be sufficient to remove the soap. Then the clothes can be hung to dry.

Your clothing should be sorted and washed in this order: whites, light colors, darker colors, then jeans and greasy clothes. As the wash water gets dirty, begin using the rinse water as the wash water, adding some boiling water, and putting clean water in the wash tub for the rinsing cycle.

Another method of doing laundry requires the same square galvanized tub (there are round ones) and a long-handled, metal plunge washer available in some stores. Grind your soap bar into shavings or powder and add one-half cup to a tub of water and clothes. Mix everything together and then apply the plunge washer to the clothes in a vigorous up-and-down motion. Grease spots or stains should be scrubbed before you use this method. Rinse one or two times as desired and hang to dry.

If you have a stove outside, clothes may also be boiled clean. If the weather is good, you can hang your clothes outside on a clothesline with clothes-pins. There are portable drying racks that can be used inside. When hanging clothes outside, wipe the line with a wet cloth. While clothes are wet, use a quick shaking motion to "snap" them. This will straighten them out, smooth the collars and sleeves, skirts, pillowcases, etc. and will save ironing time. Many garments are sufficiently smoothed in this manner. Collect and keep your clothespins indoors to prevent unnecessary weathering.

Washing Dishes

One of the best ways to insure a healthy home is by washing hands and dishes properly. Cleanliness is not difficult if you remember that germs are heat liable. You can never have too much hot water. Keep water on your heater stove, cook stove, or outdoor fire at all times. Place pre-rinsed dishes in uncomfortably hot water. Soak as many dishes as possible, especially the silverware and glassware (to kill bugs), while you put food away and wipe the counters. By the time you finish putting the kitchen in order, your wash water will be about the right temperature. When you are ready to wash dishes, fill your rinse water basin with water so hot that your dishes will quickly air dry. Many germs are transferred back onto clean dishes by wiping them dry. If the rinse water is hot enough, the first dishes placed in the drain rack are generally dry enough to put away by the time you need their space. Cleanup always takes less time if you can wash your cooking pots before the meal is served. Using ironware, this is not difficult; scrape as necessary, rinse them (in non-soapy water so as to preserve the cure), and place them on the hot stove to dry, then hang them up when cool after the meal.

Make sure anyone who washes, rinses or dries dishes have washed their hands with soap before helping. The germs that cause illness in youngsters are just as potent as those that make their parents sick!

Ironing

If you use flat irons get a set of at least two, three is better. Flat irons come with a handle to pick them up from the stove after they are heated. When they become cool again, the flatiron is placed on the stove and a hot one is used. Be sure that the irons and stove top or iron trivet on the stove is clean and that the stove top is clean.

Another easy way to de-wrinkle clothing is to hang the garment on a hanger and mist it with water from a spray bottle will straighten wrinkles. This works especially well for denim, cotton knits, and "dry-clean only" items. It is a good way to touch up garments that have acquired traveling wrinkles in your suitcase. The only disadvantage to this technique is that you must allow the garment time to dry before it is worn. The advantage is that the misting system is portable and requires no ironing.

Bathing

The equipment necessary for bathing can vary according to the amount of hot water available and the number of people. With a large number of people, scheduling bathtime will be essential. If you have a gravity-fed water system with a gas-fired hot water tank, bathing is as simple as installing a tub, shower, and drain. Should you not have gravity-fed water, or you can't buy gas for a hot water heater, there are alternatives.

As part of your basic household simple lifestyle equipment, you should have a galvanized boiler and one or two square galvanized tubs (as mentioned in the laundry section). Place the boiler on the wood cook stove or the wood heater and fill it with water. It is a good idea to keep the boiler full throughout the day for dishes, hand washing, laundry, and bathing. Let the water heat to as high a temperature as possible. This will require more dilution with cold water, allowing your hard-earned hot water to go further.

Once the water is hot, dip it out of the boiler with a pan or small bucket into your square bathtub. Dilute with cold water until comfortably hot to the touch. Have a chair or bench close by the tub in a private room.

Tub bath: Have extra water on hand in order to rinse off after this procedure. Kneel next to the tub and wash hair first. Then get into the tub and soap up. Rinse with a pan of clean, warm water. Rinsing with cool or cold water is very stimulating and will effect the release of more white blood cells to increase immunity to disease. After you have dried and dressed, the process of cleanup begins. You need to haul the bath water out to your gray water dump if you do not have a septic system. You can dip it out of the tub into a five-gallon can and carry it out.

Bird bath: Fill two washbasins with slightly diluted hot water; one for washing and one for rinsing. Wash your entire body with the soapy washcloth, starting at the face and neck and washing on down to the waist. Then rinse. Wash the lower part of the body. Rinse.

Shower: A rather enjoyable method of outdoor bathing in the summer involves a shower bucket. Commercial black solar shower bags with a hose and nozzle are available from outdoor stores. But you can make a shower bucket: the bucket must be metal and have a 4 inch by-1½ inch nipple brazed in near the bottom. On the exposed threaded end, use plumber's tape and attach a ½ inch valve and a shower head of your choosing. A shower stall may be made from tarps or wood to ensure privacy. Install a sturdy hook that will support a five-gallon bucket of water.

The showering procedure: When the bucket is full of water at the right temperature, hang the bucket in the shower stall. Step into the shower and open the valve to wet yourself down. Shut the valve off and soap yourself and shampoo your hair. Open the valve and rinse. You may refill the bucket to ½ full with cool or cold water for an excellent tonic (see The Ministry of Healing, p. 237). Don't be afraid to use all of the water. You earned it!

Simple comforts makes you feel good about yourself. In a simple lifestyle, one can be just as clean as a person who lives in a utility web. It is not difficult, but it must be planned. Your health will improve as you take time to be clean. (See Testimonies for the Church, vol. 3, p. 70.)

Study to simplify. When you are cleaning house ask yourself: Will this item be of use when there is no electricity available? Could someone use this today more effectively than I use it? Have I used this in the past year or two?

Study to be prepared. Since the Lord has told us that calamities will increase and become more disastrous, it becomes apparent that God's people should be trained in emergency response as well as having practical skills in growing and preparing food, building a house, and be able to assist in disease recovery. Most importantly, we need to prepare our hearts.

FOR FURTHER STUDY

Eat For Strength, Thrash, Calvin and Agatha, Uchee Pines Institute, Seale, AL, 36875-5703

Home Remedies, Thrash, Calvin and Agatha, Uchee Pines Institute, Seale, AL, 36875-5703

Get Well At Home, Hansen, Richard A., Shilo Publications, P. O. Box 1057, Creswell, OR 97426

Where There is No Doctor, Werner, David, Hesperian Foundation, Box 1692, Palo Alto, CA 94302

The Best of Silver Hills, a cookbook by Eileen and Debbie Brewer, 1996, Silver Hills Publishing, Lumby, British Columbia, V0E 2G0, Canada

For more information on further medical missionary training:
Eden Valley Institute: 6263 N. County Rd. #29, Loveland, CO, 80538-9519
Uchee Pines Institute: 30 Uchee Pines Rd., Seale, AL 36875
Wildwood Lifestyle Center: P.O. Box 129, Wildwood, GA 30757

For more information on how to prevent major problems such as various cancers and heart disease, Type II diabetes, etc. please contact the three institutions listed above and:
Dr. Hans Diehl
Director of CHIP (Cardiac Health Improvement Program)
c/o Better Health Productions
P. O. Box 1761
Loma Linda, CA 92354
1-909-825-1888

Chapter Fourteen

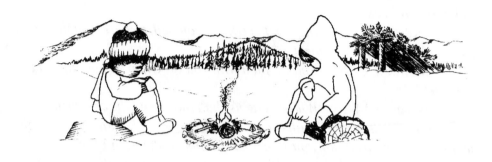

Wilderness Survival: Making a Friend of Nature

"In His written word and in the great book of nature, He has revealed the principles of life." (The Ministry of Healing, p. 115).

It has been said that the true measurement of our IQ is in how well we adapt to new situations. Very often, physical survival depends upon our ability to adapt. In this chapter we will discuss everyday, basic survival skills. Though our survival in the end time will be assisted by God, feeling at home in the wilderness may help remove our fear of the unknown. As you acquaint yourself with the great out-of-doors, keep a few pointers in mind. Being lost or injured does not mean you should panic. There are things that can be done to aid yourself and others. Consider a few verses from the Ultimate Survival Manual about being prepared.

Proverbs 22:3: *"A prudent man foreseeth the evil, and hideth himself: but the simple pass on, and are punished."*

Matthew 25:1-4: *"Then shall the kingdom of heaven be likened unto ten virgins, which took their lamps, and went forth to meet the bridegroom. And five of them were wise, and five were foolish. They that were foolish took their lamps, and took no oil with them: but the wise took oil in their vessels with their lamps."*

Proverbs 30:24-28: *"There be four things which are little upon the earth, but they are exceeding wise: the ants are a people not strong, yet they prepare their meat in the summer; the conies are but a feeble folk, yet make they their houses in the rocks; the locusts have no king, yet go they forth all of them by bands; the spider taketh hold with her hands, and is in kings' palaces."*

Psalm 34:7: *"The angel of the Lord encampeth round about them that fear him, and delivereth them."*

Matthew 28:20: *"And lo, I am with you alway, even unto the end of the world."*

Isaiah 33:14-16: *"Who among us shall dwell with the devouring fire? who among us shall dwell with ever lasting burnings? He that walketh righteously, and speaketh uprightly; he that despiseth the gain of oppressions, that shaketh his hands from holding of bribes, that stoppeth his ears from hearing of blood, and shutteth his eyes from seeing evil; he shall dwell on high: his place of defense shall be the munitions of rocks: bread shall be given him; his waters shall be sure."*

All of the things that we need to survive are available in the wilderness. Native peoples have been making use of them by "living off the land" for thousands of years, and all of the things we need for survival are still there. Wilderness survival does not necessarily have to infer an emergency. If we learn how to recognize the things we need, and learn the skills that enable us to get them, we can be "at home" in the wilderness. Though we may not think about it this way, we are all "surviving" in our present situation–otherwise we would not even be alive. We do not consider it survival, because that with which we have become familiar is not life threatening. We have surrounded ourselves with a lifestyle that provides us with the things we need to stay alive. In the process of growing up within this system, we have learned the necessary skills to obtain what we need from this system.

Whether we are in town or in the wilderness, the things that we need in order to stay alive are basically the same. In the wilderness it is considered "survival" because most people nowadays are not acquainted with the "wilderness system." When we are not familiar with the woods and wilderness systems, situations can seem more threatening. Making friends with the wilderness is essential to our relationship with nature's God. But, as beautiful and inspiring as nature is, there is nothing on earth that should attract us to stay here and miss heaven.

There will be a time when we will be forced from urban societies to a more simple existence. This is not to be feared. Living in the cities will not always be as comfortable for us as it is today.

"Often the follower of Christ is brought where he cannot serve God and carry forward his worldly enterprises. Perhaps it appears that obedience to some plain requirement of God will cut off his means of support. Satan would make him believe that he must sacrifice his conscientious con-

301

victions. <u>But the only thing in our world upon which we can rely is the word of God</u>" (<u>The Desire of Ages</u>, p. 121; emphasis supplied).

Satan would have us believe that unless we compromise our integrity, it will be impossible to survive. Learning to survive in the wilderness will require knowledge in three areas: Skills, Experience, and Trust. Although there is considerable overlap, the three areas all work together.

<u>Skills</u>: This includes the whole area of primitive skills, such as shelter and fire building, whittling, making rope cordage, cooking on an open fire, staying warm, purifying water, and finding your way in the woods. It also includes observation and identification skills such as recognizing which plants have edible and useful parts and knowing which types of rocks are good for making different types of tools. Another important observation skill is "awareness." Being aware means watching and understanding the way things in nature interact, the ways you can know what to expect from animals, plants, streams, weather, and seasons. Awareness skills allow you to act in harmony with nature.

<u>Experience</u>: The experience you get from the actual time that you spend in the wilderness is extremely valuable. Experience in the wilderness gives you a chance to learn awareness and practice your skills and trust. Spending time in nature will help you understand the wilderness better. From your experience you will realize that all the things you need to stay alive are really out there, and by being close to nature, you will have an opportunity to obtain what you need.

<u>Trust</u>: Trust is believing that the Creator has provided all the things that we need in nature. It also means that He will give us the ability to find and get them, too. The term "Sacred Hunt" was used by some Native Peoples to describe this idea. Trust grows with your experience. You are not left to just hope that the things you need might be out there somewhere. Instead, you can have the assurance that they **are** there, and that as you look for them, the Creator will help you find them.

An anthropologist may know many of the primitive skills. A naturalist may have had a lot of experience with nature and learned much about it. A believer in God may be exercising faith on a regular basis. A survivalist needs all three of these skills to be competent at living in the wilderness.

A Christian survivalist must also be sensitive to the surrounding wilderness environment. It is important for us to have the attitude of a caretaker, rather than the attitude of an exploiter or conqueror. As in life, our goal should be to leave things in a better condition than we found them. It is necessary to practice awareness and work with nature. This is possible, even when gathering live plants. For example, study the plants you want to gather. Look around; is there somewhere that the same plants are growing where they are too close together and could use some thinning? Do your gathering there, rather than taking ones that are growing by themselves. Is there some way to gather the part you need without destroying the whole plant? If so, "prune" out a crowded section. In this way you will be making room for the other plants to grow, and their growth will be healthier as a result! The area will be better off because you have been there.

Most of us, unfortunately, have the wrong idea about the wilderness and survival. The wilderness is frequently seen as something that must be conquered and/or endured. Looking at nature, and nature's Creator, in this way makes it to be an opponent or an enemy. In reality, both are quite friendly and helpful–if one is willing to be humble and accept their terms. There is nothing in the wilderness that is "out to get us." If we work with nature rather than against it, both man and nature can enjoy a symbiotic relationship. The real enemy is the natural hostility and rebelliousness of our own human nature. Survival depends more on personality than danger, weather, terrain, or nature of the emergency. If a person remains calm, trusts God, and uses common sense, he will be able to survive almost anything he encounters.

When we find ourselves in a survival situation, we all have a tendency to panic. But to panic would be the worst thing we could do. There is an acronym based on the word **STOP**. The first thing we should do when we realize that we are in a survival situation is to **STOP**, and work through these steps and develop a plan:

STAY	The opposite of running. It may not be wise to stay in that particular spot for the whole survival situation, but it is best to stay put until you have worked through these steps.
THINK	The opposite of panicking. "Your brain is your best survival tool." Relax as you can. Pray.
OBSERVE	Take note of what you have with you and what is around you. Also observe what the weather is likely to do and how many hours of daylight are left.
PLAN	Put together a plan based on the Survival Priorities and your observations.

Survival Priorities

Survival priorities are the things we need in order to stay alive. They are listed here in order of importance. Trusting that *"...my God shall supply all your need according to his riches in glory by Christ Jesus"* (Philippians 4:19).

1. SHELTER- From cold, rain, wind, or sun. Select your camp area carefully.
2. FIRE- For keeping warm, purifying water (boil 3-5 minutes), cooking, and tool making. Be sure to use fire safely.

3. WATER- Purify the water before you drink it if you have any doubts.
4. REST- Allow yourself adequate rest. It's dangerous to become exhausted.
5. FOOD- Identify and prepare wild edibles.

Priorities–Why This Order of Importance?

You can go for a couple of weeks without food; that is why it is last on the list. Under good conditions, you could even last a couple of days without water, that is why it is third–you would be okay until tomorrow. But, most likely it will get cold at night, so shelter and fire are first on the list, because you will need to avoid hypothermia. Rest is number four. You will need it too, possibly not as urgently as shelter, fire, or water, but probably before food. Before you begin your camping trip, consider including these items in your backpack. It is also recommended that the following survival kit be kept together in a "day-pack," shoulder bag, or belt pouch so it will be ready to grab in an emergency.

Suggested Survival Kit Items

Knife: Your basic tool, learn how to use it safely, and how to keep it sharp.

"Space Blanket": It will help you keep warmer, and it's waterproof.

Large Plastic Bag for Poncho: For rain covering and shelter.

7' x 7' Clear Plastic Sheet: Take with you into dry desert areas to be used for making a Solar Still or for improvising a shelter and rain cover.

Water Bottle or Canteen: At least 1 quart/liter.

Water Purification: Recommend using a .2 micron filter system.

Stainless Steel Cup or Can: 1 pint is best, can be used for cooking and purifying water. One that fits into the bottom of your canteen/water bottle would be easiest to pack.

Matches or other fire starter: Keep matches in a waterproof case. Learn how to build fires safely and efficiently.

Candle: To help start fires–it will stay lit longer than a match–and can be used for light.

Food: Something that is lightweight, nutritious, and will not be easily crushed such as sunflower seeds, nuts, whole-grain crackers, granola bars, dried fruit, etc.

Fish Hooks: There may be a body of water nearby with fish in it.

Fish Line: For fishing, but could also be used for cordage.

Bandanna: Has many uses: bandaging, slings, splints, padding, washcloth, towel, filtering water, tablecloth, headband, carrying bag, etc.

Compass: Know how to use your compass.

Map: One that shows terrain features of the area you will be in.

First-aid Kit: Keep your first-aid kit in a readily recognizable container.
Rope: About 25 feet of 1/8 inch cord. This is used for tying up shelters, improvising equipment, safety lines, etc. Learn how to tie knots properly and efficiently.
Whistle: For signaling: 3 whistle blasts, 3 flashes, 3 fires—3 of any signal is the recognized distress signal.
Metal Mirror: Also for signaling.
Flashlight: A small, lightweight flashlight may come in handy when it gets dark.
Toilet Paper: Keep it in a waterproof plastic bag.

Larger Home Survival Kit

This larger kit should be kept in a 5-gallon plastic bucket with lid. In a survival situation, it would be used for water and food storage. Keep it in a place where it could be easily and quickly grabbed in an emergency, such as an earthquake or other natural disaster. Blankets and/or sleeping bags were not included in this list because of their bulk, but you would want to take them with you when you evacuate, too. Many of these items would be useful in lesser emergencies, such as candles when lights go out. Just remember to replace them so they will be there next time. These items can be kept in or on a good backpack. Each person in the home should have their own pack.

Knife: Your most basic survival tool.
Hatchet/Machete: For heavier cutting jobs.
Hand Trowel/ Small Shovel/ Hand Pick: For digging
Whetstone: For sharpening above tools.
Water jug: Minimum of 1 gallon. A 5 gallon jug is recommended (because of its size this might not be kept in the kit, but should be close beside it).
Bucket/Washbasin: For washing, hauling water, etc.
Food: Dried fruit, sunflower seeds, hard tack, etc. Nonperishable, nutritious, and lightweight.
Cooking Pot: For cooking and purifying water.
Stainless Steel Cups: For drinking and eating utensils.
Spoons: For cooking and eating.
Aluminum Foil: For cooking.
Matches: Keep some in a waterproof container; a couple of packs of book matches will save the waterproof ones for when you need them.
Candles: For fire starting and light.
Milk Carton Strips: For fire starting.
Plastic Trash Bags: For rain covering, ground sheets, etc.
Tarp: Approximately 10' x 10' for shelter.

1/8" Rope: 25' length, some shorter lengths may also be helpful.
First-aid Kit: A well-stocked home type kit.
First-aid Manual: To provide necessary information.
Soap: For washing.
Towel and Washcloth: Bandannas may be substituted for washcloths.
Bandannas: Can be used for many things, from bandages to tablecloths.
Toothbrushes: For brushing your teeth.
Toilet Paper: Keep this in a waterproof plastic bag.
Whistle: For signaling.
Metal Mirror: For looking at yourself and signaling.
Rope: A 50' length of 1/4 or 3/8 inch rope for obstacle safety.
Compass: For route finding.
Pack: To put all of this equipment in when traveling.
Survival Book: For how-to information, ideas.
Notepad and Pencil: For writing notes, maps, messages.
Sewing Kit: For mending clothes.
Insect Repellant: For preventing bug bites.
Bible: Don't forget God when you need Him most.

Larger Basic Equipment

Water
2 Buckets (for hauling water)
Water Barrel and Dipper
Washtub (size 3)
Canning Kettle (or large pot for hot water)
Bucket for waste water
Washbasin
0.2 Micron water purification system for drinking.

Food
Pots, Pans and Cooking Utensils
Table Service for each family member
Containers for Food Storage (some sealable, metal garbage can with lid)
Ice Chest
Table (collapsible)
Grain Grinder

Clothing
Suitcase, Duffel, Chest for each family member's clothing
Warm Weather Clothing
Cool Weather Clothing
Blankets, Sleeping Bags, Foam Pads
Towels, Washcloths
Clothesline (1/4 or 1/8 inch rope)
Scrub Board
Sewing Equipment

Shelter
Tent (large size cabin-type or wall tent; a four-season tent could be selected in some areas)
Ground Cloth, Tarp
Broom and Dustpan
Lantern and Fuel Can (kerosene or white gas)

Heat
Wood Heater and Cook Stove and Stove Pipe (type that could be used inside your tent)
Ax
Bow Saw or Pruning Saw
Stove Poker
Ash Shovel

Note: The above list has been compiled with regard to utility and portability if it became necessary to evacuate your family. Primary considerations when choosing a site to set camp are availability of (1) water, (2) fuel, and (3) food.

Helpful Tools and Skills
(at home and in emergencies)

Woodworking Tools
Whittling Knife
Ax (broad hatchet)
Brace and Auger Bits (drill)
Gouge
Handsaw

Rasp
Plane
Drawknife
Tape Measure
Square
Crosscut Saw
Level
Hammer and Assorted Nails
Wood Chisel Set

Mechanical Tools
Screwdrivers
Box/End Wrench Set
Socket Wrench Set
Pliers
Cold Chisel, Punch
Crescent Wrench

Metalworking Tools
Pliers, Vise-Grips
Ball-peen Hammer
Hacksaw
Tin Snips
Vise
Anvil
File, Whetstone

Gardening Tools
Shovel or Spade
Hoe
Rake, Pitchfork
Watering Can
Wheelbarrow, Cart, or Wagon
Seed

Survival Skills
Shelter Construction
Fire Building

Identification of Edible Plants
Signaling
Knife/Tool Sharpening
Knots and Rope Safety Techniques
Route Finding (orienteering)
Cooking
First-aid
Home Nursing (natural remedies)
Woodworking (whittling)
Basket Weaving
Making Cordage (rope)
Sewing
Gardening
Pottery
Mechanical Skills
Candle Making
Weaving
Tanning
Spiritual Skills

Shelter and Rest

"And ye shall take you... the boughs of goodly trees, branches of palm trees, and the boughs of thick trees, and willows of the brook.... Ye shall dwell in booths" (Leviticus 23:40-42).

"Go up to the mountain, and bring wood, and build the house; and I will take pleasure in it, and I will be glorified, saith the Lord" (Haggai 1:8).

"He giveth his beloved sleep" (Psalm 127:2).

"The sleep of a labouring man is sweet" (Ecclesiastes 5:12).

"Love not sleep, lest thou come to poverty; open thine eyes, and thou shalt be satisfied with bread" (Proverbs 20:13).

"By communion with God in nature, the mind is uplifted, and the heart finds rest" (The Desire of Ages, p. 291).

Depending on your situation, you may need shelter from cold, rain, wind, or sun. Ideally, a shelter will provide protection from all of these, but in a survival situation you may only have time and energy to build according to your immediate needs.

First, look for a natural shelter that you could modify to suit your needs. A fallen tree, a large hollow log, an overhanging rock, or a cave. All of these have the possibility of making a good shelter. Use your imagination and ingenuity. Exercise caution when entering a natural shelter for the first time in case another animal already occupies the spot.

If possible, choose a level area with a safe place for a fire near a source of water and firewood for your camp. To avoid becoming flooded, do not make your camp in a low area or a ravine. Also avoid windswept areas if possible. However, a somewhat open area with a breeze can be helpful if insects, like mosquitoes, are a problem.

Warmth is directly related to the amount of insulation you have around you. Anything that is light and fluffy, and can provide "dead air" space can be used for insulation, even if it's wet. The thicker the insulation material around you, the warmer you will be. When lying down, insulate yourself from the ground. Because you are in direct contact with it, you will lose more heat to the ground than to the air.

Debris Hut Construction

A simple debris hut may be the best shelter for many situations. It can be easily constructed using only natural materials.

Begin making a debris hut by interlocking forks or branches, or tying together two crossed sticks and then laying a ridgepole on top of them to make a tripod. The ridgepole could also be set against a tree or rock. This framework should enclose an area about 6 inches wider and longer than the outline of your body as you lie down. Since heat rises, it should be as low as possible, yet steep enough to shed water. Think in terms of a "sleeping bag" rather than a "bedroom," realizing that you will not be able to sit up inside. If practical, have the door of your shelter facing east so you can get the morning sun. In North America, this also places the back of the shelter toward the prevailing incoming weather.

Leaving a place for the door, lay more sticks and branches against this frame to form the ribbing. Use sticks that are as big around as your forearm if possible. Thicker sticks will increase the warmth of your shelter, and the heavier sticks will be less likely to be disturbed if you bump against them during the night. If large sticks are scarce, you can use smaller branching sticks to form a lattice that will hold

Sticks

Leaves

Moss and bark

310

the thatching material. The ribbing must not extend above the ridgepole more than 1 or 2 inches, so that it will be completely covered by the thatching. If a stick pokes through the thatching, water will run down it and into the shelter.

For thatching, gather leaves, grass, pine needles, moss, or any similar debris. It does not matter if the debris is wet, it will still keep you dry. Start at the bottom and put a layer of thatching against the ribbing, laying the thatching on in layers from the bottom up like shingles so water will run out and down over each layer to keep out the rain. Keep adding debris until it is about 1 foot thick all over the shelter. In cold weather, make the debris 3-4 feet thick. Finally, lay branches or pieces of bark against the shelter to keep the wind from blowing your thatching away. Make the door just big enough to squeeze through. Save a pile of thatching material to plug the door after you crawl in for the night.

For bedding, place a 1-foot-thick layer of the cleanest and driest debris on the floor of the shelter (it will smash down as you lie on it). For warmth, it is a good idea to completely fill the inside with this clean, dry material, then burrow into it. Since bits and pieces of the thatching debris fall through the ribbing as you put it on, you will probably want to put the bedding material in the shelter last to keep it as clean as possible. Enter the shelter feet first.

The thatching will shed rain quite well. If it does leak, rebuild the shelter making the top more pointed, or the sides steeper. Be sure the thatching is "shingled" so the rain will run out and down. If rain is likely, be sure to make your camp where natural drainage will not cause flooding or puddling inside the hut.

Most thatching burns easily, so be careful with fire around the shelter! With this type of shelter you do not need a fire to stay warm, just thicker thatching. Remember: insulation equals thickness equals warmth. If you were cold during the night, improve your shelter by adding more thatching to be warmer the next night.

The debris hut shelter works best for one person. For small groups, 2- to 3-person shelters are workable. However, greater width requires greater height, so unless the shelter is stuffed with debris, it will not be as warm. One possibility is to arrange several single person shelters in a spoke-like pattern with the doors facing the center. Over the center a common vestibule could be built. This would also provide a work and storage area. For larger groups consider building a circular wickiup. The construction of a wickiup is similar to a debris hut, except that it is shaped like a tepee. A small controlled fire could be built in the center of the wickiup providing for the heat lost to the additional height. Leave a smoke hole in the top of the shelter.

YOU CAN SURVIVE!

Snow Shelters

Snow is an excellent material with which to build shelters. It provides good insulation and protects from wind exposure. It may be modified to personal need and is limited only by the imagination.

1. Mark out a suitable area and size of shelter.
2. Dig out the area including a tunnel-type entrance–leave a good amount (1 foot) of snow on the sleeping shelf/bench.
3. With small trees make roof rafters, then cover with boughs to a good depth: 6" to 1'.
4. Cover with snow–make an air vent and move in. An air vent is a must, and it may be necessary to enlarge and/or make smaller depending on inside temperature and fresh air requirements.

Another method for making snow shelters is the use of snow blocks. Gently pack an area of approximately 10' x 10'. Then with a stick or machete cut your packed area into 1' x 2' squares. Remove these blocks in whatever condition you can, and begin stacking them in the form of a shelter. Northern peoples use the igloo design by leaning the blocks toward the center of the structure. Cut a door and build an entranceway that will allow for ventilation.

Sleeping Bags

The sleeping bag is one of the outdoorsman's most valuable items of equipment. A good bag is a lifetime investment. The more it is used, the more it is appreciated. The 100 percent waterfowl down bag still holds first place as the lightest, most compact and efficient. Used properly, a quality sleeping bag will meet the manufacturer's claims; however, the effects of its misuse are cumulative and unforgiving. On a practical level, misuse robs the camper of needed sleep. If down bags are not acceptable, check Quallofil or other synthetic fiber-filled bags.

There is much that can be done to improve sleeping bag comfort and assure a good night's rest. The user, however, must be willing to put forth some time and effort if he or she expects his or her sleeping bag to perform as intended by the manufacturer.

For the attainment of a good night's rest in your sleeping bag, it might be well to consider some of the techniques that have been tried and proven over the years. "Make your bed carefully and lie in it comfortably."

1. Do not leave a sleeping bag stuffed, tightly rolled, or compressed

312

except when on the trail or transporting it. When not in use, hang it from the foot or fold loosely. A large plastic dry cleaning bag will protect the bag.

2. Do not cover your sleeping bag when in use with plastic sheeting or other waterproof fabric. Moisture will condense on the underside of waterproof materials.

3. Your sleeping bag should be insulated from the ground. Use a waterproof ground cloth first, then a foam pad, and then the sleeping bag. If extra comfort is desired and gear weight is not a factor, include an air mattress between the ground cloth and foam pad.

4. A polyfoam pad is an excellent insulator. It is preferred by many over the air mattress for cold-weather sleeping.

5. Your bag must be kept dry if you are to sleep warmly. A wet sleeping bag is difficult to dry in the field.

6. Do not cover or draw your head completely into the sleeping bag so that you breathe into it. Your nose and mouth should always be left uncovered. In very cold weather it is advisable to cover your face with a piece of woolen clothing.

7. Many who live and work on the trail in the Arctic carry two sets of two-piece long underwear. One pair for day wear and the other for night. Extra clothing for night wear, such as pajamas, only adds weight to your equipment if you are backpacking and is limited in use. A pair of loose-fitting wool socks and a loose-fitting wool cap that can be pulled down over your ears are the proven cold-weather sleeping bag wear. For those who can't endure wool underwear next to their body, consider the two-layer type such as Duofold, cotton inside and wool outside. Long underwear should not fit snugly.

8. Do not sleep in clothing that you wore during the day. Clothing worn during the day, especially long underwear, will be warm, however, it will also contain moisture which will soon chill you. If you do not have a change of long underwear, you are better off to sleep in your lighter underwear.

9. Eating a light snack, such as a candy bar, just prior to entering your sleeping bag will step up your metabolic rate and produce more body heat. A hot drink will also help.

10. Don't sleep under the stars. This practice will eventually lead to problems. Dampness, unexpected rain or snow, and wind will rob your body heat in survival situations.

YOU CAN SURVIVE!

Sanitation

"Designate a place outside the camp where you can go to relieve yourself. As part of your equipment have something to dig with, and when you relieve yourself, dig a hole and cover up your excrement. For the Lord your God moves about in your camp to protect you and to deliver your enemies to you. Your camp must be holy so that He will not see among you anything indecent and turn away from you" (Deuteronomy 23:12-14, NIV).

- "Cat holes" should be dug 6-8 inches deep. A digging stick can be used, or if the dirt is soft, the toe of your boot may be used to kick out a hole. Use the same dirt to refill the hole when finished.
- If the ground is too rocky to dig a hole, turn over an appropriate-sized rock using the cavity beneath. Replace the rock when finished.
- Clean hands: a washbasin may be made with a sheet of plastic by digging a hole and lining it with plastic, then filling with water.

Beware of Hypothermia

Hypothermia, sometimes referred to as "exposure sickness," can kill you. It occurs when the inner-core temperature of the body falls to a level at which the vital organs no longer function effectively. Hypothermia is caused by cold, wet, and/or wind chilling the body so that it loses heat faster than can be produced. Frequently the advent of hypothermia is hastened by a deficiency of energy-producing food. However, the greatest single factor to bring on hypothermia is improper clothing.

Hypothermia can occur anywhere that the environmental temperature is low enough to reduce the inner-core temperature of the body to the danger level. It occurs most frequently in rugged mountain terrain where a person on foot can pass from a calm and sunny valley into wind and rain-lashed mountains in a time lapse of only a few hours. Most hypothermia accidents occur in outdoor temperatures between -1° and 10° Celsius (30° and 50° F). It is more difficult to keep dry at these temperatures.

Fortunately, the approach of hypothermia is noticeable by its easily visible symptoms; its advance is marked by recognizable steps or stages. If the warning signs are heeded and countermeasures introduced, tragedy can be averted.

The noticeable signposts along the way to a hypothermia accident are:
1. A person feels cold and has to exercise to warm up.
2. They start to shiver and feel numb.
3. Shivering becomes more intense and uncontrollable.

4. Shivering becomes violent. There is difficulty in speaking. Thinking becomes sluggish and the mind starts to wander.

5. Shivering decreases and muscles start to stiffen. Muscle coordination becomes difficult and movements become erratic and jerky. Exposed skin may become blue or puffy. Thinking becomes fuzzy. Appreciation of the seriousness of the situation is vague or may be totally lacking. However, the victim may still be able to maintain the appearance of knowing where they are and what is going on.

6. The victim becomes irrational, loses contact with the environment, and drifts into stupor. Pulse and respiration are slowed.

7. The victim does not respond to the spoken word. Falls into unconsciousness. Most reflexes cease to function and heartbeat becomes erratic.

8. Heart and lung control centers of the brain stop functioning. A healthy person who is alert and aware of the potential danger of hypothermia can help themselves during stages 1 through 3. Once the condition has advanced to stage 4 and the person's mind starts to wander, they may not realize what is happening to them and may very well need assistance. If the condition deteriorates beyond this stage, they will definitely need help.

If a member of your party shows any of the symptoms of hypothermia—uncontrollable fits of shivering; vague, slow, slurred speech, memory lapses, incoherence; immobile, fumbling hands; frequent stumbling, lurching gait; drowsiness, apparent exhaustion, and inability to get up after a rest—he is in trouble and needs your help.

A victim of hypothermia may deny that he is in trouble, but you must believe the symptoms, not the victim. Even mild symptoms demand immediate and positive treatment:

a. Get the victim out of the cold, wind, and/or rain.

b. Strip off all wet clothes.

c. If the person is only mildly impaired, give him **warm** drinks (nonalcoholic, alcohol increases susceptibility to cold) and get him into dry clothes and a warm sleeping bag. Well-wrapped warm rocks placed near the victim will hasten recovery.

d. If the victim is semiconscious or worse, try to keep him awake and give him **warm** drinks. Leave him stripped; put him in a sleeping bag with another person (also stripped); if you have a double sleeping bag, put the victim between two warm persons. Skin-to-skin contact is the most effective treatment.

e. When the victim has recovered sufficiently to be able to eat, feed him. Make sure he is dressed in dry clothing and well rested before starting out again.

f. If the victim has to be carried out, make sure his body temperature has been brought up to normal and wrap them in a good sleeping bag before starting out. With the exception of cases involving personal body injury, most hypothermia accidents can be prevented.

Hypothermia can occur anywhere, anytime the air temperature drops low enough so that a body is exposed to the elements, leaves a dangerously reduced inner-core temperature. Wind chills the air. If you leave home or camp in a warm 5° Celsius (41° F) temperature and feel comfortable traveling at a leisurely pace, a 25 mph wind on the ridge will reduce the 5° Celsius to a cold minus 10° C or 14° F)

Wet clothing in cold weather extracts the heat from the body nearly 200 times faster than dry clothing. Wool clothing provides better protection than cot-

WIND-CHILL CHART

ESTIMATED WIND SPEED IN MPH	ACTUAL THERMOMETER READING (°F)											
	50	40	30	20	10	0	-10	-20	-30	-40	-50	-60
	EQUIVALENT TEMPERATURE (°F)											
Calm	50	40	30	20	10	0	-10	-20	-30	-40	-50	-60
5	48	37	27	16	6	-5	-15	-26	-36	-47	-57	-68
10	40	28	18	4	-9	-21	-33	-46	-58	-70	-83	-95
15	36	22	5	-3	-18	-36	-45	-58	-72	-85	-99	-112
20	32	18	4	-10	-23	-39	-53	-67	-82	-96	-110	-124
25	30	16	0	-15	-29	-44	-59	-74	-86	-104	-113	-133
30	28	13	-8	-18	-33	-48	-60	-79	-94	-109	-125	-140
35	27	12	-4	-20	-35	-49	-57	-82	-98	-113	-129	-145
40	26	10	-6	-21	-37	-53	-69	-85	-11	-116	-132	-148
(wind speeds greater than 40 mpg have little additional effect.)	LITTLE DANGER (For properly clothed person)			INCREASING DANGER			GREAT DANGER					
							DANGER FROM FREEZING OF EXPOSED FLESH					

ton clothing in wet weather.

In cold weather, an uncovered head can account for up to 60 percent of body heat loss. Carry a good wool toque or cap. The most common contributors to the development of problems during cold, wet, and windy weather are: lack of proper clothing, inadequate shelter, and exhaustion. The best defense against the advent of hypothermia is to be prepared.

1. Dress appropriately.
2. Take along rainwear, extra dry clothes, food, and matches.
3. If a member of your party is not properly dressed and equipped, bring the potential danger to his attention. It could save his life.
4. If you are the leader of a party of novices, state the basic rules of conduct for trail safety and tell them you expect these rules to be observed.
5. Travel at the speed of the slowest member of the party.
6. Break at frequent intervals for rest and gear check.
7. Distribute candies or other nibble food. It helps keep up energy.
8. If one member of your party is improperly dressed or under-equipped and you encounter adverse conditions, immediately turn back or head for shelter, build a fire, and concentrate on making your camp as secure and comfortable as possible.
9. Keep watching all members of your party for signs of fatigue or discomfort. It is far better to cancel an outing than to risk a life.

Please refer to chapter 13, "Medical Preparation," for emergency response.

Accidental Hypothermia

Predisposing Factors: poor physical condition; inadequate nutrition and hydration; thin build; non-woolen clothing; inadequate protection from wind, rain and snow; getting wet; exhaustion.

Signs (observed by others): poor coordination, slowing of pace, stumbling, thickness of speech, amnesia, irrationality, poor judgment, hallucinations, loss of contact with environment, blueness or puffiness of skin, dilation of pupils, decreased heart and respiratory rate, weak or irregular pulse, stupor.

Symptoms (felt by person): intense shivering, muscle tensing, fatigue, feeling of deep cold or numbness, poor articulation, disorientation, decrease in shivering, followed by rigidity of muscles, blueness or puffiness of skin, slow, irregular or weak pulse.

Prevention: conditioning, good rest, and nutrition prior to climb, continued intake of food, waterproof/windproof clothing (some woolen), emergency bivouac equipment, early bivouac in storm or if lost or darkness has descended, exercise to keep up body's heat production (isometric contraction of muscles).

YOU CAN SURVIVE!

Treatment/Reduce Heat Loss: shelter the victim from wind and weather, insulate them from the ground, replace wet clothing with dry, put on windproof, waterproof gear, increase exercise level if possible. **Add heat**: put in warmed sleeping bag with another person, give hot drink, provide heat from hot stones or hot canteen of water, huddle for body heat from other hikers, immerse in tub of hot water (110° F).

Six Basic Rules for Keeping Warm
1. Remember–thickness of insulating materials equals warmth.
2. Keep your torso warm so that it sends its excess heat to your less insulated extremities.
3. Avoid sweating by ventilating your insulation before you start to sweat.
4. Keep wind and rain out of your insulation by suitable outer covering or protection.
5. Keep your head covered to help force heat to your extremities. Uncover it early to avoid sweating.
6. Increase your metabolism by straining one muscle against another if you are all buttoned up and still cold.

Fire Building

A fire needs air, heat, and fuel to keep burning. Build the fire to provide for each of these.

AIR: If the pieces of wood are laid (or fall) too close together, there will not be sufficient oxygen to allow burning to take place.

HEAT: The flames that you see when a fire is burning, are actually burning gases released from the wood by the heat of the fire. (Coals are the actual burning of the wood, after all of the gases have been released.) One stick, burning by itself, may be able to generate enough heat to cause a sufficient amount of its gases to be released to keep itself burning.

In a fire, the pieces of burning wood heat each other, causing gases to be released and the fire to burn. If the sticks are too far apart, the fire will not burn well, if at all, because too much heat will be lost. This is especially true when first starting the fire, as there is very little collective heat. So, when starting a fire, it is necessary to take full advantage of all available heat in order to cause more gases to be released and the fire to burn well. Always use dry kindling.

FUEL: The size and amount of wood is of primary importance. Small diameter sticks, or kindling, can be heated quickly, releasing their gases and burning rapidly. Larger pieces of wood become heated more slowly, therefore they burn slower. So small sticks are good for starting fires, while larger pieces allow the fire to burn longer. The amount of fuel on the fire will regulate the size of the fire, assuming the fire is built in a way that it can take advantage of that fuel.

Start the fire with very small pieces, and add progressively larger pieces as the heat of the fire grows. Before you start the fire, prepare the spot by clearing away all organic matter for several feet in all directions. Make a pit or ring of rocks (16-20 inches in diameter is usually sufficient) to contain the fire. These rocks also help the fire to burn by reflecting heat back to the sticks in the fire. **Do not use river rocks**, as they may explode when the moisture inside them turns to steam when heated.

Gather at least 2-3 armloads of wood before starting the fire. (You will need about 10 armloads for an overnight fire.) Sort the sticks roughly according to sizes (fuel wood and kindling). Be sure you have a good bundle of pencil-sized sticks. Break these into 6-8 inch lengths. You will need a similar bundle of finger-sized sticks also.

Start the fire with a fist-sized ball of tinder: dried grass, pine needles, wood shavings, shredded bark–something fine, dry, flammable, and airy. Lay 2-3 layers of pencil-sized sticks over the ball of tinder before lighting. Building the fire against a large piece of fuel wood or between two large pieces (spaced 6-8 inches apart) gives something to lean the sticks on so they will stay in position. As the fire begins to burn, add larger and larger sticks until the fire is the size you want it. Then only add fuel as necessary to keep the fire going.

Fire-starting Tips

Build fire so the wind will blow the flames and heat into the sticks rather than out of them. If the wood is damp, use a candle to help get it started as it has a hotter flame and will last much longer than a match.

Here are a few objects that can be used for starting a fire without matches. Be sure to practice before you have to use any of these methods.

1. Sun and glass–camera lens, flashlight, magnifying glass.
2. Flint and steel–dry tinder, charred rags.
3. Wood friction–dry, soft-grained woods: balsa, yucca, elm, root of willow, cottonwood, cedar.
4. Bow drill

Making a fire with a bow drill is a simple matter if the apparatus is constructed correctly. It has four parts: a fire board, a drill, a socket, and a bow.

The fire board should be about one-half inch thick. A split piece from a dead branch of cottonwood is excellent. A slight depression must be drilled along one edge. The depression can be smoothed and deepened by a few turns of the bow and drill. A notch is cut in the side of the board so that it reaches to the center of the pit. This notch catches the fine powder ground off by the drill, and it is in this fine powder that the spark is formed.

The drill may be of the same wood as the fire-board, but it is often better if the wood is soft, such as willow. It should be about one foot long and about three-fourths of an inch in diameter. The top end is sharpened to a point, while the bottom is blunt.

The socket is made by drilling a depression in any piece of hardwood that fits the hand. When in use, the drill runs smoother if the socket is lubricated with grease. Rubbing the top of the drill stick through the hair or on each side of the nose will give it enough lubrication. Using water to lubricate a wooden socket only makes it swell and bind.

The bow should be 18-25 inches long and about one-half inch in diameter; a branch with a fork on one end is excellent. The best string is a strip of one-fourth inch wide buckskin or other leather. Substitutes can be made from plant fibers, shoelaces, or some other cord. The cord is attached to one end of the bow and twisted until it is tight and round before being tied to the other end. It is a good idea to fix one end in such a way that it may be loosened or tightened as needed. This can be accomplished by tying a small stick to one end of the cord and fixing it in the forked end of the bow. If the bow drill does not run smoothly, it may be that a little more twist in the cord is needed.

To use the bow drill the fire-board is placed on a flat piece of bark or wood. The spark will fall onto this piece, and it can then be placed on the tinder. Another way is to dig a small depression under the fire-board and place the tinder in the hole in a position under the board so the spark will fall directly onto it. The proper position for working the set is to get down on one knee and place one foot on the fire-board to hold it steady. The drill, with the bow cord twisted once around it, is placed in the fire-board socket. Using the hand socket to apply pressure, the bow is moved back and forth in a sawing motion with steady, even strokes until the drill tip is smoking well. Gradually the drill is spun faster and more pressure is applied with the hand socket. When a lot of black dust from the drill starts collecting in the notch and there is plenty of smoke, there should be enough heat for a spark. The drill is quickly lifted away and the black pile of dust in the notch is lightly fanned with the hand. If there is a spark, the pile will begin to glow, and then the spark is carefully placed in the tinder and blown into the flame. Always light tinder from windward side.

Four Main Types of Fires

1. The Tepee fire is easy to build, burns quickly, and can be used for cooking. Place tinder in center of fire site. Wedge a stick into the ground slanted across the tinder, the upper end pointing into the wind. Lean kindling sticks against it in circles. Add a layer of large branches. Leave an opening on the side from which the wind is coming so you can light the tinder.

2. The Trench fire is best for a windy area, the coolest on a hot day, and excellent for cooking. Dig a trench four feet long. The bottom should slope from ground level at the end from which the wind is blowing to one foot deep at the other end. Build a tepee fire in the end of the trench. Lay several logs across the trench on which to put cooking pots.

3. The Reflector fire is good for baking and roasting food and for reflecting heat into an open tent or shelter. Drive sticks into the ground several feet apart. Pile logs against these two sticks. If possible, cover the front with sod. Build tepee or crisscross fire in front of this wall. If you find a large rock, you could use this as a reflector.

4. The Crisscross fire is excellent for cooking because it produces an even bed of coals quickly. Build a tepee fire in the center of the fire site. Place two logs across them. Build up your fire by adding layers of small logs and thin branches in this crisscross fashion.

Water

Under ideal conditions, you could live up to two days without water, but expect your physical condition to steadily worsen during that time. Therefore, it is important to find a safe and adequate supply of water early in the survival experience. Isolated springs, wells, plants, and solar stills are the safest kinds of water. Other sources should be purified before drinking.

Springs: Look for areas with exceptionally lush greenery. If the water is only seeping out of the spring, dam off an area to make a catch basin. If there is no visible water, try digging a well in the dampest spot. Dig as deep as practical and remember that it may take a while for the water to seep in and fill the bottom of the well. Attempt to keep animals out of all water sources.

Wells: Shallow wells can be successfully dug in spring areas as described above. They can also be dug in the bends of dry stream beds. Choose sandy/gravelly places where the water may have pooled in the bedrock.

Tanks or Water Pockets: Natural water tanks are depressions in rocks where water pools after it rains. These are frequently found in canyon-like dry stream beds.

Streams and Lakes: Go downhill to look for streams and lakes. Though not necessarily pure, streams and lakes are frequently an abundant source of water. Very likely there will also be many useful plants and animals living in or near the water.

Dew: Early in the morning dew can be collected from grass, rocks, etc. Use your bandanna or a bundle of grass to mop it up and squeeze it into a container, or if necessary, directly into your mouth.

Plants: The pulp of some plants, such as cacti, can be pounded or shredded and squeezed through a bandanna, or in your hand, to yield usable moisture. Cottonwood trees generally have their roots in or near water.

Solar Still: Though it requires additional equipment, a solar still can give you water almost anywhere. You will need a 6' x 6' piece of plastic (clear plastic works the best), and a container in which to catch the water. Some type of tubing to suck the water out of the still is also helpful, otherwise you will have to take the still apart to get the water.

Making a solar still: Make a pit about 3 feet across and 2½ feet deep in a location that will receive full sun all day. Put the container in the center of the pit. Then lay the plastic over the pit, placing a stone or other weight on it to form a cone shape over the container. Be sure that the sides of the plastic slope steeply enough so that as the moisture forms, it will run down into the container. Be sure that nothing is touching the inside of the plastic cone or the water will be lost. The top of the plastic cone must be sealed off against the ground with a small amount of dirt all the way around.

Any moist material that is placed inside the pit will increase the amount of water collected. Expect to get only about a pint to a quart of water per day; therefore, each person will actually need several solar stills if this is your only water source.

Water Purification

There are three simple ways to purify water: boiling, chemicals, or a 0.2 micron filter. In a long-term situation, after the chemicals have been depleted, it would eventually be necessary to resort to boiling or filtering.

If your water source is not seriously contaminated, 3-5 minutes may be adequate boiling time. However, in situations in which the water is seriously contaminated, it may be wise to boil the water for up to half an hour.

Two chemicals will be discussed here: chlorine bleach (2 drops per quart) and water purification tablets (follow the directions on the bottle). **Filter purification of microbes other than viruses is preferred to chemical treatment.**

With the chemical method, it is important to treat the lid area as well as the water inside the container to avoid recontamination. This is done by first mixing the chemical with the water in the container. Then turn the container upside down, loosen the lid, and shake the container so that the treated water gets in and around the lid area. Retighten the lid, and let the water sit for the required 15-20 minutes before drinking. Follow the instructions included when using your 0.2 micron filter.

If you suspect chemical contamination, distilling the water is your only option for purification. Indications of chemical contamination may be foam or sheen. Distilling may be done by boiling the water on a fire, allowing the vapors to precipitate on a cold plate or collection tube. The droplets may be poured into another container. If the water is chemically polluted before distillation, you may have a clue that you are near help.

Rest

Strange as it may seem, outdoorsmen can perish in a very short period of time (as little as 6 hours) from hiking in wind, cold, and other hostile environments. A person away from civilization is wholly dependent upon a limited supply of usable energy and the insulation qualities of the body shelter they wear or carry. As long as a hiker's complex mass of living tissue remains quiet in a still air, room temperature-like environment, it requires little special body shelter or energy in maintaining a nearly constant internal temperature of 99° F. When muscle energy is used, it produces body heat as a by-product. Increased production of heat triggers the thermostat nerves to open the sweat glands and cool the body down by water evaporation. If the body gets too cool, the cold sensors call for the muscles to move (shiver) and produce body heat.

The use of muscle power for travel burns available energy, producing heat and some detrimental by-products. This energy is derived from food and water. Through a complex process, this food is converted to glycogen, part of which is stored as reserve in the liver. Some is converted to sugar, which is stored in the muscles for quick use.

When strenuous muscle activity produces these by-products faster than the body can dissipate them, the body can become oversaturated with waste products, causing muscle failure or exhaustion. Exhaustion will remain until the body is given time to automatically flush out the lactic acid buildup and disperse the carbon dioxide. When you rest you can get rid of about 30 percent of the lactic acid buildup in the first 5 to 7 minutes of the rest stop. But in the next 15 minutes you get rid of only about 5 percent more. The best method of preventing a buildup of by-products is to travel slower, giving the body a chance to eliminate these as you travel. Only sleep does a thorough job of regeneration. When muscle energy loss is compounded by loss of body heat through wetness and wind chill, body heat is lost faster than it can be produced. The result will first be fatigue, then exhaustion. When a person is so exhausted that they can no longer move their muscles, their body cools–possibly beyond the recovery point.

Edible Wild Plants
by Earl Qualls

There are six types of wild food that can be found in northern climates: seeds, berries, grasses, cattails, bark, leaves and nuts.

Berries
Seasons dictate the availability of berries. Berries are high in natural sugars and are an energy food, generally high in vitamin C, and a good source of moisture. Rose hips can be found most all year, but be careful to spit out the seeds as they can cause an anal rash. Most black and blue berries are edible. Red berries are sometimes edible. White berries are not edible. It is good to know the fruits in the region in which you are spending time outdoors.

Grasses
Almost everyone has chewed on the tender parts of grass stems; it's not much, but it's better than nothing. Young shoots of grass stems, leaves, and roots can be eaten in the same way. A nourishing broth can also be made from chopped grass. Probably the most nutritious part of grasses, though, are the seeds, which can be ground up and used as meal or flour. Avoid any seeds that look like they have a dark fungus growing in them.

Cattails
Cattails have been called the "supermarket of the swamps" because so many of the cattail's parts are edible. The root stems that run underground between the plant stalks can be dug up year-round. If these are young and tender, they can be washed, peeled, and cut up for stew, or cut in strips and dried for vegetable jerky. Older tough root stems can be washed, then crushed in a container of water. Let the water settle, skim off the fibers, and pour off the water to leave a white starchy layer that can be used as flour. The very young root stems that appear as "horns" around the base of the stalks can be broken off, washed, and boiled.

The centers of the base stalks can be peeled, cooked, and eaten if they are not too old and tough. If they are, they can be crushed in water to yield a flour the same as you would do the root stems. Peel the outer green leaves away from the center of the young shoots and eat the lower white part like celery. A little later

in the season, the young flower heads can be cooked and eaten. Toward autumn, the bright-yellow pollen from the mature male flower can be collected for a highly nutritious flour.

There are other uses for the cattail as well. The long leaves can be used for making baskets and mats, and as thatching for shelters. The fluffy down from the mature seed head makes excellent insulation material and can also be mixed with other shredded materials for tinder to start fires. **• Be aware that more than one person has succumbed to the roots of the poison hemlock (illustration at left), which can grow in conjunction with cattails! It grows to a height of 2-6 ft.**

Pine

Pine needles make a good tea that is high in vitamin C. In the spring when they are still young and tender, the needles can be eaten raw or cooked. The most delicious part, especially from the Pinyon, Digger, Gray, and Sugar pines, are the pine nuts, which grow between the scales of the cones, but you will have to beat the squirrels to them.

The inner bark of all evergreens is edible. Some species taste better than others, and all are quite chewy. Anytime of the year, this inner bark can be peeled in strips, dried, and ground into meal or flour.

Oak

The inner bark from the oak trees is also edible, though it is not as nutritious or as palatable as that of the pines. Acorns from the oaks, are excellent food. Unfortunately, they are available only in the fall, and most acorns contain enough tannic acid to make them too bitter to eat raw. They must be leached before eating.

Begin the leaching process by shelling the acorns and grinding them into meal. Make a bowl-shaped depression in the sand, line it with your bandana, and pour in the meal. The Native Americans sometimes lined the depression with large leaves. You could also use a basket instead of a depression in the sand. Boil some water and pour it over the meal. Continue pouring hot water over the acorn meal until it no longer tastes bitter. Cold water can be used, but it will take considerably longer. One method is to put the meal in a cloth sack and submerge it in a stream overnight. After leaching, the meal can be eaten as is, or cooked in a mush or baked.

General Rules Concerning Edible Wild Plants

1. Study ecology–interrelationship of plants and animals, typical in life zones. Example: a soaring hawk may indicate rodents such as squirrels or rabbits, which eat (and store) food used by man. Food eaten by rodents, monkeys, and raccoons is usually safe.
2. Plants on land or water have edible parts, such as seeds, pods, nuts, tubers, roots, shoots, stems, flowers, leaves, buds, sap, and bark. Edible nuts are the most nutritious.

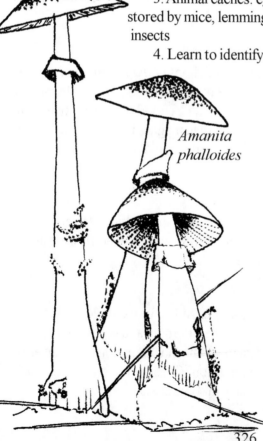

3. Animal caches: eggs, honey, fruit, nuts, seeds, and roots stored by mice, lemmings, squirrels, chipmunks and birds and insects

4. Learn to identify plants and recognize typical habitats. Never guess. If you are not a botanist, first have an expert point them out to you.

Amanita phalloides

5. Be **cautious concerning mushrooms. Amanita is deadly poisonous! Other species closely resemble edible ones. Be sure of your choice before you eat any mushroom!**

Edibility Rules

1. Most black and blue berries are edible, red berries are sometimes edible, and white berries are never edible.

2. Never eat large quantities of unknown food.

3. When in doubt, chew a berry or small portion of a plant to taste

possible bitterness or astringency, or first cook a plant 5-15 minutes. Take a teaspoonful of the plant and hold it in your mouth for 5 minutes. If no burning sensation is noted, then swallow. Wait 8 hours. If there are no ill effects such as nausea, cramps, or diarrhea, eat more and wait another 8 hours. If all is well, go ahead and eat the plant.

4. Cook all plant foods when in doubt about the edibility.
5. The growing tissues of plants are generally edible, e.g., bright-green tips, crown, or heart of grasses.
6. Most grasses are edible. Avoid grasses with fungus growth and discoloration.
7. Eat ferns only in the fiddle-head stage.
8. Gather greens. If they are bitter, cook in more than one water; changing water until greens are mild.
9. Purify (with Clorox, Halazone, or filtration) water used in washing watercress, cattail, and other raw foods from possibly contaminated water.

It is quite impossible to define all edible plants, so take time to get acquainted with the wild edibles in your area.

Edible Foods in Temperate Climates

Start simple. Everyone knows about dandelions *(Taraxacum officinale)*—well, almost everyone. All parts (flowers, leaves, and roots) are edible, raw or cooked. They are extremely high in vitamin A, and a good source of potassium, calcium, phosphorus, and other nutrients, including magnesium, manganese, selenium, zinc, and vitamin B_1, B_2, B_3, and C. In addition, dandelions have many medicinal properties.

Fruits

Many wild fruits are available in season for the picking. Blackberries, blueberries, gooseberries, persimmons, elderberries, and strawberries, are abundant and mouth-watering. Pick when ripe.

Nuts

Several kinds of nut trees grow in the wild—for example, all kinds of hickory nuts are edible except the bitternut. The bitternut has a yellow bud. Shagbark hickory has a thinner shell and is delicious. The mockernut (hickory nut also) is plentiful. Give the squirrels some competition! Other nut trees such as black walnuts, pecans, and hazelnuts are available in some areas.

Roots

Many nutritious roots can be found in the wild. Jerusalem artichokes *(Helianthus tuberosus)* grow wild or can be grown in your garden. They are very tasty either raw or cooked. Frost will kill the tops, but you can leave the tubers in the ground during winter and dig when needed.

Groundnut *(Apios americana)* is a vine that spreads over bushes and other vegetation growing near streams and moist bottom lands. As a legume, it has typical pea-like blossoms which appear mid to late summer, and are brownish-purple. The tubers grow on a string-like root, several on each string, and range in size from marbles to small eggs. They contain 13 percent protein by dry weight, almost 3 times the amount in a potato. Groundnuts may be eaten raw, but are better cooked. Use them like potatoes.

Solomon's Seal *(Polygonatum biflorum)* grows in shady woods and mountains from southern New England south to Florida and Texas. It is one of my favorites. The plant may range anywhere from one to six feet in height, depending on the richness of the soil. Several bell-shaped greenish yellow flowers hang down under the arc of the stem. These later turn into dark ball-like fruit. The white root grows horizontally. It has a number of round "seals" from previous years where the stem has fallen off. These are about one inch apart. Age is determined by counting the spaces between seals. Solomon's seal may be eaten raw or cooked. It is very mild. Roots are eaten raw or cooked. Leaves may be eaten only in the early spring.

There are many other tasty edible tubers, including Spring Beauty *(Claytonia virginica)* and false garlic *(Nothoscordum bivalve)*. As the name implies, the latter is very mild. Its leaves are narrow and grass-like. The six-petaled flowers appear in early spring, and are light greenish-yellow. There are several toothworts *(Dentaria)* belonging to the mustard family *(Cruciferae)*, which have edible roots that are whitish and shaped like a tooth. Some are rather "peppery."

Indian cucumbers *(Medeola virginiana)* are delicious. A few others might include nodding and other wild onions, chives and trout-lily *(Erythronium americanum)*.

Leafy Greens

Wild leafy greens are abundant. Lambs Quarters *(Chenopodium album)* may be eaten raw or cooked. It is high in calcium, vitamin A, and other minerals and vitamins. Pigweed *(Amaranthus retrofluxus)* which has a red root, is a common garden and field weed. It should be cooked before it gets too old. An excellent source of potassium, calcium, phosphorus, and/or vitamins A and C, it is even richer in food value than Lamb's quarters. Both of the last two are mild, and you might wish to cook a little onion with them to spice them up.

Lamb's quarters and pigweed are available in the summer, when kale and other cultivated greens don't do well because of hot weather. Another favorite is Purslane *(Portulaca oleracea)*. It contains glutathione (a common antioxidant compound), and vitamins A, C, and E. It is a good source of calcium, phosphorus, and iron, and is rich in omega-3 fatty acids. You can find it in both gardens and fields. Curled Yellow Dock *(Rumex crispus)* grows from a large tap root. The very young leaves can be eaten in a salad. Cook the larger leaves. It is also called "Sour Dock." It has almost as much vitamin A and potassium as dandelion does.

In the early spring, common chickweeds *(Stellaria media)*, and common blue violets *(Viola papilionacea)* may be gathered for salad material.

The inner bark of the Slippery Elm Tree *(Ulmus rubra)*, besides being a soothing medicine, is nutritious. It contains calcium, iron, magnesium, manganese, phosphorus, potassium, selenium, zinc and vitamins B_1, B_2, B_3, and C. Scrape the outer bark off and make a small rectangular cut in the inner bark, then peel off. Do not cut all around (gird) the tree or it will die.

With gradual experience, you will be able to see not only beauty as you walk through nature, but—a complimentary fresh market! *"From His resources, He can spread a table in the wilderness"* <u>Prophets and Kings</u>, p. 242.

Primitive Cookery

Roasting:
> Food may be roasted on a flat rock with heat under the rock, or with reflected heat.
> Place food on a stick and roast or dry over a fire or bed of hot coals.
> Wrap food in leaves and bury in sand under the fire.

Baking:
> Food can be baked in a reflector oven made of bark, rocks, or other materials.
> Bake in a clay bank oven. Preheat oven by fire kindled inside.
> Scrape fire and ashes out.
> Place food inside. Seal.
> Cover food with moist clay about an inch thick, and bake in coals.

To bake breads in ashes, make balls of dough, cover with flour and place in ashes.

Steaming:

Dig hole. Fill hole with rocks and build a hot fire on the rocks.

Rake away the fire and leave hot rocks in the hole.

Cover with wet green leaves. Lay on food.

Add another layer of damp vegetation, and fill the rest of the hole with sand or loam.

Water can be added by making an inlet with a stick. Cover inlet.

Boiling:

Water may be boiled in a bark container, green bamboo joint, or concave rock.

Put heated rocks beneath the container.

Knives

"If the ax is dull and you don't sharpen it, you'll need more strength to do the same amount of work. So it's wise to think things through before you do them" (Ecclesiastes 10:10 Clear Word).

Suppose, in a survival situation that you have only a knife. Since water is one of the priorities, you set out to find some. You realize that it needs to be purified. Therefore, you would need to make a bowl in which you could boil water. A bowl of this type can be made by burning out a piece of wood with hot coals. So therefore you would need to make a fire. To make a fire, though, you would need to carve a set of "fire sticks." To make the bow-drill set you would need a cutting tool. Since you have a knife, you can use it, but if it needs to be sharpened that may have to be done first. We would diagram this situation as follows:

Water ⇐ Bowl ⇐ Fire ⇐ Bowdrill ⇐ Knife ⇐ Sharpening

All of these survival tools are interrelated. And once you have carved a bow-drill set, it can be used to start several fires. The fire itself can be used for many things. And there is also more than one use for the bowl.

Because of the interrelatedness of almost all of the survival skills and tools, and since many of these start with a sharp knife, a knife is your most important piece of survival equipment. Therefore learning how to select a good knife, keep it sharp, and use it safely should be one of the first skills you learn.

Knife Selection

In general, be sure that the handle is firmly attached. For sheath knives, check the attachment between the handle and the blade, the blade's tang (the part that goes into the handle) should extend at least halfway into the handle and be firmly attached.

On folding knives, a quality blade should feel almost at one with the handle, moving only in the direction the blade opens and closes. It should not feel loose or "wiggle" from side to side on the pivot pin. If it is loose, this is a sign of poor construction. A lock blade folding knife is safer, as it will not close up while you are working with it. For all knives, a 2½-4½ inch blade is adequate. Longer blades can be harder to manage because you have less leverage when you are carving. A folding knife with a large and a small blade can be quite useful.

Survival knives with multiple tools are also available, but be prepared to pay a good price. The value of a Leatherman® or a Swiss Army Knife can hardly be overestimated. Beware of inferior copies.

You might also want to add a 1 inch wood gouge to your survival tools. This gouge is handy for hollowing out bowls and spoons.

Knife Sharpening

When sharpening a knife, what you are actually doing is grinding off excess metal to make a new sharp edge on the blade. In order to sharpen it, the rounded metal must be ground off with a sharpening stone.

While sharpening, the most important thing is to maintain a proper angle of the knife to the whetstone. This must be done in order to grind a keen edge. If the same angle is not maintained, it will be rounded again and the knife will not be sharp.

At first, press fairly hard using a circular motion. Work all along the knife edge from the point to the base, changing sides every so often. Rinse or wipe off the knife and the whetstone face frequently to remove the small pieces of metal and stone that are ground off. Rinsing in water works well.

When the roundness of the dull edge has been ground off, the metal at the very edge will have a tendency to turn upward rather than being ground off. This is called a "burr" or "wire edge." It is useful in that it can let you know when the roundness is removed. You can feel it by lightly rubbing your thumb or finger across the blade from the back of the knife toward the edge. The burr will catch slightly in the grooves of your fingertip. Note that it will be only on the side opposite the whetstone. Check for this burr frequently during the sharpening process. Continue grinding with the whetstone until you have this burr all along the edge. When this happens, all the roundness has been ground off, and there is a good edge all along the knife.

The last thing to do is to grind off the burr. To do this, continue grinding as

331

before, but press **very lightly** and change sides after every couple strokes. Check for the burr each time you change sides. When the burr has been ground off, the knife should be sharp.

For a superfine edge, use a leather strap. Lay the knife flat on the leather and draw it across so that the leather presses gently up across the newly ground blade, removing the last remnant of a burr from the blade. Use these same procedures for sharpening other tools such as hatchets and axes.

Knife Safety

When using your knife, always work with the sharp edge of the blade pointing away from you. Be sure, as you hold on to your work, that a finger (or other body part) is not out in front of the blade! Watch out for other people, too; keep them out of range in case you happen to slip. When you hand the knife to someone, hold on to the back of the blade and offer them the handle of the knife.

Finding Directions

Point of Reference/ Landmark Practice Activity No. 1:

Suppose that you are going on an imaginary hike (don't actually go any-where; just choose an arbitrary direction out across the landscape). Close your eyes and turn around a couple of times. Then open your eyes and face, once again, in the direction you were to go. How did you know which way to face? You probably used some point of reference or landmark that was in the direction of the imaginary hike. If there was not a landmark in that particular direction, possibly you used some landmark off to one side and remembered the angle from that landmark to the direction you wanted to go. Subconsciously, we all use landmarks or points of reference, and angles from these landmarks to determine directions. Learn to do this consciously, then you can use it as a tool whenever you need to "keep track of your tracks."

The-Star-That-Does-Not-Move Practice Activity No. 2

This activity is best done at night under a star-filled sky. Begin turning around, rotating slowly to your left. Notice how you first see objects on the left, then they move across your field of view and "set" on the right. As you continue to rotate, slowly look higher and higher. Notice how things still "rise" and "set" but make a shorter arc. Keep turning around looking higher still; high overhead you should find a spot that does not move, but everything seems to "rotate" around. When you find this spot, stop turning around. Where is this spot in relation to you? The answer is straight above you.

North Star ┤✦├

Lie face up on the ground with your arms outstretched at right angles to your body with your left arm toward the direction the sun comes up (east), and your right arm toward the direction the sun sets (west). Imagine yourself lying there for a full day visualizing what will be happening in the heavens above you. On a summer morning, you would see the sun at your far left; it would rise, and about noon be straight above you. Through the afternoon it would continue to cross the sky, and in the evening set on your far right. After sundown, it would get dark and the stars would come out. Choose a star on your far left and keep track of it through the night. What path would it take? It, too, would rise, about midnight be straight up, and toward early morning set on your far right.

Big Dipper

As you watch the sky through the night, would a certain star that the others seem to rotate around, correspond to this spot that you found above you at the beginning of this activity? Where would that star be in relation to the globe? Some Native Americans called this star "The-Star-That-Does-Not-Move." It is located almost directly above the North Pole. We call it Polaris, or the North Star. Find it by following the dipper end of the Big Dipper constellation.

For us, on Planet Earth, the North Star is an excellent reference point. Everywhere on the planet, we are affected by the rotation of the earth. The directions of the rising and setting sun are also good reference points. Because of the tilt in the earth's axis, the sun does not rise and set in exactly the same location throughout the year; therefore, neither sunrise nor sunset is as good a point of reference as the North Star. The classical way to locate the North Star is to find the Big Dipper. Having found the Big Dipper, locate the two stars on the edge of the "dipper" known as "The Pointers." The North Star is approximately in line with these two.

Earth Compass Practice Activity No. 3

With the above activities in mind, scratch a short north-south line on the ground and make an east-west line that crosses the north-south line at its center. Label the ends of the lines with N, E, S, and W, representing the four directions. Using these initials, starting with north and going around clockwise you can remember the rhyme, "Nancy Eats Shredded Wheat."

If you were only able to determine one of the four directions, can you see how easy it would be to figure out the rest of them? For example: if you were to observe the sun coming up, that would tell you which way was east. By drawing a line in that direction, then making a line crossing it and labeling the ends, you could determine all directions.

Keeping Track of Your Tracks

If you were to leave camp and go west, ask yourself which direction you would need to go to come back to camp. By keeping track of your tracks, you instinctively know which direction to return. But suppose you left camp not paying attention to which way you went, and you began wandering around. Would you know which way to go to come back? Probably not. To know your way, you need to "keep track of your tracks."

There is no such thing as an inherent "sense of direction." People who appear to have this so-called "sense" have learned, albeit subconsciously, to keep track of their tracks. They make mental notes of the direction and which way they are going at all times. When they arrive at a new location, one of the first things that they do is pick out the directions and any significant landmarks. As a result they are rarely, if ever, lost.

Orientation by the Lay of the Land

People with this so-called "sense of direction" also notice, perhaps subconsciously, which way different terrain features lie. For instance, which way does the river run? Or what direction does a mountain ridge lie? Having made mental notes of this, they are free to roam wherever they wish. For example, if we were to hike upstream, all we would have to do to get back to camp is to return downstream.

Things to remember:
1. When leaving camp, be sure you are adequately dressed and properly equipped.
2. Never leave camp alone–keep at least two in any party. The buddy system not only helps in prevention and early treatment of frostbite, but also, if you fall into the water, your buddy's efforts will probably save you. If you break a leg, you have assistance and someone who knows which direction to go for help.
3. Always anticipate accidents and have a plan for survival.

4. If lost in the wilderness, conserve your strength and body heat. Make yourself as comfortable as possible where you are and have faith.

5. If you feel cold, remember that exercise produces heat. A particularly good exercise is to tense both the extensors and the flexors of the arms and legs at the same time. This produces heat without motion. However, don't overdo it. There is a limit to work that can be done sagely, and some rest is required to avoid exhaustion and danger of freezing.

6. Perspiration is dangerous because it predisposes frostbite and freezing. Keep clothes dry internally and externally. Change and dry socks and inner sole at least daily (twice daily if on the trail). Underdress rather than overdress on the trail. Put on additional clothing when the body begins to cool.

7. Move slowly until the amount of energy available after necessary heat production is known.

8. Clothing must be kept clean and free of oils and grease. Ties, or drawstrings on parkas, etc., are put there to keep out snow and cold air, but they must **not** be tied so tight as to diminish circulation.

9. Impaired local circulation is the primary cause of frostbite of the feet. An effort should be made to avoid anything that is known to have even a mildly adverse effect on normal circulation. Do **not** wear stretch or tight top socks.

10. Shoes, and socks in particular, must not be tight. Do **not** wear too many socks unless they are successively larger in width as well as length. (Socks that are too big give folds that cause pressure points and increased tendency to cold and injury.) If your feet hurt **investigate immediately**, rewarm and exercise your feet until sensation returns, change to dry socks and dry inner soles if necessary.

11. Heavy, bulky clothing makes you clumsy and prone to accidents from lack of normal agility. Loose clothing allows freedom of movement, better insulation, and proper breathing.

12. Hot drinks add actual warmth to survival food, and they help maintain water requirements. Cook survival rations with plenty of water if possible. This makes them more palatable and far more digestible. Boiled foods are more digestible than fried foods, and the juice gives you more vitamins, minerals, and needed water.

13. Whether you eat regularly or not, be sure you take in **at least** one to two quarts of water per day. The vast majority of common ailments are prevented and treated by forcing fluids. Eating snow excessively uses body

energy. **Melt** it and drink it warmer.

14. To make a poncho from a black plastic garbage bag, cut slits in corner of sides for arms, and in center of bottom cut a T-shaped slit for the neck, the vertical cut of the "T" coming down in front. Other uses for the bag: ground cloth, "tablecloth," gathering bag, solar still, washbasin.

First-aid Kit

Ideally, every hiker venturing more than a few miles and hours from civilization should have first-aid training and a complete kit. Certainly anyone who spends much time in the back country should avail themselves of instruction offered by the Red Cross or mountaineering clubs and assemble a kit with sufficient materials to cover a wide range of eventualities.

At the very least, the novice must be equipped to handle common ailments of the trail, some of which can be disabling even though not "serious" in a medical sense. If each hiker carries a small kit, supplies can be pooled for crises; if the group (say, a family) carries only two single kits, they should be correspondingly more elaborate. The following items constitute a **one-man first-aid kit:**

Band-Aids: several, for minor cuts

Charcoal Tablets: for detoxification in case of poisoning or flu symptoms

Gauze Pads: several, 3 and 4 inches square, for deep wounds with much bleeding

Adhesive Tape: a 1 or 2 inch roll for holding bandages in place, covering blisters, taping sprained ankles, etc.

Salt Tablets: to prevent or treat symptoms of heat exhaustion (including cramps) when sweating heavily

Aspirin: for relieving pain and reducing fever

Needle: for opening blisters, removing splinters

First-aid manual: one of the booklets or books discussing diagnosis and treatment

Moleskin or Mole foam: for covering blisters

Razor Blade (single edge): for minor surgery, cutting tape and moleskin to size, and razor for shaving hairy portions of skin before taping

Gauze Bandage: a 2 inch wide roll for bandaging large cuts

Butterfly Band-Aids: for closing deep cuts that normally require stitching

Triangular Bandage: for large wounds

Large Compress Bandage: to hold dressings in place

Halazone Tablets: for treating drinking water of doubtful purity

0.2 Micron Water Filter System: best system for water purification

Antacid: for settling stomachs upset by overexertion, unaccustomed altitude, and the cook's mistakes

Wire Splint: for sprains and minor fractures

Sam Splint: for fractures of arms or legs

Elastic Bandage and safety pin: 3 inches wide, for sprains, applying pressure to bleeding wounds, etc.

First-aid Cream: for sunburn, itches, scrapes, and rashes

Antiseptic: Bactine, Zepherine Chloride, Polysporin, or other for cleansing agents in cuts and abrasions

Antihistamine: Benedryl for allergic reactions to bee stings

Oil of Cloves: for toothache

Ibuprofen: for severe pain (prescription required)

Antidiarrhetic Pills: for severe cases of liquid loss

Laxative and/or Glycerin Suppositories: for prune-resistant constipation in persons congenitally suffering this affliction

Snakebite Kit: Authorities generally advise carrying a snakebite kit, but in the unpracticed hands of semi-hysterical first-aiders the kit can be more dangerous than the bite; the rule is to seek instruction before entering an area where it may be needed.

Crazy glue: can be used to close wounds until arrival at a hospital.

Antibiotics: the use of any antibiotics is not advocated for treating sore throats or virus infections. Their use, even if a physician is a group member, should be banned, since an adverse reaction in the wilderness could be serious.

Splints, bandages, litters, and other items for extreme emergencies can be improvised from tree limbs, ice axes, clothing, pack frames, and similar available gear.

Signaling

The recognized distress signal is 3 signals of anything that would attract attention. Such as: 3 whistle blasts, 3 shouts, 3 flashes of a mirror, 3 fires, 3 blocks stamped out in the snow.

Signaling With a Metal Mirror

Hold mirror next to cheek below eye with one hand. Rotate mirror to find reflection on ground in front of you and bring other hand, with arm extended in line with the reflection so reflection falls on outstretched thumb. Now swing upper body toward object you wish to signal, keeping reflection on thumb. Sighting along mirror-thumb object line will ensure that the reflection can be seen from the object you are signaling. Move thumb out of the way for full-strength reflection.

Ground to Air Emergency Code

Make these patterns on the ground with rocks, brush, turned-up soil, stomped snow, etc. in a clear area so it can be easily seen from the air.

Signaling is the only **active** thing you can do to aid in your rescue, but praying **always** helps. Smoke is the best signal in forest. During summer, fire spotters will see it. After fire is well on, add green branches and leaves to increase smoke.

Snow Signals: Find clearing, scatter branches, rocks, dirt and/or tramp out largest possible "**X**" (minimum size 18 feet) to attract aerial searchers. They **must** be aligned north and south so that the shadows stand out in the sun moving east to west.

Desert Signals: In the desert, do the same on sand as described previously for snow. If such ground markers cannot be made and help approaches, use mylar, mirror reflector, whistle or bright-colored jacket, or any colorful contrasting moving object to attract eyes.

Summertime: Messages may be spelled out with sod blocks, logs, or rocks. The more different variety of messages the better; from smoke, flares, mirror, waving arms, or gun shots. The key with gunshots is "three in a row," but don't waste ammunition.

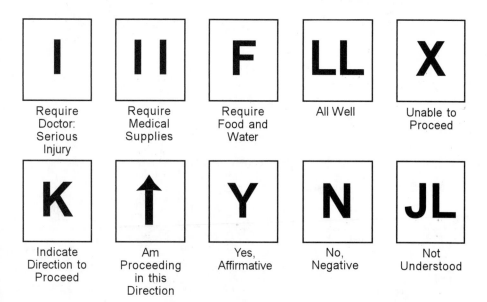

I	I I	F	LL	X
Require Doctor: Serious Injury	Require Medical Supplies	Require Food and Water	All Well	Unable to Proceed

K	↑	Y	N	JL
Indicate Direction to Proceed	Am Proceeding in this Direction	Yes, Affirmative	No, Negative	Not Understood

WILDERNESS SURVIVAL

Here is an easy way to remember the rules we have covered in this chapter.

S – Size up the situation.
U – Undue haste makes waste.
R – Remember where you are.
V – Vanquish fear and panic (positive attitude).
I – Improvise; make what you need.
V – Value living.
A – Act like you are at home.
L – Learn basic skills.

FOR FURTHER READING

The Wilderness, God's People, and the End-Time, Jim Buller, 3520 Harmon Road, Bakersfield, CA 93307. Phone: 661-366-0324. E-mail: jabuller@juno.com
Outdoor Survival Skills, Larry Dean Olsen, Brigham Young University Publications, Provo, UT 84601. 1967
Edible Wild Plants, by Miriam Kramer, c/o Outdoor Eduquip, 24414 University Ave., No. 34, Loma Linda, CA 92354. 1-800-500-7342
Earl Qualls, P.O. Box 129, Wildwood, GA 30757. Phone: 423-822-7002

Chapter Fifteen

When to Flee:
An Act of Faith

"If necessary, He would send the ravens to feed us."
(<u>Early Writings</u>, p. 56).

C orrie ten Boom tells of the time she arrived in Moscow to smuggle a suitcase full of Russian Bibles behind the iron curtain. Her big red suitcase was so heavy she could hardly lift it. The closer she approached the customs desk, the more fearful she became. Her fears were justified. Russia was closed to Christianity and smuggling Bibles was a crime severely punished. Corrie had spent time in Ravensbruck, a notorious Nazi concentration camp where she had watched her sister die. Her father and brother also died in other camps. Corrie did not want to go to prison. Panic seized her as she saw the Russian customs officers ransacking all of the suitcases of the people in line ahead of her. She feared she would be discovered. But instead of running, she prayed.

"Lord, You have promised to 'hasten and perform Your Word.' You have promised it; now You must perform it! The same moment I prayed, I saw angels surrounding that big red suitcase! When I saw who was on my side, my fear left me!"

"After my prayer the angels disappeared. Well, not really," she chuckles.

"I just couldn't see them anymore!"

"Your suitcase is a heavy one!" exclaimed the customs officer as he lifted Corrie's suitcase.

"Yes, sir," Corrie stammered.

"I have some time. I can carry it for you," he offered.

Corrie finishes her story with her unique blend of Dutch accent and Christian joy, "He not only did not inspect my suitcase, he carried it all de vay to my car!"

Think what Corrie would have missed had she fled when tempted by her fears! We have all read and perhaps coveted the experience of others who, like Corrie, have an extraordinary faith and sense of timing. They seem to know when to pray, when to stand, and when to flee. In the future, discerning these times may mean survival. The moving accounts we read of Christians who stood for the right in the face of adversity did not attain their faith by chance. True faith is learning to trust completely in God's guidance when we are in a vulnerable position; when we cannot see beyond human reasoning. Faith is learning to lean on God and maintaining our Christian integrity when human wisdom says, "Run." This kind of faith is a gift of the Holy Spirit.

Events Leading up to Flight for Christians Living at the End Time

Surviving the end times will require faith, courage, and discipline of the highest order. We shall eventually have to flee, but we must be careful to discern the time for flight. Until it is time to flee, we are to deliver His Word unto all the world.

"And this gospel of the kingdom shall be preached in all the world for a witness unto all nations; and then shall the end come" (Matthew 24:14).

Like Corrie, we may be frightened because the truth will not be popular, but angels will be with us. Though events may appear to be chaotic, we are promised that nothing will ever be out of control.

"Above the distractions of the earth He sits enthroned; all things are open to His divine survey; and from His great and calm eternity He orders that which His providence sees best" (Ministry of Healing, p. 417).

Trouble, in the end times, will also be held in check. *"At that time, while the work of salvation is closing, trouble will be coming on the earth, and the nations will be angry, yet held in check so as not to prevent the work of the third angel"* (Early Writings, pp. 85, 86; emphasis supplied).

Previously in this book we have documented several events that take place just prior to the close of probation. The Loud Cry will be given, under the power of the Latter Rain of the Holy Spirit. This is the most powerful evangelistic crusade ever experienced on earth (see Closing Events Chart, p. 458).

Subsequent to the finishing of the work will be a time of flight, and it is important to know when we should be doing evangelism and when we should be fleeing to the rocks and mountains, completely dependent upon God. We will be leaving our gardens and homes, which we have depended upon for sustenance during the Loud Cry and the time of no buy- no sell. When it is time to flee, we will be relying on the promise of Isaiah 33:16 that our bread will be given us, and our water will be sure.

Before the time for flight, we will be traveling as witnesses. As persecution increases, our movements are motivated by evangelism. We will receive special help during the last evangelistic effort.

"Servants of God, with their faces lighted up and shining with holy consecration, will hasten from place to place to proclaim the message from heaven. By thousands of voices, all over the earth, the warning will be given. Miracles will be wrought, the sick will be healed, and signs and wonders will follow the believers" (The Great Controversy, p. 612).

Angels will strengthen us today to give the message to a perishing world. They will also help us know when to flee. While in flight, they will feed us when we can no longer feed ourselves and will protect us when we must, at last, live in desolate, and perhaps unfamiliar, solitary places. Is there something we can do to prepare for this future time? Yes, there is a call for each of us today:

"It is no time now for God's people to be fixing their affections or laying up their treasure in the world. The time is not far distant, when, like the early disciples, we shall be forced to seek a refuge in desolate and solitary places. As the siege of Jerusalem by the Roman armies was the signal for flight to the Judean Christians, so the assumption of power on the part of our nation in the decree enforcing the papal sabbath will be a warning to us. It will then be time to leave the large cities, preparatory to leaving the smaller ones for retired homes in secluded places among the mountains. And now, instead of seeking expensive dwellings here, we should be preparing to move to a better country, even a heavenly. Instead of spending our means in self-gratification, we should be studying to economize" (Testimonies for the Church, vol. 5, p. 464, 465; emphasis supplied).

Time for Flight Separated from Time for Evangelism

"Decree enforcing" in the above reference, refers to the National Sunday Law. This will be our **last signal** to leave the cities and find homes in the country. It will no longer be safe to live in or operate businesses in the cities, but we will still be doing mission work because probation has not closed.

It is true that the Lord, through His servant, told us to leave the cities long ago, but "decree enforcing" refers to the **last warning; the warning to**

move to retired homes among the mountains. Since we are told that we should make no preparations for the time of flight, these "retired homes among the mountains" refer to dwellings in the country where we will live before probation closes. These outposts and homes will require preparation and planning before the enforcement of the National Sunday Law. Why not move out now and be ready, having our home in the mountain prepared?

"As the approach of the Roman armies was a sign to the disciples of the impending destruction of Jerusalem, so may this apostasy be a sign to us that the <u>limit of God's forbearance</u> is reached, that the measure of <u>our nation's iniquity is full</u>, and that the <u>angel of mercy is about to take her flight</u> never to return. The people of God <u>will then</u> be plunged into those scenes of affliction and distress which prophets have described as the time of Jacob's trouble" (<u>Testimonies for the Church</u>, vol. 5, p. 451; emphasis supplied). Jacob's time of trouble occurs after probation closes (see also <u>Early Writings</u>, pp. 284-285).

This reference, in many ways, is a parallel to the one in <u>Testimonies for the Church</u>, volume 5, page 464, but, many interesting differences occur. The terms "limit of God's forbearance," "nations iniquity is full," and "angel of mercy about to take her flight never to return" are all references specifically about the close of probation. Notice the one little key word in "the angel" phrase—the word **"about."**

When the angel of mercy takes her flight, that is the moment of the close of probation. But the word "about" indicates that probationary time is still open for yet a little while **the angel of mercy has not yet left this earth.** This reference indicates two things: first, that we are approaching the close of probation, and second, that the time of Jacob's trouble will follow shortly. The term "will then" indicates just a little more time for mercy. The NSL and its enforcement is filling up the cup of the world's iniquity. Events are happening very quickly. The total culmination of Satan's program of misery is about to occur.

The close of probation occurs after all evangelism is finished. *"When the third angel's message closes, mercy no longer pleads for the guilty inhabitants of the earth. The people of God have accomplished their work.... Then Jesus ceases His intercession in the sanctuary above. He lifts His hands, and with a loud voice says, 'It is done'"* (<u>The Great Controversy</u>, p. 613).

Preparation Necessary Prior to the Time of Flight

"Again and again the Lord has instructed that our people are to take their families away from the cities, into the country, where they can raise their own provisions; for in the future the problem of buying and selling will be a very serious one. We should <u>now</u> begin to heed the instruction given us

over and over again: get out of the cities into the rural districts" (Country Living, pp. 9, 10; emphasis supplied).

Since we are growing our own food, no buy-no sell does not signal the time for flight. While we are raising our food, we are still in probationary time. Provisions raised in our own garden will be our paycheck. When it is time to flee, we leave our gardens behind. Then God provides our food. When increased enforcement of Sunday laws escalates from fines, to imprisonment, inducements, to "no buy-no sell," and finally the death decree. The death decree is when we will need to flee. This next reference outlines a most essential preparation for last day events.

"All who are under the training of God need the quiet hour for communion with their own hearts, with nature, and with God. In them is to be revealed a life that is not in harmony with the world, its customs, or its practices; and they need to have a personal experience in obtaining a knowledge of the will of God. We must individually hear Him speaking to the heart. When every other voice is hushed, and in quietness we wait before Him, the silence of the soul makes more distinct the voice of God" (The Ministry of Healing, p. 58; emphasis supplied). (See also The Desire of Ages, p. 668.)

Steps of Sunday Law Enforcement

We are told that Sunday law enforcement will be mild at first, but will intensify as time progresses. *"The Sunday movement is now making its way in darkness…. Its professions are mild and apparently Christian, but when it shall speak it will reveal the spirit of the dragon. It is our duty to do all in our power to avert the threatened danger"* (Testimonies for the Church, vol. 5, p. 452).

"As the movement for Sunday enforcement becomes more bold and decided, the law will be invoked against commandment keepers. They will be threatened with fines and imprisonment, and some will be offered positions of influence, and other rewards and advantages, as inducements to renounce their faith. But their steadfast answer is, 'Show us from the word of God our error'—the same plea that was made by Luther under similar circumstances" (The Great Controversy, p. 607; emphasis supplied).

The next step of Sunday enforcement is the edict preventing God's people from buying and selling (Rev. 13:17). If we cannot buy or sell, we will have to raise our own food on country properties.

This reference indicates that the event of "no-buy, no-sell" is just prior to the death decree. *"Fearful is the issue to which the world is to be brought. The powers of earth, uniting to war against the commandments of God, will decree that no man may buy or sell, save he that has the mark of the beast, and, finally, that whoever refuses to receive the mark shall be put to death"* (Spirit of Prophecy, vol. 4, p. 422; emphasis supplied).

God, who loves us, knows that being located outside the cities is the safest place for us. Communion with God is vital to our preparation; He can talk to us better in the country where the noise and distractions are decreased. We will have to develop this communication with Him now in order to have it in the last days. When the Sunday law is first initiated we are told we will preach the Sabbath fully (Evangelism, p. 77: *"The cities are to be worked from outposts").*

"At the commencement of the time of trouble, we were filled with the Holy Ghost as we went forth and proclaimed the Sabbath more fully. This enraged the churches and nominal Adventists, as they could not refute the Sabbath truth. And at this time God's chosen all saw clearly that we had the truth, and they came out and endured the persecution with us" (Early Writings, p. 33; emphasis supplied).

"The commencement of the 'time of trouble,' here mentioned, does not refer to the time when the plagues shall begin to be poured out, but to a short period just before they are poured out, while Christ is in the sanctuary. At that time, while the work of salvation is closing, trouble will be coming on the earth, and nations will be angry, yet held in check so as not to prevent the work of the third angel. At that time the 'latter rain,' or refreshing from the presence of the Lord will come, to give power to the loud voice of the third angel, and prepare the saints to stand in the period when the seven last plagues shall be poured out" (ibid. p. 85; emphasis supplied).

Angels Protect and Provide

Angels will provide protection in a special way after the close of probation. There will be no more martyrdom. In Maranatha, p. 199, we are told that, *"When this grand work is to take place in the battle, prior to the last closing conflict, many will be imprisoned, many will flee for their lives from cities and towns, and many will be martyrs for Christ's sake in standing in defense of the truth."* There will be many martyrs for Jesus before probation closes. Though having faced death, these martyrs are classified as true survivors, and, at the resurrection, they have a very special place of honor, in His Kingdom. After the close of probation God's people will have finished their work, and martyrdom ceases. God will protect His people.

"So I saw that the people of God, who had faithfully warned the world of His coming wrath, would be delivered. God would not suffer the wicked to destroy those who are expecting translation and who would not

bow to the decree of the beast or receive his mark. I saw that if the wicked were permitted to slay the saints, Satan and all his evil host, and all who hate God, would be gratified" (Early Writings, p. 284).

"I saw the saints leaving the cities and villages and associating together in companies, and living in the most solitary places. Angels provided them food and water, while the wicked were suffering from hunger and thirst. Then I saw the leading men of the earth consulting together, and Satan and his angels busy around them. I saw a writing, copies of which were scattered in different parts of the land, giving orders that unless the saints should yield their peculiar faith, give up the Sabbath, and observe the first day of the week, the people were at liberty after a time to put them to death. ... In some places, before the time for the decree to be executed, the wicked rushed upon the saints to slay them; but angels in the form of men of war fought for them" (Early Writings, pp. 282, 283; emphasis supplied).

"The people of God will not be free from suffering; but while persecuted and distressed, while they endure privation and suffer for want of food they will not be left to perish. That God who cared for Elijah will not pass by one of His self-sacrificing children. He who numbers the hairs of their head will care for them, and in time of famine they shall be satisfied. While the wicked are dying from hunger and pestilence, angels will shield the righteous and supply their wants" (The Great Controversy, p. 629; emphasis supplied).

When we can no longer feed ourselves the angels will feed us. Isn't this a reassuring promise for us today, as we face the future?

Today—the Most Important Time of All

How important it is to start each day with God and to keep ourselves unspotted from the world?

"Pure religion and undefiled before God and the Father is this, To visit the fatherless and widows in their affliction, and to keep himself unspotted from the world" (James 1:27).

"The time is not far distant when the test will come to every soul. The mark of the beast will be urged upon us. Those who have step by step yielded to worldly demands and conformed to worldly customs will not find it a hard matter to yield to the powers that be, rather than subject themselves to derision, insult, threatened imprisonment, and death" (Last Day Events, p. 173; emphasis supplied).

How important is today? The decisions we make today will strengthen or weaken our preparations for this eternal decision at the time when the mark of the beast hovers over all the world. In a moment, our destiny will be decided by our answer to one question.

"The Lord has shown me clearly that the image of the beast will be formed before probation closes; for it is to be the great test for the people of God, by which their eternal destiny will be decided" (The Seventh-day Adventist Bible Commentary, Ellen G. White Comments, vol. 7, p. 976; emphasis supplied). Our eternal destiny will be decided at the enforcement of the National Sunday Law!

We can be on the right side of this decision by learning to love and obey Him now, following a "thus saith the Lord" even when it is not popular and appears extreme.

"There is a period of time just before us when the condition of the world will become desperate, when that true religion which yields obedience to a 'Thus saith the Lord' will become almost extinct" (Testimonies for the Church, vol. 5, p. 523).

If we neglect the preparation which includes spiritual, practical, geographical, and financial adjustments, we will not be ready for the times spoken of during the enforcement of the Sunday law. It is important that we do the right thing at the right time in order to be a part of God's closing work.

"It is the very essence of all right faith to do the right thing at the right time" (Testimonies for the Church, vol. 6, p. 24; emphasis supplied).

There will be no make-up time if we neglect preparation.

There are those who would have us believe that we need to lay up food and build a secret hideaway for this time of flight. But we are told that we should not make any provision for this time.

"The Lord has shown me repeatedly that it is contrary to the Bible to make any provision for our temporal wants in the time of trouble. I saw that if the saints had food laid up by them or in the field in the time of trouble, when sword, famine, and pestilence are in the land, it would be taken from them by violent hands and strangers would reap their fields. Then will be the time for us to trust wholly in God, and He will sustain us. I saw that our bread and water will be sure at that time, and that we shall not lack or suffer hunger; for God is able to spread a table for us in the wilderness. If necessary, He would send ravens to feed us, as He did to feed Elijah, or rain manna from heaven, as He did for the Israelites" (Early Writings, p. 56; emphasis supplied).

Clearly this reference refers to the time of flight, after probation is closed when we will no longer be growing our own food. While we are in flight, we trust completely in God to provide for our every need, including food and protection. Like Corrie, we may not always see our angel guides, but we can rest assured that we are never alone when we are within the circle of His will.

God Will be With Us

Elder Robert Pierson tells the story of literature evangelist Jens Hokland's difficult experience in crossing a dangerous mountain range in order to canvass homes in the valley. The path was so steep he removed his shoes and finally his socks to improve his grip on the treacherous path that clung to the side of the mountain. Anxious for his safety he asked God to send His angel to help Him. After reaching the valley safely, he called at the first cottage where an elderly couple lived.

"Where is your companion?" asked the husband.

"I have no companion; I'm alone" replied the colporteur.

"There was someone with you. We saw someone helping you down that steep place," answered the old man.

Then Jens was reminded of his prayer to God for help, and of the word of the Lord in Psalm 34:7, *'The angel of the Lord encampeth round about them that fear him and delivereth them.'* (501 Illustrations, by Robert H. Pierson)

God's people need not shrink in fear. God has promised repeatedly that He will be with us in times of trouble. Angels will guard us when it is beyond our power to protect ourselves. Even if we experience martyrdom prior to the call to flee, God will be with us (see Desire of Ages, p. 354). After the call to flight, there will be no more martyrs, for witness by death cannot advance the truth after probation is closed. Our signal for flight will be the death decree. It will take great faith to flee to the wilderness completely depending upon His promises for survival. Very troublesome times will come to us before the Lord's return. But He will return. This is a long-standing promise. **We have a choice. We can be ready.**

FOR FURTHER STUDY

Early Writings, Ellen G. White, Pacific Press Publishing Association, Nampa, ID, pp. 254-258, pp. 279-288

The Great Controversy, Ellen G. White, Pacific Press Publishing Association, Nampa, ID, pp. 61-79, pp. 563-653

The Story of Redemption, Ellen G. White, Pacific Press Publishing Association, Nampa, ID, pp. 409-413

Maranatha, Ellen G. White, Review and Herald Publishing Association, Hagerstown, MD 21740, pp. 221-312

To Look In His Eyes

A tiny black cloud in the blue eastern sky—
In wonder we gaze as it's fast drawing nigh,
As lighter, and whiter, and brighter it seems,
While ten million angels on bright shining wings
Come winging and singing a triumphant song,
Till heaven seems filled with their radiant forms.

A cloud of such glory, so dazzling white,
The bottom like fire! Oh wondrous the sight!
A rainbow above it with colors so rare,
What splendor, the glorious scene in the air!
And, Oh, in the midst rides the great King of kings!
No pen can portray how majestic the scene.

He rides forth in glory, how great His renown,
Upon His fair head many glittering crowns.
His hair is pure white, oh, as white as the snow.
His voice like the sound as when great waters flow.
His countenance shines like the sun at its height.
His eyes are like fire! Oh fearful the sight.

And now all is silent. Oh, look in His eyes!
He reads ev'ry motive and ev'ry disguise.
The secrets of life His eyes read like scroll,
And pierce to the depths, oh the depths of the soul!
Oh terrible, wonderful, awful surprise!
Oh, friend, are you ready to look in His eyes?

Are you ready for Jesus' coming,
Or would you be surprised?
He's coming in heaven's bright glory;
Oh friend, can you look in His eyes?

—Warren C. Wilson

SECTION THREE:
Our Destiny Calls

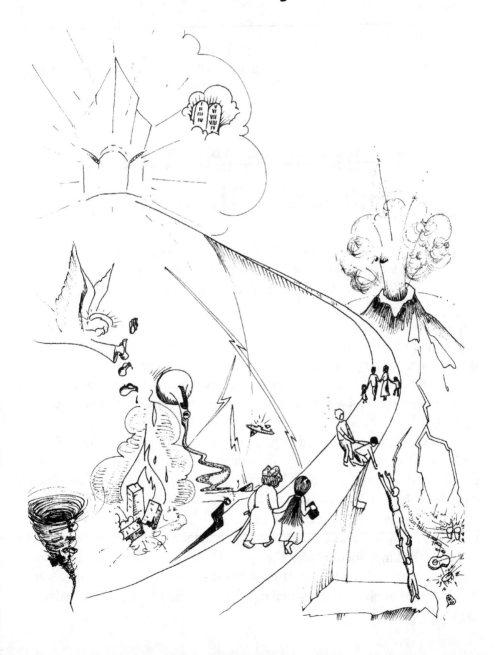

Chapter Sixteen

Treasure In the Trash: Hilkiah's Discovery

"In the reformation that followed, the king turned his attention to the destruction of every vestige of idolatry that remained" (Prophets and Kings, p. 401).

Josiah was 8 years old when he became king of Judah. Even as a very young child, he had chosen to serve God, and now that he was king he planned to carry out principles that would honor God.

When he was in his late teens or early 20s, Josiah began a program to cleanse the land of idol worship. This cleansing of the land went on until he was in his mid-20s.

A special day occurred in the providence of God when Hilkiah, the high priest of Judah, was getting money from the storehouse to pay workers who were rebuilding the temple. This rebuilding program was also part of Josiah's plan to reestablish the worship of God.

While walking through the temple, Hilkiah found a copy of the book of the Law written by Moses. He gave it to Shaphan the scribe to read. Shaphan reported to the king, not only about the progress of the work and payment to the workers, he also told Josiah that Hilkiah found a book of the Law of Moses in the debris of the temple. Josiah wanted it read to him right away, so Shaphan did as the king requested.

YOU CAN SURVIVE!

"When the king heard about the blessings and curses that were written in the book and the consequences that follow disobedience, he tore his royal robe in anguish and said to Shaphan, 'This is terrible. Go and get Hilkiah the High Priest, Achbor, the son of Micaiah, Asaiah, my personal attendant and your son Ahikam. Then go to the prophetess and find out from the Lord what all this means. The people of Judah have a right to know what is written because they haven't heard the law read to them since the days of my great grandfather Hezekiah, and that's been almost a hundred years ago. If I understand it right, the Lord is greatly displeased with us as a people because of what our fathers did, and they have passed their lifestyle of disobedience on to us'" (2 Kings 22:11-13, The Clear Word).

When Josiah sent a messenger to Huldah, the Prophetess, she told Shaphan that their king was right and that God was displeased with how they were living, especially their idol worship. She gave them words from the Lord: *"Because of this, I will destroy Jerusalem and send My people into captivity. They have even offered their children to these wretched gods that have taken My place. I am hurt that they are not showing their love to Me. Something must be done to stop this, and I will see that it is done"* (2 Kings 22:17, The Clear Word; emphasis supplied).

Then God made a promise to Josiah: *"Concerning the words you read, because you took them to heart and humbled yourself and showed your grief over what would happen to Jerusalem and to the people and wept and prayed in my presence, I will not destroy Jerusalem or bring disaster upon my people during your lifetime"* (2 Kings 22:18-20, The Clear Word).

Josiah called all of the people together at the temple and read the scrolls that were found. All of the people responded to the king by making a new commitment to God. They promised to put into practice what was written in the Book.

The king continued to tear down altars to gods, such as Molech and Baalzebub, to which infants were sacrificed. He remembered the words of the Lord, through Huldah, that God would complete the revival and reformation.

"And now, while Shaphan the scribe was reading to him out of the book of the Law, the king discerned in this volume a treasure of knowledge, a powerful ally, in the work of reform he so much desired to see wrought in the land.... But was it possible to bring about the needed reform?" (Prophets and Kings, p. 398; emphasis supplied).

Yes, the Lord did accomplish the reform through Josiah and delayed the judgments.

"This reform movement, by which threatened judgments were

averted for a season, was brought about in a wholly unexpected manner through the discovery and study of a portion of Holy Scripture that for many years had been strangely misplaced and lost" (ibid. p. 392).

"In the reformation that followed, the king turned his attention to the destruction of every vestige of idolatry that remained" (ibid. p. 401).

When he discovered the law, *"Josiah did not say, 'I knew nothing about this book. These are ancient precepts and times have changed.' He appointed men to investigate the matter and these men went to Huldah the prophetess ...In Josiah's day the Word of the Lord was as binding, and should have been as strictly enforced, as at the time it was spoken. And today it is as binding as it was then"* (The Seventh-day Adventist Bible Commentary, Ellen G. White Comments, volume 3, page 1133; emphasis supplied).

This reference draws an application, from the great revival and reformation in Josiah's time, to our day. Closely examining Josiah's call to revival we can draw some present day conclusions.

The reformation started with the Holy Spirit working on the heart of a man. *"The call of the hour is answered by the coming of the man"* (Testimonies for the Church, vol. 6, p. 332). Using his position of responsibility, even before the discovery of the scrolls, Josiah had already begun to do what he could to rid Israel of worldliness. He chose to work in harmony with those around him to accomplish the work that God had impressed him to do.

While he was taking out the trash of worldly habits and thinking, a providence occurred. A scroll of the laws of Moses was found. These laws, given by God, including commandments against idol worship, proclaimed the great blessing of following God's plan as well as the curse of the programs they were following.

In our day, the discovery and revival of the testimonies will spark a revival and reformation. *"Unless there is a breaking away from the influence that Satan has prepared and a revival of the testimonies that God has given, souls will perish in their delusion"* (Series B, No. 7, p. 63). This revival will prepare God's people for great blessing but, if rejected, judgments will fall upon His church, such as were prophesied in Ezekiel 9:4-6. God is doing this because He loves us and it hurts Him to see us damaged by the world. If we recognize that these judgments are coming it will help free us of worldly influences.

This book of the Law, discovered by Shaphan which should have been inside the ark of the covenant, was found in the debris of the unused temple. No one came to temple services—they had other things to worship. Today we need a revival and God will see that the integrity of our worship is returned.

"Truths that have been buried under a mass of rubbish are to be re-

vived, and reset in their original setting" (<u>Manuscript Releases</u>, vol. 3, p. 416).

"If the warnings and reproofs given in the Word of God and in the testimonies of His Spirit are not plain enough, what words would be sufficiently plain to bring about a revival and reformation?" (<u>The Upward Look</u>, p. 240).

God wants a revival and reformation to take place. But will it take place? <u>The Great Controversy</u>, page 464, says it will; *"Before the final visitation of God's judgments upon the earth there <u>will be</u> among the people of the Lord such a revival of primitive godliness as has not been witnessed since apostolic times"* (emphasis supplied).

This revival and reformation "will be," and it is in our power to hasten it, as did king Josiah so long ago. There will be changes in God's church and in His people! What side will we choose—to leave things as they are, or increase spirituality?

When Josiah discovered the errors, he went to the people. He was in a unique position for witnessing: he was their leader. There is a great blessing when leadership reads the scroll to the people. It will hasten our Lord's return. The king of Judah never feared or retreated from his mission of removing all idols and spurious debris covering God's plan for His people.

Molech and Ekron

During Josiah's revival and reformation initiated by the discoveries of the testimonies, several idols were destroyed. Among these was the god of Molech. The original name was "Melek," meaning "king," a name ancient Israel had originally given to the true God. Later on, the Jews felt it was shameful to call God by a pagan name, so they changed the pronunciation to "Molek." It was to this god that Israel was offering their infants as a sacrifice. The god of Ekron was also worshiped by Israel earlier as Baalzebub in the town of Ekron (2 Kings 1:2, 6). Do we worship Molech today?

The Spirit of Prophecy makes a present-day application of the worship of these idols. *"Children are not to be trained to be devotees of society. They are <u>not to be sacrificed to Molech</u>, but they are to become members of the Lord's family. Parents are to be filled with the compassion of Christ, that they may work for the salvation of the souls that are placed under their influence. They are not to have their minds all engrossed in the <u>fashions</u> and <u>practices of the world</u>. They are <u>not to</u> educate their children to attend parties and concerts and dances, to have and attend feasts, because after this manner the Gentiles walk"* (<u>Child Guidance</u>, p. 181; emphasis supplied).

As parents become willing subjects of Christ children will be safe from Molech's insatiable appetite. *"Children <u>will be</u> brought up in the nurture and* *admonition of the Lord. They will be educated and trained, not to be society devotees, but members of the Lord's family. They will not be sacrificed to Moloch. Parents will become willing subjects of Christ… They will not allow themselves to be absorbed with the customs of the world"* (The Seventh-day Adventist Bible Commentary, vol. 2, p. 1039; emphasis supplied).

No wonder the Lord is so urgent that we not follow the customs and practices of the world. It is idol worship! The god of Ekron, which was also worshiped by ancient Israel, represents many evils for God's people today.

"The idol of Ekron was supposed to give information, through the medium of its priests, concerning future events…. The predictions there uttered and the information given proceeded directly from the prince of darkness…. The history of King Ahaziah's sin [seeking the god of Ekron] *and punishment has a lesson of warning which none can disregard with impunity* [Impunity means exemption from punishment; immunity from detrimental effects].

"Though we do not pay homage to heathen gods, yet thousands are worshiping at Satan's shrine as verily as did the king of Israel….

"I have from time to time received letters both from ministers and lay members of the church, inquiring if I think it wrong to consult spiritualist and clairvoyant physicians…. So numerous are these agents of Satan becoming, and so general is the practice of seeking counsel from them, that it seems needful to utter words of warning" (Testimonies for the Church, vol. 5, pp. 192, 193; emphasis supplied).

"Cursed is the path that leads to En-dor or to Ekron" (ibid., p. 197).

If we, as followers of the true God, have allowed the world to come in, we must remove the idols or suffer judgments, just as did ancient Israel. Worldly influences have crept into our schools. If we have attached ourselves to the world by **even a thread**, the Lord says we are worshiping the god of Ekron.

"Our people are now being tested as to whether they will obtain their wisdom from the greatest Teacher the world ever knew, or seek to the god of Ekron. Let us determine that we will not be tied by so much as a thread to the educational policies of those who do not discern the voice of God and who will not hearken to His commandments" (Counsels to Parents, Teachers, and Students, p. 255; emphasis supplied). There is a need for revival and reformation and breaking down worldly altars, as in Josiah's day. May it be so, in Jesus' name. Amen.

It was during the time of Josiah's reformation movement that Elijah rebuilt the schools of the prophets that had fallen into decay. The burden of Elijah's heart was to provide an education according to God's plan.

"The heart of Elijah was cheered as he saw what was being accom-

plished by means of these schools. The work of reformation was not complete, but he could see throughout the kingdom a verification of the word of the Lord" (Prophets and Kings, p. 225).

The work of revival and reformation directly opposes idol worship. It uses true education as the basis of true character building and lasting evangelism.

Judgments During Josiah's Reign

There are some questions that we do not ask often enough; "Will God send judgments on us like He did on ancient Israel? Will He treat us differently than He treated Israel when their idol worship caused them so much grief, loss, and captivity? Is idol worship today tolerated by God more than He tolerated it under Josiah, Jeremiah, Elijah, and Ahaziah?

"He stays His judgments that He may plead with the impenitent. He who exercises 'lovingkindness, judgment, and righteousness in the earth' yearns over His erring children; in every way possible He seeks to teach them the way of life everlasting (Jeremiah 9:24). *He had brought the Israelites out of bondage that they may serve Him, the only true and living God. Though they had wandered long in idolatry and had slighted His warnings, yet He now declares His willingness to defer chastisement and grant yet another opportunity for repentance. He makes plain the fact that only by the most thorough heart reformation could the impending doom be averted. In vain would be the trust they might place in the temple and its services. Rites and ceremonies could not atone for sin. Notwithstanding their claim to be the chosen people of God, reformation of heart and of the life practice alone could save them from the inevitable result of continued transgression"* (Prophets and Kings, pp. 413, 414; emphasis supplied).

If the revival and reformation begins among us today, we may avert the judgments that could soon to fall upon us.

"What a lesson is this to men holding positions of responsibility today in the church of God! What a solemn warning to deal faithfully with wrongs that bring dishonor to the cause of truth! Let none who claim to be the depositaries of God's law flatter themselves that the regard they may outwardly show toward the commandments will preserve them from the exercise of divine justice. Let none refuse to be reproved for evil, nor charge the servants of God with being too zealous in endeavoring to cleanse the camp from evil-doing. A sin-hating God calls upon those who claim to keep His law to depart from all iniquity. A neglect to repent and to render willing obedience will bring upon men and women today as serious consequences as

356

came upon ancient Israel. There is a limit beyond which the judgments of Jehovah can no longer be delayed. The desolation of Jerusalem in the days of Jeremiah is a solemn warning to modern Israel, that the counsels and admonitions given them through chosen instrumentalities cannot be disregarded with impunity" (Prophets and Kings, pp. 416, 417; emphasis supplied).

Today these messages carry some of the most solemn counsels given by God to His church. The first part says how patient, loving, and long-suffering He is. Even His judgments are conditional. He wants to teach us the way of life, but with solemnity He says, *"Only by the most thorough heart reformation could the impending doom be averted"* (Prophets and Kings, p. 414).

Our survival is assured only as we commit our whole heart to Him. Things are not always going to be as they are now. Judgments first begin at the house of God (Ezekiel 9:6). Regardless of our claim to be the remnant, the chosen people of God, He will not wait forever on lukewarm responses. What a solemn warning! God does not regard idol worship today, in whatever form, with any less hatred than He did in days of old.

"A neglect to repent and to render willing obedience will bring upon men and women today as serious consequences as came upon ancient Israel" (Prophets and Kings, p. 416).

There are many areas in which we need to come up to higher standards. Each follower of Christ will, after committing his or her heart to God, find those things in their own lives which are binding them to false gods. Before Jesus can come, we must disconnect from all the worldly threads woven into the loom of our daily lives.

Battle Creek

In the late 1800's, God sent a judgment on the Battle Creek Review and Herald building. Before the fire, Ellen White saw an angel with a sword of fire standing over Battle Creek.

"In visions of the night I have seen an angel standing with a sword as of fire stretched over Battle Creek" (Testimonies for the Church, vol. 8, p. 97).

What was God so displeased about back then? One issue was centralization. The second was the publishing of books on spiritualism and Romanism. The third is expressed in these words: *"So Christ sorrows and weeps over our churches, over our institutions of learning, that have failed to meet the demand of God"* (ibid. p. 67; emphasis supplied).

The fourth concern is expressed on page 68: *"It [Battle Creek] has become a place where injustice and fraud have been carried on, where malice, envy, and passion have borne sway."*

YOU CAN SURVIVE!

"By rejecting God's warnings in this our day, men are repeating the sin of Jerusalem" (ibid. p. 68).

You may be wondering how deep God wants this heart reformation and repentance to reach. *"And the Lord said unto him, Go through the midst of the city, through the midst of Jerusalem, and set a mark upon the foreheads of the men that sigh and that cry for all the abominations that be done in the midst thereof"* (Ezekiel 9:4).

"In the time when His wrath shall go forth in judgments, these humble devoted followers of Christ will be distinguished from the rest of the world by their soul anguish, which is expressed in lamentation and weeping, reproofs and warnings. While others try to throw a cloak over the existing evil, and <u>excuse the great wickedness everywhere prevalent,</u> those who have a zeal for God's honor and a love for souls will not hold their peace to obtain favor of any. Their righteous souls are vexed day by day with the unholy works and conversation of the unrighteous. They are powerless to stop the rushing torrent of iniquity, and hence they are filled with grief and alarm. <u>They mourn before God to see religion despised in the very homes of those who have had great light. They lament and afflict their souls because pride, avarice, selfishness, and deception of almost every kind are in the church.</u> The Spirit of God, which prompts to reproof, is trampled underfoot, while the servants of Satan triumph. God is dishonored, the truth made of none effect" (Testimonies for the Church, vol. 5, pp. 210, 211; emphasis supplied).

Our Lord wants us to be heart to heart with Him over the sins of the world and the church. He wants us to understand why His heart is broken over these sins. *"The class who do not feel grieved over their own spiritual declension, nor mourn over the sins of others, will be left without the seal of God"* (ibid. p. 211). They will not be survivors.

Should we choose to continue on in mirth, the message is clear. *"Here we see that the church—the Lord's sanctuary—was the first to feel the stroke of the wrath of God (Ezekiel 9:6)"* (ibid. p. 211).

I know this is solemn, but God is a God of justice as well as mercy. (See Prophets and Kings, p. 413).

"The leaven of godliness has not entirely lost its power. At the time when the danger and depression of the church are greatest, the little company who are standing in the light will be sighing and crying for the abominations that are done in the land. <u>But more especially will their prayers arise in behalf of the church because its members are doing after the manner of the world.</u>

"The earnest prayers of this faithful few will not be in vain. When the Lord comes forth as an avenger, <u>He will also come as a protector of all those</u>

who have preserved the faith in its purity and kept themselves unspotted from the world. It is at this time that God has promised to avenge His own elect which cry day and night unto Him, though He bear long with them. ...

"The abominations for which the faithful ones were sighing and crying were all that could be discerned by finite eyes, but by far the worst sins, those which provoked the jealousy of the pure and holy God, were unrevealed. The great Searcher of hearts knoweth every sin committed in secret by the workers of iniquity. These persons come to feel secure in their deceptions and, because of His long-suffering, say that the Lord seeth not, and then will act as though He had forsaken the earth. But He will detect their hypocrisy and will open before others those sins which they were so careful to hide.

"No superiority of rank, dignity, or worldly wisdom, no position in sacred office, will preserve men from sacrificing principle when left to their own deceitful hearts. Those who have been regarded as worthy and righteous prove to be ringleaders in apostasy and examples in indifference and in the abuse of God's mercies. Their wicked course He will tolerate no longer, and in His wrath He deals with them without mercy" (Testimonies for the Church, vol. 5, pp. 209-212; emphasis supplied).

Judgments are coming to the church unless we experience a change in our ways and learn from the word and testimony as Josiah did. The Battle Creek fire is proof that God's judgements will not always be averted. True education plays a large part in averting these judgments and stops our worshiping at the god of Ekron. (For the whole picture of God's impartiality with sin in Battle Creek, see the Review and Herald, December 8, 1977.)

A Call to Revival and Reformation

"A revival of true godliness among us is the greatest and most urgent of all our needs" (Christian Service, p. 41; emphasis supplied).

"The time has come for a thorough reformation to take place. When this reformation begins, the spirit of prayer will actuate every believer, and will banish from the church the spirit of discord and strife" (Testimonies for the Church, volume 8, p. 251; emphasis supplied).

"There is great necessity for a reformation among the people of God. The present state of the church leads to the inquiry: Is this a correct representation of Him who gave His life for us?" (ibid. vol. 3, p. 474; emphasis supplied).

"I was shown God's people waiting for some change to take place— a compelling power to take hold of them. But they will be disappointed, for they are wrong. They must act; they must take hold of the work themselves

and earnestly cry to God for a true knowledge of themselves.... The harvest of the earth is nearly ripe" (ibid. vol. 1, p. 261; emphasis supplied).

We will either "break out" of our lethargy or "shake out" in the sifting time. His warnings, His counsel, His guidance, His plans, are pleading with us today. We have much to do, as did Josiah so long ago, to dust off the treasures within our reach. These treasures are the very tools we need for survival and revival!

"The coming of the Lord is nearer than when we first believed. What a wonderful thought it is that <u>the great controversy is nearing its end!</u> In the closing work we shall meet with perils that we know not how to deal with; but let us not forget that the three great powers of heaven are working, that <u>a divine hand is on the wheel</u>, and that <u>God will bring His purposes to pass</u>" (Selected Messages, book 2, p. 391; emphasis supplied).

God's Concern

I'd like to paint a picture
That would stir the souls of men;
But I would need a flaming brush
And iridescent pen.

How can I paint that picture
Of God's concern and care?
O'erwhelmed, I drop my brush and kneel
In penitential prayer.

For as I catch a glimpse of Him
And heaven, lo, I see
That God is bending o'er the walls—
His eyes on you and me.

Indeed "all heaven" watches us
With int'rest most intense,
To see what we are doing
In this time of dark suspense.

"All heaven" still is waiting
For us to spread the light;
When will we care enough to shine
And end earth's troubled night?

Oh, could I paint that picture
Of Heaven's true concern,
I'm sure our hearts would all respond
And hasten Christ's return!

—Adlai Albert Esteb

TREASURE IN THE TRASH

FOR FURTHER STUDY

Words of Encouragement, page 34

"In the future men in the common walks of life will be impressed by the Spirit of the Lord to leave their ordinary employment, and go forth to proclaim the last message of mercy. As rapidly as possible, they are to be prepared for labor that success may crown their efforts."

Words of Encouragement, page 36

"I have been shown that in our educational work we are not to follow the methods that have been adopted in our older established schools. There is among us too much clinging to the old customs, and because of this we are far behind where we should be in the development of the third angel's message."

Words of Encouragement, page 8

"Men may say that it is a waste of valuable time and money for strong young men and young women to go out into these hills and out-of-the-way places to labor. Some may contend that we cannot afford to allow young persons of talent to engage in this line of work. 'Cannot afford it!' If there is but one soul to be saved, that soul is more precious than all the combined wealth of this world" (emphasis supplied).

Words of Encouragement, page 11

"Let no one stand in the way. Say not, 'we cannot afford to work in a sparsely settled field and largely in a self-supporting way, when out in the world are great fields where we might reach multitudes.' And let none say, 'We cannot afford to sustain you in an effort to work in those out-of-the-way places.' What! Cannot afford it! You cannot afford not to work in these isolated places; and if you neglect such fields, the time will come when you will wish that you had afforded it. There is a world to be saved" (emphasis supplied).

Spalding and Magan Collection, page 420

"In the work being done at the training school for home and foreign missionary teachers at Madison, Tennessee, and in the small schools established by the teachers who have gone forth from Madison, we have an illustration of a way in which the message should be carried" (emphasis supplied).

<u>Last Day Events</u>, page 39

"We may have to remain here in this world because of insubordination *many more years*, as did the children of Israel, but for Christ's sake His people should not add sin to sin by charging God with the consequence of their own wrong course of action" (emphasis supplied).

<u>Sons and Daughters of God</u>, page 352

"Let us strive to be Christians (Christlike) in every sense of the word, and let our dress, conversation, and actions preach that Christ is formed within, the hope of glory and that we are looking for that blessed hope and glorious appearing of Jesus.... My affections, interest, treasure, all, is in the bright world to come."

<u>Testimonies for the Church</u>, volume 2, page 348

"They are dying spiritually because they have so long pampered their natural appetites that their power of self-government seems gone."

<u>Testimonies for the Church</u>, volume 5, page 216

"<u>Now is the time to prepare</u>. The seal of God will never be placed upon the forehead of an impure man or woman. It will never be placed upon the forehead of the ambitious, world-loving man or woman. It will never be placed upon the forehead of men or women of false tongues or deceitful hearts. All who receive the seal must be without spot before God–candidates for heaven" (emphasis supplied).

Chapter Seventeen

Hastening Our Lord's Return: Yes We Can!

"We are not only to look for, but to hasten the coming of the day of God"
(The Desire of Ages, p. 633).

When I was a boy, I had an uncle whom I loved very much. When I heard he was coming to visit, how I longed to see him! Every time he was planning to come, he would phone to let me know. He would always ask to talk to me and would inquire if I had my stuff ready. He always knew of a new place, and we just had to go there!

When he came, he would take me to places that boys love to go. We would hike, camp, and fish. We would talk together as friends. He did not speak to me as if I were a child. It seemed I could talk with him about anything. What grand times we had! Sometimes we would even catch fish!

As a boy, I wished there was something I could do to hurry the day when my uncle would arrive. I wanted to see him so badly. I wanted to be with him sooner rather than later! But, sadly, even with my ever-growing anticipation, there was no way he could come sooner. So, I got ready and stayed ready because I wanted to be ready when he came.

Over the years since those glorious days, I have reflected on those childhood events in my life which instilled in me such a great sense of anticipation. There is one event I am anticipating more than any other—Jesus' coming. He is coming, He has told us so. Is there anything we can do to get Him here sooner so that we can do things together? Through the years I have discovered that there are things we can do to hasten His return.

As a boy growing up, things were not always pleasant at home, and I am sure my uncle knew that, even though we never talked about it. We just had good times together, with no talk of bad things. As I thought about how enjoyable Uncle John's visits were to me in my childhood, a comforting thought about the great second coming of Jesus occurred to me: He is returning to earth in order to make things eternally pleasant where so much sadness and heartache now exist.

"And God shall wipe away all tears from their eyes; <u>and there shall be no more death, neither sorrow, nor crying, neither shall there be any more pain</u>: for the former things are passed away" (Revelation 21:4). He is preparing a place especially for us (John 14:1-3) for our total happiness. He alone knows what will make us truly happy. To be able to see Him, and to talk to Him, to let the care and hurt disappear, will be a great day. He says, "I am anxious to come," then He adds, "You can help Me come sooner if you want to." He doesn't lie, so I have to believe what He says.

The Sooner Everyone Knows, the Better

Matthew 24:14 says, *"And this gospel of the kingdom shall be preached in all the world for a witness unto all nations; and then shall the end come."* Jesus says that if we give the good news about Him to the whole world, He will come. By getting the work done sooner, He will come sooner!

Second Peter 3:12 tells us that His people will be found *"<u>Looking for and hasting</u> unto the coming of the day of God."* Other versions use the word "hastening," meaning to speed up the Lord's return. So, today, we can look for, expect, and hasten our Lord's return!

"By giving the gospel to the world it is in our power to <u>hasten</u> our Lord's return. We are not only to look for but to <u>hasten</u> the coming of the day of God (2 Peter 3:12). Had the church of Christ <u>done her appointed work as the Lord ordained</u>, the whole world would <u>before this</u> have been warned, and the Lord Jesus would have come to our earth in power and great glory" (<u>The Desire of Ages</u>, p. 633; emphasis supplied). We could have been in heaven before this!

"It is the privilege of every Christian not only to look for but to <u>hasten</u> the coming of our Lord Jesus Christ (2 Peter 3:12). Were all who profess His name bearing fruit to His glory, how quickly the whole world would be sown with the seed of the gospel" (<u>Christ's Object Lessons</u>, p. 69).

As Christians we have worked to spread the gospel, and have experienced church growth. Together we rejoice about evangelistic successes especially in underprivileged countries. To accomplish what needs to be done will require a power outside of ourselves. Our methods will work, only as a part of God's plan. We need overpowering manifestations of the Holy Spirit to even break the world's birth rate barrier of 80 million per year. Then we need unheard-of, undreamed-of success to reach the world population of 6 billion! God is more eager to give us this power than we are to receive it. One of the solutions to the dilemma of reaching the world is to implement God's plan for an educational system that inspires young people to be workers in evangelism as their number one career choice, rather than entering the business-as-usual work world.

Answers to our dilemma may be buried under the worldly rubbish in our homes, schools, hospitals, and in our churches, just as it was in the temple of Josiah's day (see chapter 16). Who will uncover the answers and read them to us? Josiah was a leader of God's people. Our leaders, today, do read and write to us, requesting commitments to destroy the gods of Ekron and Molech from among us and replace them with God's plan for finishing the work. Following God's plan is the only way we are ever going to finish the work, leaving heartache and sorrow behind (Revelation 21:4).

What is His Plan?

True education is vital to the finishing of God's work in the earth and in his children. It is important to understand that true education is the development of all aspects of our life; mental, physical, and spiritual.

"Education is but a preparation of the physical, intellectual, and spiritual powers for the best performance of all the duties of life" (Messages to Young People, p. 271). *"True education is missionary training. Every son and daughter of God is called to be a missionary ...to fit us for this service should be the object of our education"* (Ministry of Healing, p. 395).

The Bible mentions, in Matthew 24:14, that the gospel will go to all the world, but before that happens, before Jesus comes, we must develop true education. You may ask, "How important, then, is true education, for hastening the Lord's return?" It is vital! Notice this reference from the Spirit of Prophecy.

"Before we can carry the message of present truth in all its fullness to other countries, 'we must break every yoke.' We must come into the line of true education walking in the wisdom of God and not the wisdom of the world" (Series B, No. 11, p. 30; emphasis supplied).

Not only may we hasten the Lord's return by understanding God's plan for true education, but it will enable us to be a part of the kingdom of God. *"Now, as never before, we need to understand the true science of education. If we fail to understand this*, we shall *never have a place* in the kingdom of God" (Christian Educator, Aug. 1897; emphasis supplied).

What kind of schools will be developed in these last days?

"The plan of the schools we shall establish in these closing years of the work is to be of an entirely different order from those we have instituted in the past" (Series B, No. 11, p. 28).

"Special light has been given in regard to moving our publishing houses and sanitariums and schools out of the cities into places more favorable to their work, where those connected with them will not be exposed to all the temptations of city life. Especially should our schools be away from the cities" (Fundamentals of Christian Education, p. 492; emphasis supplied).

"If there can be found places in retired mountain regions where it would be difficult for the evils of the cities to enter, let our people secure such places for our sanitariums and advanced schools" (Manuscript Releases, vol. 10, p. 260; emphasis supplied).

"Well Done"

Would you like to hear the words, "Well done" from the Master?

"Since the Lord is soon coming, it is time to put out our money to the exchangers, time to put every dollar we can spare into the Lord's treasury, that institutions may be established for the education of workers, who shall be instructed as were those in the schools of the prophets. If the Lord comes and finds you doing this work, He will say: 'Well done, thou good and faithful servant; ... enter thou into the joy of thy Lord" (Testimonies for the Church, vol. 6, p. 441; emphasis supplied).

Are you ready to stand in your place, on the side of revival and reformation?

"The greatest want of the world is the want of men—men who will not be bought or sold, men who in their inmost souls are true and honest, men who do not fear to call sin by its right name, men whose conscience is as true to duty as the needle to the pole, men who will stand for the right though the heavens fall" (Education, p. 57).

We may hasten our Lord's return if we choose to do so according to His plan. It will be done, so we may as well be the ones to do it! It will be accomplished through a revival and reformation in our educational work. My good friend Eulene Dodson, now resting in Jesus, wrote this song about being ready for the King's return.

Do You Really Want Jesus to Come?

Is your life so full of duty
That your Lord is crowded out?
Do you neglect to study and to pray?
Or would your heart be ready
And would glory fill your soul,
If your Master would come for you today?

Do your lips say, "Come, Lord Jesus"
But if He would come today
His lovely face you could not bear to see?
Too many things unpardoned,
Cherished sins you held so dear?
Would you tremble to face eternity?

Do you really want Jesus, your Lord, to appear?
Do you long for your Savior's return?
Your lips praise His name,
Does your life show the same?
Do you really want Jesus to come?
Do you really want your Lord to come?

—Eulene Dodson

Dan and Lisa are about to make some precious discoveries about true education as Adventist College faces its greatest challenge.

Chapter Eighteen

Education for the Future:
Prisoners of Hope

*"They are prisoners of hope. ... If they will listen to His voice and
follow in His ways, God will correct and enlighten them"*
(Testimonies for the Church, vol. 6, p. 145).

D aniel believed in Jesus and His soon coming. His parents both
worked to send him to Adventist College. Now, as a freshman, he
was preparing himself for an engineering career that would pay well and
be interesting work.

Professor Paul, Daniel's first-year Calculus teacher whom the students
affectionately called "Prof.," seemed to always add a spiritual concept to each
lesson, even quoting from the Bible and the Spirit of Prophecy when questioned
about a special truth.

Daniel had spent several summers helping out on his uncle's farm. He was
pleasantly surprised at how he had gained strength by bucking hay bales and
helping to clear new land. He had helped his uncle build a new machine shed and
had learned the basics of framing and construction carpentry.

Prof. Paul also taught first-year general math for Science-Education ma-
jors. Lisa, an Elementary Education major was in one of these classes. She, too,
noticed that the professor made spiritual application to various basic math concepts. While this was an Adventist college, not all of the teachers did that. The
teacher in her Life of Christ class teacher made spiritual points, but she expected that since he was a pastor.

Lisa came from a farm in Idaho and had learned to do a lot of practical things like cooking for a crew of men, sewing, driving a tractor, changing oil, fixing things around the house. Her younger brother had promised to fill in for her while she was at college. Her older brother, Jerry, was in his third year at Adventist College.

Daniel and Lisa had benefited in a very practical way from their work experience. Although their country background didn't seem a natural fit for a college setting, their well-balanced life was a steadying influence.

Christmas Break

About midway through first semester, just before Christmas break, national news related the occurrence of several huge storms, hurricanes, tornadoes, fires, and great loss of life. These became a common topic of conversation among students and staff at Adventist College. The storms were becoming more severe. Strange diseases were occurring as a result of tainted food and the polluted air of the cities. In the country, drought and hail caused crop failures, and animal foods were causing unfamiliar ailments to threaten public health.

Many students felt that they should go home to help out and ease the financial drain their college expenses caused by these calamities. But Daniel and Lisa were encouraged by their parents to continue their career training so they could better prepare themselves for life. "This time of weather severity will pass just as it always has," they said.

When Daniel and Lisa returned to college after Christmas break things weren't quite the same. They were each impressed that their careers were not as important as what was happening in the world. They each desired to help others prepare for a crisis.

Prof. Paul, in all his classes, announced that he would be having studies at 5:30 every morning until the end of the semester. His facial expression signaled concern. "What will it be about, Prof.?" asked Daniel. Interestingly, Lisa asked the same question in her class. Prof. Paul explained, "In light of the calamities in the world, I thought we might discuss how to be ready and how we might help others get ready for Jesus' coming. I know all of you are preparing for careers, and that is important, but I sense something arising that may be even more important."

"What could be more important than earning a living for our families?" asked Daniel.

"Come to my class and see. Not just from curiosity, but from a need to be ready for the end of the world and the coming of Jesus," said Prof. Paul.

"I am so far behind in your class, I don't see how I can go," answered Daniel.

"Tell you what I will do," said Prof. Paul. "If the whole class comes, I will do away with the final. I will grade you on your midterm and daily work."

The class thought that was a good deal and agreed to come.

Early Morning Meetings

The first 5:30 a. m. meeting was attended by all of his students. Prof. Paul started out by commenting on the events of the last several months and the news of the day, revealing more and more disasters. "You know," he said, "these calamities are just a fulfillment of prophecy."

Everyone listened closely as Prof. Paul read from The Great Controversy, pages 589, 590: *"'Satan has control of all whom God does not especially guard. ... While appearing to the children of men as a great physician who can heal all their maladies, he will bring disease and disaster, until populous cities are reduced to ruin and desolation. Even now he is at work. In accidents and calamities by sea and by land, in great conflagrations, in fierce tornadoes and terrific hailstorms, in tempests, floods, cyclones, tidal waves, and earthquakes, in every place and in a thousand forms, Satan is exercising his power. He sweeps away the ripening harvest, and famine and distress follow. He imparts to the air a deadly taint, and thousands perish by the pestilence. These visitations are to become more and more frequent and disastrous.'"*

Most in the class were Adventists. Some were more committed Christians than others, but all knew in their heart that Prof. was right.

"When these things come, we should be ready," he said. The students took careful notes, writing out the sentences that he emphasized. "The following is a statement of what might have been done before now. *'Time is too short now to accomplish that which might have been done in past generations; but we can do much, even in these last days, to correct the existing evils in the education of youth. And because time is short, we should be in earnest and work zealously to give the young that education which is consistent with our faith. We are reformers. We desire that our children should study to the best advantage. In order to do this, employment should be given them which will call the muscles into exercise. Daily, systematic labor should constitute a part of the education of the youth, even at this late period. Much now can be gained by connecting labor with schools. In following this plan, the students will realize elasticity of spirit and vigor of thought, and will be able to accomplish more mental labor in a given time than they could by study alone. And they can leave school with their constitutions unimpaired, and with strength and courage to persevere in any position in which the providence of God may place them.'* That is a quote from Counsels on Health, page 183."

"'Then when I look upon the scenes presented before me; when I

consider the schools established in different places, and see them falling so far below anything like the schools of the prophets, I am distressed beyond measure. The physical exercise was marked out by the God of wisdom. Some hours each day should be devoted to useful education in lines of work that will help the students in learning the duties of practical life, which are essential for all our youth. But this has been dropped out, and amusements introduced, which simply give exercise, without being any special blessing in doing good and righteous actions, which is the education and training essential.' This quote comes from Fundamentals of Christian Education, page 228."

"What does 'essential' mean?" asked Daniel when Prof. Paul recognized his upraised hand during the pause that followed this reading.

"I am glad you asked, Daniel. We will study that very subject the next few mornings," said Prof. Paul.

Prof. Paul's Apology

There was a tear in his eye as Professor began speaking at the next meeting. His voice cracked as he said, "I am sorry, young people, I have failed you. I should have been teaching you to be ready long ago." College President Cristman and Academic Dean Matthews were in the class looking somber, as though they had something to say as well. Prof. Paul asked the two administrators to come forward and share what was on their hearts.

President Cristman told of recent happenings in the religious world. "These recent tragedies are being interpreted by other denominations as God frowning on us for desecrating Sunday. They are having large revival rallies." The dean then told of a delegation presenting a petition to Congress to pass legislation requiring people to worship on Sunday. He closed by saying, "There is a good chance it will become law. All of the churches are united on this except us. It will probably be law by the next session—a year or so from now."

Then he read from The Great Controversy, page 590: " *'The class that have provoked the displeasure of Heaven will charge all their troubles upon those whose obedience to God's commandments is a perpetual reproof to transgressors. It will be declared that men are offending God by the violation of the Sunday sabbath; that this sin has brought calamities which will not cease until Sunday observance shall be strictly enforced: and that those who present the claims of the fourth commandment, thus destroying reverence for Sunday, are troublers of the people, preventing their restoration to divine favor and temporal prosperity.'*"

Lisa could contain herself no longer. "Prof., this is the second part of the reference you read in the first meeting. Does that mean the Sunday law is upon us? Isn't this one of the signs of the end of the world?"

"Yes to both questions, Lisa," answered Dean Matthews. "Prof. Paul asked me if he could give this class. How glad we are we said yes. We will be attending as well. We have presented a contingency preparation plan to the college board," stated the dean. "We feel that the end is near and that there is still much work to do in order to be ready. We want only the essential education and what God wants"

New Curriculum

Dean Matthews also spoke of a new curriculum for the remainder of the year and on into the next: "The program will consist of using our Bible classes as prep classes for witnessing and time for personal spiritual preparation. Our Industrial Education Department will be offering practical classes such as construction, mechanics, and trades for all students. Hygiene and Emergency Response will be taught by our Nursing Department, with Dr. Luke leading out. We will have a Home Economics course for all girls to learn to cook a balanced diet. Some meals will be cooked for large groups using wood cook stoves. Any who have experience in these skills will be asked to help teach them, in some cases, students will be teaching professors. I have asked our retired agriculture teacher, Brother Samuel, to come and help us grow our own food. Any with farming experience will also be asked to help. Samuel took a retirement package when we sold the farm, and he has graciously consented to come back and help us. A friendly neighbor who bought the farm has allowed us to use 100 acres to grow food. It turns out that much of this land has already been subdivided."

Now the dean's voice was broken. "I am very sorry, young people. We have failed you. We needed that farm to help you witness in these last days." He emphasized the first sentence of his next quotation, "*The usefulness learned on the school farm is the very education that is most essential for those who go out as missionaries to foreign fields. If this training is given with the glory of God in view, great results will be seen. No work will be more effectual than that done by those who, having obtained an education in practical life, go forth to mission fields with the message of truth, prepared to instruct as they have been instructed. The knowledge they have obtained in the tilling of the soil and other lines of manual work, and which they can carry with them to their fields of labor, will make them a blessing even in heathen lands.* 'This is quoted from Series B, No. 11, page 29. We are going to present our plans to the board, in emergency session for their counsel. We will continue with degree programs for now, but I want you to know that we may very well shift our emphasis. I note that the same book, on page 28 says: '*The plan of the schools we shall establish in these closing years of the work is to be of an entirely different order from those we have instituted in the past.*'"

Lisa stood to ask Dean Matthews a question, Daniel noted that she radiated a deep Christian experience. He decided to get to know her better. But for now, he had too many questions and concerns about what his teachers had told him. Prof. Paul's reference from The Great Controversy was being fulfilled right before his eyes. He suddenly felt in great need and fearful that he and his family wouldn't be ready for Jesus' coming. He had to learn, first, what to do and then get home and tell his folks. He saw that the spirit of revival and reformation was rapidly spreading through the campus.

Sadly, Daniel observed that some of his friends left Adventist College to pursue careers at other universities. They felt that all of this excitement about the weather would "blow over," and they wanted to continue training for their careers.

Several meetings later, President Cristman told the students that the college would lose its accreditation if it insisted on this contingency plan. The accreditation board pointed out that degree programs would suffer and hence could not receive recognition. "I must say, young people," said the president, "that we are firm in our resolution to not fail you again. We thought accreditation stood in our way, but the truth is, we could have been accredited if we had chosen to follow the counsels found in the book Education. But we chose to follow certification by the world, and now we are far behind where we should be in our demonstration of true education and preparing you to give the message for this crisis."

Accreditation—by God

Dean Matthews stood up and gave a detailed study on accreditation that he had entitled "I Believe in Accreditation."

"This may seem like a strange subject to consider at first, but as it develops I think you will see why this is an important issue," he said as he introduced his study.

"In the book My Life Today, page 339, we find an interesting statement: '*Will we live the lessons given in the Word of God, Christ's great lesson book?*'

"There are many lessons in the Bible that we might consider. One is found in the first angel's message of Revelation 14. This message for the hour in which we live is to help people '*fear God and give glory to Him.*'

"The grandest purpose of our whole educational system is to bring glory to God. Reading again from the same page in My Life Today, '*Will we live the lessons given in the Word of God, Christ's great lesson book? ... It is the only book that will prepare human beings for the life that measures with the life of God. And those who make this Word their daily study are the only ones who are worthy of receiving a diploma entitling them to educate and train the children for entrance into the higher school, to be crowned as victorious overcomers.'* The study of God's Word on a daily basis is the only way a person becomes worthy of a diploma to teach young people.

"*'Constantly improve. Keep reaching higher and still higher. It is the ability to put to the tax the powers of mind and body, ever keeping eternal realities in view, that is of value now. Seek the Lord most earnestly, that you may become more and more refined, more spiritually cultured.'* This is a co-operative type of program, that you and God are entering into together. As we progress in our education, in union with God, we can be made better and better workers for Him. *'Then you will have the very best diploma that any one can have—the endorsement of God.'* This quote is from Testimonies for the Church, volume 7, page 281.

"This is the diploma we need—the endorsement of God. If we must lay aside the work of obtaining an earthly diploma in order to have the endorsement of God, that's all right. Is it not of greater value to have God's endorsement of our work than to have human endorsement?

"*'Following His example, in our medical missionary work we shall reveal to the world that our credentials are from above.'* I'm reading from page 23 of the book Medical Ministry. Notice the use of the words 'diploma' and 'credentials.' Medical missionary effort conducted according to God's plan will reveal to the world that our credentials are from above. The disciples found it necessary to say on several occasions, *'We ought to obey God rather than men.'* And likewise, today, we Christians need to decide whether or not our educational program is one upon which God can place His endorsement.

"Testimonies to the Church, volume 6, page 131, says: *'A knowledge of God and of Jesus Christ "whom He has sent" is the highest education, and it will cover the earth with its wonderful enlightenment as the waters cover the sea.'* A careful study on the subject of 'higher education' will reveal that higher education is the knowledge of God and His wonderful plan of salvation. The Christian's higher education is not what the world considers it to be—the gaining of a great amount of knowledge, information, and facts for a life on this earth. The higher education that we are constantly urged to obtain is a knowledge of our Father in heaven and Jesus Christ, His Son, and this message will cover the earth.

"I would like to share some historical knowledge with you. I trust that no one will use this information in a critical way. I present this material for two reasons. I want you to understand (1) why some of our training programs do not get involved with state accreditation, and (2) that the very materials that I present to you here are being considered by leaders in our Church. These brethren are looking for answers to problems that we have in our educational programs.

"In 1923, the question of accreditation arose in our church. Elder W. E. Howell, in a 1923 World Educational Conference, said, 'The idea has been kept before our educators of registering our colleges in a secular, standardizing association, thus tying them by much more than a thread to the educational policies of those who do not discern the voice of God and who will not hearken to His commandments.'

"Listen to this quote from Counsels to Parents, Teachers, and Students, page 255: *'Our people are now being tested as to whether they will obtain their wisdom from the greatest Teacher the world ever knew, or seek to the god of Ekron. Let us determine that we will not be tied by so much as a thread to the educational policies of those who do not discern the voice of God and who will not hearken to His commandments.'*

"Elder Howell here is telling the Educational Conference that some of the movements toward obtaining standardization and accreditation with worldly associations are going to tie us by more than a thread to their educational policies; and, he says, 'only two colleges have taken such a step on the most modern scale that could be discovered... that of registering only junior college departments. Where this step will lead these schools and any others that may take it, only He who reads the future as well as the past can predict.' Now notice what Elder Howell predicted: 'It would almost seem like tying ourselves to the tail of a kite, to be carried where the holder of the string may lead, seemingly in the direction of less efficiency to serve in the cause of God.'

"Thus, the educational secretary of the General Conference of Seventh-day Adventists appealed to our world educators, trying to help them realize the seriousness of the movements that were taking place at that very moment within the ranks of the Seventh-day Adventist Church.

"In 1931 the issue of accreditation became important enough that it had to be considered at the Fall Council of Seventh-day Adventists, and at that time it was voted that in a 'careful manner' we would go and seek accreditation. There was a safeguard established that these men felt would protect the educational program from being destroyed, which was stated as follows:

"'We recommend, that in the selection of teachers to attend the universities only persons of outstanding Christian experience and those who have been successful in Christian work should be chosen. Persons whose faith in the Bible and the Spirit of Prophecy is well grounded, and who realize that in attending the university they are being exposed to subtle and almost unconscious influences of infidelity–and persons who believe with all their hearts in the superiority of Christian education.'

"You see," continued the dean, "it would be necessary, in order to have our schools accredited, that our people go to the universities and institutions of the world to obtain the degrees and credentials necessary to measure up to the requirements of the standardizing associations. It was therefore decided to select those who possessed the characteristics of Daniel–men who could go into these institutions and yet remain true to the God of heaven. This sounds to me like it should have been a safe course, if ever there was one, but now I want to read the results of pursuing this course. The following is taken from what is now called The Branson Report. This report was brought to the Fall Council in 1935, just four years after the decision to go ahead with the plan to seek accreditation. The report was presented by Elder Branson, and others who were part of a special committee selected to study the subject. Elder Branson said:

"'We believe, Brother Chairman, as a result of our study of the situation, that the safeguards that we tried to throw around the policy of accrediting four years ago when we entered upon this course have largely broken down. Therefore we entered upon a course that we did not plan on, and we know that things have gone farther than was anticipated. We were facing dangers and perils in this matter of accrediting our colleges that were little dreamed of at that time when this action was taken four years ago.... . We have found that a large class of very young and immature people have been finding their way into the universities believing that as a highway to appointment in institutional work....

"'Our commission brought us information that from one college alone thirty had gone into the university for further training during these years. We are told that in one university there was a get-together of our Seventh-day Adventist young people for a social evening, and there were forty present at that social, and not all were reached by the invitation.... . Boards have been pressed by the accreditation bodies to put men on their faculties who have advanced degrees....

"'We believe undue emphasis is being placed upon the idea of securing degrees from worldly institutions rather than training our youth for spiritual service in the cause of God.... . Many of these will be lost, will lose their hold upon God, and will not fill the position of responsibility in this cause it was designed of God they should fill.'

"Already–after only four years–the commission realized that many who had gone out to worldly schools, studying under teachers who did not believe on Jesus as their Saviour, teachers who did not teach the things that we understand from

God's Word, were going to be forever lost. They would never see the kingdom of God. Yet he related another problem which was perhaps even worse: 'If they should fill positions of responsibility, many of them would bring to the denominational work influences that would lead farther and farther afield from the original purpose that was in the hearts of the men who established this work.' They would begin to introduce into our schools some things that were not good for our young people to learn. A good example of this is the study of evolution and of other such concepts. What a shame that we should study these things written by men that certainly have no commendation from the God of heaven! Why are these things being studied? Because we have teachers who have been educated to think, to believe, that these things are something good and perhaps even necessary for us to study.

"'Your commission believes therefore as a denomination that we are drifting and that it is entrusted to us at this Autumn Council of 1935 to endeavor to call a halt and to retrace our course and to drive down new stakes and determine by the help of God that we will rectify anything that is wrong in what we undertook to do four years ago.' I cannot help but thank God for men who are not afraid to say they have made a mistake. Elder Branson stated that it is time to retrace our course. Then he gives a comment from an educator (not a Seventh-day Adventist, but a religious educator), by the name of Andrew D. Harmon. At that time Mr. Harmon was president of Transylvania College.

"'The hitherto undisputed claim that the church college carried a more wholesome moral and spiritual atmosphere had been a compelling argument in its favor. But this claim is seriously questioned today. The requirements of standardizing agencies have compelled church colleges to shift their emphasis from morality to scholarship.... The passing of the church college is now taking place and most of its devotees are looking upon the transition; some are even players in the drama and do not recognize it.' This man did not even believe the message for this hour, yet he was wise enough to recognize that shifting the emphasis from morality to scholarship was wrong.

"Elder Branson went on to say, 'We have been in the period of transition for a period of four years. We recognize on every hand that there has been a shift of standards, a shift in the ideals, a shift in the emphasis till many of our people throughout the churches of this land are becoming alarmed.... Can we maintain our ideals in their purity and yet reach to the fullest extent the recognition from the world, and agree to being standardized by the world, which means that we must be under the domination of these worldly organizations?' This was, and is, a very serious question. 'Some of us are very much afraid of what is going on by our own inauguration four years ago that is to some degree, God only knows to what degree, destroying the foundations of this denomination and bringing into us and our work an element that is altogether unsafe.... *"Lo, the people shall dwell alone and shall not be reckoned among the nations"* (Numbers 23:9). We have been called to be a peculiar people to minister in this earth, but this earth is not our home. We must dwell alone. There is no way that we can enter into a close union with those of this earth.

"'It has become a profound conviction with us that we are drifting and that we have departed far from the blueprint that God gave to this people in the matter of establishing and operating our schools.... We are ready to admit that in our action of four years ago we went too far. We find that we made a mistake.'

"These are some of the highlights of <u>The Branson Report</u> on accreditation. This is part of the discussion that took place following the presentation of the report:

"W. A. NELSON of New Jersey: 'The Lord has counseled us not to be connected by so much as a thread and some of our schools are so bound to worldly systems that we cannot cut the rope.'

"ELDER WATSON: 'I personally believe the vote we took at that time was in the wrong direction. I have been instructed by the Word and the writings of Sister White very definitely since then.... I think we entered upon a course wrong in principle in 1931.... I think we have been mistaken in accepting standards from the world in education and in other standards.... We have entered upon a course of real peril.'

"ELDER RUSKJER: 'I believe that the entire future of the youth of this denomination is dependent upon maintaining in the institutions of education the educational policies of this denomination, and right principles, and clinging to the blueprint God has given to us.

"'Not very long ago I had the privilege of visiting with the man who stands at the head of the schools of an entire denomination. During the course of our conversation he said that he was deeply concerned over the trend of his denomination, stating that they were rapidly losing their youth, and I know his statement was correct. He stated that it seemed to him the way schools at the present time, colleges, and seminaries are drifting in a worldly direction ... if we continue to drift in this direction, ten years from now they will cease to exist. I asked him why he made such a statement. He pointed out to me that since the schools had reached out and affiliated with the universities and have employed teachers who have been trained in non-Christian universities, they have come back into the schools, he said, and have brought to the schoolroom a spirit of unbelief in the Book of all books, and we are drifting.

"'As a member of this denomination I do not want to be a party in that direction, in any plan that will make it more difficult for our youth to hold true to the fundamentals which God has given to us. I do not think that we are throwing any halo of glory upon the two institutions that we are recommending to maintain accreditation. Decidedly I think that we should eliminate these from the accrediting class also if we can.'

"It was being recommended that two colleges should have accreditation and the rest would not.

"ELDER McELHANY: 'I wish the day would come when we could rescue our entire educational system from the necessity of going to the world for any further instruction.... . I hope the Lord will lead us some day to build upon the foundation of this report to give further study in rescuing our educational system from the world.'

"My friends, I would like to have this man's wish come true."

"ELDER WILCOX: 'Four years ago I stood very decidedly against accrediting in any form. I stand on practically the same ground today.... . I hope in God that the time will come when we can take our students clear away from worldly things in our schools. While I favor this report, it is a compromise.'

"PRESIDENT ANDERSON (next day): 'I feel perplexed and confused. I cannot quite harmonize the speech of yesterday by Elder Watson and the speeches today in favor of accreditation. If we do not accredit our medical schools, we fear what can happen to us, we are told today. We were told yesterday to exercise faith. I do not honestly see how I can go back and repeat your speech, Elder Watson, and when the brethren ask me, "Are you tied by a thread?" say "not a thread." How can I harmonize that by what we are doing when we authorize accreditation of all our academies, for all of our junior colleges, and for all?

"And now we think we have saved the cause from these wicked things by eliminating three colleges from accreditation. I am afraid we will rue this day if we go ahead with this program.

"Four years ago we did make a mistake. We made a mistake, as you say. I stand for accreditation. I don't want you to misunderstand that—for the kind of accreditation the Testimonies speak of. We cannot blow hot and cold.'

"ELDER RICE: 'If we should not be tied by so much as a thread, why not cut loose?'

"H. H. HAMILTON: 'Personally, I do not believe in any accreditation at all from outside sources. If we are going out to Babylon, why not go out altogether and not have two or three schools in?'

"ELDER WATSON, president of the General Conference: 'The medical college was at one time the chief urge for accreditation. It is a large part of the urge today, and if it comes to a choice between whether we shall continue the medical college or go worldly, my vote shall be that we shall not continue our medical work, and as a leader in the denomination I am calling upon you in the fear of God to take this step to keep our principles of true education from being lost to us. That is my appeal.'

"I thank God that this man's fears were not necessary, for God would not want us to make a decision that would cause us to lose our medical work. But I cannot help but be thankful for a man who would rather have us lose that most important work from our church than have us compromise our principles.

"ELDER VOTAW: 'If this accrediting is wrong, it is wrong altogether.... I cannot see it any other way, between sending boys and girls to hell from three schools or six. If it is wrong let us quit it… If this comes up for a vote, I am going to say "NO" long enough for my vote to register "NO."'

"ELDER PIPER: 'I do not see the light in compromising with the world in any degree, and I am ready to cast my vote contrary to this recommendation, because I do not see its consistency. I do not see light in the proposition. I would like to move that it be referred back to this commission again for the purpose of being allowed to interview the commission.'

"After this, he and others privately interviewed the commission seeking to bring about a better understanding of what to do. But, unfortunately, at the conclusion of all this discussion, we find that the rush for accreditation from the world continued, unchecked. The following paragraph has been recorded by Brother Straw:

"'In the early '30's the General Conference Committee appointed a special committee to give study to recommend what should be done. (This is the committee that prepared The Branson Report.) That committee visited the different colleges and studied their situations. At the end of their investigation, the committee recommended that two of our colleges seek accreditation in the associations, and that the others continue their work in training ministers, teachers, and missionaries for foreign fields. This report was submitted to the Fall Council of the General Conference where it was reconsidered. The General Conference president urged its acceptance and pleaded with the men to accept it. But, "No," the college men said. "If some were accredited, so would they all," and all it was. From that time on a stampede set in for accreditation and university-trained teachers. Each faculty seemed to try to outdo the other in their race for accreditation and for doctor's degrees.' So in the end, even the compromise was turned down. Instead of accrediting only two schools—they voted for all schools to head in the direction of accreditation.

"Personally, it is hard for me to believe how, after the discussion I read here, such a thing could have taken place, but it did. I believe these men loved the work, but they didn't understand well enough, evidently, all that was involved.

"Elder McElhany made a speech in 1937 in which he said: 'I tell you solemnly that there are forces and influences at work which, if unchecked, will render us just as unprepared for the second coming of Christ as was Israel for His first coming.' I wonder, my friends–when I read about Israel and how they rejected Jesus, their Saviour, even though they knew all the prophecies and were Bible students–are we Seventh-day Adventists removed from falling into that problem? (See the article entitled "Why the Jews Rejected Jesus," Ministry Magazine, Dec. 1933). Could not the same thing happen to you and me today? Could we be found unprepared for the second coming of Jesus?

"Elder McElhany said in his speech: 'Make no mistake about that. I see these influences at work. The spirit of Saduceeism is working like leaven and I want to lift my voice in earnest entreaty that you may see that the door is closed against all such intrusions. I summon you all to engage in this fight against the spirit of Saduceeism. My friends, really, I am concerned about the trends and the tendencies. I confess a great anxiety about them.'

"A Sadducee did not believe in the future life; he lived only for the present. Could the people's education have something to do with the present Laodicean condition of the church predicted by Jesus? Elder McElhany was very concerned about what he saw taking place even in 1937.

"Here is what Elder A. W. Spalding was thinking as recently as 1953 in a letter he wrote to Brother Dickson of the General Conference. He had become so burdened with the problem that he couldn't sleep at night. He would have liked to keep silent. 'Twenty-five years ago, in 1928, we came to our educational Kadesh-barnea. The Promised Land was before us, but the majority of our spies brought back an evil report. We voted for affiliation and accreditation with all that it involved of affinity with the world's education.' From the history of this problem, is it clear enough what the difficulty was? Can you see why in some schools we are seeking for the accreditation of heaven? We are not seeking for the accreditation of the men of this earth, and whether or not they ever think we are doing a good work of education. I do not care. I am not interested in what they think. If God approves, I'm happy.'

"The following counsel, from Ellen G. White, comes to us now in the light of history. This counsel would be difficult to fully understand without historical background. *But let me tell you that you must not take what the world calls the higher education and bring it into our schools and sanitariums and churches. We need to understand these things. I speak to you definitely. This*

381

must not be done.' This quote is from <u>Fundamentals of Christian Education</u>, page 536. Is that clear enough–in the light of history? We must not take what the world has to offer and bring it into our schools.

"*'We are not to elevate our standard just a little above the world's standard, but we are to make the distinction decidedly apparent.'* It is not good enough to do what the world is doing. God's plan for His people is that we do something totally different–something ten times better than what is being done. *'The reason we have had so little influence upon unbelieving relatives and associates is that there has been so little decided difference between our practices and those of the world.'* You will find this quote in <u>Testimonies for the Church</u>, volume 6, pages 146 and 147.

"The same book, on page 130, further explains: *'There is no time now to fill the mind with theories of what is popularly called "higher education." The time devoted to that which does not tend to assimilate the soul to the likeness of Christ is so much time lost for eternity.'* What a sad thing it would be if in seeking the wisdom of the world we should lose our eternal life!

"<u>Counsels to Parents, Teachers, and Students</u>, page 415: *'Many are better prepared, have more spiritual discrimination and knowledge of God, and know more of His requirements, when they enter upon their course of study than when they are graduated.'* What a shame it would be if a student came to my school stronger spiritually than when he went away! How could I consider that I had done my work as a Christian educator?!"

Dean Matthews closed his address to the students at Adventist College by saying, "I want to remind you again, that I hope, as you consider this matter, you will take it in the spirit in which it was given. I love my church, but unless we understand this issue, all the spirit of dedication, all the spirit of wanting to do right, all the emphasis on evangelism, as good as these things may be, will not keep us from taking a wrong course. God has placed a burden upon my heart to help us understand the issues that were involved in our history so that we can begin looking again at the credentials of heaven, at the diploma that God gives to men and women who will follow His plan of true education.

"How does it help us to get ready for the crisis?" Dean Matthews asked. "It shows that revival and reformation are needed today. We will study other areas each morning. You may ask, 'Why is it important to study these issues?' Let me read to you a reference from Mrs. White recorded in <u>The Christian Educator</u>, August 1897, which we must always keep before us: *'Now, as never before, we need to understand the true science of education. If we fail to understand this, we shall never have a place in the kingdom of God.'*

"We need to understand this, young people, because God wants us to separate from the world," he said. "God wants us to have a place in His kingdom, so we must understand true education.

"I am sorry to announce that some of our professors have recently left Adventist College, calling us fanatics and alarmists. I want you young people to know that President Cristman and I and the remaining faculty are determined to grow along with you. Please stay with us young people," he pleaded, "and together we will see this through to the kingdom."

Location of Schools

The next morning, Dean Matthews began speaking on a topic that was even harder for him than the discussion of accreditation had been. "There has been much discussion on the Faculty Executive Committee over pages 25 and 26 of the fifth volume of the <u>Testimonies for the Church</u>: *'Our school was established, not merely to teach the sciences, but for the purpose of giving instruction in the great principles of God's word and in the practical duties of everyday life.... <u>If a worldly influence is to bear sway in our school, then sell it out to worldlings and let them take the entire control; and those who have invested their means in that institution will establish another school, to be conducted, not upon the plan of popular schools, nor according to the desires of principal and teachers, but upon the plan which God has specified.</u> In the name of my Master I entreat all who stand in responsible positions in that school to be men of God. When the Lord requires us to be distinct and peculiar, how can we crave popularity or seek to imitate the customs and practices of the world? <u>God has declared His purpose to have one college in the land where the Bible shall have its proper place in the education of the youth. Will we do our part to carry out that purpose?</u>'*

Dean Matthews emphasized the last sentence and then referred to an article, "Out of the Cities," that appeared in <u>The Adventist Review</u>, January 26, 1978, by Dr. Charles Hirsch, a former director of education for the North American Division, containing this poignant reference from <u>Selected Messages</u>, book 2, page 357, about where our schools should be located: *"'God has sent warning after warning that our schools and publishing houses and sanitariums are to be established out of the city, in places where the youth may be taught most effectively what is truth.'"*

The dean further referred to Dr. Hirsch's article noting situations where Seventh-day Adventist schools were sold and moved to country locations. "'There have been several instances where the cities have grown up around and swallowed the schools. Some of the latter committed the mistake of building off-center on a corner of their property, leaving no contiguous property surrounding the campus proper to provide a natural buffer zone. And then, to compound the error, boards sold property to pay off debts or pay for new facilities.

" 'As a result, several of these schools have relocated and still others are giving study to the development of a new campus in a rural environment.

" 'Mrs. White emphasizes in <u>Counsels to Parents, Teachers, and Students</u>, page 532: *"God bids us establish schools away from the cities, where, without let or hindrance, we can carry on the education of students upon plans that are in harmony with the solemn message committed to us for the world."* If the youth of our church are to be educated along the guidelines and the counsel given to us, then it is incumbent upon us as constituents of our schools to provide right facilities in the right places with the right teachers.' "

As Dean Matthews replaced the magazine clipping into his folder, Daniel sprang to his feet. "Dean, sir, you mean we knew all of this before and we took another route?"

The dean replied, "Many leaders have written in our church magazines concerning the need for reform in our educational work. Others, from supporting ministries, have pioneered these concepts; they were not exactly preaching to the choir. We just didn't listen, but now we work. Perhaps we had doubts that the Lord could supply all our needs if we did not conform to the world's mold. We must forgive, be forgiven, and move forward.

Our college board is studying a proposal to sell our present campus and relocate to a country-wilderness location. This is a very difficult step for many, but it is obvious that the location of our schools is important to God. We have found a property with large natural meadows, buildings and housing for 100 staff and 1,000 students. This property was a former church camp near Serenity Lake in the foothills of the mountains. It has its own hydro plant from the stream that runs through the property. It is beautiful.

"Please pray with us that the Lord's will be done and that the alumni will back us. They will have a real struggle to see us move. But if God wants us to–and we think He does–then we should move as soon as possible. Time is running out. We are convicted, as leaders of Adventist College, of Sister White's counsel in <u>Life Sketches</u>, page 351: *'Never can the proper education be given to the youth in this country, or in any other country, unless they are separated a wide distance from the cities.'*

"Notice, young people, it says NEVER can the proper education be given here, or any other place, unless we are a wide distance from the cities. Never means it just can't be done. Location is important, as we read from Manuscript Releases, volume 10, page 260: *'If there can be found places in retired mountain regions where it would be difficult for the evils of the cities to enter, let our people secure such places for our sanitariums and advanced schools.'*

"No Buy-No Sell"

"In our next meeting, we will be studying the concept of the church under 'no buy-no sell.' Please read Revelation 13 by tomorrow. God bless you all!"

The next morning, Prof. Paul began his early-morning class by quoting Revelation 13:16 and 17, *"'And he causeth all, both small and great, rich and poor, free and bond, to receive a mark in their right hand, or in their foreheads: and that no man might buy or sell, save he that had the mark, or the name of the beast, or the number of his name.'*

"Did you ever wonder, young people, what it would be like to not be able to buy and sell?" The students looked at each other as Prof. Paul continued, "No electricity, no city water, no natural gas, no grocery store, no transportation. In more detail, what would it mean to have no electricity? In fact, your homework will be to take this list and add to it. Take each category and detail what it would be like not to have it. An example: no electricity–no washing machine, etc."

"Here is my question to you and the faculty of this college." The president and Dean Matthews were in focused attention. "What have we done to prepare our church and our young people for this Revelation 13 experience? Question two is, What do we do now? And three, What is God's plan in order that we might follow it?"

"In dealing with question one, I think it is safe to say that the crisis is upon us and that we have not and are not prepared. Notice this statement from Patriarchs and Prophets, page 595, paragraph 1: *'Are there not some lessons which the educators of our day might learn with profit from the ancient schools of the Hebrews? He who created man has provided for his development in body and mind and soul. Hence, real success in education depends upon the fidelity with which men carry out the Creator's plan. The true object of education is to restore the image of God in the soul.'* Have we been true to that plan? The answer is no, we haven't, as we have heard administrators and faculty apologizing for our neglect."

Prof. Paul continued, "Question two has a simple answer; let's begin to follow the plan very closely and ask God to help us. I feel like I am in school again. During the next few sessions, we will outline the plan as best we can and we will study it with you, young people. I have asked Dean Matthews if I could bring in speakers who have had some experience with 'the plan' to study with us. Remember, we shall not have a part in the kingdom of God unless we understand true education."

YOU CAN SURVIVE!

Questions About Courtship

That evening there was a special assembly held in the auditorium for the whole campus. The rest of the college would soon hear what had been learned in the previous early-morning meetings.

Daniel was concerned how Lisa was relating to all of these rapid changes. He decided to sit so he could talk to her. Sitting down behind her, he said, "Hi!" Lisa returned the greeting, and they recognized each other from the early-morning meetings. Daniel noticed that she dressed modestly. He couldn't remember her wearing jeans to class as most of the other girls did. She seemed to have a special glow about her. The dresses she wore were neat, clean, and beautiful.

Daniel decided to ask her to go with him to a Saturday night program. She politely declined.

"Why?" asked Daniel, perhaps more boldly than he should.

"I don't date," said Lisa.

"Why?" again with too much boldness, but this time because he felt he had found someone curiously different, reserved and mysterious, not belligerent. It was as though she had some good news to share.

"I could give you a book to read," said Lisa. "It gives my reasons from the Bible and the Spirit of Prophecy."

"Really? I have been an Adventist all my life and I have never heard of such a thing," exclaimed Daniel. "I am sorry, Lisa. I didn't mean to sound all-knowing," replied Daniel sheepishly.

"Oh, it's okay. It's no surprise to me; other guys have asked me the same questions and I give them Pastor Bill's outline which is enclosed in a new book entitled God's Appointed. They give it back a few days later and say that it was too 'old-fashioned' or they didn't read it at all. Most kids think I am kind of old fashioned. I like friends, but I don't date. I have chosen to do what I feel God asks me to do."

"You mean God says we shouldn't date?" asked Daniel.

"Yes. Let me show you one reference, but it is a much deeper subject than just this one quote. Listen to this reference from Counsels to Parents, Teachers, and Students, page 100," said Lisa excitedly. Her unique combination of enthusiasm hedged by discretion increased her attractiveness: *"While at school, students should not allow their minds to become confused by thoughts of courtship. They are there to gain a fitness to work for God, and this thought is ever to be uppermost.'"*

Daniel was dumbfounded. His head was almost reeling with so many new concepts. "Is this part of the new program for the college President Cristman and dean Matthews are proposing?" he asked Lisa. She admitted that they had interviewed her and that she had referred them to Pastor Bill's outline that they were now studying.

"But, Lisa, won't that take all of the fun out of being at college?"

"Look at it this way, Daniel. It sure saves a lot of heartache if things go wrong, or the relationship gets prematurely physical. God wants us to wait for that special one–God's appointed. Please read Pastor Bill's book before you form any other conclusions. Will you?" asked Lisa, almost pleadingly.

"Yes, I will," said Daniel, "but this gets a guy right where he lives!"

"I am sure it does, but how about reserving yourself for that special one God has chosen for you—God's appointed?" Lisa suggested.

"You may be right, Lisa. Can I borrow your book?" asked Daniel.

"Sure," said Lisa. "I will bring it to our next 5:30 a. m. meeting."

"No," said Daniel. "Could I get it tonight? I want to get into it right away. I have an easier class load tomorrow, so I don't have homework to do."

"Yes, you can. Come to the dorm lobby after assembly, okay?"

"Yes, ma'am," said Daniel playfully.

Lisa blushed, wondering how Pastor Bill's outline would affect him.

"By the way," asked Lisa, changing the subject, "how are you doing with all the changes in college classes and world events?"

"I can see it all so far," said Daniel. "It really seems urgent. I don't feel ready myself, but I am really praying. It is almost overwhelming—all this information! It seems like I have been asleep and am just waking up!"

"Me too," replied Lisa, just as President Cristman began speaking.

During the next hour, the whole student body heard of the plans for a new curriculum in the light of world events. At the end, some students walked out, but the vast majority did what had never happened before in an assembly. They stood and applauded, after President Cristman and Dean Matthews apologized and asked for forgiveness. They felt they had failed to adequately provide the training necessary to be ready for the events just ahead. The applause signaled the students' openness and support of the new program.

President Cristman reported that this beginning at Adventist College was spreading to other of our church colleges with an enthusiastic reception. It seemed a revival and reformation was beginning everywhere. Truly the Holy Spirit was working.

Dean Matthews warned that many trials would come. "Some of our friends, even family, may abandon us, but I challenge you to be true to our purpose. God is working as He has never worked before." Then he read this quote from Testimonies for the Church, volume 6, page 145: "'Though in many respects our institutions of learning have swung into worldly conformity, though step by step they have advanced toward the world, they are prisoners of hope. Fate has not so woven *its meshes about their workings that they need to remain helpless and in uncertainty. If they will listen to His voice and follow in His ways, God will correct and enlighten them, and bring them back to their upright position of distinction from the world* .... *One barrier broken down will give greater ability and courage to go forward. Press in the right direction, and make a change, solidly, intelligently. Then circumstances will be your helpers and not your hindrances. Make a beginning. The oak is in the acorn.* 'You see, young people, we are prisoners. But we are prisoners of hope! Make a beginning! We need you to go with us–go with us to the kingdom. Your preparatory education is beginning now." The dean's speech was followed by more applause.

That night, Daniel was up late reading God's Appointed. "The two young people in the book, Kevin and Rachel, are much like Lisa and me," he mused. Their courtship had taken place several years before.

One reference found in Testimonies for the Church, volume 5, page 366, really caught Daniel's attention and cut across his feelings: *"In this age of the world, as the scenes of earth's history are soon to close and we are about to enter upon the time of trouble such as never was, the fewer the marriages contracted, the better for all, both men and women."*

He noted it didn't say no marriages, but the fewer the better. As he read on in Pastor Bill's book, he found that the true motive for marriage is to strengthen God's cause, not how a young person looks.

"So," he concluded as he thought it through, "if God has a work for me, then maybe He has someone for a 'helpmate.' On the other hand, any sacrifice Jesus asks me to make will make me happier, even if that includes not being married."

Daniel was truly inspired by the book that Lisa had given him. He felt at peace with his commitment. "True love waits and I will wait on God," said Daniel in silent prayer.

Even though he was up late that night, Daniel could not put the book down. It exposed a whole new level of trust in God for him. "It seems dating has us off course in two ways," he mused. "We shouldn't date in school because it sidetracks us from getting the most out of our education and it leads to a high divorce rate. Indeed," he said, clenching his fist, "there is a better way. I want that way." Daniel had decided the book contained truth as he flopped onto his bed at 1:30 a. m. and closed its pages. He knew it might mean personal sacrifice, but Daniel was at peace, and he drifted easily into sleep.

He awoke with a clear head and joy in his heart. When he arrived at Prof. Paul's 5:30 class, Lisa met him at the door. With anticipation in her voice she asked, "How did you like the book by Pastor Bill, Daniel?"

"Lisa, I couldn't put it down," said Daniel excitedly. "I read it through and finished at 1:30 this morning. I made a commitment to God. I said, 'Lord, help me, but I want to wait for God's choice for me.' I also read about fewer marriages, and I sorta got a lump in my throat, but I said, 'Thy will be done, Lord.'"

Daniel Meets an Athlete

"I am so happy, Daniel. I, too, have made those commitments." Then she said, "I want you to meet someone." She led Daniel over to a tall, muscular young man with a very reserved bearing and open face.

"Jerry is my brother, and we live on a farm in Idaho," she explained as the boys shook hands.

"Glad to meet you, Daniel," said Jerry as Lisa introduced them.

As they talked, Jerry said that he came to Adventist College after he had accepted an athletic scholarship to State University.

"Why did you quit?" asked Daniel.

"I had to, because God asked me to give it up," explained Jerry.

"But we have sports here at Adventist College," observed Daniel.

"Yes, but I think that will change soon," said Jerry. "We don't need sports to get us ready for the kingdom."

Daniel's head was spinning in confusion again. He had been interested in sports himself and had played with town kids in a summer baseball league. He was a pitcher and had helped his team make it to the finals of the state tournament.

Lisa noticed Daniel's puzzled look and asked what was wrong. "I don't know," he said, "every day it seems I am faced with putting something else in my life on the altar of sacrifice. I would like to read something on sports. Do you have anything, Jerry?"

"Yes," he said, "My dad wrote an article entitled No Sacrifice, that appeared in the Review and Herald, April 12, 1973. I have a copy in my room. I am in the corner apartment just down the hall from you. Come by when you can."

Lisa had seated herself while Jerry and Daniel talked. Jerry confessed, "My Dad was opposed to sports. It isn't easy to go against your dad, as I did when I accepted the athletic scholarship. But what he showed me from the Bible and the Spirit of Prophecy I couldn't continue at State U. Lisa was a great help to me as well," Jerry said. "She is so patient."

"Quite a testimony about his sister," thought Daniel to himself.

The meeting began with Prof. Paul offering prayer. He prayed for the meeting and world situation. He prayed for a little more time for God's people to prepare. He prayed for those making decisions; to consider God's will ahead of their own ideas and opinions. He prayed that those who were suffering might be comforted and make decisions to obey God.

Daniel's mind was elsewhere this morning. He'd had to sacrifice dating, his college major, and now sports? Where was all of this leading? Maybe his friends who had left Adventist College were right about the leaders being extremists!

Prof. Paul read a reference from <u>Fundamentals of Christian Education</u>, page 289, that refocused Daniel's attention on the word "extremist": *"When we reach the standard that the Lord would have us reach, worldlings will regard Seventh-day Adventists as odd, singular, strait-laced extremists.'"*

Then Prof. Paul balanced the challenge: "There is no benefit in being an extremist just to be different. Two things mark God's people in these last days: *'To the law and to the testimony: if they speak not according to this word, it is because there is no light in them'* (Isaiah 8:20) and from Revelation 12:17, *'And the dragon was wroth with the woman, and went to make war with the remnant of her seed, which keep the commandments of God, and have the testimony of Jesus Christ."* He also read from Revelation 19:10: *"And I fell at his feet to worship him. And he said unto me, See thou do it not: I am thy fellowservant, and of thy brethren that have the testimony of Jesus: worship God: for the testimony of Jesus is the spirit of prophecy.'"*

Daniel decided then and there that he would be on safe ground if it was in the Bible and the Spirit of Prophecy. He would try not to be bothered about being called odd or extreme. "I will leave that with God," he said to himself. But he knew he was on a steep learning curve.

He wondered about the article on sports. Oh, how he loved baseball! He wept inwardly, prematurely mourning the sacrifice that would follow his reading of the article.

Prof. Paul continued by reading from <u>Counsels to Parents, Teachers, and Students</u>, page 100, "It seems, young people, that God's purpose for our schools and colleges was *'to gain a fitness for the work of God and this is ever to be uppermost.'*

Daniel remembered this reference from the book Lisa had lent him on courtship. "Amazing," he thought to himself, "how everything is interrelated."

Spiritual Emphasis Is Number One

Prof. Paul continued with another reference from <u>Testimonies for the Church</u>, volume 5, page 14, *"'The strength of our college is in keeping the religious element in ascendancy."*

"Young people, I have already covered a lot of ground in support of a change," said Prof. Paul, "but note this one last reference this morning. It is found in <u>Fundamentals of Christian Education</u>, page 286: *'In our institutions of learning there was to be exerted an influence that would counteract the influence of the world, and give no encouragement to indulgence in appetite, in selfish gratification of the senses, in pride, ambition, love of dress and display, love of praise and flattery, <u>and strife for high rewards and honors as a recompense for good scholarship. All this was to be discouraged in our schools.</u>'* Prof. Paul spoke the last few words slowly and deliberately.

"I am recommending that we cease emphasizing the use of grades and pursue mastery of important God-given subjects for this day of earth's history. There will be no valedictorian or salutatorian. No summa or magna cum laude. We will restate our commitment to practical work as counseled by Sister White in <u>Testimonies for the Church</u>, volume 5, page 25, *"Our school was established, not merely to teach the sciences, but for the purpose of giving instruction in the great principles of God's word and in the practical duties of everyday life. This is the education so much needed at the present time.'*

"Tomorrow morning we will take up the topic of diet in these last days," was Prof. Paul's parting remark.

Daniel left with Jerry to get the sports article. On the way, he mentioned to Jerry that he would like to get better acquainted with Lisa. "How should I do that?" he asked.

"Do you remember that book you just read by Pastor Bill?" asked Jerry. "Do you remember from the outline what to do?"

"Am I really supposed to talk to my parents?" asked Daniel.

"Yes," replied Jerry, "They will ask my parents if she would like to have a courtship. This summer would be the soonest you could begin, and only if Lisa says okay. My folks need help on the farm, so you could work for us. Here's dad's phone number," he said as he gave Daniel a slip of paper. "Remember, you are both still in school."

Daniel took the sports article and went to his room to study and pray. The first reference that Daniel read was from <u>Messages to Young People</u>, page 213: *"While the youth are becoming expert in games that are of no real value to themselves or to others, Satan is playing the game of life for their souls."* The context of the reference revealed that baseball was included with other team sports. The reference closed with this solemn thought: *"Satan is delighted when he sees human beings using their physical and mental powers in that which does not educate, which is not useful, which does not help them to be a blessing to those who need their help."*

The next reference that Daniel read was from <u>Manuscript Releases</u>, volume 2, page 218: *"They act as if the school were a place where they were to perfect themselves in sports, as if this were an important branch of their education, and they come armed and equipped for this kind of training. <u>This is all wrong, from beginning to end</u>. It is not in any way appropriate for this time; it is not qualifying the youth to go forth as missionaries, to endure hardship and privation, and to use their powers for the glory of God."*

The clincher came from <u>Fundamentals of Christian Education</u>, page 229, where it says Christ our example never played sports or taught His disciples to play them. *"I cannot find an instance in the life of Christ where He devoted time to play and amusement. He was the great Educator for the present and the future life. I have not been able to find one instance where He educated His disciples to engage in amusement of football or pugilistic games, to obtain physical exercise, or in theatrical performances; and yet Christ was our pattern in all things."*

Daniel wondered about theatrics in the Drama Department for a moment, but readily dismissed it as not being a part of his own problem. It was becoming clearer why he would have to cut out sports and substitute practical work and outdoor recreation such as camping and hiking. Deep down, Daniel preferred the wilderness to the ball field anyway. He had to admit that he loved pitching because he felt like a hero, and Daniel felt he needed that sense of self-worth. Now new heroes were being "born again" every day at Adventist College and Daniel vowed to be one of them.

The Bible had an interesting slant on sports in 2 Corinthians 10:12: *"For we dare not make ourselves of the number, or compare ourselves with some that commend themselves: but they measuring themselves by themselves, and comparing themselves among themselves, are not wise."* Daniel was well aware of the extensive statistics on strikeouts, earned run averages, and win/loss records kept to in order to establish who was the best pitcher. "Much like the GPA," he mused.

John 5:44 explained athletics from another angle, *"How can ye believe, which receive honor one of another, and seek not the honor that cometh from God only?"*

Daniel thought about this for a moment. "It sounds as if our belief in God is affected if we, as humans, accept praise and honor from one another. Competitive sports do praise the best players."

Daniel remembered how he felt when the coaches and players chose him

392

to be on the all-state team. He did not feel humble and suppliant, but exalted. He saw that his pride had to go. Sports, drama, anything that contributed to his exalted feeling, would have to be sacrificed.

Daniel Calls His Dad

Later that morning, Daniel decided to call his parents and discuss Lisa. He knew he would have to explain "God's Appointed" to them, but he deeply desired to do the things that would honor God and ensure happiness.

At the end of his explanation, he asked if they would call Lisa's parents asking permission to start a courtship that would allow him to get better acquainted with her. His parents awkwardly said, "Yes." Daniel assured them that Lisa's parents knew God's plan and would talk to Lisa about it.

"Will you call me back soon?" asked Daniel anxiously.

"OK," his dad replied.

Several weeks went by and Daniel had no word from his parents regarding Lisa. In the meantime, Prof. Paul was continuing with studies in Christian education. Daniel had seen Lisa at every 5:30 a. m. meeting and they had talked. They listened intently to the speaker and his message.

One particular morning, Prof. Paul talked about essential knowledge and higher education. Daniel had the idea, as did most of the students, that essential knowledge would get a job in the work world and higher education was a graduate degree that would reinforce job security. But what Prof. read from the Spirit of Prophecy didn't seem to agree with these ideas.

In a section entitled "Essential Knowledge" he read this quote from Counsels to Parents, Teachers, and Students, page 11: "'Higher education is an experimental knowledge of the plan of salvation, and this knowledge is secured by earnest and diligent study of the Scriptures. Such an education will renew the mind and transform the character ... It will fortify the mind against the deceptive whisperings of the adversary. ... It will teach the learner to become a coworker with Christ, to dispel the moral darkness about him, and bring light and knowledge to men. It is the simplicity of true godliness—our passport from the preparatory school of earth to the higher school above.'"

"It's no wonder a knowledge of true education is essential to admittance to the kingdom of God," Daniel concluded silently.

At the next early-morning meeting, Prof. Paul discussed the negative aspects of sports. Jerry had pretty well covered all of Daniel's questions on the subject of sports, so he stayed in his room that morning and studied God's Appointed in more detail. He endeavored to digest every text and reference.

YOU CAN SURVIVE!

Near the end of the semester and the final meetings of the 5:30 a. m. study group, Prof. Paul, Dean Matthews, and President Cristman reported the progress of board approvals and implementation. More and more young people filtered into the early-morning meetings, and applause often rang out. It did not seem to break the spiritual atmosphere. It merely affirmed the leaders' plans. The applause was often followed by eager questions and testimonies of commitments to God's way.

Degrees, Prizes, Honors

Another memorable meeting had to do with the origins of many common educational practices which further tied schools to the world; tied by conformity rather than being unique, as God would want. One of the main references that caught Daniel's attention was from E. A. Sutherland's <u>Studies in Christian Education</u>, page 29: "The granting of degrees, prizes, honors, etc. is borrowed from the papal system of education." Such things as processionals, caps and gowns, were also of the same origin.

Daniel understood clearly how all unnecessary material had to be weeded from the curriculum by hearing a quote from <u>Fundamentals of Christian Education</u>, page 467: *"It is not wise to send our youth to universities where they devote their time to gaining a knowledge of Greek and Latin, while their heads and hearts are being filled with the sentiments of the infidel authors whom they study in order to master these languages. They gain a knowledge that is not at all necessary."*

Prof. Paul mentioned another reference from <u>Christ's Object Lessons</u>, page 108, *"Satan works on human minds, leading them to think that there is wonderful knowledge to be gained apart from God. By deceptive reasoning he led Adam and Eve to doubt God's word, and to supply its place with a theory that led to disobedience. And his sophistry is doing today what it did in Eden. Teachers who mingle the sentiments of infidel authors with the education they are giving, plant in the minds of youth thoughts that will lead to distrust of God and transgression of His law. Little do they know what they are doing. Little do they realize what will be the result of their work."*

Prof. Paul read a frank and lengthy reference from <u>Testimonies for the Church</u>, volume 6, pages 128-131: *"<u>The third angel's message, the great testing truth for this time, is to be taught in all our institutions</u>. God designs that through them this special warning shall be given, and bright beams of light shall shine to the world. Time is short. The perils of the last days are upon us, and we should watch and pray, and study and heed the lessons that are given us in the books of Daniel and the Revelation. ...*

EDUCATION FOR THE FUTURE

"Let our lessons be appropriate for the day in which we live, and let our religious instruction be given in accordance with the message God sends.

"'We shall have to stand before magistrates to answer for our allegiance to the law of God, to make known the reasons of our faith. And the youth should understand these things. <u>They should know the things that will come to pass</u> before the closing up of the world's history. <u>These things concern our eternal welfare, and teachers and students should give more attention to them</u>. By pen and voice, knowledge should be imparted which will be meat in due season, not only to the young, but to those of mature years also. ...

"'<u>As long as we sail with the current of the world, we need neither canvas nor oar. It is when we turn squarely about to stem the current that our labors begin</u>. Satan will bring in every kind of theory to pervert the truth. The work will go hard, for since the fall of Adam it has been the fashion of the world to sin. But Christ is on the field of action. The Holy Spirit is at work. Divine agencies are combining with the human in reshaping the character according to the perfect pattern, and man is to work out that which God works in. Will we as a people do this God-given work? <u>Will we carefully heed all the light that has been given, keeping constantly before us the one object of fitting students for the kingdom of God</u>? If by faith we advance step by step in the right way, following the Great Leader, light will shine along our pathway; <u>and circumstances will occur to remove the difficulties</u>. The approval of God will give hope, and ministering angels will co-operate with us, bringing light and grace, and courage and gladness.

"'<u>Then let no more time be lost in dwelling on the many things which are not essential</u> and which have no bearing upon the present necessities of God's people. Let no more time be lost in exalting men who know not the truth "for the time is at hand." <u>There is no time now to fill the mind with theories of what is popularly called "higher education."</u> The time devoted to that which does not tend to assimilate the soul to the likeness of Christ is so much time lost for eternity. This we cannot afford, for every moment is freighted with eternal interests. Now, when the great work of judging the living is about to begin, shall we allow unsanctified ambition to take possession of the heart and lead us to neglect the education required to meet the needs in this day of peril?

"'In every case the great decision is to be made whether we shall receive the mark of the beast or his image, or the seal of the living God. <u>And now, when we are on the borders of the eternal world, what can be of so much value to us as to be found loyal and true to the God of heaven</u>? What is there that we should prize above His truth and His law? What education

can be given the students in our schools that is so necessary as a knowledge of "What saith the Scriptures?" Prof. Paul's voice was intense.

"'We know that there are many schools which afford opportunities for education in the sciences, but we desire something more than this. The science of true education is the truth, which is to be so deeply impressed on the soul that it cannot be obliterated by the error that everywhere abounds. The third angel's message is truth, and light, and power, and to present it so that right impressions will be made upon hearts should be the work of our schools as well as of our churches, of the teacher as well as of the minister. Those who accept positions as educators should prize more and more the revealed will of God so plainly and strikingly presented in Daniel and Revelation'" (emphasis supplied).

Prof. Paul referred back to the study by Dean Matthews, where he quoted Elder McElhany, who sat with General Conference officials evaluating The Branson Report. "Young people, listen to the insight of this man back in 1935 who anticipated what we are trying to do here, today, at Adventist College. I quote Elder McElhany, 'I wish the day would come when we could rescue our entire educational system from the necessity of going to the world for any further instruction. I hope the Lord will lead us some day to build upon the foundation of this report to give further study in rescuing our educational system from the world.'

"Young people, Elder McElhany would love to be here today. Our survival depends on our fidelity to this work. In Patriarchs and Prophets, page 595, we read, 'He who created man has provided for his development in body and mind and soul. Hence, real success in education depends upon the fidelity with which men carry out the Creator's plan.'

"Elder McElhany once made this observation: 'I wonder, my friends–when I read about Israel and how they rejected Jesus, their Saviour, even though they knew all the prophecies and were Bible students–are we Seventh-day Adventists removed from falling into that problem? Could not the same thing happen to you and me today? Can we be found unprepared for the second coming of Jesus?'

"Elder F. C. Gilbert showed in an article from Ministry, December 1933, how the Jews' rejection of Jesus was due to their educational system. Could we be as unprepared for the second coming of the Messiah as were the Jews for the First Advent? Yes, we can correct our course, even though it is late, it is not too late. We must do it or we can not have a part in the kingdom of God! God has said of us we are prisoners ... prisoners of hope. Let's put actions toward the realization of these hopes," pleaded Prof. Paul. The students stood as one in affirmation.

Jerry's Testimony and Solemn News

Lisa's brother stood and read a quote from <u>Testimonies for the Church</u>, volume 6, page 179, "'*A return to simpler methods will be appreciated by children and youth. Work in the garden and field will be an agreeable change from the wearisome routine of abstract lessons, to which their young minds should never be confined.*' I think, Prof., that it will be harder for the adults to make these changes than for us as students. Personally, sir, I am looking forward to them and I welcome them. I think I speak for every one of my classmates when I say thank you for your leadership." The students applauded Jerry's testimony.

Dean Matthews was present and came forward to give a report from the emergency board meeting. The news was met with deafening silence at first, then applause. "The college, engulfed as it is by the city, has been sold and we will soon be moving out to a new mountain sanctuary." Dean Matthews continued, "The board has also decided to take selected students as additional staff. This will be done by an official call. The pay will be board, room and $1,000 per month stipend. Those students who have skills in farming, cooking, building trades, mechanics, and leadership will be called. The faculty at Adventist College decided to adopt the same pay schedule as the new student-staff. The monies then made available will be used in evangelistic endeavors. There is one providence that we as a College Executive Committee will need to see as we issue these calls. God will impress you concerning that providence. Please pray about this."

On another topic, Dean Matthews said, "The House of Representatives has voted a Rest Day Bill designating Sunday for family worship and recreation. The Senate will hear it next year. There is a provision that this new bill will have to be ratified by each state. Many feel that the approval of the states is merely a rubber stamp process. The popular opinion among the citizenry seems to be that God is frowning on us as a nation for desecrating Sunday. Referring back to <u>The Great Controversy</u>, page 590, we see this as an exact fulfillment of prophecy." Most students nodded, some voicing a solemn "Yes."

Prof. Paul then took the podium and reminded the students of their previous assignment. "Several sessions back we asked you to write a report on what it would be like to be under 'no buy-no sell.' Have you made any notes? This assignment was in conjunction with Elder N. C. Wilson's article in <u>Ministry</u>, December 1977, where he wrote about how he thought 'no buy-no sell' might affect the church. What do you think?"

Various students stood to name some things they thought would change: no salaries; can't buy food, or pay for utilities, pay taxes, buy travel tickets, fuel for cars, purchase insurance; no money for tithe, purchasing building material, and no evangelistic offerings.

"How will this affect us, and what will we do about these boycotts?" asked Prof. Paul.

One by one, possible answers were discussed. No tithe means no salaries for ministers and Bible workers. Teachers would have to be supporting themselves. This will be a hardship for some who have not accustomed themselves to practical life or learned a trade. It may test motives and calls to service. We will have to grow food, store it, and save seed for crops. We will have to build houses or cabins with no money for those who need country housing. Evangelism will no longer be dependent on money. We will have to trust in God for our needs. Suspected barriers between those who give money and those who serve will be eliminated. We will all be in the same boat, financially. Education will continue. Fundamentals of Christian Education, page 359, assures us that *"As long as time shall last, we shall have need of schools."*

Daniel asked, "Why will we need schools in the time of 'no buy-no sell,' Prof. Paul? If there is no money and we offer no degrees, why would anyone want to come to our schools?"

"Good question, Daniel. Can someone comment on his question?" His question was met with silence.

"Maybe because our schools will be of an entirely different order?" Prof. Paul suggested. "Remember the reference from Counsels to Parents, Teachers, and Students, page 532, where it says, *'The plan of the schools... is to be of an entirely different order from those we have instituted.'* We will be teaching spiritual studies, practical skills, and growing food. The reference for that is found in The Ministry of Healing, page 192, *'If they ever become industrious and self-supporting, very many must have assistance, encouragement, and instruction. There are multitudes of poor families for whom no better missionary work could be done than to assist them in settling on the land and in learning how to make it yield them a livelihood.'* "

The subject of simplifying our lives, even now, by how much "stuff" we have was mentioned. Someone from the audience stood and read the answer they had discovered in their reading the night before on page 152 of the fifth volume of The Testimonies for the Church: *"We ought now to be heeding the injunction of our Saviour: "'Sell that ye have, and give alms; provide yourselves bags which wax not old, a treasure in the heavens that faileth not." It is now that our brethren should be cutting down their possessions instead of increasing them. We are about to move to a better country, even a heavenly. Then let us not be dwellers upon the earth, but be getting things into as compact a compass as possible.'"*

"As heaven becomes more and more real to us we will see the need of further sacrifices," said Prof. Paul. One of the teachers came to the podium and read the "Impressive Dream" recorded by Ellen White in <u>Testimonies for the Church</u>, volume 2, pages 594-597: *"While at Battle Creek in August, 1868, I dreamed of being with a large body of people. A portion of this assembly started out prepared to journey. We had heavily loaded wagons. As we journeyed, the road seemed to ascend. On one side of this road was a deep precipice; on the other was a high, smooth, white wall, like the hard finish upon plastered rooms.*

"'As we journeyed on, the road grew narrower and steeper. In some places it seemed so very narrow that we concluded that we could no longer travel with the loaded wagons. We then loosed them from the horses, took a portion of the luggage from the wagons and placed it upon the horses, and journeyed on horseback.

"'As we progressed, the path still continued to grow narrow. We were obliged to press close to the wall, to save ourselves from falling off the narrow road down the steep precipice. As we did this, the luggage on the horses pressed against the wall and caused us to sway toward the precipice. We feared that we should fall and be dashed in pieces on the rocks. We then cut the luggage from the horses, and it fell over the precipice. We continued on horseback, greatly fearing, as we came to the narrower places in the road, that we should lose our balance and fall. At such times a hand seemed to take the bridle and guide us over the perilous way.

"'As the path grew more narrow, we decided that we could no longer go with safety on horseback, and we left the horses and went on foot, in single file, one following in the footsteps of another. At this point small cords were let down from the top of the pure white wall; these we eagerly grasped, to aid us in keeping our balance upon the path. As we traveled, the cord moved along with us. The path finally became so narrow that we concluded that we could travel more safely without our shoes, so we slipped them from our feet and went on some distance without them. Soon it was decided that we could travel more safely without our stockings; these were removed, and we traveled on with bare feet.

"'We then thought of those that had not accustomed themselves to privations and hardships. Where were such now? They were not in the company. <u>At every change some were left behind</u>, and those only remained who had accustomed themselves to endure hardships. The privations of the way only made these more eager to press on to the end.

YOU CAN SURVIVE!

"'Our danger of falling from the pathway increased. We pressed close to the white wall, yet could not place our feet fully upon the path, for it was too narrow. We then suspended nearly our whole weight upon the cords, exclaiming: "We have hold from above! We have hold from above!" The same words were uttered by all the company in the narrow pathway. As we heard the sounds of mirth and revelry that seemed to come from the abyss below, we shuddered. We heard the profane oath, the vulgar jest, and low, vile songs. We heard the war song and the dance song. We heard instrumental music and loud laughter, mingled with cursing and cries of anguish and bitter wailing, and were more anxious than ever to keep upon the narrow, difficult pathway. Much of the time we were compelled to suspend our whole weight upon the cords, which increased in size as we progressed.

"'I noticed that the beautiful white wall was stained with blood. It caused a feeling of regret to see the wall thus stained. This feeling, however, lasted but for a moment, as I soon thought that it was all as it should be. Those who are following after will know that others have passed the narrow, difficult way before them, and will conclude that if others were able to pursue their onward course, they can do the same. And as the blood shall be pressed from their aching feet, they will not faint with discouragement; but, seeing the blood upon the wall, they will know that others have endured the same pain.

"'At length we came to a large chasm, at which our path ended. There was nothing now to guide the feet, nothing upon which to rest them. Our whole reliance must be upon the cords, which had increased in size until they were as large as our bodies. Here we were for a time thrown into perplexity and distress. We inquired in fearful whispers: "To what is the cord attached?" My husband was just before me. Large drops of sweat were falling from his brow, the veins in his neck and temples were increased to double their usual size, and suppressed, agonizing groans came from his lips. The sweat was dropping from my face, and I felt such anguish as I had never felt before. A fearful struggle was before us. Should we fail here, all the difficulties of our journey had been experienced for nought.

"'Before us on the other side of the chasm, was a beautiful field of green grass, about six inches high. I could not see the sun; but bright, soft beams of light, resembling fine gold and silver, were resting upon this field. Nothing I had seen upon earth could compare in beauty and glory with this field. But could we succeed in reaching it? was the anxious inquiry. Should the cord break, we must perish. Again, in whispered anguish, the words were

400

breathed: "What holds the cord?" For a moment we hesitated to venture. Then we exclaimed: "Our only hope is to trust wholly to the cord. It has been our dependence all the difficult way. It will not fail us now." Still we were hesitating and distressed. The words were then spoken: "God holds the cord. We need not fear." These words were repeated by those behind us, accompanied with: "He will not fail us now. He has brought us thus far in safety."

"'My husband then swung himself over the fearful abyss into the beautiful field beyond. I immediately followed. And, oh, what a sense of relief and gratitude to God we felt. I heard voices raised in triumphant praise to God. I was happy, perfectly happy.

"'I awoke, and found that from the anxiety I had experienced in passing over the difficult route, every nerve in my body seemed to be in a tremor. This dream needs no comment. It made such an impression upon my mind that probably every item in it will be vivid before me while my memory shall continue.' "

A soft "Amen" was murmured among those present and the morning session closed with prayer by Prof. Paul that all in the assembly might be ready for Jesus' coming.

A Call For Help

At the next meeting, President Cristman requested students to make appointments with him for calls as staff members. Anyone who had experience in the skills mentioned by Dean Matthews, was asked to serve.

Daniel and Lisa both signed up, unaware of each other's desire to help. For Daniel, it had been a deep four-hour struggle before he signed up. President Cristman accepted him on the spot, partially because of Daniel's farm background at his uncle's place, but mostly because Daniel was willing to lay his engineering career aside to begin working for God.

Lisa had very little struggle, but she did want to know it was God's will. When she sensed that, she signed and was immediately accepted. She, too, had expressed her desire to work for God now and put her career in elementary education on the altar. This was the providence President Cristman wanted.

Shortly after this, Daniel's parents called to say that Lisa wanted to get better acquainted and start a courtship. She had two questions which must be answered. First, they were still in school and according to Counsels to Parents, Teachers, and Students, page 100, there should be no courtship among college students. Second, perhaps it was too late in earth's history to have plans for marriage at all.

"Well," Daniel answered his father, "I have an answer to the first question, or at least a partial answer. I have just been made a staff member. So I am not a student. I don't know about Lisa, but all in all this is good news, Dad, because I am learning so much so quickly about myself. Events are coming soon upon the earth and God's people should know to love Him and love each other."

Daniel's father replied, "You know, son, this 'plan' you told us about is a good one. It makes sense. It involves more people in your happiness. It eliminates all the fooling around as playboys and party animals and the hurts when breakups occur. But most of all, with God leading, divorce drops out of the picture. You can look back and see how God led, and it keeps the marriage bond strong."

Daniel related some of the recent developments at the college and asked that his parents keep him, Lisa, and the college in their prayers. His father assured him of their support.

"Thanks, Dad. I will be in touch again soon," said Daniel.

Drama

The next meeting had a speaker from a school that was not accredited. He was dressed simply in a black suit and tie, but his hands showed that years had been spent in manual labor. His name was brother Ron.

As he began to speak, he said that if anyone had any questions to feel free to raise their hand. He began with a Bible verse from Philippians 4:8: "*'Finally, brethren, whatsoever things are true, whatsoever things are honest, whatsoever things are just, whatsoever things are pure, whatsoever things are lovely, whatsoever things are of good report; if there be any virtue, and if there be any praise, think on these things.'* What does 'true' mean?" he asked.

Someone said, "No lies, no faking."

"What does 'lovely' mean?" asked brother Ron.

"Beautiful, colorful, peaceful, heaven-like," another student said.

"All good answers," said brother Ron. "Let me add a thought to the ones you have given. The Greek word for actor is 'hypokrites.' This is the root word for hypocrite, which again means actor.

Brother Ron took his suit coat off, his black suspenders contrasted against a crisp white shirt.

"Let me ask another question, 'Is a hypocrite someone true?'"

"No," was the loud exclamation from the students.

"Well, what about actors, are they true?" he asked.

"No," but the response was not as strong.

"Then are movies, videos, video games, and virtual reality true?" he asked.

"No," but the response was from only a few.

"Let me read you something from the Spirit of Prophecy." He held up Testimonies for the Church, volume 4, and began reading from page 578, *"'Worldly or theatrical entertainments are not essential.'"*

Then he held up the book Evangelism and read from page 137, *"Not one jot or tittle of anything theatrical is to be brought into our work. ... Let nothing of a theatrical nature be permitted, for this would spoil the sacredness of the work.'"*

"Now a promise," he said, "from Testimonies for the Church, volume 9, page 110: *'As they labor with simplicity, humility, and graceful dignity, avoiding everything of a theatrical nature, their work will make a lasting impression'"* (emphasis supplied).

As brother Ron spoke, Daniel thought he noticed a dejected look on faces all over the audience. The college had a Drama Department. Movies, plays, skits, puppets, most of TV and videos–would all these have to go?

"In closing," spoke brother Ron solemnly, "I want to reassure you that the path you have chosen for this college will not be easily followed, but God will richly bless, as the reference says, with a 'lasting impression' for eternity."

Then brother Ron read from Education, page 296, *"' "Something better" is the watchword of education, the law of all true living. Whatever Christ asks us to renounce, He offers in its stead something better.'* Christ offers something better, young people! Trust Him to do it."

The dean came forward at the close of brother Ron's brief but poignant study. As he came to the podium, he said, "Young people, I believe this is another step in separating from the world. God has promised that He will give us something better. Would anyone like to testify about movies? Use the criteria brother Ron read to us from Philippians 4:8. I will be talking to the Drama Department head, but let's consider making a pact on movies. Please pray for me as I talk to the Department chair, Dr. Jean."

One student stood and said, "Dean Matthews, I have felt for a long time that movies, because they aren't true, shouldn't be part of the Christian experience. I choose to go with God on this issue." Applause slowly gained volume as many students throughout the audience rose to their feet indicating their willingness to sacrifice pleasure for truth and secure heaven.

The dean was pleasantly surprised when he approached the Drama Department head. She, too, had been studying. "I found an interesting statement just a couple of days ago in my morning watch book," said Dr. Jean. "It's on page 159 of the book entitled In Heavenly Places: *'Often the training and education of a lifetime must be discarded, that one may become a learner in the school of Christ.'* I want to be ready. What can I do?" she asked.

"Work with others who are struggling with this, Jean."

"Okay," she said, "but before you go, may I ask one question?"

"Sure, Jean, go ahead."

"Why didn't someone show us this before we poured our lifeblood into it?"

"I don't know, Jean. I have asked myself the same question. But we can start now, can't we? The good news is, it's not too late. God is so merciful toward our ignorance and blindness."

As moving plans began to materialize, Daniel didn't see Lisa. It turned out that she had gone home to speak with her parents regarding a possible courtship with Daniel. Jerry had remained behind and was telling Daniel of her trip.

The Ribbon of Blue

The next morning meeting was on the principles of dress, and the person giving the lecture was an attractive elderly lady named Sister Ruth. She was from a nonaccredited school in supporting ministries. She began with a vivid illustration of our embrace experience with Christ resulting in our conversion. Infused with a love for Christ, we ask what He would have us do and how we may express our loyalty.

Sister Ruth then began to read from Deuteronomy 22:5: *"'The woman shall not wear that which pertaineth unto a man, neither shall a man put on a woman's garment: for all that do so are* <u>*abomination*</u> *unto the Lord thy God.'"* Then she read Numbers 15:38-40: *"'Speak unto the children of Israel, and bid them that they make them fringes in the borders of their garments throughout their generations, and that they put upon the fringe of the borders a* <u>*ribband of blue*</u>: *And it shall be unto you for a fringe, that ye may look upon it, and remember all the commandments of the Lord, and do them; and that ye seek not after your own heart and your own eyes, after which ye use to go a whoring: that ye may remember, and do all my commandments, and be holy unto your God.'"*

She paused to explain that a man and a woman must dress so as to keep a distinction plainly seen by everyone at all times. "Does the Lord ask us to have a ribbon of blue? I wonder if that could mean something today? Let's look to the Spirit of Prophecy for an explanation. <u>Testimonies for the Church</u>, volume 3, page 171, *states, 'The dress reform answers to us as did the ribbon of blue to ancient Israel.'"*

Sister Ruth challenged the students, "Young people, especially you young ladies, it is important today to show this loyalty to God. Let young ladies wear something other than the pants which are so similar to what men wear. Be women distinct from men and honor God thereby. Notice this reference in <u>Testimonies for the Church</u>, volume 2, page 66: *'The dress reform is a striking contrast to the fashion of the world. Those who adopt this dress should manifest good taste and order and strict cleanliness in all their attire.'*

"Another special principle that God has given us is in the matter of jewelry. The gems, gold, and silver are beautiful, but by far the greatest beauty is character. In First Peter 3:4, we read, *'Real beauty in a woman comes from within, that enduring charm of a gentle, tender spirit which in God's sight is priceless'"* (Clear Word).

"God wants us to demonstrate loyalty to Him by our dress and deportment. We read from <u>My Life Today</u>, page 123, *'Self-denial in dress is a part of our Christian duty. To dress plainly and abstain from display of jewelry and ornaments of every kind is in keeping with our faith.'"*

"Finally, an important question is asked by God in Romans 9:20, *'Nay but, O man, who art thou that repliest against God? Shall the thing formed say to him that formed it, Why hast thou made me thus?'* Decorating ourselves with jewelry or makeup suggests disloyalty to God and expresses unhappiness with the way He made us."

"May God help us to please our Lord with modest, distinctive dress that tells the world we are women, not dressed like men. We love the Lord by showing loyalty with this 'ribbon of blue.' One example of an abomination is a lack of distinctive dress among God's people, according to Deuteronomy 22:5."

Daniel had finally located Lisa in the audience. As usual, her dress and expression demonstrated the joy of commitment. It was rare to see such beauty combined with purity of character. It gave Lisa a powerful witness for good which was missing in the other girls with whom Daniel had been acquainted.

As Daniel began the long walk toward her, he outlined a few questions to ask about their courtship. "First, I need to find out if she is a student," he thought. "If she is staff that would be some providence," he mused quietly.

Diet for the End Times

Prof. Paul began a study on diet for the last days. It was obvious that some of the students were not vegetarians when they went home for school breaks. Some of the staff, including ministers, were not convinced that meat should be eliminated from the diet.

He began by reading from Genesis 1:29: *"'And God said, Behold, I have given you every herb bearing seed, which is upon the face of all the earth, and every tree, in the which is the fruit of a tree yielding seed; to you it shall be for meat.'* This was the diet in the beginning. "Let's read Psalm 104:14: *'He causeth the grass to grow for the cattle, and herb for the service of man: that he may bring forth food out of the earth.'* Herbs were created for the service of man. And in heaven, what will our diet be? The Lord Himself testifies in Isaiah 65:21 that the new earth will find His children building and planting, eating from their own gardens. *'And they shall build houses, and inhabit them; and they shall plant vineyards, and eat the fruit of them.'* I wonder what diet would be the best now?" asked Prof. Why, even lions will be vegetarians in heaven! We will all stop eating each other!"

"We are advised to consider the cruelty to animals that the habit of meat eating involves, both upon the animals and those whose job it is to raise and kill them." He turned to <u>The Ministry of Healing</u>, and read from pages 315-317: *'The intelligence displayed by many dumb animals approaches so closely to human intelligence that it is a mystery. The animals see and hear and love and fear and suffer. They use their organs far more faithfully than many human beings use theirs. They manifest sympathy and tenderness toward their companions in suffering. Many animals show an affection for those who have charge of them, far superior to the affection shown by some of the human race. They form attachments for man which are not broken without great suffering to them... <u>What man with a human heart, who has ever cared for domestic animals, could look into their eyes, so full of confidence and affection, and willingly give them over to the butcher's knife</u>? How could he ever devour their flesh as a sweet morsel? ... Had the use of flesh been essential to health and strength, animal food would have been included in the diet appointed man in the beginning. .... How can they take the life of God's creatures that they may consume the flesh as a luxury? Let them, rather, return to the wholesome and delicious food given to man in the beginning, and themselves practice, and teach their children to practice, mercy toward the dumb creatures that God has made and has placed under our dominion."*

"Listen to what <u>Counsels on Diet and Foods</u>, page 460, says about our diet in the last days: *'Tell them that the time will soon come when there will be no safety in using eggs, milk, cream, or butter, because disease in animals is increasing in proportion to the increase of wickedness among men. The time is near when, because of the iniquity of the fallen race, the whole animal creation will groan under the diseases that curse our earth.'*

"And on page 384: *'The light given me is that it will not be very long before we shall have to give up using any animal food. Even milk will have to be discarded. Disease is accumulating rapidly.'*

"Also on page 380: *'Among those who are waiting for the coming of the Lord, meat eating will eventually be done away; flesh will cease to form a part of their diet.'"*

Then Lisa stood and quoted a reference from a previous meeting in The Ministry of Healing, page 192, that says we should educate the poor and those who don't know how to raise and prepare their own healthy food. "We are told in Counsels on Diet and Foods, page 75, that our health message is as closely connected with the third angel's message as is the arm to the body!

Prof. Paul continued, after echoing agreement to her comments, "If we are living in the end times, we should reconsider our position about raising and taking animals for food. Meat-eating could be just one more thread, young people, and this may be a hard string for some of you to sever. Even raising animals for food is supporting a program that is not part of God's plan. It seems to me that it would be a little inconsistent to sell animals for meat, while being a vegetarian. To love my neighbor as myself would not include feeding them what we can't eat."

Lisa cited her father's example. He had already diversified from cattle to grain and soybeans. She said it would be a financial struggle for dairy farmers, ranchers, and egg producers when animal foods would eventually be unsafe to eat. She told of her father's discovery of the reference in Counsels on Diet and Foods, page 356, which had changed the focus of his farm some years before: *"'Tell them that the time will soon come when there will be no safety in using eggs, milk, cream, or butter, because disease in animals is increasing in proportion to the increase of wickedness among men.'"*

"Thank you, Lisa, for that practical insight," said Prof. Paul. "As we close this study, let's consider some spiritual aspects of our diet. Turn in your Bible to the twenty-third chapter of Leviticus. We will read from verses 27-32: *'Also on the tenth day of this seventh month there shall be a day of atonement: it shall be an holy convocation unto you; and ye shall afflict your souls, and offer an offering made by fire unto the Lord. And ye shall do no work in that same day: for it is a day of atonement, to make an atonement for you before the Lord your God. For whatsoever soul it be that shall not be afflicted in that same day, he shall be cut off from among his people. And whatsoever soul it be that doeth any work in that same day, the same soul will I destroy from among his people. Ye shall do no manner of work; it shall be a statute for ever throughout your generations in all your dwellings. It shall be unto you a sabbath of rest, and ye shall afflict your souls:*

in the ninth day of the month at even, from even unto even, shall ye celebrate your sabbath.'

"Notice the expression 'afflict your souls.' Remember, this is referring to the old Day of Atonement, which lasted 24 hours. During this special day, people sought forgiveness, made things right, did no work, and fasted. They spent time examining their lives and determined to know God better," explained Prof. Paul. "This comment from <u>Patriarchs and Prophets</u>, page 355, shows what the Israelites did on the Day of Atonement. *'Every man was to afflict his soul while the work of atonement was going forward. All business was laid aside, and the whole congregation of Israel spent the day in solemn humiliation before God, with prayer, fasting, and deep searching of heart.'*

Since 1844 we have entered upon the antitypical Day of Atonement (you can read about that in <u>Early Writings</u>, page 253, and <u>The Great Controversy</u>, page 421). What would our fast be? To not eat for many years is not an option. However, there must be a fast for this Day of Atonement.

"<u>Counsels on Diet and Foods</u>, page 188, tells of the fast that we are to make during our ongoing day of atonement. *'The true fasting which should be recommended to all, is the abstinence from every stimulating kind of food, and the proper use of wholesome, simple food, which God has provided in abundance.'* In other words, young people, our fast for this day of atonement is to follow God's plan for our diet. Our day of atonement will soon be past, for the end of all things is upon us, and we shall soon be sitting together in heaven, feeding grass to lions!" Delighted laughter met Prof's comment.

President Wilson's Call Accepted

Daniel found Lisa as the other students went to breakfast. He had an important question to ask her, but before he could speak, she said excitedly, "Daniel, President Cristman has asked me to be staff during this move and change of curriculum. They need cooks and farm workers. I will be teaching classes on dress reform and courtship and helping in the kitchen."

"Yes, they asked me too, Lisa. I will be working on the farm and teaching a courtship class for the boys. I understand, from your parents, that you consented to begin a courtship with me," said Daniel. "Is that okay with you?"

"Yes, it is, Daniel," replied Lisa. "I am looking forward to it."

"One important question remains to be answered. What about marriages in these last days? Maybe we are wasting our time doing this if nothing comes from our courtship," Daniel observed.

"Do you want something to come of it?" asked Lisa.

"Yes, I do," Daniel replied.

"Well, let's take it one step at a time," said Lisa, "and watch for God's leading. We need to select a couple of counselors for each of us and get their advice," she added.

At the next morning meeting, Daniel told dean Matthews that permission had been given by Lisa's parents and his parents to begin a courtship.

"Very good," said the dean. "I think it will help the other young people to see an example of what we have been studying. And, by the way, I am aware that you are both staff members now and not students at this college. I believe the plan is to announce your courtship. I will do that this morning."

"Dean, one more thing: would you act as a counselor to me during this time?" asked Daniel.

"Yes, I will, Daniel. I am very new at this, but I read Pastor Bill's outline some time ago. Maybe we can learn together," said Dean Matthews.

"Thank you, sir. May God bless you in your leadership. I believe there will be souls in the kingdom from this college because of your stand for God's plan," replied Daniel.

The next morning meeting was a student assembly. Dean Matthews made the announcement of Daniel and Lisa's courtship. Applause, wolf whistles, loud laughter and yelling made Daniel and Lisa uncomfortable. Dean Matthews held up his hand for attention. "Young people, Daniel and Lisa are attempting to follow God's plan for getting acquainted with each other. There are many safeguards built into this rather old-fashioned approach which some of you may be tempted to ridicule. Encourage them when you can."

When they recognized the spirituality of the occasion, the noise and laughter diminished. They responded with polite applause. Dean Matthews then announced that there would be an assembly every day, starting today, for those students and staff interested in learning more about God's methods of living healthier and happier lives and learning about spiritual survival in the end times.

Truth and Fiction

Dean Matthews spoke following prayer by Prof. Paul. "Our study this morning is on literature and fiction. Our English Department chairwoman has given me this paper as our study this morning. She received her advanced degrees in the field of Biblical literature. Dr. Helen has been an avid supporter of using Biblical literature and histories as a basis for language usage and syntax, especially as inspiration for your essays and compositions. At times, she has been criticized for that approach, but I am happy to announce to you today that those of us who criticized her academic approach to literature and composition were wrong. I am chief among those who felt we needed to be more academic."

The study began with Bible verses from Psalm 119:30: *"I have chosen the way of truth: thy judgments have I laid before me."* First John 2:21: *"I have not written unto you because ye know not the truth, but because ye know it, and that no lie is of the truth."* John 8:44: *"Ye are of your father the devil, and the lusts of your father ye will do. He was a murderer from the beginning, and abode not in the truth, because there is no truth in him. When he speaketh a lie, he speaketh of his own: for he is a liar, and the father of it."*

Dr. Helen wrote some effects of novel reading from <u>Messages to Young People</u>, page 290: *" 'Thousands are today in the insane asylum whose minds became unbalanced by novel reading.' "* Dean Matthews recalled to the audience how he had urged the use of famous novels in literature classes. He again asked specific forgiveness from the staff and students where his directives had caused a lack of unity and worldly influence.

The next reference from <u>Messages to Young People</u>, page 286, called for a housecleaning at the college. *" 'Dear youth, cease to read the magazines containing stories. Put away every novel.... We would do well to clear our houses of all the story magazines and the publications containing ridiculous pictures–representations originated by satanic agencies. The youth cannot afford to poison their minds with such things. 'What is the chaff to the wheat?' Let everyone who claims to be a follower of Christ <u>read only that which is true and of eternal value</u>.' "*

"I will be asking Dr. Helen along with our librarian to form a committee to rid our library of all the fiction and novel-type literature in this college," explained dean Matthews. "The cure for fiction addicts is found in <u>Testimonies for the Church</u>, volume 4, page 581: *'Minds that have been amused and abused by reading fiction may in nature have an open book, and read truth in the works of God around them. All may find themes for study in the simple leaf of the forest tree, the spires of grass covering the earth with their green velvet carpet, the plants and flowers, the stately trees of the forest, the lofty mountains, the granite rocks, the restless ocean, the precious gems of light studding the heavens to make the night beautiful, the exhaustless riches of the sunlight, the solemn glories of the moon, the winter's cold, the summer's heat, the changing, recurring seasons, in perfect order and harmony, controlled by infinite power; here are subjects which call for deep thought, for the stretch of the imagination.'"*

The dean then read a further explanation from <u>The Ministry of Healing</u>, page 446: *"'It is often urged that in order to win the youth from sensational or worthless literature, we should supply them with a better class of fiction. This is like trying to cure the drunkard by giving him, in place of whisky or brandy, the milder intoxicants, such as wine, beer, or cider.... The only safety for the inebriate, and the only safeguard for the temperate man, is total abstinence. For the lover of fiction the same rule holds true. <u>Total abstinence is his only safety.</u>'*

"For younger children, further counsel is also given on pages 446 and 447," said dean Matthews. "I shudder to think how far I have strayed, personally, from God's principle in this regard: *'In the education of children and youth, fairy tales, myths, and fictitious stories are now given a large place. Books of this character are used in the schools, and they are to be found in many homes. How can Christian parents permit their children to use books so filled with falsehood? When the children ask the meaning of stories so contrary to the teaching of their parents, the answer is that the stories are not true; but this does not do away with the evil results of their use. The ideas presented in these books mislead the children. They impart false views of life and beget and foster a desire for the unreal.*

"'The widespread use of such books at this time is one of the cunning devices of Satan. He is seeking to divert the minds of old and young from the great work of character building. He means that our children and youth shall be swept away by the soul-destroying deceptions with which he is filling the world. Therefore he seeks to divert their minds from the word of God and thus prevent them from obtaining a knowledge of those truths that would be their safeguard.

"'<u>Never should books containing a perversion of truth be placed in the hands of children or youth</u>. Let not our children, in the very process of obtaining an education, receive ideas that will prove to be seeds of sin. If those with mature minds had nothing to do with such books, they would themselves be far safer, and their example and influence on the right side would make it far less difficult to guard the youth from temptation.'

"Revelation 22:14 says, *'Blessed are they that do his commandments, that they may have right to the tree of life and may enter in through the gates into the city.'*

"God mercifully leads us on toward a steady spiritual growth, preparing us for entrance into heaven, as recorded in <u>Counsels to Parents, Teachers, and Students</u>, page 250: *'In the messages that have been sent us from time to*

411

time, we have truths that will accomplish a wonderful work of reform in our characters if we give them place. They will prepare us for entrance into the city of God.'

"In Testimonies for the Church, volume 3, page 171, we find that: *'If the church would manifest a greater interest in the reforms which God Himself has brought to them to fit them for His coming, their influence would be tenfold what it now is.'* Think of that! Tenfold greater!"

As dean Matthews prayed, he again asked for forgiveness, this time from God for his neglect of God's plan. He prayed that each one would dedicate their lives to Christ and be willing to sacrifice whatever He might ask of them. He then paused and asked for rededications by staff and students to God's cause of revival and reformation. Hands were raised as a sign of recommitment. He closed his prayer with a request that God would inspire loyalty and unity and to answer Christ's prayer of John 17.

Courtship Class

Daniel and Lisa soon began their staff assignments with eager anticipation. The students requested that Daniel and Lisa present the courtship class together. They were using Pastor Bill's outline, but they had very little experience in the practical application. Dean Matthews okayed the students' request.

Questions from the students about involving parents in their courtship and about their personal feelings left Daniel and Lisa feeling awkward. No one openly declared their sexual history, but there was a special interest in the concept of "secondary virginity" as explained in the book entitled "God's Appointed."

One morning, Daniel asked Lisa about her part in the courtship class. Some students had requested special counseling sessions; boys often requested to speak with Lisa and girls asked to speak with Daniel. Lisa admitted feeling awkward in these sessions, and wished Daniel was there with her. Daniel felt the same way, and because of Pastor Bill's outline, he knew that he had to be careful in counseling women. Dean Matthews recognized that Daniel and Lisa were struggling with awkward situations and proposed the plan of discussions in small groups. Daniel and Lisa presented the topics for general study during the first portion of the class period after which selected student leaders discussed the topics assigned in small groups.

That spring seemed more beautiful than any other spring to Daniel and Lisa. They were several months into their courtship, and they had discovered, to their happiness, almost complete compatibility on the course of their lives, their interests, and their chosen work for God. They had both laid their original careers aside so that they could take their places to help finish God's work and be ready for Jesus' second coming.

The spring also brought increased occurrences of natural disasters and an increased clamor for the "rest and reverence day" for the nation. Citizens were becoming frustrated with those few Christians who wanted to maintain both the principles of the Constitution of the United States and the commandments of God. Though they themselves maintained that they kept the Ten Commandments as required in the Bible, they insisted that the few Christians who kept the seventh-day Sabbath should keep Sunday. Other countries were following the popular demand in the United States for a rest day—Sunday. Daniel and Lisa felt in their hearts that new proposed amendments to the Constitution would pass in a year or so, in spite of legal snags, dictating fewer religious freedoms and more blending of church and state.

Origin of Music—Worship

Prof. Paul was continuing his early-morning studies. Nearly every student and staff member attended. This particular morning, music was the subject. Daniel had neglected this topic and became immediately concerned that here, again, he would probably have to give something up for good. But his joy of resignation opened his heart a little wider. Each sacrifice seemed only to increase his appetite for new light. Lisa, on the other hand, seemed to have been taught many of the principles at home. Daniel decided to ask her how she seemed to be living so many concepts he was just now discovering. Lisa explained by saying that she had taken home school when very young and then had attended a small school in the mountains for two years. "They had high standards and tried to educate us on God's plan. We even had a class on what to do when we can't buy and sell. I look back and see now that what they were teaching, both spiritually and academically, helped me here at college. Although I was taught many of these principles at home, that little school was a real sanctuary to me. Maybe we can go visit it together sometime." Everyone was turning to the first text, so Daniel and Lisa refocused their attention from each other to Prof. Paul's words.

"Let's read together First John 2:15-17: *'Love not the world, neither the things that are in the world. If any man love the world, the love of the Father is not in him. For all that is in the world, the lust of the flesh, and the lust of the eyes, and the pride of life, is not of the Father, but is of the world. And the world passeth away, and the lust thereof: but he that doeth the will of God abideth forever.'*

"If this were the only counsel we had on music, it would be enough to give us, with the power of the Holy Spirit, clear perceptions of good music," said Prof. "The Music Department has asked me to present the essence of their research on music. They felt that there were a few changes they needed to make. For the most part, they have taught good guidelines on music. If anyone has any input, they will be happy to hear from you. Improvements and reforms have taken place in the department regarding opera. Their emphasis will be, in the light of current events, to teach performance and appreciation of sacred music," concluded Prof as he continued to read the Music Department's prepared statement.

"What was the original purpose of music?" asked Prof. "Where did music originate?" He began to read from Selected Messages, book 3, page 334: "*Music is of heavenly origin.*' So," he concluded, "music began in heaven. Now, what was the purpose of music?" he asked. He read from Sons and Daughters of God, page 179: "*'Music was made to serve a holy purpose, to lift the thoughts to that which is pure, noble, and elevating, and to awaken in the soul devotion and gratitude to God.*'"

Again Prof. Paul concluded, "Music has a holy purpose in pointing a person to God. Any music that does not magnify Him is of no value today. Young people, you have to answer questions on music personally and honestly. There is no strict quantifiable guideline for music such as there is in diet or sports. It is of the highest importance that you answer these questions with integrity and privately. Your eternal life depends on it," said Prof. Paul with more emphasis than Daniel remembered from previous meetings.

Prof. Paul continued by reading from Testimonies for the Church, volume 1, page 506, "*'In the judgment all these words of inspiration will condemn those who have not heeded them.*' If you read the context of this reference, you will find that it refers to music," he declared. "Music is a call to examine our hearts and answer the question, 'Does my choice of music point to Christ?' We don't have time for any other priorities than to make God and His work number one. One educator put it this way, 'Music is best when words and sound are closest to nature.'

"A reference found in Testimonies for the Church, volume 6, page 358, seems to back up this idea: *'In pleasant weather let parents walk with their children in the fields and groves. Amid the beautiful things of nature tell them the reason for the institution of the Sabbath. Describe to them God's great work of creation. Tell them that when the earth came from His hand, it was holy and beautiful. Every flower, every shrub, every tree, answered the purpose of its Creator. Everything upon which the eye rested was lovely and filled the mind with thoughts of the love of God.*

Every sound was music in harmony with the voice of God. Show that it was sin which marred God's perfect work; that thorns and thistles, sorrow and pain and death, are all the result of disobedience to God. Bid them see how the earth, though marred with the curse of sin, still reveals God's goodness. The green fields, the lofty trees, the glad sunshine, the clouds, the dew, the solemn stillness of the night, the glory of the starry heavens, and the moon in its beauty all bear witness of the Creator. Not a drop of rain falls, nor a ray of light is shed on our unthankful world, but it testifies to the forbearance and love of God'" [emphasis supplied].

Dean Matthews came forward now and Prof. Paul motioned for him to take the pulpit. When the dean came forward during a meeting, it was general knowledge that he would give one of his "news flashes."

"I am thankful, young people, for our choir and the witness it has been for Jesus in our community and for our college. Some of you have been asking me some questions recently about music, so I have been studying the reference found in Patriarchs and Prophets, page 594, which states, *'Singing, as a part of religious service, is as much an act of worship as is prayer.'*

"There has been a report among Adventists that there has been a loud, irreverent use of music in worship services. As I listened to the report, I decided to do some research on music in the end of time just before the close of probation. I found this statement that I want to share with you now. It is from Selected Messages, book 2, page 36: *'It is impossible to estimate too largely the work that the Lord will accomplish through His proposed vessels in carrying out His mind and purpose. The things you have described as taking place in Indiana, the Lord has shown me would take place just before the close of probation. Every uncouth thing will be demonstrated. There will be shouting, with drums, music, and dancing. The senses of rational beings will become so confused that they cannot be trusted to make rational decisions. And this is called the moving of the Holy Spirit.'*

"I believe, young people, that this use of music is yet another fulfillment telling us where we are in the closing events. And we do not wish to have this excitement and revelry in our worship services as a substitute for the true manifestations of the Holy Spirit," Dean Matthews concluded. His presentation was met with reverent silence and then hearty amens.

As Prof. Paul took the podium, again, Daniel felt a renewed commitment to go all the way with God. He bowed his head along with Lisa and they silently asked for more of the Spirit to help them in their work of sharing God's plan with others.

YOU CAN SURVIVE!

"Young people," began Prof. Paul, "I discovered a reference that may be of interest to you from the <u>Seventh-day Adventist Bible Commentary</u>, volume 2, page 1036: *'Just before Elijah was taken to heaven, he visited the schools of the prophets, and instructed the students on the most important points of their education. The lessons he had given them on former visits, he now repeated, impressing upon the minds of the youth the importance of letting simplicity mark every feature of their education. Only in this way could they receive the mold of heaven, and go forth to work in the ways of the Lord. <u>If conducted as God designs they should be</u>, our schools in these closing days of the message will do a work similar to that done by the schools of the prophets.'*

"Another discovery I made is found in the book <u>Counsels to Parents, Teachers, and Students</u>, page 168: *'These schools, established in different localities and conducted by God-fearing men or women, as the case demands, should be built on the same principles as were the schools of the prophets.'*

"We have a school here at Adventist College. What did the students in Elijah's day do in regard to their music education? Listen to this quote from <u>Fundamentals of Christian Education</u>, pages 97 and 98: *'The art of sacred melody was diligently cultivated. No frivolous waltz was heard, nor flippant song that should extol man and divert the attention from God; but sacred, solemn psalms of praise to the Creator, exalting His name and recounting His wonderful works. This music was made to serve a holy purpose, to lift the thoughts to that which was pure and noble and elevating, and to awaken in the soul devotion and gratitude to God.'"*

When Daniel heard that, deep conviction stole over him as he returned to his room. He had excused himself, explaining to Lisa that he had something he had to do. When he arrived at his room, he began to sort his CDs and tapes. All but five he discarded and burned. Among those thrown away were some Christian rock and exciting gospel music mixed with his favorite country and rock tapes. He thought of selling them, but if he did, they would only continue to pollute others, so he took the financial loss and burned them in the school's furnace. He bowed his head and asked God to help him overcome the effects of this music he had listened to and the movies that he had seen. He desired to be pure in heart.

The College Moves

The next morning at the 5:30 meeting, President Cristman announced that all students and staff should begin to pack their personal and departmental things in preparation for the move. The use of trucks from a Christian trucking company had been donated to help with the move and could be used as long as they were needed. Remodeling crews had been working on the new "Mountain Refuge" property to allow for as smooth a transition as possible. Groups of volunteers who greeted each other with "Maranatha" worked very hard and long hours. They, too, sensed the nearness of the Lord's coming.

The next few days were a flurry of activity for Daniel and Lisa, but once their things were packed, they volunteered to help in other departments. They noticed that each department didn't pack much, but left a lot of equipment to the new buyers who wanted it for their new convenient-to-town college. At the close of one particularly hectic day, when they had done all they could to help, they decided to drive up to Mountain Refuge to look around and have a special time of prayer and fellowship together.

"I believe, Lisa, that we could be an encouragement to each other if we were together more," Daniel said awkwardly. "I feel the work that God has given us would be enhanced by...," he sighed and interrupted himself. "Lisa, I have spoken with my parents and counselors, and they have given me the okay to ask you something. But I don't want to do it until we get to Mountain Refuge."

The new campus for Mountain Refuge Adventist Missionary College (MRAMC) was beautiful in every way; 320 acres surrounded by national forest with a crystal-clear stream flowing the full length of it. There were many buildings for classes, a large lodge, nearly 100 cabins and many tent sites. There was about 100 acres of agricultural land. The mountains formed a beautiful backdrop to the quietness. Being a former church camp, it possessed many facilities and was well separated from the town that had engulfed the former campus of Adventist College.

Daniel Proposes

Along the stream were quiet pools that reflected the beauties of the mountain valley. It was at one of these deep, quiet pools that Daniel motioned for Lisa to be seated on a rock. He thought that he had never seen such beauty so simply and purely expressed. Lisa's countenance reflected an inner glow.

"What is it, Daniel?" she asked anxiously.

"Well, you see, I feel that ... I ... I mean, you know." Daniel seemed helpless to put his thoughts into words. "This is such a beautiful place to ask such an important question," he said with renewed determination. "Lisa, I believe that God's work would be furthered if we became one in Christ. Will you marry me?"

417

Daniel asked quietly. "I know our work here as staff would be strengthened if we were married."

"Daniel, I feel impressed that God had to answer our questions about marriage in the last days and He has done that for me," answered Lisa. "I would like to phone my parents and speak with them regarding your question. I can use the pay phone right over there."

When Lisa found the pay phone at the main entrance, Daniel stayed behind to give her privacy. As she was talking, he remembered the picnics and campouts the two families had had together. These pleasurable times allowed each of their parents time to get acquainted with each other and with Daniel and Lisa. Each family truly respected the choices that the young couple had made. Lisa's family really loved Daniel, and Daniel's family thought that Lisa was the most perfect match for Daniel. They loved her as their own daughter.

Lisa was smiling as she approached Daniel. She told him that her parents had given them their blessings and consent. "They spoke highly of you, Daniel."

"As for me," stated Lisa, "I have prayed much about this over the months, Daniel, and I don't need any more time. I knew quite a while ago as I watched you gain victory over every besetment that I could be your helpmate. My answer is yes, and I love you as truly as God would have me. We will continue to put God's work first in our relationship."

Daniel had never known such pure happiness as at that moment. He knew it was true joy because they had followed God's plan and providence to find "God's Appointed."

"I love you too, Lisa, very deeply," Daniel responded. "I wrote something for you." He handed Lisa a small card on which was written the words, 'Love is the depth of appreciation of communication.'

"That is beautiful, Daniel. I will treasure it always."

True Education

The next morning at the 5:30 meeting, President Cristman was the speaker. He announced, "The early-morning meetings will continue at the new campus, hopefully one week from today. And, by the way, Daniel and Lisa will be married in the Log Chapel at MRAMC." Joyful smiles spread through the audience. The absence of whistles, laughter, and applause indicated to Daniel and Lisa that their witness had encouraged the students to be more reverent about courtship. President Cristman then read for the devotional a reference from The Ministry of Healing, page 395: "*True education is missionary training. Every son and daughter of God is called to be a missionary; we are called to the service of God and our fellow men; and to fit us for this service should be the object of our education.'* This is why the board voted to reincorporate "missionary" in our name, since it is now the object of our education."

He continued reading from <u>Testimonies for the Church</u>, volume 9, page 174: *"'We hear a great deal about higher education. The highest education is to follow in the footsteps of Christ, patterning after the example He gave when He was in the world. We cannot gain an education higher than this, for this class of training will make men laborers together with God.'* This is what we desire, and as leaders of MRAMC and, as co-learners, we pledge to you, with God's help, to assist each of you in gaining that higher education.

"In closing, some thoughts from the Flood, 5,000 years ago. I know you are all familiar with the story recorded in Genesis 6:13. God told Noah to build an ark. He gave him exact dimensions, chose the wood for construction, and gave him the floor plan. Noah followed the plan exactly while people made fun of him. Sadly, not many people believed in his project. When the rains came, many believed, but it was too late then. Violent winds and eruptions from the deep threatened to destroy the ark. Noah had followed God's plan to the letter, and still the storm threatened the ark's existence. Let me ask you this, young people—where was everything that was not built according to God's plan?"

"All gone!" exclaimed a student at the back of the auditorium.

"That is correct," said President Cristman. "So we must build according to God's plan whatever the cost in money, separations, and ridicule. Soon all will want to build an ark like ours, but it will be too late. It is almost too late for us," he said solemnly. "But," he said emphatically, "don't miss this point. Even though we build according to God's plan, if we survive at all it will be only by the blessing of God. Listen to this reference describing the ark from <u>The Story of Redemption</u>, page 68:

'The beasts within expressed, by their various noises, the wildest terror; yet amid all the warring of the elements, the surging of the waters, and the hurling about of trees and rocks, the ark rode safely. Angels that excel in strength guided the ark and preserved it from harm. Every moment during that frightful storm of forty days and forty nights <u>the preservation of the ark was a miracle of almighty power</u>.'

"Young people, we, too, have an ark to build. No matter how closely we follow the blueprint, it won't be good enough to survive the coming storm. Don't ever forget that our safety is in God, and not in the ark. We must build the ark according to His plan, but we still need God's blessing and His protection in order for our ark to survive. <u>Education</u>, page 50, says: *'With us, as with Israel of old, success in education depends on fidelity in carrying out the Creator's plan. Adherence to the principles of God's word will bring as great blessings to us as it would have brought to the Hebrew people.'*

"We must build, we must follow the plan. Noah's ark would have sunk without God's blessing of protection. So will ours. God bless you as we keep His priorities prominent. Let us follow the plan. Then we can have His protection. God bless you, young people. Let us arise and build."

There was no applause but all were in agreement Many of the students stood quietly in assent. Others wept and prayed. There were a few prayer bands dotting the auditorium; some students decided to go to their rooms to pray.

"Just a couple of announcements before we leave this morning," said President Cristman. "Dean Matthews will be informing you as to specific details of the move. I will be handing out an outline of this class to each of you. It is entitled 'Prof. Paul's Notes' and Sister Helen informs me that someone has written a book entitled 'You Can Survive!' My counsel is to get a copy as soon as it is available. On behalf of Adventist College, I would like to be the first to welcome you to Mountain Refuge Adventist Missionary College."

PROF. PAUL'S NOTES
I AM THANKFUL:

1. For schools that "even at this late hour" have a balanced and systematic daily work-study program in which all teachers and students participate:

"We desire that our children should study to the best advantage. In order to do this, employment should be given them which will call the muscles into exercise. <u>Daily, systematic labor should constitute a part of the education of the youth, even at this late period</u>" (<u>Fundamentals of Christian Education</u>, p. 44; emphasis supplied).

2. For schools that do not consider athletics as a satisfactory alternative to practical training and believe in the superiority of manual labor and in the danger of spectator-type sports.

"<u>They act as if the school were a place where they were to perfect themselves in sports, as if this were an important branch of their education, and they come armed and equipped for this kind of training. This is all wrong, from beginning to end</u>. It is not in any way appropriate for this time; it is <u>not qualifying the youth to go forth as missionaries</u>, to endure hardship and pri-

vation, and to use their powers for the glory of God" (Manuscript Releases, vol. 2, p. 218; emphasis supplied).

"The physical exercise was marked out by the God of wisdom. Some hours each day should be devoted to useful education in lines of work that will help the students in learning the duties of practical life, which are essential for all our youth. But this had been dropped out, and amusements introduced, which simply give exercise, without being any special blessing in doing good and righteous actions, which is the education and training essential" (Fundamentals of Christian Education, p. 228).

"Without physical exercise, no one can have a sound constitution and vigorous health; and the discipline of well-regulated labor is no less essential to the securing of a strong and active mind and a noble character" (Patriarchs and Prophets, p. 601).

3. For schools that do not copy after the world nor allow anyone who secures a worldly education to influence their standard.

"And there are some who, having secured this worldly education, think that they can introduce it into our schools. But let me tell you that you must not take what the world calls the higher education and bring it into our schools and sanitariums and churches. We need to understand these things. I speak to you definitely. This must not be done" (Fundamentals of Christian Education, p. 536; emphasis supplied).

"How few schools are to be found that are not governed by the maxims and customs of the world" (Patriarchs and Prophets, p. 594).

"There are men among us in responsible positions who hold that the opinions of a few conceited philosophers, so called, are more to be trusted than the truth of the Bible or the testimonies of the Holy Spirit. Such a faith as that of Paul, Peter, or John is considered old fashioned and insufferable at the present day. It is pronounced absurd, mystical, and unworthy of an intelligent mind. God has shown me that these men are Hazaels to prove a scourge to our people. They are wise above what is written" (Testimonies for the Church, vol. 5, p. 79; emphasis supplied).

4. For schools that have little to say of degrees.

"In view of all this, our schools should have little to say now of 'degrees,' and of long courses of study. The work of preparation for the service of God is to be done speedily. Let the work be carried forward in strictly Bible lines. Let every soul remember that the judgments of God are in the land. Let 'degrees' be little spoken of" (Manuscript Releases, vol. 11, p. 165;

emphasis supplied).

5. For schools that help students gain a preparation for service rather than becoming confused by courtships in school.

"While at school, students should not allow their minds to become confused by thoughts of courtship. They are there to gain a fitness to work for God, and this thought is ever to be uppermost" (Counsels to Parents, Teachers, and Students, p. 100).

6. For schools that maintain that even now agriculture should be the A, B, and C of the education given.

"Some do not appreciate the value of agricultural work. These should not plan for our schools, for they will hold everything from advancing in right lines. In the past their influence has been a hindrance. Study in agricultural lines should be the A, B, and C of the education given in our schools. This is the very first work that should be entered upon" (Testimonies for the Church, vol. 6, pp. 178, 179; emphasis supplied).

7. For schools that make God's work their chief study and keep the religious element in the ascendancy.

"The strength of our college is in keeping the religious element in the ascendancy." (Testimonies for the Church, volume 5, page 14).

"God has declared His purpose to have one college in the land where the Bible shall have its proper place in the education of the youth. ... The words of God to men, which should receive our first attention, are neglected for the utterances of human wisdom... Never from cowardice or worldly policy let the word of God be placed in the background. Students will be profited intellectually, as well as morally and spiritually, by its study" (Testimonies for the Church, vol. 5, pp. 26, 27; emphasis supplied).

8. For schools that will remain small in size and are located away from the cities.

"Land should be secured at a distance from the cities, where schools can be built up in which the youth can be given an education in agricultural and mechanical lines" (Testimonies for the Church, vol. 8, p. 215).

"The school should not be in or near a city.... All schools should be located, as far as possible, where the eye will rest upon the things of nature instead of clusters of houses" (Fundamentals of Christian Education, p. 322).

"It is possible to have too many educational facilities centered in one place. Smaller schools, conducted after the plan of the schools of the proph-

ets, would be a far greater blessing" (Testimonies for the Church, vol. 6, p. 137; emphasis supplied).

"Send children to schools located in the city, where every phase of temptation is waiting to attract and demoralize them, and the work of character building is tenfold harder for both parents and children (Fundamentals of Christian Education, p. 326; emphasis supplied).

9. For schools where the highest education is taught and not merely the sciences.

"A knowledge of God and of Jesus Christ 'whom He has sent' is the highest education and it will cover the earth with its wonderful enlightenment as the waters cover the sea" (Testimonies for the Church, vol. 6, p. 131).

"Our school was established, not merely to teach the sciences, but for the purpose of giving instruction in the great principles of God's word and in the practical duties of everyday life" (Testimonies for the Church, vol. 5, p. 25).

10. For schools that understand the true science of education.

"Now, as never before, we need to understand the true science of education. If we fail to understand this, we shall never have a place in the kingdom of God" (The Christian Educator, vol. 1, No. 2, August 1897; emphasis supplied).

11. For schools that prepare students to be self-supporting missionaries.

"Students have been learning to become self-supporting, and a training more important than this they could not receive" (Series B, No. 11, p. 1).

"The lesson of self-help learned by the student would go far toward preserving institutions of learning from the burden of debt" (Education, p. 221).

12. For schools that discard novels and fiction and give a few well-chosen studies.

"In the education of children and youth, fairy tales, myths, and fictitious stories are now given a large place. Books of this character are used in the schools, and they are to be found in many homes. How can Christian parents permit their children to use books so filled with falsehood? When the children ask the meaning of stories so contrary to the teaching of their parents, the answer is that the stories are not true; but this does not do away with the evil results of their use. The ideas presented in these books mislead the children. They impart false views of life and beget and foster a desire for the unreal. The widespread use of such books at this time is one of the

cunning devices of Satan. He is seeking to divert the minds of old and young from the great work of character building. He means that our children and youth shall be swept away by the soul-destroying deceptions with which he is filling the world. Therefore he seeks to divert their minds from the word of God and thus prevent them from obtaining a knowledge of those truths that would be their safeguard. Never should books containing a perversion of truth be placed in the hands of children or youth. Let not our children, in the very process of obtaining an education, receive ideas that will prove to be seeds of sin. If those with mature minds had nothing to do with such books, they would themselves be far safer, and their example and influence on the right side would make it far less difficult to guard the youth from temptation" (The Ministry of Healing, pp. 446, 447; emphasis supplied).

"Novel and storybook reading are the greatest evils in which youth can indulge" (Fundamentals of Christian Education, p. 37; emphasis supplied).

"Thousands are today in the insane asylum whose minds became unbalanced by novel reading, which results in air-castle building and love-sick sentimentalism" (Messages to Young People, p. 290).

13. For schools that teach agriculture and are not dependant on imported produce.

"Our schools should not depend upon imported produce, for grain and vegetables, and the fruits so essential to health" (Testimonies for the Church, vol. 6, p. 179; emphasis supplied).

"Small fruits should be planted, and vegetables and flowers cultivated" (Testimonies for the Church, vol. 6, p. 176).

"The youth who shall attend our schools... are to plant ornamental and fruit trees, and to cultivate garden produce" (Testimonies for the Church, vol. 6, p. 181; emphasis supplied).

"Had the money which our larger schools have used in expensive buildings been invested in procuring land where students could receive a proper education, so large a number of students would not now be struggling under the weight of increasing debt, and the work of these institutions would be in a more prosperous condition. Had this course been followed, there would have been some grumbling from students, and many objections would have been raised by parents; but the students would have secured an all-around education, which would have prepared them, not only for practical work in various trades, but for a place on the Lord's farm in the earth made new" (Testimonies for the Church, vol. 6, p. 177; emphasis supplied).

14. For schools that are prisoners of hope, willing to pay the cost of reform.

"*Though in many respects our institutions of learning have swung into worldly conformity, though step by step they have advanced toward the world, they are prisoners of hope. Fate has not so woven its meshes about their workings that they need to remain helpless and in uncertainty. If they will listen to His voice and follow in His ways, God will correct and enlighten them, and bring them back to their upright position of distinction from the world*" (Testimonies for the Church, vol. 6, p. 145).

"*We need now to begin over again. Reforms must be entered into with heart and soul and will. Errors may be hoary with age; but age does not make error truth, nor truth error. Altogether too long have the old customs and habits been followed. The Lord would now have every idea that is false put away from teachers and students. We are not at liberty to teach that which shall meet the world's standard or the standard of the church, simply because it is the custom to do so. The lessons which Christ taught are to be the standard. That which the Lord has spoken concerning the instruction to be given in our schools is to be strictly regarded*" (Testimonies for the Church, vol. 6, p. 142; emphasis supplied).

15. For schools that do not include drama in their studies.

"*Not one jot or tittle of anything theatrical is to be brought into our work. ... Let nothing of a theatrical nature be permitted, for this would spoil the sacredness of the work*" (Evangelism, p. 137; emphasis supplied).

16. For schools that uphold the sacredness of music.

"*The art of sacred melody was diligently cultivated. No frivolous waltz was heard, nor flippant song that should extol man and divert the attention from God; but sacred, solemn psalms of praise to the Creator, exalting His name and recounting His wonderful works. This music was made to serve a holy purpose, to lift the thoughts to that which was pure and noble and elevating, and to awaken in the soul devotion and gratitude to God*" (Fundamentals of Christian Education, p. 97; emphasis supplied).

"*It is impossible to estimate too largely the work that the Lord will accomplish through His proposed vessels in carrying out His mind and purpose. The things you have described as taking place in Indiana, the Lord has shown me would take place just before the close of probation. Every uncouth thing will be demonstrated. There will be shouting, with drums, music, and dancing. The senses of rational beings will become so confused that they cannot be trusted to make rational decisions. And this is called the moving of the Holy Spirit"* (Selected Messages, Book 2, p. 36; emphasis supplied).

17. For schools that understand the importance of diet in the last days.

"Grains, fruits, nuts, and vegetables constitute the diet chosen for us by our Creator" (<u>Ministry of Healing</u>, p. 296).

"The light given me is that it will not be very long before we shall have to give up using any animal food. Even milk will have to be discarded. Disease is accumulating rapidly" (<u>Counsels on Diet and Foods</u>, p. 384).

"The true fasting which should be recommended to all, is abstinence from every stimulating kind of food, and the proper use of wholesome, simple food, which God has provided in abundance" (<u>Counsels on Diet and Foods</u>, p. 188).

18. For schools that uphold the principles of dress as a sign of loyalty to God.

"The dress reform answers to us <u>as did the ribbon of blue</u> to ancient Israel" (<u>Testimonies for the Church</u>, vol. 3, p. 171; emphasis supplied). (See also Numbers 15:38-40 and Deuteronomy 22:5.)

"The dress reform is a striking contrast to the fashion of the world. Those who adopt this dress should manifest good taste and order and strict cleanliness in all their attire" (<u>Testimonies for the Church</u>, vol. 2, p. 66).

19. For schools that have school homes.

"Teachers who are placed in charge of these homes bear grave responsibilities; for they are to act as fathers and mothers, showing an interest in the students, one and all, such as parents show in their children" (<u>Testimonies for the Church</u>, vol. 6, p. 168, continue reading to p. 175).

20. For family schools.

"They should be family schools, where every student will receive special help from his teachers as the members of the family should receive help in the home" (<u>Testimonies for the Church</u>, vol. 6, p. 152).

21. **I am especially thankful to know that God will demonstrate His ways before He comes.**

"Unless there is a breaking away from the influence that Satan has prepared, and a <u>reviving of the testimonies</u> that God has given, <u>souls will perish in their delusion</u>.... All this higher education that is being planned <u>will be extinguished; for it is spurious</u>. The more simple the education of our workers, the less connection they will have with the men whom God is

not leading, the more will be accomplished. Work will be done in the simplicity of true godliness, and the old, old times will be back when, under the Holy Spirit's guidance, thousands were converted in a day. When the truth in its simplicity is lived in every place, then God will work through His angels as He worked on the day of Pentecost, and hearts will be changed so decidedly that there will be a manifestation of the influence of genuine truth, as is represented in the descent of the Holy Spirit" (Series B, No. 7, pp. 63, 64; emphasis supplied).

"Before we can carry the message of present truth in all its fullness to other countries, we must first break every yoke. We must come into the line of true education, walking in the wisdom of God, and not in the wisdom of the world. God calls for messengers who will be true reformers. We must educate, educate, to prepare a people who will understand the message, and then give the message to the world" (Series B, No. 11, p. 30; emphasis supplied).

"The Lord would have the people warned; for a great work will be done in a short time…. Among those who were engaged in the work were young men taken from the plow and from the fields, and sent forth to preach the truth as it is in Jesus…. 'All this,' said my instructor, 'is a parable of what should be, and what will be'" (Medical Ministry, p. 305; emphasis supplied).

"Since the Lord is soon coming, it is time to put out our money to the exchangers, time to put every dollar we can spare into the Lord's treasury, that institutions may be established for the education of the workers, who shall be instructed as were those in the schools of the prophets. If the Lord comes and finds you doing this work, He will say: 'Well done, thou good and faithful servant: …enter thou into the joy of thy Lord" (Testimonies for the Church, vol. 6, p. 441; emphasis supplied).

"I will raise up agents who will carry out my will to prepare a people to stand before Me in the time of the end. In many places that before this ought to have been provided with sanitariums and schools, I will establish my institutions, and these institutions will become educational centers for the training of workers. The Lord will work upon human minds in unexpected quarters" (Counsels on Health, p. 227; emphasis supplied).

"If there can be found places in retired mountain regions where it would be difficult for the evils of the city to enter, let our people secure such places for our sanitariums and advanced schools" (Manuscript Releases, vol. 10, p. 260).

Lord, Send a Revival

The Saviour is longing His spirit to show,
As mighty in pow'r as in days long ago,
But hearts must be open and emptied of sin,
Revival is needed within.

Lord, send a revival, and let it begin with me,
Fill me, I pray—take all self away
That others Thy beauty may see.
Cleanse me now, blessed Saviour
Oh Lord, hear my heartfelt plea,
Send a revival from heaven,
And let it begin with me!

The Saviour will take away hardness of heart,
Fulfill every need, boundless strength He'll impart,
And make up our lack with His merit divine,
I'm thankful this promise is mine.

Remove ev'ry barrier that hinders today,
Oh cleanse me from sin, make me pure, Lord, I pray,
Come forth in thy beauty, and help me to be
A power filled witness for Thee.

—Eulene Dodson

FOR FURTHER STUDY

Another Ark To Build, W. D. Frazee, Pioneers Memorial, Wildwood, GA 30757

God's Appointed, Jere Franklin, Box 840, Chetwynd, BC, Canada V0C 1J0

The Branson Report, Autumn Council, General Conference of SDAs, 1935.

I Believe in Accreditation, Wilbur Atwood, Wildwood Inst., Wildwood, GA 30757.

The Canadian Union Messenger, "I Am Thankful for Schools That ...," Wadie Farag, Jan. 1, 1974.

Articles on Education and Location of Schools:

Kenneth Wood, Review and Herald, February 21, 1980.
Robert Pierson, Ministry, September 1977.
T. S. Geraty, Review and Herald, June 29, 1978.
Richard Osborn, Review and Herald, January 12, 1978.
R. L. Klingbeil, Review and Herald, March 13, 1980.
Hirsch, Charles, Review and Herald, January 26, 1978.
Neal C. Wilson, Ministry, December 1977.

Chapter Nineteen

Evangelism In the End Time: Missionary Training

"Well done, thou good and faithful servant ..." (Matt. 25:21).

Pastor Matt and his wife, Jeannie, were very successful evangelists. For several years, they had held large evangelistic campaigns resulting in thousands of baptisms. They had worked together in doing satellite evangelism to many churches in countries all over the world. This was quite a contrast to the setting in which they had received their training in the small Country School from Pastor Bill, who, in his early days, had been an evangelist and medical missionary worker. Matt and Jeannie had gained a wonderful, practical experience from him.

Recent newscasts told of terrible disasters all over the world; floods, cyclones, tidal waves, earthquakes, and unquenchable fires which were increasing in frequency and intensity. Many in North America were beginning to feel that the wrath of God was being dealt out and that their lives were threatened. These omens troubled Pastor Matt, for he knew these to be precursors to the establishment of required worship. In his evangelistic crusades, people sensed a renewed vigor in his presentations and messages, an urgency that he had never experienced. But something was still missing. This conviction troubled him and he determined to discover the source of his discomfort. He was having great success, so what could possibly be missing?

He had recently compared the number of baptisms with the birth rate and discovered that conversions were less than one percent of the birth rate. However, he also discovered that the ratio of Seventh-day Adventists to the world population in 1863 was one Seventh-day Adventist to every 367,000 non-Adventists, while today the ratio is one Seventh-day Adventist to every 512 non-Adventists. He was encouraged and impressed that when the church received increased portions of the Holy Spirit, the work would be finished. There was reason for courage because of the reduced ratio of world population to Seventh-day Adventists, but Matt could see that the church was falling further behind and that there was a definite need for greater intervention by God into the evangelistic work so that birth rate barriers could be overcome. Matt concluded that the Holy Spirit integrated into God's plan must hold the secret to greater success. Matt knew that the work would be finished in spite of any obstacles, but he urgently sought God's blessing. What was God's plan and how would it be accomplished?

"And this gospel of the kingdom shall be preached in all the world for a witness unto all nations; and then shall the end come" (Matthew 24:14).

The Search Begins

Pastor Matt and Jeannie began their search during their family worship time in the evening, by reviewing notes from Pastor Bill's evangelism class at Country School. They had completed reviewing several pages of notes but could not yet understand what was missing from their evangelistic crusades, if anything.

One evening as Sabbath began, Pastor Matt and Jeannie knelt to pray. They prayed that the Holy Spirit would enlighten their minds on the subject that had deeply concerned them these weeks and months. They prayed that God would hold the winds of strife a little while longer, until more souls could be gathered in under the umbrella of truth. They asked God for a greater measure of His Spirit, that their perplexity might be removed. They thanked God for the results they'd had, but pleaded, "Lord, give us more."

Each time they arose from prayer, a stronger sense of anticipation enveloped them—an awareness of truth covered them as a robe of light. They were strongly impressed that, whatever the wonderful revelations, it would require a complete commitment.

One evening as they opened Pastor Bill's notes, they began to read references from the Bible and the Spirit of Prophecy about the relationship between evangelism, missionary work, and God's plan for educating workers. One reference they read shocked them in its simplicity, and they sensed that it might be related to Matt's perplexity: "How can we win more souls?"

His measure of success had never been numbers of baptisms, such as were gathered by "salvation scorekeepers." He and God had long ago settled the numbers and awards question by remembering that Jesus would have come to this earth to save just one:" The *Saviour would have passed through the agony of Calvary that one might be saved in His kingdom"* (The Desire of Ages, p. 483).

Pastor Matt demonstrated his belief in the union of evangelistic and medical work by having physicians give health lectures during his crusades. This unified presentation laid a firmer foundation on which to begin building truth.

"Unity existing among the followers of Christ is an evidence that the Father has sent His Son to save sinners. It is a witness to His power; for nothing short of the miraculous power of God can bring human beings with their different temperaments together in harmonious action, their one aim being to speak the truth in love" (Testimonies for the Church, vol. 9, p. 194).

But the text he read tonight was one that he had not yet incorporated into his crusade plans. "Look at this, Jean," he said excitedly. "Isaiah 61:4: *'And they shall build the old waste places, they shall raise up the former desolations, and they shall repair the waste cities, the desolations of many generations.'* Do you remember how Pastor Bill used that text and what the Spirit of Prophecy said about this verse?" Matt asked.

"Didn't it say something about getting back to God's plan in education?" she replied.

"You are right, my dear! And look at this reference from the General Conference Bulletin, March 6, 1899. I can just hear Pastor Bill reading it to us right now" (Isaiah 61:4 quoted).

"These words of inspiration present before those who claim to believe present truth, the work that should now be done in educational lines."

"But Matt," questioned Jeannie, "how does this affect our evangelism?"

"You know, Jeannie, that has been hazy to me for a long time. But I remember how Pastor Bill often quoted that reference from The Christian Educator, August 1897: *'Now as never before, we need to understand the true science of education. If we fail to understand this, we shall never have a place in the kingdom of God.'*

"Remember, too, Jeannie, that Pastor Bill was a powerful evangelist, and yet, he was the president of a school. Maybe he understood something that we need today. I wish he were here so that I could ask him some of these questions," said Matt.

As they read together the next reference they began to see the connection with evangelism, the finishing of the work, and true education.

"Before we can carry the message of present truth in all its fullness to other countries, we must break every yoke. We must come into the line of true education, walking in the wisdom of God, and not in the wisdom of the world. God calls for messengers who will be true reformers. We must edu-

cate, educate, to prepare a people who will understand the message and then give the message to the world" (Series B, No. 11, p. 30; emphasis supplied).

"Jeannie," said Matt softly, but with strong conviction, "We need to demonstrate God's plan of true education before God will bless our evangelism in a finished work!"

"How will that ever happen?" asked Jeannie.

"I wonder," Matt mused, "Before we can have effective evangelism, according to the last reference, we must break every yoke. What yokes? We are told that we must come into line of true education, and walk in the wisdom of God, and not in the wisdom of the world. Perhaps the yokes are those of worldly favor and recognition."

Matt and Jeannie sat quietly studying their notes and then looking at each other until Matt interrupted their reverie, "How? When? Where? We need hundreds of God-educated workers; people who know the full message and have been trained in it. That takes time. Let's read on to see if there are any promises of success and triumph to answer the elusive question: Will it happen?" said Jeannie, quickly adding, "This is really powerful. Let's keep reading. Here is a reference that speaks of several things that will be.

"The next reference is Series B, No. 7, pages 63 and 64: *'I write this because any moment my life may be ended. Unless there is a breaking away from the influence that Satan has prepared and a revival of the testimonies that God has given, souls will perish in their delusion. They will accept fallacy after fallacy, and will thus keep up a disunion that will always exist until those who have been deceived take their stand on the right platform. All this higher education that is being planned will be extinguished; for it is spurious. The more simple the education of our workers, the less connection they have with the men whom God is not leading, the more will be accomplished. Work will be done in the simplicity of true godliness, and the old, old times will be back when, under the Holy Spirit's guidance, thousands were converted in a day. When the truth in its simplicity is lived in every place, then God will work through His angels as He worked on the day of Pentecost, and hearts will be changed so decidedly that there will be a manifestation of the influence of genuine truth, as it is represented in the descent of the Holy Spirit'* [emphasis supplied].

"Matt, look how many times the word 'will' is used," observed Jeannie. "Higher education **will** be extinguished and old, old times **will** be back. God **will** work through angels and hearts **will** be changed. Each one is conditional on God's people taking a stand for the truth and making true education a first priority for evangelism."

"This promise assures us it will happen and that God will be with us when we do. Pastor Bill knew this years ago," Matt said, looking a long way off, as though he were deep in thought.

"How did we miss it?" wondered Jeannie. "There are more references in this outline. Let's go on, Matt. Is your perplexity dissolving a little?"

"Yes dear, but ... Well, let's read on. The next reference comes from Medical Ministry, page 305: *'I heard the message proclaimed in power by men who had not been educated in Battle Creek. Among those who were engaged in the work were young men taken from the plow and from the fields, and sent forth to preach the truth as it is in Jesus. Unquestioning faith in the Lord God of heaven was imparted to those who were called and chosen. "All this," said my Instructor, "Is a parable of what should be and what will be"* [emphasis supplied].

"There it is, again, Jeannie!" exclaimed Matt. "It says 'what should be and what **will** be!' Pastor Bill always said that God wanted us to have a work/study program in our schools, didn't he? Remember the reference from Fundamentals of Christian Education, page 44; "We *desire that our children should study to the best advantage. In order to do this, employment should be given them which will call the muscles into exercise. Daily, systematic labor should constitute a part of the education of the youth, even at this late period.*"

"Jeannie, I can only conclude that we need outpost schools to train workers to give the message rather than training young people for business as usual. *'They are there to gain a fitness to work for God, and this thought is ever to be uppermost'* Counsels to Parents, Teachers, and Students, page 100."

Then, with these workers, trained God's way, in true education, a message is given that gains the blessing of God. We then make a tremendous impact evangelistically, much greater than we do today," concluded Matt. "I can see how effective that could be but how will it ever happen?" he questioned as he began to read the next reference from Counsels on Health, page 227; [emphasis supplied].

" '*I will raise up agents who will carry out My will to prepare a people to stand before Me in the time of the end. In many places that before this ought to have been provided with sanitariums and schools, I will establish My institutions, and these institutions will become educational centers for the training of workers*'

"It sure sounds as if God is going to raise up workers to do this," Jeannie stated emphatically.

"And He is going to help them accomplish their work," added Matt.

"Listen to this from Testimonies for the Church, volume 6, page 145: *'Though*

in many respects our institutions of learning have swung into worldly confor-
mity, though step by step they have advanced toward the world, they are prison-
ers of hope. Fate has not so woven its meshes about their workings that they
need to remain helpless and in uncertainty. If they will listen to His voice and
follow in His ways, God will correct and enlighten them, and bring them back to
their upright position of distinction from the world. When the advantage of work-
ing upon Christian principles is discerned, when self is hid in Christ, much greater
progress will be made; for each worker will feel his own human weakness; he
will supplicate for the wisdom and grace of God, and will receive the divine help
that is pledged for every emergency' [emphasis supplied].

"There," said Jeannie, "It says that God will enlighten and correct us, and that we will make much greater progress! If we will accept His plans, and seek His wisdom, He will help us turn existing institutions around as well as build new ones. I think it is obvious that a spiritual revival must work together with reformation. That will enable us to make much greater progress in evangelism"

Pastor Bill's notes also referred to Enoch's outpost as a pattern for evangelism. Review and Herald, July 5, 1906: *"The cities must be worked. The millions living in these congested centers are to hear the third angel's message. This work should have been developed rapidly during the past few years. A beginning has been made, for which we praise God. Outpost centers are being established, from whence, like Enoch of old, our workers can visit the cities and do faithful service"* [emphasis supplied].

"I'm getting the impression," said Matt, "that our evangelism should be a part of our educational system rather than separate; sort of like outpost schools teaching and doing evangelism in the cities. I have noticed these past few years that we are not producing workers who will unite with the ministers to do evangelism. Most of our graduates have other priorities; while they may be good ones, they are not specifically designed to put God's work first.

"Look at this, Jeannie! Pastor Bill is introducing another concept, which indicates that we have to make an ark as God said to make it, as Noah did, in order to have His blessing and protection. These next two references emphasize the point of God's protection resulting from following His plan:

" *'But as in the days of the great deluge Noah was preserved in the ark that God had prepared for him, so in these days of destruction and calamity, God will be the refuge of His believing ones'* (Maranatha, page 283). [emphasis supplied.]

"*They will endeavor to destroy God's people; but as Noah was shut into the ark, so the righteous will be shielded by divine power'* (Patriarchs and Prophets, page 98).

"Are we building the ark as God said to build it?" asked Matt.

"It doesn't appear so," said Jeannie, "But we are close. Fidelity to God's plan is the formula for success. Listen to this reference in <u>Patriarchs and Prophets</u>, page 595: *'Real success in education depends upon the fidelity with which men carry out the Creator's plan.'* If it was important for Noah to build the ark according to God's plan, then it would be equally important for us to build the educational-evangelistic ark according to God's plan. According to <u>The Desire of Ages</u>, page 634, *'Had the church of Christ done her appointed work as the Lord ordained, the whole world would before this have been warned, and the Lord Jesus would have come to our earth in power and great glory.'*

"If we had done our work as the Lord ordained we would have seen Jesus come before now. Since we are still here, evidently we have not done the work as God would have us do it."

Matt said, "Here's another thought that would increase our evangelistic efforts from <u>Testimonies for the Church</u>, volume 9, page 189: *'If we would humble ourselves before God, and be kind and courteous and tenderhearted and pitiful, <u>there would be one hundred conversions to the truth where now there is only one</u>. But, though professing to be converted, we carry around with us a <u>bundle of self</u> that we regard as altogether too precious to be given up. It is our privilege to lay this burden at the feet of Christ and in its place take the character and similitude of Christ. The Saviour is waiting for us to do this'* [emphasis supplied]."

"There is a hundred to one conversion rate right there!" Matt exclaimed . "You know, I have begun evangelistic series knowing that the majority, if not all, of the people sitting in the audience are brokenhearted, guilt-ridden, hopeless, and in need of something better yet I open the series with a rather deep study of Daniel 2! What if I meet them closer to their level of need? I have often thought I should make some appeals to the heart and extend hope and encouragement before I get to the doctrines. I know the doctrines are important, but I want Daniel 2 to fall upon hope-filled hearts. By giving encouragement from the Bible, people will feel more of a need to be ready, wanting to know more truth. Someone once said that the work of the gospel is like a rope. You can draw others to Christ, but as soon as you try to push, you lose your power." (See <u>The Ministry of Reconciliation</u>, James Rafferty, p. 42).

"That's true," agreed Jeannie. "Not long ago I read in <u>The Ministry of Healing</u>, page 141, that *'teaching and healing are never to be separated.'*"

"Jeannie, here's is a hard question for you. If all of our time is taken up with evangelism, when do we get our outpost center ready?" asked Matt.

"Maybe we can study that next?" Jeannie questioned, "How did Enoch actually accomplish his work?"

"I know Enoch visited the cities and then returned to his outpost. Pastor Bill's references seem to indicate that we should follow Enoch's pattern," said Matt, reaching for another book, "I think I can show you here in Evangelism, Jeannie. Yes, here it is on pages 77 and 78: *'As did Enoch, we must work in the cities but not dwell in them.'* And back on page 76, we read, *'It is God's design that our people should locate outside the cities, and from these outposts, warn the cities, and raise in them memorials for God.'*

"In The Seventh-day Adventist Bible Commentary, volume 1, page 1087, we find that, *'He* [Enoch] *did not make his abode with the wicked. He did not locate in Sodom, thinking to save Sodom. He placed himself and his family where the atmosphere would be as pure as possible. Then at times he went forth to the inhabitants of the world with his God-given message. Every visit he made to the world was painful to him. He saw and understood something of the leprosy of sin. After proclaiming his message, he always took back with him to his place of retirement some who had received the warning'* [emphasis supplied]. By giving attention to this phase of our ministry we may help strengthen the outreach of our evangelistic team."

"We need the balance. And as an added benefit, if we follow God's plan, He will bless our efforts with the plan of multiplication," said Jeannie. "Our time is so occupied with evangelism, that we don't have time to build the ark. Could our work keep us from following God's plan and being ready for Christ's coming?"

"That is a tough question, Jeannie. I don't know. But I do know that there are other areas in evangelism that we need to bring into line," said Matt.

"In Evangelism, page 137, we find this instruction, *'Not one jot or tittle of anything theatrical is to be brought into our work.... Let nothing of a theatrical nature be permitted, for this would spoil the sacredness of the work'* [emphasis supplied].

"I hope God will help us to move forward in unity on these subjects. Unity is also a great evangelistic tool. I love this quote from My Life Today, page 252: *'He prays that His disciples may be one, even as He and the Father are one; and this unity of believers is to be as testimony to the world that He has sent us, and that we bear evidence of His grace'*" [emphasis supplied].

Matt Presents His Study To the Team

Several weeks passed. Pastor Matt and Jeannie finished another evangelistic series. They discovered answers to the questions that their earlier studies had raised. They were, again, anxious over new questions and prayed earnestly for answers.

"What do we do now?" questioned Matt thoughtfully. "We have all this information that we feel would be a blessing, and yet we don't want to hurt anyone or criticize the past. *These facilities* [scientific institutions] *are not to be despised or condemned, they are ordained of God, but they can furnish only exterior qualifications'* " (Testimonies for the Church, vol. 5, p. 82).

" *'When this reformation begins, the spirit of prayer will actuate every believer and will banish from the church the spirit of discord and strife'* (Testimonies for the Church, vol. 8, p. 251). I just want to move forward. I believe the Lord wants me to present these ideas and suggestions for change to the General Conference Committee on Evangelism next month. If you agree, let's pray that God will bless these humble efforts," said Matt.

"I agree, Matt," said Jeannie solemnly. "Let's pray together right now."

They joined hands as they knelt and prayed that the Holy Spirit would bless them in their presentation; that it would be made in a noncritical, nonjudgmental way to the committee leaders in God's church. Matt was concerned about how the brethren would receive his study. He was encouraged by the promise in Matthew 28:20: *"And, lo, I am with you alway even unto the end of the world."*

Matt presented his findings in the form of early-morning studies to his evangelism team. These studies came directly from the notes Matt had taken in Pastor Bill's evangelism class many years earlier at Country School. When he asked the team what they thought of this approach to evangelism, they heartily accepted the principles Matt outlined and expressed their own convictions about making these changes as soon as possible. Pastor Matt asked them to pray for him as he presented these plans to the Evangelism Committee.

"Nothing should be done, unless approved by these brethren," Matt cautioned his team. "We will go forward in unity or not at all." The entire team volunteered to fast and pray for Matt before he presented the study to the Evangelism committee.

Trip to Silver Spring

Having been accepted on the busy agenda of the General Conference Committee, Matt arrived in Silver Spring a day early. Although he knew his material, he was concerned that his presentation properly reflect the importance he knew it deserved. As Matt walked along the sidewalk toward the committee conference room his thoughts turned to what he'd heard on the news just the night before and it had increased his intensity of conviction. There had been reports from all around the world about volcanoes, typhoons, hurricanes, great conflagrations, and severe earthquakes, all of which paralleled the events described in <u>The Great Controversy</u>, pages 589 and 590. A reference had come to mind when he heard about the disasters.

"Satan has control of all whom God does not especially guard.... While appearing to the children of men as a great physician who can heal all their maladies, he will bring disease and disaster, until populous cities are reduced to ruin and desolation. Even now he is at work. In accidents and calamities by sea and by land, in great conflagrations, in fierce tornadoes and terrific hailstorms, in tempests, floods, cyclones, tidal waves, and earthquakes, in every place and in a thousand forms, Satan is exercising his power. He sweeps away the ripening harvest, and famine and distress follow. He imparts to the air a deadly taint, and thousands perish by the pestilence. <u>These visitations are to become more and more frequent and disastrous</u>" (emphasis supplied).

The commentator had interviewed people from many denominations who were clamoring and marching in front of the Capitol buildings demanding that more respect be given to Sunday as a worship/recreation day. There were interviews with some who feared that if their demands were not met that calamities would continue to increase until Sunday was honored by legislation. Then legislators made public comments to the news media to lend support to the popular demand. Pastor Matt had said to himself as he knelt in prayer beside his hotel bed, *"Lord, it is time for Thee to work: for they have made void Thy law"* (Psalm 119:126).

Matt began to worry about what the next few minutes would bring, but found comfort in the fact that he knew his team was praying for this morning's presentation. This was an important meeting. Just as he approached the committee room two Bible texts came to his mind. He first thought of Samuel who said, *"Speak, Lord; for thy servant heareth"* (1 Samuel 3: 9), then Isaiah, who said, *"Here am I; send me"* (Isaiah 6:8).

Pastor Matt was placed first on the committee agenda, partly because it was so unusual for an evangelist as successful as Matt to take time, on his own, to visit with the committee. Matt discerned that the committee members were receptive as he began his presentation by claiming the promise in Matthew 24:35 *"Heaven and earth shall pass away, but my word shall not pass away."*

Matt took about an hour to present a condensed version of what he and Jeannie had studied. He added Elder William's experience about church funding in the last great depression from <u>The Review and Herald</u>, September 13, 1979 (see p. 143). As a parallel thought, Matt felt that God wanted this committee to begin to revive and reform evangelism. He said to the committee, "Perhaps God has a plan now for what's ahead of our church, as he did for Elder Williams back in the Depression."

At the end of his presentation, Matt emphasized that he did not want to dwell in the past, or accuse and criticize previous leaders or their plans. He only wanted to move forward with God's plan for finishing the work. "My request, Brethren, is to ask for your support to incorporate these principles into my evangelism efforts and trust God for the results. Thank you for your time," Matt concluded, as he gathered up his notes and charts.

He sensed a variety of reactions from the members of the committee; several appeared to be in shock, some surprised, others weeping. Elder Robert, the chairman, spoke in a broken voice, "Matt, many of us have studied these things and wondered how they fit together or how we would ever put them into practice. It is not something on which you can write a directive to the field. My brother, not only do you have our permission, you have our support. We can bring in our other evangelists for a few days of orientation to study the principles that you have presented. We will ask them if they would like to try them in the field. No one will be asked to do it against their will. Please send us notes and references which will allow us to further amend our policy book regarding evangelism. Thank you so much, my brother."

Some of the committee members had been evangelists themselves, others were lifetime pastors and administrators. Two members were laymen. Brother Ted, an attorney, mentioned the urgency of getting things in place in light of current events and signs of the end times.

Brother Thomas, a businessman, spoke of financial support for an outpost evangelistic school with work/study programs. "I pledge one million dollars toward your project, Pastor Matt. May God continue to bless you. And, lest you might think that those of us with money hold some sort of elevated position, I know of a reference in <u>Testimonies for the Church</u>, volume 1, pages 535, 536, which indicates that those who serve give 10 times more than those who give large sums of money. *'These persons* [those who serve] *are of solid worth. Their judgment is good, their spirit precious in the sight of God; and the amount of good which they accomplish in their unpretending way is tenfold greater than that accomplished by the wealthy, although the latter may give large sums on certain occasions.'* So please, Pastor Matt, consider my gift as a small thing, compared to the work you are doing."

Pastor Matt was overwhelmed with thankfulness. He reminded the committee that he was only building on groundwork that had been laid by Professor Paul's work in education and Dr. Luke's preparations in the field of medicine that had recently taken place at Mountain Refuge Adventist Missionary College. "We are hand in hand on our way home, brethren. God bless you for your support all these years. I love you all. My heart is overflowing with joy," Matt said humbly as he left the conference room.

Pastor Matt closed the door, knowing his church would never be the same, now that the medical, educational, and evangelistic work were uniting

Home Again

When Jeannie picked up Matt at the airport, she could hardly wait to hear about his report from Silver Spring. She was excited that the presentation had met with such a warm response from leadership. They made plans to meet with their team and extend a call to a full time physician—a partner in evangelism who would be willing to leave his practice in these last days. Matt had explained to the committee before his meeting at Silver Spring that this physician would be ordained as a minister and would share in the ministry, from the pulpit, during the large crusades. He would explain to the people how God would be honored by good health practices. Everyone was anxious to know how the Lord would fill this new position on the evangelistic team.

Although his team was excited about the acceptance of Matt's presentation at Silver Spring, they manifested a quiet confidence, which helped reassure Matt that God was in control. In the course of the meeting, Matt discovered that, while he was in Silver Spring, his team members had packed their things and given notice to their apartment house landlords. Two of the members who owned homes had listed them for sale with real estate agents. One team member explained it this way: "In light of the news events and legislative movements, we knew it was time for God to work." Acting in faith, from strong conviction, they had taken this step of commitment. Matt and Jeannie sensed God's providence in all these developments. Matt asked the team if they would travel with him and Jeannie to Mountain Refuge Adventist Missionary College (MRAMC) to visit President Cristman and the staff, especially Prof. Paul, Dean Matthews, and Dr. Luke. Matt's ministerial team all expressed an interest in coming with him.

Matt read to his team about the importance of combining the medical work, evangelism, and education from <u>Testimonies for the Church</u>, volume 9, pages 169 and 170; *"If ever the Lord has spoken by me, He speaks when I say that the workers engaged in educational lines, in ministerial lines, and in medical missionary lines <u>must stand as a unit, all laboring under the supervision of God, one helping the other, each blessing each</u>."*

"We want to offer our services in evangelistic training and then propose to unite our work in an outreach plan that would include the school and Dr. Luke's sanitarium as an outpost center," said Matt at the conclusion of his team debriefing. They had a season of thanksgiving and prayed that human nature would not interfere with progress. "If the Lord said it, that is what we will do." "Not as I will, but as Thou wilt" was their prayer.

They went home to pack in order to be ready to meet the bus for the trip to MRAMC. While the team assembled the next morning the two families who owned homes reported that they had cash offers on their properties. The buyers were waiting for their answer. Each family, without knowledge of what the other was doing, had phoned the real estate agents accepting the offers and saying they would close when they returned from this trip.

Pastor Matt had arranged to meet with President Cristman at MRAMC to discuss the possibility of his evangelistic team being a part of their training program. He briefly told President Cristman, over the phone, of the providences leading up to this visit. President Cristman commented on how recent newscasts had prompted God's people to make huge commitments of funds and services. He related to Matt how just recently many baptisms were occurring in response to the deep study of inspired instruction, and hundreds within reach of the school's influence were more earnestly seeking God's guidance. Matt and President Cristman both sensed the spirit of oneness regarding the goals of evangelism and education. *"True education is missionary training,"* from The Ministry of Healing, page 395, was the theme of their enthusiastic conversation.

Trip to Mountain Refuge

During the trip to MRAMC, the team expressed their inner feelings about this move and how these principles must make the Lord and all of heaven very happy. Every team member had experienced the peace of knowing the path of God as well as the sadness of opposition and separation. Not every church member had responded as favorably as had the evangelistic team and the staff at MRAMC to the changes proposed in evangelism. The team did not feel inferior, threatened, or in any way superior to their brethren. Those who accepted and promoted the joining of forces were eager to press on. They were convicted that Jesus was coming soon. A great sense of loss was mingled with their eagerness as some of their former associates who were not convicted on these principles separated from them. Each of them recognized that in the war of truth and error, that one puts his life on the line in total commitment to God's plan.

Pastor Matt remembered, many years back, when he had heard message after message of revival and reform. Granted, some of the messengers were openly condemning and accusatory, but some positive messages came in a more private way to church leaders, pastors, teachers, wealthy business people. There had, at times, been a temporary reviving of truth, but none of lasting impact like this present revival for the church at large.

Matt recalled a quote from <u>Manuscript Releases</u>, volume 13, on page 193: *"But when we see that message after message given by God has been received and accepted, yet no change has been made, <u>we know that new power must be brought into the regular lines</u>. The management of the regular lines must be entirely changed, newly organized. There must be a committee, not composed of half a dozen men, but of representatives from all lines of our work, from our publishing houses, from our educational institutions, and from our sanitariums, <u>which have life in them</u>, which are constantly working, constantly broadening"* (emphasis supplied).

Matt had wondered about the clause, *"which have life in them."* Now it was clear. Let people be on this management committee from institutions who were following a *"thus saith the Lord"*—people with a plan from God. He was grateful for the large volume of work in revival and reformation that had been done years ago. He felt as if he were standing upon the shoulders of mighty men of God who had recognized the need and recorded their concerns.

As the team traveled to MRAMC, they spoke in subdued tones about world events. Everywhere tragic storms were increasing in fury; fires that could not be quenched, huge earthquakes that had killed thousands, and record flooding in many places that had left scores of homeless wandering through a land they no longer recognized. Each new report of disaster inflamed those who were initiating Sunday legislation to increase their efforts in order that God's wrath might be stayed.

As the evangelistic team arrived, President Cristman greeted them in the foyer of the newly painted administration building. "I am so happy to see you, Pastor Matt," he said, clasping Matt's hand warmly in both of his. "We believe that your team brings another piece to our educational program that will help demonstrate a completeness to God's plan."

"We are convinced that we need to work from outposts," said Matt, "and we are praying that Mountain Refuge will fill our needs, too. We are also glad that we can be of assistance to MRAMC. A demonstration must be made before the work can be finished."

"Our staff would be most interested to hear the presentation you gave to the brethren at Silver Spring, Matt. We are anxious to discuss the details of how best to integrate education and evangelism on this campus. Our meeting is scheduled in Conference Room One at 9 a. m. tomorrow, up there and to the right," said the president indicating a room at the top of the stairs.

Matt's Presentation

The next morning, the staff at MRAMC listened intently to Matt's proposal of starting a department of pastoral ministry and evangelism for the students. The course offerings would include Bible and Spirit of Prophecy Studies, Practical Work, Medical Missionary Training, Sermon Preparation and Delivery. The students would apprentice with Pastor Matt in large city evangelism as well as in radio and television communication skills. Principles and practices of revival and reformation would be implemented throughout the course, including a unique training in preparation for "no buy-no sell."

The committee unanimously accepted Pastor Matt's proposal and began to discuss housing arrangements. Money could be used from donated evangelistic funds to build homes for the evangelistic team members should MRAMC be short of housing.

The committee was particularly interested in Pastor Matt's references stating that revival and reformation must take place and will take place before the work of God could be finished and Jesus come. Matt read the references from Medical Ministry, page 305, Series B, No. 11, pages 29 and 30, and Series B, No. 7, pages 63 and 64, as he had at the General Conference meeting a few days earlier. Matt added a few more references that he had discovered at the conclusion of his research.

"The next references explain further the relationship of higher education which is not on the altar, and being ready for Jesus' return. The first is in Evangelism, page 613: *'The day of God is coming with stealthy tread, but the supposed wise and great men are prating about "higher education." They know not the signs of Christ's coming, or of the end of the world.'*

"The second reference is found in Testimonies for the Church, volume 5, page 80: *'God has never made the flock wholly dependent upon human instrumentalities. But the days of purification of the church are hastening on apace. God will have a people pure and true.... Those who have rendered supreme homage to "science falsely so-called" will not be the leaders then. Those who have trusted to intellect, genius, or talent will not then stand at the head of rank and file'* [emphasis supplied].

"I love this next reference not only because it does not condemn what has been done," said Matt, "But because it proposes that we move forward as a result of our spiritual growth. Testimonies for the Church, volume 5, page 82: *'God will work a work in our day that but few anticipate. He will raise up and exalt among us those who are taught rather by the unction of His Spirit than by the outward training of scientific institutions. These facilities are not to be despised or condemned, they are ordained of God, but they can furnish only exterior qualifications. God will manifest that He is not dependent on learned, self-important mortals'* [emphasis supplied].

"In spite of our past, our education, our proud hearts, our worldly wisdom, and our old practices, God will take charge if we allow Him and we will be successful in the completion of the work that God has given us. We must determine to humble our hearts, place our lives on the altar, and practice God's plan. God has His leaders already in training. They know His plan, and they want to honor Him by putting that plan into practice at the cost of ridicule, accusations, and derision," explained Pastor Matt.

"We read in <u>Counsels to Parents, Teachers and Students</u>, pages 511, 512, *'In the common walks of life there is <u>many a toiler</u> patiently treading the round of his daily tasks, unconscious of latent powers that, roused to action, <u>would place him among the world's great leaders</u>. <u>The touch of a skillful hand is needed</u> to arouse and develop those dormant faculties.... There were many learned and honorable men who believed the teaching of Christ. Had these fearlessly obeyed the convictions of their consciences, they would have followed Him. Their abilities would have been accepted and employed in the service of Christ, had they offered them. But they had not moral power in the face of the frowning priests and jealous rulers, to confess Christ and venture their reputation ...'* [emphasis supplied].

"You see," explained Pastor Matt, "we just need to bow to superior wisdom and plans. These plans are plainly stated in His Word and in His testimony. Let us all, regardless of our background or training, humble our hearts knowing that God has His workers ready to fulfill His plans and that we might be of use to Him in accomplishing His goals.

"I am sure most of you are familiar with this next reference in <u>The Great Controversy</u>, page 464: *'Before the final visitation of God's judgments upon the earth, there <u>will be</u> among the people of the Lord such a <u>revival of primitive godliness</u> as has not been witnessed since apostolic times'* [emphasis supplied].

"Think of it, brothers and sisters!" said Matt excitedly. "God has promised to bring about a revival and reformation. He is just waiting for our willingness to have it! Notice how God pleads with us to become active for Him. The prophet uses the words 'will be,' indicating that it **is** going to happen. The 'when' is up to us, as we read in <u>Counsels on Stewardship</u>, page 52: *'When we have entire, wholehearted consecration to the service of Christ, <u>God will recognize the fact</u> by an outpouring of His Spirit without measure; but this will not be while the largest portion of the church are not laborers together with God'* [emphasis supplied].

"God will recognize our commitment and give us His Spirit without measure. This puts the responsibility upon us as a people to hasten the outpouring of the Holy Spirit and the latter rain," explained Matt. "This quote from <u>Education</u>, page 263 explains how our deviations from His plan bring Him grief: '*Every departure from right, every deed of cruelty, <u>every failure of humanity to reach His ideal, brings grief to Him</u>* ' [emphasis supplied].

"The Lord is grieved that we don't come up to His ideal. Remember the reference in <u>Patriarchs and Prophets</u>, page 595, that says '*real success in education depends upon the fidelity with which men carry out the Creator's plan*'? It is important to God that we respect His blueprint for finishing His work.

"In Isaiah 63:9 we can see how diligently God works to redeem us when we deviate from His plan: '*In all their affliction he was afflicted, and the angel of his presence saved them: in his love and in his pity he redeemed them.*'

"When we hurt from the results of our ways, He hurts. With such great love He is our example of intercession. When we are unsuccessful, He feels our disappointment as though it were happening to Him. Judges 10:16: '*And his soul was grieved for the misery of Israel.*' When we are in prison, He feels our imprisonment. Never forget, the words of inspiration in <u>Testimonies for the Church</u>, volume 6, page 145, that we are **prisoners of hope!**

"Praise the Lord!" Matt exclaimed, lifting both arms in a victory signal. He paused, his face aglow in the anticipation of his next thought. Matt loved the church so much, he was jealous that it have the best things said about it, and have the greatest influence possible. A smile began to break, slowly at first, finally spreading over his face like a sunrise as he began to read.

"'*If <u>the church</u> would manifest a <u>greater interest in the reforms</u> which God Himself has brought to them to fit them for His coming, <u>their influence would be tenfold what it now is</u>*'[emphasis supplied]. This reference from <u>Testimonies for the Church</u>, volume 3, page 171, shows how to increase the church's influence tenfold! Ten times more power for soul winning, if we adopt the reforms that God Himself has given us, is a tremendous increase! Combine this with the counsel from <u>Testimonies for the Church</u>, volume 9, page 189 where we read that we would experience a hundredfold increase in conversions if we were '*kind and courteous and tenderhearted and pitiful....*'

"Do the math! Just by practicing kindness and reforms, we can increase our evangelistic impact a thousandfold! Remember, though, unless these reforms fall on a converted heart, broken into selflessness, no lasting success will be realized. We read the truth of this in <u>Selected Messages</u>, book 1, page 128: '*Revival and reformation are to do their appointed work, and in doing this work they must blend.*'

Revival is based on repentance and evidence of a broken heart; selfishness is gone. Reform means a change in the life because of a change in motives.

"We cannot have revival without reformation or reformation without revival. When this work is being accomplished, the providences and truths of God will be clearly discerned, easily distinguished from the spurious. This blending will bear fruit of a wonderful peace, joy, and love. You remember that the Pharisees in Christ's time had reformed and looked to be good men, but were called 'whited sepulchres' by Jesus."

"You may ask the question," said Pastor Matt with a thoughtful expression, "'Are revival and reformation necessary?' Let's look at <u>Testimonies for the Church</u>, volume 7, page 285, which answered this question for me, *'God's people will not endure the test unless there is a revival and reformation.'*

"We have to endure the test, we must survive, and God says that revival and reformation are the preparation for passing the final test. Listen to this statement from <u>Manuscript Releases</u>, volume 20, page 43: *'When will men cease to depend upon the same routine which has left <u>so much work undone</u>, so many fields unworked? <u>Is not the present presentation enough to make men see that a revival is necessary and a reformation essential?</u>'* [emphasis supplied].

"There is no doubt in my mind that revival and reformation are essential to our survival. Here is a blessed promise of completed work," continued Pastor Matt, "We find it in <u>Manuscript Releases</u>, volume 17, page 18: *'"I counsel thee to buy of Me gold tried in the fire, that thou mayest be rich; and white raiment, that thou mayest be clothed, and that the shame of thy nakedness do not appear; and anoint thine eyes with eyesalve, that thou mayest see"* (Revelation 3:18). <u>But that message will do its work, and a people will be prepared to stand without fault before God</u>'* [emphasis supplied].

"I believe it because God said it," said Pastor Matt. "We know that this work of obtaining the eyesalve is connected with a demonstration of true education. Part of the work of this eyesalve is to help us establish schools and sanitariums. *'<u>I will instruct the ignorant and anoint with heavenly eyesalve the eyes of many who are now in spiritual darkness.</u> I <u>will</u> raise up agents who <u>will</u> carry out My will to prepare a people to stand before Me in the time of the end. In many places that before this ought to have been provided with <u>sanitariums and schools</u>, I <u>will</u> establish My institutions, and these institutions <u>will</u> become educational centers for the training of workers'* (<u>Counsels on Health</u>, page 227). [Emphasis supplied.]

"In closing, brothers and sisters, I submit the goal to be reached; the affirmation that means more to me than any other reward, and it is offered by

Jesus. *'Since the Lord is soon to come, it is time to <u>put every dollar</u> we can spare into the Lord's treasury, that institutions may be established for the <u>education of workers</u>, who shall be instructed as were those in the schools of the prophets. If the Lord comes and finds you doing this work, <u>He will say</u>: "Well done, thou good and faithful servant: ...enter thou into the joy of thy Lord"'* (<u>Testimonies for the Church</u>, volume 6, page 441). [Emphasis supplied.] I want to hear that 'well done,' don't you?"

"Matthew 28:20 gives us clear instruction that what we have learned from God we are to teach to others, *'Teach them everything I've taught you. I'll always be with you, even unto the end of the world'* [Clear Word]. All of this revival and reformation that we have learned from the law and the testimony we need to share with others."

As Matt closed the meeting with prayer, there was a reverent hush throughout the room. Hearts burned with an urgency to begin that for which Jesus was waiting: a true revival and reformation. Confessions and pleas for forgiveness began with members of the committee and soon spread over the campus. The spirit of faultfinding, jealousy, criticism, and condemnation were laid aside. Forgiveness was urgently sought and given. There was an outpouring of the Holy Spirit at MRAMC.

Many wept in contrition and with heartfelt thanks and expressed their total commitment to new directions and goals. Instead of their own agenda, they became more concerned about each other. Those who humbled themselves sensed a great peace within their heart.

"And they overcame him [Satan] *by the blood of the Lamb, and by the word of their testimony; and they loved not their lives unto death"* (Revelation 12:11).

Chapter Twenty

Heaven:
The Ultimate Survival

*"And God shall wipe away all tears from their eyes; and there shall be no
more death, neither sorrow, nor crying, neither shall there be any more
pain: for the former things are passed away"* (Rev. 21:4).

There is a majestic mountain valley not far from our home in northern
British Columbia where we once stepped back a hundred years in time.
In this remote valley there was a grand herd of pack horses who knew only
friendly hands. Water was drawn by a rope and bucket from the clear river, and a
fresh pot of water simmered at the back of an old wood cook stove in a quaint log
cabin. It was a place where the Canadian geese announced the seasons and a forest
of stately spruce trees embraced a picturesque natural meadow. Through this pris-
tine beauty the sands of time slowed their rapid flight to the quiet flow of the Wolverine River. This was the home of trapper John Terry, whose friends nicknamed him
"Johnny Sundown" after he tacked the ten commandments on his cabin door. But I
should go back to the beginning of the story.

We first visited the J Bar W back in the summer of 1975. John was bringing in his hay with a big team of black Percherons, Dan and Pride, who were
hitched to his hay wagon. My wife and I, and the friends we'd brought with us, ate

our picnic lunch beneath the tall spruce trees on the bank of the Wolverine River and then helped John bring in his hay. A few days after our visit to the Wolverine, John made an uncustomary visit outside his valley, and knocked at the door of our cabin at Sanctuary Ranch. After a cup of wild mint tea, John began unfolding a story that had started nearly twenty years before. We sat, spellbound, as he told us of his dream.

"I recognized you right away as my 'Happy People,'" he said, shyly caressing his ancient brown cowboy hat. "I saw you in a dream many years ago, and I saw heaven, too."

Here, in his own words, is John's vision of heaven which came to him one night in the late 1950s. "My guide said, 'I have come to take you on a trip.' But he told me I should stop smoking so that I could travel with him. He took my arms and seemed to pump all the tobacco out of my system and for the next two days I had no desire to smoke! Then he took my hand and we floated away. He took me close to the moon and said, 'Man will soon be on the moon, and you will know what it looks like.' The surface of the moon looked kind of like a pancake ready to be turned.

"We traveled past the moon, through the stars and arrived at a Light; a light so beautiful it is beyond explanation. I saw heaven. I felt like a little bee coming down through the huge trees. I saw a beautiful city full of happy people, waving to each other and singing as they floated around. Ever after this I called them my 'Happy People.'

"Before my dream ended, I asked my guide if I could tell anyone. 'You can if you wish,' he said, 'But they won't believe you. You will know the time.'"

As John finished relating his dream to us, he looked at Linda and I and said, "So now you know what I mean when I say, 'You are my Happy People.'" I've seen you before.

"My guide told me during my dream, 'You will know the truth when you find the church that believes that each day stands for a year.' Jere, over the last 17 years, I have inquired of many churches about this, and the people either laugh at me, accuse me of drinkin' too much, or else they just look blank. I think you can tell me what it means, can't you?" asked Trapper John

"Yes, Sir!" I replied. We showed him Numbers 14:34 and Ezekiel 4:6 where we are told that in Biblical prophecy each day stands for a year. He was noticeably relieved as I promised to give him Bible studies over the next few months during which time he decided to lay his cigarettes aside (he had smoked for over 50 years) and asked to be baptized.

When John finished his story, I was reminded of Ellen White's vision, so I reached for a little red book on the shelf behind me and read to him:

"I saw another field full of all kinds of flowers, and as I plucked them, I cried out, 'They will never fade.' Next I saw a field of tall grass, most glorious to behold; it was living green and had a reflection of silver and gold, as it waved proudly to the glory of King Jesus. Then we entered a field full of all kinds of beasts—the lion, the lamb, the leopard, and the wolf, all together in perfect union. We passed through the midst of them, and they followed on peaceably after. Then we entered a wood, not like the dark woods we have here; no, no; but light, and all over glorious; the branches of the trees moved to and fro and we all cried out, 'We will dwell safely in the wilderness and sleep in the woods'" (Early Writings, p. 18).

When I finished reading, John looked at me and with tears in his eyes and said, "That's what I saw! I've been there, Jere. That's where I want to be." I knew this tough mountain man who sat before me had never seen the book from which I read. Neither had I ever been part of someone's dream! It was a foretaste of heaven to those of us gathered in our cabin.

Trapper John now rests in peace, beside his beloved Wolverine River, awaiting his guide to meet him and give him a tour through heaven.

Another John Saw Heaven

Jesus called John "the beloved" disciple. He and John must have shared some enlightening and heartwarming times together. John learned to love Jesus so much that even when he was banished to the Isle of Patmos, after Jesus' crucifixion, he was blessed with a vivid vision of heaven.

"And I saw a new heaven and a new earth: for the first heaven and the first earth were passed away; and there was no more sea. And I John saw the holy city, new Jerusalem, coming down from God out of heaven, prepared as a bride adorned for her husband. And I heard a great voice out of heaven saying, Behold, the tabernacle of God is with men, and he will dwell with them, and they shall be his people, and God himself shall be with them, and be their God. And God shall wipe away all tears from their eyes; and there shall be no more death, neither sorrow, nor crying, neither shall there be any more pain: for the former things are passed away. And he that sat upon the throne said, Behold, I make all things new" (Rev. 21:1-5; emphasis supplied).

If heaven were a desert, and there were no more tears, sorrow, pain, nor death, I would still want to be there, wouldn't you? But along with all those beautiful promises of peace, it is such a spectacular place of beauty that it is far beyond our human ability to imagine.

"And he carried me away in the spirit to a great and high mountain, and shewed me that great city, the holy Jerusalem, descending out of heaven from God, having the glory of God: and her light was like unto a stone most precious, even like a jasper stone, clear as crystal. ... And the building of the wall of it was of jasper: and the city was pure gold, like unto clear glass. And the foundations of the wall of the city were garnished with all manner of precious stones.... And the twelve gates were twelve pearls.... The street of the city was pure gold, as it were transparent glass. And I saw no temple therein: for the Lord God Almighty and the Lamb are the temple of it. And the city had no need of the sun, neither of the moon, to shine in it: for the glory of God did lighten it, and the Lamb is the light thereof. ... For there shall be no night there. ... " (Rev. 21:10-25).

Can you see the city in your mind's eye? Or is it just too bright to bring into focus? Then let's turn to the landscape.

"And he shewed me a pure river of water of life, clear as crystal, proceeding out of the throne of God and of the Lamb. In the midst of the street of it, and on either side of the river, was there the tree of life, which bare twelve manner of fruits, and yielded her fruit every month: and the leaves of the tree were for the healing of the nations.... And he said unto me, These sayings are faithful and true: and the Lord God of the holy prophets sent his angel to shew unto his servants the things which must shortly be done.... Blessed are they that do his commandments, that they may have right to the tree of life, and may enter in through the gates into the city" (Rev. 22:1, 2, 6, 14).

Isaiah's vision of heaven reveals an agrarian society; a place of beauty filled with busy, happy people who grow their own food and build their own homes.

"For behold I create new heavens and a new earth.... And they shall build houses and inhabit them; and they shall plant vineyards, and eat the fruit of them. They shall not build, and another inhabit; they shall not plant, and another eat; for as the days of a tree are the days of my people, and mine elect shall long enjoy the work of their hands" (Isaiah 65:17-22).

What we have learned to love here in our country homes we will continue to enjoy in heaven. The faithful will see Eden restored!

"Let them remember that the home on earth is to be a symbol of and a preparation for the home in heaven." (Ministry of Healing, p. 363).

Jesus Assured Us of Heaven

Many times Jesus assured His followers of something better in the hereafter. Just hours before His crucifixion, He reiterated the promise of His return to earth and that heaven awaited those who remained faithful. He said that He would have told us if there was anything better. He gave explicit directions on how to get there and told us that we would be with Him forever.

"Let not your heart be troubled; ye believe in God, believe also in me. In my Father's house are many mansions; if it were not so I would have told you. I go to prepare a place for you. And if I go and prepare a place for you, I will come again and receive you unto myself; that where I am, there ye may be also. And whither I go ye know, and the way ye know" (John 14:1-4).

We need not fear to make heaven every bit as real as it is.

"A fear of making the future inheritance seem too material has led many to spiritualize away the very truths which lead us to look upon it as our home. Christ assured His disciples that He went to prepare mansions for them in the Father's house. Those who accept the teachings of God's word will not be wholly ignorant concerning the heavenly abode. And yet... human language is inadequate to describe the reward of the righteous. It will be known only to those who behold it. No finite mind can comprehend the glory of the Paradise of God. In the Bible the inheritance of the saved is called a country. There the heavenly Shepherd leads His flock to the fountains of living waters. The tree of life yields its fruit every month, and the leaves of the tree are for the service of the nations. There are ever-flowing streams, clear as crystal, and beside them waving trees cast their shadows upon the paths prepared for the ransomed of the Lord. There the wide-spreading plains swell into hills of beauty, and the mountains of God rear their lofty summits. On those peaceful plains, beside those living streams, God's people, so long pilgrims and wanderers, shall find a home. ...

"None will need or desire repose. ... We shall ever feel the freshness of morning, and shall ever be far from its close. ... The light of the sun will be superseded by a radiance which is not painfully dazzling, yet which immeasurably passes the brightness of our noontide. The glory of God and the Lamb floods the Holy City with unfading light, The redeemed walk in the sunless glory of perpetual day. ...

"The loves and sympathies which God Himself has planted in the soul, shall there find truest and sweetest exercise. The pure communion with holy beings, the harmonious social life with the blessed angels and with the faithful ones of all ages, who have washed their robes and made them white in the blood of the lamb, the sacred ties that bind together 'the whole family

HEAVEN

of heaven and earth'—these help constitute the happiness of the redeemed.

"There, immortal minds will contemplate with never-failing delight the wonders of creative power, the mysteries of redeeming love. ... There the grandest enterprises may be carried forward, the loftiest aspirations reached, the highest ambitions realized; and still there will arise new heights to surmount, new wonders to admire, new truths to comprehend, fresh objects to call forth the powers of mind and soul and body. All the powers of the universe will be open to the study of God's redeemed. ... From the minutest atom to the greatest world, all things, animate and inanimate, in their unshadowed beauty and perfect joy, declare that God is love" (The Great Controversy, pp. 674-678; emphasis supplied).

Ralph Waldo Emerson discovered, "As a man begins to live more seriously within, he begins to live more simply without." God's call to His remnant, the end time Christians, is to simplify. Is there something here on earth for which we are willing to sacrifice eternal happiness? The forested wilderness is beautiful, the best we have on this earth, but neither our love for it, nor our desire to preserve it, should have a higher priority than attaining our heavenly home.

Nothing is so easy, nor so difficult, as trusting ourselves to the God of Abraham, Isaac and Jacob. By submission, this great gift of heaven is ours.

We have seen in previous chapters that God's call to a simple lifestyle rings true down through the ages from man's first home, through to modern Israel. Laodicea still resists committing totally to God who can supply for her that which she cannot supply for herself. Our survival is not in our own hands, although there are decisions we can make to help answer the call of the hour. No matter how well we physically prepare for the end times, our human survival is with God. He tenderly holds in His powerful hands, our hopes, our plans, our loves, and our lives.

What Can We Do?

Jack Benny, a comedian who was known for his penny-pinching attitude, tells about the time he was held at gun point by a man who demanded all his money. Jack did not respond, so the man yelled, "I said, your money or your life!"

"I'm thinking! I'm thinking!" Jack replied.

This illustration so aptly portrays how humanity too often weighs the incomparable riches of the unseen world against the things we have learned to value here. How we spend our time, either in pursuit of the things of time or of eternity, will determine our destiny. Is it too easy, or is it too difficult? The answer is yes. We are so often caught up in the things of time that we cannot even lift our eyes to

453

things eternal. We often tend to feel that life is out of control; that there is no purpose, no design to the haphazard occurrences in our lives. But nothing could be further from the truth.

"Above the distractions of the earth He sits enthroned; all things are open to His divine survey; and from His great and calm eternity He orders that which His providence sees best" (Ministry of Healing, p. 417).

Mysterious Farewell

At sunset, on a hill overlooking the gleaming domes of Jerusalem, Jesus wept. These were not tears of joy, nor of appreciation of her outstanding beauties. He was looking at the city with deep longing for the people who lived there. Many of them were unwilling to see the kingdom of heaven. Many would listen. A few would believe, but most who did believe on Him were intent only on making Jesus an earthly king. Yet He lived among them, willing to die, that they might know heaven. Inspiration calls this mysterious farewell to Jerusalem Jesus' separation struggle.

"He [Jesus] exclaimed, 'O Jerusalem, Jerusalem, thou that killest the prophets, and stonest them which are sent unto thee, how often would I have gathered thy children together, even as a hen gathereth her chickens under her wings, and ye would not!' This is the separation struggle. In the lamentation of Christ the very heart of God is pouring itself forth. It is the mysterious farewell of the long-suffering love of Deity" (The Desire of Ages, p. 620; emphasis supplied). (See Matthew 23:37.)

When Jesus wept, He had spiritual insight into the destruction soon to come upon Jerusalem and He felt the deepening sorrow. We, too, are to weep, just as Jesus did for those who have not yet been gathered. But, we are not called upon to say farewell to anyone, as long as time lasts. The time had come for Jesus to say good-by to many in Jerusalem when they would hear no more appeals, not because they **could** not, but because they **would** not listen.

"When we see one err from the truth, then we may weep over him as Christ wept over Jerusalem" (Testimonies for the Church, vol. 5, p. 345).

We do not have that insight and cannot judge whether the message we give will be received or rejected; but the day is coming when no more appeals will be given for time will run out. Our concern, as part of the remnant, is to be ready for the angel who will set the mark on the foreheads of the true believers.

"Set a mark upon the foreheads of the men that sigh and that cry for all the abominations that be done in the midst thereof" (Ezekiel 9:4). *"The class who do not feel grieved over their own spiritual declension, nor mourn over the sins of others, will be left without the seal of God"* (Testimonies for the Church, vol. 5, p. 211).

To those who weep, as did Jesus over Jerusalem, the seal of God will be given. We don't want to miss this seal.

The Work Will be Finished

Though it may sometimes seem as if all things are continuing as they always have, great changes are being orchestrated for the world, and for men. All heaven is waiting and watching; the wheels are in motion, time is running out. The arena of politics, the occurrence of natural disasters, and the persecutions of the beast will soon intermingle to form a world in which survival will be a concern to those who are loyal to Bible truth. Only members of the remnant, aware of eternal consequences, will choose spiritual survival over the apparent sacrifice of their daily bread. Only those who recognize the gift of time and begin applying their heart unto wisdom will be prepared. Revival and reformation must begin among us.

"This church will never prosper until the members commence the work of reform in their own hearts.... There is no halting place for us this side of heaven" (Testimonies for the Church, vol. 5, p. 308).

Thank God we are not left to think about failure through lack of reform. We have promises that tell of large changes in our church. Consider this one, *"There seemed to be a great movement—a work of revival—going forward in many places. Our people were moving into line, responding to God's call"* (Last Day Events, p. 58).

"She [the church] *will appear in her God-given simplicity and purity, separate from worldly entanglements, showing that the truth has made her free indeed. Then her members will indeed be the chosen of God, His representatives"* (Last Day Events, p. 60; emphasis supplied).

The Lord has told us that only one thing must occur before He returns in glory; the truth must go into all the world. We have learned that it is within our power to hasten his coming (see chapter 17). Nothing can bar the way of those who have seen a vision of the heavenly land and who have so learned to love it that they are willing to make any sacrifice ensuring that they, their families, and others might experience heaven. To refuse the next step in our commitment to character development or spiritual growth is to commit spiritual suicide. If only we could see, with the eye of faith, the great cloud of witnesses hoping, praying, longing for our eternal survival, we would be strengthened to come into line.

"Before we can carry the message of present truth in all its fullness to other countries, we must break every yoke. We must come into line of true education, walking in the wisdom of God, and not in the wisdom of the world. God calls for messengers who will be true reformers. We must educate, educate, to prepare a people who will understand the message, and then give the message to the world" (Series B, No. 11, p. 30; emphasis supplied).

I want to break every yoke that binds me to the world. I want to come into line of true education. I want to meet Trapper John Terry under the Tree of Life. He'll grasp my hand in his, and say, "This is what I saw! Come let me show you my new cabin!" And I will know that whatever I had to pay for heaven, it was cheap enough!

And all the survivors will agree.

THE END

Appendix

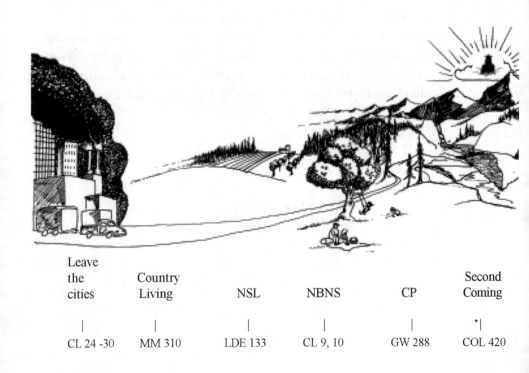

Leave the cities	Country Living	NSL	NBNS	CP	Second Coming
|	|	|	|	|	•|
CL 24 -30	MM 310	LDE 133	CL 9, 10	GW 288	COL 420

CLOSING EVENTS CHART *

| NATIONAL SUNDAY LAW | CLOSE OF PROBATION | SECOND COMING OF CHRIST |

TODAY

HOLY SPIRIT WITHDRAWN
(GC 614)

HEAVENLY SANCTUARY
CLEANSED *(DANIEL 12:1,
GC 423-432, 613-
614)*

THE LATTER RAIN... *(EW 279)*
THE LOUD CRY... *(EW 277)*
THE SHAKING... *(EW 269)*

SUNDAY LAW ENFORCEMENT

GROWING INTENSITY OF

DEATH DECREE *(EW 283)*
JACOB'S TIME OF TROUBLE
(5T 451)
Flight into desolate and
solitary places *(5T 464)*

PREPARATION:
(5T 452)

Spiritual and
practical skills
are developed

FINES, IMPRISONMENT AND
INDUCEMENTS *(GC 607)*
"NO BUY-NO SELL" *(Rev. 13:17)*
(4SP 422)

GREAT TIME OF TROUBLE
(GC 613)

TROUBLES
INCREASE
(EW 282)

SHORT TIME OF TROUBLE
(EW 33, 85)

(EW 52)

(REV. 16)

MARTYRDOM
(Maranatha 199)

Eternal Decision *(7BC 976)*

SEAL OF GOD
(Rev. 7:3)
(EW 67-71)

| 1 | 2 | 3 | 4 | 5 | 6 | 7 |

P L A G U E S

MARK OF
THE BEAST
(Rev. 13:17)

SIGNS OF DELIVERANCE

• Small black cloud in the east.
• Bright star at midnight.
• Sun appears at midnight.
• 10 Commandments appear
  in the clouds.
• Rainbows appear at
  midnight and encircle
  praying companies.
• Voice of God declares day
  and hour of Christ's return.

(Great Controversy 635-652)

The NSL is the CP
for Sabbath-keepers:
I Peter 4:17
Ezekiel 9:4-6
5T 211
9T 97
2SM 16
7BC 976

Millenium: Rev. 20:2,4; Saints reign with Christ 1000 years in heaven. Satan bound on earth (GC 653)

** This chart does not include all events prophesied.
Please contact the author for a more complete teaching chart.*

The "Ready or Not" List

Here is a list of events and experiences that **will occur** among God's people before Christ returns. They **will happen** whether we are ready or not!

Sunday Law Development

Natural disasters will become more and more frequent

"These visitations [catastrophes] *are to become more and more frequent and disastrous"* (The Great Controversy, p. 590; emphasis supplied).

God's people will be blamed for these disasters

"It will be declared that men are offending God by violation of the Sunday-sabbath; that this sin has brought calamities which will not cease until Sunday observance shall be strictly enforced; and that those who present the claims of the fourth commandment, thus destroying reverence for Sunday, are troublers of the people, preventing their restoration to divine favor and temporal prosperity" (The Great Controversy, p. 590; emphasis supplied).

There will be fines, imprisonment, inducements in Sunday Law enforcement

"As the movement for Sunday enforcement becomes more bold and decided, the law will be invoked against commandment-keepers. They will be threatened with fines and imprisonment, and some will be offered positions of influence, and other rewards and advantages, as inducements to renounce their faith" (The Great Controversy, p. 607; emphasis supplied).

Final stages of enforcement of the National Sunday Law

"Fearful is the issue to which the world is to be brought. The powers of earth, uniting to war against the commandments of God, will decree that no man may buy or sell, save he that has the mark of the beast, and, finally, that whoever refuses to receive the mark shall be put to death" (Spirit of Prophecy, vol. 4, p. 423; emphasis supplied).

No buy no sell

"He causes all, both small and great, rich and poor, free and slave, to receive a mark on their right hand or on their foreheads, and that no one may buy or sell except one who has the mark or the name of the beast, or the number of his name" (Revelation 13:16-17, NKJV; emphasis supplied).

YOU CAN SURVIVE!

Death decree

"And he had power to give life unto the image of the beast, that the image of the beast should both speak and cause that as many as would not worship the image to the beast should be killed" (Revelation 13:15, KJV; emphasis supplied).

Revival and Reformation

Key to endurance

"God's people will not endure the test unless there is a revival and a reformation" Testimonies for the Church, vol. 7, p. 285; emphasis supplied).

Revival of primitive godliness

"Before the final visitation of God's judgments upon the earth, there will be, among the people of the Lord, such a revival of primitive godliness as has not been witnessed since apostolic times. The spirit and power of God will be poured out upon His children. At that time many will separate themselves from those churches in which the love of this world has supplanted love for God and His word. Many, both of ministers and people, will gladly accept those great truths which God has caused to be proclaimed at this time, to prepare a people for the Lord's second coming" (The Great Controversy, p. 464; emphasis supplied).

Increase of the church's influence

"If the church would manifest a greater interest in the reforms which God Himself has brought to them to fit them for His coming, their influence would be tenfold what it now is" (Testimonies for the Church, vol. 3, p. 171; emphasis supplied).

Greater progress will be made

"When the advantage of working upon Christian principles is discerned, when self is hid in Christ, much greater progress will be made; for each worker will feel his own human weakness; he will supplicate for the wisdom and grace of God, and will receive divine help that is pledged for every emergency. Opposing circumstances should create a firm determination to overcome them. One barrier broken down will give greater ability and courage to go forward. Press in the right direction, and make a change, solidly and intelligently. Then circumstances will be your helpers and not your hindrances. Make a beginning. The oak is in the acorn" (Testimonies for the Church, vol. 6, p. 145; emphasis supplied).

Truth Will Triumph

Can't overestimate the work God will do

"It is impossible to estimate too largely the work that the Lord will accomplish through His proposed vessels in carrying out His plan and purpose" (Selected Messages, book 2, p. 36; emphasis supplied).

The message will do its work

"From those who have rejected truth, the light of God had departed. They did not heed the message of the True Witness, 'I counsel thee to buy of me gold tried in the fire, that thou mayest be rich; and white raiment, that thou mayest be clothed, and that the shame of thy nakedness do not appear; and anoint thine eyes with eyesalve that thou mayest see'" [Revelation 3:18]. *But that message will do its work, and a people will be prepared to stand without fault before God"* (Manuscript Releases, vol. 17, p. 18; emphasis supplied).

"While they are consecrating themselves to God, a convincing power will attend their efforts to present the truth to others, and its light will find access to many hearts" (Testimonies for the Church, vol. 5, p. 454).

Preachers will be called from the plow

"Among those who were engaged in the work were young men taken from the plow and from the fields, and sent to preach the truth as it is in Jesus. Unquestioning faith in the Lord God of heaven was imparted to those who were called and chosen. 'All this,' said my instructor, 'Is a parable of what should be, and what will be'" (Medical Ministry, p. 305; emphasis supplied).

Truths buried will be revived

"Truths that have been buried under a mass of rubbish are to be revived, and reset in their original setting" (Manuscript Releases, vol. 3, p. 416; emphasis supplied).

He will bring His purposes to pass

"The coming of the Lord is nearer than when we first believed. What a wonderful thought it is that the great controversy is coming to its end! In the closing work we shall meet with perils that we know not how to deal with; but let us not forget that the three great powers of heaven are working, that a divine hand is on the wheel, and that God will bring His purposes to pass. He will gather from the world a people who will serve Him

461

in righteousness" (<u>Selected Messages</u>, book 2, p. 391; emphasis supplied).

Schools

Schools of the Prophets will be revived

"*If conducted as God designs they should be, our schools in these closing days of the message <u>will do a work</u> similar to that done by the schools of the prophets*" (<u>Bible Commentary</u>, vol. 2, p. 1036; emphasis supplied).

Prisoners of hope

"*Though in many respects our institutions have swung into worldly conformity, though step by step they have advanced toward the world, <u>they are</u> prisoners of hope. Fate has not so woven its meshes about their workings that they need to remain helpless and in uncertainty. If they will listen to His voice and follow in His ways, <u>God will correct and enlighten</u> them, and <u>bring them back</u> to their upright position of distinction from the world*" (<u>Testimonies for the Church</u>, vol. 6, p. 145; emphasis supplied).

Educational centers in the end times

"*Thus saith the Lord.... 'I <u>will instruct</u> the ignorant and anoint with heavenly eyesalve the eyes of many who are now in spiritual darkness. I <u>will raise</u> up agents <u>who will carry out My will</u> to prepare a people to stand before Me in the time of the end. In many places that before this ought to have been provided with sanitariums and school, <u>I will establish my institutions, and these institutions will become educational centers for the training of workers</u>'*" (<u>Counsels on Health</u>, p. 227; emphasis supplied).

Education most essential

"*The usefulness learned on the school farm is the <u>very education that is most essential</u> for those who go out as missionaries to many foreign fields. If this training is given with the glory of God in view, <u>great results will be seen</u>. No work will be more effectual than that done by those who having obtained an education in practical life, go forth to mission fields with the message of truth, prepared to instruct as they have been instructed. The knowledge they have obtained in the tilling of the soil and other lines of manual work, which they carry with them to their fields of labor, <u>will make them a blessing</u> even in heathen lands. <u>Before we can carry the message of present truth in all its fulness to other countries, we must first</u>*

462

break every yoke. We must come into the line of true education, walking in the wisdom of God and not in the wisdom of the world. God calls for messengers who will be true reformers. We must educate, educate, to prepare a people who will understand the message and then give the message to the world" (Series B, No. 11, p. 29; emphasis supplied).

Schools should be out of cities

"Never can the proper education be given to the youth in this country, or in any other country, unless they [schools] are separated a wide distance from the cities" (Life Sketches, p. 351; emphasis supplied).

God will bless those schools

"The plan of the schools we shall establish in these closing years of the message is to be of an entirely different order from those we have instituted. For this reason, God bids us establish schools away from the cities, where without let or hindrance, we can carry on the education of students upon plans that are in harmony with the solemn message committed to us for the world. Such an education as this can best be worked out where there is land to cultivate and where the physical exercise taken by the students can be of such a nature as to act a valuable part in their character building and fit them for usefulness in the fields to which they shall go. God will bless those schools that are conducted according to His design" (Counsels to Teachers, p. 532-533; emphasis supplied).

Higher education will be extinguished

"Unless there is a breaking away from the influence that Satan has prepared, and a reviving of the testimonies that God has given, souls will perish in their delusion. They will accept fallacy after fallacy, and will thus keep up a disunion that will always exist until those who have been deceived take their stand on the right platform. All this higher education that is being planned will be extinguished; for it is spurious. The more simple the education of our workers, the less connection they have with the men whom God is not leading, the more will be accomplished. Work will be done in the simplicity of true godliness, and the old, old times will be back when, under the Holy Spirit's guidance, thousands were converted in a day. When the truth in its simplicity is lived in every place, then God will work through His angels as he worked on the day of Pentecost, and hearts will be changed so decidedly that there will be a manifestation of the influence of genuine truth, as is represented in the

463

descent of the Holy Spirit" (Series B, No. 7, pp. 63-64; emphasis supplied).

    "As we draw near to the close of time the cities will become more and more corrupt, and more and more objectionable as places for establishing centers for our work. The dangers of travel will increase, confusion and drunkenness will abound. If there can be found places in retired mountain regions where it would be difficult for the evils of the cities to enter, let our people secure such places for our sanitariums and advanced schools" (Manuscript Releases, vol. 10, p. 260; emphasis supplied). This counsel will help us today.

Success depends on fidelity

    "Real success in education depends upon the fidelity with which men carry out the Creator's plan. The true object of education is to restore the image of God in man" (Patriarchs and Prophets, p. 595; emphasis supplied).

God's Judgments Today

Our claims will not defer judgments

    "Nothwistanding their claim to be the chosen people of God, reformation of heart and of the life practice alone could save them from the inevitable result of continued transgression" (Prophets and Kings, p. 414).

    "Let none refuse to be reproved for evil, nor charge the servants of God with being too zealous in endeavoring to cleanse the camp from evil-doing. A sin-hating God calls upon those who claim to keep His law, to depart from all iniquity. A neglect to repent and render willing obedience will bring upon men and women today as serious consequences as came upon ancient Israel. There is a limit which the judgments of Jehovah can no longer be delayed. The desolation of Jerusalem in the days of Jeremiah is a solemn warning to modern Israel, that the counsels and admonitions given through chosen instrumentalities cannot be disregarded with impunity" (Prophets and Kings, p. 416; emphasis supplied).

Past Judgments of God

    "But I was not surprised by the sad news, for in visions of the night I have seen an angel standing with a sword as of fire stretched over Battle Creek" (Testimonies for the Church, vol. 8, p. 97; emphasis supplied).

Family Safety Net

    "It is time for our people to take their families from the cities into more retired localities, else many of the youth, and many also of those

older in years, will be ensnared and taken by the enemy" Testimonies for the Church, vol. 8, p. 101; emphasis supplied).

"Only Safety" List

"*The only safety for us is in trusting implicitly and following faithfully the instruction of the word of God. The Bible is the only chart that marks out the narrow path which shuns the pitfalls of destruction...*" (This Day With God, p. 247; emphasis supplied).

"*The instruction that was given in the early days of the message is to be held as safe instruction to follow in these its closing days. Those who are indifferent to this light and instruction must not expect to escape the snares which we have been plainly told will cause the rejecters of light to stumble, and fall, and be snared, and be taken*" (Selected Messages, book 1, p. 41, emphasis supplied).

Our Children's Safety and Our Own

"*The only sure safety for our children against every vicious practice, is to seek to be admitted into the fold of Christ, and to be taken under the watch care of the faithful and true Shepherd, He will save them from every evil, shield them from all dangers, if they will heed His voice*" (Child Guidance, p. 467; emphasis supplied).

"*Instead of the crowded city, seek some retired situation where your children will be, so far as possible, shielded from temptation, and there train and educate them for usefulness*" (Testimonies for the Church, vol. 5, p. 232; emphasis supplied).

"*It is time for our people to take their families from the cities into more retired localities, else many of the youth, and many also of those older in years, will be ensnared and taken by the enemy*" Testimonies for the Church, vol. 8, p. 101; emphasis supplied).

Living Like a Watchman

"*Prayer and watching thereunto are necessary for advancement in divine life. ... Your only safety is to live like a watchman. Watch and pray always. Oh, what a wonderful preventive against yielding to temptation and falling into the snares of the world*" (The Faith I Live By, p. 224; emphasis supplied).

Ancient Landmarks

"*The passing of time in 1844 was a period of great events, opening to our astonished eyes the cleansing of the sanctuary transpiring in heaven, and having decided relation to God's people upon the earth, the first and second angels messages and the third, unfurling the banner on which was inscribed, 'The commandments of God and the faith of Jesus.'*

One of the landmarks under this message was the temple of God, seen by his truth-loving people in heaven, and the ark containing the law of God. The light of the Sabbath of the fourth commandment flashed its strong rays in the pathway of the transgressors of God's law. The non immortality of the wicked is an old landmark. I can call to mind nothing more that can come under the head of the old landmarks. All this cry about changing the old landmarks is all imaginary" (Counsels to Writers and Editors, p. 30; emphasis supplied).

"Our only safety is in preserving the ancient landmarks. 'To the law and to the testimony: if they speak not according to this word, it is because there is no light in them'" Counsels on Health, p. 459; emphasis supplied).

Thus saith the Lord

"Thus he [Adam] gained an experimental knowledge of disobedience to God's commandments. Thus he knew good and evil; thus he lost his fidelity and loyalty to God and opened the floodgates of evil and suffering to the whole human family. How many today are making the same experiment! When will man learn that the only means for his safety is through a full confidence in a 'thus saith the Lord'?" (Manuscript Releases, vol. 18, p. 34; emphasis supplied).

Seed of Vital Truth

"No one should be indifferent on this subject, saying, if we are honest, it is no matter what we believe. You cannot with safety surrender any seed of vital truth in order to please yourself or anyone else" (Selected Messages, book one, p. 299; emphasis supplied).

God's Peculiar People

"Our only safety is to stand as God's peculiar people. We must not yield one inch to the customs and fashions of this degenerate age, but stand in moral independence, making no compromise with its corrupt and idolatrous practices" (Testimonies for the Church, vol. 5, p. 78; emphasis supplied).

"Wherefore come out from among them, and be ye separate, saith the Lord, and touch not the unclean thing; and I will receive you, and will be a father unto you, and ye shall be my sons and daughters, saith the Lord Almighty" (II Corinthians 6:17,18).

THE "ONLY SAFETY" LIST

"<u>Our only safety is in separation from those who live in its darkness</u>. The Lord has enjoined upon us to come out from among them and be separate, and to touch not the unclean thing, and He will receive us and will be a Father unto us, and we shall be His sons and daughters. If we wish to be adopted into the family of God, to become children of the heavenly King, we must comply with His conditions; we must come out from the world and stand as a peculiar people before the Lord, obeying His precepts and serving Him" (<u>Testimonies for the Church</u>, vol. 4, p. 109-10; emphasis supplied).

Secret Prayer

"There is need that much time be spent in secret prayer, in close communion with God. Thus only can victories be won. Eternal vigilance is the price of safety" (Counsels to Teachers, p. 258).

Walk in Christ's Footsteps

"Now is our time of peril. <u>Our only safety is in walking in the footsteps of Christ</u>, and in wearing His yoke. Troublous times are before us. In many instances, friends will become alienated. <u>Without cause, men will become our enemies</u>. The motives of the people of God will be misinterpreted, <u>not only by the world, but by their brethren</u>. The Lord's servants will be put in hard places. <u>A mountain will be made out of a molehill to justify men in pursuing a selfish, unrighteous course</u>. The work that men have done faithfully will be disparaged and underrated, because apparent prosperity does not attend their efforts. By misrepresentation, these men will be clothed in dark vestments of dishonesty because circumstances beyond their control made their work perplexing. <u>They will be pointed to as men that cannot be trusted. And this will be done by members of the church</u>" (<u>Spalding Magan Collection</u>, p. 370; emphasis supplied).

No Place for the Devil

"<u>Our only safety</u> is in giving no place to the devil; for his suggestions and purposes are ever to injure us, and hinder us from relying upon God" (<u>Our High Calling</u>, p. 95; emphasis supplied).

In Saving Others We May Save Ourselves

"I read of a man who journeying on a winter's day through the deep, drifted snow, he became benumbed by the cold which was almost impercep-

tibly stealing away his vital powers. As he was nearly chilled to death by the embrace of the frost king, and about to give up the struggle for life, he heard the moans of a brother traveler, who was perishing with cold as he was about to perish. His humanity was aroused to rescue him. He chafed the ice-clad limbs of the unfortunate man, and after considerable effort, raised him to his feet; and as he could not stand, he bore him in sympathizing arms through the very drifts he had thought he would never succeed in getting through alone. When he had borne his fellow traveler to a place of safety, the truth flashed home to him that in saving his neighbor he had saved himself also. His earnest efforts to save another quickened the blood which was freezing in his own veins and created a healthful warmth in the extremities of the body. These lessons must be forced upon young believers continually, not only by precept, but by example, that in their Christian experience they may realize similar results" (Testimonies for the Church, vol. 4, pp. 319-320; emphasis supplied).

SUBJECT INDEX

SUBJECT INDEX

SUBJECT INDEX

SUBJECT INDEX

SUBJECT INDEX

About the Author

Jere Franklin has enjoyed teaching science and math to high school and college students. He was president of a youth ranch for several years, is a member of ASI, and active in the supporting ministries of the Seventh-day Adventist Church. He enjoys addressing groups concerned about being ready as the end time approaches. He is convinced that an attitude of business-as-usual will soon be replaced by a spirit of preparation among believers.

Jere's hobbies include prayer, family, teaching, camping, hiking, photography, natural history, and log cabin building.

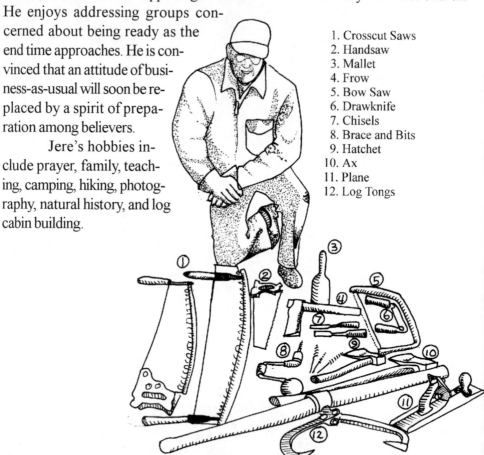

1. Crosscut Saws
2. Handsaw
3. Mallet
4. Frow
5. Bow Saw
6. Drawknife
7. Chisels
8. Brace and Bits
9. Hatchet
10. Ax
11. Plane
12. Log Tongs

For information about an end time events seminar at your church phone or write:

Jere Franklin (home: 250-788-2944)
Box 840
Chetwynd, BC Canada V0C 1J0
youcansurvive.org